The Gothic Line

THE GOTHIC

MARK ZUEHLKE

LINE

CANADA'S MONTH OF HELL
IN WORLD WAR II ITALY

DOUGLAS & McINTYRE
Vancouver/Toronto

03 04 05 06 07 5 4 3 2 1

Douglas & McIntyre Ltd.
2323 Quebec Street, Suite 201
Vancouver, British Columbia
Canada V5T 4S7
www.douglas-mcintyre.com

National Library of Canada Cataloguing in Publication Data
Zuehlke, Mark
The Gothic Line : Canada's month of hell in World War II Italy / by Mark Zuehlke.

Includes bibliographical references and index.
ISBN 1-55365-023-9

1. World War, 1939–1945—Campaigns—Italy. 2. Canada. Canadian Army—History—World War, 1939–1945. I. Title.
D763.I8Z83 2003 940.54'215 C2003-910595-4

Library of Congress information is available upon request

Editing by Elizabeth McLean
Jacket design by Peter Cocking & Jessica Sullivan
Jacket photograph: NAC PA-173437
Interior design by Peter Cocking
Maps by C. Stuart Daniel/Starshell Maps
Typeset by Rhonda Ganz
Printed and bound in Canada by Friesens
Printed on acid-free paper

All photos were supplied by the National Archives of Canada, and, unless cited, were taken by unspecified Department of National Defence photographers.

We gratefully acknowledge the financial support of the Canada Council for the Arts, the British Columbia Arts Council, and the Government of Canada through the Book Publishing Industry Development Program (BPIDP) for our publishing activities.

It is just a rough hard job, which must be carried through.

WINSTON CHURCHILL

Oh, what with the wounded, and what with the dead.
And what with the boys, who are swinging the lead.
If this war isn't over, and that goddamn soon,
There'll be nobody left in this bloody platoon.

UNKNOWN CANADIAN SOLDIER IN ITALY

I can't see us getting out of here alive.

PRIVATE STAN SCISLOWSKI,
PERTH REGIMENT OF CANADA

[CONTENTS]

PREFACE

THIS IS THE FINAL VOLUME of what has developed into a trilogy of books detailing the experiences of Canadians in the largest, most decisive battles of World War II's Italian campaign. Following the publication of both *Ortona: Canada's Epic World War II Battle* and *The Liri Valley: Canada's World War II Breakthrough to Rome,* an ever growing number of veterans of this long, brutal, and terribly costly campaign contacted me to share their personal memories of the Gothic Line Battle. I have drawn on veteran memories by letter, E-mail correspondence, telephone calls, and personal interviews. The willingness of these old soldiers to frankly discuss what for many was a painfully grim part of their young lives has made these three books possible. It is their ability to vividly recall many details—sifted together with the official records, regimental diaries and official histories, autobiographies and biographies, and other archival materials—that enabled a dramatic and detailed depiction of the combat experience of Canadians at the Gothic Line during the late summer of 1944.

Some military historians are skeptical of incorporating veteran memory into the examination of battle. This skepticism becomes most keenly honed when one is asking a person to reach back across the span of almost a lifetime. Such historians tend to argue that it is only to the official records that we can turn for accurate accounts of events. Another, generally smaller number of historians turn only to the oral history of those who lived through the war—choosing to present in unvarnished form the accounts of veterans, without placing these experiences into the larger historical context of the battle in which their tale unfolded.

I follow a middle path between these two groups—shaping a detailed narrative of the Canadian experience of battle by weaving together the accounts of veterans and the official record. Such an approach is fraught with its own intrinsic difficulties, the most challenging being how to handle those times when historical record and veteran memory conflict. Fortunately, these situations arise far less than might seem probable at first blush. I have often been amazed at how clearly many veterans recall a specific incident and can peg it to an exact date or even hour. Go back to the official record, particularly the regimental war diaries, and there is a short description that aligns well with the veteran's recollection.

There are, however, times when memory and record do not mesh so cleanly. Most of these instances occur where the perception of regimental honour or the reputation of an individual—most probably a senior officer—might be compromised by the reality of events and behaviour during the course of combat. At such times, the regimental histories and official contemporary military records become suddenly vague or highly sanitized to avoid the hint of aspersion. My approach in these instances is to consult as many sources as possible, both by contacting more veterans who were present at the time and by checking every possible document. This approach usually makes it possible to develop an accurate depiction of how that event transpired. At other times, however, the matter remains obscure and it is necessary to finally make a calculated judgement call as to how a situation likely played out. In these rare circumstances, I have tended to accept veteran memory over the official record, for it is, after all, their story that I present here. The veterans lived through the battle, buried friends who did not, and have carried the memory of war's experience through the rest of their lives.

As the years have passed, memories have generally dimmed. There are few veterans still able to extensively recall the twenty-six days of combat that was the Gothic Line Battle. What they impart are fragments, anecdotal incidents that burned so deeply into consciousness they remain there still. Seldom are these moments that bathe the remembering veteran in a heroic spotlight. That light they direct elsewhere, onto friends and compatriots they served alongside. Often the memories are humorous, because there is little pain in such stories. These are generally the only tales that veterans will tell wives, children, and grandchildren. When asked—as I have asked—for them to relate the darker events, some refuse, but surprisingly most do their best. One veteran's small fragment linked to those of other veterans is then tied together with the historical and official record to yield a credible account. An account that does honour to those who lived through a terrible test of spirit.

ACKNOWLEDGEMENTS

My greatest thanks to the many veterans who contributed to this book, all of whom are listed in the bibliography. There are a few, however, who I would like to recognize specifically. Tony Poulin took great care to provide many personal experiences, often translating thoroughly from French to English for my non-bilingual edification the accounts he had written years before. Strome Galloway has been a wonderful, gracious source for the duration of my research work on all three books. John Dougan, Jack Haley, David Kinloch, J. Milton Gregg, and Ted Shuter were also extremely patient and helpful.

At the regimental museums and archives, staff and volunteers were always generous with their time and willing to provide material that otherwise would not have been available. Special thanks to Tony Walters of the Rocky Mountain Rangers and Howard Hisdal of the British Columbia Dragoons. Thanks also to Dr. Steve Harris and others at the Directorate of History, Department of National Defence, staff at the National Archives of Canada, Chris Petter and the two Terrys at University of Victoria's Special Collections, and Debbie Lindsey at the Canadian Broadcasting Corporation's Radio Archives.

In Italy, Amedeo Montemaggi was a wonderful resource and I cannot say enough kind things about Oviglio Monti. Both shared their wartime stories and local knowledge. Monti drove much of the battlefield with me and, when he could not, loaned his car to this virtual stranger from Canada for solo outings. His Hotel Levante in Rimini was a pleasant base for operations. My thanks to his family, too, for their help.

Alex McQuarrie translated the German paratrooper Carl Bayerlein's account into English and has always been supportive of my work. Dr. Bill McAndrew pointed me to several valuable sources and provided sound counsel on other matters of relevance. Ken McLeod previously opened many doors to the homes of veterans in Vancouver and kindly shared his oral history collection with me.

Literary agent Carolyn Swayze worked very hard on my behalf, making it possible for me to focus on the research and writing while she dealt with the burdensome contractual and financial complexities that sometimes seemed destined to sink this entire project. That it is here today is in no small measure due to her efforts. As was the case with my other two books on the Italian campaign, C. Stuart Daniel contributed his mapmaking excellence and Elizabeth McLean her precise editorial eye. Finally, I have been fortunate indeed to have the support and companionship of Frances Backhouse, *mi amore.*

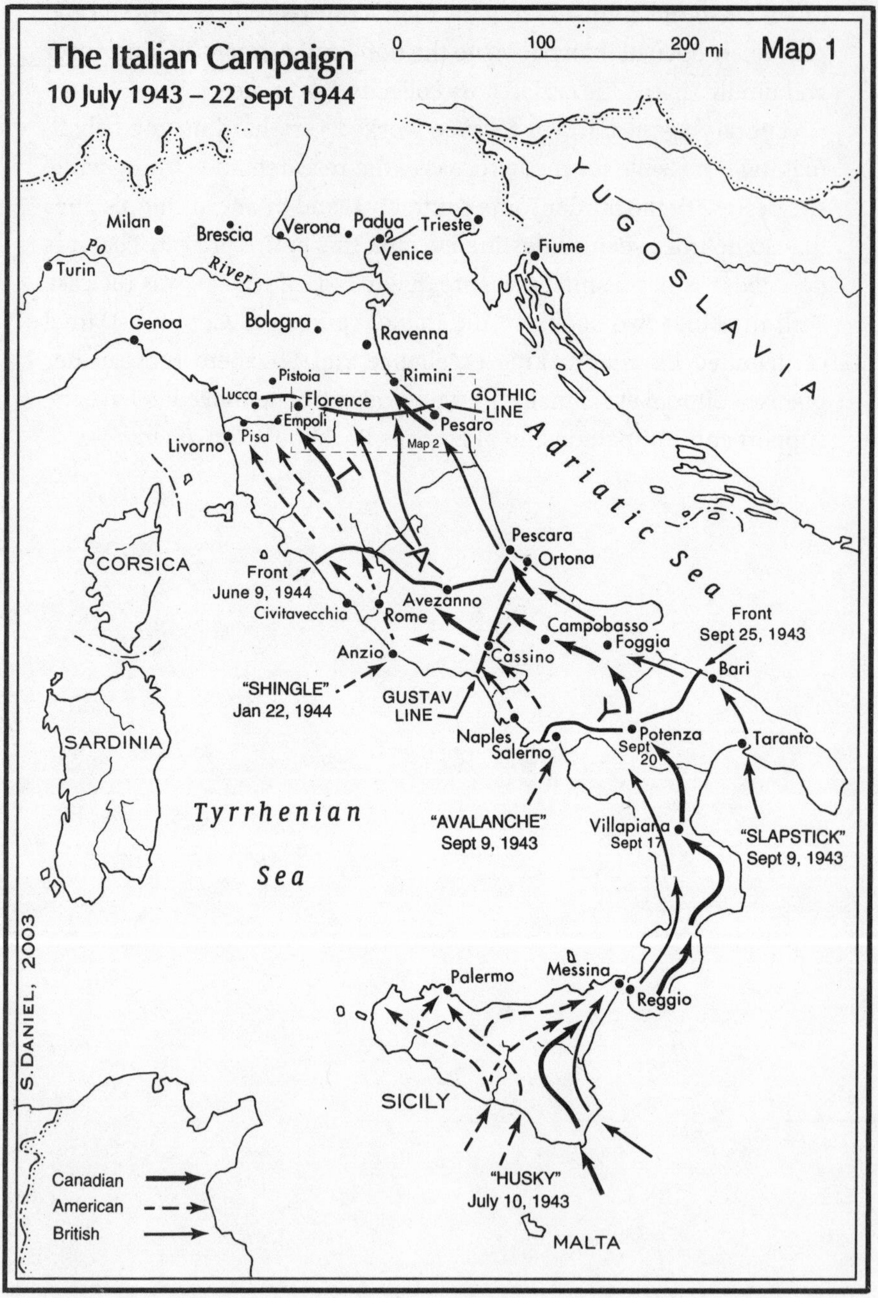
The Italian Campaign
10 July 1943 – 22 Sept 1944
0
100
200 mi
Map 1
YUGOSLAVIA
Milan
Brescia
Verona
Padua
Trieste
Turin
Po River
Venice
Fiume
Genoa
Bologna
Ravenna
Pistoia
Rimini
Lucca
Florence
GOTHIC LINE
Empoli
Pesaro
Livorno
Pisa
Map 2
Adriatic Sea
ITALY
Pescara
Ortona
CORSICA
Front June 9, 1944
Avezanno
Civitavecchia
Rome
Campobasso
Foggia
Front Sept 25, 1943
Anzio
Cassino
Bari
"SHINGLE" Jan 22, 1944
GUSTAV LINE
Naples
Salerno
Potenza
Sept 20
Taranto
SARDINIA
Tyrrhenian Sea
"AVALANCHE" Sept 9, 1943
Villapiana
Sept 17
"SLAPSTICK" Sept 9, 1943
S. DANIEL, 2003
Palermo
Messina
Reggio
SICILY
Canadian
American
British
"HUSKY" July 10, 1943
MALTA

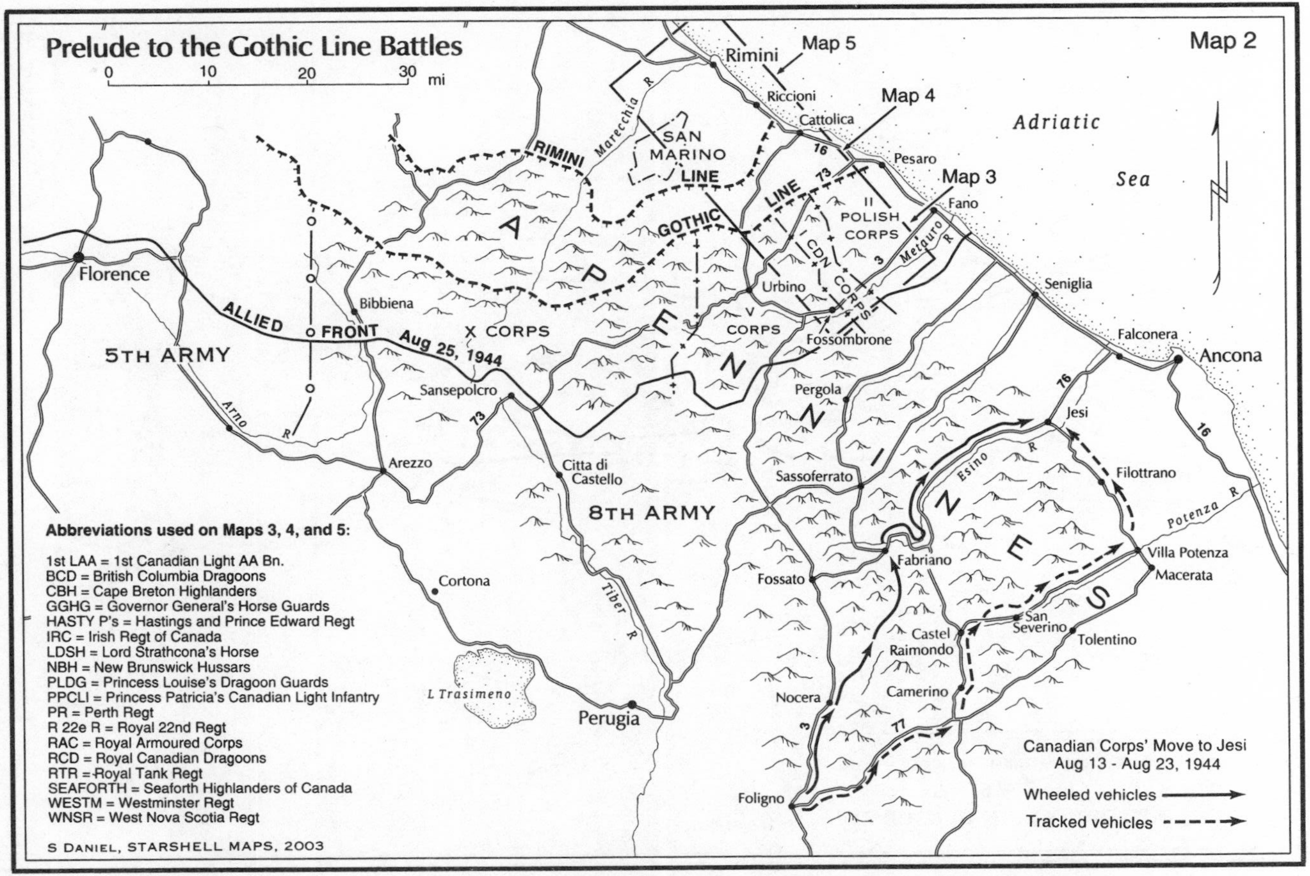
Prelude to the Gothic Line Battles
Map 2
0 10 20 30 mi
Adriatic
Sea
Map 5
Map 4
Map 3
Rimini
Riccioni
Cattolica
Pesaro
Fano
Seniglia
Falconera
Ancona
SAN MARINO
Marecchia R
RIMINI LINE
GOTHIC LINE
II POLISH CORPS
I CDN CORPS
V CORPS
X CORPS
Metauro R
Urbino
Fossombrone
Pergola
Sassoferrato
Fabriano
Fossato
Nocera
Foligno
Castel Raimondo
Camerino
San Severino
Tolentino
Macerata
Villa Potenza
Potenza R
Filottrano
Jesi
Esino R
Florence
Bibbiena
ALLIED FRONT Aug 25, 1944
5TH ARMY
8TH ARMY
A P E N N I N E S
Arno R
Sansepolcro
Arezzo
Citta di Castello
Tiber R
Cortona
L Trasimeno
Perugia
16
73
76
77
3
Canadian Corps' Move to Jesi
Aug 13 - Aug 23, 1944
Wheeled vehicles
Tracked vehicles
Abbreviations used on Maps 3, 4, and 5:
1st LAA = 1st Canadian Light AA Bn.
BCD = British Columbia Dragoons
CBH = Cape Breton Highlanders
GGHG = Governor General's Horse Guards
HASTY P's = Hastings and Prince Edward Regt
IRC = Irish Regt of Canada
LDSH = Lord Strathcona's Horse
NBH = New Brunswick Hussars
PLDG = Princess Louise's Dragoon Guards
PPCLI = Princess Patricia's Canadian Light Infantry
PR = Perth Regt
R 22e R = Royal 22nd Regt
RAC = Royal Armoured Corps
RCD = Royal Canadian Dragoons
RTR = Royal Tank Regt
SEAFORTH = Seaforth Highlanders of Canada
WESTM = Westminster Regt
WNSR = West Nova Scotia Regt
S DANIEL, STARSHELL MAPS, 2003

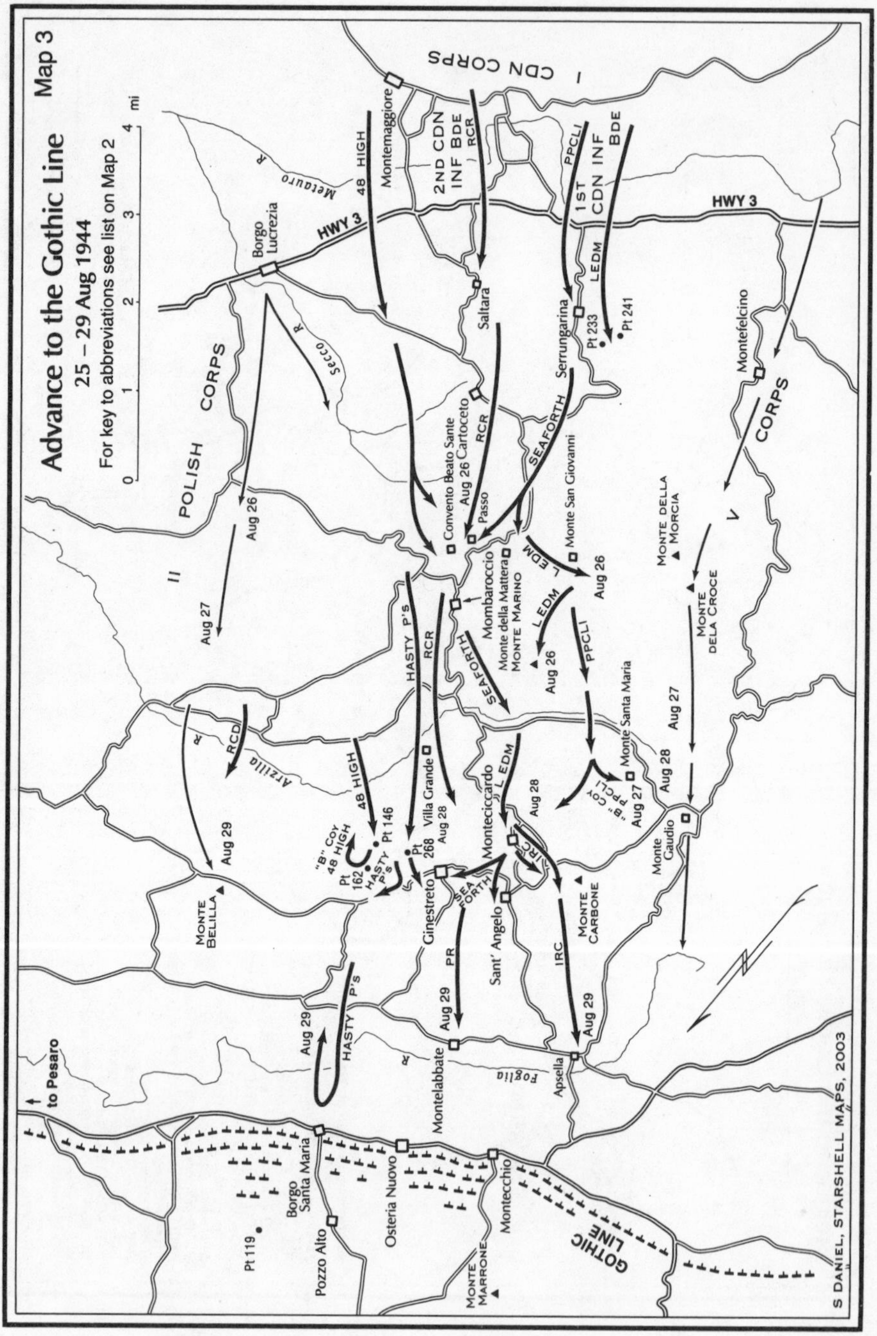
Map 3
Advance to the Gothic Line
25 – 29 Aug 1944
For key to abbreviations see list on Map 2
0 1 2 3 4 mi
I CDN CORPS
2ND CDN INF BDE
1ST CDN INF BDE
II POLISH CORPS
V CORPS
HWY 3
Metauro R
Secco R
Arzilla R
Foglia R
Borgo Lucrezia
Montemaggiore
Saltara
Serrungarina
Pt 233
Pt 241
Montefelcino
Cartoceto
Convento Beato Sante
Passo
Monte San Giovanni
Mombaroccio
Monte della Mattera
MONTE MARINO
MONTE DELLA MORCIA
MONTE DELA CROCE
Monte Santa Maria
Monte Gaudio
Villa Grande
Monteciccardo
Pt 146
Pt 268
Pt 162
"B" COY 48 HIGH
"B" COY PPCLI
Ginestreto
Sant' Angelo
MONTE CARBONE
MONTE BELILLA
Montelabbate
Apsella
to Pesaro
Borgo Santa Maria
Pt 119
Pozzo Alto
Osteria Nuovo
Montecchio
MONTE MARRONE
GOTHIC LINE
48 HIGH
RCR
PPCLI
LEDM
SEAFORTH
HASTY P'S
RCD
IRC
PR
Aug 26
Aug 27
Aug 28
Aug 29
S DANIEL, STARSHELL MAPS, 2003

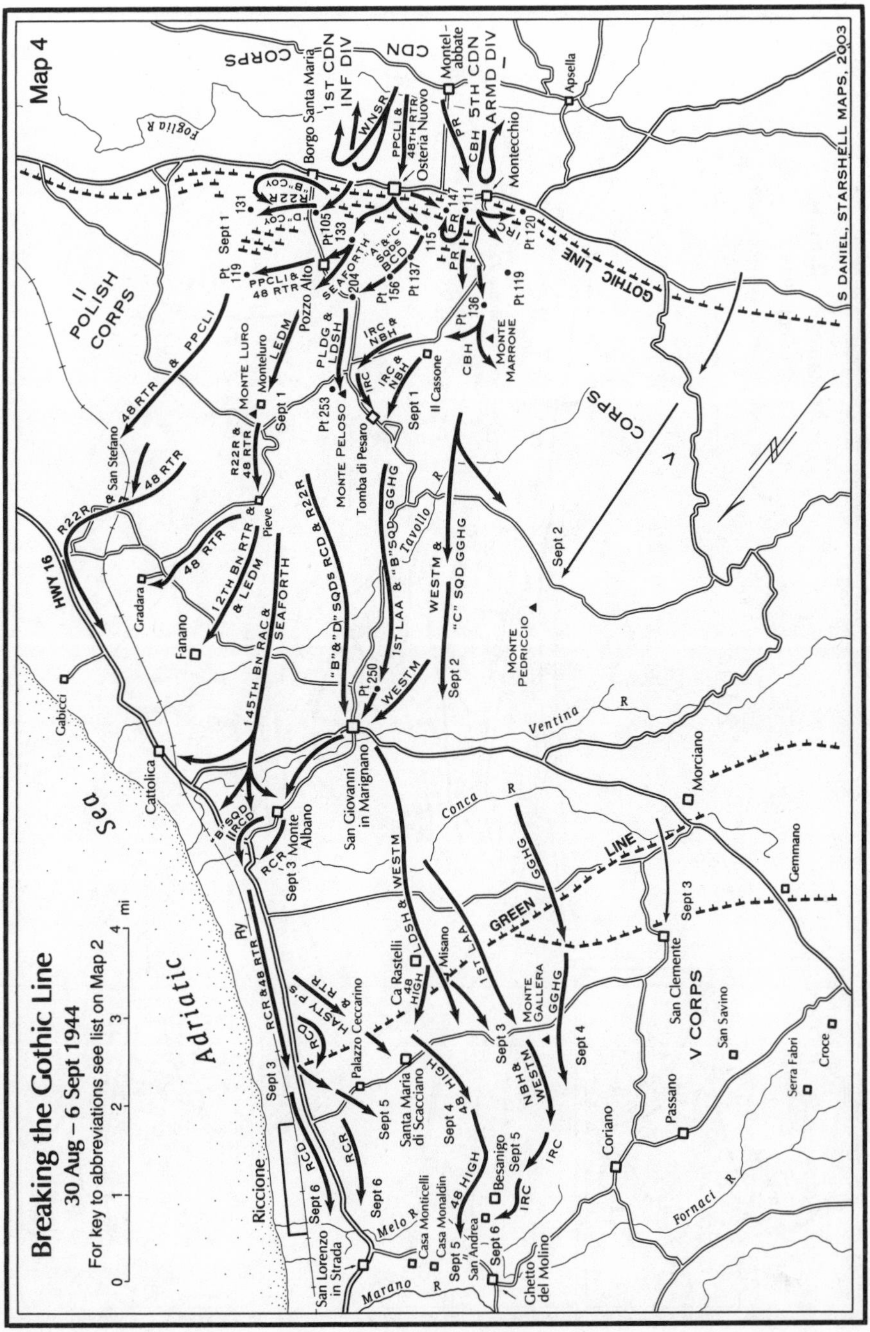
Map 4
Breaking the Gothic Line
30 Aug – 6 Sept 1944
For key to abbreviations see list on Map 2
0 1 2 3 4 mi
S DANIEL, STARSHELL MAPS, 2003
Adriatic Sea
II POLISH CORPS
1ST CDN INF DIV
CDN CORPS
5TH CDN ARMD DIV
V CORPS
GOTHIC LINE
GREEN LINE
HWY 16
Foglia R
Conca R
Ventina R
Tavollo R
Melo R
Marano R
Fornaci R
Rv
Gabicci
Cattolica
Fanano
Gradara
San Stefano
Pieve
Monteluro
MONTE LURO
Pozzo Alto
Borgo Santa Maria
Osteria Nuovo
Montelabbate
Montecchio
Apsella
Pt 253
MONTE PELOSO
Tomba di Pesaro
Il Cassone
MONTE MARRONE
Pt 119
Pt 120
Pt 136
Pt 137
Pt 156
Pt 204
Pt 105
Pt 133
Pt 115
Pt 147
Pt 111
Pt 131
Pt 250
MONTE PEDRICCIO
San Giovanni in Marignano
Monte Albano
Morciano
Gemmano
San Clemente
San Savino
Serra Fabri
Croce
Passano
Coriano
Riccione
San Lorenzo in Strada
Casa Monticelli
Casa Monaldin
San Andrea
Ghetto del Molino
Besanigo
Santa Maria di Scacciano
Palazzo Ceccarino
Ca Rastelli
Misano
MONTE GALLERA
48 RTR & PPCLI
R22R
48 RTR
R22R & 48 RTR
12TH BN RTR & LEDM
145TH BN RAC & SEAFORTH
"B" & "D" SQDS RCD & R22R
1ST LAA & "B" SQD GGHG
WESTM & "C" SQD GGHG
PPCLI & 48 RTR
LEDM
PLDG & LDSH
IRC & NBH
SEAFORTH
WNSR
PPCLI & 48TH RTR
PR
CBH
GGHG
LDSH & WESTM
1ST LAA
48 HIGH
NBH & WESTM
IRC
RCR
RCD
RCR & 48 RTR
HASTY P's & RTR
"B" SQD 1RCD
Sept 1
Sept 2
Sept 3
Sept 4
Sept 5
Sept 6

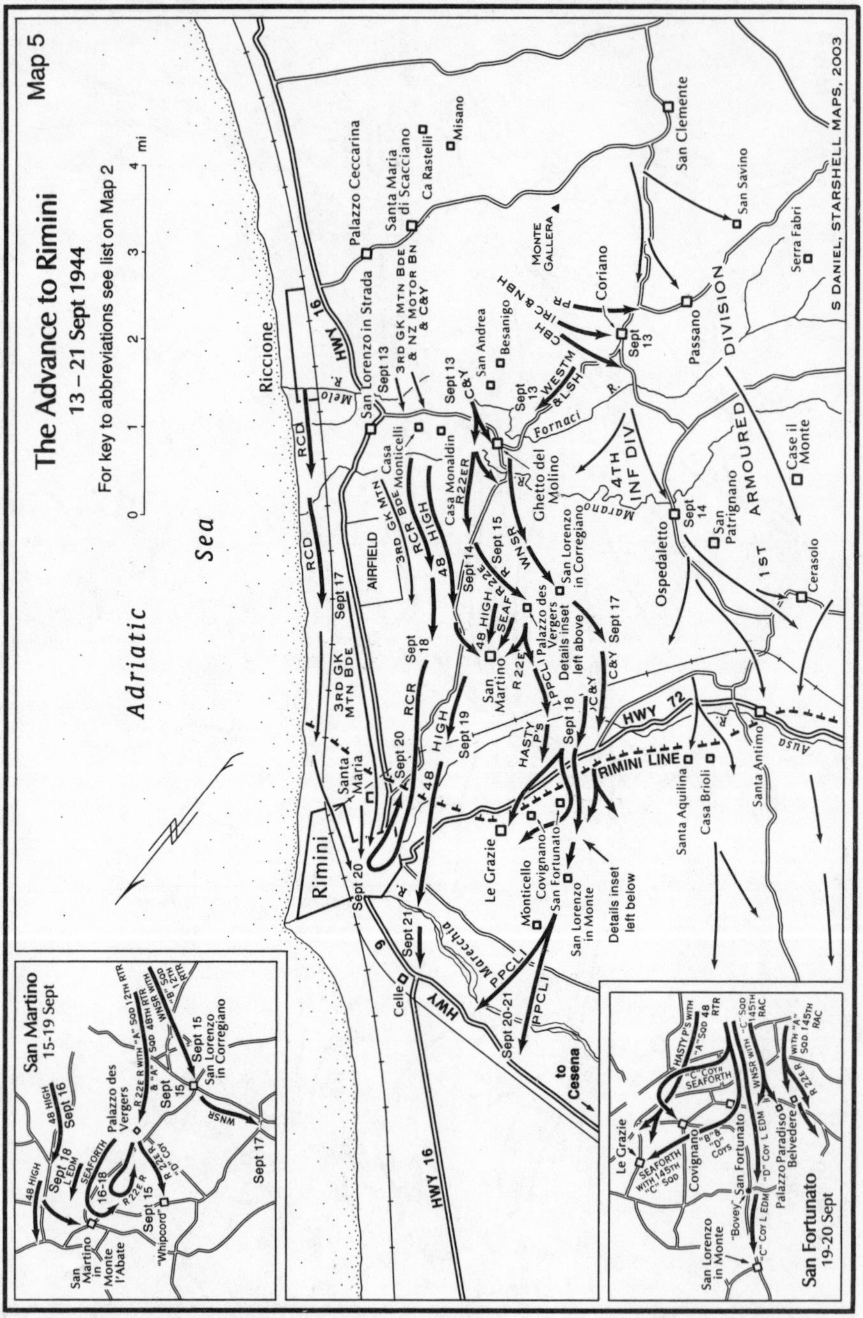
Map 5
The Advance to Rimini
13 – 21 Sept 1944
For key to abbreviations see list on Map 2
Adriatic Sea
San Martino
15-19 Sept
San Fortunato
19-20 Sept
S DANIEL, STARSHELL MAPS, 2003

[INTRODUCTION]

Long March To the Gothic Line

THEY WERE the forgotten soldiers. Some thought themselves forsaken. They marched amid an Allied army in a Canadian corps that had largely disappeared from the consciousness of Canadians back home. "Where are you? We never hear about you in the newspapers!" was a common refrain in letters received from parents, siblings, wives, and lovers. The short, grim answer: "In Italy."

For almost a year, until early June 1944, the eyes of the Western world had been rivetted on the slow, bloody Allied advance up Italy's long, hard boot to Rome. On June 6, 1944—D-Day—history's largest armada hove to off the shores of Normandy and a great amphibious invasion gained the Allies a decisive toehold in northern France. D-Day transformed the Western European theatre of combat. Once it had been thought that the outcome of the Western Allied war against the Axis powers might depend on driving up the length of Italy to pierce into Austria, and then break into Germany through the back door north of Vienna. British Prime Minister Winston Churchill called this the offensive against "Europe's soft underbelly."

Italy had, however, proven to be more hard, sinewy muscle than tender tissue. An unforgiving land, divided in the centre by the Apennines, crisscrossed by ravines and spiny ridges, Italy was ideal for defence and hostile to the offence. In summer, it was sun-scorched and dust-choked; in winter, drenching rains transformed the soil into a muddy quagmire. Despite the terrain, the Allies in Italy had slowly, relentlessly prevailed.

From the Canadian perspective, the Italian campaign had served initially as a proving ground for an army largely untested. Although by early 1942 Canada had deployed 465,000 soldiers to Britain, none had undergone a baptism of fire. While thousands of British soldiers fought and died in North Africa, the Canadians in Britain trained and waited for a great invasion of Western Europe that drew no closer with each passing season. Between training schemes, they drank, went sightseeing, fell in love with and married British women, and fathered children. Along with growing numbers of Americans, they behaved somewhat like an occupation force. "The problem with the Americans," went a British saying of the day, "is they're overpaid, oversexed, and over here." Canadians were only slightly more popular.

On August 19, 1942, the Canadians finally did fight. Operation Jubilee was an amphibious raid on the small French port of Dieppe. Of the 6,000-strong attacking force, 4,963 were Canadians. Jubilee was a disaster. In a matter of hours, the attackers were cut to pieces on the beaches. Only 2,210 Canadians returned to Britain and 28 of these died of wounds. Of the rest, 807 were killed during the battle and 82 of the 1,946 taken prisoner of war perished while in captivity.

Rather than dampen Canadian military ardour, Dieppe fuelled the growing demand at home that Canada's army get into the fight. The government agreed and saw its opportunity when Operation Husky, the invasion of Sicily, was proposed in early 1943. Initially, no Canadian units were assigned to the operation. But the Canadian government lobbied hard and the Combined Chiefs of Staff finally agreed to attach 1st Canadian Infantry Division and 1st Canadian Armoured Brigade to the British Eighth Army for the invasion.

On July 10, 1943, the Canadians waded ashore on the extreme tip of the Pachino peninsula, Sicily's southernmost point. From here, they marched 130 miles, fought several small, fierce engagements, and took 2,310 casualties. Of these, 562 died and 490 were buried in a small Canadian-only cemetery on the outskirts of Agira in the hardscrabble Sicilian interior. It was at Agira and nearby Leonforte—two dun-coloured mediaeval hilltop fortress towns—that a majority of the Canadian casualties were suffered.

Sicily served as a stepping-stone for an invasion of Italy. It was an invasion the British wanted and the Americans agreed to only half-heartedly, fearful such a campaign would weaken the Allied ability to proceed with the invasion of Western Europe. Canada wanted to be in the fight, if there was to be one. On September 3, Eighth Army crossed the Strait of Messina with the Canadian veterans of Sicily leading the way.

Even as these Canadians started the long trek up the Italian boot, plans were underway in Ottawa to expand the Canadian presence in Italy from a mere division and brigade to a full, entirely Canadian corps. By November 1, I Canadian Corps was a reality brought into the strength of Eighth Army. It comprised the seasoned troops of 1st Canadian Infantry Division and 1st Canadian Armoured Brigade, as well as the newly arrived 5th Canadian Armoured Division. By the end of 1943, about 75,000 Canadians were in Italy, including the many support personnel necessary to keep a corps operational.

The 5th Canadian Armoured Division was spared the first prolonged Canadian battle in Italy. From December 6, 1943 to January 4, 1944, 1 CID and 1 CAB slugged it out with the elite 90th Panzer Grenadier and 1st Parachute divisions for control of a few miles of ground extending from the Moro River to just beyond the Adriatic port town of Ortona. The Moro River, Villa Rogatti, San Leonardo, Casa Berardi, Cider Crossroads, The Gully, Torre Muchia, and Ortona became battle honours for the regiments engaged at each place. Inside Ortona, an eight-day street battle between the German paratroopers and the Loyal Edmonton Regiment, the Seaforth Highlanders of Canada, and the Three Rivers Tank Regiment was one of the most intense and costly battles ever fought by Canadian soldiers. At month's end, 2,339 Canadians were casualties, including 502 dead.

Although Ortona fell, the broader offensive that had brought about the fight for this town stalled in the face of Italy's intense winter rains. The mud reduced the battlefield to one eerily reminiscent of the Great War trench lines found in Belgium's Flanders. On the

Adriatic coast, Eighth Army was stalemated. Across the Apennines, the U.S. Fifth Army was even more hopelessly deadlocked before the heavily fortified Gustav Line, which ran from the impregnable Benedictine monastery atop Monte Cassino across the Liri Valley to the mountains of the coast.

Repeatedly during the winter of 1943–44, the Americans tried to break through this line. The casualties incurred in these failed attacks were devastating. An attempt to outflank the Gustav Line by launching an amphibious landing sixty miles to its rear at Anzio on January 22, 1944 resulted in VI U.S. Corps, a combined American-British force, being trapped inside a narrow, perilous beachhead. By spring, the situation on the Italian west coast was bleak and even the shifting of an entire corps from Eighth Army to this front had failed to yield a breakthrough.

General Harold Alexander, Deputy Supreme Commander, Mediterranean, decided that victory in Italy would only come on the west coast. To achieve such a victory, he needed the combined strength of his two armies. Accordingly, I Canadian Corps marched west in April to face the Liri Valley. Its role in the forthcoming Operation Diadem was to be a decisive one—the gatecrashers, who would spearhead the Allied charge up the fertile Liri Valley towards Rome. On May 11, the great offensive began with British infantry divisions and armoured brigades, including 1st Canadian Armoured Brigade, punching a hole in the Gustav Line. This time, the German fortifications were breached. By May 18, 1st Canadian Infantry Division approached the next defensive line—the formidable Hitler Line. After a series of costly failed attempts to break the line with hasty attacks, a set-piece attack was launched on May 23. For 2nd Canadian Infantry Brigade, fighting on the division's right flank, this was the single most costly day of battle. By day's end, 160 of its men were dead, 438 wounded, and 79 either missing or lost as prisoners. On the left flank, however, 3rd Canadian Infantry Brigade's Carleton and York Regiment had broken through. The brigade soon opened a narrow gap through which 5th Canadian Armoured Division's lead elements squeezed.

Even while withdrawing, the Germans mounted a fierce resistance that denied Alexander a quick advance and foiled his plan to link up with the Allied divisions breaking out of the Anzio beachhead, thus encircling and then crushing the retreating enemy divisions. Despite the unfaltering bravery of Canadian units such as the Westminster (Motorized) Regiment and the Lord Strathcona's Horse reconnaissance unit, which jointly won and held a bridgehead across the Melfa River on May 24, the advance faltered. When U.S. Fifth Army commander General Mark Clark independently changed the axis of his advance to ensure American divisions reached Rome first, the German divisions successfully melted away. Although mauled, they regrouped, refitted, and returned to the fight as they had so often in the past.

The Allies had incurred terrible casualties during May 1944. The Fifth and Eighth armies collectively suffered 43,746 casualties in exchange for losses estimated at slightly more than 50,000 on the German side. Of these Germans, 24,334 were taken prisoner. Total Canadian battle casualties during this time were 3,368: 789 killed, 2,463 wounded, and 116 missing. Illness incapacitated a further 4,000.

Although Clark undertook a triumphal parade into Rome on June 4, the victory was hollow. It was rendered even more so two days later by Operation Overlord, which put thousands of troops ashore on beaches in Normandy. The Germans in Italy, meanwhile, slowly withdrew northward towards yet another heavily fortified defensive line that stretched from south of Rimini on the Adriatic coast to Pisa on the western coast.

Even as the Canadians moved into rest camps in the Volturno Valley, southeast of the Liri Valley, and started refitting and rebuilding the corps, everyone from general to private knew another major offensive must soon follow. Many who had been part of the campaign since Sicily believed death or a debilitating wound inevitable before the fighting in Italy would finally end. It was during this time in the rest camps that these soldiers first heard themselves referred to as D-Day Dodgers.

According to the instant legend that grew up around this intended aspersion, Britain's first female Member of Parliament, Lady Nancy Astor, directed the derogatory term their way because she thought the soldiers in Italy enjoyed an easy war compared to those fighting in Normandy. Derogation was quickly transformed into mark of honour, as the men in Italy made up various versions of a song. "We are the D-Day Dodgers" was sung to the tune of "Lili Marlene." As the campaign continued, new verses were added, but in the early summer of 1944 the most common Canadian version ran five simple verses.

We are the D-Day Dodgers, out in Italy,
Always on the vino, always on the spree.
Eighth Army skivers and their tanks,
We go to war in tie and slacks,
We are the D-Day Dodgers, in sunny Italy.

We fought into Agira, a holiday with pay;
Jerry brought his bands out to cheer us on the way,
Showed us the sights and gave us tea,
We all sang songs, the beer was free.
We are the D-Day Dodgers, in sunny Italy.

The Moro and Ortona were taken in our stride,
We really didn't fight there, we went there for the ride.
Sleeping 'til noon and playing games,
We live in Rome with lots of dames.
We are the D-Day Dodgers, in sunny Italy.

We are the D-Day Dodgers, way out in Italy.
We're always tight, we cannot fight.
What bloody use are we?

If you look around the mountains and through mud and rain,
You'll see the rows of crosses, some which bear no name.
Heartbreak and toils and suffering gone,

The boys beneath, they linger on.
They were some of the D-Day Dodgers,
And they're still in Italy.

Some of the Canadians marched to this song as I Canadian Corps returned to active operations in the middle of July. The corps marched towards Florence for what was an anticipated major offensive in the central Apennines against the Gothic Line. Within a month, I Canadian Corps was—as it had been in the Liri Valley—again tasked with the primary role in a decisive Allied offensive. It fell to the Canadians to spearhead the breakthrough of the Gothic Line. This is the story of that bitter and costly battle.

PART ONE

RETURN TO THE ADRIATIC

[1]

Sojourn in Florence

FROM INSIDE the Galileo Observatory, Major Strome Galloway, Royal Canadian Regiment second-in-command, gazed down upon the great spires and domes of Florence's multitude of cathedrals, churches, and abbeys. The gentle, muted Tuscan light cast the city's elegant buildings in soft hues of terra cotta and dappled the broad, slow-flowing waters of the Arno River—almost directly below—with sparks of gold. Spanning the river was a single bridge—the fourteenth-century Ponte Vecchio—and this reminded Galloway that he looked down upon the city not as a tourist but as a soldier.[1]

Just prior to 1st Canadian Infantry Division's August 5–6 move into the line fronting the Arno River, the engineers of the German 4th Parachute Division had blown the city's five other ancient bridges. Among those destroyed was Santa Trinità, completed in 1569 and supported by a revolutionary, near vertical, elliptical-shaped arch system. The bridge design was believed to have been sketched by Michelango, but the master architect and sculptor Bartolomeo Ammanati had completed the actual construction. Now the renowned arches, upon whose scientific design bridges around the world had been based, were just so many heaps of debris lying in the river between the piers that had supported them for centuries. Even Ponte Vecchio had not escaped unscathed. Although the two- and three-storey tall shops that formed the bridge's distinctive outer walls and confined its crossing span to a narrow lane barely wide enough for an ox cart to pass through appeared intact, the approaches and the buildings that had fronted these had all been demolished. This rendered the bridge virtually impassable.

The destruction of the bridges and approaches seemed an unnecessary act of vandalism. Ostensibly, Florence was an open city, so declared by both the Germans and Allies in order to prevent its many architectural and other historic and artistic treasures being damaged. Having declared that "the whole city of Florence must rank as a work of art of the first importance," the Allies had taken pains to spare the city aerial or artillery bombardment.[2] Front-line troops were unable to shell obvious German targets and were restricted to the use of only rifles and machine guns. Discharging their projector infantry anti-tank (PIAT) launchers or mortars was strictly prohibited.[3]

Targets there were aplenty. Not two feet from where Galloway stood, the colossal barrel of the observatory's main telescope had been fully depressed and was being used by a Royal Canadian Regiment soldier to scour the streets and buildings for signs of the enemy. Unaware that the telescope's astrally intentioned optics pinned them as neatly as butterflies mounted on a collector's board, German paratroopers sauntered down streets hundreds of yards north of the Arno in tempting bunches that a salvo of mortar or artillery fire would savage. Although they reported the targets, no clearances for such shoots resulted. So the men in the observatory contented themselves primarily with using the telescope for sightseeing, including detailed examinations of the intricately lavish facades of Florence's trove of Renaissance buildings.[4]

Sometimes they used the telescope to monitor the goings-on of the other regiments holding the ten-mile-long Canadian sector. Immediately to the RCR's right, the Hastings and Prince Edward Regiment—a fellow 1st Canadian Infantry Brigade unit—was positioned. To the rear of the brigade's two forward regiments, the 48th Highlanders of Canada stood in reserve. Beyond the Hasty P's were the regiments of 2nd Canadian Infantry Brigade: the Seaforth Highlanders of Canada, the Princess Patricia's Canadian Light Infantry, and the Loyal Edmonton regiments. Farther south, and out of view of the telescope because of intervening hills, the 3rd Canadian Infantry Brigade stood some distance back from Florence to serve as divisional reserve.

After the bloody fighting in the Liri Valley, the division's veterans welcomed the quiet of this battleground. Since the end of the Liri Valley Battle in early June, the division had been refitting, reorganizing, and conducting training exercises to integrate newly arrived reinforcements, but the soldiers remained battle-weary. For the reinforcements, however, the sporadic German shelling, searching machine-gun fire, and sniper activity served as their first introduction to combat. The veterans were quick to remind any reinforcement unnerved by these minor hazards that they were fortunate their first taste of war occurred in such a "peaceful" setting.[5]

Not that the front was entirely inactive. Around the clock could be heard the fitful chatter of machine guns and the crack of rifles. Down along the riverbank, Canadians and Germans traded gunfire on a regular, if desultory, basis. Snipers from both sides posed a constant threat. When a German sniper killed a soldier in the Hasty P's, the regiment's snipers were duly unleashed to exact revenge. A deadly game of cat-and-mouse in this built-up area followed until the German sniper was killed.[6]

When the Loyal Edmonton Regiment had entered the line, it relieved the 2nd New Zealand Division's 28th Maori Battalion. During the hand-off, Edmonton commander Acting Lieutenant Colonel Jim Stone noted that the Maoris had loaded their trucks with a vast stock of ladies' shoes that they obviously intended for barter with civilians. Stone later visited a large villa with an eye to turning it into his headquarters. An American woman, who had married an Italian prior to the war, answered the door. The woman embarked immediately on a tirade about the indignities she had suffered by having to house "black people." Stone, suspecting that she and her husband were a couple of closet fascists, cut her off in mid-sentence and harshly lectured the woman about the Maoris and her own questionable Allied patriotism. "Who's your superior officer?" she demanded. Stone declared, "Madam, there's no officer in the world superior to me."[7]

That evening, the ever aggressive Stone ordered fighting patrols from 'A' and 'D' companies across the shallow Arno to test the 4th Parachute Division's alertness. One of the patrols bumped into some paratroopers and a firefight ensued that left Lieutenant J.C. Butler and two other ranks dead. Another three men were wounded.[8]

The next day, Stone was notified that the Edmontons' stay in the line was to be a short one. Even as other regiments from 2 CIB were still taking up positions in the front lines, Stone was out with a reconnaissance party to find a staging area for the Edmontons' forthcoming move to the rear. The party used the regiment's pioneer and engineering platoon's jeeps, one of which towed a trailer loaded with beehive bombs. Containing powerful plastic explosives, these bombs were beehive shaped to focus the blast against the wall of concrete pillboxes or other structures.

Stone told Captain R.S. Stephens and a lanky private named J.A. Foster to take the jeep with the trailer and check the suitability of some nearby buildings for concealing the regiment's vehicles. Stone then carried on in another jeep. He was about a half-mile down the road when a mighty explosion came from behind him. Stone U-turned and raced back. In the middle of the road was a house-sized hole. All he could see of the jeep and trailer was a jeep wheel lying on top of a nearby roof. Several Italians were wandering around dazed, with bleeding arms. Stone asked an old woman what happened.

"Tall boy, *minnen*," she replied, indicating that Foster had tripped a mine.

For the first time, Stone noticed stacks of Italian box mines lying alongside the road. A small wooden box packed with explosives, such mines detonated if the closed lid was opened. Alternatively, the detonator could be rigged to explode if an open lid was closed. Set up in this way, the mine could be buried in a road and any vehicle running over it would slam the lid shut and detonate the mine.

Foster had taken a mine and, while standing on top of the trailer containing the beehive mines, had opened one to examine the box's contents. The exploding mine had set off the entire stock of beehives. Stone thought a half-ton of explosive had gone off at once.

Stephens's body was lying nearby, head and one leg blown off. Of

Foster nothing remained but some hair and little bits of flesh. No trace of his identity tags could be found. Stone's men gathered what they could of the private in a pail. "We called it Foster and buried him," Stone said later.[9]

ON AUGUST 7, the day after the RCR moved into the line, 'A' Company was mortared. Major Sam Liddell, Lieutenant F.K. Wildfang, Regimental Sergeant Major D.P. Duffey, and several other men were wounded. The incident was a stark reminder that Florence's comparatively modern southern outskirts were not to be spared the destruction of German mortaring and shelling. Still, they were somewhat judicious about the selection of targets. The RCR's headquarters was a modern villa no more than nine hundred yards from the river. Despite the constant comings and goings that clearly betrayed the building's current use, the villa drew no German fire. Galloway was glad of this, for it was a lovely sixty-four-room mansion with so many lavishly comfortable bedrooms that most of the regimental staff had one to themselves.[10] A huge four-poster bed all but filled Galloway's bedroom. There was also "an immense wall portrait of a luscious nude reclining with all her ample charms revealed in full, living colour. The bathroom next door was the sunken pool variety in a beautiful marble environment, with erotic artwork to beguile the sensuous mind." There was also a library with "thousands of books, hundreds of them in English."[11]

The four staff officers took their meals "at a mammoth dining room with high-backed baronial chairs which gave the necessary post-prandial panache, as we sipped our cheap *vino rosso,* pretending in our minds, though not with our palates, that it was the best port."[12] Galloway wished life on the Florence front would not end too soon.

Not only the headquarters' staff enjoyed luxurious accommodations. Line companies were also comfortably fixed. 'A' Company was established in a Medici palace dating back to 1430, while 'B' Company occupied Aldous Huxley's Florence residence.[13]

Scout platoon commander Lieutenant Jimmy Quayle thought this the strangest war he had yet seen. Having waded ashore in Sicily, having survived Ortona and the Liri Valley, and having been twice wounded, he was a seasoned campaigner. Yet he had never before attempted to conduct surreptitious scouting operations on a riverbank opposite German positions while, all around his furtively moving scouts, Florentines thronged the streets, totally unconcerned for their personal safety. Stunningly attractive women wearing bright print dresses strolled with typical Italian haughtiness past Quayle as he crouched in a shop doorway for protection.

The peaceful atmosphere was illusory. When Quayle was on the verge of joining the throngs—rather than creeping along like the cautious combat veteran he was—there was the sudden scream of an incoming shell. As the smoke rolled up from the street, women, children, and old men lay on the cobblestones bleeding and dying before his eyes. An hour or two later, the casualties had been picked up, the street washed clean, and the Florentines meandered again with careless abandon. Soon a shot was fired from a nearby apartment building roof and someone pitched dead to the sidewalk. This time everyone fled for cover, but they didn't stay there long.

This urban battleground's surrealism made it hard for the soldiers to keep vigilant. One of Quayle's men got shot in the upper arm while carelessly looting a camera store situated on the Arno's south bank in plain view of the Germans. When Quayle visited him at the Regimental Aid Post, the painstricken soldier grinned at him sheepishly. "That was a kind of dumb thing I did," he said.[14]

Quayle knew that the man meant getting shot was dumb, not the act of looting. In impoverished Sicily and southern Italy, there had been little worth taking, except food and wine. The pickings improved greatly, however, once the Canadians marched north of Rome. Although army regulations prohibited looting, Eighth Army's military police and most of its officers generally turned a blind eye so long as the thievery was kept somewhat in check. Suffering a chronic shortage of reinforcements, commanders were loath to send men off to the stockades for such infractions as looting.

Captain Howard Mitchell of the Saskatoon Light Infantry—the regiment that provided heavy machine-gun, 4.2-inch mortar, and anti-aircraft gun support to 1 CID—spent his second day on the Florence front censoring his company's mail. Usually this consisted of simple letters home. This day, however, there was a small stack of identically sized small soft parcels. Dismayed at the thought of unwrapping and rewrapping each package, he simply franked them all and sent them off uninspected. The next day, a virtually identical stack of small parcels awaited his attention.

Mitchell demanded an explanation from the company sergeant major, who shrugged and said, "The boys found a warehouse of silk, Sir. They are sending some of it home." Mitchell offered no rebuke; he only wished he had procured some of the silk for himself.[15]

Soldiers didn't just limit themselves to stealing civilian property. En route to Florence, 1 CID had debussed near Siena and advanced to the front in a series of night marches in order to avoid detection by enemy spies. Night marches were unpopular because the men could only rest during the day and many, like Quayle, found it impossible to sleep when the sun was up. This was particularly true in the intense Italian summer heat. A couple of days into the march, Quayle was so tired he discovered that it was possible to catnap while actually marching, so long as he ensured that one of his men reined him in whenever he wandered off the road towards the ditch.

If the scouts only had a jeep, he lamented, they could take turns sleeping in the jeep and marching. The day after the RCR relieved the South African Division in Florence, some of his men appeared with a rattletrap jeep. "Found it, Sir," the sergeant in charge of the group said, totally deadpan. One man pointed at the jeep. "Someone has even filed off all the markings, Sir. Must have been stolen."

Quayle said gravely, "Must have been. No doubt at all." Quayle soon delighted in driving by foot-bound RCR captains and majors while he, a mere lieutenant, possessed a private limousine.[16]

QUAYLE WAS CAREFUL to stay out of areas of Florence where Italian anti-Fascists and Fascists were still fighting each other. For in the midst of the conventional war being fought by the Allies and the Germans, there waged a fierce guerilla war.

On July 25, 1943, the Italian government's Grand Council had arrested Benito Mussolini and reinstated the monarchical regime under King Vittorio Emanuele III. The king empowered seventy-one-year-old Marshal Pietro Badoglio, a suddenly reformed ex-Fascist, to form a new government and officially dissolved the Fascist Party. Realizing their Italian ally was planning to capitulate to the Allies, the Germans had immediately imposed an occupation force. On September 8, Italy had surrendered and the king, Badoglio, and other key members of the government fled Rome to avoid imprisonment. Boarding a ship at Ortona in the early morning hours of September 11, they escaped to a port behind the advancing Allied front lines.

The next day, German paratroopers, under command of SS Hauptsturmführer Otto Skorzeny, freed Mussolini from a remote jail in the Gran Sasso Mountains and spirited him to northern Italy. On September 17, he assumed leadership of the Republican Fascist Party and the presidency of a pro-German puppet nation—the Italian Social Republic—that claimed to be Italy's legitimate government.

Meanwhile, in Rome on September 9, an anti-Fascist coalition had formed the Committee of National Liberation and called for a general uprising against the Nazi-Fascist forces. A partisan resistance movement was born that immediately undertook guerilla and clandestine intelligence operations against the German occupation forces and those Italians serving in Fascist military and police units. With the liberation of Rome on June 4, 1944, partisan morale soared and thousands of Italians joined their ranks.

Advancing north from Rome, the Allies entered ground in which many partisan bands operated. Previously, Canadians had seldom met partisan forces, but on Florence's southern outskirts they were numerous. Partisan snipers routinely exchanged rifle fire with Fascist infiltrators. The two Italian factions also tangled in fierce melees for control of buildings within the Canadian perimeter.[17]

The Seaforth Highlanders of Canada saw their first partisan fighters on the second day in the line. Rugged, bearded men, wearing a raggle-taggle assortment of civilian and military clothing, the partisans used their local knowledge to assist Seaforth operations against the Germans across the river. The partisans provided intelligence on the strengths and identities of opposing German forces, their dispositions, and locations of minefields. They also accompanied reconnaissance patrols that slipped across the river to gather intelligence and take prisoners. The partisans sought little in exchange. "Food and supplies of arms and ammunition sufficient to enable them to carry on their underground war against the Germans were their prime requisites, and given these they would infiltrate back through the enemy's lines to harass *Tedeschi* in their own unique way."[18]

Back in the RCR sector, Quayle lined up behind some partisans in the regimental kitchen for a meal. A bearded partisan wandered in casually with a submachine gun under his arm and emptied a full magazine into one of the waiting men. "As the bleeding, dying victim lay on the floor, the machine-gunner said, 'Fascist,' and walked off."[19] The other partisans continued calmly waiting for their food, ignoring the regimental cook's demands that the executioner be brought back to clean up the mess he had made of the kitchen. No pursuit was attempted and it was Canadians who carried off the corpse and scrubbed the blood off the floor and walls.

BEFORE MOVING to Florence, the Canadians had been ordered to remove all their unit identification patches and markers so spies would have no idea which Eighth Army division was in the line. Upon arrival, however, the men were ordered to sew everything back on again. This made little sense if Florence was, as the rumour mill insisted, the base for the next major offensive—the much anticipated attack on the Gothic Line. Most everyone in I Canadian Corps expected to play a key role in any Eighth Army offensive against the reportedly formidable final German defensive line. Yet after 1 CID had spent three days on the Florence front, boldly displaying its identity, there could be no question that the Germans were aware of their presence. Which would mean the enemy knew precisely where the major offensive would be launched.

On August 7, Seaforth Sergeant Bill Worton was left baffled by his superiors when several divisional staff officers started deliberately throwing Canadian cigarette packages and other items bearing distinctive Canadian markings into the sluggishly flowing Arno. As the packages drifted slowly across to the German side of the river, there was no doubt they would be quickly retrieved as a valuable intelligence find.

Worton was equally perplexed by an order for his three-inch mortar platoon to prepare a fire mission against a German target on the other side of the river, seemingly in defiance of the open-city policy. Dutifully, after dinner, the mortar platoon drove its trucks out into the middle of a field that stood in plain view of the German defences. The truck ran over a small mine and Sergeant Al Warrington, who was walking alongside it, was blown over a wall into a small courtyard. To his surprise, he suffered only a few bruises.

The men started hacking firing pits out of the sun-hardened ground. Worton's hands were soon blistered and bleeding as he banged away at the unyielding earth with a shovel. "I hope we got shells for this fucking pit," he grumbled to Lance Corporal Gordon Winning. "I hope we got some real targets to fire on after this." He also hoped that the Germans wouldn't see them out there on the bald prairie digging this absurdly exposed position. It took all night to get the holes dug, the mortars squared away, and the ammunition stowed in adjacent holes. Exhausted, Worton and the others flopped down an hour before dawn to get what sleep they might. As the sun started edging over the horizon, an officer woke Worton and ordered the mortars broken down. "We're moving out," he said.

"What about the shoot?" Worton demanded.

"Forget the shoot. Move it." When asked where they were going, the officer replied, "We'll all know when we get there."[20]

An hour later, the mortar platoon drove away from Florence with no idea where they were bound. As he bounced along in the front seat, Worton started unstitching the regimental, divisional, and other identification insignia that distinguished him as Canadian. Once more, it appeared, I Canadian Corps was supposed to disappear into the midst of Eighth Army, leaving no trace of its movements to be detected by German intelligence. The sojourn of 1st Canadian Infantry Division in Florence was over and the Canadians were once again marching off in secret towards an unknown battlefield.*

* Three days after the Canadians left Florence, the 4th Parachute Division evacuated the rest of the city and withdrew to the north.

[2]

A Very Happy Family

BASED ON THE COLOUR of their shoulder patches, 1st Canadian Infantry Division and 5th Canadian Armoured Division were respectively nicknamed the Red Patch Devils and the Mighty Maroon Machine—each moniker considered by the Canadians serving in its numbers as due recognition of their fighting prowess. Together, the two divisions constituted the fighting teeth of I Canadian Corps. While General Harold Alexander, Deputy Supreme Commander, Mediterranean, and Eighth Army's General Sir Oliver Leese genuinely admired and respected the combat record of the two divisions, the same could not be said of their overall commander. Both wanted to get rid of Lieutenant General E.L.M. (Tommy) Burns.

No sooner had the last shots been fired in the Liri Valley than Burns found himself fighting to save his career and his command. The opening skirmish in this struggle came on June 5, the day after Rome fell, when he reported to the Eighth Army commander. Both Burns and Leese were decorated World War I veterans, but that was where any similarity between the two men ended. Burns was small, intensely introverted, and rather shy. The forty-seven-year-old appeared to be in deadly earnest about everything and was seldom known to either laugh or even crack a smile. Leese was Burns's polar opposite—a big, rangy, forty-nine-year-old Coldstream Guards veteran noted for his outgoing manner, big-toothed guffawing laugh, ribald sense of humour, informal style and dress, and somewhat uncharacteristic interest in botany. In his usual blunt, straightforward manner, Burns asked Leese directly whether the rumours that the general was dissatisfied with his performance were true. Leese, taken aback by the directness of Burns's approach, dissembled, asking instead whether Burns thought himself up to the job. Burns replied that he doubted his own ability not at all.[1] There the conversation rested.

"Neither Burns nor his Corps staff are up to [Eighth] Army standards," Leese wrote within days of the meeting.[2] Then, on June 28, Leese took his complaints to Alexander, who duly fired off a cable to Chief of the Imperial General Staff, Field Marshal Sir Alan Brooke. "I am very concerned about the future of the Canadian Corps," Alexander began. "There is no doubt at all that the present position regarding Command is most unsatisfactory.... I am not sure you know Burns well. He is intelligent and easy to work with but he is sadly lacking in tactical sense and has very little personality and no (repeat no) power of command. It might be possible in time to develop a tactical sense in him but personality and power of command are as you know qualities which simply cannot be taught to a man of his age. Burns's shortcomings as a Corps Commander place Leese in a very difficult position regarding the employment of the Canadian Corps since he must either give them a task beyond the powers of the Commander or below the capacity of the troops.

"These are the facts. The conclusions are obvious," Alexander ended, and he proposed that I Canadian Corps be disbanded. "Between ourselves," he added, "I believe the Canadian Divisions out here have no opinion or feeling for their Corps, and would I am sure, though they might not admit it if questioned, as soon be in a British Corps, if they would not in fact prefer it."[3]

Alexander and Leese had always opposed I Canadian Corps's creation because it would restrict their ability to deploy the two Canadian divisions in Italy in whatever way most benefited Eighth Army operations. If the corps could now be disbanded or brought under British command, flexible use of the Canadian divisions would be assured.

Standard British Army corps strength was three divisions. I Canadian Corps had just two divisions. This reduced strength meant it must always fight on a narrower front than other Eighth Army corps. The obvious solution to this problem was to add another division to I Canadian Corps's strength, but Canadian Military Headquarters (CMHQ) in London had no interest in sending another Canadian division to the secondary Italian front. And Leese and Alexander were "loath to put a British or Indian Division under a headquarters in which [Leese] did not have full confidence."[4]

The substance of Alexander's cable reached First Canadian Army commander General Harry Crerar in London. Recognizing that Burns's alleged shortcomings were being used to justify I Canadian Corps's dissolution, he decided an investigation of the problems in Italy was necessary. Crerar dispatched CMHQ Chief of Staff Lieutenant General Ken Stuart to determine if Burns had the confidence of his subordinates. If he did not, then Burns would have to be replaced. At the same time, Stuart was to inform the British "at the outset... that the dissolution of I Canadian Corps is not a prospect even worth discussing."[5]

A VETERAN MILITARY INTRIGUER, Stuart, together with Crerar, had been deeply complicit in bringing about former First Canadian Army commander Lieutenant General Andrew McNaughton's forced resignation in December 1943, paving the way for Crerar to succeed him. The fifty-two-year-old officer had graduated from Royal Military College a couple of years behind Crerar and had seen World War I service in the Royal Canadian Engineers. He had become CMHQ Chief of Staff on the heels of McNaughton's resignation.

Stuart faced an extremely delicate task. He must interview two Canadian divisional officers regarding their superior's fitness without creating a situation that could leave Burns beholden to them for not forcing his replacement.

Arriving in Algiers on July 9, Stuart was joined by Lieutenant Colonel John Buchan, Lord Tweedsmuir, the Canadian liaison officer to Eighth Army. The next morning the two men flew to Eighth Army HQ at Lake Trasimeno, north of Rome. Leese spent three hours detailing the failings of I Canadian Corps in the breakout from the Hitler

Line phase of the Liri Valley Battle, as well as Burns's supposed shortcomings. He suggested that Major General Charles Keightley, presently commanding the British 78th Division, replace Burns.

Stuart agreed that if the allegations Leese made against Burns were proven then he must be replaced, but he flatly rejected any British officer being given command unless a suitable Canadian could not be found. In his final report, Stuart wrote: "I said, however, that I was not entirely satisfied that the picture painted to me about Burns was an accurate picture. I said that I proposed to proceed to Canadian Corps at once and make my own investigation. I pointed out that Burns was not lacking in power of command but admitted that he had perhaps been diffident about exercising it in the recent operation." Stuart suggested that during a first operation in which the divisional generals were both more battle experienced than the corps commander such diffidence was perhaps appropriate. He further rejected the accusation that Burns lacked tactical sense. Both Stuart and Crerar had served alongside Burns for years and knew him well. "I said that . . . perhaps General Leese was confusing lack of operational experience with lack of tactical sense." He also found suspect the accusation that divisional commanders and other principal staff officers had lost faith in Burns. Stuart intended to get to the heart of that allegation.

Flying to Caserta, he joined Burns in the I Canadian Corps officers' mess for dinner and then the two men adjourned to Burns's quarters for a conversation that lasted well into the night. Burns, who had thought Leese in agreement that he could correct the corps's weaknesses and "make a success" of it, was dismayed to hear the extent of his commander's lack of confidence in him. The only way to address the "alleged lack of confidence issue," Stuart said, was for him to meet the two divisional commanders and two principal staff officers to find out if they believed Burns up to the job. If not, either Burns or the dissenting subordinates would have to go. He promised to inform Burns of the results of his inquiry as soon as the interviews were concluded.[6]

Stuart interviewed four officers individually on the morning of

July 13: I CID's Major General Chris Vokes; 5 CAD's Major General Burt Hoffmeister; corps general staff officer Brigadier Desmond Smith; and Burns's senior administrative staff officer, Brigadier J.F. Lister. Vokes found Stuart "sitting behind a desk looking for all the world like the headmaster at a school about to chastise a naughty pupil." Instead of discussing the Italian campaign, Stuart set about heaping lengthy praise upon 3rd Canadian Infantry Division's performance during D-Day and the subsequent fighting in Normandy. Vokes inferred that Stuart believed "the Canadians in Italy had seen no fighting to compare." Then, abruptly, Stuart demanded: "What is your opinion of General Burns?"

Vokes was taken aback. The forty-year-old officer had graduated from Royal Military College in 1925 and throughout his military career had been taught that it was both improper and unethical for a junior officer to openly criticize a senior officer, or to be asked to do so. He said as much to Stuart, who ordered him to comply. After registering a formal protest, Vokes expressed his opinion bluntly. Burns "seldom appears cheerful and his 'sad sack' manner repels subordinates and senior commanders alike," he said. Nothing seemed to spark any enthusiasm in Burns and he was incapable of making subordinates feel enthusiastic about performing their duties or conducting operations. "He seems to lack the human touch ... necessary in the successful command of fighting troops. All the British corps commanders in Italy are cheerful extroverts as part of their stock-in-trade. By comparison General Burns is a drab commander. It may arise from his excessive shyness, but he is known throughout the hierarchy of the Eighth Army as a general who lacks personality."

Vokes thought Burns—who had never held divisional or even brigade command—lacked the tactical perspective such battle experience would have provided. "As time goes on, he may better this tactical perspective but I doubt it, as he seems unwilling to accept advice from, or to give sound advice to, his subordinate commanders." He concluded that he felt Burns "will never make a good corps commander."

Stuart looked to Vokes as if he had been kicked with a fork. "Generals Alexander and Leese have expressed a similar opinion," Stuart said icily. "They have requested General Burns be replaced. I disagree with them and I disagree with your opinion. Will you give Burns your loyal support?"

Unhesitatingly, Vokes answered that, "so long as I think he is performing in an adequate manner as corps commander," he would support Burns.[7] Vokes left certain that Burns's command was assured, but the decision wrong-headed. He thought Burns should be replaced and, in the absence of a suitable Canadian officer, the replacement should be "an experienced British general in whom both Alexander and Leese reposed confidence."[8]

Also under protest, Hoffmeister, who at thirty-seven was the youngest Canadian general officer in Italy and one of the youngest in the Canadian army, similarly damned Burns's abilities. Stuart's written report to Crerar on July 21, however, gave an entirely different account of his meetings with these two officers. "Each [divisional commander]... was quite outspoken about the Corps Commander," he wrote. "They respected his tremendous fairness in all his dealings with their Divisions. They respected his tactical knowledge and found no fault whatever in any tactical decision he had made during the last operation... They expressed themselves as being quite happy to go into the next operation under Burns and his present staff. They both hoped that I would speak to Burns regarding his manner and personality, and such was the only criticism I got from either.

"My conversations with the two principal staff officers were productive of exactly the same results except that both were even more emphatic... regarding their complete confidence in the ability of the Corps Commander to make sound tactical and other decisions."[9]

When Stuart presented this sanitized version of his discussions to the corps commander, Burns promised solemnly that, "if given another chance, he would make a success of any operation entrusted to the Canadian Corps." Stuart said he would propose to Leese and Alexander that Burns be allowed to prove himself in another operation. Should his performance at that time be found wanting, however, Stuart would "initiate action to have him replaced at once."[10]

En route to Lake Trasimeno, Stuart wrote: "As a result of meeting these officers and talking with them I was more convinced that there was nothing wrong with the Canadian Corps and that they would give an excellent account of themselves in any future operations. They were, I felt, a very happy family. There were excellent relations between Corps and Divisional staffs and the Corps staff itself was, I felt, a congenial and happy staff. In these circumstances, the alleged lack of confidence issue was a washout in so far as I was concerned."[11]

STUART REPORTED THAT his final meeting with Leese on July 14 "began in rather a stormy fashion." Leese "lost his temper and accused me of criticizing many of the decisions he had made in respect to the Canadian Corps and even went so far as to suggest that I was trying to command the Eighth Army." Stuart welcomed Leese's loss of control, for it made it "easy to refute in turn every statement he had made. Also he was obviously rather ashamed of his outburst, which made the remainder of the conversation much more useful. I cannot say that he accepted the decision in good part, but he accepted it because he felt there was no alternative. We parted the same good friends that we have been for a number of years and I promised to return and see him if possible during, or immediately after, the next operation in which the Canadian Corps is engaged."[12]

Politeness aside, Leese was still fuming. No sooner was Stuart out the door than Leese fired off a letter to him summarizing Stuart's purported findings from his visit to Canadian Corps headquarters and his proposals for the future. "I am therefore left with no alternative except to carry on with Burns, in whom I have no confidence," he declared. "It is, of course, you and your Government alone who can appoint the Commander of a Canadian Corps, yet your decision cannot relieve me of the ultimate responsibility for the lives of Canadian troops serving with this Army . . . The decision to retain Burns makes my task as Army Commander more difficult. It makes my Army inflexible, since at any rate at first I shall not be able to employ Burns on any task which I consider beyond him. This is a further serious handicap, as through my lack of faith in their Commander, I may be prevented from employing my best troops on the most critical task. As I promised, everything in my power will be done so that the great prestige of Canadian troops may not be prejudiced.

"While I will do my very best to train Burns, I must frankly say this with very little confidence." Leese, ever the British gentleman, then closed: "I so much enjoyed having you to stay and do hope you will come to see us again whenever you can."[13] To his wife, Leese complained that Stuart "was not helpful about Burns. I shall, I am afraid, have to keep him, which will make this much more difficult as he is not up to standard & I do not believe in him." He added that Stuart was "tiresome" and "very odd." Leese thought Stuart had come to Italy with the intention "of forcing me to give Burns a second chance, rather like a second helping of suet pudding!"[14]

AT BEST, Lieutenant General Tommy Burns was on probation. If I Canadian Corps fought its next battle well, Burns would keep his command. If it faltered, he would be dismissed. The psychological burden on Burns's shoulders was, he wrote General Harry Crerar, "pretty shaking to me personally.... However, I look to the future to put the matter out of question."[15] Masking his inner anxieties, the dour lieutenant general betrayed no outward behavioural change. He continued to obsess over meticulous administrative details best left to subordinate staff officers and remained a stickler for the display of correct military form and protocol.

Yet Burns was no fool. His assessment of the root causes of the corps's failure in the pursuit phase that followed the breaching of the Hitler Line on May 24 was typically thorough. The prime requisite, he wrote, was speed. This called for "*bold* action—taking risks which in other circumstances might be reckless" in order to prevent the enemy from breaking off contact and having sufficient time to establish new defensive lines or to mount a counterattack. During the pursuit phase, 5th Canadian Armoured Division, particularly 11th Canadian Infantry Brigade, plodded forward while spending far too long building firm bases to meet counterattacks rather than plunging ahead to maintain contact with the Germans and deny them time to reorganize.[16]

Burns was gravely concerned about 5 CAD's inherent combat organization, which conformed to traditional Commonwealth doctrine regarding strength and unit composition. This meant that 5 CAD fielded two brigades—5th Canadian Armoured Brigade and 11th Canadian Infantry Brigade—supported by four artillery regiments, a motorized reconnaissance regiment (the Westminsters), engineering companies, and other miscellaneous specialized units. Neither tanks nor infantry could long survive on the modern battlefield without the support of the other, so the two brigades were equally balanced in size.

There was, however, another organizational tenet fundamental to armoured divisions. Being a corps's cavalry, they were supposed to dash through breaches opened by infantry divisions and cause chaos in the enemy's rear. The armoured division's raison d'être was to be extremely mobile and to deny the enemy opportunity to undertake an orderly withdrawal or to regroup. By cutting enemy units off from each other, overrunning artillery and headquarters units, and seizing bridge crossings, the division was to create general panic that reduced orderly withdrawal into rout.

5th Canadian Armoured Brigade's Shermans provided the division's speed and hitting power, while the Westminster (Motorized) Regiment, with its Bren carrier- and armoured-personnel-carrier-borne infantry companies, could operate alongside the tanks. If necessary, the footsloggers of 11 CIB could ride atop the tanks in the manner the Soviet Army used to good effect in the open steppe country of the Eastern Front. Generally, though, 11 CIB's role was to open holes for the tanks to drive through and then to mop up enemy units or strongpoints that the armoured brigade bypassed.

While this composition of armoured divisions might have been sound during the North African campaign, the British quickly realized that it ill suited operations in Italy. The rugged hills, narrow valleys crisscrossed by endless series of rivers and irrigation canals, and dense foliage of olive orchards and vineyards made it virtually impossible for armoured divisions to function in accordance with standard operating doctrine. Tanks advancing without infantry protecting their flanks were routinely shot to pieces by hidden antitank guns or infantry armed with Faustpatrone antitank rocket launchers.

Infantry perched precariously on tanks faced slaughter by enemy machine-gunners. When 5 CAD broke out from the Hitler Line, its armoured brigade was unable to charge forward on its own and the division was too weak in infantry regiments to quickly overcome determined German opposition.

Burns had soon recognized the problem and rushed regiments from 1st Canadian Infantry Division forward to help. But these regiments were badly depleted by casualties suffered at the Hitler Line. When the battle was over, Burns knew that what 5 CAD really needed was more inherent infantry. On June 3, he advised Canadian Military Headquarters in London that 5 CAD needed two Canadian infantry brigades to work in succession with the armoured brigade, a reorganization that would mirror the constitution of British armoured divisions in Italy. In the British case, the 61st Infantry Brigade had been attached to the British 6th Armoured Division, while the 24th Independent Guards Brigade had joined the 6th South African Armoured Division.[17]

General Oliver Leese and General Harold Alexander supported Burns's suggestion. The Chief of the Imperial General Staff, Field Marshal Sir Alan Brooke, however, scuttled this plan. He insisted that any reinforcement units coming from Canada must serve in Western Europe.[18]

Leese then suggested that Burns create a second infantry brigade out of units already in I Canadian Corps. The Westminster (Motorized) Regiment could serve as the brigade's senior regiment and the Royal Canadian Dragoons—the corps's reconnaissance regiment—could be unhorsed from their armoured cars to form another regiment. The light anti-aircraft regiment, little utilized now that the Luftwaffe had been largely chased from Italy's skies, could be converted into the third regiment to form a complete brigade. Leese did not think it problematic that this plan actually only provided 5 CAD with two new regiments, since the Westminsters were already inherent to the division.[19]

Burns sought a more radical reorganization that would also reunite all Canadian units in Italy under his command. On February 9, 1944,

1st Canadian Armoured Brigade had been removed from I Canadian Corps and attached to the British XIII Corps in response to criticism by Major General Chris Vokes that this brigade had poorly supported his division's operations on the Ortona front. Burns now proposed that this brigade be returned to 1st Canadian Infantry Division. One of Vokes's three infantry brigades would then be transferred to 5 CAD. This reorganization would transform 1 CID into an armoured division, while simultaneously giving 5 CAD the extra infantry brigade necessary to align it with Eighth Army's new organizational model.

Leese refused to release the Canadian tankers from XIII Corps. He considered 1 CAB "the most experienced armoured brigade in Italy and therefore in great demand."[20] Stonewalled by Leese, Burns had to abandon his plan and implement the alternative proposed by the Eighth Army commander.

However, rather than dismounting the Royal Canadian Dragoons, Burns ordered 1 CID's reconnaissance regiment, the 4th Princess Louise Dragoon Guards, unhorsed to serve in 5 CAD's new infantry brigade alongside the Westminsters. The 89th and 109th Light Anti-Aircraft Batteries of the 1st Canadian Light Anti-Aircraft Regiment would provide the personnel for the third infantry regiment. With no infantry heritage to draw upon, the new unit provisionally retained its anti-aircraft regiment designation while taking on an infantry role. Burns, meanwhile, transferred the RCD from his direct control to Vokes, so that the divisional commander retained a reconnaissance regiment.[21]

The new brigade—12th Canadian Infantry Brigade—was officially formed on July 13. Burns estimated that it added 79 officers and 1,269 other ranks to 5 CAD's immediate fighting strength—less than a tenth of the division's normal established strength of 750 officers and 14,219 other ranks. However, as the brigade's personnel were all to serve as front-line combatants, the division's fighting strength was increased by a full third.[22]

Least affected by assignment to 12 CIB was the Westminster Regiment, which kept its motorized nature and simply shifted from independent status to being under brigade command. It was another matter for the Princess Louise Dragoon Guards. They not only lost their treasured armoured cars, but were also transferred from one division to another. Major General Chris Vokes was infuriated. He considered the Dragoons "a first-class, well-trained and experienced unit. I vehemently protested the removal of this unit from my command but received very short shrift."[23]

The regiment's officers and other ranks were stunned by the news. Of the armoured cars, the regiment's war diarist wrote: "Those were our homes for a long time, and no cavalryman ever felt sadder at losing a faithful and tried mount."[24] That very night the officers held a wake where "much vino was consumed in an effort to neutralize the pains of frustration, despair, and complete loss of morale." A barrage of Very light signal flares, fired off in protest, soon lit the night. Tipsy officers were at a loss to control the demonstrating soldiers, but fortunately no casualties or damage resulted.[25]

July 13 was dubbed "Black Thursday" by the PLDG. The next day, when Vokes attended a regimental farewell parade, a fresh grave stood in front of the mess. Painted on a cross were the words: "R.I.P., 4 Cdn Recce Regt. (4 P.L.D.G.) 13 Jul 44—STABBED IN THE BACK."[26] The PLDG officers invited their counterparts from other divisional regiments to a final cocktail party that evening. Again the men expressed their feelings by setting the sky red, white, and green with flares. And, recorded the war diarist, "our ... celebration was augmented by the L.A.A. Regiment [1st Canadian Light Anti-Aircraft Regiment], whose barrage of Bofors ammunition considerably added to the display."[27]

Although the anti-aircraft regiment was already slated for disbanding, its men had served as gunners for four years. Now they were to fight as infantry, the most dangerous role on the battlefield and one for which they were untrained. Lacking a regimental name, they coined their own prophetic one—the Slaughterhouse Battalion.[28]

On July 15, the two regiments joined 5 CAD at Ciaizzo, its base in the Volturno Valley. This was the last time the PLDG travelled in their armoured cars. Two days later, the vehicles were surrendered and they began infantry training. For twenty-three-year-old Sergeant Gordon McGregor, the transition from armour to infantry was particularly difficult. While working as a logger near Kamloops, B.C.,

McGregor had severed a tendon in his ankle with a chainsaw blade. The injury made it agonizing for McGregor to march more than about ten miles at a time. It was because of this injury that he had been transferred from the Seaforth Highlanders of Canada to the PLDG. Now he was back on foot and marching was proving as painful as ever.[29]

BURNS KNEW THAT IF 12 CIB were to be melded into an effective fighting force it needed a veteran brigadier in command. He decided on 1st Canadian Infantry Brigade's Brigadier Dan Spry. Noted for Boy Scout politeness and a gentlemanly manner, Spry had proven himself both concerned about the men under his command and an extremely capable fighting commander.

Allan Calder, a Saskatoon Light Infantry brigadier, replaced Spry as commander of 1 CIB. Vokes didn't know Calder and was concerned that the officer had no battlefield experience. However, he took an instant liking to Calder and decided that "although I might have to lend a helping hand during his first battle or two, it seemed . . . he had the makings of a good brigade commander."[30]

The Westminsters had a steady, proven hand in Lieutenant Colonel Gordon Corbould, while the Princess Louise Dragoons Guards were slated to lose Lieutenant Colonel Fred Dean Adams to promotion elsewhere. He was to be replaced by the regiment's second-in-command, Major Bill Darling. As for the 1st Canadian Light Anti-Aircraft Regiment, the veteran infantry commander Lieutenant Colonel W. Clement Dick took charge. Dick faced the difficult task of not only transforming the gunners into infantrymen, but also instilling a sense of esprit de corps unsupported by any links to traditional regimental pride.[31]

Dick knew one thing for certain—this regimental name problem needed immediate addressing. He wanted a highland designation because the trappings of kilts, bagpipes, and other Scottish garb would provide an instant regimental identity. Lieutenant Colonel Ian Johnston, commander of the 48th Highlanders of Canada, endorsed the plan and suggested that the welfare organization of the 48th Highlanders back in Canada "could very well look after a second battalion overseas." At a practical level, Spry noted in a July 20 letter, "shoulder titles and cap badges are available in this theatre" if the regiment became a 48th Highlander one. Dick liked the idea, but wanting a backup plan, he suggested the new unit might alternatively be designated the Lanark and Renfrew Scottish Regiment, after an unmobilized Ontario regiment.[32]

Although Spry and Dick tried to push the name issue through, CMHQ and Ottawa had to grant final approval and dragged their heels over the matter. It soon became evident that the new regiment would fight its first infantry battle wearing the shoulder flashes of an anti-aircraft regiment. Although the majority of its men were former 1st Light Anti-Aircraft Regiment gunners, a nucleus of experienced infantrymen was attached to provide the infantry knowledge necessary to quickly instil infantry skills and experience. The veteran infantrymen were drawn from convalescent centres and reinforcement depots.

SERGEANT FRED CEDERBERG of the Cape Breton Highlanders had been struck down in late May by both jaundice and malaria. Since his recovery, the tall twenty-one-year-old had been sent to the replacement depot in Avellino. When Cederberg was ordered to the anti-aircraft regiment, he groaned at the news.

"I have no choice, my boy," the assigning officer said sympathetically, "none at all. My orders—along with every other holding unit CO—is to ship up one battle-experienced sergeant and one corporal at a minimum. And you're the only three-striper I've got on strength."[33]

When Cederberg asked if his friend Corporal Albert MacNeil could go as the corporal, the captain agreed. That night, the two soldiers polished off a bottle of Seagram's VO on the grass outside their barracks. The next day, they trucked to their new assignment. "Welcome to the outfit without a name," Sergeant Scotty Morrison said, as he logged them in. "According to headquarters we're supposed to get 10 officers and 156 men. You're among the first." He handed the men each a Thompson submachine gun and showed them to their quarters in the Bren carrier platoon, which was Morrison's own unit. "Like I said," Morrison reiterated, "we got no name, so we're kind of screwed up. But it'll all fall into place."[34]

Cederberg and MacNeil reported for duty to Sergeant Eddie Kerr, an antitank regiment veteran, who said that the duty the gunners had seen previously had been one of endless tedium waiting to drive off German Luftwaffe planes that never came because the Allies dominated the Italian skies. It was up to the infantry veterans, like them, to show the gunners how to be infantrymen. "What's it all about?" he asked.

MacNeil, who had been wounded by shrapnel in the Liri Valley, picked up a handful of dirt and tossed it into the humid air. "Mostly an awful lot of fuckin' noise. You get used to it."[35]

A sergeant's mess party that night, which was intended to bring the infantry sergeants and artillery sergeants together, proved disastrous. Cederberg noticed "an invisible, frigid wall . . . between the newcomers and the remaining old battery sergeants. . . . The former line regiment infantry three-hookers were neatly but almost casually turned out, wearing their former unit patches. But those from the ack-ack batteries looked like British guardsmen. You could cut butter with the creases in their summer drill trousers. Their shoulder lanyards and hooks had been white-ohed, each tiny herringbone stripe done individually."

Sergeant Tommy Graham, a stocky newcomer who had won a Distinguished Conduct Medal during the Dieppe raid as a Royal Hamilton Light Infantry soldier, tossed loud jibes at the gunners that were cuttingly returned by a regimental sergeant major named Stinson. "You guys will forget all that chicken shit stuff," Graham growled, as he casually flicked one of the artilleryman's stripes with a finger.

Stinson snapped, "It's too bad you infantry people never learned to dress like proper soldiers. When I look at you, I sometimes think..." Graham's fist smacked into the man's mouth and the flood of words was replaced by blood.[36]

"You're all Canadians, you're all on the same side, and you all know what you have to do—help win a war we didn't start," a disgusted Lieutenant Colonel Dick scolded the sergeants in the morning. Hoping to mollify the men, he added that plans were afoot for the battalion to become the "second" battalion of the 48th Highlanders. The sergeants all disliked that idea. "We may be a bastard unit," Sergeant Morrison said to Cederberg, "but I don't like being called a 'second' battalion."[37]

AS JULY TURNED into August, the no-name battalion learned the infantry trade from its experienced draft of officers and non-commissioned officers. They spent hours doing bayonet drill, learning how to cope in the hell of a minefield, practising on crudely constructed firing ranges to competently fire Lee Enfield rifles, Bren guns, Thompson submachine guns, PIATS, and two-inch mortars, and to handle grenades. Cederberg thought this training missed some essentials and said as much to Sergeant Eddie Kerr. The sergeant told him to do whatever he thought necessary to ready the Bren carrier platoon for combat.

"Every man's going to need a slit trench," Cederberg told them. "You should know how to convert a tank rut into a slit in twenty seconds. Or know that a lousy little fold in the ground can save your ass when the 88s or mortars come whistling in." Someone asked about ditches. Cederberg said he didn't like them. "They're too friggin' wide open at both ends. Like if a mortar slams into one, the shrapnel will slice the shit out of you. And there's always the chance some Jerries have them covered with machine guns."

Cederberg and MacNeil hammered home their lessons on getting down into the ground for shelter. MacNeil told the men, "Most of you guys think your weapon is your key to survival. Well, it isn't. And don't laugh when I tell you it's your friggin' shovel. Don't go anywhere without it."

"What about bayonet fighting?" one man asked.

In the ranks was veteran Loyal Edmonton Regiment Private Alex Greenwood. He was a thirty-one-year-old general store owner, father of three children, and a University of Alberta graduate. Greenwood said, "I never saw a bayonet fight. And I never took part in one. I've walked a long way. I've been shot at with a variety of deadly weapons. And I was wounded in the Hitler Line. But I don't know anything about bayonet fighting."

MacNeil added, "If I was that close to a Jerry, where we could use bayonets, one of us would have already surrendered."

The gunners fretted about what to do when confronted by a German tank, particularly the massive Tigers that were so feared by Allied soldiers. "If you got time," MacNeil said, "get your ass out of the area. Right quick."

But if you had a PIAT, one of the men persisted. "It depends on your choices," Cederberg said. "If it lumbers by you, like only twenty or twenty-five yards away, and your PIAT is loaded and there are no German infantry with it, take a shot. Go for the shoulder. Or better still, get it in the rear after it's gone by. Then, get your ass out of the area like Corporal MacNeil said."

Cederberg and MacNeil took No. 4 Platoon (Carriers) out that night on an exercise. The mosquitoes were so bad the men wore netting over their faces. Throughout the night, they showed "how to move up silently, cross a crest on their bellies, dig in and take up all-round defensive positions. To a man, they took it seriously, learning that loose shovels and weapons can make one helluva lot of noise in the stillness."

After the exercise was over, Cederberg told platoon commander Lieutenant Claude Nadeau, "They're going to make one damned good platoon."

The chain-smoking officer replied that he always knew they would. Cederberg said, "I bet you didn't notice they're beginning to walk like infantrymen, Mister Nadeau, did you?"

"How's that?" Nadeau asked.

"Well," Cederberg replied, "you know how artillerymen walk. Like they take themselves seriously. Like they'd like to know who owns the place. Infantrymen swagger a bit, like they don't give a goddamn who owns the place."[38]

BY THE END of July, the new brigade was as combat ready as was possible after such a short, intensive training period. From July 28 to August 7, I Canadian Corps had concentrated south of Florence, with 1 CID moving into the southern outskirts of Florence itself on August 5 and 6. The entire corps movement northward was undertaken with great secrecy, as all identifying markings on uniforms and vehicles were covered or removed.

That Eighth Army was massing divisions south of Florence for a major offensive against the Gothic Line seemed clear. A fiery pronouncement by General Alexander was read to 1 CID's troops just before they entered the Florence line. "Now we are completing an extensive regrouping in order to bring about the collapse of the enemy. This is taking place according to plan and it is my intention to proceed with the second and perhaps final stage of the destruction of the German forces in Italy. The eyes of the world and the hopes of all at home are upon us—we shall not disappoint them. We shall continue as we have begun to destroy the enemy wherever we find him and to march along the road to the last battles where final victory awaits us."[39]

While 1 CID deployed outside Florence, 5 CAD concentrated south of Lake Trasimeno. On August 1, Hoffmeister's headquarters and 11th Canadian Infantry Brigade had just arrived when new orders were circulated directing the division to relocate to a concentration area near Foligno and take over this sector from the 10th Indian Division. No sooner had 5 CAD started assembling there, however, than the division was instructed to remain in its concentration area and conduct such "intensive training . . . as security would permit."[40]

On August 8, 1 CID left Florence under "the strictest security regulations" and moved by truck thirty miles south to a staging area outside Siena. Two days later, the division rejoined I Canadian Corps in the Perugia-Foligno area. The Canadians were baffled as to the point of all this manoeuvring.[41] Chris Vokes just wanted a battle. "We came to Italy to fight, not to sit on our asses!" he declared.[42]

[3]

Inevitable Wrangles

WHERE TO FIGHT, or even whether to fight at all, was precisely the issue plaguing the Allied high command in Italy. By early summer, the pursuit of the German Tenth and Fourteenth armies to the north of Rome had slowed to another grinding, costly contest of attrition. Having quickly regrouped, the Germans defended every river crossing, mountain pass, and hill town lending itself to fortification. The past months of fighting up Italy's boot had proven the Germans to be masters of this form of strategic fighting withdrawal. This time, the Allies raced against a clock, for every day they were delayed south of the Apennines granted the Germans more time to transform the Gothic Line in the mountain range's heart into an impenetrable fortress.

When the U.S. Fifth and British Eighth armies first swept north from Rome and chased the Germans into Latium and Tuscany, General Harold Alexander, Deputy Supreme Commander, Mediterranean, had expected no serious opposition to be offered in front of the Apennines. As for the mountains themselves, he anticipated they would pose only a minor obstacle to the advance into the Po Valley beyond. At worst, Alexander expected to quickly breach the Gothic Line with a hasty frontal assault that would send the Germans reeling.[1]

This early optimism was dashed in late June, but not by German action. Instead, the culprit proved to be the Allied Combined Chiefs of Staff, who decided to rewrite the entire Allied Mediterranean strategic plan on the spur of the moment. Up to now, Alexander had been doggedly working towards an outcome far more ambitious than just winning Italy's liberation and destroying the German divisions there. Having drawn his two armies together on the western flank of Italy in order to capture Rome, Alexander believed that he now had "two highly organized and skilful Armies, capable of carrying out large scale attacks and mobile operations in the closest co-operation.... Neither the Apennines nor even the Alps should prove a serious obstacle to their enthusiasm and skill."[2]

Alexander envisioned achieving the grand design that had first prompted British Prime Minister Sir Winston Churchill to advocate invading Italy. If the two armies could drive through the Ljubljana Gap into Austria, Churchill and Alexander believed the war could be shortened and Austria denied to the advancing Soviet hordes. Churchill rightly feared that any Soviet-liberated country would be transformed into a Communist puppet state. But if Alexander's armies won the race to Vienna, a key central European nation would be preserved as a democratic bastion that would significantly weaken the Communist spectre.[3]

Churchill's post-war concerns, however, were little shared by the Combined Chiefs of Staff. They were more anxious to break the deadlock in Normandy, where the invading Allies had bogged down in the face of determined counterattacks from a gathering number of German infantry and panzer divisions. The chiefs had always envisioned launching an invasion of southern France on the heels of Operation Overlord. By mid-June, they decided this invasion was urgently required to relieve pressure on the forces in Normandy. To quickly cobble together an invasion force of sufficient strength to be assured of winning a beachhead and developing it, the chiefs decided that many divisions currently fighting in Italy must be reallocated to this purpose. On June 14, they ordered Alexander to detach the U.S. VI Corps and the Corps Expéditionnaire Français for the southern France invasion—codenamed Operation Dragoon. Virtually overnight, seven divisions were stripped from the U.S. Fifth Army, slashing it from 249,000 men to 153,000. Because mastery of the air over southern France had yet to be won, seventy per cent of Alexander's fighter and bomber squadrons were also assigned to Operation Dragoon.[4] With one sweeping order, the combined chiefs dealt a stunning blow to the Allied forces in Italy.

Sir Henry Maitland Wilson, Supreme Allied Commander, Mediterranean, Alexander, and Churchill all loudly protested the decision in vain. Notably, they were all British and Operation Dragoon was an American idea. It was as much a political stratagem as a military one, for it was intended to frustrate British intentions in the Mediterranean. President Franklin D. Roosevelt, U.S. Army Chief of Staff General George C. Marshall, and Supreme Commander, Allied Expeditionary Force General Dwight D. Eisenhower were in agreement that Britain's proposed Mediterranean strategy sought more to rebuild empire than defeat Germany. Not sharing Churchill's suspicion that the Soviet Union was intent on creating a post-war empire of its own, the Americans neither thought Austria a worthwhile objective nor the liberation of Italy militarily important.

In the American mind, the purpose of Allied forces in Italy was simply to tie down the German divisions there, preventing them from being shifted to Normandy. This narrow American focus had always resulted in a rift between the Americans and the British regarding the Italian campaign's grand scheme. As early as October 1943, Eisenhower, who served as Supreme Allied Commander, Mediterranean from the invasion of Sicily until January 8, 1944, had dismissed the Italian campaign as "a distinctly subsidiary operation."[5] His opinion remained unaltered in June. Marshall had no interest in Italy at all. What he wanted was the liberation of Marseilles, one of France's largest ports. Forty American divisions were whiling away the days in the United States for want of a major French port that could handle the unloading of the hundreds of ships required to carry such a massive military force across the Atlantic. Several French divisions were similarly stalled in place in North Africa.

Marshall also believed the Germans in Italy no longer constituted an effective fighting force capable of defending the Gothic Line. He expected they would retreat to the Alps, leaving Alexander punching only air. If Alexander advanced to a line running from Pisa to Rimini, he would control the Apennines and be standing on the edge of the Lombardy Plain. From here, the Allies could simply watch the Germans slink out of Italy without further bloodshed. By then, the German divisions leaving Italy would also be too depleted and late in withdrawing to have any effect on Allied operations in France.[6]

On June 23, Eisenhower endorsed Marshall's arguments. "France," he wrote, "is the decisive theater.... In my view, the resources of Great Britain and the U.S. will not permit us to maintain two major theaters in the European War, each with decisive missions."[7] Time was of the essence, he said. Either Dragoon must be launched by the end of August or the divisions assigned to this task should be diverted directly to the Normandy beaches.

No amount of contrary intelligence reports would dissuade the Americans from believing that Marshall's appreciation of German plans in Italy was correct. In mid-June, Hitler had declared in a message to Commander-in-Chief Southwest Generalfeldmarschall Albert Kesselring that the Gothic Line was the "final blocking position." If the Gothic Line were breached, he said, "an Allied entry into the plain of Lombardy would have incalculable military and political consequences." Hitler cautioned that "the misconception, existing in the minds of commanders and men alike, that there is a fortified Apennine position, must be scotched once and for all." It would, Hitler added, take "mighty labours for months to come" to get the line into full readiness. Kesselring was ordered to slow the Allied advance to buy time for completion of the fortification work. Duly intercepted by the top secret Ultra operation—which had broken the codes used by Germany's Enigma encryption machines—the message was forwarded to the Combined Chiefs.[8]

When Field Marshal Sir Alan Brooke saw the intercepted signal, he decided it was "all-important... the most marvelous information." Now, he confided to his diary, "there could be no argument that the Germans were about to retire in front of us."[9] The Americans, however, dismissed the message as unimportant. At the end of June, Roosevelt threw his weight behind his generals in a strongly worded memo to Churchill. Operation Dragoon must continue.

On July 1, Churchill registered a formal protest against siphoning off almost 100,000 men from the Italian theatre. Roosevelt's reply was icy. "I always think of my early geometry: 'A straight line is the shortest distance between two points.'"[10] That line ran from Normandy to Berlin. It did not zig from Rome to Vienna and then zag to Berlin. Churchill grumbled to the British Chiefs of Staff on July 6: "Let them take their seven divisions. Let them monopolize all the landing-craft they can reach. But let us at least have a chance to launch a decisive strategic stroke with what is entirely British and under British command. I am not going to give way on this to anybody. Alexander is to have his campaign.... I hope you realize that an intense impression must be made upon the Americans that we have been ill-treated and are furious.... If we take everything lying down there will be no end to what will be put upon us."[11]

Alexander did have one surprising American backer—Fifth Army commander General Mark Clark. An unapologetic anglophobe, Clark was also a glory hound. He realized there would be scant glory for an American general commanding an army whittled down to a mere five divisions and three tank battalions. Worse, the men he was losing—both French and American—represented 40 per cent of his most experienced combat strength. Word that his strength would be bolstered by a regimental combat team from the recently formed and unblooded 92nd U.S. Negro Infantry Division little raised his spirits.* He was even less impressed when the untried Brazilian Expeditionary Force was attached to his army.

Clark frantically tried to save his veteran American divisions. On June 17, while meeting with Marshall, Clark argued that the French corps alone could take Marseilles. General Alphonse Juin, the highly respected commander of Corps Expéditionnaire Français, agreed. Marshall refused to back down. The American divisions must be transferred.

* The American military was still segregated in World War II, with African Americans generally restricted to service in support roles, such as truck drivers. By 1944, however, manpower shortages led to the formation of segregated combat divisions in which black personnel could serve. Most of their officers were white.

When circumstances in Normandy suddenly improved, Churchill, Wilson, and Alexander renewed the debate. On July 25, General George Patton's Third U.S. Army broke out on the right flank of the Normandy salient, raising the prospect of the liberation of several channel ports. Churchill cabled Roosevelt on August 4, suggesting cancelling Operation Dragoon.

The British prime minister pressed his case vigorously with Eisenhower the following day. The American general "continued to say no all afternoon and ended up saying no in every form of the English language at his command," Churchill wrote.[12] Eisenhower informed Washington that under no circumstance would he agree to Dragoon's cancellation.

Indeed, cancelling Dragoon was no longer practicable. The assigned divisions were already boarding ships and the invasion was set for August 15. Five days before the first troops hit the beaches in Provence, Churchill wrote the British Chiefs of Staff. "We are not prepared in any circumstances to have it [Italy] regarded as a lesser operation than Dragoon or that Dragoon should have priority over its essential needs."[13]

This was mere bluster. The shortage of manpower and resources remaining in Italy necessitated that future operations be limited in scope. Alexander's task in Italy was to push the Germans back to a line running from Venice through Padua, Verona, and Brescia. Only when this line was reached would Alexander be given further instructions.[14] To reach this line, however, Alexander must crack the Gothic Line.

HAVING LOST the diplomatic skirmish with his American allies, Alexander turned his attention to winning the forthcoming offensive against the Germans. His instinct was to go for the jugular. The most strategically important city immediately to the north of the Apennines was Bologna. Florence and Bologna were separated by some of the highest Apennine peaks, but running through these was Highway 65. This narrow road provided the shortest route by which the Allies could reach Bologna. Alexander's remaining forces had been concentrated around Florence with this knowledge in mind. If he struck quickly, Alexander believed the Germans would be denied the time they sought to strengthen the Gothic Line. A bold dash should enable his armies to break through with barely a pause.

His plan called for both Fifth Army and Eighth Army to strike simultaneously, as they had in the Liri Valley. Eighth Army had two rested corps—I Canadian Corps and V Corps. Together they fielded five divisions. He also had a newly arrived reinforcement division, the 1st British Armoured Division, to back up V Corps's infantry divisions. By July 17, an operational appreciation had been drafted that called for these two corps to attack with two divisions forward. Meanwhile, II Polish Corps would continue its slow slog up the Adriatic coast and a detailed deception plan would be carried out there to mislead the Germans into thinking the offensive was coming on the Allied extreme right flank rather than out of the centre.

The U.S. Fifth Army, reduced to four infantry divisions and one armoured division all much battered in recent fighting, currently stood in front of the massive Monte Pisano. Alexander had learned the costs of attacking such features head-on at Monte Cassino in the Liri Valley. He therefore suggested Clark assume a defensive posture, but concentrate his forces so that, at Alexander's signal, they could drive east of Empoli and fan outward to capture both Lucca and Pistoia. Clark agreed and Alexander set the offensive's start date for between August 5 and 10.[15]

Alexander wanted not only to break out into the Po Valley, he wanted to trap the Tenth and Fourteenth armies south of the Po River and destroy them before they could escape to the other side. On July 12, Mallory Major—an air operation intended to destroy all key bridges crossing the Po and subsidiary rivers—was launched. In three days, nineteen bridges were rendered unusable. Fears that the Germans might repair them before the Allies reached the Po prompted more raids through to July 27, after which the bridges were reported to be irreparable without major work.

On August 4, with the clock ticking down to the launch date, Eighth Army commander General Sir Oliver Leese asked Alexander for a hasty meeting. Alexander and his Chief of Staff, General Sir John Harding, flew from Rome to meet Leese at Orvieto airfield. It was scorching hot, so the three generals hunkered in the shade cast by the wing of a Dakota transport. The day before, Leese had visited the headquarters of Lieutenant General Sir Sidney Kirkman, commander of XIII Corps, at Casciano near Florence. Kirkman, Leese reported to Alexander, believed the offensive could not succeed because the fighting would occur in narrow mountain valleys and passes.[16] Having learned its trade in North Africa, Eighth Army had hardly any experience in mountain fighting. There was little ground in these confined valleys for massing tanks and thousands of artillery pieces. Kirkman had urged Leese to persuade Alexander to switch Eighth Army's offensive to the Adriatic coast, where he believed the ground open enough for fighting the set-piece offensive at which Eighth Army was adeptly skilled.[17]

Leese said he agreed with Kirkman, hence this emergency meeting.[18] On the Adriatic coast, Leese summarized, "Eighth Army would have fewer mountains to contend with, the chance of employing its artillery in controlled and concentrated 'set-piece' attacks and the hope of flat country ahead for its desert-trained armour; above all it would be fighting its own battle without the distractions of day to day consideration of the progress of another Army moving on the same objective."[19] Pressed by Harding, Leese agreed that his concerns were largely psychological in nature. But he argued that the topographical problems also compellingly weighted the issue in favour of redirecting the offensive towards the Adriatic front.

Harding flatly disagreed. Having been the chief architect behind Alexander's original plan, he stuck by it; but the final decision rested with Alexander. Whatever he decided, Harding said he would support. Equally reluctant to put his commander's back to the wall, Leese tempered his remarks by assuring Alexander that should he decide the offensive must be directed at the centre Eighth Army would make sure it succeeded.

Fifty-three-year-old Sir Harold Rupert Leofric George Alexander was no autocrat who would impose his will on subordinates. If his own arguments were not sufficiently persuasive to win a subordinate over to his plan, Alexander generally acceded to the subordinate's alternative proposal. He had demonstrated this tendency in May 1944 when Clark openly defied Alexander's orders by breaking away from his assigned line of advance in order to ensure that American troops were first into Rome. A furious Alexander had nonetheless avoided confronting Clark or insisting that the general follow orders. This resulted in large numbers of the Fourteenth and Tenth armies escaping the very encirclement that had been the primary raison d'être behind the entire Liri Valley offensive. Clark claimed Rome as his prize even as he rendered the victory a hollow one.

Now, after patiently hearing Leese out and weighing Harding's objections, Alexander, "realizing how impolitic it would be to persuade an Army Commander to fight a battle against his inclination and judgement," agreed to the Adriatic switch.[20] Right there, Alexander recast his plan. Instead of Eighth Army driving through the mountains in Italy's centre, it would carry out a swift, secret movement to the Adriatic. Once there, the army would roll up the German left flank at a point where the enemy enjoyed the poorest advantage of terrain along his entire front. Once this attack was underway, the U.S. Fifth Army would launch a subsidiary attack from the Florence area and advance on Bologna.[21] Leese said the plan—largely what he had proposed—suited him completely. Harding reluctantly nodded approval.

Leese was delighted. Eighth Army would now fight where he preferred and he also would not have to fight alongside Clark, whom he despised. Clark believed Leese and the Eighth Army were ineffectual and that the British had left the Americans to suffer the heaviest casualties throughout the course of the Italian campaign. No evidence to the contrary was going to sway his opinion.

Clark took every opportunity to publicly snub Leese. When the Americans occupied Rome, he issued orders putting the city off limits to Eighth Army personnel. Even the British divisions fighting alongside the Americans as part of Fifth Army were denied access except for one 1st British Infantry Division battalion assigned to garrison duties for form's sake.[22] In the end, Clark's order did not hold and the Americans opened the city to limited numbers of Eighth Army personnel carrying a suitable pass. But Rome remained a largely American furlough base.

On hearing that Alexander had approved Leese's plan, Kirkman wrote: "Oliver Leese must have been delighted to be well separated from 5th Army and to get away from the inevitable wrangles and the unpleasant spirit of competition between the two armies, which was always encouraged by Mark Clark."[23]

LEESE DID NOT GET everything he wanted, however. When Alexander met Clark on August 10, the American general raised the tactical point that, while an Eighth Army division would be covering his right flank, its army commander would be on the other side of the country directing a major offensive. Therefore, all of XIII Corps, to be left in the centre to form a line bridging the distance between Fifth Army and the Eighth Army's main body on the Adriatic, should come under his command. This would boost Fifth Army's strength by four divisions—also bringing some of the most experienced Eighth Army divisions under Clark's control. Although he had little but contempt for the Eighth Army, Clark would be able to use these divisions to cover his flanks. He could then concentrate his American divisions to spearhead any offensive. As with Leese, Alexander deferred to Clark's arguments and agreed to put XIII Corps under Clark's command.[24]

By giving Clark Kirkman's corps, Alexander denied Leese the ability to siphon off any of those divisions—two being veteran armoured divisions—to form a reserve for his Adriatic offensive. Alexander's entire force was now almost evenly distributed between Fifth Army and Eighth Army. There could be no concentration of force against a specific point of the Gothic Line.

Yet Fifth Army was assigned no significant role in the initial offensive. Instead, Alexander intended to use it later to deliver the second punch in his preferred offensive style. He called this a "two-handed punch" where two points, equally vital to the Germans, were attacked, forcing the enemy to split its reserves. Initially, Clark's VI Corps would carry out highly visible manoeuvres in the direction of Lucca to mislead the Germans into thinking an offensive there was imminent, while at the same time covertly concentrating II Corps and XIII British Corps in front of Florence for a follow-on drive up Highway 65 to Bologna. This advance would only proceed once the Germans were forced to leach divisions from this front in order to reinforce the Adriatic sector in an attempt to stem Leese's offensive.[25]

[4]

With the Greatest Energy

"IF I ONLY KNEW where the Canadians are!" Generalmajor Friedrich Wentzell, Tenth Army Chief of Staff, lamented to Army Group Chief of Staff Generalleutnant Hans Röttiger in early July.[1] For nearly two months, the Germans had unsuccessfully sought the whereabouts of I Canadian Corps, but some 85,000 men had seemingly dropped off the face of the earth. Tenth Army intelligence staff feared the Canadians were concentrating, gathering to spearhead the next Allied offensive. I Canadian Corps's performance in the Liri Valley had fixed in the German mind the belief that the Canadians were Eighth Army's crack shock troops and would surely lead any major attack. "One of these days," LXXVI Panzer Corps Chief of Staff Oberst Henning Warner Runkel confided to Wentzell, "the Canadian Corps is going to attack and then our centre is going to explode."[2]

One clue to the Canadians' location seemed to emerge in July when II Polish Corps paused unexpectedly outside Ancona to regroup. Tenth Army Commander Generaloberst Heinrich von Vietinghoff telephoned Commander-in-Chief Southwest Generalfeldmarschall Albert Kesselring. Casting himself in Alexander's shoes, von Vietinghoff postulated: "This may mean several things. The Poles are getting nowhere; 'we might take them out and put in the Canadians.' Or he may also say to himself, 'It seems to go well in the centre. I will take the Canadians there and push ahead.'"

"Which centre do you mean?" Kesselring asked.

"The Tiber Valley."[3] Kesselring and von Vietinghoff were just speculating. Neither had the slightest idea where I Canadian Corps was or where the inevitable Allied hammer blow would fall.

Born into a middle-class family of Bavarian farmers and beer brewers, the fifty-eight-year-old Kesselring had entered the German army in 1904 shortly after his eighteenth birthday. "I wanted to be a soldier," he said later. "I was set on it, and, looking back, I can say that I was always a soldier heart and soul."[4] After two years of World War I service on the Western Front, Kesselring had been appointed to the General Staff. In the 1930s, during Adolf Hitler's military rebuilding, he transferred to the Luftwaffe and, under the patronage of Reichmarschall Herman Göring, became Chief of Air Staff. In 1940, he was promoted to Generalfeldmarschall and had commanded units in the Battle of Britain and the Siege of Malta before assuming responsibility for Germany's defence of Italy. Even the Allies conceded that Kesselring was a brilliant defensive strategist. Although forced to surrender one defensive line after another, Kesselring had always denied the Allies the chance to destroy his two armies. And every battle had exacted a bloody toll in Allied casualties.

Kesselring's cheerful nature, unfailing optimism, and iron willpower enabled him to rebound from each defeat with amazing alacrity. These personality traits also ensured that he was able to draw the best out of subordinate commanders. Kesselring had proven himself the perfect German commander for the Italian theatre, a man who could almost without fail use his limited resources and manpower to best effect.

He did, however, have one flaw—a tendency to ignore or discount unpleasant realities. In May, for example, he had refused repeatedly to accept that Monte Cassino and the Hitler Line must soon be lost. He then decided that the Melfa River could be turned into a new defensive line that would hold until winter mud and rain ground Allied operations to a standstill. This despite the fact that it was spring and the Allies had before them many months of good campaigning weather. Such optimism in the face of reality led Kesselring to believe his army always on the verge of decisively stalemating the Allies.[5]

Kesselring was also fettered in his handling of the Italian theatre by Hitler's increasingly deluded operational meddling. When Rome fell, Kesselring had planned a speedy and orderly withdrawal to the Gothic Line. His decision was supported by Oberkommando der Wehrmacht (Armed Forces High Command, acronymed OKW) Operations Staff Officer, General der Artillerie Walter Warlimont. The OKW staff officer had flown from Berlin to tour the Italian front on June 7. Everything Warlimont saw over the next few days convinced him that retreating into the defensive works of a significantly strengthened Gothic Line was essential.

Before flying back to Berlin on June 10, Warlimont had telephoned Operations Chief Generaloberst Alfred Jodl and offered his conclusion. "If... despite the greatest efforts the enemy cannot be brought to a halt, it will be necessary to fall back to the Gothic position in three weeks."[6]

Jodl cautioned him: "I can only advise you most emphatically to be most careful when you get back here and make your report."[7] Every OKW officer understood the subtext of this kind of warning. Hitler was obviously in no mood to hear of surrendering ground without a fight. Warlimont argued his case anyway. Hitler refused to even glance at the officer's supporting maps, charts, and organizational tables. Adequately fortifying the Gothic Line would take at least seven months, he declared. Kesselring must hold south of the Apennines until then.

On June 11, Hitler sent an order to Kesselring that stated: "Delaying resistance must not be continued till the Apennines are reached. After reorganization of the formations the Army Group will resume defence operations as far south of the Apennines as possible."[8] German tactical doctrine made a precise distinction between delaying resistance and defence. The former involved gradually yielding ground, the latter holding out to the last man and bullet.

A dismayed Kesselring complained to Jodl that defending unprepared positions south of the Gothic Line raised the spectre of entire divisions being encircled and destroyed. An even greater danger was that his divisions would become so reduced in strength that they would be incapable of adequately garrisoning the line when it was occupied. Another risk was that the Allies might reach the line simultaneously with the retreating Germans and bounce it before a defence could be organized.

Ironically, five days later, Hitler slipped into one of his increasingly common funks and issued an order renaming the Gothic Line the innocuous-sounding Green Line.[9] The Allies, having just a few days before discovered from a captured map the designation of Gothic Line, paid the name change no attention. As when Hitler ordered the Adolf Hitler Line in the Liri Valley renamed the Senger Line to avert an Allied propaganda victory, the order came too late to prevent the Allied propaganda value of the original designation.[10] The Germans would defend their Green Line while the Allies would attack a Gothic Line.

HITLER'S ORDERS ASIDE, holding the Allies south of the Apennines was not viable because Kesselring's armies were simply too weak after the Liri Valley Battle to engage in protracted battle without benefit of a fortified line. On June 2, Kesselring advised OKW that he had 38,024 dead, wounded, or missing and that "the figure keeps mounting."[11] Considering both personnel and weapons, the fighting strength of the divisions of Tenth and Fourteenth armies had been reduced to between 50 per cent and 10 per cent of their strengths prior to the battle. Kesselring's most elite formations, the 1st Parachute Division and the 90th Panzer Grenadier Division, could muster only about 15 per cent of their normal strength. On June 10, the paratroopers numbered just 902 men.

Obergefreiter Carl Bayerlein, serving in the 3rd Company of the 1st Fallschirmpionier (Engineer) Battalion of the 1st Fallschirmjäeger (Parachute) Division, had missed the fighting at Cassino and the Hitler Line, enjoying instead a rare and welcome period of leave in Germany. When the nineteen-year-old fallschirmpionier rejoined his company near Rieti, he was shocked to see how few men survived. His platoon's flame-thrower operator had gone missing amid the ruins of Cassino and machine-gunner Arno Köhler was dead. All the company's officers and sergeants had also been either killed or wounded. "A large part of our 'new' platoon," he later wrote, "were strangers, and I had to get used to new faces and new names. Some were older soldiers, but most were younger."[12] His commander, Unteroffizier Reinhard Schumacher, who had been wounded in a minefield at Cassino but since recovered, had Bayerlein assigned to his gruppe (a platoon with a normal strength of twelve). The section commander was Feldwebel Heinz Schumacher, Reinhard's younger brother. After eight days' rest in Rieti, the battalion boarded their Henschel engineer vehicles and drove north.

"Now the real retreat began," Bayerlein wrote. "It went all the way back along the route I had travelled just a few days before [when returning from leave]. We were deployed all over the place on our mining and demolition missions. It often happened we would not see each other all day long. Sometimes you were alone, sent all by yourself for several days and nights in some demolition site, under bridges, in houses, or in the open. Then, when the last German unit passed the site, it could be detonated and the retreat continued. We used commercial explosives like Donarite or Ekrasite, and dynamite. Later, aircraft bombs were used for demolition, since there were no longer aircraft to use them. Even mines and shells were used. Anything that had military significance was regarded as a target: roads, bridges, towers, defiles, railway installations, fuel and ammunition dumps, factories, and various workshops and tunnels. The important point was to hold up the oncoming enemy as long as possible and to weaken him."[13]

On July 17, the engineers reached Piegaro, a small town south of Lake Trasimeno. Several houses adjoining an arched gateway through which the main road exited the town were to be blown up to form an obstacle. While Unteroffizier Gutheil's gruppe rigged the gate and houses for destruction, Bayerlein's team was south of Piegaro planting explosives on each of the switchback curves that wound up to the edge of the hill town. Bayerlein was drenched in sweat from wielding a pick under a searing sun. Not for the first time, he "cursed the life of a combat engineer."[14]

Holes dug, the engineers planted explosives in them, lit the fuses, and drove through the town. As they passed under the gateway, Gutheil's party was finishing setting the demolitions that would destroy the gateway. So that everyone could see the fireworks, the driver of Bayerlein's truck paused at a curve five hundred yards beyond the town walls. Soon the cry of "Fire in the hole" was heard. Gutheil's men jumped into their truck and pulled away, but no explosion followed. When it was obvious the fuse must have had time to burn through, Gutheil's men walked back. Just as they passed through the gateway, a powerful explosion collapsed it and the adjoining houses. A great cloud of dust swallowed the engineers. Although Bayerlein's gruppe dug frantically through the rubble, they found no trace of survivors. Gutheil and his troops, all recent paratroop reinforcements, were initially assumed killed. But everyone agreed it was odd that no bodies were unearthed. Later, Bayerlein learned that they were believed to have deliberately rigged the demolition so it would not explode and then, under the guise of investigating, had dashed through the gateway and set off the explosives behind them to prevent being followed. In this manner, they had been able to desert and surrender to the Allies, an increasingly frequent course of action taken by demoralized German troops.[15]

Bayerlein's engineers were working to Kesselring's orders that the Tenth and Fourteenth armies do everything possible to delay the Allied advance. But these orders were much less strident than Hitler had envisioned. Nobody was fighting to the last man or bullet to hold every inch of ground south of the Gothic Line. Kesselring's ability to defy Hitler's initial order arose from a compromise he had pried out of the Führer during a personal meeting on July 3 at the German leader's personal retreat high atop a Bavarian mountain in the village of Obersalzberg.

For the first hour of the meeting, Kesselring and his operations chief Oberst Dietrich Beelitz suffered silently through one of Hitler's lengthy lectures, delivered in a quiet and modulated voice. "The only area which offers protection against the enemy's superiority and restricts his freedom of movement," Hitler concluded, "is the lower gut of Italy."[16]

Ever the dutiful toady, Jodl, who was also present, noted in his personal diary that this was: "A graphic description of the situation by the Führer, and insistence on the necessity of fighting for every square mile of ground and every week of time."[17]

Kesselring's response was heated. "The point is not whether my armies are fighting or running away. They will fight and die if I ask it of them. We are talking about something entirely different, a question much more vital: whether after Stalingrad and Tunis you can afford the loss of yet two more armies.... If I change my plans to meet your ideas, sooner or later the way into Germany will be opened to the Allies. On the other hand, I guarantee, unless my hands are tied, to delay the Allied advance appreciably, to halt it at latest in the Apennines, and thereby to create conditions for the prosecution of the war in 1945, which can be dovetailed to your general strategic scheme."[18]

Surprisingly, Hitler was mollified by Kesselring's promise to stop the Allies in the Apennines. "Hitler said no more—or rather, he muttered a few words which ... were not uncomplimentary. Anyhow, I had won my point," Kesselring wrote.[19]

Kesselring never doubted he could keep his promise, despite the daunting nature of the task. Somehow Kesselring must conduct a slow fighting withdrawal south of the Apennines and simultaneously find the manpower and resources to build up defensive works sufficient to enable his Tenth and Fourteenth armies to pin the Allies down in front of the Gothic Line until early 1945.

Kesselring did receive some modest reinforcements in the form of three fresh, although inexperienced divisions—the 356th Infantry Division, the 162nd Turcoman Division, and the 20th Luftwaffe Field Division. The latter was shipped to Italy from Denmark and consisted mainly of underutilized Luftwaffe aircraft mechanics lacking any infantry training. The Turcoman division was composed of enforced conscripts from Eastern Europe more inclined to surrender or desert at first opportunity than to fight for Germany. All that kept such divisions fighting were the guns pointed at the men's backs by their German commanders and sergeants.

Although these divisions were of poor quality, they allowed Kesselring to withdraw three of his most battered Fourteenth Army divisions for regrouping, rest, and absorption of reinforcements outside a combat zone.[20] He could offer his other divisions little respite. They must continue to suffer the inevitable casualties for as long as possible in order to buy time for the Gothic Line's completion.

THE GOTHIC LINE took advantage of a major Italian topographic feature. From the toe of Italy, the Apennines run like a hard spine virtually up the peninsula's centre to the upper Tiber River. Here, abruptly, the mountains turn northwest to cut across the peninsula and join the Maritime Alps on the French border. This sharp dogleg separates central Italy from the great basin of the Po River Valley and Lombardy Plains to the north. Cutting as they do across the breadth of Italy, the mountains present a natural strategic barrier. Only on the east coast do they fall away sufficiently to allow relatively straightforward north-south passage. Even here, though, a series of spurs juts out from the mountains in the form of ridges, like the fingers of splayed hands, to touch the Adriatic Sea.

The Apennines' northwest dogleg is about 140 miles long and varies in depth from 50 to 60 miles. In 1944, only eleven, mostly poor roads transected the mountains from south to north. Carved out of the flanks of narrow valleys and crossing steep passes, these roads were subject to heavy winter snowfall and torrential year-round rains. To the west, the passes soared to heights of 4,300 feet. In the centre, where Highway 65 linked Florence and Bologna, the highest pass was only 2,900 feet and the distance through the mountains just 50 miles. It was, however, a rugged route with many easily defended choke points.[21]

Even before the Allies invaded Italy, the Germans had been so impressed by the defensive potential of the northern Apennines that OKW believed no more than a delaying operation should be fought to their south. Hitler had advised Mussolini of this on July 19, 1943, while the Sicilian campaign was still being fought.[22] On August 18, OKW had issued an operations order to the effect that, should Italy surrender, "Southern and Central Italy will be evacuated, and only Upper Italy, beginning at the present boundary line of Army Group B (line Pisa–Arezzo–Ancona) will be held."[23]

Initially, Kesselring had only been responsible for operations in the southern part of Italy, while Generalfeldmarschall Erwin Rommel commanded Army Group 'B' in the north. Increasingly pessimistic after the destruction of his Afrika Korps and the loss of Sicily, the Desert Fox became the leading proponent for maintaining the August 18 plan. Within weeks of the Allied landings in Italy, however, Kesselring began advocating a different strategy—development of a series of fortified lines in southern Italy to check the Allied advance south of Rome. Ultimately, Kesselring prevailed and the Allies were forced to pay a high price in both casualties and long delays in order to fight their way through one defensive line after another.

The strategy exacted a price from the Germans as well, for they had to divide their efforts to construct defensive lines. Such dispersion of resources meant that by early August 1944 the Gothic Line appeared far more formidable on paper than it was in reality. Kesselring had realized this deficiency the previous January when Allied landings at Anzio threatened the rear of the Gustav and Hitler lines. Near the month's end, Kesselring had issued an order, intercepted by Ultra, to "develop the Apennine position with the greatest energy," with special attention to the eastern flank at Pesaro because of the lack of inherent physical features favourable to the defence.[24]

Despite Kesselring's desire for haste, construction progressed slowly throughout the winter and early spring of 1944. In April and May, Ultra code-breakers provided General Harold Alexander, Deputy Supreme Commander, Mediterranean with the contents of detailed engineering reports on Gothic Line progress. The reports revealed that the line's readiness state varied greatly from one sector to another, with the eastern flank less developed than the western flank and the interior mountains having received the least attention of all.

On June 2, with the fall of Rome imminent, OKW took renewed interest in the work and issued a comprehensive order that set out point-by-point tasks and the means that would be provided to ensure their completion. Sectors that provided the most open ground for tank manoeuvre, such as the eastern flank on the Adriatic coast, were to be protected by the deadly Panzerturms that had destroyed so many Allied tanks during the May 24 breaching attack on the Hitler Line. Each

Panzerturm was a fabricated steel-and-concrete shelter dug into the ground and mounted with a turret from a disabled Panther Mark V tank. The turret could rotate through a 360-degree field of fire and its powerful 75-millimetre gun had a maximum range of 1,200 yards. These well-camouflaged gun positions were difficult to detect by aerial reconnaissance. They were also virtually immune to Allied tank or artillery fire. Thirty Panzerturms were to reach Italy by July 1, the order stated, and one hundred steel shelters (most capable of housing a machine-gun post or antitank gun) were also en route. Extensive tunnels were to be dug into the rocky terrain and fire embrasures carved out to protect artillery from aerial or counter-battery fire.

The Gothic Line's front approaches were to be blocked by swaths of minefields and a six-mile-deep obstacle zone created "by lasting demolition of all traffic routes, installations and shelters." All civilians living within a twelve-mile area to the front of the line, and to a depth of six miles behind, were to be evacuated. About two thousand German troops were assigned to enforce this evacuation and forcibly recruit male Italians for civil labour construction teams.[25]

On August 1, Obergefreiter Carl Bayerlein's engineer battalion was transferred from the interior to Fano on the Adriatic coast. "Our assignment was the demolition of the coastal railway, plus coast surveillance, preparing positions and mining the coastal strip. The Gothic Line already had many bunkers, minefields and dugouts, but most of them were still under construction. Between Fano and Pesaro, as a defence against enemy landings, we laid a new kind of mine. These were made of concrete in which nails, screws and miscellaneous bits of scrap iron had been cast. They were stuck on wooden poles just above the ground and connected with trigger wires. They were to be used against landing troops, and were all painted green so as to be invisible in the grass. The effect of these mines was devastating."[26]

After completing their work at Fano, the parachute engineers moved northward to Pesaro, home to the Benelli motorcycle production plant and several other large industrial factories. Most of the machinery, tools, and production materials from these installations had already been stripped and transported to factories north of the Gothic

Line or to Germany itself. Bayerlein's team blew up any equipment that could not be removed.

Bayerlein was next put in command of an Italian labour group of thirty civilians and ordered to prepare some fighting positions at the very front of the Gothic Line. The heat and bugs were terrible. Mosquitoes posed a particular hazard. The German soldiers slept under mosquito netting at night and took Atabrine to ward off malarial infection.

More threatening than the hovering mosquitoes were the Allied fighter-bombers that circled high overhead searching for prey. Any detected vehicle or work party was bombed or strafed. Bayerlein's Italian workers apparently feared being killed by the Allied planes more than being shot by him, for within a week he had only eight men left. The rest had run away one by one when his back was turned. Confiscating the identity papers of the next batch of rounded-up civilians stopped further desertions.

The Allied bombing not only disrupted the rate of work on the line, but also destroyed much that had been completed. When one fighter-bomber attacked a minefield, its bombs detonated hundreds of the mines that had taken days to plant. Nearby, Bayerlein's party was constructing a dugout in the side of a sandy hill. Suddenly Bayerlein "heard a howling in the sky, and when I looked up, there was a fighter-bomber diving on us. At the last moment, I was able to push two men inside the dugout, and I finally found cover. Already the cannon were hammering away. The projectiles struck the earth right above the entrance—it was work made-to-measure."[27] When the attack ended, the Italians immediately fled en masse, despite Bayerlein's possession of their identity papers.

On August 20, 1st Parachute Engineer Battalion moved a few miles north to Cattolica to assume coastal watch duties and form an immediate ready reserve for the LXXVI Panzer Corps divisions holding the Adriatic sector of the Gothic Line. A popular seaside resort prior to the war, Cattolica's beach was lined with hotels. Since its civilian population had been evacuated, the German troops had the run of the place and little to do but maintain a casual eye on the Adriatic horizon for an amphibious invasion nobody really expected. Bayerlein and his comrades spent many hours floating nude in the blue, warm sea or playing about on pedal boats. From the nearby fields they gathered tomatoes for salads and picked grapes and melons. In one small hotel, Bayerlein found a letter written by two German women some months before Italy became a war zone. They inquired whether nude bathing was permissible. Bayerlein duly wrote a reply stating that "everyone was bathing in the nude." By now bored with endless swimming, Bayerlein happily discovered some artist's paints in a house and set to trying to portray the blue sea and the boats. It was, he thought, "an idyll come true."[28]

Meanwhile, other German and Italian labour and engineering teams worked on. By August's end, Tenth Army's sector of line, stretching from just north of Vicchio east to Pesaro, boasted 2,375 machine-gun posts; 479 antitank gun, mortar, and assault-gun positions; 3,604 dugouts and shelters that included 27 caves; and 16,006 riflemen's positions that consisted of embrasures constructed of fallen trees and branches. The Germans had also laid 72,517 Teller antitank mines, 23,172 S-mines, 73 miles of wire obstacles, and dug 9,780 yards of antitank ditches. Only four Panzerturms, however, were complete. Another eighteen were under construction and seven more planned. Eighteen of forty-six smaller tank gun turrets mounting 1- and 2-centimetre guns were ready. While twenty-two steel shelters were under construction, none was as yet complete.[29]

[5]

Under the Boot Heel

German efforts to fortify the Gothic Line were greatly hindered by an increasingly hostile populace. Many Italians living inside German-occupied Italy refused to recognize the legitimacy of Benito Mussolini's puppet government. Mussolini and his cabinet ruled from the Fascist capital city of Salò on Lake Garda—near Verona—but they functioned entirely at the behest of their German overseers.

With every passing day, as the Allies advanced northward, growing numbers of guerillas were launching hit-and-run ambushes against German installations and supply routes. The partisans became so well organized and numerous that in May 1944 General Harold Alexander's headquarters staff reported: "There are three Allied armies in Italy. The Eighth and Fifth in front of the enemy need no introduction but the Partisans fighting in the enemy rear have been the subject of... much tainted enemy propaganda."[1] Partisan strength was estimated at about 100,000. The report claimed that, except for the main roads and railways, the partisans effectively controlled all mountain areas from Genoa to the Po River and from Bologna to the Gothic Line.

Even these transportation corridors were far from safe. "The toll of bridges blown, locomotives derailed, odd Germans eliminated, small groups of transport destroyed or captured, small garrisons liquidated, factories demolished, mounts week by week. The German nerves are so strained, their unenviable administrative situation taxed so much further, that large bodies of German and Italian Republic troops are constantly tied down in an effort to curtail Partisan activity. Occasionally pitched battles have been fought, with losses to the enemy comparable with those they might suffer in a full-scale attack."[2] Commander-in-Chief Southwest Generalfeldmarschall Albert Kesselring's decision to impress thousands of civilians into labour battalions to work on the Gothic Line construction and to repair transportation links damaged by partisan activity and Allied aerial bombardment prompted hundreds more Italians to join the resistance.

Nothing the Germans did could bring the partisans to heel. After each raid, the guerillas melted back into the mountains beyond the reach of the manpower-short German forces. Kesselring estimated that between June and August 1944, the partisans inflicted German losses of "5,000 killed and 7,000–8,000 killed or kidnapped, to which should be added a maximum total of the same number wounded.... The proportion of casualties on the German side alone greatly exceeded the total partisan losses."[3]

The Germans responded savagely. Hostages were shot or hanged in reprisal for every German soldier killed. Some villages were burned to the ground. Yet the partisan numbers and the boldness of their strikes merely increased. Reprisals and counter-reprisals spawned a circular pattern of brutality that touched almost everyone.

Situated atop a high ridge, Coriano lay about ten miles south of Rimini. Most of its one thousand citizens were poor farmers, eking a living out of nearby plots of land. The village's houses clustered around a small church square. With his parents and two brothers, sixteen-year-old Oviglio Monti lived in one home. A short walk away was a Catholic school, where his language studies consisted of both French and German. His father, Paulo, and mother, Eda, were not political and had adopted a live-and-let-live attitude towards the Italian Fascists and German occupation forces. It was a common attitude in Coriano, where the people were poor and had to work hard simply to survive. Few ever possessed cash. Instead, they traded produce and livestock for other consumables. A skilled craftsman who could earn money through construction work in Rimini, Paulo Monti was more fortunate.

Remaining neutral in the middle of a land being fortified proved increasingly difficult in the summer of 1944. When the Germans tried to draft some of the men and older youths for work parties, most fled to the hills. Then the oldest son of a family living near the Montis joined the partisans and was quickly identified as participating in a raiding party that killed a German soldier. In reprisal, the Germans seized the man's younger brother, Ciavatta Aristodemo, and announced that either the older brother surrendered the next day or the boy would be executed. When the accused partisan failed to surrender, the townspeople were forced to gather in the village square. There, Ciavatta Aristodemo was shot by a firing squad.[4]

IN NEARBY RIMINI, conditions steadily worsened during the summer of 1944. Ever more civilians were being impressed into labour parties, while each day brought Allied bombers overhead to hammer the city's railway marshalling yards, docks, and highway intersections. For twenty-one-year-old Amedeo Montemaggi, the destruction of his beloved city felt like a personal wound to the heart. The first raid on Rimini had come on November 1, 1943 when about three hundred U.S. 12th Airforce B-25 Mitchell bombers struck. It was All Saint's Day. The bombers returned the following day, which was All Dead's Day. Montemaggi thought the date appropriately macabre, for the raid killed many civilians and destroyed several historic buildings.

Originally founded by the Etruscans, Rimini had become a Roman colony in 268 BC. Situated on what was then called the Ariminus River, the Romans knew it as Ariminium. Finding the northern Apennines impassable, any travel by land between Rome and Gaul passed through the city. The great highway Via Aemilia ran from Gaul to Ariminium, where it linked to the Via Flaminia, which followed a pass through the Apennines to Rome. In 48 BC, after leading his troops south of the Rubicon in defiance of a Senate edict, Julius Caesar made his famous address to the soldiers in the city's main plaza. The Arch of Augustus, at the southern end of the city, was started in 27 BC and completed in 22 AD by Tiberius. The Roman ruler also built Ponte de Tiberio (Tiberius's Bridge) in 21 AD.

Following the Roman Empire's collapse, Byzantines, Goths, Lombards, and Franks variously controlled Rimini before it became an independent commune in the twelfth century. In 1334, the Malatesta family was declared the city's ruling lords. Malatesta lord Sigismondo Pandolfo built an extensive fortification around the city in the fifteenth century. He also murdered his first two wives to clear the way for his marriage to Isotta degli Atti. When Isotta died shortly thereafter, the grief-stricken Sigismondo transformed the city's thirteenth-century cathedral into a personal chapel dedicated to her memory. The intricate and lavish architecture and interior artwork rendered the renamed Tempio Malatestini one of the most significant creations of the Renaissance. Sigismondo's rebelliousness against Papal rule resulted in Pope Pius II condemning him to hell in 1461. Eventually forced to submit to the pope, Sigismondo surrendered most of his land beyond Rimini. In 1509, the city became a Papal state.

Rimini's conversion into a modern city with tourism as its economic mainstay came in the late nineteenth century when businesspeople expanded outside the decaying fortress walls to erect seaside resorts on the Riviera del Sole of the Adriatic, Europe's longest continuous beach. By 1920, a series of satellite towns lined the coast for a ten-mile stretch from Torre Pedrera in the north to Miramare to the south. Summer saw the white sand densely crowded with rows of beach umbrellas backed by shoulder-to-shoulder hotels.

His father had taught Montemaggi a passion for history. A railroad engineer who also edited the local newspaper, *Cronaca di Rimini,* Montemaggi's father instilled in his son a strong anti-fascist sentiment, a love of freedom, of newspapers, of the racehorse Muscletone, and the toreador Manolete. When his father died of cancer on January 1, 1941, Montemaggi, then only eighteen, took over the newspaper editorship and simultaneously began studying journalism at the university. *Cronaca di Rimini* focussed on local stories. Montemaggi's correspondents, who were mostly unpaid, submitted reports on the happenings of such nearby localities as Riccione, Cattolica, Coriano, and Morciano.

Italy was under the boot heel of Mussolini's Fascists, so Montemaggi was careful not to print anything obviously political in nature. Any anti-fascist display had to be printed discreetly to avoid denunciation by local party officials. Before becoming a newspaper editor, Montemaggi's most public anti-fascist act had occurred at age twelve when he was unwillingly declared a member of Rimini's "Guard of Honour" by the city's Fascist authorities. Young Guards of Honour were supposed to stand guard beside various Rimini memorials to demonstrate the nation's martial vigour. Montemaggi had simply failed to report for duty, an act that resulted in no formal repercussions from the authorities.

In the summer of 1943, however, Montemaggi met the forty-nine-year-old renowned anti-Hegelian Marxist philosopher Galvano della Volpe and helped him type the first draft of *Communism and Freedom*. Montemaggi was now flirting dangerously close to subversion. With Italy's surrender in September and Mussolini's temporary imprisonment, Montemaggi wrote a critical article focussing on the former Il Duce's many romantic interludes with mistresses in Riccione and, in particular, with his mistress Claretta Petacci at the Rimini Grand Hotel. After the Germans freed Mussolini and installed him as head of the Salò Government, Giorgio Pini, Mussolini's biographer and now a government minister, notified Montemaggi that he was banned from continuing as a newspaper editor. Montemaggi was grateful that Pini had not denounced him as a Communist, for that would have resulted in his arrest and probable deportation to a German concentration camp or forced labour factory.

The increasing danger from Allied bombing raids and his shaky political status convinced Montemaggi that he should flee to the country, but before he could act a draft notice arrived, ordering him to report for service in the Fascist army Mussolini was forming to fight the partisans and Allies. Montemaggi had no intention of reporting. Instead, along with his mother and younger brother, he set off on foot the next day and walked fifteen miles across country to a village called Pecchiano, just a little cluster of houses a few miles outside the somewhat larger village of Sogliano. The villagers were poorly educated peasants, who took no interest in events beyond their farms and neighbours. Montemaggi's family rented a small house.

Montemaggi owned a small crystal radio set that was about the size of a box camera. By running an aerial wire across the roof from one side of the house to the other, he was able to tune in to BBC Radio for news. Clad as a peasant, he then roamed from farm to farm and to other nearby villages, reporting the news he had heard on the radio and spreading other anti-fascist propaganda. He won their trust by being able to talk with them in the local dialect.

A few weeks after his arrival in Pecchiano, Montemaggi's anti-fascist activity was made riskier when a German supply transport unit occupied the little village and a sergeant major moved into the house with Montemaggi's family. The German told Montemaggi that his wife and two children had been killed during a bombing raid on Bremen. He also advised Montemaggi that if partisans attacked his unit it would be nothing personal, but the Germans would shoot Montemaggi and his brother.[5]

The sergeant major's warning echoed standard German practice. On June 20, 1944, Kesselring had issued an order stating: "Whenever there is evidence of considerable numbers of partisan groups a proportion of the male population of the area will be arrested, and in the event of an act of violence these men will be shot. The population must be informed of this. Should troops be fired at from any village, the village will be burned down. Perpetrators or ringleaders will be hanged in public."[6]

Further German orders drafted on August 9 added that local "Prefects, Party Secretaries, and other Fascist Headquarters are instructed to prepare lists of all Communists in the area, so that these elements are always at their disposal. Hostages may be taken from the circles which produce these criminals, so that, should shooting be necessary, a blow is dealt at others of the same ideology."[7] When acts of violence were committed by partisans, "an appropriate number of hostages will be hanged. In such cases the whole population will be assembled to witness the execution. After the bodies have been left hanging for 12 hours, the public will be ordered to bury them without ceremony and without the assistance of any priest."[8]

IN CORIANO, Oviglio Monti spent the first weeks of August engaged in a dangerous game of deception with the Germans, who, learning that he spoke German, had ordered him to interpret for requisitioning parties that were rounding up farm oxen, mules, and horses to use for transport. Despite its reputation for carrying out lightning-fast *blitzkrieg* invasions, the German army had always been heavily dependent on animal-drawn wagons to move supplies and munitions beyond the reach of railway lines. A typical infantry division until 1943 fielded a total of 1,133 horse-drawn vehicles as opposed to 942 motor vehicles. While such a division consisted of 17,000 men, it also numbered 5,375 horses. The daily food requirement of the men was fifty-four tons (including cooking fuel) while the horses consumed fifty-three tons of hay and oats per day.[9] In 1943, the number of motor vehicles assigned to an infantry division was slashed and the number of horse-drawn vehicles increased. Finding enough stock to meet demand, however, became a critical challenge for the Germans in Italy and civilian stock became highly prized. Italian farms little used horses or mules. The ox was the draft animal of choice.

Monti was sick with anxiety the first morning when three Germans collected him from his home. He knew that for the farmers to lose their precious oxen and mules would inflict terrible hardship, for they would then have to plow their fields entirely by hand—an almost impossible task. As the soldiers stomped into each farmyard, the desperate farmers turned to the sixteen-year-old for help.

"Tell them these animals are no good for transportation, Oviglio," they urged him. "Tell them they are sick, old, diseased. Anything."

Monti duly concocted one dire story after another. As it turned out, the German soldiers with him were all city raised, so accepted this plague of pitiful farm stock at face value. At day's end, they all trudged back to Coriano empty-handed and reported that no suitable stock was to be found on any of the farms.

Their officer turned a skeptical eye on Monti. "Tomorrow, Monti," he said, "you come with me and we'll keep the oxen and horses."

Monti knew there would be no fooling this steely eyed officer whose gaze had seemed to pierce right into his soul and recognize the deceit there. He also could not rid his mind of the image of his friend being executed in Coriano's square. Monti wanted nothing to do with the Germans. "No more Germans," he said to his parents. "I'll speak no more German for them. This is no good for Italy. It's no good for our people. I have to go to San Marino."[10]

That night, Monti walked west through the fields to San Marino. Situated on the slopes of Monte Titano, ten miles inland from Rimini, San Marino was Europe's third-smallest independent state. Only 23.5 square miles in size, it was also the world's smallest republic. Settled originally by the Dalmatian stonecutter Saint Marinus and a group of Christians escaping persecution by the Roman emperor Diocletian in 301 AD, the huge triple-summited limestone mass of Monte Titano provided a perfect refuge. A relic of the Italian self-governing states, San Marino's independent status had been repeatedly ratified down through the ages. Surprisingly, when the Germans occupied Italy, they acknowledged San Marino's independence and left it unmolested. In recent months, it had become a refuge for civilians fleeing the bombing of Rimini and the German impress gangs. It was also a base for partisan operations. The small nation was linked to the outside world by road and also by a railroad that ascended through a series of tunnels to the capital city of San Marino.

When Monti reached the tunnels, he found more than 200,000 civilians from the Rimini area already sheltered there. They slept on blankets shoulder to shoulder and he could see nowhere for another body to lie. So he slept outside in the company of hundreds of other boys who had also fled their homes. He discovered various friends from Coriano. Two days later, his parents and younger brothers arrived, carrying with them sacks of food. The family pitched a rough camp on the ground outside the tunnels. Monti's father said he believed they would have enough provisions to wait out the German occupation of their village. It would not, he thought, be long.

Monti agreed. For from their lofty perch on the heights of Monte Titano the family heard the rumbling thunder of the Allied cannon to the south and could sometimes see the rise of dust clouds churned up by exploding shells. Allied planes droned and circled overhead and then suddenly swooped down on unseen targets like hawks. At night, the southern skyline glowed red and orange with the flashes of the artillery and the fires their shells caused. The Allies were coming. Monti thought that soon these days of trouble would pass his family by.[11]

[6]

A Tremendous Nut To Crack

EIGHTH ARMY faced a daunting task just to move two corps to the Adriatic front for the planned offensive. The day after General Harold Alexander, Deputy Supreme Commander, Mediterranean formally agreed to move the main thrust from Florence to the Adriatic, General Oliver Leese issued a warning order to lieutenant generals Tommy Burns and Charles Keightley. All divisions of I Canadian Corps and V British Corps were to immediately concentrate in the Foligno area, southeast of Perugia. From here, a major highway crossed the Apennines to intersect coastal Highway 16 north of Ancona.

On August 9, Leese, Burns, Keightley, and the deputy commander of II Polish Corps huddled at the Canadian corps's headquarters to hammer out an operational plan. Leese wanted a three-corps attack in line that would entail II Polish Corps pressing up the coast, V Corps through the low land in the centre, and I Canadian Corps marching through the rugged foothill country. The Canadians were to "break the Gothic Line, secure the dominating ground on the left of the sector and protect the left flank of the breakthrough."[1] At its disposal, V Corps had four divisions of infantry, the recently assigned 1st British Armoured Division, and an armoured brigade. Leese sensibly enough intended this corps to serve as the breakout force. Neither the Canadians with two divisions nor the Poles with three battle-worn divisions compared. Leese wanted V Corps positioned to punch a gaping hole in the German defensive line and then pursue the demoralized and routed German defenders deep into the Po Valley. Although Keightley endorsed Leese's plan and Burns offered no objections, the Polish deputy commander cautioned that "progress along the coast road axis was generally slower than inland" because the Germans conducted extensive demolitions on the highway while tending to leave the interior roads less sabotaged.[2] Thinking that the Poles, having clawed a path up the Adriatic coastline for almost three months, should know their business, Leese immediately swapped the Canadian and British positions in the line.

He did not, however, change their roles. V Corps was still the breakthrough unit, despite the fact that it must advance through mountainous terrain "ill-suited for vehicle movement of any kind. Stretching ahead was a continuous succession of high hills rising to the massif on which perched the Republic of San Marino. Only minor roads ran through [V Corps's] sector, and these could easily be blocked by Germans holding the peaks," one commentator later wrote.[3] Leese seemed to believe he could break through the German defences wherever he pleased without regard to topography.[4]

Leese's instructions for the overall offensive were short and to the point. The line, he said, must be broken quickly. Consequently, the largest city in the line of advance—Pesaro—would be bypassed and left to the Poles to mop up. Beyond Pesaro, the Canadians would extend their line to the coast, effectively pinching the Poles out of the advance and freeing them for the mopping-up operation. The key obstacles in the Canadians' path were expected to be a series of three heights standing between the Foglia and Metauro rivers and the Monteluro–Tomba di Pesaro ridge feature to the west of Pesaro and immediately behind the Gothic Line's main fortifications. The sooner the Canadian Corps' armour reached Cattolica the better. Leese wanted to hit the Germans hard, pierce the line, and bull ahead so quickly the enemy had no time to regroup.[5]

While Leese started moving his two other corps to the Adriatic, the Poles were to continue their slow advance. Leese expressed the hope they might reach the Metauro River before the other two corps arrived. Ideally, they would have forced a crossing and seized the Monteluro–Tomba di Pesaro ridge. As the Poles were noted for reckless assaults that incurred heavy casualties, Leese cautioned the Polish deputy commander not to win a crossing over the Metauro at a price that left the corps too weak to isolate and mop up Pesaro.[6] Leese left it to the respective corps commanders and their staffs to work out actual plans for both the attack and the movement from Foligno to the Adriatic.

After Leese and his staff departed, Burns and Keightley met privately. The forty-three-year-old Keightley had just been promoted from command of the British 78th Division to corps command on August 3—replacing Lieutenant General Charles Allfrey. Keightley's promotion made him the British army's youngest lieutenant general and the only one not to have seen service in World War I. Burns found the ability of the two men to always agree quickly on matters "a most happy circumstance."[7] Both generals were skeptical that the Poles could even reach the Metauro River, let alone win a crossing. Shifted from the west to the Adriatic coast after the conclusion of the Liri Valley Battle, the Poles had followed a bloody trail north from Ortona to Ancona. Between heavy losses suffered during the fighting for Cassino and Monte Cassino and those since incurred on the Adriatic, they were very diminished. And the Poles had no reliable source of reinforcement. Instead, they drew most reinforcements from Polish conscripts captured from German formations. Although II Polish Corps had rebuilt itself several times in this unorthodox manner, there were never enough liberated Poles to bring the corps to even an approximation of full strength.

Despite the fact that Leese's quick change of plan left the entire Eighth Army offensive curiously weighted so that its greatest strength was concentrated in the foothills and lower mountains on the left flank, neither Burns nor Keightley questioned the decision. Clearly, I Canadian Corps was now attacking the sector of Gothic Line most suited for winning a rapid breakout—the very terrain advantage gain that had led to the decision to move the offensive from the central mountains to the Adriatic. Because of Leese's adamant refusal to put

British divisions under Burns's command, however, the Canadians must break through here with nothing in reserve. At the same time, Keightley had "a small army" of five divisions and one armoured brigade, but faced a line of advance over rugged country ill suited for rapid exploitation of any hole it created in the German line.[8]

During the following week, Burns met several times with II Polish Corps commander General Wladyslaw Anders. As Anders spoke no English and Burns no Polish, they conducted their meetings in French. Neither spoke that language particularly well, so their sentences were liberally sprinkled with fractured grammar. Somehow each officer managed to make himself understood. These meetings reassured Burns that the plucky Poles would in fact reach the Metauro River before the main offensive began.[9]

Meanwhile, corps headquarters was abuzz with activity. "The general air of smug satisfaction among the informed staff personnel," stated the official operational account, "contrasted sharply with the studied indifference of those who could only guess at the details of the impending operation. The weather remained hot and dry and the troops, barred from the pleasant little towns of Umbria which had been very little damaged by the rapid German retreat and which were inhabited by a class of people much superior to those of the southern towns, felt none too inclined to embark on the strict courses of training which were laid down for the remainder of their stay in the concentration area."[10]

The ban on entry by Canadian personnel into any villages was imposed to prevent the Germans learning the whereabouts of I Canadian Corps. In truth, Eighth Army intelligence staff worried that they might have previously been too clever by half. When Alexander had originally planned to drive through the central Apennines, a deception plan had been launched to convince German intelligence that the Canadians were forming up on the Adriatic coast to attack the Gothic Line. Canadians from various units had visited the Polish corps, making a point of flashing their regimental and corps shoulder flashes and the stitched marking of "Canada" on their shoulder straps before all and sundry. German spies and Italian informers duly reported what they saw. Now, the Canadians were to move precisely where Eighth Army's intelligence officers knew the Germans probably expected them to appear.

Hoping to throw the Germans off the scent, a counterdeception was initiated that saw 1st Canadian Infantry Division, then serving in the Florence line, suddenly don their identity patches and again become Canadians. This was also why all the telltale Canadian clues, including cigarette packages and the like, had been carelessly strewn into the Arno River for certain recovery by the Germans. This deception plan somehow failed, but it mattered little. The Germans not only missed the clues sown in Florence but also had earlier discounted the validity of the Adriatic deception. Instead, German intelligence believed the Canadians to be in reserve somewhere to the south.[11]

WHILE LEESE AND his corps commanders were finalizing their plans, the divisional commanders raced to prepare for the forthcoming movement to the Adriatic coast. Major General Chris Vokes received a general briefing from Burns while his 1st Canadian Infantry Division was still in the process of withdrawing from the outskirts of Florence to a new concentration at Foligno, so could do little in the way of immediate preparations. His counterpart, Major General Burt Hoffmeister at 5th Canadian Armoured Division, however, was able to immediately put his men back on a combat footing. The much cherished afternoon siesta was cancelled and a demanding fitness regime instituted.[12]

Hoffmeister had been grimly impressed by the preliminary information on the actual strength of the Gothic Line. "It was represented to me to be a particularly heavily fortified line," he later said, "possibly even more so than the Hitler Line, with a huge antitank ditch running across the front of the whole thing, and the ground rising up and forming an ideal defensive position.... One thing about the Gothic Line was that it was in great depth, so it was fairly obvious that this was to be a set-piece attack, preceded by an air program using some heavy aircraft, followed by a very comprehensive artillery program using everything in the book.

"It just shaped up as the major operation—the Hitler Line had been bad enough, but after all we'd broken through it. Other battles that we'd had we had won, but this one looked ... a tremendous nut to crack."[13]

Before the operation could begin, however, I Canadian Corps and V British Corps had first to reach the Adriatic coast. This would be no mean feat. Each Canadian division had to manoeuvre about 450 medium tanks, 240 smaller tanks, 50 self-propelled guns, 320 armoured cars, 200 cars and jeeps, 2,000 half-tracks, and 10,000 trucks over the narrow winding mountain roads.[14]

Initially, both corps were to have crossed the Apennines via Highway 3 running from Foligno to Fossato, then proceed down the eastern slope on Highway 76 to concentrate at Jesi, fifteen miles inland from Ancona. Eighth Army engineers quickly discovered that so many bridges on Highway 3 had been expertly demolished by the Germans, a diversion from Nocera to Fabriano had to be constructed that crossed the main Apennine ridge by "a series of hairpin bends" and extremely steep grades. Although this diversion was suitable for wheeled vehicles, it could not sustain tank and Bren carrier traffic because the tracks would tear up the hastily constructed road surface. Nor could the thirty-four-wheeled tank transporters easily negotiate the tight corners, so these massive juggernauts were largely eliminated from the movement scheme.[15]

An alternate tank route was required. By August 8, no suitable road had been found, so I Canadian Corps's chief engineer, Brigadier Colin Campbell, was instructed to build one forthwith and have it ready for use by August 15. He was to do so without jeopardizing the movement of wheeled vehicles via the already completed route and without any Bailey bridge material—all of this already in use on the other route.

Before construction could begin, Campbell had to search the mountains and discover a suitable pass over which a one-way road capable of bearing hundreds of tracked vehicles could be hastily constructed. Two Canadian engineers, Lieutenant Colonel R.E. Wilkins and Lieutenant Colonel J.D. Christian, reconnoitred possible options and reported back in just a few hours. They believed a track could be constructed that ran from Camerino over a narrow pass to Castel Raimondo in the heights of the Apennines. From there, the Canadians could follow the Potenza River from its headwaters eastward to San Severino and then to Villa Potenza. A rough road could then cut north through a jumbled series of foothills to reach Jesi. Over the next three days, Canadian engineers traversed as much of the route as possible in jeeps in order to design a rough engineering plan. Some areas proved impassable even to jeeps, so Campbell and a few senior engineers studied these sections by plane and then worked up plans based on their observations.

On August 9, even as this work was underway, 13th Field Company rushed equipment to Camerino and started improving the first section of track. The following day, 12th Field Company leapfrogged past them to start cutting a path from Castel Raimondo to San Severino. Campbell quickly realized these corps headquarters' engineering companies were too small to finish the job on deadline. Accordingly, 5 CAD's 14th Field Company was transferred to Campbell's command and on the late afternoon of August 10 joined the road-building effort. Three days later, Campbell reported that he still had insufficient numbers of men and equipment to meet the August 14 completion deadline.[16]

On the sunny Sunday of August 13, 1st Canadian Infantry Division's engineers were enjoying a quiet day of rest at their base near Perugia. Lieutenant Colonel Ted Webb, 1 CID's chief engineer, was away from headquarters when a frantic call demanded that he report immediately to the Chief Engineer's Office at corps HQ and that all the division's engineering companies must immediately prepare to execute a long move. "This was startling news," the divisional engineer's war diarist noted, "as all companies had unloaded their vehicles completely and were in the process of checking their equipment. The Divisional Bridging Platoon was also unloaded as 1 Canadian Field Company [was] attempting to get some Bailey bridge training."[17]

By the time Webb returned to his headquarters at noon, the division's engineers were in a complete dither, wondering whether they should be loading gear into trucks or continuing with their inventory. After calling corps headquarters for instructions, Webb scheduled an

Orders Group of company commanders for 1600 hours and advised everyone that the moment this meeting was completed all the division's engineers would immediately move out on a major operation. At the O Group, Webb explained that the engineers were to head immediately to the Villa Potenza area to help complete the tank track. By nightfall, everyone except the headquarters unit was on the move. The latter remained to gather up stragglers "left behind as a result of the rapid move." When these stragglers were all pulled in early the next morning, the last of the engineers decamped.[18]

Webb had rushed ahead with the main body. As the engineering companies of 5 CAD and corps headquarters had already discovered, the actual roadwork proved easier than anticipated. The narrow, winding trails used as the base for the track's construction were generally wide enough to accommodate Sherman tanks. There were, however, many small creeks and ditches requiring bridging. The engineers either slammed in culverts or cut diversions with bulldozers. By August 14, Webb reported 1 CID's sections completed—the last engineering unit to get the job done. As darkness fell, the first tanks started rolling.[19]

The exhausted engineers of 1 CID received no respite from their labours. They set off in a truck convoy for the coast that very night, following a tortuous side route mapped out by corps headquarters in order to keep their heavy construction vehicles from damaging the precious wheeled-vehicle route. The engineer's war diarist described the route as involving "numerous steep grades and sharp curves. The road itself degenerated into a mere goat track. Finally the heavy transporters [bearing bulldozers and other heavy construction equipment] of the field park company had to be turned back and sent along a better road."[20]

On the night of August 16, corps headquarters and the Royal Canadian Engineer Corps troops moved to the area of Jesi. Like all the other convoys rolling over the Apennines, they travelled without using headlights in order to avoid German detection. Hour after hour, the road ahead worsened. At dawn, the road abruptly petered out and the convoy found itself stranded atop a mountain summit. The track was too narrow to turn the vehicles around. With no option but to go onward, the engineers unloaded a couple of bulldozers and proceeded to cut a rugged cross-country trail overland to where it could link into another road.[21]

Security during the move was exceptionally tight. Once again, everyone had removed uniform badges and flashes and concealed all identification markers on vehicles. Any communication with Italian civilians was prohibited. The 3rd Field Regiment, Royal Canadian Artillery war diarist noted that, "with the prospect of smashing Hun resistance in Italy in the forthcoming battle ahead of them," everyone was more than willing to abide by the security measures."[22]

The movement across the Apennines by V British Corps and I Canadian Corps took ten days to complete. Every night, units formed long lines and drove into the gathering gloom. Winding nose to tail, the convoys snaked over the hills at a standard pace of twelve miles per hour. Any vehicle breaking down on the single-lane track was pushed over the edge and abandoned. Each driver could barely see the vehicle ahead, which was illuminated only by sidelights. Sudden stops resulted in bumpers colliding and muffled curses. Sometimes the vehicles ahead speeded up on descents, leaving the following truckers scrambling to catch up, but also fearful of rounding a turn and colliding with the truck ahead. Route markers were few and lit only by shielded lanterns. Wrong turns, such as that taken by corps headquarters, inevitably dead-ended. Every evening, some of the hastily constructed culverts collapsed. On nights cursed by a thunderstorm, mucky clay and sliding gravel rendered the road surface treacherous. Engineering parties frantically repaired washouts and cleared away slides during daylight hours, then spent the nights watching the trucks roll past, causing yet more damage. At dawn, the entire process began anew.[23]

Near the end of the Canadian move over the Appenines, Staff Sergeant Thomas A. Loten of 1 CID's 5th Field Ambulance found himself inching along in a truck that was well short of Jesi when predawn light started washing over the route of passage. The tortuously winding route had kept Loten and his driver on edge throughout the night. Just after sunrise, the convoy entered a series of extremely sharp

S-bends. The truck in front plunged off the road, but both men in the front cab managed to jump clear. As Loten's truck edged past, he could see no trace of their vehicle at the bottom of the steep cliff. A few minutes later, the convoy ground to a brief halt at the pass's summit. Looking back the way they had come, Loten thought the following convoy had "the appearance of a huge caterpillar, with its stop-and-go movement, inching its way up the steep grade. Looking east, down towards the Adriatic, the sun was just a golden dot with a single ray of light shining straight up into the heavens."[24]

It took three nights for the tanks and Bren carriers to make the move. The British Columbia Dragoons started on August 17. In addition to their normal loads, each Sherman tank had two forty-four-gallon drums of petrol strapped on the back and the lighter Honey tanks carried one drum each. These were to refuel the tanks en route. Before setting out, Major Jack Turnley, commanding the BCD's tank column, was told that some sections of road had been cut into cliff faces and three tanks had already been lost to landslides off the cliffs.[25]

Although the move was supposed to happen entirely under cover of darkness, huge bottlenecks built up on both the tank and wheeled-vehicle routes. Each passing day saw ever more convoys waddling into their predesignated concentration areas after hours of daytime travel. Massive dust clouds rising off the roads were visible for miles. Everyone assumed that the Germans must have noted this and deduced that a major buildup of forces was underway on the Adriatic front. When 5th Canadian Armoured Brigade's headquarters moved on August 18, it got tied up behind a long column of British tank transporters that were forced to shift back and forth repeatedly in order to get the long trailers around the tight corners. It took the column fifteen hours to travel a mere seventy-five miles.[26]

Because of the traffic backups, some regiments made the entire journey by day. The recently unhorsed Princess Louise Dragoon Guards departed at 0815 hours on August 21 and were soon snarled in long traffic jams. Many of the diversions over streams had been washed away by storms. What had started out as an orderly column, with the Canadians travelling as one continuous unit, became hopelessly broken up as British truckers barged out of side roads to bully their way into the column.[27] The British drivers seemed to take it for granted that the colonials would give way, while the Canadians were equally convinced of their own priority right to the road. Where the traffic control officers were was anybody's guess.

Somehow all the convoys managed to get through with a remarkably small number of vehicles lost and very few punches thrown. Most regiments reported only two to three trucks abandoned to breakdowns. The Canadians, wrote the corps engineering unit's war diarist, "had mushroomed into being on the Adriatic front."[28]

Some Canadian units were more pleased with their new homes than others. The 3rd Field Regiment, Royal Canadian Artillery was directed to an area too small for all of its guns, trucks, ammunition stores, and tents. There was little shade and scant cover, so almost everything had to be concealed with camouflage nets. There was, however, "a pleasant little stream" on the edge of their rear boundary and "since a bath seemed even more important than food and sleep many made it their first stop."[29]

The Governor General's Horse Guards "set up under a great spreading [stand of] evergreen with a magnificent view of the valley to the south." Just behind the area stood a small white villa that the officers considered using for their headquarters until it was found to be swarming with bugs and mosquitoes. Medical officers, fearful of malaria infestations, put it off-limits instead.[30]

On August 18, the Royal Canadian Regiment set up six miles behind II Polish Corps's front lines and just completed digging in and concealing the vehicles with camouflage by nightfall. Three days later, Major Strome Galloway set off to try purchasing eggs, green vegetables, and other provisions to break the regular diet of bully beef or Spam and dehydrated potatoes. In a little house, he encountered "a really beautiful blonde, either a patrician or a prostitute, lolling about in a yellow silk gown with a magnificent full-length green Chinese dragon embroidered or appliquéd on its back. She spoke good English and when I complimented her on it she demonstrated her French, German, and native Italian. I thought afterwards she might have been a spy left behind by the Germans, perhaps with a radio set to tell them what was going on.... The cottage was remote from anywhere. It was little more than a hovel and certainly a very strange place for a woman of her apparent education and refinement to be living."[31]

Galloway duly reported the woman's presence to Lieutenant Colonel Jim Ritchie, "who immediately set out to investigate the blonde enigma. After much skillful parrying in both English and French [he] found that the woman spoke German, French, and some English and that to all intents and purposes was of Italian parentage. Many enemy agents had been operating behind our lines and it was thought that she may be one of them. Needless to say, [Ritchie] arrived at no definite conclusion regarding the blonde menace and it was hoped that the matter would be investigated more fully at a later date."[32]

Aside from having a possible Mata Hari in their midst, I Canadian Corps staff were satisfied with the manner in which the hastily organized move to the Adriatic coast had been executed. The engineers' war diarist claimed, "The rapid and comparatively unobtrusive movement of such a ponderous force over long distances across mountainous country was a tribute to the staffs concerned and a true example of the mobility of the modern Army."[33] Corps staff estimated that the Canadians had moved "a million shells ... and 12 million gallons of petrol. The Canadian Corps alone moved some 280 carriers, about 650 tanks, and some 10,700 wheeled vehicles."[34] It was a significant achievement for any army and it was completed none too soon. For even as the last Canadians concentrated around Jesi, Burns and his divisional commanders were scrambling to prepare for an attack that was to begin in just thirty-six hours.

PART TWO

DRIVE TO THE GOTHIC LINE

[7]

We Begin the Last Lap

NEVER BEFORE had Eighth Army carried out such a grand offensive on such short notice. Having scrapped weeks of careful preparation for a central Apennines operation after one brief consultation carried out under the wing of a small airplane, General Harold Alexander, Deputy Supreme Commander, Mediterranean and Eighth Army's General Oliver Leese could spare not a moment reconsidering the wisdom of the new scheme. Neither could the corps commanders charged with carrying off this risky gamble.

While, as the British official history would later relate, "changing plans at so late a stage took great moral courage," it also required digressing from the methodical operational planning process that had distinguished Eighth Army's previous battlefield successes.[1] The invasion of Sicily had taken months of planning. So, too, had Operation Diadem, which had carried the previously deadlocked Allies up the Liri Valley. Every imaginable contingency had been studied and prepared for before the attack order was drafted.

Operation Olive, as the present operation was codenamed, was to be altogether different. The involved divisions would have just a few scant hours to study the ground and probe enemy positions with patrols. Despite this lack of deliberate planning, an air of heady optimism prevailed.

As I Canadian Corps's Lieutenant General Tommy Burns and V British Corps's Lieutenant General Charles Keightley got down to work, Leese took a noticeable back seat. Burns and his staff were primarily concerned with the six-mile-wide corridor or defile that was bordered by II Polish Corps on the right and V British Corps in the foothills of the Apennines to the left, for this was to be the Canadian area of operation.[2]

Their first obstacle was the Metauro River. Burns gave the 1st Canadian Infantry Division—which would initially lead the offensive—the task of establishing a bridgehead across the river in the face of inevitable German opposition. The 21st British Tank Brigade's three regiments would support the Canadians. Fortunately, the corps had spent the past two months training for opposed river crossings, so Burns believed 1 CID "could accomplish this task rapidly and without heavy loss."[3]

Once across the river, the division faced a twelve-mile advance through broken, hilly country to reach the Foglia River. Immediately behind this river lay the Gothic Line proper. About midway between the Metauro and Foglia rivers, a ridge rose in front of the village of Mombaroccio. Approximately 1,200 feet high, the ridge constituted the highest ground the Canadians would have to traverse during this first phase of the operation.

Facing Eighth Army were three divisions of the Tenth Army's LXXVI Panzer Corps. This corps had another two divisions in reserve. Despite the corps's panzer designation, its divisions were all infantry. On the seaward flank, the 278th Infantry Division had been badly battered following almost three months spent trying to check II Polish Corps's advance. In the centre, the 71st Infantry Division stood opposite the Canadians. This division was reportedly demoralized and only at half strength. Holding the line in the foothills through which V Corps was to attack was the 5th Mountain Division. Lurking behind the 71st Infantry Division was the 1st Parachute Division and 162nd (Turcoman) Division. The latter division was of poor quality, but the same could not be said for 1st Parachute Division. The Canadians had fought the paratroopers on many occasions, most notably at Ortona and the Hitler Line, and knew they would offer a tough fight whenever they entered the front line. Burns ruefully noted that 1st Parachute Division had become a legend, "even described by some enthusiastic Allied journalists as the best fighting division in any army—Allied or enemy. This became rather a sore point with [Major] General Chris Vokes, who used to point out, not without some heat, that whenever his 1st Canadians had met the parachutists the latter had had the worst of it."[4]

Burns fully expected 1 CID to quickly bludgeon the Germans back to the Gothic Line fortifications. Here the battle should reach its climax. Through aerial photographic reconnaissance, intelligence officers had provided Burns with a fair appreciation of the defensive fortifications. If a slugging match were required to breach the line, there was no question it would be costly. But Burns "hoped that our advance would be rapid enough to reach the position before [the fortifications] could be completed, and before the German garrisons could be settled down in them ready for a protracted defence."[5] Indeed, Burns hoped to arrive before any German reinforcements and "bounce" the line "through quick thrusts by tanks and infantry. Otherwise, there would have to be a set-piece attack, with an elaborate, coordinated plan involving heavy artillery preparation and support."[6]

This actual breakthrough was to be 5th Canadian Armoured Division's job. Just before 1 CID reached the Gothic Line, 5 CAD would form up to its left and press right on through. The armoured division would then drive to Cattolica on the coast and run up Highway 16 to Rimini. It was at Cattolica that II Polish Corps would be pinched out of the advance and left behind to mop up Pesaro.

Burns was confident the Canadians could carry out their assigned tasks without requiring reinforcements—a necessity because Eighth Army had no reserves the Canadians could draw upon if the attack bogged down. After XIII Corps's transfer to the U.S. Fifth Army, Eighth Army had only eleven divisions and all but two of these were committed to the forthcoming attack. As Alexander noted later, "We had all our goods in the shop window and it was impossible for me to create a central reserve with which to influence the battle."[7] Although

2nd New Zealand Division was concentrated near Jesi as a floating reserve, Leese had made no allowance for it to support I Canadian Corps. As in the Liri Valley, the Canadians were left with just two divisions that must succeed or fail on their own.

ON AUGUST 22, I CID began moving from Jesi to assembly areas for the Metauro River assault. The Royal Canadian Regiment tromped through the night to a midpoint position that lay five hours of cross-country marching from their final assembly point two hundred yards south of the hilltop village of Montemaggiore. Although it was night, temperatures hovered in the nineties; the air was lifeless and heavy. Underfoot, the ground was cracked and fissured from weeks of exposure to baking hot sun. Staggering under the weight of their heavy packs, the men sweated and quietly cursed every time they had to climb another of the steep slopes in this crazily rolling countryside.

At first light, the column stumbled into a cluster of olive groves. While the troops flopped under the scant cover of the trees to wait until nightfall and the last leg of the march, Major Strome Galloway and several other officers went ahead in a jeep to scout the final assembly area. They were soon standing out in the open on a small hill, looking down on the virtually dried-up Metauro. Galloway calculated that the water trickling over the stony-looking riverbed was no more than ankle depth. While the river itself wound oxbow fashion towards the coast, parallelling it at a distance of between three hundred and five hundred yards was the Via Flaminia Highway. Centuries might have passed, but the Roman engineering that had created the original great highway was still obvious. As Galloway started pointing out the various positions from which the RCR's rifle companies would launch their attacks, Lieutenant Geoff Wright remarked casually, "I feel as though some bloody Jerry is staring at me through a pair of Zeiss field glasses."[8] No sooner had he spoken than an artillery shell struck a house to the front of the officers.

As two more shells shrieked down, the men scattered. Flinging himself into a pigsty, Galloway pressed his trembling body against "the filthy hide of a huge, squealing sow."[9] Captain Ted Maxted ran towards the beckoning safety of an open door belonging to the house struck by the opening round. Just as he reached the door, however, an Italian peasant inside slammed it in the officer's face. No other cover available, Maxted jumped into a ditch. The other officers had meanwhile wormed their way into a small cave. The Germans pounded the hill for six minutes with what Galloway estimated must have been seventy-five shells.[10]

If the Germans had this forming-up position so well registered that they didn't hesitate to waste that much ammunition on five officers, Galloway realized a deluge of explosives and shrapnel would greet the regiment's arrival here. He raced back in the jeep to 1st Canadian Infantry Brigade headquarters and warned commander Brigadier Allan Calder of the danger. Calder said it was too late to dramatically shift the regiment's forming-up position. All he could do was give the RCR a slightly wider front line so that it could disperse the rifle companies farther afield to take advantage of available cover inside the farm buildings. Being almost all built of stone, these could withstand some battering by artillery.[11]

On the night of August 23, 1st Canadian Infantry Division's headquarters arrived at its planned forward position to find the area likewise subject to random artillery and mortar fire. Everyone was so exhausted by the move, however, the divisional war diarist wrote, that "we nevertheless go to sleep and the night is relatively quiet."[12]

In the morning, the headquarters staff discovered itself on "the side of an easy sloping hill. The fighting front moves with us [so] we are still some five miles from our Forward Defence Lines. However, though a multitude of trees offer good cover, this piece of ground is under enemy observation. Movement on routes must be kept at a minimum, no queuing is allowed for meals, slit trenches must be dug under trees and even latrines have to be camouflaged!"[13]

Reconnaissance parties from many of the division's regiments received equally rough treatment from German artillery as they scouted their new forward positions. As a patrol from 3rd Field Regiment, Royal Canadian Artillery was descending a long hill towards its assembly position, the men belatedly realized their jeep was fully exposed to anyone on the opposite side of the Metauro. Lieutenant D.W. Chute jumped from the jeep and started guiding the driver into a sheltered position between two buildings only seconds before a salvo of shells crashed down. The officer was killed. "Lefty," as he was known in the regiment, had been an immensely popular veteran who had served with 3rd Field Regiment since 1942. "Imperturbable and cheerful in action or out," the regiment's war diarist declared, "he was the friend of all and a competent officer. It is hard to think of 'B' Troop without him."[14]

Another artillery unit, 5th Canadian Armoured Division's 17th Field Regiment, was plagued by tragedy from the moment it arrived on the Adriatic front. On August 19, its commander, Lieutenant Colonel R.W. Armstrong, was seriously injured when his jeep overturned. He died four hours after the accident. On August 21, four officers suffering from either jaundice or malaria were hospitalized. "The regiment will go into action short of officers unless reinforcements arrive very soon," the regiment's war diarist lamented.[15] The following day, Lieutenant G.W. "Cass" Garnett was killed trying to clear a mine blocking a road scheduled for use during the August 25 attack. Noted the war diarist, "Cass ... was not only a willing war horse but did his job with a cheerfulness and efficiency you enjoy in a person. His memory will live on in this regiment not only because he was a soldier, but also a man who knew men and loved to work with them and for them."[16]

At 2030 hours on August 23, the regiment headed for its forward gun position near Montemaggiore. All went well until the regiment left the main road for the gun positions. In the darkness, with only sidelights switched on, the long, twisting track they followed proved extremely hazardous. Four vehicles rolled over into ditches or broke down. Despite using the cover of night to slip into their position, the Germans opened fire as the regiment's vehicles pulled up. An exploding shell killed the regiment's new commander, Lieutenant Colonel F.T. McIntosh, and Lance Corporal T.A. Kennedy.[17]

The new position clustered the entire regiment together on a half-acre shelf in the bottom of a deep valley. About four hundred feet above their position, Montemaggiore perched on its hill. To the front of the village was the Metauro River.

Lieutenants Alexander Ross and Fred Cooper arrived here in the morning from a reinforcement depot. Ross was soon taking the roll call of seventy strangers serving in his new home, the 76th Battery. Shells were exploding all around the battery position. Between salvos, Ross dashed from slit trenches to crannies inside a house to find the gunners, so he could introduce himself and check them off as present and accounted for. Ross suddenly realized his training days were done. This was the real thing. As this reality sunk in, Ross saw a burial party carry McIntosh towards a freshly dug grave. The body was "wrapped in a grey army blanket secured with signal wire, just his carefully polished high boots showing." A piper followed along playing a Toronto Irish lament, "The Flowers of the Forest."[18]

Ross was assigned to command 'F' Troop. The troop's four 25-pound guns were all well camouflaged and positioned in deep revetments. His men had also dug their slit trenches in more deeply than normal because of the persistent shelling. Ross's command post was a coffin-shaped hole covered over crudely with planks and a tarpaulin to prevent the escape of light at night.[19]

Like everyone else, Ross was frustrated by the regiment's inability to fire back at the German artillerymen. The Canadian gunners were under strict orders to maintain gun silence until they were to open fire in support of the infantry attack. The German shelling was so intense that the resulting dust made it difficult for Ross to see his guns from the command dugout. Fortunately for everyone, most of the shells exploded harmlessly in olive groves behind the regiment's position. When one shell, however, set fire to camouflage covering one of the troop limbers—a trailer loaded with cartridges of high explosives, Ross and his men had to brave the incoming fire to quell the blaze before the trailer's load of explosives detonated. A terrified Ross was grateful that he had found the courage to join his men in suppressing the fire. Failing to have done so would have left a damning first impression. Ross was greatly impressed by his men, who were mostly prairie farm boys; muscular, large framed, and spare of speech.[20]

Three of them were wounded during shelling on August 24. The war diarist wrote, "It is a difficult job for gunners to sit for a period and receive the shelling we are catching in this area and yet not fire back." But, he added, "It is our silence period before all hell breaks loose on the Hun."[21] That a hellishly heavy artillery fire program was certain was evidenced that night when trucks unloaded three hundred rounds per gun. The shell delivery was, of course, carried out under enemy fire and one Royal Canadian Army Service Corps driver was killed and two wounded. Several vehicles turned over trying to hurry down the winding track and a few others were destroyed by direct artillery or mortar hits.

On the morning of August 25, the regiment's new commander Lieutenant Colonel G.A. Rankin arrived. "We can't say the CO is taking the regiment over at its peak," the war diarist confided, "but we do know he will get full support and cooperation of all ranks." Throughout the gun positions, the regiment girded itself for action. Soon the gunners would be released from their enforced silence. That night, at 2359 hours, the attack was to go in and at 0013 hours of August 26, 17th Field Regiment would open fire with the rest of I Canadian Corps's gunners. "The spirits and anticipation of all ranks was unbounded," noted the war diarist, "as we all said to ourselves, 'At last we get our own back.'"[22]

GIVEN THE SHORT TIME available to plan his attack, Major General Vokes believed the division was as well prepared as possible. Not until August 16 had Vokes been able to provide his general staff and brigadiers with details of their objectives, so they could begin planning for a contested river crossing and advance over hilly terrain.[23]

Fortuitously, 2nd Canadian Infantry Brigade's commander, Brigadier Graeme Gibson, and Brigade Major A.F. Macdonald had both visited Rimini before the war and retained some memory of the nature of the ground. Drawing from personal memory, topographical maps, and aerial photographs, the two officers constructed a sand model. To maintain security they gave the indicated towns false names, but the ground detail was rendered as accurately as possible.[24] For two days, the brigade's regimental commanders and the commanders of all supporting units worked out the details of a theoretical attack based on the sand model. Only the day after the study group broke up did Gibson inform the officers that "the ground studied during the past two days ... was a model of the actual ground which [2 CIB] would shortly ... attack."[25]

Vokes planned a two-brigade-strong attack delivered across a four-mile-wide front. Each brigade would commit two regiments and hold its third in close reserve. II Polish Corps's 5th Kresowa Infantry Division was on the Canadian right flank and V British Corps's 46th British Infantry Division on the left. Left of this division would be the 4th Indian Division, while the Kresowa Division would have the 3rd Carpathian Infantry Division to its right. These five divisions were to simultaneously strike the Metauro River.

Because it was a night attack, the infantry would have to fight until dawn without tank support. Once it was light, six tank regiments of the 7th British Armoured Brigade and the 25th British Tank Brigade would support the British infantry divisions, while three regiments of the 21st British Tank Brigade would support the Canadians. The 2nd Polish Armoured Brigade was inherent to the Polish division.[26]

Having lost most of his air power to the invasion of southern France, Alexander could not offer Leese as many aircraft as either general would have wished. Still, the British Desert Air Force promised that one hundred medium bombers would hit the Gothic Line with fragmentation bombs delivered in a series of staggered raids. Weather permitting, these bombers would return the following day for a repeat performance while another five hundred medium bombers pounded Pesaro's outskirts. Night raids by six squadrons of Wellington bombers against the Gothic Line would follow. Fighter-bombers would also be available each day, circling overhead in cab ranks for fast deployment.[27]

The cab rank system had proven itself during the Liri Valley Battle. Normally this entailed a group of fast planes, usually consisting of three to six Kittyhawk fighter-bombers forming up overhead. These planes were on call to hit targets assigned by the air staff captain stationed at each divisional headquarters. Depending on the target, a single plane might be called out of the rank or the entire cab rank might be unleashed.[28]

Eighth Army would depend on the weight of its artillery, more than air power, to destroy enemy defensive works. The three attacking corps had at their disposal 1,052 guns. Just under half were assigned to V Corps, with the majority of the others dedicated to the Canadians. This included 1 CID's inherent artillery regiments, the guns of 1st Army Group Royal Canadian Artillery, the artillery regiments of the 4th British Infantry Division, 5th Canadian Armoured Division, and several batteries from II Polish Corps. In all, this amounted to ten field regiments—of which two were self-propelled—four medium regiments, one heavy regiment, and a heavy anti-aircraft battery.[29]

At the Liri Valley, Brigadier Bill Ziegler, 1 CID's chief divisional gunnery officer, had decided that the standard Eighth Army tactic of supporting infantry advances with creeping barrages had failed. These barrages entailed the infantry following a general line of shelling that advanced one hundred yards every two to five minutes according to a preset schedule intended to match the rate of the infantry's forward movement. Ziegler had found such barrages incapable of eliminating well-dug-in German defensive works, such as the four attacking Canadian regiments now faced. He felt that firing heavy concentrations against specific preset targets or target areas was more effective. Each concentration would be fired in "belts of 400 to 500 yards in depth and timed to agree with the proposed rate of advance of the infantry (100 yards in six minutes).... The concentrations would in effect provide curtains of fire in direct support of the infantry, moving up and along each of the four ridges in advance of the assaulting troops until the outer perimeter of the prepared bridgehead was reached at approximately 0200 hours, an hour before the infantry were expected to arrive on their objectives. During the succeeding hour the belt of fire on pre-arranged targets would assist the infantry in recognizing the limit of penetration for Phase 1."[30]

That penetration was to be three thousand yards. Ziegler's plan would utilize a total of 280 guns. The 25-pounders, medium guns, and 4.2-inch mortars would each have three hundred rounds per gun or tube. The heavy anti-aircraft guns would have five hundred rounds apiece.[31]

ON AUGUST 24, the 1st Canadian Infantry Brigade and 2nd Canadian Infantry Brigade brigadiers issued their orders for phase one of the attack—the river crossing and bridgehead establishment. This was 1 CIB's Brigadier Allan Calder and his headquarters staff's first battle together. Although confident, Calder fretted nonetheless that some overlooked detail might jeopardize his attacking regiments.[32]

Divisional intelligence staff had advised Calder that "enemy opposition to crossing... the Metauro and the advance to Via Flaminia would probably be light and confined to small arms fire, with possible mortaring and shelling of likely crossing places. It was believed that opposition would be stiffer about the towns and on high features, which lay between the Metauro and the Foglia. It was expected the 'silent' crossing would achieve at least a measure of surprise."[33]

The two brigades would attack with 1 CIB on the right and 2 CIB on the left. Calder's left-hand regiment would be advancing across rough ground where several sheer escarpments would have to be circled around. Royal Canadian Regiment drew this duty. On 1 CIB's right-hand flank, where the 48th Highlanders of Canada would advance, the terrain sloped down into a somewhat rolling coastal plain that offered better going, particularly for tanks. As usual in Italy, small creeks and irrigation ditches cut the entire front from west to east to form natural tank obstacles. The 48th Highlanders would start crossing the river at 2310 hours, with the RCR following five minutes later. Once the leading companies of both regiments crossed the river, engineering parties would start constructing crossings. The Hastings and Prince Edward Regiment would provide security for the engineers and then go forward when the 48th Highlanders and RCR finished securing their objectives. Calder warned Hasty P's commander Lieutenant Colonel Don Cameron that, because the two leading regiments were attacking at night, some German pockets of resistance would likely be missed and require mopping up during the follow-up advance.[34]

The more Calder thought about the plan, the more convinced he was that the need for mopping up possible German pockets would significantly delay the Hasty P's. Consequently, he cancelled the original plan that would have seen them jump through the two leading regiments once these had consolidated on the other side of the Via Flaminia and drive out to the three-thousand-yard point that was to mark the outward boundary of the initial bridgehead. Instead, Calder ordered the RCR and 48th Highlanders to go the entire distance with the Hasty P's following along as best they could.[35]

Over at 2 CIB headquarters, Brigadier Graeme Gibson planned to send the Princess Patricia's Canadian Light Infantry forward on his right flank with the Loyal Edmonton Regiment on the left. Unlike Calder, Gibson saw no reason for a change in plan in order to mop up bypassed Germans. The PPCLI would cross the river at 2235 hours and the Loyal Eddies at 2305 hours. The Edmonton regiment would seize two high points beyond Via Flaminia that dominated the left flank of the brigade's forward lines—Point 233 and Point 241—while the PPCLI would gain control of the hamlet of Serrungarina. When these objectives were secure, the Seaforth Highlanders of Canada would pass through to secure the bridgehead boundary.[36]

That the two brigades would succeed in crossing the river and gaining the initial objectives was considered a given. The German 71st Infantry Division facing them was known to be small in number and badly organized. Resistance would more likely stiffen as the Canadians moved towards the bridgehead's outward boundary and the Germans brought up reinforcements. For this reason, it was vital that the supporting tanks crossed the Metauro by dawn at the latest in order to catch up to the infantry before the German reinforcements arrived. This meant the Royal Canadian Engineers had little more than four hours to build tank crossings. Although largely dry in summer, the Metauro's banks were steep and its wide riverbed soft enough to mire tanks trying to cross unaided by a properly constructed diversion. In 1 CIB's sector, three such fords were planned. The sappers also had to clear the minefields on both riverbanks and those blocking several roads and rough tracks that approached the Metauro from the south.

Mine clearing had started on August 20. It was slow, dangerous work compounded by German mine-laying ingenuity. In the past, German engineers had generally used heavy explosives to blow large craters in roadbeds. This time, they had gone a step farther by lessening the size of explosive charges and stringing them out in a line so that instead of one crater, a series of smaller, interlocked craters was created. These took longer to fill. To add a dash of danger to the mix, the Germans had also buried 'S' mines, Schümines, and Italian box mines in the roadbed near where the explosives had gouged out crater strings. The explosions that opened the craters also rained thick coatings of debris over the emplaced mines, leaving them too deeply buried to be seen by the Canadian sappers, discovered by their mine detectors, or found by the methodical probing of ground with knife blades. All the sappers could do was hope the cratered roadbed was free of mines and set to work filling the holes in with bulldozers. But, as the bulldozers scraped one layer of debris after another away from the covered mines, the triggering devices were eventually depressed and the bulldozer disabled or destroyed. The only recourse for the sappers was to halt the clearing process after each pass by a bulldozer and sweep the ground for mines, resulting in long delays. Despite these problems, by nightfall on August 25, the roads were declared ready for traffic and the four regiments leading the attack moved quietly through the darkness to their jumping-off points.[37]

Earlier, the troops had listened to their officers read messages from Leese and Burns. "You have won great victories," Leese's announced. "Now we begin the last lap. Swiftly and secretly, once again, we have moved right across Italy an Army of immense strength and striking power—to break the Gothic Line.

"Victory in the coming battles means the beginning of the end for the German Armies in Italy.

"Let every man do his utmost, and again success will be ours."[38]

Burns bluntly set out the task. "Let every one of us go into this battle with the determination to press forward until the enemy is destroyed; to strike and pursue until he can fight no longer. Then, and only then, shall we have won what we, as Canadians, have been fighting for—security, peace and honour for our country."[39]

This immediately prompted some sardonic wag to compose a new verse for singing to the ever popular melody of "Lili Marlene."

We will debouch into the Valley of the Po
We will deal the Hun a mighty, mighty blow
We will debouch into the Po
This we know, for Corps says so
Onward to Bologna, onward to the Po.[40]

[8]

Ah, Cannon!

THE DAY'S TERRIFIC heat had barely lessened by nightfall, when a gentle breeze began to blow in off the Adriatic. A waning moon quickly set behind the mountains, leaving the sky awash with glittering stars. On the Canadian right flank, the 48th Highlanders of Canada marched along a gravel road towards the Metauro River. Earlier that day, Lieutenant Colonel Don Mackenzie had reconnoitered this line of approach and realized the gravel crunching under his men's boots would betray their presence. Accordingly, he ordered them to slip their boots inside oversized socks in a crude attempt to muffle the noise their footsteps must make. With insufficient standard-issue socks to go around, some soldiers, with whispered apologies to moms and aunts, resorted to using woollen stockings knitted by relatives. Although most had been dubious, the Highlanders discovered the socks did effectively mask the sound of their boots.[1]

While the Highlanders employed stealth, other units cast aside all discretion. Lieutenant A.D. Egan's Royal Canadian Regiment marched towards battle garishly wrapped in colourful silk scarves purloined from the same Florence factory Lieutenant Jimmy Quayle's scouts had plundered.[2] The RCR's 'B' and 'C' companies were leading. At 2315 hours, these two companies began descending a gentle slope towards the river.

To their left, the Princess Patricia's Canadian Light Infantry's 'A'

Company, under Major E.W. Cutbill, and Major Colin McDougall's 'B' Company led, while 'A' and 'D' companies of the Loyal Edmonton Regiment formed on their left flank. A heavy silence hung in the air. No trace of sound or sign of movement could be detected on the German side of the river.

The PPCLI were to cross at an oxbow that pushed to within mere yards of the Via Flaminia—the first objective of the Canadian attack. Elsewhere river and road were separated by several hundred yards, but here the Germans could fire directly into the riverbed with any machine guns set up on the higher ground north of the road. To improve the PPCLI's odds of achieving complete surprise, this regiment was given a head start. Cutbill and McDougall's men reached the edge of the Metauro's south bank at 2230 hours, paused just five minutes to hastily reorganize, then started creeping across the gravel riverbed. Although the Loyal Eddies reached the river simultaneously with the PPCLI, its two leading companies remained hidden in the tree line bordering the southern bank. They were to wait until 2305 hours before crossing, by which time the PPCLI were expected to have cleared the Germans from in front of, and immediately behind, their sector of the Via Flaminia.

Neither gunshot nor cry of alarm greeted the PPCLI during the river crossing. Climbing out of the riverbed, the men advanced in line across a field lying between the river and the highway. They expected any moment to hear a rifle crack or the dreaded sheet-tearing sound of an MG42 followed by the thump of a mortar firing and the piercing white glare of an illumination flare exploding overhead, but there was only silence. At the roadside, the leading platoons hesitated in disbelief at their good fortune for a moment before bounding across by sections to enter a maze of gunpits that all proved empty.[3] Thirty minutes later, the Edmontons, also meeting no resistance, formed up beside them.

The 48th Highlanders and RCR enjoyed similar success—the only resistance encountered being some deep pools in the riverbed that sucked the socks off their boots. As they slipped into a cluster of olive groves and headed towards the highway, one soldier tripped and dropped his Lee Enfield. A sergeant hissed at him to mind his footing.

They soon realized the man's clumsiness didn't matter. There were no Germans to hear.[4]

Five minutes after the first Highlanders were already coming up the other side, RCR Lieutenant Jimmy Quayle's scout platoon crossed. The previous night, Quayle and two of his men had probed the river's other side and detected no signs of German occupation. But the scout officer had dismissed this discovery as resulting simply from their not having stepped into the wrong spot at the wrong time. Night patrols could pass within a few feet of hundreds of Germans hunkered in fighting holes without either side being aware of the others' presence. So he could scarcely believe the Germans were well and truly gone.[5] Spreading out north of the Via Flaminia, the four Canadian regiments waited for 2359 hours and the onslaught of the guns.

AT ROYAL CANADIAN Horse Artillery's 'C' Battery, Canadian Press correspondent Doug How stared fixedly at the movement of his watch's second hand. Earlier the battery commander, Major D'Arcy Doherty, had briefed him on the mechanics of artillery fire. "It had all been there on paper," the reporter wrote afterwards, "sheet after sheet of mathematics, of map references, of target heights, of plus and minus signs, of times from and times to, of rates and types of fire." There were eight 25-pounder artillery pieces in 'C' Battery, with each gun dug into a deep pit in front of the farmhouse that served as Doherty's command post. During the day, camouflage netting had rendered the guns virtually invisible. Now the netting had been stripped away and the starlight silhouetted the big barrels reaching towards the sky. The shadowy shapes of the gunners moved purposefully around their weapons. Then How's second hand swept up to midnight. "There had been silence over these farmlands between the Apennines and the Adriatic," he wrote. "But now, as one, the hundreds of guns hurled forth their shells and for three hours they dominated the night."[6]

The reporter had witnessed other Eighth Army massed artillery operations, but none such as this. "For three hours the medium and field and self-propelled and the heavy anti-aircraft guns gave their thunderous interpretation of the concentrations and counter-battery task tables. There was no barrage this night. For once stealth had ruled out that violent prelude to an infantry attack. They had given the infantry an hour to get across the river. Then the guns beat forth their assistance ... to establish a bridgehead."[7]

Just minutes after the first mighty gun blasts rent the air, How's ears were battered numb by the concussion and noise. He retreated to the command post. Here lieutenants J.B. Black of Kingston and D.F. Ryan of Ottawa calmly and quietly passed orders by phone to the gun crews. They worked from a fixed schedule. "Their targets were marked on an artillery board gridded like the map of the area they were shooting at. Their eight guns would fire 1,700 rounds in the three hours. Everything was precision and experience and drill. Lieutenant Black would say the word and eight guns would fire 312 rounds in 13 minutes into an area 150 yards long and 80 yards wide. That was a 'murder' concentration in close support of the infantry timed in advance on spots picked by aerial reconnaissance and plotting of enemy ... gun flashes.

"If Lieutenant Black said 'intense' the guns would fire five rounds per gun per minute. If he said 'slow' they would fire two.... In a matter of seconds he could have all hell pouring down on one machine-gun post, then switch it to another. They could support their own division or the divisions on their flanks. Everything was simplicity and certainty and violence in expression. That is modern artillery."[8]

Much farther behind the front lines than How, Eighth Army commander General Oliver Leese watched the artillery light up the sky with none other than British Prime Minister Sir Winston Churchill at his side. Churchill had arrived in Italy three days earlier and General Harold Alexander, Deputy Supreme Commander, Mediterranean, had flown with him to Jesi airport just that morning to enable the prime minister to witness Operation Olive's launch. Leese and his guests had dined late that evening, enjoying a festive, optimistic spirit. There had been whiskey before dinner, champagne during, and Kümmel, an anise-caraway flavoured liqueur, as a postprandial. Churchill held forth throughout the evening on a wide variety of subjects that repeatedly circled back to the folly of the southern France invasion. "We then sat out—a glorious starlight night," Leese wrote his wife the next day, "and he was thrilled to see the barrage open. In some ways the flashes that rent the whole sky reminded me of Alamein." Churchill watched the artillery "flashes [while] smoking his enormous cigars" until shortly after 1:00 a.m. and then went to bed.[9]

While Churchill and CP correspondent Doug How recognized only well-orchestrated professionalism at work on the night of August 25–26, neither was aware of how closely the artillery operation had come to proving a fiasco. For most of the day prior to the attack, the artillery regiments—such as 3rd Canadian Field Regiment—had been incapable of firing a single round with any accuracy. "Still no fire plan, no registration ... and no indication as to what will be required of us," the regiment's war diarist complained late that morning. By early afternoon, he noted, "we were getting worried about the fire plan. We didn't know what we were going to shoot.... Finally, early in the evening a [fire plan] arrived ... and there it was: hostile mortar and hostile battery lists, target lists, prearranged [defensive fires] and—one copy of the concentration task table." The single copy was frantically copied and rushed to each battery to "get the command posts working. FOOS [Forward Observation Officers] ... had to rely on the infantry—who received large numbers of copies—for their knowledge of the fire plan. At any rate, when the infantry pushed off across the valley and shallow stream at 2300 hours, the guns were ready, and the first rounds crashed into the hills on the other side at 2359 hours. From then on the guns blazed steadily. We waited for news of the attack."[10]

On 17th Field Regiment's gun lines, the 25-pounders opened fire at 0013 hours and shooting was continuous until 0300. "It was a good feeling," wrote the regiment's war diarist, "to hear the guns roaring forth again and the sky a red glow with flashes of 25-pounder, mediums, and heavies."[11]

THE CANADIAN INFANTRY'S immediate task was to strengthen the small toehold they had established north of the Metauro. At 0120 hours, PPCLI commander Lieutenant Colonel David Rosser sent 'C' and 'D' companies over to link up with his leading element. 'D' Company was accompanied by the regiment's machine-gun platoon, which broke down its 40-pound Vickers .303 Mark I medium machine guns and carried them up on their shoulders and backs. Although following the same route used by the two leading companies, one of 'D' Company's platoons stumbled into a field of Schümines—small, wooden box-type mines fitted with pressure-triggered igniters. Nine pounds of pressure was all it took to set off the seven-ounce charge of TNT or picric acid packed within. The resulting explosion usually amputated the leg of the man triggering the mine just below the calf. Three men were so wounded in mere seconds. Despite this, the two companies quickly leapfrogged 'A' and 'B' companies and, by 0300 hours, reached their preliminary objectives. While 'D' Company and the machine-gunners covered them, 'B' Company started up a winding track towards the small village of Serrungarina—the PPCLI's final bridgehead objective. At 0345 hours, after filtering through the smouldering wreckage of the shell-blasted village, 'B' Company set up a perimeter on the northern outskirts, still without firing a shot.

Back at the river, engineers had opened one diversion and the company's jeeps and Bren carriers were jockeying for priority. Fearing a bottleneck, Rosser jumped out of his jeep to direct the vehicles over in single file. The third vehicle Rosser signalled across was his own, driven by his signals officer, Lieutenant J. Rachlis. As the jeep entered the stream, it struck an Italian box mine that the first two vehicles had somehow missed, and was blown apart. The blast threw Rachlis into a roadside ditch, from which he emerged shaken but otherwise unscathed.[12]

Across the entire Canadian front, the bridgehead was being rapidly expanded. By first light, all four regiments had reached their final objectives. The Edmontons detected no sign of recent German habitation on Points 233 and 241. At Saltara, the RCR entered a hamlet as badly worked over by artillery as Serrungarina. It fell to the 48th Highlanders, at the very end of the longest Canadian advance, to trip the first German gun position. When they were within two hundred yards of the road running from Borgo Lucrezia to Cartoceto, a machine gun opened up on their right and three men in one section fell wounded. A flurry of gunshots erupted from the darkness ahead.

After hitting the dirt, the Highlanders formed for a hasty attack only to see the Germans beat a hasty retreat. The Canadians crossed the road and started digging in.[13]

A few teenage German stragglers were rounded up who said they had somehow been left behind when their companies had withdrawn the previous night.[14] On hearing this news, 48th Highlander Captain Pat Bates shouted triumphantly to one of his platoon leaders, "They've gone right back to the Alps!"[15]

THE GERMANS WERE actually close by, digging into a series of linked ridges and hills running out of the foothills through the village of Mombaroccio almost to the Adriatic. Commander-in-Chief Southwest Generalfeldmarschall Albert Kesselring had ordered a withdrawal to this rugged terrain on August 20. By the time the Canadians struck, almost a week later, the 71st Infantry Division and the 4th Regiment of the 1st Parachute Division were in the final stages of conducting an orderly withdrawal.[16]

Although propitious for the Germans, the move had not been ordered in response to the imminent Eighth Army offensive, of which Kesselring had had no inkling. He merely sought to shorten the German line so that half of LI Mountain Corps's 334th Infantry Division could drop back from its front-line position well west of the Adriatic and be formed into a small mobile reserve—something Tenth Army presently lacked. The Germans deemed the front so quiet that Tenth Army's commander, Generaloberst Heinrich von Vietinghoff, went on leave. So, too, did General Richard "Papa" Heidrich, the eccentric but brilliant tactician commanding 1st Parachute Division.[17]

On the morning of August 25, Tenth Army Chief of Staff Generalmajor Friedrich Wentzell reported to Kesselring that not much was happening and it was unclear what mischief the Allies might be making. His main concern was the army's supply situation, which had been badly disrupted by Desert Air Force's destruction of the Po River bridges. Wentzell told Kesselring that the ordered withdrawal was underway.

"Otherwise nothing of importance?" Kesselring asked.

"Otherwise nothing," Wentzell responded.[18]

Even on the morning of August 26 with the Allies across the Metauro, Wentzell remained calm. Eighth Army's massive artillery assault had struck vacated ground and consequently inflicted few casualties. As for the reported river crossings, LXXVI Panzer Corps commander, General der Panzertruppen Traugott Herr thought this a localized tactical operation intended to drive a wedge between 1st Parachute Division and the 71st Infantry Division.[19]

As the day developed, however, Herr and Wentzell became increasingly suspicious that something bigger might be afoot. Wentzell duly called Kesselring. "It seems that it is going to be quite an affair on the Adriatic coast," he said. "The English have appeared on the front . . . and at this very moment I have received the report that the Canadians have appeared at the joint between [1st Parachute and 71st Infantry divisions]."

"What is the situation and what do you make of it?" Kesselring demanded.

"I feel that we have been lucky with our withdrawal since it preserved us from being caught in the artillery barrage. I expect that he will follow with strong forces."[20]

Kesselring was less sure. Everywhere along the German line reports indicated heavy Allied movement. In the central Apennines, the U.S. Fifth Army was reported massing and air activity there was intensifying. Even more confusing, a just captured document appeared to be ordering a major offensive on the Adriatic front. "We have moved right across Italy an Army of immense strength and striking power—to break the Gothic Line," the alleged order began. Kesselring could scarcely believe Eighth Army could have done so undetected. He suspected this was a clever deception and the real attack—if there was to be one at all, given the invasion of southern France and the resultant stripping of Allied divisions from Italy—was forming elsewhere.[21]

DECEPTION OR NOT, the Adriatic attack had caught 71st Infantry Division and 1st Parachute Division still engaged in the act of redeploying in their new ridgeline positions. Suddenly the two divisions had to whirl around and face a determined attack. Barely pausing for breath after the night's successful advance, 1 CID's leading regiments were on the march again by 0730 hours. Speed was paramount, Major General Chris Vokes warned both 1 CIB's Brigadier Allan Calder and 2 CIB's Brigadier Graeme Gibson.[22] Vokes hoped to catch the Germans so off-balance that he could drive right up to the Gothic Line and bounce it without pause, something he had tried and failed to achieve at the Hitler Line in May. That failure had forced the division to break the line in a bloody set-piece attack. Perhaps this time fortune and circumstance would be on his side.

The country ahead promised rough going. Blocking the left-hand flank of the advance was the 1,600-foot-high Monte della Mattera with a lesser summit—Monte San Giovanni—guarding its western slope. The eastern slope of Monte della Mattera was equally covered by Point 393, atop which perched an old convent—Convento Beato Sante. Vokes ordered 1 CIB to seize the convent, with the 48th Highlanders out front and the RCR behind and off to the left. Meanwhile, 2 CIB's Seaforth Highlanders of Canada would strike directly at Monte della Mattera while the Loyal Edmontons hooked out from behind the Seaforths' line of march to deal with Monte San Giovanni. Once these three positions fell, the Canadians would be on the southern edge of the Arzilla River valley. Beyond this river lay one more spur of land and then the Foglia River and the Gothic Line.[23]

On a map, the whole enterprise looked relatively straightforward, the stuff of staff college exercises. The Canadians knew that, unfortunately, Italian terrain seldom correlated with the maps. On August 26, this proved as true as ever. The infantry pushed into a confusing maze of hills and ridges. It was anybody's guess which hill corresponded with which map reference. Gullies and an endless number of unmarked roads and tracks crisscrossed their path. Streams and irrigation ditches followed seemingly random paths little related to a general flow seaward. The ground was thickly overgrown with olive groves, small woods, vineyards, and pocket-sized grain fields. Had there not been a war on, had there not been a pressing need for haste, had there not been the constant danger of German ambush, the chaotic countryside would have been charming. Instead, the men cursed it. They moved forward warily, wanting to go slowly and carefully, but always their commanders goaded them to make haste.

The infantry also moved this morning without support from the promised tanks. At the river, the engineers had run into problems. First, a bulldozer working on the south bank had triggered a mine and been disabled. Then the riverbed proved too mucky for a graded diversion to suffice. A bridge was needed. Not until 0700 hours was the work finished. The 12 Royal Tank Regiment squadrons assigned to the 48th Highlanders started rolling north only to run afoul of concealed mines and road demolitions.[24] The tanks did not marry up with the infantry until noon, four-and-a-half hours after Calder had ordered the Highlanders to advance on the first objective.[25]

Lieutenant Colonel Don Mackenzie learned at 0730 hours that the tanks would be late, but he had his orders. So he simply turned to 'C' Company commander Major Ed Rawlings and said, "Clean them out in front of us."[26]

Up ahead, a large red building stood on a hill to the south of a sunken road. Rawlings thought it a good initial objective. With two platoons out front and two in trail, the company started walking. At first, it looked like a repeat of the night's uneventful exercise, but then a section from Lieutenant Court Benson's platoon on the right flank was fired on at close range by a well-camouflaged self-propelled gun. While this section took cover in a fold of ground, Benson brought Sergeant Joe Gauthier's section up on the left in support. Through a thicket of bamboo, Benson noticed a small house that might be a German fortification and charged it with Gauthier's men following. They went in firing from the hip, ignoring the return fire pouring from fighting pits dug into the base of the building. The gun battle ended abruptly when the eight Germans who survived the initial Canadian volley promptly surrendered. Private Rex Waddell had, however, been shot in the nose. Six more Germans were sprawled out dead in the pits. The fall of the house convinced the nearby SPG crew to flee. Refusing evacuation, Waddell had a mate cover his nose with a field bandage, picked up his rifle, and rejoined his section.[27]

Meanwhile, on the company's left flank, a five-man section under Corporal Jack O'Brien's command flushed another SPG. The panicked crew fled without offering a fight. As O'Brien's party checked out their prize, German infantry counterattacked. The ensuing firefight left all five men wounded. While the two least injured managed to escape, the others were taken prisoner. Later that day, however, they were liberated by Hastings and Prince Edward Regiment troops mopping up the area.

Although he could hear the gunfire from his right flank platoon, Rawlings had no information on how the fight there was developing. Lieutenant Stew Reid's platoon and the company commander's tactical headquarters had reached the red building without incident and that led Rawlings to think the advance was proceeding pretty much as expected. He set up a tactical HQ in a covered German trench near the building, while Reid set off to clear three buildings on the hill's north slope. No sooner had Reid's platoon departed than Rawlings's section came under fire from previously hidden positions on his left flank.

Meeting no opposition at the first house they cleared, Reid's platoon headed towards the second one up the slope. They were just approaching it when a large number of Germans erupted from the third house and launched a counterattack. The platoon scattered. Cornered in the courtyard of the second house, Reid was taken prisoner along with Private Bill Heasman.*

With everyone pinned down, Rawlings tried to withdraw his infantrymen behind a covering screen of smoke rounds fired by the company's two-inch mortar. But the yellow smoke blew the wrong way. When Rawlings reported 'C' Company's situation, Mackenzie told him to sit tight. The Highlanders must wait for the tanks, after all.

---

* The two men were subsequently interrogated by intelligence officers from the 1st Parachute Division, but refused to answer any questions. The paratroopers were convinced they were Canadian, but when this was reported to Wentzell, he was less certain. Consequently, it was another day before Tenth Army realized that the Canadians were without doubt involved in the Adriatic sector offensive. (Beattie, 609–10)

AS THE HIGHLANDERS' advance ground to a halt, Lieutenant Jimmy Quayle's RCR scouts wandered the rolling landscape with only the vaguest idea of their whereabouts. Quayle's situation struck him as bizarre: here he was, a scout leader who lacked any sense of direction, but was walking point for the regiment with a platoon that officially didn't exist.

According to Ottawa's War Establishments regulations, which dictated the nature and size of regimental units, there was no allowance for a regimental scout platoon. Early on, however, many regimental commanders had realized the utility of having a small unit of soldiers that could range across the battleground and serve as their personal eyes and ears. As every regimental headquarters was authorized a Regimental Support Company, which consisted of a mortar, pioneer, carrier, and antitank platoon, it was easy enough to create an unofficial scout platoon by drawing personnel from the other support company platoons.

As for Quayle's lack of directional sense, he had learned that the veteran scouts in his platoon could be relied on. "Time and again," he later wrote, "we would be returning from a night patrol, with shells falling, buildings burning and tracer rounds streaking across the sky, and we would come to a crossroads. I would hesitate, 'Let's see, is it the right or left turn we take?'

"For chrissake, Sir, it's the left road," one of his men would hiss.[28]

This morning, the three men accompanying Quayle were almost as disoriented by the confused terrain as he was. They considered themselves fortunate to have not yet stumbled on any Germans. There were, however, many Italian civilians about, part of a tragedy that Quayle had often witnessed during his long march northward from Sicily. As Quayle's platoon walked along a dusty track, they passed farmers in their black clothing loading dead adults and children into open carts for transfer to the nearest cemetery. These were the casualties caused by the night's artillery barrage. Women and children wept, some of the older women beseeched heaven to explain this suffering, while the men—mostly old—grimly carried out their gruesome task.

After passing the civilians by, Quayle's party crested a hill and walked right into a group of six Germans strolling along with their guns slung over their shoulders. Seeing the Canadians had their weapons at the ready, the Germans promptly surrendered. Quayle immediately appropriated a German sniper rifle from one man. The gun was the standard German issue—a World War I vintage 7.92-millimetre Mauser 98—far inferior to the Commonwealth-issue Lee Enfield. The Germans transformed this old weapon into a sniper rifle, however, by fitting it with a four-power scope with optics superior to anything the Allies produced. Quayle slung the gun over his shoulder, determined to take it back to Canada as a souvenir.

He thought it would have been more dramatic if he could have written to his family with the claim that he had won the gun following a long duel with an opposing sniper. The truth, he knew, however, was that "both groups were lost, but we were less lost."[29]

Quayle's scouts were not the only RCR troops lost that morning. RCR Lieutenant Colonel Jim Ritchie had no idea of the whereabouts of any of his rifle companies beyond the fact that they were somewhere out to the front of Saltara. After setting his tactical headquarters up amid Saltara's ruins, Ritchie and his intelligence officer, Lieutenant Gordon Potts, set off with 'C' Squadron of the 12th Royal Tank Regiment to link the tanks up with his riflemen. Ritchie, aware that the Highlanders were pinned down on his right flank, planned an infantry-cum-tank attack against the hill topped by Convento Beato Sante, for it was from positions in and around the convent that the heaviest fire against the Highlanders was originating. If the RCR could capture "Convent Hill," the pressure on the Highlanders would be relieved. Having arranged for an artillery concentration to first soften up the German positions, Ritchie now fretted that his companies might be so far forward that they would get caught in the shellfire. Unable to raise any of his company commanders by radio to ascertain their precise locations or to order them to fall back to escape the impending artillery, Ritchie had hopped a ride with the tanks. He hoped to get past the intervening high terrain blocking his radio signals and then guide the tanks to the rifle companies.

Although Ritchie didn't know it, his companies were all pinned down near the base of the convent's hill by intense German artillery and mortar fire. They had quickly dug in and were now awaiting the tanks, which they had no idea Ritchie was bringing forward.[30]

WHILE RITCHIE AND the tankers searched uncertainly for Convent Hill, a small convoy of cars and motorcycles barrelled into Saltara in a boiling cloud of dust at 1630 hours. Out of a large convertible stepped Prime Minister Winston Churchill with General Harold Alexander at his side. As the headquarters was still being established, the situation was confused. Only the regimental padre, Major Rusty Wilkes, was on hand to receive the illustrious pair. Churchill asked after the tactical situation and Wilkes, somewhat flustered at having one of the most powerful men in the world at his side and being no tactician, sent a runner scrambling to find the nearest "combatant officer."[31]

A few minutes later and some two hundred yards away, Captain Ted Shuter saw platoon sergeant Jack Napier jogging towards him. The commander of the antitank platoon had been trying to get all the regiment's vehicles concealed from German observation inside an old gravel pit, but the sudden kicking up of a plume of dust back at the headquarters had drawn mortar fire down on the pit itself. When Napier told him some visitors had arrived who wanted his immediate presence, Shuter was thrown into a foul temper. He stalked back towards the party standing around Padre Wilkes.

As he got closer, Shuter forcefully swallowed his temper when he recognized General Alexander. Without looking at anyone else, Shuter crisply saluted the general. Alexander then turned to the portly civilian by his side and said, "You know Mr. Churchill, of course."

Churchill was wearing a pith helmet and tropical kit uniform with no rank insignia. He gave the flabbergasted captain's hand a hearty shake, while Alexander asked if "there was a possibility of seeing troops in action from the top of our sheltering hill?" Shuter warned that using the hill was dangerous, for the area was under German observation. Alexander told Shuter to lead on anyway. As they climbed the slope, Churchill continuously sucked on one of his trademark cigars. From the hilltop, Shuter could "see some troops running diagonally across our front, about eight hundred yards away." Having no idea of the real identity of the soldiers, he told Churchill "they were RCR in an attack."*[32]

Suddenly, Ritchie's artillery started shelling the general area of Convent Hill. Churchill beamed with pleasure as plumes of dirt were thrown up and the black smudges of airbursts appeared. "Ah, cannon," he exclaimed and lowered his binoculars.[33] Shuter could tell that Alexander was getting increasingly twitchy about their situation and so too was Shuter. The British Prime Minister should not be so close to the front lines, exposing himself to this kind of danger. Alexander finally coaxed Churchill off the hill. After thanking Shuter for his kind assistance, the party roared off in another dusty trail.

A few minutes after Churchill's departure, a breathless Major Strome Galloway arrived asking if it were true that the Prime Minister and Alexander had visited. Shuter was amused by Galloway's obvious mortification at having missed the august twosome.[34]

Churchill was duly excited by his experience. He later wrote: "This was the nearest I got to the enemy and the time I heard the most bullets in the Second World War."[35] Leese noted in a letter that Churchill "was all the better for his visit—He went out with [Alexander] yesterday and went well up to the front line, in fact on to ground shortly captured. Luckily he was not shelled or blown up on a mine!"[36]

---

* Some accounts have said that this was 'B' Company, RCR attacking Convent Hill. However, the distance between Saltara and the convent make it unlikely that any RCR companies would have been visible at the time.

[9]

Quite an Affair

UNLIKE THE DISORIENTED RCR, the Seaforth Highlanders of Canada were able to direct their advance unerringly towards their final objective—the 1,600-foot Monte della Mattera. Because the engineers here had opened 2nd Canadian Infantry Brigade's river crossing at dawn, 'A' and 'C' companies also enjoyed the close tank support of the 145th Royal Tank Regiment's 'C' Squadron from the moment they left the bridgehead at 0815 hours.

Lying between the bridgehead and Monte della Mattera were two lesser summits, bearing the map designations of Point 382 and Point 394, that the regiment was to secure en route. 'A' Company headed for the first objective; 'C' Company the second. A troop of 40-ton British-made Churchills accompanied each company. At 0930 hours, 'A' Company climbed and descended Point 382 with nothing lost but some sweat, and pressed on for Monte della Mattera. Forty-five minutes later, 'C' Company, commanded by Major Haworth Glendinning, reached the crest of Point 394 and flushed twenty-four Germans from the 71st Infantry Division's 211th Panzer Grenadier Regiment. Facing a company of infantry supported by three Churchills, they wisely surrendered. As the prisoners were marched past Lieutenant Colonel Syd Thomson's tactical headquarters, he thought they looked "a very poor type of soldier . . . very badly shaken by our artillery concentrations."[1]

By the time they reached the base of Monte della Mattera, the Seaforths were well ahead of schedule and beginning to think the exercise a pleasant walk in the country on a hot summer's day. Those thoughts were rudely dispelled when two British spitfires dived out of the sun with machine guns blazing. Even as the infantrymen dived for cover, the planes broke off and vanished over the horizon. Fortunately, the pilots were poor shots and no casualties resulted.[2]

Shaken by the experience, the two companies paused briefly to regroup. Then, at 1140 hours, Glendinning's 'C' Company started slogging up Monte della Mattera with No. 13 Platoon leading. Barely had the platoon started climbing when several Spandau machine guns and a self-propelled gun opened fire from positions on the summit. With the hillside too narrow to allow more than one platoon to form a line, Glendinning ordered No. 13 to carry on with the tanks advancing alongside it.[3] Tracks clawing for traction on the hill's steep rocky slope, the Churchills inched upward with 75-millimetre guns thundering in an attempt to keep the SPG crew ducking. The infantry dashed and slithered on their stomachs from one scrubby bush to another, following a zigzag path meant to throw off the aim of the machine-gunners. Three men fell with wounds. It took fifty minutes for the attackers to reach the summit, and there the fight abruptly ended with fifteen Germans surrendering. The rest, including the SPG, had apparently scampered just before the Canadians came over the crest. 'A' company quickly reinforced 'C' Company on the summit. The men spread out, dug in, and waited for further orders.[4]

Monte della Mattera was linked to Convent Hill by a curving half-mile-long ridge with a saddle lying between the two summits. About four hundred yards below the convent was Passo, a cluster of shell-blasted homes. From their hilltop vantage, the Seaforths could see German machine-gun positions dug in around Passo and the convent raking 1st Canadian Infantry Brigade's Royal Canadian Regiment and 48th Highlanders of Canada. They could also see the flashes of mortars and artillery firing from German gun positions running all the way north to Monteciccardo. Glendinning suspected that artillery spotters in the convent were directing this fire on 1 CIB's two regiments. If the Seaforths tried advancing northward from

Monte della Matera, their right flank would be exposed to the convent and the same German fire. The attack was stalled until somebody kicked the Germans out of the convent.

Thomson reported to 2 CIB commander Brigadier Graeme Gibson, who conferred with his 1 CIB counterpart, Brigadier Allan Calder. Gibson suggested the Seaforths attack across the saddle, but that meant entering the other brigade's area of operations. Calder told him to wait because he had just ordered the Hastings and Prince Edward Regiment to conduct a right hook around the 48th Highlanders' flank to get behind Convent Hill and hit its northern slope.[5]

This plan had been hastily cobbled together by Calder minutes before Gibson's call when the 1 CIB commander visited Lieutenant Colonel Don Cameron's headquarters.[6] The Hasty P's cook trucks had also just arrived with a hot meal for the men, so Calder agreed to a short delay of the attack to allow the men to eat. As Calder drove off in his jeep, the troops gathered outside an old church in the welcome shade cast by its bell tower.[7]

Five minutes later, the food line was smothered in flame and smoke as dozens of artillery shells exploded in a single, violent salvo. Seventeen were wounded, including the regiment's staff officer, Lieutenant J.S. Farewell. Three were dead: Lance Sergeant L.J. Richardson and privates A.J. Stoneberg and H.G. Smith. At 1345 hours, 'B' Squadron of the 12th Royal Tank Regiment arrived to support the Hasty P's attack and, despite this battering, the companies formed up and marched towards battle.[8]

After some thought, Calder decided Gibson should have the Seaforths mount a patrol in force towards the convent to distract German attention away from his attack. Gibson ordered Thomson to strike at 1400 hours, and the plan was anything but a diversion. Major Frederick D. Colquhoun's 'B' Company was instructed to ride on top of several Churchills to the outskirts of Passo, sweep the buildings clear, and then attack the convent.[9]

A combination of demolitions on the narrow road and the steep terrain on either side stalled the tanks a few hundred yards short of the village.[10] The Seaforths dismounted and Colquhoun sent No. 11 Platoon, commanded by Lieutenant Dave Fairweather, to secure Passo while his other two platoons and the tanks provided covering fire. Fairweather's men entered the olive groves and vineyards to the right of the road and worked carefully towards the village. As No. 11 Platoon disappeared into the foliage, a self-propelled gun fired at the covering force. Five men, including Colquhoun, died instantly and another twelve were wounded. Although injured, Lieutenant John Thirwell took command. Heavy machine guns weighed in alongside the SPG. The muzzle flashes of the guns betrayed their position to Thirwell, who ran to the Churchills on the road and pointed them out. The fire from the tankers thinned out the German fire, and when Thirwell showed them where the SPG was hiding it was knocked out or driven off—either way, it ceased firing.

While this action was underway, Fairweather's platoon dashed out of the vineyards into Passo and bagged six prisoners among the ruins. From a hasty interrogation, Fairweather learned the convent was held by at least sixty Germans. Receiving this information, Thomson ordered 'B' Company to pull back so the slope running from Passo up to the convent and the structure itself could be shelled.[11] When Thirwell reported his company still pinned under machine-gun fire, Thomson decided to delay further action until after dusk so that the withdrawal could be covered by darkness.[12]

With the Seaforth attack stymied, Gibson decided to broaden 2 CIB's offensive front. This would increase the pressure on the defending Germans, who had concentrated their forces on Convent Hill. He ordered the Loyal Edmonton Regiment to pass behind the Seaforths and advance about five thousand yards northwestward towards Monte Marino and the lesser feature of Monte San Giovanni. At 1800 hours, Lieutenant Colonel Budge Bell-Irving called his officers to an O Group. The thirty-one-year-old former Seaforth Highlander of Canada was a relatively unknown commodity to his new regiment. His grandfather, Henry Ogle Bell-Irving, had built Anglo-B.C. Packing Company into one of the world's largest tinned salmon exporters, and his ten children had been born into one of Vancouver's leading families. Henry Pybus "Budge" Bell-Irving was university educated, fine mannered, sardonically minded, and deliberately "British" in both mannerisms and speech. He was a stark contrast to

Major Jim Stone, from whom the Eddies generally believed this rather prissy young officer had usurped the regiment's command.

Almost to a man, the Edmontons admired the thirty-six-year-old, six-foot-five bear of a man. English-born, Stone had no discernible accent. Before the war, he had worked at forestry camps in northern Alberta's great expanses of boreal forest and had ridden on horseback from a camp near Blueberry Mountain to enlist as a private the moment war was declared. Possessed of a keen intelligence and great determination of will, Stone was soon fast-tracked into officer training.[13]

Bell-Irving served gallantly with the Seaforths in Sicily and during the march up the Italian toe until October 1943, but a lieutenant colonel's promotion had resulted in a transfer to command an officer's training school in Britain. Consequently, he missed the bitter battles of Ortona and the Hitler Line. Shortly after the Liri Valley Battle concluded, Bell-Irving returned to Italy to assume command of the Edmontons. Stone, who had passed through Bell-Irving's school in Britain and had poor relations with the commander there, was initially surly and uncooperative as Bell-Irving's second-in-command. He even demanded a transfer. Bell-Irving had shaken his head and said Stone "*was* the Edmonton Regiment" and must stay. After a moment's reflection, Stone promised to do his best as second-in-command and the two were soon fast friends.

Despite their disparate backgrounds and ways, Bell-Irving and Stone were much alike. Each loved to play and to work hard. Whenever opportunity permitted, Bell-Irving organized lavish parties. But he was also first man up the next day and would march the regiment relentlessly through one training scheme after another.[14]

Now Bell-Irving was determined the Eddies would vigorously advance towards Monte Marino by a semi-circular route that followed the line of a ridge from Monte della Mattera to a first objective of Monte San Giovanni and then to the final objective. 'C' Company would lead off at 1930 hours and secure Monte San Giovanni. Then 'B' and 'D' companies would carry on to Monte Marino.[15]

WHILE THE EDMONTONS teed up this attack, the Hastings and Prince Edward Regiment formed up behind the 48th Highlanders.

Leading the regiment was 'D' Company, commanded by Major Alan Ross, with support from a troop of Churchills. Ross could see that the German fire against the Highlanders was coming primarily from buildings on a low shoulder of Convent Hill immediately ahead. He could see no enemy movement on the right flank, which boded well for the planned hook approach. Despite these favourable signs, Ross hesitated to order the advance.

The ground his company was to cross was bare of vegetation, leaving his men badly exposed to German fire. A deep creek cut across the line of advance, which Ross doubted his supporting tanks could negotiate. Those gullies that might serve as covered lines of advance were being subjected to regular artillery and mortar fire in an obvious effort to cut up any units trying to use them. Ross thought it logical that the Germans on the hill facing the Highlanders would have the open ground also covered by antitank guns hidden in the dense foliage that matted the hill's eastern slope. He knew any element of surprise would be thrown away the instant his company stepped out into the open.

The company commander chewed the problem over with Cameron by radio. Forget flanking the hill, the lieutenant colonel decided. Instead, he ordered Ross to drive through to the Highlanders' pinned-down 'C' Company, extricate it, and then, if possible, go right up the front of the small hill. Cameron promised him not only the support of the troop of Churchills, but the continuous covering shellfire from a troop of Sherman tanks that would stand to his rear.[16]

Ross struck quickly with the infantry out front and the Churchills grinding along close behind. Whenever a German machine gun opened up, the infantry hit the ground, and the tanks knocked out the enemy position with 75-millimetre shells and bursts from their machine guns. If a German antitank gun engaged the tanks, the infantry, firing from the hip as they ran, swarmed it. In short order, 'D' Company swept past the weary Highlanders of 'C' Company straight through to the buildings, where they rooted out any Germans who had yet to retreat up the slope to Convent Hill. Within minutes, the action was over. The Hasty P's lost one man killed and two wounded, compared to a good number of German dead and six prisoners. A few minutes later, a couple of the tanks rolled up with about twenty more prisoners marching out in front. 'D' Company also captured a 75-millimetre antitank gun, a 20-millimetre self-propelled gun, two trucks, a half-track carrier, and a broken-down motorcycle. With the light fast failing, the other companies formed around 'D' Company, while the tanks withdrew to a safer place to spend the night. The Hasty P's settled down much pleased with having rescued the Highlanders—with whom they enjoyed a friendly, but intense, rivalry.[17]

All across the Canadian front the supporting tanks were withdrawing from the front lines because it was considered too risky to leave them in exposed forward positions at night. Among those leaving were the tanks with which Royal Canadian Regiment commander, Lieutenant Colonel Jim Ritchie and his intelligence officer, Lieutenant Gordon Potts, had been vainly searching for his four missing rifle companies. Having dismounted and watched the tanks clatter off into the gathering gloom, the two men walked towards the front lines. Each man had a grenade and Potts carried a Thompson submachine gun. Expecting to use the tank's radio for communications, neither man had thought to bring a portable set with them. For the next three hours, the two officers stumbled around in the ever deepening darkness, climbing up and down cliffs, until finally giving up and groping their way back to their headquarters.[18]

Meantime, the commanders of the RCR rifle companies had decided that with no orders coming from headquarters they had better do something on their own. Major Sandy Mitchell of 'B' Company took charge and established radio contact directly with Calder at Brigade HQ.[19] He proposed infiltrating up the slope of Convent Hill. With no idea what had happened to Ritchie, Calder told Mitchell to proceed on his own initiative. The RCR went up the hill in an arrowhead formation with 'A' Company on the tip, 'B' Company right and 'C' Company left. They scooped up ten German prisoners found dozing in slit trenches and then, after slipping and sliding blindly up the steep last stretch, the three companies burst onto the summit only to find that the Germans had fled minutes before. The Canadians dug in for the night around the convent.[20]

ON THE CANADIAN far left flank, the Loyal Edmonton Regiment crept through the dark towards Monte San Giovanni with 'C' Company in the lead and 'B' and 'D' companies close behind. Also in trail and travelling in a couple of Bren carriers was a detachment from the three-inch mortar platoon and the medium machine-gun platoon. Meeting no opposition on the approaches, the Eddies quickly secured the summit. When some men jumped off one of the carriers and swept through a pair of bypassed houses, they captured two Germans manning a wireless set. The house with the radio was determined to have been an artillery observation post and likely the one responsible for calling down much of the accurate fire that had plagued the Seaforths on Monte della Mattera.[21]

'B' and 'D' companies took over the lead and headed for Monte Marino. It was 2035 hours when the two forward companies rushed the summit. One company came onto the objective right in the heart of two companies of completely surprised Germans. A short firefight ensued before the German defenders were driven off. Eight Germans were awakened at bayonet point in a house that turned out to be a possible regimental headquarters.[22] Another wireless set, engineering equipment, and some medical supplies were captured. The Edmontons also rounded up seven horses and nine carts. They suffered no casualties and reported Monte Marino secure at 0030 hours, August 27.[23]

Although the advance had bogged down before Convent Hill, the Canadians had made excellent overall progress. They were now about seven miles north of the Metauro River. On their flanks, II Polish Corps and V British Corps had been similarly successful. Eighth Army had advanced so rapidly that it had managed to prevent the Germans from breaking contact. The task for August 27 was to maintain the chase.

In the past, Eighth Army had often frittered away opportunities gained like this by pausing to regroup and thus allowing the Germans to fall back to their next defensive line. Major General Chris Vokes believed that next line was probably based on Monteciccardo—a hill town overlooking the "muddy trickle" of the

Arzilla River.[24] The nine-hundred-foot hump upon which the town stood was the high point of a rugged ridge that ran from the village of Monte Gaudio in V Corps's sector near the Canadian left flank to Monteciccardo. From here, the ridge dropped off into a low three-hundred-foot-high saddle that contained the villages of Sant' Angelo and Ginestreto. Beyond these villages, the ground rose sharply again to the summit of Monte Belilla, which lay in the Polish sector. These features constituted the last physical obstacle between the Allies and the Foglia River. North of this ridge, the land sloped gradually towards the Foglia save for a small secondary ridge that skirted the southern edge of the river's flood plain.

Intelligence reports supported Vokes's theory. His spirits were further buoyed by the fact that these reports stated that the prisoners taken in the day's fighting indicated that "unit strengths [were] much reduced, weapons scarce, but small-arms ammunition sufficient. Enemy morale bad and many deserters." Vokes "ordered the leading brigade commanders to push ahead on their own initiative to the ... Foglia without respite, and to avoid giving the enemy a breathing spell."[25]

THE GERMAN SITUATION was not as dire as Vokes thought, but it was precarious. The defending 71st Infantry Division had already been in an exhausted state before falling back to the Metauro River and was rated by Tenth Army headquarters as only "fit for defence within limits." Overtaken by the Canadians in what was supposed to have been an orderly, uncontested withdrawal, the division's regiments had crumbled, with many men surrendering without offering even token resistance, while others fled at the first sign of Allied troops. In the early morning hours of August 27, Tenth Army Chief of Staff Generalmajor Friedrich Wentzell telephoned Kesselring's Chief of Staff, Generalleutnant Hans Röttiger, and described Generalleutnant Wilhelm Raapke's 71st Division as "weary."[26] The LXXVI Panzer Corps did not, however, plan to relieve this division. Instead, Raapke was told he must continue fighting until September 15, by which time 1st Parachute Division would have completed absorbing two thousand reinforcements that had arrived only on August 26.

Despite the fact that even after taking in these reinforcements the paratroop division would still be seventy-five per cent understrength, Wentzell knew it remained one of the crack German units. The reinforcements were young, but relatively well trained. By mixing them judiciously alongside seasoned veterans, the division would soon, he thought, be "in good condition and fully qualified for any operational task."[27] Already, despite the original intention to keep the division from renewed operations until September 15, the weakened state of the 71st Division had forced commitment of 1st Parachute Division's 4th Regiment in front of the Poles. During the retirement from the Metauro River, this regiment had been caught in the open by artillery fire and suffered heavy casualties. It also remained hard-pressed, as the Poles continued their advance towards Pesaro.[28]

This was the kind of frittering away of strength that Kesselring and Wentzell wanted to avoid, preferring to save the paratroops for the day when a firm defence must be mounted within the Gothic Line fortifications. In the streets of Ortona and Cassino, and at the Hitler Line, the paratroops had displayed an astonishing ability to inflict heavy casualties with thinly spread forces if they were able to fight from inside prepared positions. If the paratroops were again to work their magic at the Gothic Line, they must not be cut up piecemeal in the ever chaotic battlefield conditions inherent in a fighting withdrawal.

For the 71st Infantry Division, the grim task was then to regroup on the northern side of the Arzilla River, dig in, and fight. Its job was simple. To hold the Allies south of the Foglia until the paratroops and other divisions were ready to defend the Gothic Line. Kesselring remained unworried. Despite all evidence to the contrary, he still clung to the belief that the Adriatic offensive was a diversion intended to panic him into reinforcing this sector to the detriment of the line north of Florence.

Wentzell was less sure. He warned Kesselring that if the Eighth Army had shifted its main strength to this coast—and if the Canadians were here, this was entirely likely—that the German's left wing could collapse. Kesselring took the issue up with his Army Group staff, who agreed that, if true, this would certainly be a worst-case scenario. Evaluating the situation from the Allied side, they concluded that an offensive on the Adriatic front, given the weakness of the German divisions in that sector, would be "the right one, all right." Kesselring remained dubious, but he decided to err on the side of caution and issued orders recalling Tenth Army Commander Generaloberst Heinrich von Vietinghoff and General Richard Heidrich from their leaves. If a major battle was shaping up on the Adriatic front, he wanted his best commanders there to fight it.[29]

[10]

A Gallant Do

THROUGHOUT HIS first day of commanding a brigade in combat, 1st Canadian Infantry Brigade's Brigadier Allan Calder had constantly moved from one regimental headquarters to another, issuing orders on the spot to keep the momentum going. This had left his staff back at brigade headquarters "completely out of touch with both events and [his] intentions."[1] Deep valleys and intervening ridges had wreaked havoc on radio communications, so that Calder could seldom get through to his headquarters on his jeep's No. 18 set. The radio problems further convinced Calder that to exercise command control over his regiments he needed to be up front with them. Yet Calder also knew he should be available to receive intelligence information and instructions from divisional and corps headquarters in order to ensure 1 CIB's operations conformed to the overall offensive plan. Needing to be everywhere at once, Calder had raced back and forth from brigade headquarters to his three regiments at an exhausting pace.[2]

Roving the battlefield, as Calder did, was anathema to 2nd Canadian Infantry Brigade's commander, Graeme Gibson. He seldom strayed from a headquarters habitually sited well back from the front lines. If he needed to consult one of his lieutenant colonels, they were summoned to his headquarters. Although 2 CIB operated in even hillier country than 1 CIB, radio signals here had proven more reliable. So, even though his forward regiments were a good four miles from his headquarters at Serrungarina, Gibson seldom lost contact with them.[3]

Not that August 26 closed with Gibson controlling a seamless operation. Following the Seaforth Highlanders of Canada's failed sally against Convent Hill, a worrisome gap had opened between his brigade and that of 46th British Division's 128th Brigade as his line had drifted farther to the east than planned. At 0100 hours, August 27, Gibson ordered Princess Patricia's Canadian Light Infantry commander Lieutenant Colonel David Rosser to carry out a night move from its reserve position in Serrungarina to plug the gap. By dawn, the PPCLI was to have reached the small summit of Monte Altiero behind the Loyal Edmonton Regiment's position on Monte Marino. From here, it would then drive around the Loyal Edmontons' left flank to move through rugged hill country to the Arzilla River. The regiment would be supported by the tanks of 'B' Squadron of the 145th Regiment, Royal Armoured Corps.[4]

By 0230 hours, Rosser had his more than four hundred men on the march, while he and his staff remained at PPCLI headquarters hammering out a plan of attack. They had three hours before Rosser must get his headquarters moving by jeep and truck to rendezvous with the rifle companies at the base of Monte Altiero. A briefing of company commanders was scheduled for 0630 hours, with the attack starting an hour later.[5]

The PPCLI were not the only Canadians going without sleep this night. At 0330 hours, Loyal Edmonton Lieutenant Colonel Budge Bell-Irving began briefing the acting commanders of 'B' and 'D' companies. The normal company commanders had been rotated to headquarters as Left Out of Battle. This was a standard army practice that required holding back a small group of officers and men from every company. If the company were decimated, they would form a nucleus around which it could be rebuilt by reinforcements. By intermittently designating company commanders as LOB, opportunity was also provided for second-in-commands, in this case, captains Gordon Armstrong and Alon Johnson, to gain valuable command experience.[6]

It was over snaking roads such as this that I Canadian Armoured Corps made its secret move from the central Apennines to the Adriatic coast.
NAC PA-204147.

above · A dispatch rider sews his regimental shoulder flaps back onto his uniform at the end of one of several attempts to deceive the Germans as to the Canadians' whereabouts. NAC PA-185005.

top right · Royal 22e Regiment troops engaged in a training scheme prior to the advance to the Gothic Line. J. Ernest DeGuire, NAC PA-190299.

right · The 1st Canadian Light Anti-Aircraft Regiment (the so-called "No Name Regiment") antitank platoon pose with their six-pound antitank guns. NAC PA-135903.

COMMANDER
I CDN CORPS

left · Major General Chris Vokes (left) and Lieutenant General Tommy Burns in discussion just prior to the attack on the Gothic Line. NAC PA-185006.

above · Rimini had the sad distinction of being Italy's most heavily bombed community. NAC PA-173439.

above · Artillery crew readying for the August 25–26 barrage to open the drive to the Gothic Line. NAC PA-185004.

top right · Canadian 25-pounders fire on targets at the Metauro River on the night of August 25–26. NAC PA-129762.

right · An artillery captain, his plotter, and signalman provide targets and ranges to the guns just before the barrage begins. NAC PA-185003.

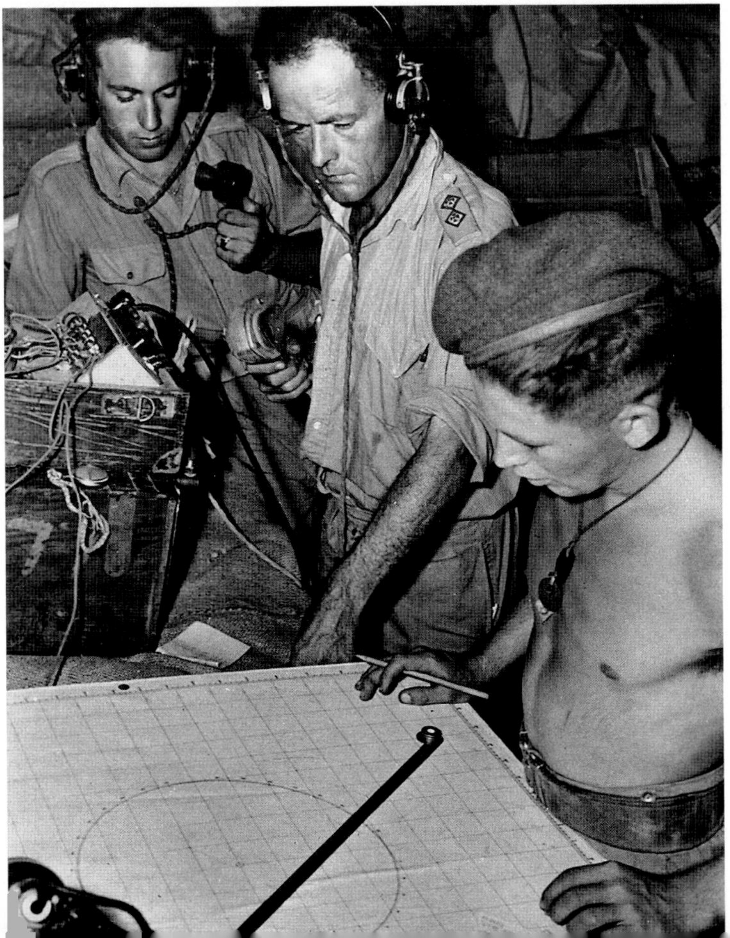

above · Tanks of the Governor General's Horse Guards are cheered as they advance towards the Metauro River. NAC PA-168022.

top right · Private L.V. Hughes, 48th Highlanders of Canada, snipes at German positions near the Foglia River. NAC PA-116842.

right · German prisoners are marched to the rear just after the fall of Mombaroccio. NAC PA-185007.

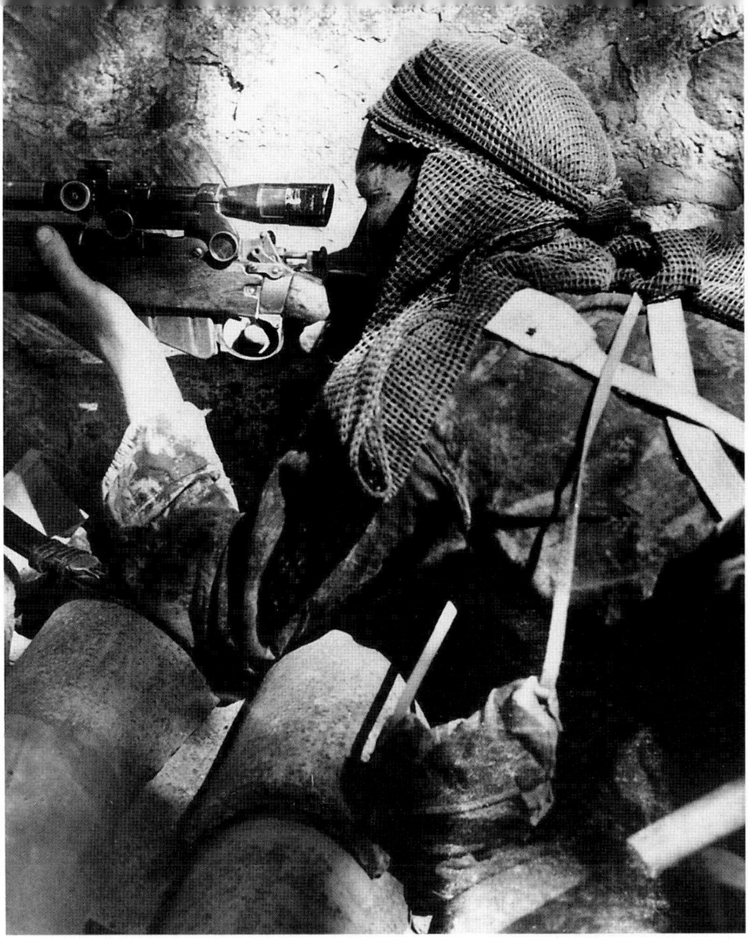

top left · A file of 48th Highlanders of Canada marches towards the Foglia River on August 29. NAC PA-177533.

left · A B.C. Dragoons Sherman tank with its turret blown off near Point 204. NAC PA-176300.

above · German tank knocked out near Tomba di Pesaro. NAC PA-144728.

above · Canadians look out from the castle ramparts of Gradara at the view German artillery spotters had enjoyed during the battle for the surrounding terrain before the breakthrough to Cattolica. NAC PA-173612.

top right · The relentlessly hot sun that Canadians experienced through most of the Gothic Line Battle was scarcely cut by the camouflage netting used to conceal artillery positions. NAC PA-177532.

right · Canadian soldiers on the march during the breakout from the Gothic Line. NAC PA-168941.

above · Churchill tank on the move towards Cattolica. NAC PA-184997.

top right · Lance Corporal J.A. Weston of Fairfield, New Brunswick, mans his Bren gun. NAC PA-184999.

right · Self-propelled gun advances up a narrow track. Note the dust cover draped over the main gun. NAC PA-184998.

Privates P. Saulnier and L.L. Little take cover in a shell crater they hastily transformed into a weapons pit near the Foglia River. NAC PA-185000.

Bell-Irving's plan appeared straightforward. With Armstrong's 'B' Company on the left and Johnson's 'D' on the right, they "were to head right out a mile or two miles into enemy territory." Bell-Irving ended his briefing with a sardonic smile. "Well, good-bye chaps," he said. "It's going to be a gallant do. I do hope to see you again."[7]

Before this attack started, however, Armstrong was to send a platoon out "for the purpose of killing the enemy and, if possible, holding the ground" to the front of the company's start line.[8] Setting off at 0530 hours, the platoon became disoriented in the dark and confusing terrain and ended up wandering lost until it stumbled upon a small German outpost. Having killed two Germans in the process of routing the enemy, the platoon commander radioed Armstrong for further instructions. Deciding this action fulfilled the "killing the enemy" part of his orders, Armstrong told him to bring the platoon home.

At 0615 hours, the two companies launched the main attack. Johnson's 'D' Company led off and headed towards a height of ground identified as Point 302. The company slipped onto the summit at dawn by platoons and found two bewildered Germans just waking up. Johnson put them under guard and the two companies started digging in on another easily secured objective.[9]

HAVING SPENT THE night securing their hold on Convent Hill and the ground to its immediate east, 1 CIB's regiments were beginning to feel the effects of lack of sleep. The men also knew there would be no rest any time soon, for at 0600 hours Brigadier Calder arrived by jeep at the Royal Canadian Regiment's headquarters with orders for an immediate attack on Mombaroccio. Calder's arrival came mere minutes after Lieutenant Colonel Jim Ritchie finally wandered out of the hills into his regiment's position. An exhausted Ritchie said he still had to reorganize his regiment and—always prone to being careful, slow, and methodical—would need until noon to organize the attack. Calder agreed to the delay.[10]

In a brief moment of radio clarity, Calder had also managed to contact Lieutenant Colonel Don Cameron during the night to give the Hastings and Prince Edward Regiment its orders for the morning. Cameron then held an O Group of his company commanders at

0400 hours and arranged for the men to be served a hot breakfast at 0710 hours. They gulped the food down and at 0730 hours 'C' Company led the advance with a squadron of tanks in support. The other companies followed with 'A' directly behind, then 'D', and finally 'B' bringing up the rear of the column. The regiment's task was to "move forward in pursuit of the enemy" by crossing the Arzilla River at Villa Grande and then advancing to capture points 268 and 146.[11] Both lay four miles from the start line, with the latter hill a few hundred yards east of the former.[12] On this clear, blue morning the villages of Monteciccardo, Sant' Angelo, and Ginestreto "stood out white and crenellated against the skyline."[13] To the immediate right of Monteciccardo, a monastery's tall bell tower rose high above the other buildings. Monteciccardo and Sant' Angelo lay about a mile to the west of the Hasty P's line of advance, Ginestreto just a few hundred yards west of Point 268. Both villages were on summits about one thousand feet high, only a bit lower in elevation than either Point 268 or Point 146. The Hasty P's could see that whoever controlled these two points also dominated the surrounding ground and the Foglia River valley below.[14]

No sooner was the regiment across the start line than the supporting Churchills were stalled by a maze of craters blocking the road. They headed back to the start line to find an alternate route forward, leaving the infantry to carry on alone. The soldiers advanced warily into a devastated landscape. German demolition teams had blown every bridge and cratered long stretches of the roads and tracks. Mines were a constant threat and every vineyard, olive grove, stout-walled church, monastery, or farmhouse potentially hid a sniper or machine-gun position. Sporadic shelling and mortaring repeatedly forced the companies to ground. Progress was slow and the tanks, having finally discovered that the safest route forward was to follow in the infantry's footsteps, were unable to keep up as they lurched perilously across the rugged, stone-strewn country that threatened to break their tracks.[15]

Crossing the three miles of country between the start line and the southern edge of the Arzilla River took three hours. While the men started digging slit trenches among the vineyards and olive groves hugging the edge of the ridge, Cameron stared down at the valley floor. Almost a mile wide, the country down there was open and through it the little stream wound like a snake. Cameron recognized the ground for what it was—an ideal kill zone for any Germans manning positions on the valley's northern flank. There was no sign of movement there, but Cameron sensed the Germans watching and waiting. For infantry to move down into the valley unsupported by tanks would be asking for a mauling, so Cameron knew the Hasty P's must wait on the badly lagging tankers.[16]

CALDER'S PROPENSITY for being constantly on the move was frustrating Major General Chris Vokes. When he pulled up in a jeep outside 1 CIB headquarters at 1100 hours, he was told Calder was still up front. Vokes stared at his map and then radioed Calder with orders for the brigadier to meet him at a specific map reference point near Convent Hill. Calder raced to the rendezvous and waited there until 1230 hours, but Vokes never appeared. Giving up on the major general, the brigadier drove to a forward observation point from which he could see the ground between the convent and the Arzilla River.[17]

Having apparently overshot the rendezvous point, Vokes drove up to the convent at 1200 hours. The general complimented Ritchie on the RCR's performance since the crossing of the Metauro River and then went back to searching for Calder.

After bidding adieu to the major general, Ritchie ordered 'A' Company to lead off towards Mombaroccio with 'B', 'C', and 'D' companies following in line. Meeting no resistance, the regiment passed through the little village's ruins, and pressed on towards the Arzilla River.[18]

About the time the RCR left Mombaroccio, Vokes returned to 1 CIB headquarters and found I Canadian Corps commander, Lieutenant General Tommy Burns, also waiting on Calder. The two officers were finally briefed on 1 CIB's operational plan by the brigade major "in absence of the brigade commander."[19] From here, Vokes and Burns travelled to 2 CIB's headquarters to discuss the operation with

Gibson. Both "seemed well pleased with the progress that had been made," the brigade's intelligence officer, Captain Ed Bradish, noted in the war diary.[20]

Although generally satisfied with the development of his division's offensive, Vokes worried that the advance was being dangerously slowed by a combination of the problems the tanks faced traversing the rugged ground and the slowly stiffening German resistance. Champing at the bit to get closer to the action, Vokes ordered his divisional headquarters moved just north of Passo.[21] Captain H.B. Gourlay and Captain C.J.A. Hamilton from 2 CIB were meanwhile locating a new brigade headquarters for occupation in the morning that was, in a curious development resulting from Gibson's tendency to hang well back, several miles to the rear of the divisional headquarters.[22]

Burns was even more anxious than Vokes about the increasingly sluggish pace of the advance. Before visiting 1 CIB headquarters, he had conducted an aerial reconnaissance of the front, "but little was to be seen of what was happening."[23] That had led to his trip to brigade headquarters, which left him certain that the "advance was taking much longer than had been anticipated [and] that the enemy might have time to occupy the Gothic Line in strength." Hoping to hurry things up, Burns ordered Vokes to prepare his reserve brigade—3rd Canadian Infantry—to take over the right-hand portion of the line from Calder's brigade. He then issued a warning order to 5th Canadian Armoured Division's Major General Bert Hoffmeister to be ready to pass through 2 CIB on the night of August 28–29. By then, Burns hoped both 1 CIB and 2 CIB would have reached the south bank of the Foglia River. If not, the fresh units would have to finish this job before immediately following up with an assault on the Gothic Line.

Hoffmeister, Burns knew, would have to relieve 2 CIB with his experienced 11th Canadian Infantry Brigade, supported by one of 5th Canadian Armoured Brigade's tank regiments. This would weaken I Canadian Corps's ability to take advantage of the breakout from the Gothic Line by advancing rapidly into the German rear, which was his main strategic purpose. Lacking a third division, Burns also knew he had no alternative but to draw down his armoured division's fighting strength in front of the Gothic Line should Vokes's division require reinforcement.[24]

Burns also had to watch his flanks. General Oliver Leese warned Burns that II Polish Corps and V Corps were both trailing behind the Canadians. The Poles, Leese said, could not possibly reach the Foglia until August 28 and that meant the Canadians were now "the spearhead of the attack."[25] The Eighth Army commander, previously betting on V Corps effecting the breakthrough, had now decided the odds favoured I Canadian Corps winning the race to the Gothic Line. He hoped Burns could get his divisions there in time to surprise the Germans and "gatecrash" the Gothic Line, which would avoid a set-piece attack.[26]

EVEN AS LEESE and Burns indulged themselves in this optimistic scenario, the Canadian advance was banging into ever more determined opposition, particularly on the far left flank where the PPCLI were attempting to cross the Arzilla River. At noon, 'C' Company, commanded by Major S.A. Cobbett, had sent a fighting patrol over the river to test the German defences. The patrol quickly overran and captured five Germans defending a small gun position. By 1245 hours, the entire regiment had crossed the river and was pushing north, the men sweating heavily in the sweltering early afternoon heat.[27]

Behind them, the tanks of 145th Regiment's 'B' Squadron were descending in a line down a spur that cut from the overlooking ridge to the riverbank when shells started exploding around the tanks. The squadron commander spotted the muzzle flashes of 88-millimetre guns firing from the village of Monte Santa Maria, almost a mile to the northwest of their position, and quickly directed artillery fire against the hilltop village. As the first shells exploded among the houses, the German fire ceased. But now the tanks stood on the edge of the river and could find no suitable crossing, for, although the Arzilla was shallow and narrow, its steep banks presented a natural tank obstacle. A delay ensued while 'B' Squadron's reconnaissance troop searched for a viable crossing point. Finally one was located and the tanks continued "over steep mountainous slopes and razor-back ridges" that caused many tanks to throw tracks, become stuck, or break down as they tried to catch up to the infantry.[28]

The PPCLI was having its own problems moving through the countryside north of the Arzilla. Each company had been given a series of preliminary objectives in the form of hills or other significant landmarks that were to serve as marking points guiding them to the final objective. For three of the companies, this scheme worked well and they stayed on course. 'D' Company under Captain R.G.M. Gammell, however, overshot its final objective by about one thousand yards. The mistake proved costly, as this brought them into range of German artillery and mortar positions on a hill to the northeast of Monte Santa Maria. A salvo of shellfire killed four of Gammell's men and wounded eleven others. When the Germans continued heavily bombarding the company, Gammell's men were unable to withdraw. They could only frantically dig slit trenches and hunker down.[29]

Major Colin McDougall's 'B' Company, some distance back from 'D' Company and to its left, paused for a short break at 1530 hours next to a church that had been one of its guiding points. Just as the men began to brew some tea, German rifle and machine-gun fire started whipping around them. The fire was coming from two points—Monte Santa Maria, about six hundred yards northwest, and a farmhouse four hundred yards to the company's front. When two of 'A' Squadron's tanks rolled up, McDougall had them shell the house while a platoon rushed it. The house was quickly cleared, with several Germans killed and twelve taken prisoner in exchange for one wounded Canadian.

Hoping to escape the German fire from Monte Santa Maria, McDougall rushed the rest of his company over to the house. If anything, the fire only intensified. McDougall knew the hilltop village lay within V Corps's sector and was an objective for the 46th British Division's 128th Brigade, supposedly operating on the PPCLI's left flank. But there was no sign of the British. McDougall had another problem. His radio had failed and, with dusk approaching, the tanks withdrew. Unable to contact Rosser for instructions, McDougall decided to rid the regiment of the threat Monte Santa Maria posed to its left flank.

Fortunately, McDougall had the PPCLI's medium machine-gun platoon following him on foot. Captain J.R. Koensgen immediately set his men to reassembling the forty-pound Vickers water-cooled guns that they had broken down for carrying purposes. As the machine-gunners started linking belts of .303 ammunition into the breeches, McDougall sent one platoon of riflemen to circle around the village to attack it from the rear. Once that platoon attacked, McDougall then led the rest of the company in a direct assault, with the medium machine guns providing covering fire. Although the small German force inside the village was well equipped with machine guns, resistance quickly collapsed in the face of the two-pronged attack. When McDougall managed to establish radio contact with Rosser at 1715 hours, he was able to report the village secure and that the company had suffered no casualties. Koensgen's medium machine-gunners had been less fortunate. As they had been approaching the hill to rejoin the company, a stonk of shellfire had caught one gun team, wounding two men and knocking the gun out.

McDougall left a platoon under Sergeant Frederick William Snell—who had won a Distinguished Conduct Medal at the Hitler Line—to temporarily garrison the village until the British arrived. The rest of the company then cut back to its assigned advance line and marched through to the final objective to the southwest of Monteciccardo. Soon 'B' Company was setting up near 'C' and 'A' companies for the night. While 'A' Company had suffered no casualties during the day, 'C' Company had reported four men wounded and one missing after a single hit by artillery fire. 'D' Company remained isolated well to the front of the rest of the regiment.[30]

ON THE PPCLI'S RIGHT, the Loyal Edmonton Regiment had renewed its advance at 1400 hours towards the base of the hill leading up to Monteciccardo. 'C' Squadron of the 145th Regiment supported them. The infantry made the journey without incident and were in position by 1700 hours. As had become the norm in this rough country, the tanks had fallen well behind. One by one, the tanks were immobilized until only two Shermans remained operational. These were ordered to circle back around Mombaroccio and join 'A' Squadron, which was to support a planned advance by the Seaforths the next morning.[31] The Edmontons, meanwhile, were warned to be ready to pass through the RCR during the night, following that regiment's capture of Monteciccardo.[32]

Like the PPCLI, the RCR had been keeping on track by advancing from one identifiable landmark to another. Lieutenant Jimmy Quayle and his scout platoon were moving "up a dry, parched slope, leading 'A' and 'D' companies, when brown-clad people entered a house on our left." Sergeant Roy Greenough, who habitually carried his Thompson submachine gun "at waist level, with index finger curled around the trigger," and Corporal Muller "rushed the building and called out to surrender. There was some hesitation, so Greenough fired a tommy gun burst through the window. Four Germans came tumbling out, hands high in the air. They had been about to set up an MG42 which would have given them a lethal enfilade sweep of 'A' and 'D' companies as they climbed the long slope. Our new prisoners told us there were more Germans ahead and they were ready to surrender. Four of us raced on, full of confidence, until another MG42 opened fire from the crest of the hill. Now the shoe was on the other foot, with a vengeance."[33] The enemy fire killed one of Quayle's men.

'D' Company's Captain G.C. Hungerford was preparing to assault the hill with 'A' Company providing covering fire, when Ritchie radioed an order cancelling the attack. As the day had progressed, the boundary between 1 CIB and 2 CIB had been increasingly pinched with the Edmontons and RCR both closing on Monteciccardo. Assessing the situation, Vokes had decided the RCR should shift several hundred yards to the right, widening the Canadian front in an easterly direction. This would close a gap that was developing between the Canadians and the Polish 5th Kresowa Polish Infantry Division, as this division drifted eastward in an attempt to bypass positions being stiffly defended by the 4th Parachute Regiment. Instead of attacking Monteciccardo, the RCR was instructed to "side slip a considerable distance to the right" and become 1 CIB's reserve.[34] The Loyal

Edmonton Regiment was ordered to capture Monteciccardo in a night attack. Divisional intelligence warned Lieutenant Colonel Bell-Irving he would probably face stiff opposition, for the Germans were believed to have turned the village into a major strongpoint. All afternoon, Allied planes had been bombing Monteciccardo, so the Canadians expected "to find the enemy at least shaken" by the experience.[35]

On the RCR's right flank, the Hastings and Prince Edward Regiment descended into the Arzilla River valley at 1535 hours, following the arrival of its supporting tanks. 'A' Company led with a squadron from the 12th Royal Tank Regiment in support and the other infantry companies close behind. The infantry again crossed the river easily, while the tanks were unable to find a passable crossing. Caught in the open, the tanks presented perfect targets for German antitank guns firing from concealed positions on the northern heights. Two tanks were knocked out. Finally, unable to find a crossing point, the tankers pulled back. They were to return to the riverbank at first light, by which time engineers would either have located a crossing or created one.[36]

The Hasty P's marched on towards their objectives, with 'D' Company aiming for Point 268 and 'A' Company heading to the right to outflank a cluster of buildings perched on a spur of ground jutting out into the valley. As the companies started ascending the long gradual slope leading to the ridgeline, they came under mortar and artillery fire. Spreading out, the men pressed on. Just two hundred yards short of Point 268, 'D' Company was raked by heavy machine-gun and rifle fire coming from the hilltop and from hidden trenches located on both flanks. Forced to ground, the troops quickly scraped out slit trenches and began returning fire.

Having reached the buildings on the spur, 'A' Company's leading platoon found the first building empty. Outside, somebody blew a tinny whistle that sounded like a child's toy. Then the building was struck by machine-gun fire from three directions. The rest of the company scattered into the cluster of houses, breaking down doors and crawling through windows to find cover from the deadly fire. Artillery rounds directed against the Germans struck the Canadian positions instead. Then two Churchill tanks on the south side of the river started taking potshots at the buildings, presumably thinking them still German-held. Hearing planes approaching, the men looked up and were horrified to see two Spitfires vectoring in on them. A quick-thinking platoon commander hurled a yellow air-recognition smoke canister out a window just in time to warn the pilots off. The planes turned tightly and dropped their payloads on two German tanks that had been clanking towards 'A' Company's position.[37]

When darkness fell at 2100 hours, 'A' Company tried to renew its advance, but was immediately forced back into the buildings by heavy small-arms fire. Cameron ordered his rifle companies to stay put for the night and sent the scout platoon forward to reconnoitre routes that could be used to move rations up to the men and to evacuate the dead and wounded. The two leading companies had lost five men killed. Sporadic mortar and small-arms fire continued throughout the night.[38]

In the late afternoon, Calder had realized that the Hasty P's faced a protracted fight. He therefore ordered the 48th Highlanders of Canada to close up just behind the Hasty P's tactical headquarters, which was on the south ridge overlooking the Arzilla River, in preparation to relieve the embattled regiment. Calder told the Highlanders' commander, Lieutenant Colonel Don Mackenzie, that he would rendezvous with him there to plan the operation. When it took Calder longer than expected to arrive, Mackenzie warned his companies that the relief attempt would have to take place at night. He then established radio contact with Calder, who told him to come back and be briefed at brigade headquarters. Mackenzie said he was on foot and couldn't get there in time. Calder snapped, "Get your battle adjutant back here, if you can't make it yourself!"[39]

Mackenzie contacted Major Jim Counsell by radio with Calder's instructions. The officer, who was back at the regimental headquarters, rushed to a jeep and raced to brigade HQ, arriving just in time for the briefing. He then hurried back to the companies and briefed the officers on the job ahead. The regiment was to rally at the Hasty P's tactical headquarters, where a final O Group would be held before the attack jumped off in the early morning hours of August 28.[40]

It was a moonless night and the marching companies fumbled through the inky blackness. Mackenzie, having gone on alone, arrived at the Hasty P's headquarters well ahead of his regiment. Cameron had not been informed that his headquarters in a farm outbuilding that contained two steers was to be the Highlanders' forming-up point. So he was a bit perplexed when Mackenzie asked if he had "seen his battalion anywhere."[41]

Cameron's men had rendered the building functional by hanging a blanket over the door to conform to blackout regulations and then scrounging an old kitchen table on which a candle had been fitted into an empty bully-beef tin. The headquarters staff had just been sitting down to stew earlier that evening when somebody coughed outside the entrance. Thinking it one of his men, Cameron pulled back the blanket and faced a six-foot German wearing the camouflaged smock of a parachute corporal. Impatient to return to his dinner, Cameron glowered at the man and said, "You are in the wrong camp. Go away."

Apologetically, the German explained that he was lost. Cameron pointed out a footpath and said that if he followed that four hundred yards he would likely soon find his comrades. Then the ever solicitous Cameron asked if the man had eaten. When the corporal said not for twenty-four hours, Cameron invited him to the table. Politely, the German excused himself first to wash up and then returned and ate a healthy serving of stew. While the German dined, Cameron's officers debated whether the Geneva Convention would consider the corporal a prisoner or a social guest. The corporal, who had some command of English, ventured that he was tired of the war and was content to be a prisoner. Cameron retorted that this was nonsense because the corporal had arrived at his headquarters by mistake and that he posed nothing but an "administrative nuisance." The German pounded the table, "But I tell you, I am your prisoner. The Geneva Convention says I am!"

Cameron responded in kind. "You are a soldier absent without leave from his unit and your CO will be looking for you. You may even be charged with desertion. You go along, and when you get back, tell your CO that we're going to beat the hell out of him come the dawn." The German still refused to leave and finally Cameron, needing to hammer out the details of the forthcoming attack with Mackenzie, accepted the corporal's surrender.[42]

Surreal the circumstances surrounding the German corporal's surrender might be, but his presence at Cameron's headquarters confirmed intelligence reports trickling in that indicated the 71st Infantry Division was being reinforced by two battalions of 1st Parachute Division's 4th Parachute Regiment. On the 71st's eastern flank, this reinforcement had begun during the early afternoon, resulting in the Hasty P's coming up against strong positions established earlier by the paratroops. Elsewhere during the night of August 27–28, other elements of the 71st were handing the line to the parachutists.[43]

As word of the presence of the paratroops reached I CID headquarters, a sense of gloom settled in. Not only had the 71st Division proven a tougher nut to crack than expected, the arrival of their old foes served as a warning that the worst of the fighting south of the Foglia was still to come. When Burns called Vokes to ask if there was any hope his brigades might reach the Foglia by morning, Vokes curtly replied, "Seems unlikely."[44]

[11]

Most Difficult and Unpleasant

THE LOYAL EDMONTON REGIMENT was first to test the mettle of the paratroopers on August 28. Although a narrow road with a sharp hairpin corner approached Monteccicardo from the south, Lieutenant Colonel Budge Bell-Irving wanted to avoid using such an obvious approach. Instead, 'A' Company started up the slope well to the right of Monteciccardo at 0130 hours with instructions to enter it from the east flank. 'B' Company simultaneously advanced on a point of high ground three hundred yards right of where the road switched back eastward on its steep climb to the village. Ready to support the flanking attack if required, 'C' Company was in trail behind 'A' Company. 'D' Company was held in reserve.

'A' Company crept up to the edge of the village without being detected and Captain W.G. Roxburgh slipped his troops in among the buildings. Neither the streets nor the houses showed signs of life. Men spread out to search buildings and to establish defensive points. Meanwhile, 'B' Company cleared the heights without incident and struck out for the village's western flank.

Roxburgh's company had been in Monteciccardo a scant ten minutes when the heavy tramping sound of men on the march was heard to the immediate north of the town. Moments later, a column of German infantry marching three abreast, with weapons slung on shoulders, materialized out of the darkness. The captain realized that the

71st Infantry Division must have withdrawn without waiting to hand off the village to the paratrooper relief force. Now that force was tromping towards the village and 'A' Company scrambled to give them a surprise welcome. The two Bren gunners quickly set up on either side of the street and opened fire the moment the German column reached the village's main square. Each man ripped off a couple of magazines in rapid succession, killing or wounding sixty to seventy paratroopers in seconds. A handful of Germans managed to run back the way they had come without being shot.

When the two guns fell silent, 'A' Company had no time to celebrate its initial success, for the grinding sound of tank tracks cut through the night. A large tank materialized in the centre of the road and behind it a pack of paratroopers started spreading out into the buildings. Moments later, small-arms fire began snapping at the Canadians from various nearby buildings, rooftops, and street corners. Roxburgh ordered a hasty retreat and 'A' Company fled.[1]

Captain Alon Johnson's 'D' Company had just crossed the Arzilla when the rattle and crack of gunfire erupted in Monteciccardo. He ordered his men to establish a firm defensive base in front of the river in case the leading companies had to retreat. The ground alongside the riverbank was strewn with German corpses, as if an artillery or aerial bombardment had caught a platoon or company in the open. Johnson saw one of his Bren gunners casually stretch out behind the cover of one of the bodies and brace his gun across the corpse. A few minutes later, 'A' Company came streaming back with its platoons all hopelessly jumbled together.[2] Once Johnson and the other officers got everyone calmed down, they discovered that Roxburgh, Company Sergeant Major E.H. Morris, and eight other men were missing. Thirty of the men who had made it back were wounded.

Up the slope, 'B' and 'C' companies were engaged in a hot skirmish with the Germans on the edge of the town. Although they took eighteen prisoners, it was soon evident that the battle was stalemated until tanks could be brought up at dawn. The two companies dug in and spent the rest of the night exchanging sporadic fire with the paratroopers.[3]

ON THE CANADIANS' far right flank, the 48th Highlanders of Canada had started their advance at 0200 hours with the companies marching in single file towards Point 146, a hump of ground about five hundred yards east of Point 268. The Hastings and Prince Edward Regiment was simultaneously taking another stab at capturing this latter point.[4]

The Highlanders walked along the outside edge of a narrow track descending towards the Arzilla River, with 'B' Company leading. Nobody expected any trouble crossing the river. Lieutenant Colonel Don Mackenzie and his intelligence officer, Lieutenant N.H. McMurrich, were walking at the very front of 'B' Company in order to guide the regiment to the forming-up point for the actual attack against Point 146. Mackenzie became uneasy, though, when he saw the red glow of ashes smouldering in a ditch beside the road. "Jerries," he whispered to McMurrich and drew the officer off the road into some bushes to check their map references with a hooded flashlight. Mackenzie was worried that they may have somehow drifted off course.

As the two men consulted the map, 'B' Company passed them and continued on towards a cluster of houses on the riverbank. 'A' Company followed and 'C' Company was halfway past Mackenzie when a storm of rifle and machine-gun fire from ahead and to either side ripped into the regiment, followed immediately by the explosions of mortar rounds in their midst. The Highlanders had walked into an ambush and could do little but take cover in the buildings of the small hamlet or dive into the ditches on either side of the road. Even as they sought cover, the platoon sections stuck together.

The Germans had sprung the ambush just as 'B' Company passed beyond the main body of houses, leaving it nowhere to hide initially but in the roadside ditches. Captain Gordon Proctor managed to slowly withdraw two platoons into the buildings of a farm, but any attempt by the lead platoon to pull back was met with withering machine-gun fire. 'A' Company and Mackenzie's headquarters section found shelter among the buildings, while 'C' Company set up just to the rear of the nameless village. 'D' Company was back far enough that its position lay outside the German ambush's pincers.

Although the situation was critical, the paratroopers seemed reluctant to press their advantage by directly attacking the elongated Canadian line. Instead, they held their ground, continuing to rake the Highlanders with gunfire. This allowed Mackenzie and the other officers to reorganize. Inside what the Highlanders would later refer to as simply The Village, Battle Adjutant Major Jim Counsell and McMurrich established an advance tactical HQ in a stone building on the southern outskirts. The old building was a combination farmhouse and grain mill. About a dozen Italian peasants were hiding in a cellar below the building and immediately outside a terrified cow bawled continuously. Miraculously, the animal remained unscathed by the mortar and machine-gun fire lashing the courtyard. After ensuring that 'A' Company had taken up a sound defensive perimeter within the village, Mackenzie and McMurrich withdrew to the location of the less heavily engaged 'D' Company. Captain L.G. Smith had established a strong defensive position on a small rise that looked down on the rest of the regiment. Mackenzie figured he would be better able to direct the battle from here than if he remained inside the embattled village.

Although 'D' Company's position was now secure, it had been won only after a hard fight. 'D' Company had already passed this rise by when the Germans had sprung their ambush, and the company was scattered every which way by the incoming gunfire. Smith realized immediately that he must get his company back to the ridge in order to regroup. He bellowed orders to his lieutenants and sergeants to get their men moving back, but not a soul emerged from the cover of whatever hole, ditch, or cluster of brush they hid in. Noting that the German fire seemed to be either falling short or snapping well overhead, Smith decided a desperate, possibly suicidal gamble was required to get his men moving before the Germans found their range. He shouted for Company Sergeant Major Leitch to order the men to form up on the road in parade order of three abreast.

"In threes?" the stunned CSM stammered.

"Fall them in! Line them up! Get going!" Smith bellowed.

Troopers and officers alike emerged from their hiding points wearing dazed, fearful expressions. But they responded to the familiar orders instinctively, forming precisely as if on a drill field back in Canada. Maintaining this formation, Smith marched his company up the centre of the road to the low ridgeline. Only when they passed the crest did he shout the order for the parade to fall out and quickly got his men digging trenches. Not a single soldier had been hit by the wildly inaccurate German gunfire that had continued seeking the marching column as it proceeded to the ridge.[5]

From the vantage of 'D' Company's position, Mackenzie quickly realized there was no way to improve his regiment's position until tanks could come to the rescue and he could start directing artillery and mortar fire against the well-concealed German positions. His men would have to hunker down until dawn.[6]

When all hell had broken loose around the 48th Highlanders, the Hastings and Prince Edward Regiment had just started probing once again towards Point 268. The leading companies were halted by fire from the same well-prepared German positions as had been encountered the day before. Like the Highlanders, they could only wait for daylight and some tanks.[7]

FAR OUT ON THE Canadians' left flank, the 'B' Company platoon of the Princess Patricia's Canadian Light Infantry garrisoning Monte Santa Maria collectively tensed at the sound of men marching towards them from the west. It was 0430 hours. Sergeant Frederick Snell motioned everyone to bring weapons to bear, including the medium machine-gun section that was still with the platoon. Out of the gloom, twenty-five Germans nonchalantly traipsed towards the village. The Canadians opened fire, knocking down many of the Germans with the opening volley. After a short firefight, the surviving enemy retreated. Snell's platoon had suffered two men wounded.

An hour later, Lieutenant Colonel David Rosser, planning to establish his regimental headquarters in Monte Santa Maria, led a column of vehicles to the village. The four PPCLI rifle companies were also moving westward to strengthen the Canadian hold on the little mountain town, which divisional headquarters had decided the Canadians must hold until the British could come up on line.

As Rosser's column neared the village, it came under fire from some well-dug-in Germans. Rosser and his driver bailed out of the lead jeep to take cover in a ditch. The regiment's snipers and scouts rushed past to close with the enemy. They quickly captured one German, killed six more, and drove the rest off. By 0830 hours, the PPCLI were concentrating in and around the village when a salvo of artillery struck 'A' Company, wounding one soldier. Three trucks were also damaged. Sporadic shelling proved the order of the day, but no further casualties resulted.

To the PPCLI's left, the 128th Brigade of 46th British Division was slogging towards Monte Gaudio, a hill almost parallel to Monte Santa Maria. When the brigade launched its assault on the feature at 1600 hours, the Germans started conducting a hasty withdrawal that took them right across the PPCLI's front. The Vickers of the medium machine-gun platoon ripped into the fleeing troops, forcing them to take cover wherever they could. With the retreating soldiers pinned in place by the machine-gun fire, the PPCLI's artillery Forward Observation Officer (FOO) calmly started directing accurate artillery fire on their heads. Desperate, those Germans who survived the initial bombardment made a break for it, but were further chewed up by an onslaught of artillery shells fired from their own lines when they were obviously mistaken for attacking Allied troops. All in all, the PPCLI spent the day wreaking havoc on the Germans at little cost to their own ranks.[8]

WHILE AUGUST 28 offered a day of easy victories for the PPCLI, dawn had only rendered the 48th Highlanders' position more precarious by enabling the Germans to fire at any movement inside the regiment's badly extended linear perimeter. 'D' Company's position south of The Village was separated by a stretch of about five hundred yards of open ground. Trying to cross it on foot invited near certain death. This left Mackenzie dependent on radio contact to communicate with his other companies. Out front of the village, 'B' Company remained completely trapped either in the roadside ditch or in the farm buildings. Mackenzie was unable to raise Captain Gordon Proctor on the radio.[9]

Proctor had been caught by the sudden onset of first light trying to creep from the farmhouses to where his forward platoon was trapped in the ditch. With bullets cracking all around him, and lacking any entrenching tools, the officer had frantically carved out a one-foot-deep hole with a celluloid protractor that was part of his map-reading equipment. Proctor was soon hungry, thirsty, and terrified. Above his head, fat bunches of grapes dangled enticingly from a vine, but every time he reached for them rifle and machine-gun fire showered bits of the vines down on his head. Finally, he just lay in his shallow trench, virtually motionless, enduring what he later called the longest day of his life.[10]

The 12th Royal Tank Regiment reached the southern ridge overlooking the Arzilla River at 0615 hours. Hearing heavy volumes of gunfire ahead, its commander, Lieutenant Colonel H.H. Van Straubenzee, proceeded on foot to Lieutenant Colonel Jim Ritchie's Royal Canadian Regiment headquarters. Ritchie informed him that the 48th Highlanders were held up "just in front of the river" and directed Straubenzee to both Mackenzie's headquarters and that of the Hastings and Prince Edward Regiment. The British officer met and discussed the situation with both regimental commanders. It was decided that the tank regiment's 'A' and 'C' squadrons would provide fire support from the south side of the river until the situation stabilized sufficiently to allow 'A' Squadron to cross the river and provide the infantry with direct support.[11]

As the two tank squadrons began pounding various targets with their main guns, Canadian artillery and mortar units also fired on suspected German positions. The intensity of the shelling caused an immediate slackening of the German fire, prompting 'A' Squadron to begin its move forward. The moment the leading tanks came off the slope en route to the Arzilla River, however, antitank guns started blazing away from covered positions on the northern ridge. Two tanks were knocked out and the rest had to duck for cover in an olive grove or hastily withdraw behind the ridgeline.[12]

Lieutenant Colonel Don Cameron of the Hasty P's called a heavy concentration of artillery down upon Point 268, hoping to assault the position with his infantry alone. Although the artillery fire was accurate, the leading companies were driven to ground before they could even kick off the attack. At 1210 hours, Brigadier Allan Calder ordered his regiments to sit tight and directed the commanders to send back representatives to 1st Canadian Infantry Brigade's headquarters to receive instructions for a new attack.

Calder told the assembled officers that he wanted the Hasty P's to swing towards the 48th Highlanders' left flank to relieve pressure on the embattled regiment. The Highlanders would then proceed with a drive up to Point 146. Once that objective was secure, the Hasty P's would wheel northwestward and strike out against Point 268 under the cover of darkness. At the same time, the RCR would attack Point 268 from the southwest and then pass through the Hasty P's on the summit to continue northward. During the initial phase of the attack against Point 146, artillery would fire smokescreens to cover the supporting tanks, which would then cross the Arzilla River and advance to the Highlanders. The attack was to begin at 1745 hours.[13]

The 12th Royal Tank Regiment squadron assigned to the Highlanders counted eleven tanks, a mix of three Shermans and eight Churchills. According to the plan, they would back up 'A' Company as it pushed off from the village at the head of the regiment towards Point 146. Things started to go badly from the outset, however, when one Churchill was knocked out by antitank fire from the northern ridge while crossing the river and another Churchill and two Shermans became hopelessly mired in the water. As the remaining seven tanks entered the village, a German mortar round or a rifle grenade dropped directly into a Churchill's open turret hatch and killed the entire crew. An antitank shell knocked off another Churchill's track and the massive machine slewed into a ditch, nearly crushing two Highlanders who just managed to roll clear of its treads.

One of the surviving tanks was the squadron commander's Sherman, which had to remain in the village so its radio could be used to coordinate the attack. That left only four to support the Highlanders. 'A' Company set off regardless at 1930 hours with the four Churchills in the vanguard. Lieutenant Harry Kilgour's No. 9 Platoon was forward on the right, Lieutenant Frank Girdlestone's platoon to the left, and Captain Bob Murdock's platoon followed closely behind the two leading platoons, with Captain George Beal and his company headquarters unit behind that.

The Germans met the advancing force with heavy artillery that struck down the leading section in Kilgour's platoon, killing or wounding every man. The fire also knocked out one of the Churchills. With his sights set on reaching the summit, Kilgour failed to notice that German fire had driven his men to ground just short of the crest. He rushed onto the hilltop alone and then, realizing his predicament, scuttled over to where Lieutenant Girdlestone was forming up on the left-hand side of the hill. Kilgour's platoon linked up with this force a few minutes later.

Thinking Point 146 now secure and unable to contact Beal for instructions, the two platoon commanders decided to press on to their next objective—another small hill a short distance to the north that was identified as Point 162. As they closed on this position, a heavy concentration of artillery bracketed the hill. Beal, unaware his men were virtually on top of the objective, was softening it up for the attack. The two platoons took cover while Kilgour yelled into his radio for the artillery to break off. No sooner had he managed to get the shelling lifted than heavy, determined small-arms fire from the summit of Point 162 proved that this position was held in strength. The two platoons retreated towards Point 146 but, as they approached, came under fire from paratroopers who had infiltrated back onto the hill after the Highlanders had departed.

Although the Churchills hammered the handful of buildings on the summit of Point 146, Beal lacked sufficient strength to clear out these newly arrived German defenders. He ordered his company to dig in on the southern slope of the hill to await reinforcement.[14]

To the left of the Highlanders, the advance by the Hasty P's was stalemated because the Germans on Point 146 could slice into their exposed flank should they try moving forward. They were also still wondering where their tanks were.[15] Repeated attacks on Point 146 by the remaining Highlander companies and the tankers were repelled. The Germans set haystacks on fire and used the light from the resulting bonfires to aim their machine guns and antitank weapons. One Churchill was knocked out by a Faustpatrone, and when the crew bailed out the Germans killed them with a blast from a flamethrower.[16] At dawn on August 29, the two surviving Churchills withdrew for lack of ammunition and 'A' Company fell back on the village. Of the August 28 fighting, the regimental war diarist wrote: "This day in its entirety, will ... go down as one of the most difficult and unpleasant that this battalion has had to experience."[17]

AUGUST 28 HAD PROVEN equally unpleasant for the Loyal Edmonton Regiment, which was attempting to renew its attack on Monteciccardo. Even while the infantrymen waited for elements of 'A' and 'C' squadrons of the 145th Regiment, Royal Armoured Corps, fire from the German lines intensified. 'B' Company was so plagued by gunfire from a position three hundred yards off that a platoon was sent to clear it out. This it did at a cost of two Canadians wounded in exchange for one German prisoner and two others wounded. Clearing the outpost, however, failed to lessen the rate of German artillery and mortar fire harassing the company. A direct hit on 'B' Company's headquarters killed two men and wounded a further eight.

At 0700 hours, the tanks ground up to the rear of 'D' Company's position. Lieutenant Colonel Budge Bell-Irving called tank commander Captain R.F. Grieve and Captain Alon Johnson of 'D' Company together to discuss the attack. Given the open terrain between the Arzilla River and Monteciccardo, there were few options other than to charge straight at the village.[18] Bell-Irving told Johnson to concentrate his company and enter Monteciccardo directly in front of the monastery tower, for it appeared this was the only spot where a street entering the village was wide enough to admit the Churchills.[19]

Before the attack went forward, Bell-Irving had the regiment's antitank platoon blast the tower apart. As the antitank gunners were blowing great chunks of masonry out of the tower, four of 'A' Company's missing men managed to use this distraction to escape from their hiding place in the town and dash to the Canadian lines. All were suffering from light wounds. They brought with them four German prisoners, of whom two were also wounded.[20]

At 1315 hours, Johnson's company and the tanks headed for Monteciccardo. Johnson's men were well spaced out, so the constant artillery, mortar, and machine-gun fire caused few casualties and failed to slow their advance. Liaison between the tankers and the infantry quickly became a problem, however, as the infantry officers were unable to attract the tankers' attention and direct them to fire on specific targets.[21] Still, by 1400 hours, 'D' Company reached the village outskirts. The lead platoon charged into the monastery garden and entered the structure itself, of which only the ground storey still stood. A wild melee broke out between the Canadians and ten Germans inside the building. When the bullets and fragments of grenades stopped, the Germans were all dead. The Canadians had suffered no casualties.[22]

As the other platoons came up to the edge of the garden, however, they were subjected to heavy fire from tunnels extending from underneath the monastery. These were large enough to hold two companies of German infantry and proved immune to artillery or aerial bombardment. Although 'D' Company remained unaware of the origin of this fire, it had unwittingly discovered where the Germans had been able to hide during the air raids that had savaged Monteciccardo on August 27.[23]

From the edge of the monastery grounds, Johnson watched Captain Grieve's Churchill roll up close to the monastery and fire on suspected German strongpoints. Suddenly, several Germans stepped out from the corner of a nearby building. One shouldered a Faustpatrone and fired. When the explosive charge struck, the tank exploded into flame.[24] Grieve and three of his crew bailed out, but the officer and two of the men had suffered wounds during the explosion. The men no sooner hit the ground than several Germans surrounded and quickly hustled them all into a cellar that was part of the tunnel network running under the monastery.[25]

The other tanks were still struggling to find a route up the final bit of slope leading to the edge of town and were further slowed by the heavy artillery fire buffeting their armoured hides. Figuring he faced a protracted fight for the monastery, Johnson slipped his web belt off in order to lighten his load and make it easier for him to dash quickly back and forth between platoons. As he straightened up, a bullet slammed into the front of his helmet, passed through the thin steel, and opened a gash down the centre of his skull. Johnson was knocked flat on his back by the impact, and when he sat back up blood gushed down all sides of his head.

His first concern was to regain control of his company, but a stretcher-bearer ran up and said, "Sir, you're hurt bad." The words startled Johnson far more than had the sight of his blood or the rapidly increasing pain of his wound. He suddenly felt dizzy, verging on fainting. Forcing himself to concentrate, Johnson turned over company command to Lieutenant H.F. "Fritz" Hansen and then walked back to the Regimental Aid Post. It would be two months before Johnson returned to duty.[26]

The fight around the monastery degenerated into complete confusion when several Churchills got up to within one hundred yards of the monastery wall and started hammering the building with high-explosive rounds. Inside, 'D' Company's lead platoon watched the building shake and tremble under the explosive impact of each round, but its stout walls withstood the battering. When the tanks ceased fire fifteen minutes later, the platoon scrambled out of the building and rejoined the rest of the company on Monteciccardo's outskirts. 'D' Company set up in a semi-circle facing the monastery. The other Edmonton companies were still well back, waiting for instructions.

Bell-Irving realized that only a much more coordinated and heavy concentration of artillery would shift the odds into his favour. He hammered out a plan that called for 25-pounders to fire on the village from 1915 to 1950 hours, whereupon two regiments of heavier medium artillery would take over for ten minutes. Under the cover of this fire, 'B' Company and a squadron of tanks would close on the monastery. At 2000 hours, the artillery would abruptly cease firing and 'B' Company would rush the building. Companies 'C' and 'A' would immediately pass by the monastery, enter the town, and clear it.

When the 25-pounders finished their scheduled fire plan at 1950 hours, the explosions inside Monteciccardo suddenly ceased. No fire came from the medium artillery. Bell-Irving radioed for an explanation of the delay. Finally, even as the clock ticked up to 2000 hours and the scheduled time for the infantry companies to begin their assault, he was told the guns had been required elsewhere. The Edmontons would have to attack without the promised support. They also had only two tanks instead of the promised squadron, for the others had unexpectedly withdrawn without telling anyone they were leaving. Bell-Irving went ahead with his plan.

'B' Company rushed the monastery and swept into it without meeting any resistance. The other companies passed by and within minutes had driven through to the other side of Monteciccardo. The Germans had fled. They had left Captain Grieve and his three crewmen behind in a cellar under the monastery. A patrol mopping up the town soon discovered the body of Captain Roxburgh lying in an alley. No trace of the other missing Edmontons was discovered and they were assumed captured. At thirty minutes after midnight, Monteciccardo was declared secure.[27]

The moment the Edmontons broke into Monteciccardo, the Seaforth Highlanders of Canada, who had been following their fellow 2 CIB regiment, passed by the village on the right and started marching towards the villages of Ginestreto and Sant' Angelo to the east and north of Monteciccardo respectively. 'D' Company led the way, with 'C' immediately behind and 'A' following farther back. 'B' Company remained in reserve. Only slight opposition was met during the night's advance and by dawn of August 29 Ginestreto was in the regiment's hands. 'A' Company then moved on to Sant' Angelo and pronounced it secure at 0830 hours.[28]

On the Canadian right flank, 1 CIB's regiments had reorganized and resumed the attacks against Points 146 and 268 at 0330 hours. Where resistance had been strongly offered by the Germans scant hours before, the advancing Hasty P's and 48th Highlanders now met little opposition. By 0430 hours, the Highlanders reported Point 146 secure and the Hasty P's and RCR walked through the abandoned German fighting positions on Hill 268 to advance a mile along the road leading out of Ginestreto.[29] The Hasty P's had suffered forty-three casualties in the protracted fight for Point 268, of whom seven men were killed. For the Highlanders, the toll paid for taking Point 146 was eight dead and twenty-four wounded. The ease of the subsequent advance indicated that, having lost Monteciccardo and other strongholds west of where 1 CIB had been stymied, the Germans had decided to withdraw behind the Foglia River.[30]

As the Germans pulled out, the two leading brigades of 1st Canadian Infantry Division were directed to prepare to be relieved. Both the Hasty P's and the RCR, however, pushed patrols through to the Foglia River. Calder was discussing turnover of his sector with Brigadier Paul Bernatchez of 3rd Canadian Infantry Brigade when the RCR reported by radio that a patrol had found the Foglia "fordable to infantry practically anywhere" and probably passable in many spots to tanks.[31] While pleased with this information, Bernatchez asked Calder to immediately instruct his units to cease further patrolling as his own troops would soon be patrolling near the Foglia and there was a risk of patrols exchanging fire. Only one patrol by the 48th Highlanders on the extreme right boundary was authorized.[32]

The order to cease patrolling came too late for Cameron's Hasty P's. The lieutenant colonel had already dispatched a patrol at 2230 hours with instructions to cross the Foglia and test the German defences. Sergeant E.R. Leroux led his men across the river and then a mile northward to a road running inland from Pesaro. Leroux returned from the patrol at 0430 hours and reported encountering not a single German, despite the fact that the Canadian front lines continued to be battered by German artillery and mortar fire throughout the night. Leroux's patrol proved that the paratroops, believed to be taking over the entire front facing the Canadians, were still thin on the ground.[33]

[12]

Something Radically Wrong

IN A FORTNIGHT'S TIME, the Perth Regiment of Canada's commander had said in a rousing pre-battle speech delivered while standing on the hood of a jeep, they would "be riding the watery streets of Venice in gondolas." Private Stan Scislowski had wanted to believe Lieutenant Colonel William Reid, but the man was a newcomer from the Irish Regiment and had yet to win the trust of his new command. The twenty-one-year-old conscript from Windsor was not alone in thinking that the regiment's own Major M.W. Andrew should have got the regiment when in August Lieutenant Colonel J.S. Lind was promoted to brigadier of the new 12th Canadian Infantry Brigade. "Butterballs," as the men called Andrew, was from Stratford, whereas Reid shared no links to the Ontario farm country and small towns from which most of the regiment's ranks hailed. A nice-enough-seeming fellow, Reid, like many high-ranking officers, appeared to think he could rally the ranks by sounding "like a high school football coach whipping his team up for the big game, with all the rah-rah stuff."[1]

Scislowski and his mates in 'D' Company's No. 18 Platoon had heard this folderol before at the Arielli River north of Ortona and again at the Liri Valley. Butchered and shamed at the Arielli, the Perths and other regiments of the 11th Canadian Infantry Brigade had then endured a long, cruel march up the Liri Valley. One look at a map showed a hell of a lot of Italy to cover before anyone should indulge in gondola-riding fantasies.

Today alone, the men faced a thirty-five-mile march to relieve the Seaforth Highlanders of Canada. They started out at 1000 hours on what the regiment's war diarist declared was "one of the warmest days we had." Except for a small advance party sent ahead to scout the assigned concentration area, most of the regiment's 37 officers and 795 men were marching.[2]

"Sweat dripped off our foreheads in a steady stream, brought on not only by the heat absorbed by our steel helmets, but also by the pace of the march," Scislowski later wrote. "Whoever was up at the head of the column was clipping along too fast for our liking, and it took a lot out of us just to keep up. And that's when the cursing and the complaining got going. 'What the hell's the bloody hurry?' someone behind me rapped out, and then more voices began to echo rude sentiments. They came thicker and faster by the minute. 'I'll shoot the son of a bitch if I ever get my hands on him! I'll cut his balls off, the bastard!'"[3]

Lieutenant Colonel Reid was setting the cadence.[4] He pressed on relentlessly, unmindful or uncaring of the complaints and threats brewing in his wake. Reid was tough and a seasoned infantry officer, but he also marched light. He did not carry a heavy pack, a Lee Enfield rifle or Bren gun, and web belts crammed with ammunition that added up to a hundred pounds or more of weight, on a day when the temperature was crackling just under one hundred degrees Fahrenheit.

Men started falling out, staggering off the track and flopping down under any kind of shade. The rest tromped past. "Sweat poured down our faces, soaked the collars of the denim we wore, and the constant rubbing of the coarse, salt-laden cloth against our necks chafed us something terrible—but there was nothing we could do to ease the irritation except swear and keep on going.

"A thick layer of dust, as fine as talcum powder, swirled upward like white smoke from under our boots. It settled into the corners of our mouths, and with every intake of breath the dust built up in the mucous of our nasal passages and coated the soft tissue of our throats. Breathing came in laboured gasps, and all along the way it was a spit, gag and cough affair. Sweat dripping off our foreheads ran into our eyes and blurred our vision. And to make matters worse, salt in the sweat mixed with gritty dust irritated our eyes to such a degree that we had to constantly use the water in our canteens to wash it away. A steady demand for water brought on by extreme thirst, rinsing out dust-contaminated mouths, and washing out our eyes had soon drained our water-bottles dry."[5]

Every hour there was a five-minute break. The men spent it frantically refilling canteens from farm wells before the column started moving again. Scislowski verged on delirium, his only bearing being the back of the man ahead. Where that soldier went, so went Scislowski. In time, each forward step also rendered the sounds of a battle ahead clearer to the ear—the pop of rifle fire, the angry sharp rip of a German MG42 answered by the slow thudding of a Bren gun.

Finally, after twenty miles, and with the long shadows of evening slipping down the hills, the Perths halted behind a ridge lined by umbrella pines and cypress. There was a pool, fed by "crystal-clear cold water from an underground stream." Men tore off their clothes and leapt in naked, "shouting, laughing, splashing and dunking in the cooling depths." The pain and feverish heat literally washed out of Scislowski's body, as the refreshing water revived his spirit and strength.[6]

They were not to linger here. At midnight the orders came and, groaning under the weight of their packs, the Perths resumed the march, moving through a night so black Scislowski was unable to see the man ahead. If anyone hesitated, the man behind banged into him and the column would collapse inward like an accordion that left men cursing and shoving each other.

Then Reid, still out front, lengthened his stride and unbelievably the Perths were nearly jogging. "It went something like this: walk faster, break into a run a few paces, walk again, jog five or six paces, walk. It was like this all the way right up until first light."[7]

As August 29 dawned, they entered Mombaroccio, where they paused for four and a half hours as the Loyal Edmonton Regiment finished clearing Monteciccardo and the Seaforth Highlanders of

Canada the other villages overlooking the Foglia River. Jeeps arrived, carrying welcome corned-beef sandwiches. Scislowski bit into his and almost gagged on the thick, waxy margarine slathered on the bread. Ravenous, he wolfed the sandwich down anyway and sucked tea gratefully from a cup. At 0900 hours the march began anew. By noon, "the Perths were strung out for miles on the dust choked road stretching back over hillocks and down valleys. Man, but was it ever hot! Steel helmets by now had become brain-baking ovens. Pack straps had taken on knife-edges, cutting sharply into aching shoulders. Thigh muscles strained at every incline, and feet throbbed from the pounding they'd been taking over the past twenty-four hours."[8]

The column left the road, heading cross-country. Scislowski initially thought this might offer easier marching than the hard, dusty road surface. "Brambles tore our knees. Potholes, field stones, and erosion ruts on the slopes added another dimension of discomfort as we plodded sullenly and bleary-eyed towards the sounds of battle, now little less than a mile away." Scislowski tripped on a root and sprawled face first into the dirt. "I cursed the army. I cursed the officers. I cursed my NCOS and I even uttered a few choice words of profanity up to God for having chosen the infantry to serve in."[9] There was another hill, steep and covered in scrub. Men sobbed aloud that they couldn't go up another, only to do so anyway.

Entering a cluster of houses, they stopped behind a low cinderblock wall following the ridgeline. This was Ginestreto. The Perths' gruelling route march was over. Scislowski's platoon sprawled on a patch of pavement, each man panting as if he had just crossed the finish line after a flat-out 880-yard dash. When Scislowski's heart rate steadied, he tottered over to the wall to look down at the new battlefield. It seemed unremarkable, like any other Italian valley. There was no sign of the dugouts, trenches, and amoured cupolas reported as forming the backbone of the Gothic Line.[10]

THE MILE-WIDE Foglia Valley was almost entirely flood plain, vegetated by reedy grass and low brush. Where the ground rose slightly to form narrow shelves, there were fruit trees and vineyards. The Germans had felled any tall trees to open fields of fire, and the gentle slope running up from the valley to a low ridge on the north was sparsely vegetated. Just beyond the ridgeline, a deep antitank ditch ran westward from the village of Osteria Nuova to Montecchio directly in front of a parallel road. West of Montecchio, the valley walls steepened to form a natural tank obstacle.

North of the road that parallelled the Foglia River, the ground rose sharply into the low, broken hills of the Monte Luro–Tomba di Pesaro feature, which thrust several spiny ridges towards the valley like the fingers of a splayed hand. At 948 feet, Monte Luro formed the highest point.

I Canadian Corps headquarters staff had divided the slightly more than three-mile Canadian frontage into two roughly even lanes. The eastern lane would be 1st Canadian Infantry Division's responsibility and the western one 5th Canadian Armoured Division's. Monte Luro lay in the centre of 1 CID's ground. Running southwestward from its peak, a ridge cut sharply across 5 CAD's front and extended well into V Corps's sector. Tomba di Pesaro perched on the crest of a spur that jutted northwest from this ridge. Immediately southeast of the village was Monte Peloso, also identified as Point 253. The village and Point 253 dominated alternate flanks of a vital north-south running road and both were believed heavily fortified. Two other spurs extended south from the main ridge. One ran about a mile southwest of Point 253 before dividing into three fingers that reached the edge of the lateral road and were separated by deep gullies. The most easterly of these terminated at Borgo Santa Maria, the centre finger midway between this village and Osteria Nuova, and the longer, more irregular, third finger passed just east of Montecchio. Two points of high ground dominated the latter spur—points 147 and 115. On the far left, another narrow, steep-sided ridge curved in a southwesterly direction and culminated in a three-hundred-foot promontory, identified as Point 120, which overlooked the road immediately west of Montecchio. A small summit called Monte Marrone rose up out of the ridgeline at the point where it started trending more sharply southward towards Point 120. The promontory was thought to be heavily fortified and enjoyed a clear two-hundred-degree field of fire that commanded both the flats to the front and the deep draws on either flank.

The only decent road in 5 CAD's entire sector followed a narrow draw from Montecchio towards Tomba di Pesaro, and Point 120 served as a roadblock to any force trying to enter this road from the south. This made the promontory a key objective.[11]

But before there could be any assault on Point 120, 11th Canadian Infantry Brigade must win a bridgehead across the Foglia River. The same held true for 1 CID's planned drive towards Tomba di Pesaro. While the Foglia presented no significant natural obstacle to either infantry or armour, the forward teeth of the Gothic Line followed the riverbank from Pesaro to a point twelve miles inland. Behind this line, more defences were layered in rows back at least as far as Monte Luro.

Fronting the defensive works were thousands of mines that had been sown in overlapping panels, each about fifty feet wide. Inside each panel were six to seven rows of mines. The rows and the mines inside them were methodically spaced between seven to eight feet apart. The zigzagging antitank ditch just south of the lateral road was fourteen feet wide and only broken for a one-mile stretch of steep embankments between Borgo Santa Maria and Osteria Nuova. Backing the antitank ditch was a long string of machine-gun, antitank, and field-gun emplacements linked by a communication trench that had been protected by a wood roof covered in a thick layer of dirt and sod.

The Germans had also braced this section with great amounts of concrete. "Approximately twenty casemates large enough to contain antitank guns or light field guns are placed out among the other defences and all of them cover the river, the antitank ditch, or the minefield west of Montecchio," 1 CID intelligence staff noted. "Numerous pillboxes of various sizes ranging from the two- to three-man types to those capable of containing light guns are seen along the entire length of this sub-sector, the majority of which also fire south to cover the anti-tank obstacles."[12]

Positioned immediately behind the front band of defences was another broad belt of barbed wire, in turn covered by a second system of pillboxes and emplacements. Well sited on the Monte Luro–Tomba di Pesaro feature were several concrete-based Panther V turrets—Panzerturms. These faced a wide skyline against which any Allied tank crossing the ridgeline south of the Foglia River would be immediately silhouetted and remain exposed during the entire one- to two-mile advance to the base of the feature.

To construct this detailed report on the Gothic Line's defences, Canadian intelligence had relied on reports by Italian partisans, interrogations of German prisoners, and, most importantly, photo intelligence provided by the Mediterranean Air Interpretation Unit (MAIU). Since early August, MAIU had flown hundreds of reconnaissance missions that meticulously photographed the Gothic Line from the Adriatic to a point fifteen miles inland. By following a precise grid pattern, they were able to develop a detailed interlocking photographic map on a scale of 1:15,000.[13]

SEEING THE FOGLIA RIVER valley for the first time, Saskatoon Light Infantry Captain Howard Mitchell felt a chill of despair run through his body. "I fervently wished," he later wrote, "that my God would take me or do anything to spare me this. The Hitler Line was in fairly flat country between two mountain ridges. This was different." Here there was a mile-wide valley and a high crest behind which the German artillery and mortars could remain hidden and invisible to the Canadian artillery gunners, mortarmen, and medium machine-gunners. In the river valley itself, Mitchell saw "no trees, no bushes, no houses. It was a bare valley and every inch of it from our side of the river to the far side of the valley was covered by everything the Germans had. The Hitler Line was terrible. This could only be a stupid slaughter."[14]

Lieutenant General Tommy Burns shared the same worries; hence his earlier desire to "gatecrash" the line. But he now figured the advance from the Metauro to the Foglia had taken too long for this to still be possible. As 11 CIB and 3 CIB took over the corps's front lines on August 29, Burns was discussing with Eighth Army commander General Oliver Leese the need to heavily bomb the German defences the next day. He also wanted twelve regiments of field artillery available to support an inevitable set-piece attack. Leese assured Burns that by September 1 he would have his artillery, as well as two naval destroyers mounting either four or six 4.7-inch guns apiece and a gunboat bearing two six-inch guns standing offshore.[15]

The aerial attack on August 30 would kick off several days of artillery concentrations and air raids that would culminate in the launching of the set-piece attack on the night of September 2–3 under the light of a full moon.[16]

Even as Burns was teeing up a set-piece offensive, a new exciting possibility was gelling in the mind of 5 CAD's Major General Bert Hoffmeister. Never one to hang back at divisional headquarters, he spent the afternoon of August 29 touring the front in the company of 11 CIB's Brigadier Ian Johnston. Crawling on their bellies up to a point where they could look at the valley undetected by the Germans, the two men examined the antitank ditch and the ridge. Hoffmeister thought the ridge was "just a real fortress in itself, this great rocky thing." He noted several concrete gun emplacements, the swaths of barbed wire, and the obviously extensive minefields. But Hoffmeister noticed something else that made his pulse quicken. "There was no life around the place," he later said. "I didn't expect German officers to be swanking up and down, but the whole thing looked terribly quiet. There wasn't a shell coming over our way." A dirt road running from one side of the valley to the other showed obvious signs of recent use, but amazingly the bridge crossing the Foglia was still intact. He would have expected it to be blown.

Hoffmeister turned to Johnston and said, "There's something wrong with this whole situation. It just doesn't sit right with me. There's something radically wrong."[17]

Rushing to corps headquarters, Hoffmeister told Burns what he had seen and asked permission to send some patrols across the river. Burns agreed. At 1500 hours, several Cape Breton Highlanders scouts crossed the Foglia in a brazen daylight test. They climbed Point 120 and captured one lonely German manning a position there. Private Paul MacEachern discovered a couple of German antitank guns in an emplacement. Their breech blocks had both been removed, a sure sign that the Germans had abandoned the position. When a nearby Italian woman waved her white apron, the patrol—thinking she might be signalling the Germans—scooped her up as a prisoner. They then hurried back to the Canadian lines and excitedly reported that Point 120 was clear. The captured woman was found to have been merely calling her domestic geese back to their pen and was quickly released.[18]

At 2200 hours, Perth scout officer Lieutenant D.L. Thompson and two men crossed the Foglia. In six hours, they circled up to the anti-tank ditch and back without seeing a single German. It took them so long to reach the road because the ground through which they passed was lousy with mines, mostly the Italian wooden box and Schümine varieties.[19]

During the night, the Cape Breton Highlanders sent out another patrol consisting of a party of engineers and a platoon from 'A' Company commanded by Lieutenant W.F. Dean. Once across the river, they slowly wove through a series of minefields to the lateral road. Creeper vines had grown out of the ditches to cross its twelve-foot macadam width and some melons were also growing out on the road from vines rooted in the verges. Dean started leading the patrol down the road, but called an abrupt halt and signalled everyone into the ditch when he saw a wooden cart moving about fifty yards ahead. It lurched another ten yards towards them, halted, and then a voice barked out, "Hallo, Hallo, Hallo." Dean's men slowly slinked back the way they had come, trying not to betray their presence. Leaving the road, they had moved about five yards into the bordering minefield when there was "a challenge from [the] knoll, 'Halt, Halt,' imperious and gutteral." Dean and his men froze for ten minutes and then moved on to the river without further incident. The lieutenant noted carefully that the stream was only twenty-five feet wide and just ankle deep.[20]

These details were quickly passed to Hoffmeister, who hurried to Burns's corps headquarters. But the lieutenant general was away, attending a meeting at Eighth Army headquarters. Leese, Burns, II Polish Corps commander General Wladyslaw Anders, and Leese's chief of staff were finalizing the planned attack for the night of September 2–3.

Even as they ground on with the task of setting out movement schedules and determining artillery assignments, Leese was receiving other evidence that the Gothic Line was not held in strength. Based on this information, he ordered the aerial bombardment that had begun at dawn halted at midday and moved the set-piece attack forward to the night of September 1–2. Meantime, the Canadians were to carry out more patrols to gather further intelligence.[21]

When Burns returned to his corps headquarters at noon on August 30, he found Hoffmeister waiting impatiently. "I think there's just something very strange about this whole situation," the major general said. "I think the Germans are possibly unprepared for anything other than a set-piece attack for which they'll get plenty of warning. Whether they know we've concentrated in this area in front of them or not, we don't know." But Hoffmeister suspected the Germans had been caught flat-footed and a great opportunity to actually "gatecrash" the Gothic Line existed.

Hoffmeister proposed lining 11 CIB into two columns, with the Cape Breton Highlanders leading the left column and the Perth Regiment the right column. Both columns would have inherent support from a regiment of 5th Canadian Armoured Brigade and backing by artillery batteries organized so that one section of guns could be laying down covering fire while the other was moving up on the column's rear. Sappers would be right up front with the infantry to pull mines in order to open sufficient room for the tanks to slip through gaps and keep pace. If needed, the supporting tail of artillery and additional tanks could be switched quickly from one column to reinforce the other in order to effect a breakthrough wherever opportunity best presented itself. In reserve, Hoffmeister would still have the 12th Canadian Infantry Brigade and most of his division's tank regiments. The entire action could begin that very night.[22]

Intrigued and inclined towards the innovative attack plan, Burns told Hoffmeister to ready his division. At 1345 hours, Burns issued an order to both Hoffmeister and Major General Chris Vokes to start immediate vigorous patrolling north of the Foglia River to determine once and for all whether the line was a paper tiger. "Should results of the patrols indicate that the line is only lightly held, both divisions will send through strong fighting patrols, strength equivalent to at least one battalion per divisional sector. These patrols will penetrate the line and the necessary gaps and crossings through minefields and antitank ditches will be prepared. Should these patrols succeed in getting forward without heavy opposition both divisions will establish a bridgehead night of 30–31 August.... These bridgeheads will be established so that at first light both I Canadian Infantry Division and 5 Canadian Armoured Division will be able to advance through them and continue the advance in their respective divisional sectors."[23]

Hoffmeister had originally thought the attack would be a night operation and knew that was what Brigadier Johnston wanted because of the wide-open valley the attacking regiments must cross. But Burns had upped the ante by ordering the attack to begin as quickly as possible.

Hoffmeister and Johnston worked frantically through the mid-afternoon to move the designated regiments to their jumping-off positions. Behind the Perths and the Cape Breton Highlanders, the Irish Regiment of Canada and the Princess Louise Dragoon Guards—borrowed from 12th Canadian Infantry Brigade—stood in reserve and offered a firm base of support in case the entire operation turned sour and the leading regiments had to retreat. Squadrons of the 5th Canadian Armoured Brigade's 8th Princess Louise New Brunswick Hussars hovered close by, ready to move forward on a moment's notice. Self-propelled antitank batteries were also positioned in the trail of the two columns and the 17th Field Regiment, RCA had its guns at the ready.[24]

But there would be no initial artillery fire on either Canadian division's front. This was to be a surprise attack hurled into the valley at 1730 hours. And it was an attack that had been thrown together in a few short hours. Hoffmeister wasn't worried by the haste. He felt in his gut that II CIB could break right through. If not both columns, then surely one.

Despite the fact that Major General Chris Vokes had tried and failed with this kind of operation at the Hitler Line, he shared Hoffmeister's and Burns's enthusiasm. "If we attempted a breakthrough with all possible speed, we had every chance of quick success. Following this we should be able to turn the operation into the pursuit phase readily," he later wrote.[25] For the pursuit phase, Vokes formed an ad hoc armoured task force comprised of squadrons from the 21st Royal Tank Brigade supported by infantry regiments and the

Royal Canadian Dragoons—his divisional armoured reconnaissance regiment. He planned for 3rd Canadian Infantry Brigade to establish a bridgehead across the Foglia through which he would pass the rest of the division in successive stages to the Conca River, which was just under seven miles away and drained into the sea a bit north of Cattolica. Once 1 CID reached the Conca it would be halfway to Rimini. Vokes "hoped to be able to effect this break-out during the night 30–31 August."[26]

For such a grand design, Vokes's initiation of the plan was strangely tentative. He assigned just one company of the West Nova Scotia Regiment to conduct the first probing of the Gothic Line at a point midway between Borgo Santa Maria and Osteria Nuova. "When this was successful," Vokes wrote, "remainder of the WNSR was to cross the river and join this company and establish a bridgehead. [Royal 22e Regiment] was then to relieve WNSR and effect the break-in."[27] Brigadier Paul Bernatchez, commander of 3rd Canadian Infantry Brigade, told Lieutenant Colonel Ron Waterman by phone that his West Novas were to take Point 204, a high point on the ridge behind the two villages. If successful, the remainder of the brigade would follow. Waterman could arrange for some artillery support if he wished, but there would be no tanks. Bernatchez told Waterman to issue the company with extra PIATS and ammunition for the men's personal weapons. Waterman said he could strike at 1600 hours.[28]

PART THREE

THE GATECRASH

[13]

Go Down, Boys

TO A MAN, the soldiers of the West Nova Scotia Regiment knew about the minefield that started three hundred yards north of the Foglia River. The previous night, a patrol had probed quietly into the field and returned with a frightening report on how thickly the Germans had sown the explosive charges. Then, at 1330 hours on August 30, regimental intelligence officer Captain R.E. Campbell listened to two Italian farmers describe in grim detail how the ground across the river was literally riddled with mines.[1] A worried Campbell feared the intelligence on the threat of the minefield was too late arriving. Thirty minutes later, Lieutenant Colonel Ron Waterman convened his final O Group. The attack was on and must start in just two-and-a-half hours.

Waterman selected Captain J.H. Jones's 'B' Company to spearhead 1st Canadian Infantry Division's attack. Its task was to cross the river and push up to Point 133, midway between Borgo Santa Maria and Osteria Nuova and about seven hundred yards north of the lateral road. Once this objective was secure, the West Novas' remaining three rifle companies would establish a bridgehead extending from the riverbank to 'B' Company's position. They would hold this small triangle of ground until relieved by the Royal 22e Regiment and then renew the northward advance. During his briefing, Waterman never mentioned the minefields. Nor did he assign sappers from 4th Field

Company, Royal Canadian Engineers to clear a path for 'B' Company through the mines.[2]

The West Nova commander had started the war as a Princess Patricia's Canadian Light Infantry lance corporal, working his way up to officer's rank. On December 12, 1943, he had been the second-in-command of the West Novas when Lieutenant Colonel Pat Bogert was wounded. Waterman had commanded the regiment since. At the Hitler Line he had led the West Novas bravely and wisely, consequently being awarded the Distinguished Service Order. In the past couple of months, however, the strains of war had taken their toll on this once fine officer. He had become self-indulgent to a fault, lounging about in a caravan of the type normally the preserve of only divisional and corps commanders. There were rumours of excessive drinking. And there was Waterman's mysterious disappearance from the regiment for several weeks after the Liri Valley campaign ended. Eventually, he was discovered shacked up in a mansion with an Italian contessa. Major General Chris Vokes had wondered then if he should not replace Waterman, but had hesitated because to do so would inevitably scuttle the man's career.[3]

'B' Company walked down the slope towards the valley bottom in extended order with two platoons forward and one back. Right on time at 1630, the soldiers stepped down into the riverbed.[4] Ten minutes later, the first soldier trod on a Schümine concealed beneath a one-inch covering of turf and was badly wounded. Captain Jones sent men to find a route around or through the minefield. Several of these scouts triggered mines and were maimed or killed. Jones radioed Waterman that he was going to "continue cautious advance."[5] Again and again, there was the sharp booming of mines exploding under men's feet. Unconscious soldiers sprawled brokenly on the ground, while others writhed and screamed in agony or stared in shocked horror at the blood pumping out of a stump where a leg had been just moments before.

Despite the punishing losses, 'B' Company pressed on. Thirty minutes later, the remnants exited the minefield and stood at the base of the ridge. A gully cut up to the lateral road on the crest, offering a covered approach. Jones signalled his men to move up it.

The leading section was just about at the top when intense volleys of small-arms fire ripped into the most forward platoons. Men dodged for cover only to find that the banks and rim of the gully had been sown with Schümines. More men died or were wounded. 'B' Company froze and went to ground just south of the road. Jones radioed Waterman at 1850 hours that he desperately needed reinforcement.[6]

Ten minutes later, Vokes was chivvying Brigadier Paul Bernatchez to get the West Novas to hurry up with establishing the bridgehead. He was anxious to get the breakout going. Bernatchez called Waterman and was told that 'B' Company was on Point 133. Waterman soon radioed back with a correction. 'B' Company, he said, was "moving very slowly through the minefield under MG fire."[7] He assured Bernatchez "that the company would be able to get through the minefield and to the lateral beyond" and that his plan for the rest of the regiment to cross into the bridgehead was "all arranged."[8]

It was not until 1930 hours, however, that Waterman ordered his other three rifle companies to establish the bridgehead. They moved across and took up positions just in front of the minefield. Meanwhile, the beleaguered Jones requested permission to withdraw to the bridgehead at 2000 hours. Waterman approved. Jones's men spent the next forty minutes extracting themselves slowly and fearfully back through the minefield. They were dogged by intense German small-arms fire almost the entire way.[9]

Bernatchez knew nothing of the company's withdrawal. He still thought that 'B' Company was "just short of the main lateral road... and still trying to get forward.... Since it had previously been reported that all arrangements for this move were complete it was expected that the remainder of the battalion would shortly be up to the leading company. At 2220 hours it was reported that the battalion was complete in the bridgehead positions but there was no indication that any move forward of that area was in progress."[10]

Exasperated, Bernatchez grabbed his artillery liaison officer, Lieutenant Colonel H.E. Brown of the 1st Field Regiment, RCA and headed for Waterman's headquarters. Half an hour later, Bernatchez observed that "the situation was confused and that orders for the attack by the battalion had NOT been issued."[11] He immediately radioed brigade HQ to advise that he was organizing a new attack, but it would be 0200 hours before it could proceed.

Bernatchez and Waterman agreed that this attack should entail a second company moving up alongside 'B' Company, which Bernatchez still understood was "close to the lateral road." Even now, he "was NOT aware that it had been withdrawn," Bernatchez later wrote.[12] Brown arranged a short, simple artillery-fire plan to support the two companies in crossing the lateral road and establishing a firm defensive base immediately on the other side. A third company would then jump through and seize Point 133. One company would remain inside the bridgehead. Bernatchez, having found it difficult to get the strangely sluggish Waterman to coordinate the attack, was forced to set the start time back to 0300 hours. Believing everything now in order, he and Brown returned to brigade HQ.

At 0235 hours, Waterman notified Bernatchez that the attack would have to be delayed because "difficulty was being experienced in gathering company commanders for an O Group."[13] Not until 0420 hours did Waterman report the O Group underway and that the regiment would attack at 0530 hours. At 0505 hours, Waterman pushed it back to 0600. Twenty minutes later, he again reported 'B' Company as being 250 yards short of the road and held up by mines. In what seemed pure fantasy, considering that 'B' Company was tight inside the bridgehead and nowhere near the road, he said the Germans were dug into a bunker along the road that "would have to be broken down, but that there was no antitank ditch." Bernatchez ordered him "to mop up the area of the road on either side of the gap once his battalion reached the main lateral road."[14] Although concerned about Waterman's apparently muddled reports, Bernatchez had no idea how badly misinformed he was as to the true state of affairs.

Beyond the bridgehead a small, heroic group was at work. Led by regimental chaplain Captain Laurence Frank Wilmot, a party of stretcher-bearers had ventured into the unknown hazards of a minefield subjected to searching artillery and machine-gun fire from the German positions on the ridge. Dead and wounded West Novas were scattered throughout the field, requiring Wilmot and his men to warily zigzag about to reach them. Wilmot never hesitated. Showing amazing calm, he directed the evacuation of the wounded. Few of these men were capable of walking because of mangled legs. Wilmot scoured the minefield in advance of the following stretcher-bearers, marking the wounded men for evacuation. After spending a few moments talking softly with each man in order to calm him down, Wilmot renewed his quest. Throughout the night, he continued this work until satisfied that all the casualties were evacuated. Wilmot's selfless actions resulted in his winning a Military Cross.[15]

ON THE WEST Nova Scotia Regiment's left flank, two regiments of the 5th Canadian Armoured Division crossed the Foglia River in the late afternoon of August 30. The Perth Regiment was immediately left of the West Novas and the Cape Breton Highlanders farther to the west. Two squadrons of the 8th Princess Louise New Brunswick Hussars were ready to follow the infantry once the engineers established river crossings. The Perths headed for the grassy knoll of Point 111, about a half-mile east of Montecchio. From here, the regiment would press northward to Point 147, which lay about a third of a mile beyond Point 111. For the Cape Breton regiment, the job was to capture the village of Montecchio and then the pine-studded promontory of Point 120 to the west.[16]

Lieutenant Colonel Boyd Somerville told the Cape Breton officers at 1515 hours that resistance should be light to nonexistent. Company 'B' was to secure Point 120 and then 'A' Company would advance to the nearby target of Point 136 while 'C' Company secured Point 119. 'D' Company would remain in reserve.

'B' Company crossed the Foglia at 1730 hours with No. 12 Platoon leading. At first there was no opposition. When II CIB commander Brigadier Ian Johnston asked Somerville for a situation report at 1806 hours, he was told that 'B' Company was not yet on its objective "but everything is going OK."[17]

The infantry company reached the summit, passed through Montecchio, and started up the slope towards Point 120 without incident. As the leading platoon closed on the summit at 1840 hours, however, streams of tracers from well-sited heavy machine guns dug in on the hill to the company's front, and from Point 111 to its rear, ripped into the Canadians. No. 12 Platoon was overrun by a strong counterattack. Just five men and the platoon commander reeled back to rejoin the rest of the beleaguered company. Hoping to reclaim the initiative, the company commander shouted for the two-inch mortar team to get its tube firing. Before the men could set up the weapon, they were shot down and killed.

Retreat was now the only option, but breaking off contact with the closing Germans proved impossible. Realizing the entire company faced destruction, twenty-four-year-old Private Alphonse Hickey of Whitney Pier, New Brunswick volunteered to cover the retreat with his Bren gun. Everyone knew there were scant odds of the young man surviving. Showing no visible signs of fear, Hickey said: "Go down, boys. But leave your Bren gun magazines with me."[18] Each man dropped every Bren magazine he carried at Hickey's side as they ducked by and dashed towards the ruins of Montecchio. Behind, they heard the hard thumping of Hickey's Bren covering their withdrawal. The company escaped without suffering any further casualties.

From behind Montecchio a group of 8th Hussars's tankers watched a lone figure silhouetted in the fading light near the top of Point 120. The soldier stood with machine gun braced into his shoulder like it was just a Lee Enfield rifle, firing in a semi-circle at the closing Germans. Hickey's bullet-riddled body was found the next day amid a cluster of dead Germans. Five spent magazines lay beneath his Bren gun. Because the only medal a Canadian could be awarded posthumously was a Victoria Cross and no application for such an award was made on his behalf, Hickey's heroism went largely unrecognized. He received only a Mention in Despatches.[19]

Pinned down inside the village, 'B' Company remained snarled in a cauldron. When 'A' Company attempted to come up on the left of Montecchio, the enfilading fire from Point 111 tore into the advancing men. They hugged the ground, unable to either advance or withdraw.[20]

Somerville called for an artillery smokescreen to blind the Germans on Point 111, but even with that position shrouded in grey-white smog the two companies were unable to renew the advance.

Somerville told Major Howard Keirstead of the Hussars 'B' Squadron that he wanted immediate tank support for his trapped infantry.[21] Keirstead, who had come up to Somerville's HQ to better monitor events, sent a dispatch rider racing back to his second-in-command, Captain Bob McLeod, with orders for him to "move the tanks up."[22] McLeod led the tanks into the valley, but as the column approached the Foglia River a provost party blocked the road and signalled a halt. Another tank regiment that was "going straight through to Rimini" had priority on the crossing, the provost officer excitedly claimed. McLeod engaged the officer in a shouting match, but he steadfastly refused to budge or to recognize that he awaited a phantom tank regiment.

Unable to raise Keirstead on the radio, a frantic McLeod jumped on the back of the dispatch rider's motorcycle and told him to get them both up to Somerville's HQ, but a salvo of German shells bracketed the road and forced the two men back. By now, the provost officer had ordered McLeod's Shermans to get off the road and wait in a neighbouring field. The movement into the field resulted in two Shermans throwing tracks and a third becoming stuck. McLeod was furious at having lost these tanks because of sheer stupidity. Ordering the remaining tanks to form behind his Sherman in column, McLeod ground towards the crossing. The provost officer shouted orders and waved his arms, but McLeod, sitting high in the turret, ignored him. When the red cap realized he must give way or be run down, he scampered aside.[23] The tanks reached the Cape Breton Highlanders' HQ at 1930 hours.

Somerville was by now realizing he needed to regroup before renewing the attack. He asked permission to pull 'A' and 'B' companies back from Montecchio, so that it could be blanketed with artillery fire. Johnston agreed. When the two companies fell back, they brought with them five German prisoners, identified as members of the 26th Panzer Division. The prisoners said their division had relieved the 71st Infantry Division just that afternoon and had been moving into their positions when the Highlanders attacked.[24] The Canadians knew they now faced a fresh, tough division on their left flank. Furthermore, the ground in front of Tomba di Pesaro was believed defended by the 3rd Regiment of the 1st Parachute Division with this division's 4th Regiment holding the right-hand flank where I Canadian Corps's boundary adjoined that of the II Polish Corps. It was going to be a tough gatecrashing operation.

SIMULTANEOUS WITH the Cape Bretoners' attack, Major Harold Snelgrove had signalled the Perths' 'B' Company to cross the Foglia and advance up a narrow gravel track towards the antitank ditch and the lateral road. Immediately beyond the road a twenty-degree slope ascended to Point 111. Lieutenant D.L. Thompson of the Perths' scout platoon walked alongside Snelgrove as the company advanced. Thompson had reconnoitered the attack route that morning and was to guide the company through the minefields he had earlier identified. The company advanced in line with a platoon commanded by Lieutenant A.W.D. Robertson several hundred feet ahead of the company's other platoons.

As Robertson's men reached a T-junction where the track joined the lateral road, they were engaged by heavy machine-gun and rifle fire from Germans dug in on Point 111. An intense barrage of mortar and machine-gun fire that swept the lower slope and valley floor struck the rest of Snelgrove's company. The company fell back to the river to reorganize, but the intense fire quickly broke every renewed attempt.[25] By 1900 hours, the Perth attack appeared as stalemated as those mounted by the Cape Breton Highlanders and the West Nova Scotia Regiment.

Lieutenant Colonel William Reid sent a runner barrelling into 'D' Company's position in a shell-torn vineyard south of the river behind Montelabbate with orders for Captain Sam Ridge to take over the attack at 2030 hours with 'A' Squadron of the 8th Hussars in support. Private Stan Scislowski was, like everyone else in the company, buttoned down inside a shallow slit trench. When he heard the breathless runner repeating the order, Scislowski "felt a hard knot of fear hit the pit of my stomach."[26]

Off to the right, he could hear the constant explosion of mortar rounds, mines, and the screeching rip of German machine guns. Scislowski knew the West Novas were taking a hell of a beating. To the front, 'B' Company was receiving similar treatment. Now 'D' Company must enter the bloody fray.

Ridge led the men at a dogtrot along a road littered by foliage scythed from the bordering trees by shrapnel, blast, and bullets. After 150 yards, they came to the river crossing in front of Montelabbatte. 'A' Squadron was milling in front of the crossing point; great clouds of dust and exhaust fumes boiled up around the Shermans. Snarled among the tanks were dozens of jeeps, trucks, and transporter flatbeds all competing for access to the crossing. Men were running about shouting and flapping their arms ineffectually.[27] Tangled among the Hussars were elements of 5 CAD's Governor General's Horse Guards reconnaissance regiment, which were also trying to get forward, and the supporting arms of the Cape Breton Highlanders and the Irish Regiment of Canada. When the Hussars finally extracted themselves from this tangle and crossed the river, a wrong turn further delayed the tanks.[28]

As Scislowski trotted towards the crossing, he could make no sense of the chaos ahead. Ridge didn't bother slowing to find out whether his tanks were across the river or not. He led the men at a run into the riverbed, where the stream was merely a three-foot-wide trickle that the soldiers jumped without even getting damp feet.

'D' Company tore through the dazed-looking ranks of 'B' Company and up the road past the three tanks of a troop that was deploying on the right-hand side of the road. Ahead lay the slope up to the ridge—a thousand yards of open ground. Ridge signalled for Scislowski's platoon, No. 18, to lead the way in extended order up the right side of the road. In front of the men was a wire fence and strung along it "at eight-foot intervals were these triangular signs with the death's-head insignia and the words '*Achtung! Minen!*' painted on them. Mines! 'Holy Jeezus!' I blurted out. They're not sending us in there! We're as good as dead!"[29] Even as he thought this, Scislowski and the rest of the platoon climbed the fence. Ridge was gambling that the extensive marking of the minefield was a ruse and there were no mines inside the fenced area. Scislowski prayed his captain was right.

Private Jimmy Heaton was on point just ahead of Scislowski as the eight-man section entered the field in single file. Scislowski's heart was in his mouth. It was getting dark, making the ground difficult to see. All he could do was take one step after another, trying to place his feet precisely in Heaton's footsteps. Off to the left, there was a sharp explosion as somebody tripped a Schümine. Two more explosions and two more men down with mangled legs. Heaton froze. Everyone in the section was afraid to go on. From behind them Sergeant K.M. "Blackie" Rowe bellowed, "Get your goddamn asses moving! Come on! Move! Move! Haul your asses!" Scislowski looked over his shoulder at Private Gord Forbes and hissed, "Holy shit! The crazy son of a bitch is determined to get us all killed!" They crept forward. "I can't see us getting out of here alive," Scislowski whispered back to Forbes just as the man tripped a mine and went down. Scislowski instinctively began stooping to help his friend, but Rowe admonished the men to keep moving. Reluctantly, Scislowski left Forbes lying there.[30]

Three more men were lost on mines covering another thirty yards. Scislowski was angry at having to die this way, terrified at the inevitability of being maimed, proud that he pressed on in the face of terrible danger. And then the platoon crossed another band of wire and the minefield was behind it. The men passed the "twisted and torn bodies lying scattered on the road" of 'B' Company's leading platoon. Rowe directed his company off the road into a narrow channel of ground bordered on one side by the road's drainage ditch and on the other by a fence line. Scislowski realized the sergeant hoped the German machine guns only had the road and adjoining drainage ditches zeroed in.

They came up to the wide antitank ditch and saw that the road crossing it had not been blown. Scattered in front of the road crossing were more bodies of 'B' Company troops, grim testimony to the dangers facing anyone trying to use the road to get over the ditch. The platoon lay down behind a wire fence and waited for Rowe to decide what to do. A burst of MG42 fire from Point 111 ripped across the road, plucking the dead soldiers with bullets. Twenty seconds passed and nobody moved. Another burst of fire raked up and down the length of the crossing. Twenty seconds later, the machine gun spoke again. Each burst lasted about three seconds. In typical Teutonic manner, the German gunner was following a fixed routine.

Rowe passed the word. The moment the next burst of searching fire stopped, two men would run like hell across the fifteen-foot-long crossing. Ray Welsh and Johnny Humphrey went first. They made it. Scislowski and Heaton were next. By twos, No. 18 platoon crossed. Then Ridge fed the other two platoons over the same way. In fifteen minutes, the entire company had crossed the antitank ditch and were huddled in the protection of a steep embankment at the bottom of the slope running up to Point 111. Ridge spent fifteen more minutes forming up his assault. As the men waited, a Sherman tank rolled up close to the ditch crossing and started pumping 75-millimetre shells towards the summit.

Ridge blew his whistle and the platoons ran up the slope with bayonets fixed—the regiment's first charge. On the right was No. 17 Platoon, led by Lieutenant Bill Hider, to the left Lieutenant Dooley's No. 18 Platoon. Lieutenant George Till's No. 16 Platoon followed. Fifty yards from the summit, a German machine gun opened fire. All three platoons hit the dirt. Scislowski could hear Ridge yelling at them to keep the charge going. For a few seconds the men remained frozen. Then, as one man, the platoons were up, screaming at the top of their lungs, charging the chattering gun, while firing their own weapons from the hip. Beside Scislowski, Private Jim Heaton ripped off a couple of bursts with his Bren.

Just as Scislowski neared the summit, an exploding grenade bowled him and Private Walt Thomas over like tenpins. The two men were so high on adrenaline they bounced right back onto their feet and took up the charge again. By the time they followed the rest of No. 18 Platoon over the ridgeline, thirty Germans were standing up in a trench with their hands up and shouting, *"Kameraden!"* repeatedly. Point 111 was taken.[31]

Major Jack Tipler quickly brought 'A' Company into 'D' Company's position. A half-mile north of Point 111 lay Point 147. Between the two points was a spiny ridge and to the right a draw. Tipler realized that the Germans must have machine guns covering both the draw and the spine. Off to the left, however, was a rugged series of cuts and draws too numerous to easily defend. He led his company that way, executing a left-hook manoeuvre that brought his platoons up on the hill from behind. At 2300 hours, his company surprised the defending Germans and cleared the objective.

Major T.H. White then moved 'C' Company out onto the spine towards Point 115, but was forced to retreat to a point just ahead of 'D' Company by heavy machine-gun fire.[32] Snelgrove brought the survivors in 'B' Company up behind Ridge's men. By midnight, the regiment formed a strong salient deep inside the Gothic Line, although its flanks were, noted the Perths' war diarist, "threatened... due to the failure of our friends on the right and left."[33] The Perths were the first Allied unit to break into the Gothic Line.[34]

At 0200 hours, 'A' Squadron of the 8th New Brunswick Hussars clanked up onto Point 111. Their commander, Major P.M. "Frenchy" Blanchet, was deathly ill with jaundice. But he refused to relinquish command. A mine had disabled one tank en route. Lieutenant George Cahoon took a troop off to the left of the Perths' position and set up in a sunken road. When the tankers tried climbing out of their Shermans, they came under fire from Germans hiding inside haystacks scattered around the tanks. Thinking Point 115 had been taken by the Perths, Cahoon tried going there on foot. Hearing loud German voices on the summit, he beat a hasty retreat back to his tank and buttoned up tight for the night.[35]

AS A PALE, nearly full moon rose over the battlefield, a massive artillery concentration, summoned by Cape Breton Highlander Lieutenant Colonel Boyd Somerville, poured down on Point 120. The shelling stopped at 0115 hours on August 31 and Captain O.J. Price's 'A' Company and 'D' Company, under Major T.M. Lowe, marched towards the enemy. Even as the artillery fell silent, 'B' Squadron of the 8th Hussars started firing from just behind the Highlanders. 'A' Company advanced on the point with two platoons up and one in reserve. 'D' Company was to press on past the summit and seize a house about four hundred yards to the northeast.

The attack proved a repeat of the earlier effort, with 'A' Company driven to ground by heavy machine-gun fire at the hill's base. From his position behind the leading company, Lowe determined from the tracer flight patterns that the Germans were firing their Spandaus on fixed lines. He tried to advise Price of this by radio, but 'A' Company's No. 18 set had failed. Lowe pushed his company forward, intent on assisting. When he tried to contact Somerville to report, he was unable to raise a response on the company radio. Lowe passed his company through Price's and pressed up the hill despite the German fire. His leading platoon was just thirty yards from the crest when it confronted a sheer cliff draped in tangles of barbed wire with mine-warning signs posted beside it. Germans started dropping stick grenades down on the Canadians. Lowe sent men to find a route up the cliff but all they found were more tangles of wire and mine-warning signs. Finally, Lowe was forced to fall back to the base of the hill and rejoin Company 'A'. As dawn was approaching, Somerville decided to pull the badly battered companies back to consolidate for another all-out try by daylight. The regiment had suffered sixty-three casualties, nineteen fatal.[36]

VOKES AND HOFFMEISTER both realized that I Canadian Corps was locked in a race with their German counterparts. They had struck just as the 26th Panzer Division and the 4th Regiment of the 1st Parachute Division had begun relieving the 71st Infantry Division. Some German companies were well emplaced, others still getting settled, and even more not yet in their assigned positions. If the Canadians moved quickly, Eighth Army commander General Oliver Leese's gatecrash could just happen. But more men were needed.

Vokes had expected the West Nova Scotia Regiment to open up a salient, but the minefield they had stumbled into and Lieutenant Colonel Ron Waterman's apparent failure of command had scotched that plan. He had the Princess Patricia's Canadian Light Infantry from 2nd Canadian Infantry Brigade on hand awaiting a signal to push through to Osteria Nuova and from there onto Point 115, which lay about four hundred yards beyond. From Point 115, he wanted the

PPCLI to drive over another height of ground identified on military maps as Point 137 and advance to Point 204 astride a lane that extended from the lateral road behind the Foglia north to Tomba di Pesaro. It was an ambitious plan and Vokes kicked it into action just before midnight.[37]

The failure of the Cape Breton attack on Point 120 had thrown Hoffmeister's original plan into disarray. Originally, once the Cape Bretoners had cleared Point 120, the Irish Regiment of Canada was to have passed through Montecchio and secured Monte Marrone, part of the rearmost extent of the Gothic Line. Realizing that continued frontal attacks against Point 120's defences must only end in further fruitless slaughter, he directed Lieutenant Colonel Bobby Clark to cross the brigade's front and hook through the Perth Regiment on Point 111 to attack Point 120 from the rear. Marching across the brigade front brought Clark's Irish Regiment into the midst of the traffic jam building on the south side of the Foglia, resulting in his companies becoming separated. A frustrated Clark told Hoffmeister he could not reach Point 111 until after daybreak.[38]

The PPCLI meanwhile was set up in Ginestreto, ready to advance forward on signal from division. Lieutenant Colonel David Rosser would not be in command. At 1400 hours the previous day, his staff had noticed that he was shivering, sweating, and nearly delirious—suffering an outbreak of malaria.[39] Rosser was confined to bed and Major R.P. "Slug" Clark—the brother of the Irish Regiment's commander—took over.

Five minutes after midnight, Major Clark sent Captain L.G. Burton's 'C' Company off with 'D' Company in trail. Both companies crossed the river and headed up a track that led almost to Osteria Nuova without mishap or betraying their presence. Clark then ordered 'B' Company, under Major Colin McDougall, to pass through and secure Osteria Nuova. McDougall was warned he must be snug in the village by first light. The Germans had demolished Osteria Nuova weeks earlier in order to clear fields of fire, but the scattered piles of rubble would provide his company with good cover from which to launch further advances after dawn.

Lieutenant E.E. Chambers and his No. 11 Platoon were leading when the company came upon a marked minefield about four hundred yards deep, lying just in front of the lateral road. This was part of the same massive minefield that had crippled the West Nova Scotia Regiment. Some of the mines in this section were poorly concealed and, from the visible pattern they presented, it seemed there was a mine planted in every two-foot square of ground. The only way to reach Osteria Nuova was to cross the field. Chambers led the entire company into it, everyone following him in single file by platoons and trying to put their feet precisely in his footsteps. There was a narrow dirt path, which Chambers followed despite the fact that it was heavily mined. But so too was the rest of the minefield, and at least the path was free of roots and branches. Three men who strayed from Chambers's footsteps triggered mines. The rest pressed on, passing through the minefield and across the also-mined antitank ditch paralleling the road. They entered the town's ruins without meeting serious resistance, the handful of defenders surrendering the moment their commander was shot in a short exchange of gunfire.[40] It was 0600 hours. With the village in its hands, the PPCLI had succeeded by first light in adding more weight to the Canadian presence inside the Gothic Line.

[14]

A Definite Breach

IN THE PREDAWN light of August 31, the West Nova Scotia Regiment renewed its efforts to reach Point 133. Major Allan Nicholson's 'D' Company led, followed by 'C' Company, under Captain S.D. Smith. As these companies passed the apex of the bridgehead held by Captain J.H. Jones's shredded 'B' Company, German mortar and machine-gun fire smothered the entire front despite the effort of supporting artillery to force the enemy to take cover. Jones's men fired their rifles and Bren guns at the German positions, desperately trying to support the two advancing companies.[1]

Nicholson headed up a narrow gully that petered out just short of the road. Although protected from the worst of the heavy fire, several men tripped Schümines in the trenchlike channel. As 'D' company emerged at the gully's end with 'C' Company still in trail, they became tangled in the minefield that had earlier maimed so many 'B' Company men. They were also nakedly exposed to the Germans on Point 133. Bullets cut men down, shrapnel from mortar rounds tore into bodies, and mines exploded underfoot. Schümines tore legs off both Nicholson and Smith. Soldiers hugged the ground or sought any bush or depression for cover. When some men hit the dirt, they landed on mines that detonated, ripping their chests or stomachs open or tearing off arms. Others were similarly wounded trying to crawl to safety.[2]

Waterman ordered a withdrawal at 0630 hours, but the men were unable to comply. They lay helpless under the German fusillade for two and a half more hours until Waterman, still behaving with unusual sluggishness, finally arranged for a smokescreen to cover their withdrawal to the gully. At 0840 hours, the Royal 22e Regiment finished forming up in the bridgehead's rear and received orders to take over the attack from the chewed up and utterly demoralized West Novas.[3] In just over twenty-four hours, the West Novas had lost three men killed, seventy-two wounded, and three men missing. Three of the wounded subsequently died. Everyone thought it a miracle that so few soldiers had actually been killed in the debacle.[4]

Arriving at the West Novas' tactical headquarters to meet with both Brigadier Paul Bernatchez and Lieutenant Colonel Waterman, Van Doo commander Lieutenant Colonel Jean V. Allard observed that Waterman "was severely rattled."[5] Virtually ignoring the West Novas commander, Bernatchez and Allard decided that Waterman's surviving soldiers must sit tight in their currently badly exposed positions until a well-laid plan for the regiment's withdrawal through the Van Doos to the south bank of the Foglia could be implemented. Waterman, however, maintained that despite having lost their commanders, 'D' and 'C' companies remained "ready to advance again immediately." Morale was high and, as the regimental war diarist noted, there were no cases of battle exhaustion reported.[6]

Allard disagreed with this assessment of the readiness of the West Novas to renew the attack. He believed that Waterman was burned out and no longer fit to command. When he voiced his concerns to his old friend, former regimental commander, and now brigadier, Bernatchez agreed with Allard's assessment.[7]

Notified that the West Novas could not possibly continue the attack and the Van Doos were still getting prepared in the bridgehead, Major General Chris Vokes decided the Princess Patricia's Canadian Light Infantry would have to widen the breach in the Gothic Line. The Canadians must complete the breakthrough quickly or the Germans would get organized and stiffen their opposition. Vokes and 5th Canadian Armoured Division's Major General Bert Hoffmeister were hampered by the fact that they were dealing with a tactical situation neither had previously faced. During the Liri Valley offensive, the two divisions had leapfrogged each other, one taking over the advance as its opposite number ran out of steam due to casualties and overall unit fatigue. Now the two divisions fought shoulder to shoulder on a very narrow front—little more than three miles in width. One divisional commander's plans inevitably affected his counterpart. Fortunately, the two men had worked closely together in the past, respected each other's judgement, and were good friends. Hoffmeister had served directly under Vokes when the latter had commanded the Seaforth Highlanders of Canada, then the 2nd Canadian Infantry Brigade, and finally 1 CID. As Vokes had moved up the ladder, Hoffmeister had followed his footsteps into two earlier commands before getting his own division.

The two divisional plans were also becoming increasingly confused by the battle's rapid development. Both Vokes and Hoffmeister were trying to launch flying columns of armour and supporting infantry into the narrow breach that had been won the previous day. While Vokes's column was still being cobbled together on the morning of August 31, Hoffmeister had formed his column almost the moment he had intuited the German lack of readiness to meet the Canadian offensive and was ready to go.

When 11th Canadian Infantry Brigade failed to break through to Tomba di Pesaro, as Hoffmeister had planned, he calmly altered the scheme. With only the Perth Regiment inside the Gothic Line in any depth, he feared this narrowly opened gate was in the process of swinging shut. If that happened, a costly, time-consuming set-piece offensive would have to be forced on I Canadian Corps. Hoffmeister and 5th Canadian Armoured Brigade commander Brigadier Ian Cumberland decided that if they struck hard with a powerful armoured force they could knock the gate right off its hinges and steamroll through to Rimini. Consequently, at 0200 hours, orders were issued for the British Columbia Dragoons to cross the Foglia and link up with the Perth Regiment. The Dragoons and the Perths would then mutually attack Point 204. They would be supported in this effort by one troop of the 82nd Anti-Tank Battery and a section of the 5th Canadian Assault Troop. Right on the heels of this advancing force would follow the Lord Strathcona's Horse Regiment, the Westminster (Motorized) Regiment, a second troop from the 82nd Anti-Tank Battery, and another section of the 5th Canadian Assault Troop.[8]

The 82nd Anti-Tank Battery squadrons were equipped with M10 Tank Destroyers—a standard Sherman M4 tank with its turret and main gun replaced by a high-velocity 17-pounder gun mounted in an open-top revolving turret. Assault troops were specialized teams that operated out of Stuart tanks, known as Honeys, from which the turret had been removed. Each Honey was loaded with one hundred pounds of various explosives, an array of minesweeping equipment, probing irons, and other mine-clearing devices. The crews were highly trained in conducting demolitions, constructing temporary bridges, blowing riverbanks, and in other ways overcoming obstacles that might delay or block tanks.[9]

Lieutenant Colonel Fred Vokes was told his Dragoons must quickly get through to Point 204, the fingertip of the ridge that extended south from Tomba di Pesaro. That kind of order was just fine by Vokes. A permanent force officer in the Lord Strathcona's Horse before the war, Vokes had a reputation as a hard-driving, brash, profane, and abrasive officer. Many a B.C. Dragoon blamed the heavy casualties in the Liri Valley, particularly at the Melfa River, on his leadership. Another matter that rubbed many Dragoons wrong was that, despite the ferocity of the fighting during these engagements, Vokes had failed to cite for possible decoration any officers or troopers who had fought heroically. Although the squadron commanders had submitted several such recommendations, none were sent upstairs from regimental headquarters for approval. Troopers muttered amongst themselves that Vokes intended to be the first medal-winning Dragoon and until that happy event materialized, the rest of the regiment could go hang.[10] Even his older brother, Chris, thought Fred Vokes dangerously impetuous.[11]

Although the current orders differed greatly from what his squadron commanders had expected, the lieutenant colonel failed to brief them on the new plan. So when the order came at 0545 hours for the tanks to roll, most of the tankers believed they moved not to battle but to an assembly point north of the Foglia River. The gun muzzles on the Shermans were still covered in canvas to prevent their being clogged by dust kicked up by the tracks of the tanks ahead—a standard cautionary procedure followed when a column was on the move behind friendly lines. The regiment moved in a long chain with 'A' Squadron in front, then 'C' Squadron, Vokes and his regimental headquarters section, and 'B' Squadron playing tail-end Charlie. 'B' Squadron commander Major David Kinloch "expected nothing more than a long, slow, boring move. We ground slowly along a road congested with all sorts of vehicles going both ways; but suddenly, just after first-light things began to change, and a sense of urgency began to develop," he later wrote. "Our speed increased; vehicles were being moved to the side of the road, and Traffic Control was waving us through. It seemed that the message was, 'Clear the road and let the B.C. Dragoons go by.'"[12]

Kinloch was surprised to see the Governor General's Horse Guards lined up on the verge as the Dragoons rumbled down the winding road leading towards the river. He had thought the reconnaissance regiment was already well up in the front lines. When the column momentarily lurched to a halt, Kinloch's tank stopped directly opposite that of Guards' commander Lieutenant Colonel A.K. Jordan. The GGHG commander walked over and handed a freshly harvested peach up to the major. "If I were you," Jordan said, "I wouldn't be going down into that valley with your muzzle covers on. I think they've had trouble there and you're going into action immediately."[13]

That was the first Kinloch had heard about heading into a fight and he was unsure whether to credit Jordan's opinion. Surely if they were going into immediate action, Vokes would have briefed the squadron commanders before the regiment started out or would have at least done so by radio during the move. Wireless traffic was increasing, but not in the form of signals from Vokes. Kinloch was getting sporadic signals from 'A' Squadron, which was pulling into the designated assembly area. It sounded as if they might be engaged there. At the back of the column, Kinloch could only keep grinding along. He was increasingly glad that during the short stop he had followed Jordan's advice and ordered his troop commanders to strip the muzzle covers off the 75-millimetre main guns. If there was going to be a fight, Kinloch wanted to be ready.

THE DRAGOONS WERE not the only Canadian tankers driving towards imminent battle. The 8th Princess Louise New Brunswick Hussars were heading in support of the Irish Regiment of Canada. The primary job for these two units was to take Point 120, the fortified promontory on I Canadian Corps's extreme west flank from which the Cape Breton Highlanders had been so bloodily repelled the previous day. Capturing Point 120 would leave the German garrison, which had reoccupied Montecchio when the Highlanders had withdrawn, so isolated that it could be mopped up at leisure. The plan was for the Irish to start the attack from Point 111 with 'C' Squadron of the Hussars under Major Cliff McEwan in support.

Although the Perth Regiment had captured Point 111, its hold was far from uncontested, so this was not as secure a jumping-off point for the attack as the Irish expected. Private Stan Scislowski's section in No. 18 Platoon had set up for the night in an outpost about fifty yards down the steep forward slope. The sun-baked ground proved so hard the seven men could barely scrape out slit trenches. Private Jim Heaton and Scislowski were in one shallow trench, with Heaton manning his Bren gun and Scislowski serving as his loader. The Perths were still hacking at the ground to make their trenches when a party of men blundered past the section leader, Corporal Jimmy Eves, and Private Walt Thomas. Eves, unsure if the men were Canadian or German, had called out the night's password and then repeated it when no countersign was returned. Suddenly the men in the passing party threw down their packs and raised their arms in surrender. One man, however, snapped a shot just past Eves's head. Thomas grabbed Eves's Thompson from the ground and blew the man's stomach out with a long burst of .45-calibre rounds. The other four Germans, who had been carrying ammunition forward to the garrison they believed held Point 111, stood quietly through this exchange with their arms held high. The dead German was identified as the resupply party's commander.

At daybreak, Scislowski's section had fallen back to a more secure position on the summit of Point 111. Heaton and Scislowski set up the Bren in a trench barely wide enough for the two men to lie down side by side and only two feet deep. They were both exhausted, giddy from lack of sleep. Fifteen minutes after the two men closed their eyes, a battery of 25-pounders across the river started pitching shells over the top of the hill. The rounds shrieked past no more than a few feet above the ground. "Goddamn it, Jim, they're pretty damn close," Scislowski mumbled to Heaton.

"Yeah, they sure are, the bastards better raise their sights a notch or the next one's gonna land right on top of us," Heaton replied.[14]

Just then a 25-pound high-explosive shell struck the corner of their trench, right above Scislowski's head where he had piled his rifle, web pouches stuffed with Bren magazines, battle pack, and helmet. Perhaps because the shell had already passed them by, its blast and shrapnel were thrown forward. Scislowski's rifle snapped in two like a twig, his pouches and pack were shredded, and the helmet vapourized. Knocked unconscious, Scislowski awoke lying in a fog of high-explosive smoke and almost vomited on its stench. His head rang as if someone had struck him with a wooden plank. Private Vern Gooding, a stretcher-bearer, helped him stand. He tried to thank Gooding, but could hear no words coming out of his mouth even though he was moving his lips. Gooding's mouth was also working, but Scislowski heard only a ringing noise. He was nauseated, barely able to stay on his feet. Finally Scislowski understood that Gooding was asking if he could make it back to the field dressing station south of the Foglia. He nodded that he could and stumbled off the hill towards the river. On the way down, he passed a squadron of Hussars moving up towards Point 111.

When he finally arrived at the dressing station, Scislowski witnessed a horrifying scene of war's carnage. "Bandaged men were everywhere, some soaked with blood, others with their faces and bush-shirts or denim flecked or blotched red, heads swathed, uniforms ripped open at the sites of injuries, bandages and shell-dressings applied in several places on their shrapnel-ravaged bodies. I looked into the drawn faces of the wounded, eyes dulled with pain;

some were half asleep under the soporific effect of the morphine they'd been injected with. The pale upturned faces of the gravely wounded had taken on a greyish, waxen quality, the appearance not unlike that of the dead I had seen so many times lying about on the battlefield. I knew as I turned my back and walked away, that some of the boys lying here wouldn't make it through the day.

"Most of the walking wounded congregated loosely around the dressing station appeared to be, like myself, little the worse for wear. I did notice on some, however, the familiar blank stare of men suffering from battle neuroses.... A few yards away lay the blanket-covered bodies of six of our boys who had succumbed to wounds."[15] Scislowski walked over to some Perths grouped near a low-slung building across the road from the dressing station. "They looked hopelessly beaten and shorn of pride," probably battle-exhaustion cases. More men, looking as bad as those outside, sat around inside the building. Retreating outside, Scislowski bumped into the regimental padre, Crawford Smith. Scislowski told the padre what had happened to him on Point 111. The man listened patiently. Then, he said, "Stanley, the boys need you up on the hill. Don't let them down. Please join them, won't you?"[16]

Scislowski knew what he had to do. He scrounged a rifle, a couple of ammunition bandoliers, some webbing with pouches, a bayonet, water bottle, and a helmet that fit badly and set off towards the hill, sucking on a Lifesaver the padre had given him. When he got back to the hill, Scislowski found only men from the Irish Regiment and these had no idea where the Perths had gone. After wandering about for thirty minutes, Scislowski stumbled upon 'D' Company on the east slope of a low hill. The other men in his section, including Heaton, had all been unharmed by the exploding shell. But the new position was under almost continuous mortar and artillery fire. Despite the dangers, Scislowski was relieved to be back with his comrades in arms.[17]

THE IRISH REGIMENT and Hussars of 'C' Squadron started being machine-gunned and mortared from Point 120 and the ruins of Montecchio the moment they took Point 111 over from the Perths. One already undermanned company was caught in the open by a stonk of mortar bombs and suffered several casualties, reducing its strength to only fifty men. Major Cliff McEwan wheeled 'C' Squadron's Shermans to face Point 120 and ordered it pounded by high-explosive shells. Soon the promontory was blanketed in a cloud of smoke and churned-up dust. When Lieutenant Colonel Bobby Clark arrived aboard a Bren carrier, the Irish commander and McEwan started planning their attack.[18]

Meanwhile, with the Cape Breton Highlanders and the Perths still too beaten up to immediately return to battle, 11 CIB's Brigadier Ian Johnston ordered the Hussars's 'A' Squadron to advance without infantry support two miles northwestward from Point 111 to Monte Marrone. This was an unorthodox, always risky strategy. Johnston told Major P.M. "Frenchy" Blanchet that the Cape Bretoners would catch up to his tanks shortly.[19]

Following a quick briefing by Blanchet, 'A' Squadron's officers started climbing back into their Shermans. The soft pop of a distant German rifle was heard and a single round hit and mortally wounded Lieutenant S.B. Henderson.[20]

The squadron took the officer's loss in stride and moved out at 0835 hours with one troop under Lieutenant George Cahoon hanging back on Point 111 to provide covering fire. 'A' Squadron's other three troops and command section travelled across a rough landscape of steep, naked slopes that so increased the risk of throwing a track that the crews concentrated more on avoiding this event than on detecting German positions. They were thirty minutes out when an antitank gun, mounted in a concrete emplacement concealed inside a haystack, fired. The first Hussar tank started to burn.

Spotting the concealed gun position, the jaundice-plagued Blanchet ordered his driver to charge the Germans while his gunner brought them under fire. At the same time, he shouted into his radio mouthpiece for Battle Captain Doug Lewis, following right behind, to cover his advance. Back on Point 111, Cahoon had also spotted the enemy gun and his three tanks fired at the haystack, which burst into flames. Blanchet's Sherman ground right over top of the burning position, only to find that Cahoon's fire had already destroyed the gun and killed its crew.

With this action over, Lewis looked back to the burning Sherman in time to see Sergeant Bill McIntee and his crew bailing out safely, only to come under fire from a nearby machine gun. One man was killed instantly and everyone but McIntee wounded. Then several German infantrymen ran out and started bayoneting the wounded. McIntee, who had run past his wounded men before the machine gun opened fire, spun around, and, armed only with his fists, rushed the Germans. They shot him down. Two of the crewmen were bayoneted to death. But the other, named McGrattan and nicknamed "Muscles," wrestled the German trying to bayonet him to the ground and strangled him to death.

Knowing his gunner would be unable to rotate the turret in time to prevent McGrattan being killed by the other murderous Germans, Lewis stood up in the turret and shot one in the head with his pistol. That prompted the rest, including the machine-gun crew, to abandon their weapons and surrender. But they received no mercy from the Canadians. Lewis's gunner raked the Germans with the co-axial machine gun, killing them all.

'A' Squadron renewed its advance, soon losing another Sherman to an antitank gun firing from the northeast front of Tomba di Pesaro. When the tanks approached a small hill, designated Point 136, Blanchet called a halt so he could go ahead on foot and spy out whether the hill was defended. Staggering with weakness, the major no sooner dismounted than the Germans opened up with rifles, machine guns, and mortars in an attempt to kill the exposed officer. Blanchet clambered back inside his tank and called artillery down on the hill. The moment the shelling ended, 'A' Squadron charged Point 136. First onto the summit, Sergeant Billy Bell's tank had its left-side suspension immediately torn away by a German 88-millimetre round. The tank was bowled off the hillcrest and rolled slowly end over end down the hill. Whenever the turret turned upright for a few seconds, one crewman bailed out of the hatch. All escaped unharmed.

Having rushed his tank troop over to join the charge, Lieutenant

Cahoon's Sherman was also struck by an antitank round and started sliding backward. Fearing this tank was about to overturn and follow Bell's down the hillside, the crew bailed out. When the tank skidded to a halt, Cahooon got his men back inside. Of the nineteen tanks that had started out for Monte Marrone, only nine remained operational. Having lost radio contact with regimental headquarters, Blanchet sent one tank back to Point 111 for reinforcements. Another, which had been struggling up the hillside, staggered to a halt as its engine broke down. Left with just seven tanks still in the fight, and fearing an imminent counterattack, he circled them on the little hilltop so they could meet an attack from any direction. Blanchet was red-eyed and sunken faced, almost debilitated by his illness.[21] 'A' Squadron had knocked out one Mark V Panther, two antitank guns, and killed about twenty-five Germans in exchange for ten dead, six wounded, and four tanks destroyed. At 1900 hours, the tankers were relieved to see Canadian infantry marching up the hill instead of Germans.[22] The Cape Breton Highlanders arrived with 'B' Squadron in support.

A few minutes later, the infantry and tanks of the new squadron pressed on towards Monte Marrone, while Blanchet led his weary squadron back to Point 111. Before the attacking force really got moving, however, brigade ordered it to assume a defensive position because of a feared German counterattack. The infantry dug in around the tanks, but after a three-hour wait the enemy failed to materialize. In the late afternoon, tanks and infantry set out again, but the going was slow over rough ground. At 2200 hours, 'B' Squadron withdrew because of the approaching darkness and the Cape Breton Highlanders marched on alone.[23] At midnight, they climbed Monte Marrone and found an extensive system of abandoned fortifications.

WHEN THE REMNANTS of 'A' Squadron rumbled into the Hussars' harbour on the reverse slope of Point 111, Major G.R.H. Ross strolled over to Blanchet's tank for a chat. Finding Blanchet huddled on the ground beside the Sherman, "so sick he could hardly raise his head," Ross had him taken immediately to the Regimental Aid Post.[24]

While 'A' Squadron's foray towards Monte Marrone had met fierce German resistance, an equally determined defence of Point 120 failed to deter the Irish Regiment's attack there. At noon, 'D' Company had struck from Point 111 in a straight-on frontal attack while 'A' Company hooked around to the north to take up position on a low hill from which it could bring fire to bear on the German positions. 'A' Company would also block the German line of retreat. Meanwhile, 'C' and 'B' companies remained in reserve on Point 111 and provided covering fire for the two attacking companies.[25]

By running hard on the heels of an artillery barrage and using all available ground cover to conceal their movements, 'D' Company, under Captain F.E. Southby, crossed the half-mile gap between Point 111 and the objective without being detected and gained complete surprise. The Germans surrendered with barely a shot fired and the company took four officers and 117 enlisted men prisoner.[26]

Having to follow the road, 'C' Squadron's Shermans had swept right through Montecchio en route to the hill and destroyed two anti-tank guns and a self-propelled gun along the way. Six of the squadron's tanks were disabled by thrown tracks, but there were no other casualties. Although the Irish had pulled off the attack on Point 120 with the loss of only one man, the regiment's total casualties for the day were eighteen killed and thirty-two wounded. Most of these were in 'A' Company, which had been hard hit by the German shelling of Point 111. Of the attack on Point 120, the Irish war diarist wrote: "31 August was a day in which the Irish proved they need take second place to no other infantry regiment."[27]

AT 0930 HOURS, the PPCLI's 'C' Company headed due west out of Osteria Nuova to secure the junction point where one of the best roads running north from the Foglia met the lateral road. A hundred yards to the east of this junction, a deep natural re-entrant was overlooked by Point 115. The ground inside the re-entrant was the designated assembly area for the B.C. Dragoons to form for their scheduled attack in support of the Perth Regiment against Point 204. The re-entrant and junction, through which the tanks must pass to reach it, were still in German hands. Even as the Shermans of 'A' Squadron, which led the column of Dragoons, approached from the south, the PPCLI advanced on the junction from the east.

Captain L.G. Burton's riflemen were caught in a short, intense firefight with several Germans as they came up to the junction. Schümines and small-arms fire wounded five men, but the company quickly seized the vital intersection. The situation remained anything but secure, though, as German paratroopers held positions both in the re-entrant to the company's left and on Point 115 above it. Burton could see no way of clearing the area without the assistance of tanks.[28] The 48th Royal Tank Regiment that was supposed to have supported the PPCLI had yet to start crossing the river, so he figured it would be afternoon before they arrived.[29]

Shortly after the PPCLI seized the junction, however, a jeep bearing an advance party of Dragoons intent on preparing the assembly area for the regiment's imminent arrival drove through their hidden positions too quickly for the infantry to flag them down. The jeep contained Captain Jack Letcher, Lieutenant H.J. Russell, Sergeant Bill Grainger, and Trooper George Bentley. Blocked by a heavy barbed-wire entanglement at the re-entrant, the men calmly cut an opening sufficiently wide to permit the passage of tanks.

While they waited for the first tanks to arrive, Letcher walked over to several PPCLI soldiers holding a nearby position. They told him they had some wounded men about a hundred yards away who needed to be evacuated. Letcher and Russell followed one soldier towards the wounded men, but suddenly the infantryman "let out an ungodly scream of pain" as a mine exploded underfoot. When Russell jumped to the stricken man's side, he tripped another Schümine that tore his leg right off. A fragment struck Letcher above his left eye and knocked him unconscious.[30]

Major Gerald Eastman's 'A' Squadron was meanwhile passing the junction en route to the re-entrant. Eastman noticed some infantrymen lying in ditches alongside the road and saw that the Bren gunners were firing short bursts as if engaging enemy infantry. Eastman stopped and called down to them for directions to the Dragoons' reconnaissance party. A frazzled-looking soldier shrugged, said nobody had passed by, and went back to his measured shooting. Puzzled, Eastman signalled his squadron to follow, turned right onto the lateral and clanked towards the assembly area. As the tanks rolled up to the wire fence, Eastman was relieved to see Grainger and Bentley waving them in. The two men then returned to their work of checking the ground with minesweepers. The re-entrant was riddled with German trenches and dugouts that Eastman presumed were abandoned. All seemed calm. Eastman's orders were to assemble his squadron on the left, and 'C' Squadron would form to his right. As the squadron moved to the left, a Faustpatrone charge exploded against Captain Richard Sellars's Sherman. The burning tank rolled back several feet to collide with the Sherman immediately behind it. The two tanks locked tracks and the fire quickly spread from one to the other. Both crews managed to escape without serious injury.

Sellars, who had armed himself with a Thompson submachine gun before abandoning his tank, "started blazing away at the trench in front of him."[31] When Eastman tried depressing his main gun to fire into the trench, he realized his tank was too close. The Germans in the trench hurled stick grenades at Eastman, who sat up high in the open turret hatch to lob Type 36 grenades back at them. A lot of grenades were going off, but neither Eastman nor the Germans seemed able to hurt the other. Finally, Eastman had his driver back up a few yards and the gunner punched a couple of high-explosive rounds into the trench. Out popped a white handkerchief fixed to a long pole and Sellars quickly accepted the surrender of forty paratroopers.[32]

As the firefight ended, Letcher stumbled out of the minefield into the assembly area. He had awakened to find the maimed Russell and the similarly injured infantryman gone, presumably evacuated by the PPCLI. Whoever evacuated the two men must have either not seen him or had assumed the unconscious man was dead. Seeing the tanks blasting away at Germans in trenches he had thought empty, Letcher realized the paratroopers must have remained hidden while his party cut the wire and started sweeping for mines, in the hopes of bagging bigger game. Letcher thought it had probably been a rude surprise when the bigger game proved to be a squadron of Shermans.[33]

A Sherman tank commanded by Sergeant Weber escorted the prisoners back to the river. On the return trip, an armour-piercing round punched into the tank turret and exploded inside. Everyone but the driver, Trooper Tom Blake, was killed. Shrapnel had, however, penetrated the driver's compartment and passed through his chair, peppering his back with a mix of metal and shredded horsehair from the seatback. Painfully dragging himself towards the open turret hatch, Blake saw the tank's main compartment was lathered in blood and gore. Arms and legs lay everywhere. Only Weber seemed in one piece, his corpse sort of leaning in a sitting position against the back wall. Blake crawled out of the turret and fell to the ground. Because of infection from the horsehair, his wounds would take two months to heal.[34]

In the re-entrant, 'A' Squadron was now being fired on by German infantry in positions on their flanks and to the front. The tankers shot back with their main guns and machine guns.[35] When 'C' Squadron arrived, it joined the fray. Soon the Dragoons silenced the opposition in the re-entrant and started ranging out of the assembly area to assist the PPCLI at the road junction and at Osteria Nuova, where Major Colin McDougall's 'B' Company was trying to repel a German counterattack. The tanks, McDougall wrote, "got behind the enemy and copped them."[36] A total of ninety-six prisoners were rounded up in the wake of this brief action.

At 1030 hours, the PPCLI's 'D' Company jumped off from Osteria Nuova towards Point 115, which looked down upon the Dragoons' assembly area. A sharp gunfight broke out between the Patricias and the defending Germans that lasted until 1330 hours, when twenty-three paratroopers surrendered. The PPCLI suffered six casualties.[37]

Once Point 115 was reported secure, PPCLI Major R.P. Clark ordered 'A' Company to advance to the right and seize Point 133—the last feature in this sector that dominated both the lateral road and the Foglia River. Its capture would "create a definite breach in the Gothic Line through which spearheads could be pushed and the famous Gothic Line rolled up," wrote the regiment's war diarist.[38] Supported now by 'B' Squadron of the 48th Royal Tank Regiment, Major E. Cutbill led his company forward. No sooner had the tanks crossed the road than Teller mines disabled two. The infantry marched doggedly onward through a hail of artillery and mortar fire, with the remaining tanks following close behind. They climbed a thousand-yard-long forward slope into the face of the Germans' defending fire. As the infantry and tanks rolled over the crest onto Point 133, ninety-seven Germans threw down their guns and surrendered. The position that the West Nova Scotia Regiment had tried to reach at terrible cost was finally taken. Despite the murderous fire they had passed through, the PPCLI suffered only six casualties.[39] Their triumph was soured, however, by news that the regimental chaplain, Captain Kenelm Eaton, had been fatally wounded near Osteria Nuova when he knelt on a Schümine while trying to assist an injured soldier. Originally too young to qualify for a chaplaincy, Eaton had signed up as a stretcher-bearer and served in that capacity until reaching the required maturity.[40]

[15]

A Bitter Day

IN THE RE-ENTRANT, the situation by mid-morning of August 31 was still chaotic, with the British Columbia Dragoons trying to group by squadrons in the midst of persistent heavy mortar and artillery fire. As Sergeant Eric Waldron of No. 4 Troop rolled the last 'C' Squadron tank through the gap in the wire, a mortar round exploded on his Sherman's front deck. The concussion banged Waldron's face against the hatch rim, breaking his nose and blackening both eyes. Blood gushing from his nostrils, Waldron fell to the bottom of the tank in a heap. "Are you dead, sarge?" his loader/signaller called down softly. Waldron moaned that he was okay and crawled back into the turret's cupola. When he looked out of the hatch, Major Jack Turnley, his squadron commander, was standing nearby. "You all right?" he called up to the sergeant. "I think I'll live," Waldron replied. Turnley told him to move his tank up to the top of the eastern ridge to guard the regiment's flank.

From a position hull-down behind the ridgeline, Waldron observed some kind of German depot—heavily camouflaged in netting—set up in an open basin. Waldron suspected it was an ammunition dump. He radioed Turnley for permission to fire on the depot, but the major curtly refused. Waldron cursed his major's consistent reluctance to permit 'C' Squadron to fire on unidentified targets. While seconded for six months during the North African campaign to the British 5th Lancers, Turnley had once shot up several armoured cars that turned out to be British. He had been at pains since not to repeat that mistake.[1] Waldron sat in his tank, sweating under the hot sun, German shells exploding nearby, and glared impotently down at the depot.

Down in the re-entrant, Lieutenant Colonel Fred Vokes waited impatiently for the Perth Regiment. He had been advised the Perths would soon join the Dragoons for a joint assault on Point 204.[2] Perth commander Lieutenant Colonel William Reid, meanwhile, was near Point 111 still waiting for the Princess Louise Dragoon Guards to relieve his regiment and did not expect to rendezvous with the Dragoons until after 1000 hours.[3] The Perths were going to be coming, but definitely not as quickly as Vokes expected.

Vokes paced outside the regimental command tank, his headset linked by a long wire to the turret, so he could communicate with his signaller without being hemmed up inside the Sherman. From his nearby tank, 'B' Squadron commander Major David Kinloch watched Vokes's growing restlessness. Finally, in what Kinloch thought was an independent action, Vokes ordered 'C' Squadron to head for Point 204 with 'A' Squadron in trail. The lieutenant colonel would remain in the re-entrant with Kinloch's squadron and the regimental HQ tanks until the Perths arrived and then bring them forward at the double.[4] Back at brigade headquarters, 5th Canadian Armoured Brigade commander Brigadier Ian Cumberland had no idea that the Dragoons were going to attack without infantry support.* In fact, one of his general staff officers, Lieutenant Colonel Harry Angle, who had commanded the Dragoons until being transferred to brigade headquarters, understood that Cumberland had told Vokes that the combined operation would not begin until early morning of September 1.[5]

---

* All contemporary accounts written by 5 CAB HQ staff, including the brigade's war diary, cite the attack as having been launched as a joint tank-infantry operation with the Perths accompanying the B.C. Dragoons towards Point 204, and the two units eventually becoming separated.

'C' SQUADRON HEADED out in an arrowhead formation with Lieutenant R.W. "Bud" Green's No. 4 Troop right, Lieutenant Tony Romanow's No. 1 Troop left, and Lieutenant Z.M. "Zeke" Ferley's No. 3 Troop centre. Tucked inside the arrowhead was No. 2 Troop under Lieutenant Jack Saville and Turnley's HQ section.[6] The squadron rolled down the ridge into a wide valley of grain fields, where the shoulder-high wheat provided excellent cover for snipers and gun emplacements. A confusing array of ridges and hillocks cut across the valley this way and that, making it difficult for the tankers to keep their objective in view. Halfway between Point 204 and the re-entrant stood a hill marked on their maps as Point 156. Once 'C' Squadron reached this initial objective, 'A' Squadron was to leapfrog to the lead.[7]

The ground under Ferley's tank tracks was "loose and dry. On the least slope, one had to be extremely careful, or the tank would slip sideways and throw a track, immobilizing the tank. It was necessary to hit each upward or downward slope square on with the tank," he wrote.[8] Saville's troop had started out with only two tanks, having lost the third to a breakdown. Now one of the two remaining tanks threw a track. Turnley ordered Saville to attach himself and the remaining Sherman to Ferley's troop, which was also a tank short. The loss of these tanks reduced the squadron to twelve Shermans, four below standard strength.[9]

Not only was the terrain difficult to traverse, but the advancing squadrons were being intensely shelled by the Germans and sporadically, it seemed, also by Canadian artillery. When the shelling grew too severe, the tank commanders buttoned up their hatches and resorted to using their periscopes to guide the drivers forward—a difficult undertaking in even the best tank country. Despite these problems, 'C' Squadron reached Point 156 without serious difficulty at about 1100 hours.[10]

The ground ahead, Ferley saw, "was undulating and irregular—there was no definite pattern to the rise and fall of the ground. This even applied to the squadron position." Ferley was unable to see either No. 1 or No. 4 troops, despite the fact that he knew they should be just off respectively to his left and right. He sensed the Germans were out ahead, barring the way to Point 204. "I knew that they would probably get the first crack at us—they were hidden, we were not, a usual situation."[11]

About six hundred yards ahead, a two-storey farmhouse stood on the long slope running up to Point 204 with a large green tree growing fifty yards behind it. The tree had a wide base and a trunk that tapered off very gradually like a child's drawing might. To the left of the farmhouse was a dense grove of trees. From his map, Ferley knew Point 204 was obscured from view by these woods. Beyond the trees rose another higher hill, identified as Point 253 or Monte Peloso. This hill was a bit to the southeast of Tomba di Pesaro.

As Ferley scanned the ground to the front, his attention kept being drawn back to the tree behind the farmhouse. It seemed so out of place there, almost surreal. As he considered what was odd about the tree, the bright flash of a heavy gun jetted out of the tree's base. The muzzle flash and gun recoil shook off some of the camouflaging and suddenly the tree was transformed into a cleverly concealed self-propelled 88-millimetre gun. Ferley called out firing coordinates to his gunner and laid the tank's 75-millimetre on the SPG. The first shot was high, the high-explosive shell exploding far beyond the crest of the facing hill. While Ferley's crew reloaded, the German gun fired another shot at some target the troop commander could not see. Ferley's gunner snapped off another round, which exploded below the German position. Once again the German gun fired, still apparently seeking the same invisible target. Ferley's gunner raised his sights a bit and this round struck home, causing the German gun barrel to tilt slightly upward.

"Three rounds HE, rapid fire!" Ferley shouted. "Fire, fire, fire." The shells blasted out. "One round AP. Fire." The armour-piercing round shrieked down on the German SPG. Ferley then had the gunner rake the position with the co-axial machine gun. Scratch one German gun, Ferley reported to Turnley.[12]

By the time Major Gerald Eastman's 'A' Squadron clanked up onto Point 156, the hill was under fire from German artillery and self-propelled guns and antitank guns that were largely invisible to the Canadian tankers because of excellent use of camouflage. Eastman sidled his Sherman towards a stand of trees that offered a little cover. As the big tank shoved aside some scrub trees, it slid into a hole and tipped on its side. Eastman and his crew scrambled out. Leaving his men there to wait until a recovery team could pull the tank out of the hole, Eastman commandeered another tank in his headquarters section. He could see only one of his tank troops and had no idea where the others had gone.[13] Radio communication was hopeless. According to the plan, Eastman's squadron was to leapfrog 'C' Squadron. But it looked as if Turnley's Shermans had already gone ahead.

'C' Squadron was indeed headed for Point 204, but its formation had fallen to pieces even before the full squadron shoved off from Point 156. After Ferley reported knocking out the antitank gun, Turnley bellowed over the radio for Lieutenant Romanow to advance on the farmhouse. Turnley's voice was hoarse from shouting. Ferley noticed this always happened in combat. It was as if the major "wanted to be sure that we would be able to hear him even if his radio set had gone dead. Sometimes I think we could have."[14]

Romanow confirmed that he saw the house and was on his way. His troop would be the first to enter the open ground between the two hills. It was a dangerous assignment and Ferley wondered how the officer was feeling, for this was Romanow's first battle. He "watched the low ground ahead and to the left—waiting for 1st Troop to come into view" off to his left. No tanks showed. Turnley asked Romanow if he was moving. "Roger, are well on the way," Romanow responded.

Ferley reported that he couldn't see any tanks. Turnley checked with Romanow again. "Roger, we have almost reached the objective," the lieutenant replied. Ferley realized that Romanow "was lost, badly lost, and very far to the left of his objective. And he was in a desperate situation—completely isolated from any support." Staring at his map, Ferley thought Romanow's troop was probably nearing the road from Montecchio to Tomba di Pesaro. The amount of German antitank fire coming from that flank was such that the troop might very well be wiped out at any moment.

Turnley must have realized the same thing, for he ordered Romanow to stop, find some cover, and wait while the squadron located him. Attempts to fix his location by having him describe the terrain failed to help. Ferley was heartened by Romanow's radio manner. "He did not seem unduly worried, which was a good sign. He was not the type to become easily rattled." Finally, Romanow tried firing a Very light, even though this would betray his location to the Germans. The rest of the squadron "peered into the sky to our left, but it was a clear, hot day, and the sun was shining brightly, and we saw nothing."[15]

Turnley decided they could wait no longer. No. 1 Troop would have to fend for itself. The squadron, now only nine tanks strong, growled towards Point 204. Far to the left, No. 1 Troop had indeed come into the firing sights of several German antitank guns. Seconds after the Very light was fired, German gunners ripped into the three Shermans with armour-piercing rounds. Only Romanow and one of his crew survived. Both men were unhurt and managed to remain hidden until being able to slip back to Canadian lines on the night of September 2.[16]

Ferley's three tanks, which included Lieutenant Jack Saville's Sherman, made for a position to the right of Point 204, while No. 4 Troop under Lieutenant Bud Green headed for the summit itself with Turnley's headquarters section following. They picked their way slowly and carefully down the slope despite the excellent targets this presented to any German gunners dug in on the facing hill. Ferley was using the house that had been close to the phony tree position for a reference point. As he drew closer to the building, a cluster of Germans darted out and ran towards Point 204's summit. Before they could reach the safety of the trees, Ferley's gunner cut most of them down with a long, hard machine-gun burst.

When No. 3 Troop reached the slope leading up the hill, Ferley thought the ground immediately in front of him too steep and loose to climb safely. Guiding the tanks to the left to where the slope rose more gradually, Ferley led the way towards the top. Behind him, Sergeant S. Foster and Lieutenant Jack Saville's respective tanks both slipped sideways and lost their tracks. Ferley carried on alone. "My other two babies have lost their shoes, I have only my own baby left," Ferley advised Turnley.[17]

Looking over to where the rest of 'C' Squadron was clawing its way up the hill, Ferley thought they were blessed with better ground under their tracks than he was encountering. He also noted their line of advance was drawing them ever farther from his tank. Ferley and his crew were truly "out in the blue."

AS THE SURVIVING REMNANT of 'C' Squadron closed on Point 204, Lieutenant Colonel Fred Vokes paced constantly back and forth, listening to the confused jumble of messages from the two squadrons closing on the objective. Finally, he could stand it no longer and told Major David Kinloch that 'B' Squadron should continue waiting for the Perths. Meanwhile, Vokes would take the regimental headquarters section forward.

Kinloch thought the decision cavalier because Vokes's Sherman and one other in the headquarters section were equipped with so much radio equipment the 75-millimetre guns had been removed and replaced with a fake wooden barrel mounted to the tank's exterior to disguise its status as a command tank. This meant that only two of the tanks could fight. But Kinloch knew there was no reasoning or arguing with Vokes.

Not long after the lieutenant colonel headed for Point 204, he was on the radio to Kinloch with the suspicion that the Perths must have missed the assembly point and were probably somewhere between the objective and the re-entrant. Kinloch should go look for them. 'B' Squadron chewed a path up the steep slope leading out of the re-entrant, dropped down into the valley, and started rolling across open ground. Then Vokes came back on the radio.

He had established contact with the Perth Regiment and "the flat-footed friends" were now in the assembly area. Kinloch must wheel 'B' Squadron around and fetch them. As the major swung the column around, a German shell knocked out one of his squadron headquarters tanks. German fire from an unseen gun disabled two more Shermans in one of the troops and two more tanks lost tracks while turning around.[18]

The uphill grade they had so easily descended proved so steep on the return that his driver shifted into bull low, reducing the Sherman to a crawl. German artillery and antitank guns were blazing away. Great spouts of earth erupted all around Kinloch's tank. Finally, the column of Shermans crossed the crest and skidded precariously down the steep reverse slope. Getting out of his tank, Kinloch walked over to Perth commander Lieutenant Colonel Bill Reid. "Are you ready to move, sir?" he asked.

"No," Reid replied. "My men have been marching and fighting all day and all night and they are utterly exhausted. We can't move until they've had some food and water and a short rest." It was early afternoon and the temperature in the re-entrant was at least 110 degrees Fahrenheit, which certainly wasn't helping the infantry recover. Kinloch had his men break out water from the jerry cans they carried on the Shermans and scrounge together whatever food they could manage for the infantry.

Kinloch was now in Vokes's earlier predicament. Should he wait for the Perths or hurry on alone? The other squadrons desperately needed help and there was the added worry that he had lost radio contact with Vokes. Before Kinloch reached a decision, Reid announced the Perths were ready to go. It was only half an hour since they had arrived in the re-entrant.[19]

'C' SQUADRON WAS meanwhile grinding up towards the summit of Point 204, with Lieutenant Bud Green's tank leading. Ahead he saw what looked to be a German Regimental Aid Post, from which four armed Germans emerged, jumped into an ambulance, and drove off to the northeast. Ambulance drivers and medical personnel were forbidden under Red Cross conventions from being armed, so Green asked Turnley for permission to blow the truck to pieces. Turnley scotched that idea. "Move on," he snapped. A few minutes later, they reached the final sharp upgrade to the summit and halted. Green and Sergeant Eric Waldron, who by now looked like a raccoon from the bashing his eyes and nose had earlier taken, jumped down from their Shermans and crept up to the summit to see if there were any German antitank guns or tanks skulking about in ambush.[20] A north-south running road passed directly over Point 204; to its immediate left, the big gun of an abandoned Panzerturm pointed the way the Dragoons had come. Had it been manned, they would have all been shot to pieces coming up the slope.

Seeing no obvious traps, the tankers rolled onto Point 204 and started jockeying for hull-down positions that would allow each tank to mutually support the others. Captain Raymond E. Stubbs was the squadron battle captain, which meant it was him rather than Turnley who maintained a constant radio link back to Vokes. This practice enabled the squadron commander to focus on running his squadron while the battle captain kept Vokes informed of events and took charge of calling in artillery and other supporting arms. As 'C' Squadron's six remaining Shermans crested the summit, Stubbs reported they were on the objective.

"Consolidate," Vokes said.

Radio mike turned off, Stubbs muttered: "With what?"[21]

A few minutes later, six 'A' Squadron tanks arrived. Major Eastman reported that was all of his squadron that was left.[22]

The Dragoons on Point 204 knew they had bypassed large numbers of hidden paratroopers and were now surrounded. But the enemy didn't seem in a hurry to try wiping them out. Except for one soldier, who crept up through a hedgerow bordering the east flank of the hill and tossed a grenade into the hatch of an 'A' Squadron tank, managing to kill the entire crew.

Sergeant Waldron's gunner quickly traversed the turret to bring the co-axial machine gun into play against the lone German. Waldron was happily watching .50-calibre tracers walking towards the paratrooper when the gun abruptly jammed and the German ducked down the steep, densely vegetated slope. Rolling his tank up to the edge of the hill, Waldron chucked about twenty grenades out in a pattern he hoped would do the paratrooper some harm.

Having driven the German off, Waldron scanned the horizon for enemy targets. South of Point 204 there was a high-walled cemetery adjoined by some woods. About forty Germans emerged from the trees and marched northward in close formation along a road. Waldron's crew couldn't believe their luck. While his gunner carefully sighted in on the slow-moving target, his loader gathered a lap full of high-explosive shells. The gun crew slammed rounds out so fast there was almost no gap between the first explosion and those that followed. Waldron thought he saw only three Germans stagger clear. The rest lay like so many torn-up bundles of rags in the middle of the road.

Green suddenly came up on the radio alerting Waldron to dust clouds approaching from Tomba di Pesaro. The two tank commanders dismounted and ran to the forward crest of the hill, where they lay on their stomachs peering through binoculars. Eventually, the dust parted to expose a Panther Mark V and two self-propelled guns headed directly towards Point 204. The Panther was a deadly Sherman killer, with a more powerful 75-millimetre gun, and armour so thick it was largely impervious to anything the Canadian tanks might throw at it.

The two men scrambled back to their tanks and advised Turnley that the Germans were a mile off. Ever cautious about firing on distant targets, Turnley told them to wait until the vehicles were closer and they were "positive they could not be our own." Waldron was disgusted and scared. "Hell of a lot of good it does to study German vehicle profile charts," he groused. Green and Waldron braced inside their tanks for trouble. They could only catch brief glimpses of the German armoured group as it moved across the wildly undulating terrain. The Germans were going to come right in on top of the Dragoons and there would be little chance to get in good shots before their presence was betrayed to the enemy. Then, just as the Panther in the lead was about four hundred yards off, the three armoured vehicles swung to the right and headed off behind a little ridge. The tank battle every Sherman tanker feared had, for now, been averted.[23]

TO THE RIGHT of the main position, Lieutenant Zeke Ferley's Sherman—the lone survivor of Troop No. 3—was still headed towards a solitary farmhouse. He advised Turnley that he was almost there and it appeared clear of enemy. Turnley said, "Roger, go round objective to the right and explore further."[24] Ferley could hardly believe the order. Had the major forgotten he was alone out here? "This was no spot, and no assignment for a single tank," he later wrote. The lieutenant was certain Turnley knew his other two tanks had been disabled. He wondered if he should remind the major, but instead—good soldier that he was—said only, "Wilco, out." Then Ferley directed his driver to pass the house on the right-hand side at a good distance in case there was an antitank gun hidden inside.[25]

On the crest of a small hill, Ferley paused to survey the country ahead through his binoculars. Beyond this hill, another slope led up to yet another hilltop upon which a large farmhouse stood. The ground out to his front was mostly covered by low shrubbery, but about three hundred yards to the left a pocket of trees ran up Point 204's east flank. Off to the right, the ground levelled somewhat and was less vegetated. Ferley didn't think there was anywhere over there for the Germans to hide guns or tanks. Things were so quiet it was eerie. Swivelling, Ferley looked back the way he had come and could see all the way to the ridge fronting the assembly area. "There was a great void—no tanks, no infantry, nobody."

Turning his attention back to the front, he said: "Driver advance. Slowly." The Sherman ground down the slope into a little draw between the hills. "As we did so," Ferley remembered, "I realized that we were in a rather hopeless situation and could not expect to accomplish much. . . . If we had company within sight, it could only be German and they were probably watching us closely from their usual invisible positions."[26]

Near the bottom of the draw, Ferley halted again to scan the ground ahead. The tank was like an oven and the lieutenant was dripping with sweat from the heat and his increasing anxiety. Nothing moved. Then abruptly, fifty yards off something did. Ferley swung the turret to bring the gun to bear just as a German soldier stepped clear of some shrubs holding a Red Cross flag mounted on a long pole. The lieutenant told the gunner to hold his fire. Although apparently unarmed, the German soldier also had no Red Cross markings on his sleeve. Holding his flag aloft, the man started walking up the far hill. From a small thicket, another unarmed soldier emerged to join the first. The two men walked very slowly, "as though expecting to be cut down at any moment." But Ferley entertained no such thought. They had abandoned their weapons; they were under the protection of a

Red Cross flag. Ferley let them go and a minute later they disappeared behind the large house.

Ferley knew the jig was up. It was time to retreat to Point 204. The lieutenant thought the shortest and safest route was likely to follow the tree line until he found a way up the slope. Having gone only fifty yards towards the slope, however, the tank suddenly lurched to the right and halted. "Good God, not here," Ferley hissed. The Sherman had lost a track and was "immobile in the palm of the German's hand." Fortunately, the tank had slewed sideways so that its front armour, which was thickest, faced northward. There was nothing to do but "tough it out here, even though we were sitting ducks, lonesome ones at that." Ferley had no intention of abandoning his tank to the enemy. They would man it until a recovery team arrived to help repair the track.

Something gave the tank a hard-rattling whack. Ferley realized the Sherman "had probably been hit a glancing blow by an 88 or a long-barreled 75 and that we had between ten to fifteen seconds to clear the tank or we would be blown to bits with it." As the round had struck the left front corner near the driver's station, he asked if the man was okay. When the driver replied that he was fine, Ferley ordered the crew to bail out.

"With one motion, I brushed off my tank helmet, grabbed my ground helmet, flipped myself up and onto the turret, and leaped to the ground on the right side of the tank and rolled and crawled into a small ditch some twenty-five or thirty feet from the tank. At the ditch, I turned to check on the rest of the crew. Hughes, the gunner, was right on my tail. Rogers, the driver, was right behind him. The operator-loader was hitting the ground en route. But Campbell, the co-driver, was up on the outside of the tank, leaning into the turret."

"Campbell! Get off the tank," Ferley yelled.

Pulling a Thompson from the turret, Campbell jumped down and scurried over to join the rest of the crew in a ditch. "He had hardly hit the ground, when the second shot hit the tank and the ammo started to go." The men cowered in the ditch as another shot slammed into the tank. Ferley and his crew belly-crawled away from the German gun. "There was a god-awful commotion coming from the tank, as the ammo was exploding every which way." The ditch petered out and Ferley, not sure what to do next, halted.

He "was awfully tired, hungry, and very, very thirsty. I suppose I had been standing in the turret of the tank for some eight hours or so. I hadn't eaten since supper the evening before, and it was very hot." Ferley decided to call a rest where they were, while he tried to figure out what their next move should be. The nearest cover beyond the ditch was three hundred yards away. Meanwhile, the Germans were still firing at Ferley's Sherman. They "sure wanted that tank badly. They hit it eight times in all. The turret blew off and it was exploding and burning wildly. They were so busy pounding our baby, they didn't drop a shell or mortar bomb on us, nor did a single rifle or machine-gun bullet come our way." Ferley couldn't understand it. They must have seen the crew evacuate the tank and would know they had been unable to flee the area.

The lieutenant could see no way to get across the open ground safely without the cover of darkness. Campbell had his Thompson and Ferley a pistol that he couldn't hit "a barn door at thirty paces with," so he figured they could at least offer a token resistance if it came to that. The men lay in the ditch for thirty minutes, sweating and listening to the ammunition cooking off in the tank. Then over that racket, Ferley heard the approach of a wheeled vehicle. It was coming down the hill from Point 204, following a narrow track. A few seconds later, a German ambulance appeared and stopped about eight feet away from Ferley and his men. The driver of the vehicle and Ferley stared at each other for a long time before the ambulance drove off to the north.

As Ferley started drifting off to sleep, Campbell nudged him. "Here come some paratroopers," the co-driver said. Ferley woke up smartly. Sure enough, marching along the same route followed by the ambulance were four paratroopers. In their wake was a Dragoon by the name of Garnett from Green's No. 4 Troop. He had a Thompson casually pointed at the Germans' backs.

After carefully calling out in a way that identified himself in order to avoid panicking Garnett into shooting him, Ferley asked: "Where are you going with those prisoners?" The trooper said he was taking them back to the Foglia. Ferley observed that Garnett was heading towards enemy lines rather than the Canadian rear. Realizing the Germans were unlikely to fire on the party for fear of hitting the prisoners, Ferley had the paratroopers clasp their hands on their heads and the Canadians all marched off to safety. Once they were safely behind the crest of a hill, the lieutenant sent Garnett back to Green's troop. Garnett was to tell Turnley that Ferley's tank had been destroyed and he and his crew were escorting the prisoners to the rear.[27]

WITH EACH PASSING HOUR, the situation for the twelve tanks on Point 204 worsened. Several had either run out of fuel or were so low that the engines were kept turned off unless a move to a new firing position was required. The interiors of the tanks were like dust-choked steam rooms. Sweat showered off the tankers. From Tomba di Pesaro, mortar and artillery fire constantly hammered Point 204, making it extremely hazardous to venture outside the Shermans.

Eastman and Turnley had lost contact with Vokes, so they took turns imploring brigade "to get additional troops forward, telling them that there was nothing in front of them of any consequence and that any attack in strength would be successful." They asked for help from Kinloch's 'B' Squadron, but brigade headquarters replied that this squadron was "pinned by antitank gun fire some mile or two behind."[28]

Just before 1300 hours, Waldron heard growling engines and clanking tracks approaching from the south to the hill's left flank. The sergeant recognized the four tanks running along a narrow track that cut across the base of Point 204's left flank as those of the regiment's headquarters section. It looked as if Lieutenant Colonel Fred Vokes's tank was in the lead, followed by his adjutant's Sherman. Neither of these had a functioning gun. The two tanks mounted with real 75-millimetres were in trail, so that the two Shermans lacking guns blocked their firing forward.

Waldron reported Vokes's coordinates to Green and warned that the regimental commander was headed directly towards where the Panther and self-propelled guns had last been seen. Green called

Turnley. "Senior Sunray is passing us on our left," he said. "Suggest you stop him if possible as the road is covered by a gun we cannot locate as yet." Turnley acknowledged.

But it was too late. Vokes led his section directly into an ambush, presumably mounted by the Panther and self-propelled guns. The first round set the third tank in line ablaze, effectively blocking the line of retreat for the two forward tanks. Unable to either return fire or withdraw, these two tanks were in turn knocked out. The last tank had become separated from the rest by a space of about fifty yards. It immediately reversed and fell back to Point 204.

Green could see two of the headquarters tanks burning and frantically fired smoke rounds in front of them, hoping to cover an escape by the crews. He was unable to see any trace of survivors.[29]

A few minutes later, Major Eastman saw Vokes running up alone towards his position. The lieutenant colonel had lost his helmet and pistol and been forced to leave all the maps behind. Vokes told Eastman and Turnley that everyone else was either dead or captured. Eastman, who had earlier taken a P38 Luger from a prisoner, gave the pistol to Vokes so he would have a weapon.[30]

Vokes set up shop next to Captain Stubbs's tank because it was the only one with a radio link to brigade. The tank was parked on the road where a steep cutbank rose up from the left-hand ditch. Vokes called brigade and asked for immediate reinforcement, but received the same response that Eastman and Turnley had been getting. Phantom German antitank guns were still pinning down 'B' Squadron, which in reality was at this point still awaiting the Perth Regiment. Eastman, Vokes, and Turnley huddled in the ditch at the base of the cutbank and in the lee of the tank while they discussed what to do next. Stubbs was nearby with his earphones and microphone on a long lead from the tank. The tank itself was out of fuel because a gas line had been severed by German fire during the advance up to Point 204. Inside the tank, the fumes were so strong it was almost unbearable. Stubbs was happy to be outside, despite the sporadic shelling.[31]

Suddenly a mortar round exploded directly behind where Vokes crouched. The three officers were knocked to the ground. Eastman saw that Vokes had been struck in the back by shrapnel. Lying next to the wounded officer was the P38 that Eastman had given him. The pistol grip had been ripped off the gun. At first, as Eastman looked Vokes over, he thought the man's wound not too serious. Then the major saw blood flowing from Vokes's abdomen and realized some shrapnel had gone clear through his body.[32]

As Stubbs climbed up on the tank and retrieved a syringe of morphine, another mortar round exploded nearby. Shrapnel severed the cord of his headset and a small chunk of metal penetrated his hand.[33] Turnley was making a frantic effort to arrange for the lieutenant colonel's evacuation, but the ground between the regiment's assembly area at the Foglia River and Point 204 was so hotly contested no ambulance could get through safely. At last, Trooper A. Bonnifant from Halifax drove off towards Point 204 in his reconnaissance unit Honey. Although the Honey was fired on several times by artillery and mortars during the one-hour journey, Bonnifant managed to get through.

While they waited for the evacuation vehicle, Vokes told Eastman that he "had no chance of survival. He continued discussing the operation."[34] Vokes ordered Turnley "not to withdraw but to hold the position until it was consolidated with the Perth Regiment." Turnley was amazed at the man's calm and ability to concentrate "while he was in great pain."[35] Vokes's entreaties for reinforcements at this time must have finally had the desired effect. At 1430 hours, 5th Canadian Armoured Division commander Major General Bert Hoffmeister ordered Brigadier Ian Cumberland to immediately relieve the embattled Dragoons with the Lord Strathcona's Horse Regiment, then exploit to Point 253, and onward to Tomba di Pesaro with the Perths in support. Realizing that the Dragoons had kicked a hole almost two miles deep into the direct centre of the Gothic Line, Hoffmeister was anxious to exploit the opportunity to effect the breakthrough.[36]

The shelling of Point 204 continued. Shrapnel from one exploding round knocked Stubbs flat. He got up, checked the numerous spots on his body embedded with shrapnel, decided he was okay, and then "carried on." His gunner was less fortunate. Shrapnel tore one of his eyes out. When the Honey arrived, Turnley ordered Stubbs evacuated. The captain ignored the order, loaded his gunner aboard, and then helped strap the by now unconscious Vokes onto the Honey's back deck.[37]

Although still alive when he arrived at a casualty clearing station in Sant' Angelo, Vokes died several hours later. The news of his wounding and subsequent death soon reached his older brother, Major General Chris Vokes. The 1st Canadian Infantry Division commander found no comfort in one of his own philosophies of war. "From the day a soldier is born," he believed, "his fate is written, and likewise the manner of his going, and also there is nothing he can do about it, nothing."[38] Vokes managed to get to the casualty clearing station before his brother's burial. "It was a very sad thing," he wrote, "to see this only brother of mine, whom I loved very much, balled up in a blanket and put into a hole in the ground. In fact, I broke down. I cried."[39]

AS THE AFTERNOON dragged on, the Dragoons on Point 204 continued to wait in vain for the promised relief. By early evening, the sixty men manning twelve tanks were extremely anxious. They had no radio contact with brigade, so were uncertain any attempt was underway to relieve them. If nobody came before nightfall, they would be hard pressed to stave off any German counterattack. While the paratroopers had obviously been caught off guard by the Dragoons' unsupported armoured attack, they were no doubt already recovering. During the day, the Germans had seemed mostly lacking in the deadly Panzerfausts that enabled infantry to wreak havoc among tanks unsupported by infantry. If they now got among the tanks under cover of darkness with such weapons, there would be little the tankers could do to defend themselves.

Waldron had wondered from the beginning of this risky assault if Vokes had been acting without orders. Now he was certain of it. He noted "that there was never any timing to the advance. It just happened as people gave orders to push on. It was just a series of errors piled one on the other. They [the orders] were so stupid even the Germans were surprised and because of our penetration into the line we disorganized what should have been a complete kill. They just didn't take advantage of our lack of organization."[40] That would surely change. Waldron feared they would be slaughtered on Point 204.

Yet help was on the way. Lieutenant Colonel Bill Reid had told 'B' Squadron commander Major David Kinloch that his men were ready to move at 1500 hours. Kinloch's squadron and the infantry had immediately set off, the tanks clawing their way once more out of the re-entrant and the soldiers scrambling up the steep slope under the weight of their weapons and gear. But just as the force topped the crest, squadrons of tanks from the Lord Strathcona's Horse Regiment met them. Lieutenant Colonel Jim McAvity, the Strathconas' commander, told Kinloch that his regiment was to relieve the Dragoons on Point 204. Kinloch handed off the Perths and led his squadron back into the re-entrant to await the return of the rest of the regiment. For the major, it had been a bitter day. He "had lost good men killed and wounded, not a shot was fired by my squadron, and we accomplished nothing."[41] He was also desperately worried about what was happening on Point 204, but also knew there was now nothing he could do to help his comrades there.[42]

[16]

Pure Bloody Murder

Lieutenant colonel Jim McAvity, the Lord Strathcona's Horse Regiment commander, had no intention of slowing his dash from the Foglia River to Point 204 to match the pace of the infantry. He told Lieutenant Colonel Bill Reid that his Perth Regiment should follow in the tracks of the Shermans at its best rate. At 1600 hours, with 'C' Squadron leading and 'A' and 'B' squadrons following, the tanks sallied out from the start line towards a small hill that McAvity had designated the regiment's intermediate objective. Once 'C' Squadron reached the hilltop, it moved into hull-down positions from which the main guns could provide a base of supporting fire for the advance's second phase. 'B' Squadron, guided by the reconnaissance troop's Honeys, passed by on the right flank and drove towards Point 204. Within minutes of passing 'C' Squadron's position, a Panther tank engaged 'B' Squadron. Massed fire from all the squadron's Shermans ripped the Panther apart before the German tank could cause any damage with its heavier, more lethal gun. Then the squadron pressed on for Point 204. Major Bill Milroy and his tankers arrived there at 1900 hours.

Observers from divisional headquarters, who were sitting on a ridge back by the Foglia River, later told McAvity that the advance "looked rather like a sand-table demonstration of fire and movement."[1] Despite his intention to execute the manoeuvre quickly, the regiment had ended up taking twice as long to cross the ground as had the British Columbia Dragoons. When the Strathconas arrived on Point 204, Major Gerald Eastman of the Dragoons' 'A' Squadron thought they had taken far too long getting there and that brigade command had entirely fumbled the operation. "Had they proceeded at the speed which we were able to make, it would have taken them perhaps at most an hour, even under fire, to get to where we were and they would have had time to go much farther." By 1900 hours night was falling, rendering a further advance infeasible. Eastman thought the opportunity to deal the Germans a stunning, decisive blow had been frittered away.[2]

When the rest of the Strathconas arrived, McAvity deployed 'C' Squadron on a spur running southeast towards the village of Pozzo Alto to cover the right flank, 'A' Squadron on another spur running to the northwest, and 'B' Squadron tight on Point 204 itself.[3] Not knowing if the Perths would soon arrive, Milroy deployed his troops so each tank could fire across the others' bows. Machine guns were dismounted and set up to protect the tanks from infiltrating German infantry.[4]

While the Strathconas prepared their defensive perimeter, the weary Dragoon survivors returned to the re-entrant near the Foglia River. At dawn, the regiment had fielded fifty-four Shermans. By day's end, only eighteen remained operational.[5] Fifty-one officers and men were either dead or wounded.[6] But the B.C. Dragoons had done their duty. They had kicked a deep hole in the Gothic Line that could now be exploited by the rest of 5th Canadian Armoured Division. Despite the haphazard manner of the battle's development, it proved to be the regiment's finest day of battle. Eighth Army commander General Oliver Leese was quick to praise the Dragoons for "their dash and determination in the fighting [which] largely helped us gain decisive results during the day."[7]

The Dragoons received the welcome news that, upon hearing of Lieutenant Colonel Fred Vokes's death, Lieutenant Colonel Harry Angle had immediately demanded command of the regiment and Brigadier Ian Cumberland had agreed. Whereas Vokes had refused to recommend any officers or men for decorations during his tenure, Angle, in the immediate wake of the fighting, submitted the names of two men for medals. Captain Richard Bartley Sellars received a Military Cross for his attack on the German bunker in the re-entrant assembly area and Sergeant Frank Alexander Glover received a Military Medal.

Glover's Sherman suffered a direct hit near Point 204 that blew the sergeant, his gunner, and his loader/radio-operator out of the turret. The explosion killed both the driver and co-driver. Because the gunner was badly injured, the surviving crewmen were unable to make a hasty escape. In fact, Glover could find no means by which to evacuate the wounded man from the immediate area of the tank and quickly appreciated that the Germans must soon overrun the position. Leaving the unwounded crewman to tend to the gunner's wounds, Glover scrounged several abandoned German and Canadian rifles and light automatic weapons scattered about the surrounding battlefield. He then dug three well-spaced slit trenches in an arc uphill from the disabled tank and placed several weapons in each trench. When the German attack came, Glover dashed from trench to trench, firing off rounds from the guns stashed there to create the illusion that more than one man defended the tank. The Germans gave up after Glover repelled three attacks.[8]

During their withdrawal from Point 204, the Dragoons passed the Perth Regiment marching towards the hill. 'D' Company was on the right and 'B' Company on the left, with 'C' Company close behind. 'A' Company had remained on the north ridge of the Foglia Valley in reserve. Private Stan Scislowski of 'D' Company's No. 18 Platoon welcomed the long late-afternoon shadows cast by the heights to the west, figuring they partially hid the Perths from the German gunners dug in on the various surrounding hilltops.[9] The regiment made the crossing without incident and by 2030 hours was digging in around the Strathconas' tanks.[10]

The infantry were desperately thirsty; their canteens long since drained. At a well next to the road leading from Point 204 towards Pozzo Alto, Scislowski joined some men lined up with their canteens at the ready while one man lowered a bucket into the hole. Suddenly Sergeant K.M. "Blackie" Rowe waded into their midst, pushing and shoving them away from the well. "Get the hell back where you belong, you dumb bastards!" the sergeant bellowed. Griping and cussing, the men sullenly complied. Scislowski belatedly remembered that the Germans liked to zero wells in with mortars, wait for a cluster of thirsty men to gather around, and then flay the position with explosives. Rowe told the still angry men that later, when they had finished digging in and darkness had fallen, one man from each section would be allowed to fill all of its canteens.

Even then, the Perths made the fatal error of bunching around the well before it was fully dark. When the smoke from the German mortar rounds cleared, six men lay dead, including Company Sergeant Major Bob Johnston from 'D' Company. Scislowski felt lady luck had been on his side, for he had volunteered to refill his section's canteens. Because he wanted Scislowski and Bren gunner Private Jim Heaton to set up a forward position on the north-facing slope, Rowe had sent another man instead.[11] So someone else had died at the well.

LIKE HIS COUNTERPART Major General Bert Hoffmeister at 5th Canadian Armoured Division, 1st Canadian Infantry Division's Major General Chris Vokes had sought a breakout in depth by pushing a combined armoured-infantry column through a narrow gap in the German forward defences. His column consisted of the 21st British Tank Brigade, the armoured cars of the Royal Canadian Dragoons, and two companies of infantry detached from the Royal 22e Regiment. Brigadier D. Dawnay, 21st Tank Brigade commander, was in overall command and given authority to call on regiments of the 2nd Canadian Infantry Brigade as required for additional strength.[12]

Vokes's immediate problem had been to open the gap through which to unleash the armour. In the wake of the West Nova Scotia Regiment's bloody debacle amid the forward minefields, the only gains by his division on August 31 had been those won by the Princess Patricia's Canadian Light Infantry on the left flank. Vokes decided to use the PPCLI-held Point 133 as the launch pad for a night attack by the Seaforth Highlanders of Canada on Pozzo Alto. Once the Seaforths seized this village, he would feed other 2nd Canadian Infantry

Brigade regiments through to capture Monte Luro and Point 119. This latter objective was on the division's far right flank, where his divisional boundary adjoined that of II Polish Corps. While 2 CIB effected this penetration in depth, it would fall to the two companies of the Van Doos remaining unattached to Dawnay's breakout force to seize the ground that had been denied to the West Novas. Once through the forward defenses, the Van Doos would execute a hard right turn, fall on Borgo Santa Maria from the rear, and drive east to Point 131—sweeping the Gothic Line's entire front lines clear. To make up for the lost companies assigned to Dawnay, one company of the Carleton and York Regiment was placed under Van Doo command.[13]

The developments on the Canadian front and Vokes's operational plan were the focus of discussion when I Canadian Corps commander Lieutenant General Tommy Burns met with Eighth Army staff at 1700 hours on August 31. With the Strathconas and Perths snug on Point 204, only the barrier of the Tomba di Pesaro–Monte Luro feature now stood between the Canadians and Highway 16. By cutting across II Polish Corps's front immediately south of Gradara—a hilltop village with a thirteenth-century castle—Vokes's flying column could gain the highway and drive straight up the Adriatic coast into Rimini.[14]

Seaforth commander Lieutenant Colonel Syd Thomson assigned the capture of Pozzo Alto to 'B' and 'D' companies. Both companies crossed the Foglia at 1726 hours and, once across, 'D' Company mounted the tanks of the 145th Regiment, Royal Armoured Corps. When the tanks entered the shell-battered ruins of Osteria Nuova, the infantry dismounted and, together with the tanks, advanced along a narrow track towards Point 133 and the jump-off point for the attack.

The commander of 'B' Company meanwhile had strayed off to the right as he tried to lead his men through the confusingly rough terrain. Infantry and supporting tanks drifted east along the lateral road until finally bumping into a pocket of paratroopers. A short fight ensued, ending when twenty-one Germans surrendered. 'B' Company's commander led his men onward along the lateral road until finally stumbling into the outskirts of Borgo Santa Maria, which was a full mile and a half off course from where they were supposed to be. Still in German hands, the town and surrounding terrain were being subjected to Canadian artillery and mortar fire that left the Seaforths dodging their own shells until the company commander realized his mistake. Swinging northward, 'B' Company managed to disengage from the Germans defending the village and get back on track towards the regiment's objective.[15]

'D' Company meanwhile had pushed off from Point 133 towards Pozzo Alto, with its supporting tanks using main guns to pound suspected enemy positions before the infantry went in to clear them. The company plan was to hook into the village from the north and thereby catch the defending Germans by surprise. At 2045 hours, the company attacked the village but was repulsed by an alert and well-prepared force of about one hundred paratroopers. A second attack was similarly repelled. The company sustained twelve casualties. One platoon commander, Lieutenant F. Henderson, who was twice wounded in the attacks, braved the open field in front of the village to gather one of his wounded men up and carry him to safety.[16]

With no idea where 'B' Company and its supporting tanks were, the 'D' Company commander pulled back to a position about eight hundred yards from the village to await reinforcement. When 'B' Company and its tanks straggled in a while later, the infantry formed a perimeter around the armour in case the Germans counterattacked. Thomson told the two company commanders to await the dawn before renewing the attack.[17]

ON THE SEAFORTHS' right flank, the Royal 22e Regiment spent the night teeing up its plan for attacking Borgo Santa Maria in the early morning of September 1. Determined to keep casualties as light as possible, Lieutenant Colonel Jean Allard approached the planning with methodical care. There was to be no sending his Van Doos blundering into the vast minefield. Instead, sappers from 4th Field Company, Royal Canadian Engineers were ordered to use the cover of darkness to clear three lanes through the mines.[18]

It was a hazardous mission for the engineers, who were clearly illuminated by the light of a bright moon as they moved out at 0100 hours onto the bald ground in which the mines were concealed.

Major E.A.N. Prichard and Lieutenant A.C. Ferguson were in command. Just as the sappers started lifting mines, a concentration of misdirected Canadian artillery fire crashed down on them.[19] Several sappers were so badly wounded that stretcher-bearers and other sappers had to evacuate them even while the minefield was being torn by exploding shells that were also igniting some of the mines.[20] Despite the casualties and the hazards faced by the continuing erratic shelling and their exposure to German fire, the sappers had the lanes completed by 0415 hours.[21]

While the sappers toiled in the minefield, Allard was finalizing his attack plan. With two of his companies seconded to Brigadier Dawnay's flying column, the thirty-one-year-old commander had no reserves other than one company drawn off from the Carleton and York Regiment. Knowing it was dangerous to mix together units that had never fought together, Allard wanted to restrict this company's use to a purely support role. There was the further complication of language—the Van Doos were French Canadian, the Carleton and Yorks English-speaking Nova Scotians. Although Van Doo officers were generally bilingual, most of the men, including the sergeants, were not. So Allard knew he must send 'B' and 'D' companies into the attack together. If they failed, there would be no reinforcement available and the entire breakout might falter.

Allard planned to push out of the minefield towards a hill designated Point 105, then wheel southeast to take Borgo Santa Maria from the rear. From there, the regiment would strike northeast to a pivotal hill on the outer right boundary of I Canadian Corps's front. This was Point 131, a feature that dominated the proposed line of advance for the 3rd Carpathian Rifle Division's cooperative assault against Monte Luro. Gaining control of Point 131 was therefore of critical importance.[22] At 0200 hours, Allard convened an O Group. Once the sappers finished clearing the lanes, he said, Captain Yvan Dubé's 'B' Company would carry Point 105 while Major Tony Poulin brought 'D' Company up onto a height of land to Dubé's left. With these points secure, Dubé would attack Borgo Santa Maria from the rear, seize it, and continue his drive through to a secondary objective designated Point 137 that lay southeast of the village. Poulin meanwhile would move cross-country north of the lateral road in a virtual beeline from Point 105 to Point 131.

Allard stressed that Point 131 was vital because it commanded the roads running northward on the Canadian right flank. Its capture, he said, would be "the most difficult of these operations." He later wrote: "It was an enormous task to undertake with such limited resources. In fact, this 425-foot mountain was the principal point of defence for the sector. It had a number of works which were well dug in and camouflaged and gave the defenders a marked advantage. Since I had no choice at this stage, all I could do was consider how to provide Poulin with the support he would need."[23] That support would consist of artillery concentrations Poulin could call for by radio. Captain Bill Howarth, a Forward Observation Officer from the Royal Canadian Horse Artillery Regiment, would travel with Poulin to direct this fire.

As the Van Doos in 'B' and 'D' companies started getting ready in the early morning darkness, they could hear gunfire and explosions coming from the direction of Point 204 where 5 CAD had won a deep lodgement in the heart of the Gothic Line the previous day. The French-Canadian soldiers murmured back and forth that it sounded like the German paratroopers were launching a hellish counterattack against the Canadians there.

THE COUNTERATTACK at Point 204 came just a few minutes after midnight. In their forward observation point on the front slope, privates Stan Scislowski and Jim Heaton were trying to determine if some voices coming from below them were speaking German or English. A few seconds later, a Faustpatrone charge "swished like a Roman candle no more than two feet over our heads, following the angle of the hill in its upward passage. Startled, we whipped our heads around and watched it zoom high up into the starlit sky and then it disappeared as its solid fuel burned up. Now," Scislowski later wrote, "we had no doubt as to who was down in the valley."[24]

Snatching up their weapons, the two infantrymen beat a hasty retreat up the hill to 'D' Company's perimeter. They found everyone there so deep asleep that the passing Faustpatrone round had gone by unnoticed. Nor was the increasingly heavy mortar and artillery fire hitting the hilltop causing anyone to stir. Scislowski and Heaton started shaking men awake, even as rifle grenades began exploding throughout the position in an obvious prelude to the German infantry rushing the position. The exploding grenades seemed to wake everyone in a hurry. The exception was Private Hugh Detlor from Niagara Falls, who was to sleep undisturbed through the entire counterattack.

Sergeant Blackie Rowe quickly ordered the fifteen men of 'D' Company's No. 18 Platoon to occupy a zigzag trench that looked down from the brow of the hill upon the north-facing slope. "I'm not going to holler, 'Fire,'" Rowe said softly. "When my rifle goes off, you guys open up, d'ya get that?" Scislowski pressed the butt of his Lee Enfield rifle into his shoulder and waited for the Germans to silhouette themselves against the skyline as they crested the hill. Beside him, Heaton manned his Bren gun.

When several shells exploded behind the trench, the dirt wall crumbled and Scislowski's boots were filled with grit. Then the guns stopped firing and immediately a line of Germans started jogging up the slope. It was the first time Scislowski had seen "the enemy so close, and the first time I was in a position to get in some dead-on shooting. Fifteen fingers twitched on triggers, but not a shot rang out. It was fire discipline at its very best. It surprised me how cool we were as the enemy came towards us in that peculiar half crouch of the infantry. One wave, a second, and then a third emerged from the valley, each about five yards apart. I swallowed hard, but there was nothing to swallow. My throat was dryer than burnt toast, and it wasn't from thirst."[25]

Scislowski wondered what the hell Rowe was waiting on. The first Germans were now only yards away. Then Rowe's rifle cracked and "an explosion of small-arms fire blazed away at the hapless enemy. The first volley chopped the lead wave down in their tracks. The second wave went to ground but got no shots off as .303 and .45 slugs slammed into their bodies. They were out in the open with no cover. It was pure bloody murder! The third wave was somewhat luckier. Since they were only a few yards away from the lip of the valley, most of them were able to duck down out of the line of fire. Only a few from the second wave were lucky enough to escape. Round one to 18 Platoon, round two coming up."[26]

The paratroopers charged head on at No. 18 Platoon a few minutes later and when Rowe's men hit them with another storm of fire, a rifle slug set off a phosphorous grenade attached to one German's belt. "He fell to the ground screaming and thrashing about in hellish agony as the chemical slowly consumed his flesh in a phosphorescent glow. His agony lasted only fifteen seconds, because one of our recent reinforcements, Lloyd Querin, let fly a five-second burst from his Bren. The bullets slammed into the screaming man's smouldering body, ending his agony."[27]

As this latest German assault crumbled, a runner from regimental headquarters told Rowe to pull back into the Strathconas' perimeter. The ground outside the ring of the tanks was going to be smothered by artillery concentrations and No. 18 Platoon was in the line of fire. The platoon was furious about having to surrender the high ground, for, whatever the outcome of the artillery fire, the Germans would surely manage to occupy the trench and then the shoe would be on the other foot for whoever drew the duty of taking it back.[28]

ALL AROUND THE embattled Canadian perimeter on Point 204, Germans were moving, testing, probing for a weak point. A German self-propelled gun managed to take up a position on a convex slope that was hull down from 'B' Squadron's tanks but provided a line of fire against Lieutenant Colonel Jim McAvity's headquarters' section, positioned next to 'A' Squadron. McAvity had a perfect bead on the SPG, but a useless wooden gun in his turret. 'A' and 'C' squadrons were unable to fire on the German target because it stood so close to the tanks of 'B' Squadron. Fortunately, although it fired more than a dozen rounds, the SPG gunner proved a hopeless marksman and failed to score a hit.

Then another vehicle crashed directly into the Canadian lines, drawing fire from tankers and infantry alike. The vehicle was a burning wreck by the time everyone realized it was just a farm tractor that the Germans had for some reason rigged so that it would run unmanned down into the position.

The most determined probing, both by infantry and several SPGS or tanks, was directed at 'B' Squadron's perimeter. For the tankers buttoned up inside their Shermans here, it quickly became impossible to sort out among all the infantry milling about who was friend or foe. At times, some of the tankers clambered out of their tanks armed with rifles, submachine guns, and pistols and joined their infantry counterparts in fighting off attacking Germans in vicious hand-to-hand melees.

Hardest pressed were Lieutenant Wayne Spencer's three Shermans. Manning the tank's bow gun, which was set up in a slit trench near his tank, Trooper Harold Boettcher held off a number of Germans until the gun stopped working. Drawing his pistol, Boettcher emptied the clip and then ran to a tank commanded by Corporal J.B. Matthews. Boettcher wanted the tank to direct its main gun on the closing German infantry, but Matthews and his gunner were locked in a duel with an SPG that was in a position where its line of fire threatened the entire troop. However, unlike most Canadian Shermans that had the pintle-mounted, .50-calibre Browning anti-aircraft machine gun removed to avoid its tangling in the wires supporting Italian grapevines, Matthews's tank still possessed the gun. Jumping onto the rear deck, Boettcher yanked the charging lever back on the Browning and ripped off long, measured bursts at the enemy. He stuck to the gun despite being dangerously highlighted by a tank and a haystack that were both burning nearby and suffering several bullet wounds. Finally, his fire drove the paratroopers off. Boettcher was awarded the Military Medal.

'B' Squadron's battle exacted a terrific toll on its officers. All but Spencer were killed or wounded. When the firing finally ceased, Major Bill Milroy, Captain D.G. Munro, lieutenants E.A. McIlwaine and R.A. McKay-Keenan were all wounded. Lieutenant H.V. Gar, who had seen his first combat this day, was mortally wounded. Trooper A.G. Roper was also killed. Another twelve men—most from 'B' Squadron—were wounded, Trooper Jacob Kippenstain Funk mortally.[29]

On the left-hand flank of Point 204, meanwhile, the Perths fought a tangled, deadly battle. When several self-propelled guns seemed on the verge of getting in among the Shermans, Lieutenant Colonel Bill

Reid gathered up all the PIAT men he could from 'B' and 'D' Company and went hunting German armour. Although they scored several hits on the SPGS with the anti-tank weapons, none were knocked out. Reid, however, was struck in the face by shrapnel. Refusing to be evacuated, he carried on fighting until suffering another wound. This time he agreed to leave the battlefield. Reid won the Distinguished Service Order.[30]

With the battle on the left-hand side of Point 204 winding down, the attempt to recapture the brow of the hill to the north that Scislowski and his platoon mates had feared got underway. 'D' Company, less its PIAT men, was given the job. Captain Sam Ridge put No. 18 Platoon out front with No. 16 Platoon in skirmish order behind and No. 17 Platoon ten yards farther back. The men fixed bayonets and started up the slope. Scislowski hoped to hell that the Germans had been swept right off the hill by the artillery, but he knew better than to bank on this. As they neared the crest, Scislowski realized the entire platoon was starting to bunch up. This was a common but deadly problem common to night attacks, where the ingrained desire to find security among friends outweighs the knowledge that well-dispersed soldiers make less inviting and easy targets. Just as Scislowski turned to caution his comrades to spread out, "a bluish white flash went off close to my right foot, bouncing me half around as though there were coil springs under my boots. In the next instant another flash went off in the air only inches off the top of my helmet." Scislowski heard no explosions. The next thing he knew he was face down on the ground and waking up. "My helmet was gone and blood was running freely down my face and the side of my head. I felt little pain, but at the rate the blood was flowing I was afraid I was bleeding to death." Staggering to his feet dizzily, he almost passed out but somehow remained conscious.[31]

Later he learned that two German grenades had knocked down five men from No. 18 Platoon. Bob Wheatley was dead. The others were all wounded and evacuated. At the 1st Field General Hospital in Jesi, Scislowski was advised his head wound was only superficial. He would, however, need two weeks' hospitalization.[32]

Back at the slope, Sergeant Rowe had pressed on with No. 18

Platoon's remaining nine soldiers. Rowe led the platoon into the midst of the Germans and, after emptying his Lee Enfield, started stabbing men with the rifle's fixed bayonet. Having bayoneted two men to death, he advanced on another who was trying to fire his rifle from hip-level at the sergeant. Just as the German squeezed the trigger, Rowe nimbly jumped out of the way, danced back again to dodge a second bullet, and then brought his assailant down with a hard bayonet thrust.[33] When he turned from this task, the hill was back in Perth hands and Rowe had earned a Distinguished Conduct Medal. Also standing tall on the hill was Private R.D. Saunders, who had assumed command of his section after both section leaders had fallen wounded. Saunders had led the section into the zigzag trench and cleared a long strip of it in a fierce melee. He was awarded a Military Medal.[34]

Only when the brow of the hill was clear did somebody from No. 18 Platoon check the spot where Private Hugh Detlor had last been observed sleeping deeply. They feared finding a corpse or an empty slit trench, evidence that the private had been taken prisoner. Detlor was still there, however, and only just now stirring. Amazed, the survivors of No. 18 Platoon could only think that the Germans mistook this Rip Van Winkle for a corpse.[35]

Between the dawn of August 31 and the early morning hours of September 1, when the battle for Point 204 ended, the Perth Regiment suffered fifty-two casualties. Among the dead were the regiment's intelligence officer, Lieutenant J. Henderson, and Lieutenant G.S. Hall. Lieutenants Bill Hider, George Till, and signals officer J. Morgan were wounded.[36] But the Perths and Strathconas had clung on to Point 204. Come morning, the Strathconas counted forty dead Germans scattered about on their left flank. When Major Gerald Eastman of the B.C. Dragoons returned to the hill on September 2 to recover some knocked-out tanks, he estimated that there were approximately two hundred dead Germans spread across a five-acre area on the north side of Point 204. He had never before "seen so many dead men in such a small area."[37]

[17]

A Greater Sorrow

A COUPLE OF HOURS past midnight on September 1, Major Tony Poulin turned to his fellow Royal 22e Regiment company commander, Captain Yvan Dubé. "It's all or nothing! What do you think?"

Dubé shrugged Gallic-style. "It'll be a real slugging match."

With that, the two men parted. Poulin was dead tired. In the past forty-eight hours, the Van Doos had barely slept as they hastened towards the front lines. So once back at his company headquarters in an abandoned German redoubt, the major fell into an exhausted slumber that lasted just two hours before someone shook him awake. Poulin was surprised to see Lieutenant Colonel Jean Allard sitting on the dirt beside his shoulder. His watch said it was 0415 hours, time for 'D' Company to assemble for the attack. "Is everything ready?" Allard asked softly.

"Yes, sir," Poulin replied, as he gathered his equipment and checked his pistol.[1] An hour earlier, Allard had wakened Dubé and now 'B' Company was already out in the minefield. In order to prevent the two companies becoming intermingled while passing through the narrow lanes the engineers had cleared in the minefield, Poulin's company was to follow at 0515 hours.

Poulin's simple equipment was characteristic of what an officer carried into battle. Personal kit stuffed into a small battle pack, including a medium-sized towel; a wool sweater, either military issue or homemade; apack of cigarettes; two pairs of socks; bar of soap;

emergency rations consisting of a bar of sickeningly sweet high-calorie chocolate and a few hard tack biscuits. The food was to be eaten only if headquarters granted permission. His battle pack also contained a small notebook, some envelopes, and a pen. Strapped to the bottom of the pack, so that it rested against the base of his spine, was a tightly rolled gas cape. Also hooked to the pack was an entrenching tool Poulin considered better suited "to making sand-castles on a sandy beach than for digging a slit trench in rocky terrain." In one hand he carried a map case, the maps therein considered by the twenty-six-year-old officer as a company commander's most vital weapon. His pistol was stuffed into the front of his pants. No officer of sound mind wore a holster or made a show of waving his pistol about, for that invited a sniper's bullet.[2] Some officers carried a Lee Enfield rifle or Thompson submachine gun, but Poulin "figured either was just too awkward" and that he "had a bigger job than firing a rifle." He controlled men and so "didn't have time to muck about with a hollow stick."[3]

This time, Poulin controlled just 85—well under the regulation strength of 120. Nothing surprising there. Rifle companies in Italy were chronically understrength. Reinforcements never matched losses due to casualties and sickness. Poulin worried less about numbers than about the fact that neither his men nor he knew each other. While the Van Doos had fought their way through Sicily and up the Italian boot, Poulin had been on detached duty for fourteen months rebuilding the Les Fusiliers Mont-Royal—almost wiped out at Dieppe. After the Liri Valley Battle gutted the Royal 22e Regiment's officer ranks, Poulin was recalled and assigned to 'A' Company's command. But mere days ago, Allard had transferred him to 'D' Company. "You're kidding," Poulin had protested. "I've trained 'A' Company. I've taken them from zero to what they are. They know me, know what we are."

Allard replied that 'D' Company had become a disciplinary problem. Before the Liri Valley it had been the regiment's best company under Major Ovila Garceau's inspired leadership. But a sniper had mortally wounded Garceau at the Hitler Line and the company had suffered heavy losses among its most senior men. Morale had crashed. "They've become a bunch of bandits and bums. I think that only you can handle them in battle."[4]

Poulin admired Allard too much to argue. He was also a proud Van Doo. If these men were bandits, they had lost that pride. Poulin would not tolerate that. The major had enlisted on August 30, 1939 direct from university into the Van Doos. He would have probably signed up even if there had been no war. The military seemed right for him. Although he had initially fretted as to whether the regiment would accept him, a commission was offered. The commander at the time, Irish Quebecer Lieutenant Colonel Percy Flynn, had served with Poulin's father in the Great War. When the younger Poulin reported for duty, Flynn stared at him, thoughtfully drumming fingers on his desk. "You're as tough looking as your father," he said finally. "We'll get along."[5]

Now Poulin had to prove he was tough enough to ready 'D' Company for a battle just three days away. The major sat down immediately with the company's other two officers, lieutenants Hector Pelletier and François "Fritz" Laflèche and the Company Sergeant Major Irénée Roy. All good men, willing to do their bit to straighten out the company if led by a good company commander. Poulin ordered a parade for 0700 hours the next morning. "Tell the men," he said, "you can get drunk. You can do what you damned well like, but at 0700 you will be there and fit for duty."

Right on schedule, Poulin faced his new company. The men stood at attention with their field kits and weapons. Among them was a former corporal with a reputation as a good combat soldier but a problem in rest areas. Four times he had been promoted to corporal only to be subsequently busted back to private. This morning the corporal was obviously drunk, slouching somewhere between a stance of being at attention and at ease. A wine bottle dangled from a string tied to his belt. The man wore a cheeky grin. "You're drunk," Poulin said flatly.

"Yes, sir," the man slurred.

"You heard what I said about being fit for parade?"

"Yes, but."

Drawing his pistol, Poulin barked, "There are no buts." From a distance of five feet, he shattered the bottle hanging from the corporal's belt with a single shot. "That sobered him up right away," Poulin later commented, "and I never had trouble with the company after that."[6]

At 0500 hours on September 1, Poulin led 'D' Company up to the start line. Heavy concentrations of artillery fire were battering Point 105, Borgo Santa Maria, and Point 131. The latter hill was 'D' Company's final objective. The first two were Dubé's responsibility. Ten minutes later, Dubé reported from the other side of the minefield that his company was crossing the lateral road and moving towards Point 105. At 0535 hours, 'B' Company reached the summit unopposed.[7] Five minutes later, Poulin signalled his men into the minefield. With his company headquarters section directly behind him, Poulin led one platoon up the middle lane. The other two platoons were in the lanes on either side. A strip of white cotton tape marked the outer edges of the cleared areas. Each lane was only wide enough to be passed through single file. The ground underfoot was rough with holes and exposed roots. Progress was slower than Poulin liked. His men were nakedly exposed in the morning light.

Scattered throughout the minefield were the bloated and dismembered bodies of unrecovered West Novas. Then, to Poulin's horror, some of the men he had thought dead started calling out. "Weakened by loss of blood, afraid to move for fear of setting off other mines, tortured by hunger and thirst, they called weakly for stretcher-bearers and for water and implored us not to let them die like animals. But we were on a mission; we gritted our teeth and went on."[8] Later that morning the engineers swept paths through the field to reach each wounded man and those who had survived their ordeal were rescued. Before this help arrived, however, some had bled to death or succumbed to shock.

Twenty feet short of the lateral road the white tape marking the cleared lane petered out. Poulin stared at the space ahead. What the hell had happened? Did the engineers run out of tape? Had they bolted after being fired on and figured the lane was close enough to the road that the Van Doos could get through with only a few casualties? The company had been in the minefield for ten minutes and so far had attracted not a single shot from the Germans. But retracing his steps to use one of the other lanes would unreasonably tempt fate. From behind, CSM Roy and the company wireless operator were taking turns asking if he saw mines up ahead. "I don't goddamned know," Poulin replied. Then he started walking carefully forward. "If you see me go up, you'll know," he hissed.[9]

There were no mines. 'D' Company crossed the road, formed in line, and headed for Point 105. 'B' Company meanwhile was already jumping off from this hill to move southeasterly towards Borgo Santa Maria. Poulin's 'D' Company reached the summit of Point 105 at 0610 hours. By this time, Dubé was back on the lateral road and just short of the village. Neither company had so far met any opposition. After a six-minute rest, Poulin headed towards Point 131. Everything remained quiet.

Not until Dubé's men entered the village's outskirts did they come under sporadic small-arms fire, but the officer led his men forward so aggressively that in less than fifteen minutes Borgo Santa Maria had been swept clear. Two Germans were captured, while a few others fled eastward along the lateral road. The village was a ruin, with only one house standing.[10]

Even as Dubé reported Borgo Santa Maria secure, "a deluge of machine-gun fire" hit Poulin's company on the slope of Point 131. "There were concealed fortifications on the side of the slope and at its summit and they delivered a crossfire that left little untouched."[11] Poulin had the platoons under lieutenants Pelletier and Laflèche out front and these immediately engaged the closest German positions. Royal Canadian Horse Artillery Forward Observation Officer, Captain Bill Howarth, called for an artillery concentration to plaster the entire hill.[12] Although the two forward platoons managed to wipe out the machine-gun positions to their front, they started taking heavy fire from another position on their right flank. Several men went down dead or wounded.

As this German machine gun was only about fifty yards from the platoons, Poulin knew it was too risky to try neutralizing it with artillery. Instead, he pointed out to his two-inch mortar team where the gun was hidden behind the corner of a wrecked brick house. The mortar man fired five rounds before hitting the building. As Poulin turned to encourage the man to pump out the bombs, he saw the mortar man "fling up his arms and slump to the ground. A spreading red stain marked the spot where a bullet had struck his chest. I leaped over, picked up his mortar and fired the seven remaining bombs, shouting to Sergeant Roméo Vézina to get his reserve platoon ready to attack with grenades and bayonets.

"Before the last bomb had struck, I threw the mortar aside, and, clutching my pistol, dashed towards the machine-gun position. Vézina's platoon followed me. The attack was fierce and pitiless. Firing from the hip, throwing grenades, howling like demons, we ran ahead. Many of my men fell. Those who survived had no mercy. Firing point-blank, we didn't even give the Germans time to raise their arms to surrender."[13] The Van Doos discovered the position consisted of "two sunken steel casemates" connected by a trench system. They flung phosphorescent and fragmentation grenades into the casemate ports, killing or wounding the Germans inside. Those who tried to come out were gunned down. No prisoners were taken.[14]

For twenty-five minutes, Poulin's company cut a deadly swath up the hill through one enemy emplacement after another. They took thirteen in all before being stopped cold about seventy-five yards from the hillcrest by a torrent of machine-gun fire. Poulin could see four concrete emplacements from which a number of MG42s blazed away. The casemates were linked by trenches; the "position seemed impregnable."[15] Pelletier and Laflèche's platoons were pinned down, trying desperately to form a defensive line along the embankment of a sunken road that would be capable of throwing back a German counterattack. Poulin tried to lead his headquarters section across to them. As he burst through a vineyard and out into a stretch of open ground, Laflèche yelled, "Watch out, you're in their line of fire!"

Bullets whizzed around Poulin. He and his men hit the dirt just as a stonk of German mortar rounds exploded practically on top of them. Clouds of dirt kicked up by the explosions blinded Poulin. Wiping grit from his eyes, he scrambled towards the sunken road. "The cracks of machine guns filled my ears, then a hard blow spun me around twice. I landed about fifteen feet away. I got up angrily and tried to reach the embankment. Before I had taken two steps I felt a sharp burn on my right leg. I was sure I'd been hit. I made it to the road and found myself near a redoubt the Germans had left. Inside, I found that four bullets had gone through my haversack but my leg was only scratched."[16]

Several of Poulin's HQ section had been wounded in the crossing. But Sergeant Vézina had managed to get his reserve platoon up on the right flank of the other two platoons, so the company now "formed a crescent around the Germans at the top of the hill." Next to Poulin, Captain Howarth peeked over the top of the embankment to try spotting the German positions. His helmet flew off and he slumped forward. Poulin dragged him by his feet into the roadside ditch. There was a small red hole in the FOO's left temple. Howarth's war was over.[17] Poulin's situation was now critical. His company radios had all been knocked out by German fire, so he was unable to call for support. Howarth's artillery signaller reported this set also malfunctioning.

'B' Company, meanwhile, was moving east from Borgo Santa Maria towards where I Canadian Corps's boundary met that of II Polish Corps. Once this move was complete, Dubé was to swing northward to reinforce Poulin. At 0800 hours, Dubé reported by radio to Allard that he was held up by two machine-gun positions and would be en route to Point 131 once these were eliminated. By this time, Allard, always eager to be close to the action, had relocated his tactical headquarters to Borgo Santa Maria's sole surviving building.

At 0845 hours, 'B' Company reported Dubé down and wounded. Second-in-command Captain Gérard Payette was hit minutes later. Allard sent operations officer Captain Côme Simard to take over even as he realized the battle was becoming stalemated.[18]

Back at Poulin's position, the artillery radioman had succeeded in getting his radio back on the air. Although tempted to call for artillery support, Poulin doubted the twenty-five-pound shells would even scratch the concrete fortifications. He could summon a barrage by the more powerful medium or heavy guns, but that would necessitate pulling his company back to avoid the great shells striking his men. Any ground he gave up would just have to be won all over. Alternatively, he could request tank support. When he pursued that option, however, Allard said none was immediately available. With the German mortaring of his position increasing rapidly—a sign that a counterattack was likely only minutes away—Poulin knew he was rapidly losing the initiative.

Quickly, he ordered Pelletier's platoon on the left flank to assault the two casemates there while the rest of the company covered the move. Even with Poulin firing smoke rounds from the two-inch mortar to screen Pelletier's men, the platoon's two attacks were driven back. Several wounded men had to be left in the open. Wounded by a bullet when he was just fifteen yards short of the casemates, Corporal Veillette was unable to move on his own. The company's two stretcher-bearers approached him under the protection of a Red Cross flag they held aloft, gave him first aid, and then carried the wounded soldier safely back to the company lines. The whole time, Poulin waited with his "heart in his mouth," for fear the Germans would cut the men down. He later noted that the opposing paratroopers "were ferocious and merciless in combat, but they respected the Red Cross and stretcher-bearers."[19]

Poulin knew his only option now was to call in medium or heavy artillery. But damned if 'D' Company would give up the ground won, so he ordered his men to get as low as they could in hastily dug slit trenches. The first salvo dropped in the open atop Point 131. "Southwest fifty," Poulin instructed over the radio, knowing that by shifting the fire accordingly the next salvo would either hit the western casemates on target or stray right down on top of his company. Poulin heard over the radio an artillery officer shout, "Fire!" Seconds later, the shells exploded in front of the Van Doos. "Peering through the smoke and dust, it seemed two or three shells had struck the casemates."

"Repeat and maintain fire for ten minutes," Poulin shouted. "A deluge of fire and steel followed. The air was filled with the smell of gunfire and pulverized masonry. Shock waves whipped my face. The blasts were so strong I thought my head would be blown in. Several shells went astray, killing one man and wounding another."[20]

When the last shell exploded, Poulin ordered a charge. Although the shelling had killed all the Germans in one of the casemates, the remaining three were still intact and the men inside opened up with a hail of machine-gun fire. The attack crumbled. Poulin had run out of ideas. Then Laflèche crawled over. "Major, we are almost out of ammunition," he reported, and there were no more grenades or mortar rounds. The men were counting out and sharing the remaining bullets.

When Poulin cast about frantically for CSM Roy, intending to send him back to Borgo Santa Maria for ammunition and reinforcements, he could find no trace of the man. So he sent two privates instead. It was 1042 hours and 'D' Company had been engaged more than three and a half hours. Under Allard's operation's officer, Captain Simard, 'B' Company was crawling painfully towards Poulin's company through persistent sniper fire and one encounter after another with hidden machine-gun positions.[21]

Meanwhile, the men sent to get ammunition returned empty-handed, having been driven back by snipers lurking in the woods behind 'D' Company. Lieutenant Laflèche volunteered to run this gauntlet and Poulin, knowing "nothing but death could stop" the twenty-one-year-old lieutenant, agreed.[22]

Ten minutes after Laflèche set out, Captain Guy Vaugeois, Poulin's towering six-foot-two friend from Montreal and commander of the Bren carrier platoon, calmly walked out of the woods. When he recognized Poulin, the captain's mouth dropped in surprise. "Aren't you dead?"

"Sorry to disappoint you," Poulin laughed. "But you'll be the dead one if you don't take cover." Dashing into Poulin's little redoubt, Vaugeois dropped down on the earth floor and handed the major a cigarette. Poulin took a grateful drag that relaxed him despite the exploding mortar rounds and the machine-gun slugs hammering against the surrounding walls. There was nothing more to do. 'D' Company could only wait for Laflèche to return with ammunition and reinforcements. Out of the original eighty-five men, Poulin figured he had at most fifty capable of fighting and most of these sported one or more minor wounds.[23]

At 1240 hours, CSM Roy strode into Allard's HQ and demanded some tanks. Having realized the peril of 'D' Company's position and unable to reach Poulin safely to get permission to seek reinforcement, the old veteran had set off on his own initiative. He had crawled and dashed through German sniper fire and now offered to guide tanks back to Poulin.[24]

Allard said he had no tanks. The best he could offer was the regiment's four Bren carriers. Fifteen minutes later, the carriers, mounting Vickers medium machine guns, rattled out of Borgo Santa Maria stuffed to the brim with ammunition and with instructions to break through to Poulin at all costs. Roy and Laflèche were both aboard. Meeting virtually no opposition, the carriers clanked into Poulin's position just before 1400 hours.[25]

A delighted Poulin ordered the carriers "to deploy in a half-circle and advance gradually until their machine gunners could shoot right into the firing ports of the casemates. The hail of two hundred bullets a minute would keep the Germans from firing. With this support, we would attack in two waves with automatic weapons and grenades. Before the Germans could recover from the carriers' fire, we would dash up, throw our grenades at the ports and fire into them at point-blank range."[26]

The attack went precisely as planned. At 1425 hours, after a fierce firefight of less than twenty-five minutes, Point 131 was taken. Seven prisoners were captured and an unknown number of paratroopers killed. Poulin's battered company dug in atop the hill while the carriers set up in nearby defensive positions. When a German Panther Mark V started pounding the hill with its heavy gun from a range of just three hundred yards, Allard hastily reinforced Poulin with the six-inch guns of the regiment's anti-tank platoon. The Van Doos had paid in blood to capture Point 131 and Allard was determined not to lose it. In the aftermath of the battle, the Van Doos were surprised to find their casualties were not as bad as originally feared. The two companies had suffered only six men killed, twenty-seven wounded, and two men missing, with one of these believed killed. They had captured thirty-one prisoners.[27] The French Canadians had also cleared a mile-and-a-half-wide swath of the Gothic Line's front defences to a depth of about a half-mile. Allard recommended Poulin for a Military Cross, but by the time the recommendation wended its ponderous route up the chain of command the award was reduced to Mentioned in Despatches.

FROM A HILLTOP south of the Foglia River, U.S. correspondent Martha Gellhorn had watched the Canadian battle on September 1. Ernest Hemingway's wife was a leading war correspondent for the magazine *Colliers*. She sat amid a patch of thistles near 2nd Canadian Infantry Brigade's headquarters, watching the fight in the company of Brigadier Graeme Gibson and some staff officers. Gibson had been told Gellhorn would be with the brigade for several days.[28]

Through binoculars, Gellhorn viewed a battle rendered in miniature. Beetle-sized tanks scuttled up hills or ducked behind a crest for cover. Occasionally, one flared into a ball of flame. Overhead, airplanes circled like dragonflies and then zipped down to unleash their bombs on the breadloaf-shaped Monte Luro. Cottonball-shaped smoke puffs marked the explosion of fresh artillery rounds. "The battle, looking absolutely unreal, tiny, crystal-clear, spread out before us. But there were men in the tanks, and men under those trees where the shells landed, and men under those bombs. The noise was so exaggerated that nothing like it had been heard since the movies," Gellhorn later wrote. "All that day . . . the noise of our guns was physically painful."[29]

Gibson entertained his guest by describing an imaginary postwar garden party. Dinner would be served on a long wooden table over which a dirty, white cloth was carelessly tossed. A monotonic voice would drone incessantly from a radio transmitter placed in one corner of the garden. Bulldozers in another corner would clank back and forth to simulate the racket and vibration of tanks. A Hollywood dust-machine would create the illusion of a dusty Italian road. Just before dinner was served, a waiter would set a thousand flies loose in the garden. Then cold bully beef appetizer would precede a lukewarm dish of meat and beans with hardtack on the side. Dessert? More hardtack, but with jam and tea that had been brewed that very morning. Being as this was virtually the meal Gibson offered this evening, Gellhorn was suitably amused.

But it was hard to remain gaily chatting with this seemingly carefree brigadier when a battle raged before her. Gellhorn found herself thinking, "It is awful to die at the end of summer when you are young and have fought a long time and when you remember with all your heart your home and whom you love, and when you know that the war is won anyhow. It is awful and one would have to be a liar or a fool not to see this and not to feel it like a misery, so that these days every man dead is a greater sorrow because the end of all this tragic dying seems so near."[30]

WHILE GIBSON ENTERTAINED his thirty-six-year-old correspondent, his brigade spent September 1 deepening 1st Canadian Infantry Division's breakthrough. Stymied the night before from capturing the village of Pozzo Alto, the Seaforth Highlanders of Canada's 'B' and 'D' companies had tried again at 0900 hours and taken the village in just fifteen minutes. While Lieutenant Colonel Syd Thomson moved his tactical headquarters and 'A' and 'C' companies into the town, the two leading companies drove several hundred yards northward to secure a low ridge and again met virtually no opposition.[31] As had been the case throughout the gatecrashing Canadian offensive, the Germans were proving incapable of meeting I Canadian Corps's offensive with a consistent, sustained, and interlocking defence. So while some regiments, like the Van Doos, faced fierce resistance from a determined and well-positioned defender, others, like the Seaforths, encountered only slight, easily eliminated pockets of resistance.

On the extreme left flank at Monte Marrone, the Germans seemed to have no infantry to throw against the Cape Breton Highlanders and 'B' Squadron of the 8th Princess Louise New Brunswick Hussars. Instead, they resorted to constant artillery fire and probing the hilltop position with several tanks and self-propelled guns.

Private Bill Metcalfe and his buddy had dug a slit trench during the night and covered it with a crude straw roof to create some shade. The two men were still sound asleep just after dawn when an SPG started raking the ground around them with machine-gun fire. Gazing out from under the improvised roof, a startled Metcalfe realized they had dug the trench slightly downhill on a slope directly facing the German lines. Blinded by the sun, the private couldn't see the SPG. But there was no mistaking the tracers striking the ground just forty feet away and slowly, methodically, creeping his way. Then a tracer plowed into the ground in front of their trench and ricocheted up through the overhead straw. There was a sizzling sound and flames started engulfing the roof over their heads. Metcalfe and his friend rolled out of the trench and hugged the ground nearby, hoping to hell the straw would burn up quickly so they could reclaim their trench.[32]

Close by, two Shermans in Lieutenant Bill Spencer's No. 3 Troop burst into flames after the SPG hit each in rapid succession with armour-piercing rounds. Two of the tankers, unable to bail out, burned to death. The tank squadron's strength was reduced to just nine tanks. An armour-piercing round struck the main gun on Captain Bob McLeod's Sherman, bounced off the side of the turret with a mighty clang, but failed to penetrate. As blinded by the rising sun as Metcalfe had been, the Hussars were unable to bring the SPG into their sights. They fired into the general area, frantically hoping for a lucky hit.[33]

Suddenly at 0930 hours, the sun rose a little higher and the SPG was brought into plain view. The Hussars opened fire, quickly reducing it to a smoking wreck. A Panther Mark V was also exposed and knocked out by a storm of armour-piercing shot fired almost simultaneously by several Shermans.[34]

'B' Squadron commander, Major Howard Keirstead, could now see Tomba di Pesaro off to the northeast of Monte Marrone. Thought to be the last key Gothic Line fortification in 5th Canadian Armoured Division's way, this was the objective that other Hussar squadrons and the 11th Canadian Infantry Brigade infantry were scheduled to soon attack. Hoping to soften up the German defence there, Keirstead ordered McLeod to take command of No. 2 Troop and lead it out 1,000 to 1,500 yards to a ridge that would enable the Shermans to range in on the village.[35]

McLeod set off at 1000 hours in his tank *Byng*, with Sergeant "Tug" Wilson and Corporal H. Sheppard in tow. The tankers took no chances. They raked every passing bush and clump of trees with machine guns and blasted any houses or haystacks with high explosive.

When a high-explosive round in McLeod's gun stuck in the bore, he realized the German round that had earlier hit the gun must have damaged the barrel. It took his gunner five minutes to finally remove the shell. Then McLeod's radio ceased functioning just as Sheppard spotted a 75-millimetre antitank gun to the left and rear of his captain's tank. The corporal smashed the gun with a high-explosive round before its crew could fire.

Momentarily halting the column, McLeod ran over to Sheppard and ordered the corporal to switch tanks with him so he could restore a radio link to the squadron. The day was another scorcher. McLeod gulped water so quickly that he immediately vomited most of it back up. When they reached the ridge at 1100 hours, the Shermans lit into Tomba di Pesaro with their 75-millimetre guns.

After about an hour of blazing away, McLeod advised Keirstead he was running low on ammunition. The troop was going to stop shooting so there would be some ordnance left for their return trip to Monte Marrone. Keirstead sent another No. 1 Troop under Lieutenant Wally Manley to take over the shelling operation.

While the captain awaited his relief, he decided to check a farmhouse on the opposite side of the crest. When McLeod raked the building with the co-axial machine gun from the rise, a flurry of white sheets appeared in various windows. With McLeod covering him, Sheppard rolled his Sherman down the slope to investigate. The house proved full of Italian civilians, none of whom had been hurt by the machine-gun fire.

Manley arrived at 1330 hours and McLeod briefed him in the shade of some overhanging grapevines. As No. 2 Troop rolled back towards the squadron along the southwest edge of the ridge, McLeod spotted some German infantry off to his right. Simultaneously, Manley called up on the radio to report that one of his men, Trooper F.A. MacDonald, had crushed his hand in the breech of his 75-millimetre gun and required immediate evacuation. McLeod dispatched Sheppard to fetch the injured soldier. While he and Sergeant Wilson waited on Sheppard's return, three German infantrymen blundered out of the nearby brush and immediately surrendered when McLeod fired his pistol at them. One carried a sniper's rifle. McLeod searched the Germans and relieved them of a Luger pistol, a cigarette lighter, and a pen and pencil set.

Things were starting to get dicey, McLeod realized, as a lot more German infantry were moving around the vicinity of his position. Things came to a head just as Sheppard's tank returned and a concealed antitank gun suddenly opened fire on McLeod's Sherman. The first round struck just to the left, the second to the right, and the third ricocheted off the turret. McLeod ordered the three prisoners to jump on the back of his tank and told his driver to get moving. The tank sped along a trail that had a steep bank on the left side. When the trail suddenly narrowed, one of the Sherman's tracks climbed steeply up the embankment and nearly upset the tank.

Safely back with the squadron, a shaken McLeod told Keirstead: "After two hits on my tank it looks like I was born to be hanged, not shot." As the adrenaline generated by combat rapidly burned away, the captain felt suddenly dead on his feet. Somebody passed him a mug of coffee and a bowl of soup. The food helped somewhat. But McLeod realized he had been going full-tilt for more than forty-eight hours. Everyone in the squadron was exhausted. When Keirstead had McLeod radio regimental headquarters and request relief, however, Lieutenant Colonel George Robinson "wasn't complimentary."[36] The entire regiment, Robinson said, was in similar straits and 'B' Squadron would just have to soldier on.

[18]

Absolute Bedlam

THE BATTLE's relentless pace was wreaking havoc on 5th Canadian Armoured Division, particularly 11th Canadian Infantry Brigade. The Cape Breton Highlanders were so beaten up, Major General Bert Hoffmeister decided to leave them on Monte Marrone to rest up while still serving to anchor his left flank. That meant giving the Irish Regiment of Canada the job of assaulting Tomba di Pesaro.

Hoffmeister's original plan had also assigned the Perth Regiment, supported by the Lord Strathcona's Horse Regiment, to capturing Monte Peloso (Point 253 on military maps). Repelling the counterattack on Point 204 had, however, left its commander wounded and the surviving infantrymen exhausted. The general had no option but to commit some of 12th Canadian Infantry Brigade's regiments—so far kept out of battle to keep them fresh for the anticipated rapid breakout from the Gothic Line—to complete breaching that line. All hopes of winning a breakout now hung in the balance. Accordingly, Hoffmeister ordered Lieutenant Colonel Bill Darling to march the 4th Princess Louise Dragoon Guards to Point 204 and attack Point 253 from there.[1]

At 0900 hours on September 1, Darling arrived at Point 204 by jeep to conduct a preliminary reconnaissance while the regiment followed on foot. The PLDG was going into battle for the first time since being reduced from an armoured car unit to infantry. Most of its men still resented being subjected to what they viewed as a demotion in regimental status. In a quiet act of defiance, the regiment had retained armoured designations, so its men served in squadrons broken down into troops rather than companies comprised of platoons.

Darling found the situation on Point 204 vague and confused. Lieutenant Colonel Jim McAvity, the Lord Strathcona's Horse commander, had no intelligence on how many Germans defended the PLDG objective. When his troops arrived, Darling held them on Point 204's reverse side and called the officers up to an observation post on the hilltop that afforded a good view of the ground over which they would attack. After a quick briefing, the officers headed back to their companies, but had taken only a few steps when an artillery salvo caught them in the open. 'B' Squadron's Major J.B. Lawson was killed. A combination of losses due to sickness and artillery-inflicted shrapnel wounds had so diminished this company's officer ranks that a junior platoon commander, Lieutenant P.M. Moore, was left as the only fit officer. He took over the squadron's command.[2]

At noon, Darling warned the attack would start in just forty minutes. But as he started to brief the surviving officers on the details, the entire regiment was caught in a devastating artillery bombardment. "Absolute bedlam reigned," Darling wrote afterwards, "while we were subjected to an extremely heavy concentration of shelling and mortaring which kept up continuously for half an hour. I should think five hundred heavy shells landed within our immediate area. Three tanks and numerous vehicles were destroyed and burning. Grass fires were raging and the men had scattered to find cover as best they could. All this somewhat interrupted the O Group but worse still, three officers and about thirty [other ranks] were hit, about a hundred more were 'off their rockers' from the merciless pounding, and there was a considerable amount of confusion." Darling had to delay the attack by thirty minutes.[3] At 1310 hours, 'A' Squadron, which was to have led off on the left flank with 'D' Squadron on its right, was still sorting itself out from the shelling. Darling swapped it for 'C' Squadron. The Strathcona's 'C' Squadron, under command of Major Jack Smith, followed in waves behind the two advancing infantry squadrons.

No sooner had the Dragoons started down the side of Point 204 than snipers began harrying them from the front and their flanks.

"Progress," wrote the war diarist, "very slow due to inexperienced men, lack of officers and NCOs. Houses dotted all along the line of advance were each, in turn, an enemy post and had to be dealt with. Casualties soon began to mount, as did the number of POWs."[4]

Lieutenant Moore was wounded minutes after he led 'B' Squadron across the start line. Individual sergeants assumed command of each troop and nobody exercised any overall control over the squadron itself, but the men kept pushing forward. Infantry and tanks struggled slowly downhill for about eight hundred yards into a saddle running between Point 204 and Point 253.

The tanks "sprayed every hedge and wheat stook with machine-gun fire—and reaped the heaviest toll of German paratroopers ever credited to the regiment."[5] One paratrooper, armed with only a rifle, popped out from behind a stack of wheat and squared off against an advancing Sherman. Standing in full view with his rifle shouldered as if he were on a shooting range, the German fired one shot after another that harmlessly pinged off the armour of the tank's turret. The tankers chopped him down with a burst of .45-calibre machine-gun fire and then ground the corpse under their tracks.

McAvity, who had been directing the tankers from his vantage on Point 204, suddenly heard his voice collapse to a hoarse whisper that made issuing further orders impossible. He handed command to Major Lee Symmes.

Meanwhile, the attack had bogged down in the middle of the saddle when the infantry were driven to ground by heavy machine-gun fire from a stoutly built farmhouse. When Captain D.J. Burke attacked the house with several sections from 'A' Squadron with tanks backing him up, the Germans were quickly wiped out. Inside, the troopers found the rooms strewn with corpses of paratroopers and well stocked with machine guns and Faustpatrones.

The PLDG started a slow, bloody push up the eight-hundred-yard steep slope towards the summit of Point 253. Darling paused on the edge of a plowed field that covered the last two hundred yards leading up to the hillcrest to organize a final charge. He had only forty men. Burke's section numbered only eight. Darling jogged over to Major Smith's Sherman and asked him to deploy his squadron halfway across the field and to go there without infantry support. If the tanks met only light opposition along the way, Darling would put in his charge. The Shermans entered the field in an arrowhead formation and started wallowing through two-foot-deep furrows. Drivers dumped their transmissions into bull low and the Shermans lurched slowly through the crumbling clay while the gunners hammered any houses or clumps of vegetation that might hide enemy positions with 75-millimetre and machine-gun fire.

When the tanks reached the halfway point, Darling and his forty men charged out into the open field.[6] Bullets whipped around them and some struck flesh. Fifty yards from the summit, only fifteen men still followed Darling. These went up the last, steeper stretch on hands and knees right into the face of the Germans. At the last minute, when it seemed this small group of attackers would surely all be killed, the paratroopers broke and fled. Darling staggered onto Point 253 at about 1600 hours. The PLDG had won its first infantry battle and Darling would receive a Distinguished Service Order for gallantry.[7]

When Strathcona Lieutenant W.J. Brown's lead troop joined the Dragoons a few minutes later he pulled out a bottle of whiskey, offered a toast to the hard-won victory and passed the bottle down to Darling. After savouring the fiery liquor, Darling got to work establishing a defensive perimeter around the hilltop. With every passing minute, more infantrymen filtered in to boost the ranks. Some had been pinned down in small firefights with isolated pockets of paratroopers, while others had been unable to keep up. A few had hidden, cowering in fear until the fighting ended.

Corporal Gordon McGregor, the Kamloops logger, was in terrible shape. Over the past few days, he had marched twenty miles on the damaged tendon in his leg. He had arrived at Point 204 barely able to continue walking, only confirming the wisdom of his decision to request a transfer to the division's assault engineers, who always moved by truck. Then had come the uphill attack and all the terror and pain that had entailed. During the advance, a piece of shrapnel had embedded itself in his forehead, but he yanked it out and kept limping up the hill.

The next day, McGregor learned his transfer had come through. "You want to go or you want to stay?" a major asked him. "I don't want to stay," McGregor replied. "I don't like to walk." As the assault engineers were at full strength, he was shunted off to a reinforcement depot and then assigned to a tank delivery squadron where his job was delivering replacement tanks to the front lines.[8]

Within an hour of Point 253's capture, Darling had about one hundred men on the hill. He radioed brigade headquarters: "Objective captured," and urgently requested ammunition, supporting arms, and most immediately water for his parched troops.

The PLDG paid a bloody price for this tiny bit of real estate—129 casualties, of whom thirty-five died, while the Strathconas counted six dead and twenty-four wounded.[9] An estimated 120 Germans were believed dead and as many were taken prisoner.[10] Within a couple of hours, one Perth Regiment company reinforced the hilltop and a Princess Louise Fusiliers platoon brought several Vickers medium machine guns to stiffen the defence.[11] Shortly thereafter, four M10 Tank Destroyers arrived and the Strathconas withdrew to the reverse slope to reorganize, rearm, and refuel out of sight of the Germans who constantly shelled the summit.[12]

On hearing the details of the PLDG's attack, Eighth Army commander General Oliver Leese shot off a congratulatory message to Darling. "My congratulations to you and all ranks of your battalion on your hard fighting at Tomba di Pesaro. The Regiment may be proud of its part in a great and hard-fought victory. With many thanks and best wishes to you all. Well done, Canada."[13]

LEESE WAS MISINFORMED. Tomba di Pesaro still remained in German hands; a fact the Irish Regiment of Canada hoped to change with a night attack. Zero hour for the Irish was 1945 hours.[14] That afternoon, the Irish and the 8th Princess Louise New Brunswick Hussars' 'C' Squadron passed through the Cape Breton Highlander lines on Monte Marrone and three-quarters of a mile eastward to Il Casone. This was a large farm situated on a low ridge that arced gradually northeastward to meet the heights upon which Tomba di Pesaro stood.

Leading the way, the Hussars entered a small valley just short of

Il Casone and were suddenly among a group of German infantry on the march. Surprise was complete for both sides, but the tankers recovered more quickly and raked the infantry with machine guns. After unsuccessfully trying to return fire with a few Faustpatrones, about seventy Germans surrendered and were quickly passed back to the Irish.[15]

During the climb up the rough, steep slope to Il Casone, several Shermans lost tracks, leaving the squadron with only ten serviceable tanks by the time it reached the farm buildings.[16] Lieutenant Colonel Bobby Clark marched his infantry into the position shortly thereafter. From the large farmhouse's upper storey, Clark, Hussars Major Cliff McEwan, and the company and troop officers gazed out at their objective. "It was another town of stone and mortar, brown and quiet on its hilltop, and mysterious because there was no way of knowing, after Montecchio's lesson, what resistance lurked behind its walls."[17]

Clark had an all too rare advantage during this gatecrashing battle—time to plan his attack. From their excellent vantage, Clark pointed out the routes each officer was to follow to the objective. It would be a two-pronged attack. Captain Bill Elder's 'B' Company would drop into the valley fronting Tomba di Pesaro and ascend the slope to enter the village's left-hand side. Meanwhile, 'C' Company, under Captain Bill Mitchell and riding atop five tanks, would follow the ridgeline leading to the town's right flank and break in there. The remaining five tanks would force the Germans to keep their heads down with fire support from Il Casone. A short artillery bombardment supplemented by fire from the Irish mortar and antitank platoons would precede the attack at 1945 hours, with the antitank guns specifically targetting the village's church steeple.[18]

Soft evening light lit Tomba di Pesaro gently as the first shells started to fall. To the Canadians watching from the farm, the picturesque nature of the scene was oddly disturbed by the plumes of black smoke and flashes of flame caused by the artillery, tank, and antitank fire. Soon the village was entirely obscured by a thickening haze of smoke that drifted along the ridgeline to completely obscure the battlefield. Then 'C' Company was told to board the five tanks commanded by Captain Lloyd Hill and, when they were all crouched on the back deck or lying against the turret, the Shermans rumbled forward. They headed for Tomba di Pesaro at top speed with the infantry clinging grimly to whatever handholds they could find. 'B' Company meanwhile bolted into the valley, swept across the narrow bottomland, and then started sweating up the steep slope.

The Shermans rolled right through to the edge of the village without attracting any opposition. Captain Mitchell's infantry company piled off the tanks and warily slipped in among the shell-battered buildings. On the opposite side of Tomba di Pesaro, Elder's men did likewise. Although they tumbled a few Germans from the 1st Parachute Antitank Battalion, these immediately surrendered without a fight. By 2000 hours, Clark was informed the village was secure.[19]

The ecstatic infantry commander walked over to McEwan's tank and handed the major a gallon jug of rum to share with the rest of 'C' Squadron's tankers as a token of good old Irish appreciation. Next morning, when Clark marched the rest of the regiment into the village, he was greeted by a large, hastily created sign painted crudely on the whitewashed side of a building next to the main street entrance that declared: "Bobby Clarksville—In Bounds to All Canadian Troops." This was a jibe at I Canadian Corps's provost officers, renowned for constantly erecting signs designating every village out of bounds to Canadian troops within hours of their capture. A smaller sign nearby read: "Out of bounds to Provost." Clark let the latter remain for a few hours before ordering it painted over.[20] September 1 was a hallmark day for the Irish Regiment. Its war diarist wrote: "The First day of the month found the Irish Regiment completing the breakthrough of the Gothic Line."[21]

Regimental pride aside, however, the breakthrough achieved by the Canadians on September 1 had been the work of many regiments. And on the Canadian right flank, 1st Canadian Infantry Division had been trying to drive even more deeply that day than had 5 CAD.

WITH THE PLDG protecting that division's left flank from Point 253, Pozzo Alto and the low ridge behind clear of Germans, and his right flank secured by the Royal 22e Regiment, Major General Chris Vokes believed the time was right to unleash his flying column towards the

Adriatic coast. Brigadier D. Dawnay, whose 21st Royal Tank Brigade provided the column's armoured teeth, was equally anxious to win a deep penetration before day's end. The objective was Monte Luro, about two miles to the north. Once the Canadians controlled that mountain, they would dominate a pivotal intersection of roads leading east towards the Adriatic and thereby deny the Germans the ability to easily reinforce or maintain any cohesive defence south of Cattolica. The Loyal Edmonton Regiment, supported by the 12th Royal Tank Regiment, was ordered to immediately seize Monte Luro.

Lieutenant Colonel Budge Bell-Irving sat down with his armoured regiment counterpart, Lieutenant Colonel H.H. Van Straubenzee, to hammer out a plan. Theirs was a tall order, particularly as the two officers would not reach their jump-off point on the ridge held by the Seaforth Highlanders of Canada until 1730 hours. It was impossible to predict how stiffly the Germans would defend the ground between the ridge and Monte Luro. And the mountain was believed to be strongly fortified and ideally suited for defence.

In the event, the drive to the foot of the mountain proceeded smoothly. 'A' and 'C' companies led the way by bounds, with men riding on the backs of tanks until German opposition was encountered. Twenty-three-year-old Captain John Dougan had just been given command of 'C' Company after serving several months as its second-in-command. When 'A' Company, which was leading, bumped into some Germans holding a house halfway to the base of the summit, the infantry piled off the Shermans and tackled the position with rapid fire. Dougan's men then rolled up and dismounted to finish the mopping-up phase while 'A' Company reboarded its tanks and hurried on. The two companies repeated this procedure twice more before reaching the base of the mountain and were delayed only a few minutes at each stop.[22]

The infantry dismounted for the attack on the mountain and went up the slope with 'C' Company left and 'A' Company right. The tanks were right behind, and directly in front a creeping artillery barrage preceded the infantry. Everyone was riding high on adrenaline because of the pace at which the advance was progressing. Lieutenant Keith McGregor, one of Dougan's platoon commanders, charged uphill so quickly that he and his men outran the barrage and were forced to desperately take cover when shells chased across their position. As the Edmontons burst onto the summit, several large blobs about twenty inches in diameter screamed over Dougan's head to disappear far off in the valley to the south. It took several minutes for the puzzled officer to realize the Germans were firing at the mountain with huge Italian coastal guns positioned either at Rimini or Cattolica. Fortunately, their aim remained high. Standing on the summit, with the sun setting behind the mountains to the west so that the rugged coastal plain was cast in a gentle golden glow, Dougan could see the Adriatic beyond the coastal towns of Fano, Pesaro, and Cattolica. Nowhere north of Monte Luro was there any sign of German movement. To the young officer it seemed that 1st Canadian Infantry Division could go as far as it liked if it just kept moving as quickly as it had this day.[23]

The Edmontons took twelve prisoners on Monte Luro. Among them were six Germans who surrendered their Panzerturm without firing a shot from its powerful 75-millimetre gun.[24] Had they offered a fight, the tanks grinding up the slope would have presented perfect targets. At the Hitler Line, a single Panzerturm had systematically knocked out thirteen North Irish Horse tanks in minutes.

With Monte Luro in Allied hands, Brigadier Dawnay was eager to sustain his flying column's momentum. His immediate targets were the seaside resort of Cattolica and a number of other small villages lying south of the Conca River. Pieve, Gradara, and Fanano perched on spurs that stretched down from Monte Luro. In the flats before the Conca were San Giovanni in Marignano and Monte Albano. Dawnay ordered the Princess Patricia's Canadian Light Infantry and 'B' Squadron of the 48th Royal Tank Regiment to conduct a night attack northeastward towards Point 119, which was quickly and successfully executed.[25]

THE SPEED AND FEROCITY of the Canadian attack had sent the Germans reeling. Desperately, German commanders attempted to re-establish some semblance of a linked defensive line with badly disorganized units. On the eastern flank, a large number of battalions of 1st Parachute Division were still pulling out of Pesaro as II Polish Corps fought its way into the city. Dawnay was in a position to effect an encirclement of these paratroopers if he could sever the highway that was their main line of retreat.[26]

Throughout I Canadian Corps, spirits were running high. One corps intelligence staff officer's summary concluded: "In the Liri Valley Heidrich's [1st Parachute] division were able to escape through the mountains, but this time, if we succeed in cutting him off, he will have to use rowboats."[27] Another declared the battle "all over but for the pursuit."[28]

The advantage still lay with the Germans, however, because they controlled the coastal highway while Dawnay's column must travel overland in order to cut both the road and railway in front of the retreating Germans. On the corps's western flank, Hoffmeister's 5 CAD was seriously depleted after the terrific battles fought to crack through the Gothic Line. Hoffmeister told Burns that 11th Canadian Infantry Brigade was exhausted and required thirty-six hours to reorganize, as did the Princess Louise Dragoon Guards.[29] The 5th Canadian Armoured Brigade's three regiments were in similar straits.

Not that Hoffmeister proposed standing still. While he had available formations, Hoffmeister remained in the game. And the major general had two fresh battalions from the 12th Canadian Infantry Brigade and the Shermans and armoured cars of his reconnaissance regiment—the Governor General's Horse Guards. Hoffmeister ordered these two battalions to pass through Tomba di Pesaro, each with a squadron of the GGHG in support, and run hard and fast to the Conca River. The units would advance in two columns. As the left-hand column had farthest to travel, Hoffmeister assigned the Westminster (Motorized) Regiment that task. This regiment had proven its battle worth at the Melfa River in the Liri Valley. Originally attached to 5 CAB to provide the armoured brigade with inherent infantry that could match the tanks' pace during a pursuit or breakout operation, the regiment was equipped with armoured personnel carriers and Bren carriers.

As for the right-hand column's infantry element, nobody knew what it was capable of. This was the "No-Name Regiment," still denoted as either the 89th/109th Battalion or 1st Canadian Light Anti-Aircraft Battalion while it waited confirmation from Canadian Military Headquarters of its name change to the Lanark and Renfrew Scottish Regiment. Would a battalion of former anti-aircraft gunners stiffened by a core of randomly assigned infantry veterans be capable of a rapid advance during battle? Hoffmeister had no choice but to find out the hard way.[30]

Both columns had the immediate objective of a ridge about one mile south of the Conca that overlooked the second objective of San Giovanni. The two columns would approach this village by different routes, merge there, then race northeastward on a road running from San Giovanni through Monte Albano to a junction with the coastal highway just before the Conca.[31] In effect, Hoffmeister and Dawnay would be taking different routes towards the same final destination. Whoever got to San Giovanni first would press on to the coast and it mattered not who won this race as long as one reached the coast quickly. Having made the Germans run, Lieutenant General Burns was determined to keep them panicked and disorganized.

He arrived at Eighth Army Headquarters in a very satisfied mood late on September 1 to report that the Gothic Line was broken across the entirety of his sector. Leese, who had been issuing one congratulatory note after another to Canadian regiments throughout the day, was meeting with General Harold Alexander, Deputy Supreme Commander, Mediterranean. "They were highly pleased," Burns wrote, "and, I thought, a little surprised at the speed of the Canadians' advance."[32] After delivering his report in his usual terse, no-nonsense style, Burns took his leave. Leese called him back just as the lieutenant general was stepping into his jeep. Alexander told Burns he was personally recommending him for the Distinguished Service Order. Burns was stunned. "I considered the decoration as an honour for the corps whose bravery and sacrifice had won the victory. But I also took it as a sign that the generals had decided that I could handle my command and that confidence had replaced the doubts that had formerly existed."[33]

Leese also offered Burns the 3rd Greek Mountain Brigade and its supporting field artillery regiment, both currently serving with the 2nd New Zealand Division. The object of doing so, Leese said, would be to give the Greeks some "battle experience." Burns took this as a further sign that Alexander and Leese, having earlier sought his dismissal from corps command, had revised their opinion of his abilities. He agreed to discuss with New Zealand commander Lieutenant General Bernard Freyberg how the brigade might best be utilized.[34]

Burns left Eighth Army HQ cheerfully, but he also left lacking the very thing he most needed. Having cracked the Gothic Line wide open, I Canadian Corps desperately required reinforcement in the form of a fresh armoured division capable of shoving the disorganized Germans aside and plunging straight through to the Po Valley. The opportunity existed. The Canadians had created a gaping hole. Leese had the 1st British Armoured Division positioned to the south in readiness to carry out just such a breakout. But Leese had set his strategy in mid-August and predicated his operations on the supposition that the Germans would crumble in front of V Corps. The Eighth Army commander therefore offered Burns nothing more than the Greeks—an infantry brigade of dubious value.

Leese's failure to seize the initiative won by the Canadians was all the more puzzling in view of V Corps's sluggish advance through the mountains to the west. To the immediate left of I Canadian Corps, the 46th British Infantry Division was managing to keep more or less abreast of the Canadians. But in the higher country left of this division, Lieutenant General Charles Keightley's V Corps was bogging down and a dangerous gap had opened between the 46th Infantry Division and the 4th Indian Division on its left. This gap was so wide that Keightley had decided he must bring his reserve division—the 56th Infantry Division—up to fill the centre.

While briefing the 56th's Major General John Whitfield, Keightley emphasized the need for haste. Whitfield later recalled how he could "still see the way the corps commander kept putting his hand on the map and saying, 'We mustn't get involved in the hills. We can get along on this flat bit and the army commander reckons that we might get a race up that right-handed side.'"[35] Keightley referred here to the narrow strip of ground immediately bordering the Canadian Corps's left flank. Significantly, this was country through which no roads other than local tracks passed. It was hardly ideal tank country even by Italian standards.

Not only was Leese still banking on breaking out through a corps beginning to founder, but he made no effort on September 1 to move 1st Armoured Division rapidly north from its holding position to where it could enter any breach that was opened. In a curious attempt to reduce traffic on the few and heavily congested roads in Eighth Army's rear, Leese had positioned the division one hundred miles from the front. His initial instructions to its commander, Major General Richard Hull, were to be ready to start operations on September 7. These instructions went unmodified, even after Leese had approved the attempt to gatecrash the Gothic Line. Only on the night of August 31 did Leese order the division to start a ponderous approach towards the Metauro River. No haste was urged and no accelerated timetable was proposed for the division's breakout operation.[36]

Hull believed his division would not be called into battle until the Germans had been thrown all the way back to the Rimini Line and a gap created in that final defensive position before the Po Valley. Hull told his officers they would "pass through the Rimini gap... and then... go on, and on and on, day and night, until we are too exhausted to see the target."[37] An enticing vision for tankers trained to believe that an armoured division's primary role was exploitation deep into the enemy rear.

That such a dramatic strategic development was improbable on V Corps's front was obvious. And, although the Canadians had opened such a gap, it was equally evident that Leese had no intention of taking full advantage of this opportunity. So Hull continued to await developments on V Corps's front while moving northward at an unhurried pace. Hence, even as the Canadian Corps won its finest victory in Italy, the decisive opportunity this success offered Eighth Army was beginning to slip away.

[19]

A Long Chance

On August 31, 104 Canadians had been killed and 271 wounded, followed by another 97 dead and 202 wounded the next day. Hardest hit was the Canadian 5th Armoured Division. During the height of the battle, staff from hospitals farther back had to reinforce its No. 24 Field Ambulance at Monteccicardo.[1] In the Corps's field dressing stations and surgeries, doctors and medical orderlies worked nonstop. Chaplain Waldo Smith, formerly the Ontario Regiment's padre, had joined No. 16 Field Dressing Station just five days before the battle began because he thought himself too old for the hard duty demanded of regimental chaplains serving in fighting units.

Among the casualties that passed before him on August 31 was Captain Kenelm Eaton, the young Princess Patricia's Canadian Light Infantry chaplain who had knelt on a mine while tending a wounded soldier. "Now I can get home," the chaplain told Smith while orderlies prepared to take him into the surgery. The chaplain had lost much blood and was in shock. Citing a passage from the 23rd Psalm, Smith told his friend: "Surely goodness and mercy shall follow me all the days of my life."

"And I shall dwell in the house of the Lord forever," Eaton responded wearily. Five hours later, an orderly summoned Smith. "I think the padre is dying," he said. Smith hurried to the man's side, but he was already gone.[2]

On September 1, the surgical teams started operations at 0700 hours and worked twenty-four hours straight with only brief pauses for meals. By 1900 hours, despite their efforts, a twelve-hour backlog had developed between the time a wounded man arrived and when he entered the surgery. The doctor in command ordered further admissions stopped until the backlog was shortened, with the wounded who were turned away transported by ambulance to medical facilities farther from the front lines.

Smith helped nurses to bathe post-operation patients and get them into beds. As the anaesthetic wore off, some of the wounded regaining consciousness would thrash about wildly as if still in combat. To keep the men from tearing intravenous or transfusion needles from their arms or clawing their bandages off, Smith had to hold "down restless arms and fix a glittering eye upon semi-conscious lads."[3]

In the resuscitation room where blood transfusions were given, Smith watched many soldiers bleed to death as the blood pumped out of wounds faster than it could be transfused. He came "to know by the amount of blood on the floor under the stretcher whether the soldier was to die."[4]

The resuscitation doctor's job was a thankless one, Smith thought. The man had to monitor blood pressures and then decide which wounded should be operated on and in what order of priority. "Here was a man so badly wounded that there seemed no chance that he should live. Was he to be left lying there while others who came in after him whose wounds appeared less severe were taken in and dealt with? It was a medical decision and I had no word to say. All one could do was try to keep up men's faith in their God and trust in His care. One tried to assure them all that the doctors were very anxious about them and were working as hard as they could, taking first those whose need was greatest."[5]

THE FLOW OF WOUNDED was unlikely to abate any time soon, for the battle still raged with I Canadian Corps renewing its drive northward in the early morning hours of September 2. Expectations ran high throughout the corps that the Canadians would manage to breakthrough to the Po Valley in just a few more days, vindicating all the bloodshed by winning a decisive victory.[6]

The 21st British Tank Brigade's Brigadier D. Dawnay, who commanded 1st Canadian Infantry Division's flying column, ordered the Royal Canadian Dragoons and one company of Royal 22e Regiment to cut the coastal highway and railway southeast of Cattolica. From there, he hoped to send an armoured car squadron north to seize a bridge crossing the Conca River. Meanwhile, another company of Van Doos would advance with a 48th Royal Tank Regiment squadron in support to capture Pieve. Both columns were to strike out from a position parallel to Monte Luro. En route to this forming-up position, the rugged, confused country through which only ox-cart trails passed proved impossible to navigate quickly in the early morning darkness. It was soon obvious that the attacking units could not reach their forming-up positions before dawn, but attempts to relay this information by radio to Dawnay failed.[7]

At 0200 hours, the British brigadier was still anxiously awaiting the arrival of the two columns and more fearful with each passing minute that the opportunity to block the escape of the 1st Parachute Division units withdrawing from Pesaro was trickling through his fingers. Looking for an alternative plan, Dawnay noted that the Princess Patricia's Canadian Light Infantry was well out on the corps's right flank at Point 119 with 'B' Squadron, 48 RTR, in support. He immediately ordered 'A' and 'D' companies to board the tanks and proceed by the fastest route possible to cut the railroad line where a bridge crossed a deep ditch at San Stefano, two thousand yards southeast of Gradara. Progress was swift, and by 0400 hours the small force was digging in astride the steel tracks to form a defensive right-flank position for 1 CID and to secure the bridge for use by Allied armour.[8] Only a single self-propelled gun had offered any resistance, firing one round at a Sherman conducting a dawn reconnaissance on the north side of the bridge. Although the shell glanced harmlessly off the hull of the tank, the concussion somehow caused a fire to break out inside the turret. PPCLI Major E.W. Cutbill, who was riding inside, suffered serious burns.[9]

Even as the bridge crossing was secured, the Van Doos aboard a squadron of 48 RTR tanks finally jumped off towards Pieve. Dawnay ordered the Loyal Edmonton Regiment holding Monte Luro to get ready to leapfrog through that village the moment it was captured. The flying column was on Pieve's outskirts before an antitank gun and several snipers inside the village offered the first German resistance. The infantry quickly broke into the small village and swept it clear.

Developing his strategy on the fly, Dawnay tried to sustain the rapid pace of advance. He ordered the Van Doos to sit tight in Pieve to prevent the Germans filtering back into the buildings while the 48 RTR squadron raced by road towards Gradara.[10] Meanwhile, the Loyal Edmontons were ready to proceed with their leapfrog operation but were left waiting on the arrival of the 12th Royal Tank Regiment, upon whose armoured hides they were to ride forward. This regiment was slogging along the same ox-cart tracks that had delayed the flying columns and did not marry up with the infantry until 1100 hours. The force set off immediately towards Fanano, slightly less than two miles north of Pieve.[11]

After a grinding, slow trip cross-country, the tanks reached a position looking up towards Fanano at about 1300 hours. While trying to scan the village from a nearby hilltop, 12 RTR's commander, Lieutenant Colonel H.H. van Straubenzee, came under mortar fire and was knocked unconscious when a chunk of shrapnel struck him in the head.[12] Assuming command, Lieutenant Colonel Budge Bell-Irving ordered Captain John Dougan's 'C' Company to attack the town the moment a scheduled artillery bombardment lifted. Dougan looked at the six hundred yards of open ground that ran up a steep slope to the hilltop town and called for the artillery to lay down smoke screens on his flanks at the same time as it shelled the village.

When the smoke shells and high-explosive rounds screamed in, Dougan immediately led his men out into the open ground with No. 13 and No. 14 platoons out front and No. 15 Platoon close behind. Running as hard as they could, the company got in among the houses just as the barrage started to lift and caught the Germans emerging from sheltered positions before they could reenter their fighting positions. Surprise was complete and after the Edmontons killed several Germans in a fusillade of gunfire, the nineteen survivors surrendered. Captured intact was a self-propelled gun whose crew had been unable to get from the shelter of a building to man it before being overrun by the Canadians.

Dougan told his radio signallers to set up a company headquarters in a nearby house while he organized the platoons in defensive positions. When the unarmed signallers walked into the building, they found themselves face to face with seven heavily armed paratroopers. The Germans, Dougan recalled, "gave themselves up like sheep."[13] Bell-Irving moved the rest of the regiment up and by 1830 hours reported Fanano secure.[14] The village soon proved itself a surprisingly pleasant billet. Everywhere the men looked there seemed to be chickens and other domestic fowl scuttling about. Soon every squad had a pot of water boiling and several plucked birds ready for cooking.[15]

The Loyal Edmontons were not the only 2nd Canadian Infantry Brigade regiment to leapfrog through Pieve that day. So too had the Seaforth Highlanders of Canada aboard tanks of the 145th Regiment, Royal Armoured Corps. Their objective was Monte Albano, which lay just south of the Conca and was about three and a half miles distant. The trip passed with only a few minor skirmishes, although one self-propelled gun managed to knock out four Shermans before being destroyed by other tankers. Because there were no roads to follow, the journey was relatively slow, however, and it was early evening before Lieutenant Colonel Syd Thomson set up his headquarters inside a church in the heart of the hilltop village. Dawnay ordered him to spread his companies out along the road leading towards the Conca so it was kept open for a squadron of Royal Canadian Dragoons to use as a route leading to an intersection with the coastal highway and a bridge crossing over the Conca there.[16] Thomson immediately did as instructed, but it was an unnecessary action, for the Dragoons had already come and gone.

DAWNAY HAD ORDERED the Royal Canadian Dragoons to split up into two prongs and push out from the division's flanks to deepen the break won by his combined tank and infantry columns. The main

RCD prong passed through the PPCLI position at San Stefano and headed towards the coastal highway with instructions to drive to Cattolica. Dawnay's secondary prong was intended to provide both protection for the Seaforths' exposed left flank and to find a route past San Giovanni by which the armoured cars could cut to the northeast through Monte Albano and secure the coastal highway bridge crossing the Conca.[17]

At first light on September 2, the RCD's 'A' Squadron, accompanied by a company of the Royal 22nd Regiment and a squadron of 48th Royal Tank Regiment, had departed San Stefano and driven up a bush-covered track that proved hard going for the British Shermans. Their numbers rapidly diminished as tanks bogged down or threw tracks. Then German self-propelled guns and mortars firing from inside the stoutly walled Gradara castle brought the column under heavy fire, which came as a surprise because the castle was to have been taken earlier by another squadron of 48 RTR that had been assigned that task by Dawnay. That squadron, however, had been unable to enter the narrow, winding streets of the ancient town without covering infantry and so could only cut the road leading up to Gradara and then subject the Germans inside the castle to harassing fire.[18]

Seeing that the British tanks were incapable of keeping up, the Dragoons transferred the Van Doos who had been riding on the Shermans over to their armoured cars and raced ahead. All went well until the large Staghound armoured cars were unable to get around a crater blocking the track. The leading edge of the column cut itself even finer as the smaller, nimbler Canadian-made Lynx II Scout Cars—called Dingoes—continued alone with a few of the infantry clinging to their hulls. Intended more for speed than combat prowess, the eleven-thousand-pound Dingo had a two-man crew—the driver and the car commander. A fifty-mile-per-hour top speed was made possible by a combination of power provided by its eight-cylinder Ford engine and light weight-reducing armour that was only thirty millimetres thick in front and in some points dropped to a mere twelve millimetres. Its only armament was a Bren gun operated by the commander. The Dingo's five-foot, eight-inch height gave it a low profile, while its relatively narrow six-foot width provided agility and manoeuvrability normally lacking in armoured vehicles.[19]

By comparison, the U.S.-built Staghound was more tanklike in design, weighing 26,600 pounds and measuring seven feet nine inches high by eight feet ten inches wide. It had a top speed of fifty-five miles per hour provided by two six-cylinder Chevrolet engines, a maximum armour thickness of 4.4 centimetres and a minimum thickness of 63.5 millimetres. The five-man crew was armed with a 37-millimetre M6 main gun in the turret, a .30 calibre co-axial machine gun, and a .30 calibre bow-mounted machine gun.[20]

As the RCD war diarist noted: "Nothing whatsoever was known of the situation, either enemy or our own troops, but advance on Cattolica was ordered and advance on Cattolica was made."[21] Leading the Dingoes was Corporal W.J. Swan of Lieutenant J.C.R. Waddell's troop. Just as his car entered a road running from Gradara to the coastal highway at a point where the railroad line crossed it, Swan came face to face with a motorcycle with a sidecar attached "bowling briskly along" with three Germans aboard. The motorcycle skidded to a halt; Swan aimed his Bren and ordered the Germans to surrender. A feldwebel went for his gun, but Swan put a burst into him and the other two men quickly threw their hands up.[22]

When Waddell paused to interrogate the wounded German non-commissioned officer, 'A' Squadron's Staghounds under command of Major Charles Vickers managed to catch up. Vickers decided that whatever might be learned from the German was not worth delaying the advance over, so he spurred the Dragoons onward. Soon the squadron came upon two 88-millimetre guns and several anti-aircraft weapons that the 4th Parachute Regiment had abandoned, which the major took as evidence that the appearance of his small squadron in the German rear was spreading panic in the manner of cavalry operations of old. "The crews," he later noted, "had simply fled, probably in the belief that they had been enveloped in an advance from the flank." The RCDs took this as "significant of the disorganization that armoured cars appearing suddenly at many points in the rear of the enemy can cause."[23]

That any German panic was localized, however, soon became evident when 'A' Squadron broke out onto the coastal highway at 1420 hours and turned in the direction of Cattolica only to be immediately fired on by a Panther. Armoured cars ducked every which way to find cover while the mighty Panther swatted away at them with eleven shells. None struck home and the tank finally turned its back disdainfully on the Dragoons and growled off into the distance.[24]

Proceeding with subdued caution, 'A' Squadron got to within two miles of Cattolica before several heavy machine guns and antitank guns opened up from a narrow band of ground that stood between the road and a series of steep cliffs fronting the sea. As the squadron was driving through a cutting when the ambush was sprung, the fire largely passed overhead, although the bullets and exploding antitank rounds threw branches and stones down on the cars. 'A' Squadron pressed its cars up against the east bank of the cutting for shelter, while Vickers and the Van Doo company commander sized up the German position. The two men quickly realized that the paratroopers were trying to keep the band of ground between the road and the sea open for use by their comrades withdrawing from Pesaro and the position was too strong for their force to eliminate this blocking force.[25]

Before the two officers finished their discussion, however, several Dragoons from the Dingo troop tried probing the German position on foot. Armed with a PIAT, Sergeant H.B. Lewis crept up on one machine-gun position and knocked it out with an explosive round. But one Dragoon was killed and another wounded before Vickers could order the squadron to pull back to a position opposite Gardara and dig in for the night. The attempt to reach Cattolica by the coastal highway had for now failed.[26]

ON I CID's far left flank another Royal Canadian Dragoon squadron was intent on seizing the Conca River bridge crossing just north of the seaside resort. At 1000 hours, Major Allen Brady's 'D' Squadron slipped past Monte Luro, followed by 'B' Squadron with a Van Doo company riding on top of its armoured cars. The Dragoons were carrying out a long left hook, which they knew "was a long chance and required skilful execution and a good measure of luck for success."[27]

Corporal Charles James Paterson of Lieutenant E.M. Jones's troop led. So rapidly did the column move that before noon it was already descending along a road towards San Giovanni, when a German truck turned out of a side road directly in front of the corporal's Dingo. For a few minutes, the truck rumbled unawares towards the village with the entire Canadian column breezing along behind until a glance in the side mirror by the driver revealed Paterson staring at the man over his Bren gun's sights. The driver tumbled out of the truck without bothering to stop first, arms high over his head. Paterson quickly understood the German's haste in surrendering when he discovered the back of the truck was full of ammunition that a burst from his Bren would have certainly ignited.[28] No sooner was the column moving again than a German staff car nearly collided head-on with Paterson. The officers inside managed to escape into a cornfield before any Dragoons could bring them under fire.[29]

By 1400 hours, 'D' Squadron looked down on San Giovanni from a steep rise and saw that the road ran directly through the heart of the undoubtedly German-occupied village. The Dragoons had no option but to fight their way through, but between them and the village was nothing but open fields, so Lieutenant Donald Telfer and his troop of Staghounds was ordered to lead the way in a straight-out charge down the road. The Staghound drivers raced at full throttle towards San Giovanni and managed to get in among the buildings without a shot being fired their way. The village was a warren of old buildings with overhanging balconies on the second and third storeys looking down upon narrow streets, which the Staghounds could barely squeeze up without scraping their sides. The doors and windows of the houses were all shuttered and the village appeared empty.

Slowly, 'D' Squadron approached the town's plaza, with the individual troops following streets. Corporal Paterson's Dingo arrived first. As he edged out into the open square, a Panther emerged across the way. The tank crew's commander was perched atop the turret, guiding the huge tank down the narrow street. Paterson let loose with his Bren, the tank commander fell with an agonized cry, and there came "a clashing of tracks as the tank driver panicked and swung. The tank wallowed sideways, lurched ahead, quivered and came to a halt. With a deafening clang the left track writhed clear of the bogeys and fell to the cobblestones. For a moment the great hulk lay there motionless; then the huge gun began to swing ponderously towards its tiny opponent."[30] Paterson ordered the Dingo reversed smartly into the street from which it had come and pressed the armoured car up against a wall. Then he and his driver waited anxiously "for the end of the street to disappear in smoke and flying bricks as the tank shelled it. But nothing happened."[31] Black smoke started streaming overhead. Paterson cautiously moved his Dingo back up the street to where he could peek into the square. The Panther was engulfed in flames, obviously destroyed by the crew who had then fled.

The short engagement with the Panther proved the only resistance the Dragoons met in passing through San Giovanni and renewing their drive towards Monte Albano and then on to the Conca. Corporal Paterson was once more well ahead in his advance scout role. Monte Albano was nothing more than a dozen buildings perched on a crest overlooking the river, and as Paterson drove up the main street he thought it was abandoned. But as his Dingo rounded a corner he suddenly confronted another Panther. Its crew was standing beside the tank and talking with a group of about forty infantrymen. Realizing that if the tankers manned the Panther they could easily tear the Dragoon column apart, Paterson ordered his driver to charge the Germans with the Dingo while he brought them under fire with his Bren gun. A sustained burst of fire knocked down about ten Germans before the Dingo raced past and zoomed out the other side of the village.

Paterson could see the Conca River ahead and also that the bridge had been blown up. But beside this torn jumble of concrete, German engineers had erected a temporary crossing that a steady progression of German infantry was retreating over either on foot or in any manner of vehicle.[32] And guarding the crossing from positions down in the valley were two more Panthers. Despite the Panthers, Paterson figured if the Dragoons acted quickly enough they could capture the temporary crossing and that therefore it was imperative he report to Major Brady.

Between the corporal and his commander, however, a Panther

lurked inside Monte Albano. Undeterred, Paterson and his driver raced back into the town with the hope they could slip through safely by avoiding the main street. Although they avoided the Panther, they encountered two German infantrymen who opened up with rifles. Paterson cut them down with his Bren and the armoured car dashed on to where 'D' Squadron was just closing on the village. Paterson gave his report, and for his actions at both San Giovanni and Monte Albano would subsequently win a Military Medal.[33]

Well-briefed on the opposition ahead, Brady ordered 'B' Squadron and the company of Van Doos to take the lead, move through the village, and then attack the temporary bridge crossing. No trace of any Germans was discovered in the village and, with evening settling in, the Panthers guarding the crossing were found to have also fled. The Dragoons and Van Doos seized the crossing without a fight and dug in on the north bank of the Conca, concluding a six-mile advance, the longest achieved by any unit that day. September 2 marked the first time the Canadians had been able to turn armoured cars loose in the "midst of a withdrawing, if still resolute, enemy and the Dragoons had been able to add to his confusion"[34] at the loss of only two men killed.

BOTH THE Royal Canadian Dragoons and the Seaforth Highlanders–48 RTR columns had reached San Giovanni ahead of the two 5th Canadian Armoured Division columns also assigned to capturing this village. The 5 CAD formations met stiffer opposition, primarily in the form of intense, well-directed artillery and mortar fire that doggedly pursued the advancing columns with an eerie accuracy. It soon became apparent that German artillery officers must be directing the fire from positions on the hills to the west. And with the 46th British Infantry Division lagging well behind, 5 CAD's left flank was completely exposed.

The 1st Canadian Light Anti-Aircraft Battalion left Tomba di Pesaro for Point 250, a spur of high ground that overlooked San Giovanni and the Conca Valley. About a mile south of the village, this was their preliminary objective. 'B' Squadron of the Governor General's Horse Guards was to provide close support, but tanks and infantry both missed the marrying-up position and so proceeded independently.

Sergeant Fred Cederberg, the former Cape Breton Highlander commanding a section of the no-name regiment's Bren Carrier platoon, was painfully aware that it was the first time most of his men had been under shellfire and fighting as infantry. He wondered how they would cope and who would crack. At his shoulder, the veteran anti-aircraft gunner Sergeant Eddie Kerr pointed out quietly how one fellow, Corporal Howie MacLeod, seemed to wince visibly after each thunderous roll of artillery fire. Cederberg cautioned Kerr that it was impossible to tell from physical behaviour who would break and who wouldn't. "It's uncanny," he said. "One guy you think is a shit-hot soldier, he just can't tolerate it. But most can, somehow. If you're asking me about the platoon, hell, they'll do fine." The more he looked at these fifty men from the prairies, the valleys, the cities—from all over Canada—the better he felt. "They'll do just great. And they know it in their own way," he told Kerr.[35]

Point 250 was home to several typical stone farm buildings; the carriers parked behind their south-facing walls at 1845 hours. The infantrymen, who had arrived well ahead of the tankers, started digging slit trenches on the north side of the buildings so they could defend the hill against any counterattacks. But not everyone set to this work as enthusiastically as Cederberg would have liked and more than one complained that it was unnecessary. So far, they had seen little indication of the enemy.

Cederberg thought of the map he had consulted on the journey to Point 250 and how the hill was designated clearly as the junction of two dirt tracks. "The Jerries probably have the same friggin' maps," he warned the men. Then the first shells started ranging in. Everyone dived for cover, Cederberg ending up under one of the carriers. "The ground heaved as the 88s exploded one behind the other in sheets of pale yellow flame, spraying the platoon area with shards of white-hot metal."[36]

Amazingly, the platoon's only casualty was a steel pot in which one of the men had been boiling some chickens they had killed for dinner. The pot was riddled with holes. Cederberg's men suddenly became enthusiastic diggers.

Not everyone in the regiment was as fortunate as the carrier platoon. Shellfire that dogged 'A' Company throughout the advance to Point 250 killed nine men and wounded twelve others. 'B' Company's Lieutenant E.J. Pritchard and Sergeant Tommy Graham, who had previously won a Distinguished Conduct Medal, were killed and four men wounded. Total casualties for the day were twelve dead and twenty-one wounded.[37]

The battalion put several patrols into San Giovanni in the early evening and, unaware that the Royal Canadian Dragoons had already swept through, reported it empty of Germans.[38]

On 5 CAD's extreme left flank, the Westminster (Motorized) Regiment also spent September 2 pressing deep into the enemy rear. The Westminsters encountered little resistance beyond intermittent shelling of their advancing companies, until they were approaching the ridge overlooking the Conca River at 1600 hours with 'C' Squadron of the Governor General's Horse Guards and a squadron of M10 Tank Destroyers in support. 'B' Company, under Major George Johnson, and Major Ian Douglas's 'C' Company went in behind a heavy curtain of covering artillery fire and after a short firefight succeeded in driving a small force of Germans off the high-ground objective by 1710 hours.[39]

Unaware that one of Major General Chris Vokes's flying columns had already succeeded in capturing the crossing over the Conca, Hoffmeister ordered Westminster commander Lieutenant Colonel Gordon Corbould to assemble a raiding party and break through to the coastal highway via the road running from San Giovanni through Monte Albano. Captain Vern Ardagh's 'A' Company, supported by 'C' Squadron of the GGHG and an M10 Tank Destroyer troop, was given the task. At the last minute, the GGHGS substituted 'B' Squadron because 'C' Squadron had lost too many tanks during the advance to breakdowns and artillery fire.

The raiding party left at 2000 hours in a long, snaking line with 'A' Company in the lead aboard its armoured personnel carriers. As it passed through San Giovanni, gaps opened between platoons. Lieutenant J.E. Oldfield and the first seven carriers were well out in front when they roared into Monte Albano and found themselves staring down the rifle barrels of a company of Seaforth Highlanders. Oldfield radioed back to Ardagh, who became convinced that the presence of the Seaforths meant the lieutenant had gone badly astray and the column was south of their assigned road. Oldfield insisted he was on course and that he had no idea what the Seaforths were doing there.[40]

Pressing on to the Conca River, Ardagh was even more surprised to find the RCD already on the other side of the crossing. Minutes later, he was confronted by 1 CID provost marshals who angrily ordered the Westminster officer to get all his vehicles off the road because they were hampering the forward movement of that division's traffic. This order was quickly endorsed by 1 CID headquarters, who made it clear to both 12th Canadian Infantry Brigade commander Brigadier J. Lind and Hoffmeister that this kind of "swanning" into their sector was unappreciated. It would be late afternoon of September 3 before the raiding party's various elements were able to regain the roads and rejoin their parent units.[41]

SEPTEMBER 2 WAS the culmination of three disastrous days for the German Tenth Army's LXXVI Panzer Corps. Tenth Army Commander Generaloberst Heinrich von Vietinghoff was trying to get the badly disorganized 1st Parachute Division safely over the Conca River in a desperate bid to establish a defensive position along the so-called second Green Line, which ran from the west at Gemmano through San Clemente to Riccione. On September 1, a German report concluded that after losing points 204, 253, and Tomba di Pesaro, "the situation of 1 Para Div was precarious in the extreme, as there was imminent danger of its being cut off in the coastal sector Cattolica–Pesaro."[42] Only von Vietinghoff's authorizing 1st Parachute Division commander General Richard Heidrich to abandon Cattolica and the surrounding ground and withdraw to the Conca River during the early morning hours of September 2 prevented this disaster. The parachutists had to scramble back rather than conduct an orderly fighting withdrawal to the river. While 1st and 3rd regiments were able to escape in relatively fair condition and take most of their artillery with them, the 4th Parachute Regiment lost seventy per cent of its strength either killed or captured. They also had to abandon most of their anti-tank and heavy anti-aircraft guns.[43]

If the British V Corps had been able to match the rate of I Canadian Corps's September 2 advance, the paratroops might have been thoroughly mauled or even surrounded. A German after-action report concluded that the 26th Panzer Division and elements of 1 Parachute Division on the German right flank facing the 46th British Infantry Division enabled "the units of 1 Para Div committed in the middle and left divisional sector . . . to escape the threatened encirclement."[44]

Many individual paratroopers did not escape. Among these was Obergefreiter Carl Bayerlein. The nineteen-year-old fallschirmpionier's Cattolica idyll had ended abruptly in the late afternoon of August 31 when his 1st Combat Engineer Battalion was trucked towards the Monte Luro–Tomba di Pesaro feature. Unloading in a sunken road, the battalion came under heavy and accurate mortar fire that wounded several men. Then they went into a confused attack where some of their own artillery rounds fell short and killed a number of soldiers. Morning of September 1 found the battalion in hilly terrain "interspersed with vines, luxuriant fields of grain, and vineyards. Everywhere strewn about were farmers' sheds. Alongside a dusty road, stooks of grain had been collected on a harvested field, and since these offered us cover, we collapsed in them."[45]

Several skirmishes followed and there was always much confusion before the fighting began, for the paratroopers were wearing their yellowish tropical kit that closely matched Commonwealth khaki. To avoid firing on their own men, the Germans waited until they could clearly see the helmet outlines. In the late afternoon, the battalion received a fresh issue of ammunition and Bayerlein gratefully slung a Faustpatrone across his back. Having antitank weapons, he figured, ensured that "the greater part of the battalion was saved from annihilation!"

The munitions came none too soon, for in short order the paratroops heard "the noise of engines and the clatter of tracks. Enemy tanks were coming!" The tanks approached in single file and far behind some infantry followed. Unteroffizier Maffika "fired his MG42 at the hatches, shooting from the hip," Bayerlein later wrote. "When I saw that my comrade, Richter, right alongside me, was running away, I became enraged. I stood up and aimed at a tank rolling towards me. There was an officer standing in the turret with a revolver in each hand. He fired at me without hitting me. Now I triggered the [Faustpatrone] and, in a jet of fire, the round streaked for the tank and hit it in the turret. At the same moment, I felt a powerful blow in my right arm, so that the barrel of the [Faustpatrone] was knocked away. I had been hit. The sleeve of my uniform was ripped open and blood was spurting out. I pressed on the artery with my left hand and ran back."[46]

After having the wound rudimentarily bandaged by the unit medic, Bayerlein set out to find a field dressing station. All around him paratroops were scattering under the fire of the tanks. A shell went off and a shrapnel splinter pierced Bayerlein's lung. Weak from loss of blood, he stumbled into a farmhouse where several other German wounded lay on some straw. Bayerlein lost consciousness, only to be awakened later by intense heat. The straw around him was on fire, the house ablaze. He crawled outside, but many of the others were too weak to escape and perished inside the burning building. Hearing foreign voices, Bayerlein surmised that these soldiers had set the straw on fire. Later he was driven before a Canadian soldier, who struck him with a rifle butt whenever he slowed, through a tangled vineyard to a crossroads and then locked into a house. A captured German medic gave him a morphine injection to ease the pain. Finally, the German prisoners were put on stretchers and set out on the ground preparatory to being loaded on trucks. But the position was hit by German Nebelwerfers (six-barrelled mortars). The Germans were abandoned by their guards and several were killed or suffered additional wounds. As Bayerlein was slowly evacuated to the rear he kept meeting other men from his unit, also taken prisoner in the aftermath of their skirmish with the tanks.[47]

Bayerlein's engineering battalion was largely wiped out or captured. His commander, Leutnant Heinz Schuhmacher, was missing and presumed dead. One veteran wrote later that on September 1 "many of the old, staunch soldiers, who had been fighting and bleeding in all theatres of war ever since 1940, were finally lost to the battalion."[48]

The confusion in the German ranks was such that it was not

known until much later that Bayerlein had been taken prisoner. In a letter to Bayerlein's father, written on December 12, 1944, the company's new commander confirmed that on September 1, "despite fierce resistance, a number of our company, including your son Carl, were taken by the enemy. Since owing to the considerable disintegration of the company it was not possible to determine accurately who was taken wounded to a field hospital, or captured or missing, your son was reported wounded on the basis of individual reports by members of the company.

"We therefore did not notify you because we were still waiting for a report from the field hospital. Since nothing has been reported to you in the meantime either, it must be assumed that your son, too, has been taken prisoner. A number of comrades have already reported from captivity."[49] Bayerlein would not be released and returned to Germany until September 1945.

Those paratroops who escaped to the second Green Line were directed by Generaloberst von Vietinghoff on the evening of September 2 that the line was to be defended at all costs, "above all in order to gain time for the reinforcements to arrive."[50] Commander-in-Chief Southwest Generalfeldmarschall Albert Kesselring was scrambling to find reinforcements and rush them to the Adriatic coast. Generalmajor Fritz Polack's crack 29th Panzer Grenadier Division was pulled from the central mountains. But because of the distances it must travel, this division could not reach the area in any strength until September 4.[51] The partly trained 98th Infantry Division, which was possessed of an as yet undetermined "fighting value," and the 162nd Turcoman Division, comprised of unreliable, forcibly impressed conscripts, were also ordered to the Adriatic.[52]

These three divisions constituted Kesselring's last reserves. By throwing them into the fray, he hoped to stem disaster. But if the battered paratroopers holding the line on September 3 proved incapable of checking I Canadian Corps's advance, the reinforcements would arrive too late to prevent an Allied breakthrough to Rimini and the Po Valley. The forthcoming day's fighting was to be decisive.

PART FOUR

THE DOG FIGHT

[20]

All This Unpleasantness

BETWEEN THE Conca River and Marecchia River, whose northern bank rested on the edge of the Po Valley, lay twelve miles of low foothills and coastal plain. I Canadian Corps's Lieutenant General Tommy Burns planned to cover this ground in four bounds. The first would carry the Canadians to a finger-shaped ridge running northeastward from the mountains through San Clemente and Misano to Riccione. In front of the ridge stood the prepared fortifications of the second Green Line. The second bound would be to the Marano River—midway between the Conca and Marecchia rivers. Then would follow the securing of the last ridge south of the Marecchia, San Fortunato Ridge, two miles southwest of Rimini. From here, the final bound would carry the corps north of the river to the Rimini-Bologna Railway.

Burns retained the same divisional alignments, with 1st Canadian Infantry Division closely following the coastal highway and 5th Canadian Armoured Division pushing through the more rugged inland terrain. With II Polish Corps having been pinched out of the offensive at Pesaro, Major General Chris Vokes's right flank rested on the Adriatic Sea. Major General Bert Hoffmeister's 5 CAD still had V Corps's 46th British Infantry Division coming up on its left flank.

The fierce fighting to reach and then break through the Gothic Line had serioiusly reduced the combat effectiveness of 1 CID's 2nd and 3rd infantry brigades, so Vokes ordered the relatively well-rested and recently reinforced 1st Canadian Infantry Brigade to pass through 2 CIB on the night of September 2–3. The armoured division handicap of having only two infantry brigades meant that Hoffmeister lacked any fresh reserves. The best he could muster was the beat-up regiments of the 5th Canadian Armoured Brigade supported by the Westminster Regiment's motorized infantry. Close behind, 12th Canadian Infantry Brigade's 1st Canadian Light Anti-Aircraft Battalion would mop up bypassed German pockets.[1]

The coastline from Cattolica to Rimini featured long stretches of sandy beaches and dunes behind which a continuous line of seaside resorts and villas paraded. Fearful of an amphibious operation, the Germans had previously fortified the beachfront with concrete pillboxes either festively disguised as beachside gelateria or concealed inside existing buildings. Running behind the resorts was the coastal highway, with an average setback from the beach of five hundred to a thousand yards. West of the road lay farmland, mostly dense, closely planted vineyards. The highway crossed numerous canalized streams. Between Riccione and Rimini, the major streams were, respectively, the Melo, Marano, and Ausa. By blowing the bridges, the Germans had transformed each stream into a deep, steeply banked tank obstacle. Nearby buildings and drainage ditches provided excellent defensive cover. Tanks attempting to flank the canalized portions of the stream would have to travel cross-country through the dense vineyards—ideal concealment for infantry armed with Faustpatrones or antitank guns. In the event of rain, the deeply plowed fields would become quagmires that the narrow-tracked Shermans, unlike the wider-tracked German Tigers and Panthers, were ill equipped to wade through.

For its part, Hoffmeister's division faced a chaotic series of ridges and hills soon to be known simply as Coriano Ridge, after the small village atop the primary feature. Immediately north of the Conca River was a ridge running from the Apennines to the sea. Three spurs extended north from here like narrowly spaced fingers reaching towards Rimini. The most westerly and highest spur was Coriano Ridge, home to the villages of San Savino, Passano, and Coriano. Just past Coriano, this ridge descended slowly towards the Fornaci and Marano rivers—the former draining into the Melo River just south of Ghetto del Molino. The seven-thousand-yard ridge formed a hulking height of land that bordered 5 CAD's left flank. Scattered all along the ridge's eastern edge were farmhouses and small hamlets, ideal for use as either fighting positions or observation posts. The ridge's western reverse slope was laced with roads and tracks, enabling the German forces to move easily while remaining invisible to the Canadians.

About two thousand yards closer to the sea, the second spur reached out two miles from San Clemente before ending abruptly in a steep bluff at Ca Rastelli. The last spur, known to Canadians as the Besanigo Ridge, curved from Monte Gallera to a church at San Andrea and then descended into the Melo River valley.[2]

AT 2100 HOURS on September 2, the Lord Strathcona's Horse moved with a troop of M10 Tank Destroyers from the 89th Anti-Tank Battery of the 4th Anti-Tank Regiment towards San Giovanni to link up with the Westminster Regiment. Their orders were to execute a joint night attack over three miles of rough terrain to reach the high ground north of Misano. At first light, the 8th Princess Louise New Brunswick Hussars, with another Westminster company, would then pass through this position and establish a bridgehead across the Marano River. The total advance for the day would be five miles.[3]

Strathcona commander Lieutenant Colonel Jim McAvity set the tanks and tank destroyers lumbering towards the Conca River and then hurried to confer with his Westminster counterpart, Gordon Corbould. Bursting into the Westminsters' tactical headquarters at 0310 hours, McAvity was astonished to find that Corbould knew nothing of the planned attack or even that Hoffmeister had placed the Westminsters' temporarily under 5th Canadian Armoured Brigade command. With one company sidelined at the Conca River crossing and the others exhausted from the previous day's fighting, Courbould could only promise to get 'B' and 'C' companies moving as soon as possible.[4]

Then McAvity's second-in-command, Major Lee Symmes, radioed to report that heavy traffic, poor roads, and being sent in the wrong direction by a confused provost marshal had so delayed the armoured column that it would not reach San Giovanni until 0400 hours.[5] As soon as the armour was in position, McAvity convened a candlelit O Group in a farmhouse. The weather was deteriorating, with heavy thunderclouds obscuring the moonlight that was to have illuminated the attack, and jagged lightning was jamming radio transmissions so that McAvity was unable to communicate with 5 CAB headquarters.[6] Just before the O Group concluded at 0540 hours, Brigadier Ian Cumberland strode into the house and agreed to push the attack back to first light. He also put the entire Westminster Regiment under McAvity's command.[7]

At 0600 hours, the Strathconas' Shermans clanked off with the reconnaissance troop leading in its Honeys, followed in order by 'C' Squadron, 'A' Squadron, McAvity's regimental headquarters, the battery of M10s, and finally 'B' Squadron. Overhead, the thunderstorm was intensifying, seriously disrupting radio communication. As McAvity's tank left the assembly area, his signaller reported that the link to brigade was lost but the radio appeared to be working fine. Moving to the spare command tank proved equally futile, with the signaller reporting the signal strength at a "bloody awful" level of two. Then the tank banged across a ditch and the brigade radio's master switch short-circuited. McAvity changed to yet another tank, which had a functioning gun and therefore space for only one radio instead of two. Adjutant Captain R.J. Sutherland stationed himself in the other headquarters tank with an operational radio and tuned his set to brigade while McAvity netted in to the regiment. The lieutenant colonel would direct the advance and Sutherland would maintain communications with brigade—a far from desirable way of maintaining command and control.[8]

Having fallen out of column to sort out the communication problems, the headquarters section had to race cross-country to catch up. When the four tanks suddenly popped up on a rise a thousand yards off to the flank of 'C' Squadron, a spooked gunner opened fire on them. As McAvity's tank scuttled for cover in a farmyard, it plunged through a cellar's dirt-covered roof and became hopelessly stuck. While McAvity glared down helplessly at the mired Sherman, he heard the hard thump of main guns and rattle of machine guns. The Strathconas' were in a fight, but his disabled tank's radio was malfunctioning so he was completely out of touch. With only one of the three operable tanks in the section mounting a gun, he was reluctant to roar off along a line of travel that would dangerously silhouette the Shermans to possible German antitank guns. The lieutenant colonel decided to leave the tanks where they were and find a safe route on foot to his embattled squadrons. Trooper G.W. Mills, armed with a Thompson, accompanied the officer.

The two men were following a track running along a hedge when they spotted a German on the other side. A burst from the Thompson and two bullets from McAvity's pistol struck the paratrooper before he could react. McAvity dived into a ditch on one side of the track and Mills into a ditch on the other side just before a fusillade of Schmeisser and Spandau fire tore through the hedge. A following potato-masher grenade exploded next to Mills and killed him. McAvity's ditch was directly below the raised hedge, so the remaining paratroopers were unable to fire down at him without exposing themselves. But he was also pinned down and could be easily killed if the paratroopers thought to roll grenades onto him.

Seeing his commander's predicament from his vantage beside the farmhouse, Sutherland directed the one Sherman with a 75-millimetre gun to fire rounds over McAvity's head into the hedge. The covering fire enabled McAvity to crawl safely on his stomach back to the farm. But the tank fire alerted the paratroopers to the whereabouts of the headquarters section and they popped a white flare over the building, which directed German artillery and mortar fire onto the position. Seeing a nearby haystack hidden from the view of the paratroopers, McAvity set it alight with several matches. The smoke and flame that soon boiled up from behind the farmhouse tricked the Germans into thinking the tanks had been knocked out and the shelling ceased.

Stripping the machine guns from the tanks and armed also with rifles and submachine guns, the headquarters section established a defensive position inside the house and around it. From an upper-storey window, McAvity could see the paratroopers dug in near the track where Mills's body lay in the ditch. It was a complete standoff. McAvity was effectively out of the Strathconas' battle.

The fight McAvity was hearing started when an antitank gun outside Misano confronted Corporal George McLean's lead Honey. Swinging the turretless tank off the road and behind some cover, McLean jumped down with a PIAT and stalked the gun on foot. He crept up and fired a charge, but the resulting smoke and dust made it impossible to tell if the gun had been destroyed. Seeing 'C' Squadron's Shermans approaching, the corporal ran back and pointed the antitank gun out to the lead tank commander, who pounded the position with his main gun. Running through fire from several light machine guns and rifles, McLean returned to his Honey only to see several enemy transport trucks about two thousand yards away and fleeing downhill towards the German rear. Zigzagging back through the German small-arms fire, McLean pointed out the new targets to the tanker and at least two were destroyed by his troop's fire. McLean was awarded the Military Medal.[9]

The Strathconas shoved on, with 'C' Squadron bypassing Misano to gain the high ground beyond by 0930 hours. 'A' Squadron came up a bit to the west, while 'B' Squadron settled in to the rear of 'C' Squadron. From these positions, they could support the Westminsters, who were attacking the village itself. But the high ground the squadrons occupied proved to be under observation by Germans on Coriano Ridge and the tankers were soon being heavily mortared and shelled. To avoid providing a static target, they kept "waltzing" their Shermans a dozen or more yards back and forth.[10]

With McAvity and his headquarters section missing, Major Lee Symmes had assumed command and roamed in a Honey between the Strathconas and the advancing Westminsters. Symmes hated travelling in the open, light-skinned Honey and yearned for the chance to get back inside "a nice big fat Sherman," so he could "be safe from all this unpleasantness." Like most tankers, Symmes failed to comprehend why "most infantrymen abhorred the idea of riding around in one of our 'fire-traps.'"[11]

The Westminsters meanwhile alternately cursed and praised the Strathconas. Cursing was loudest when Captain Vern Ardagh's scout car approached the tankers' position opposite Misano only to have one of the Shermans swing its turret and draw a bead on him. Only by shouting at the top of his lungs and waving his arms frantically did Ardagh manage to stop them from doing "a very horrible thing." But the shellfire from the Shermans also enabled the Westminsters to win Misano at about 1500 hours without suffering a single casualty.[12]

As the Westminsters established a sheltered defensive area near Misano in which their armoured cars and Bren carriers could park for the night, two German Panthers roared into their midst. While a Westminster transport sergeant thought the two tanks were "friendlies" and tried waving them into appropriate parking slots, the equally surprised Germans gunned the two tanks and barrelled through the Canadian position without firing a shot. A blown bridge north of the village forced the German tankers to creep along the edge of the stream in search of a fording, which gave the Westminsters' antitank platoon sufficient time to deploy its six-pounder guns and knock the tracks off the Panthers. The German crews then meekly surrendered.[13]

Determining whether an area was under German or Canadian control was increasingly difficult. At 1600 hours, still thinking Misano was German-held, an 8th Princess Louise New Brunswick Hussars' squadron shelled the Westminster's 'B' Company. Fortunately, no casualties occurred during the time it took Lieutenant Colonel Gordon Corbould to frantically radio Brigadier Cumberland and get the Hussars warned off.[14]

Just before dusk, a German quartermaster truck drove into 'C' Company's position out front of the village and was captured. The truck carried mess tins of hot food that was happily distributed. General consensus afterward held that the food was not "a damn bit better than ours," and the watery beer tasted like "low grade spring water." Still, it was a change, something always appreciated by troops on campaign.[15]

The German shelling and mortaring of Misano was constant and proving uncannily accurate. At 1700 hours, Lieutenant Ralph Fountain's support platoon set up its Vickers machine guns on high ground east of the village and fired on several draws being used by the paratroopers to form up for planned counterattacks against the Strathconas and Westminsters. Before the guns let off more than a single burst, German artillery rounds rained down, killing Fountain and wounding five others.[16]

The paratroopers counterattacked twice, but fire from the Shermans and artillery concentrations called in by Westminster Major Ian Douglas broke the attacks almost before they started. Just before nightfall, the Princess Louise Dragoon Guards relieved the Westminsters, who pulled back to regroup for the forthcoming morning advance. Darkness also enabled McAvity to hoof it across country to where some Canadians from 1st Canadian Infantry Division's Hastings and Prince Edward Regiment were digging in about a mile from the farm. Major Alan Ross detached a platoon from 'D' Company to bolster McAvity's defensive position protecting the disabled tank.[17]

WHILE THE STRATHCONAS and Westminsters had gained a lodgement in the heart of the German's second Green Line, the Governor General's Horse Guards had punched right through. Based on an intelligence report that the Germans were withdrawing behind the Marano River, Lieutenant Colonel A.K. Jordan had ordered 'A' Squadron to find a crossing over this river with all haste. The squadron crossed the Conca River at 1220 hours and charged towards a hilltop objective three and a half miles west of San Giovanni. A thousand yards out from the Conca, No. 1 Troop scattered a force of German infantry at a large farm.

A few minutes later, Sergeant Humphries, aboard a Honey, spotted an 88-millimetre antitank gun covering a crossroads just ahead of the approaching squadron. He radioed its location to No. 1 Troop commander Lieutenant Gordon Base, who shelled the gun position with high-explosive rounds, causing the gun to burst into flames and explode. No sooner was this gun destroyed than three German Mark IVs flushed from cover and fled with Base's tankers futilely trying to score hits on the speeding tanks before they disappeared. When No. 1 Troop reached the crossroads, they found the four-man crew of the antitank gun still alive and eager to surrender.

The troop carried on, shooting up every house and haystack it approached. Noticing some "very wide tank tracks" in a spot of mud next to a roadside hedge, Humphries slowed his Honey in the protection of a farmhouse. As the sergeant's vehicle crept around the corner of the building, he saw two Mark VI Tigers twenty-five yards ahead. The behemoth tanks, which mounted a powerful 88-millimetre gun, weighed forty-five tons, and had armour one hundred millimetres thick, were virtually immune to anything a Sherman could throw at them. Fortunately, the Tigers were withdrawing with their guns pointed away from the Canadians, giving Base time to bring his three Shermans up to join Humphries.

Not really caring if he scored a hit or not, Base fired the 75-millimetre high-explosive round in his gun so his gunner could reload with armour-piercing shot. The rattled gunner accidentally stomped on the floor pedal that fired the co-axial machine gun and ripped off a long burst. Base, figuring the main gun was jammed and fearing the Tigers would at any moment rotate their deadly guns, yelled at his driver to reverse into the cover afforded by the farmhouse. He then brought the other two Shermans in the troop up alongside his tank and the three crept out in line to engage in a bloody close-range shootout. But the Tigers had used the moment of confusion to scamper.

By 1500 hours, 'A' Squadron had scattered the few German infantry defending the hilltop objective. Lieutenant Colonel Jordan instructed the squadron to set up a defensive perimeter on the hilltop and wait there until 'C' Squadron and his regimental headquarters arrived. Predictably, as 'A' Squadron began digging in, it was subjected to intense and prolonged mortaring. Three men were wounded.

At 1900 hours, Jordan radioed 'A' Squadron and ordered it to renew the advance towards the Marano, as 'C' Squadron and a troop of M10 Tank Destroyers from the 82nd Anti-Tank Battery would soon reach the hilltop position. Lieutenant Base's No. 1 Troop led 'A' Squadron along a road running northwest of Monte Gallera, with Sergeant Humphries out front in his Honey. Progress was good until one of the Honey's tracks suddenly blew off and the machine slewed to one side of the road. Base thought the Honey must have struck a mine, but a second later an armour-piercing round slammed into the left side of his Sherman, tore the driver's cupola off, and pitched it up over the turret. When a second round ripped through the drive train and stopped just forward of the ammunition bin, the Sherman veered out of control and crashed into a haystack.

The crews of both the stricken Sherman and Honey bailed out and crawled to cover while No. 1 Troop's remaining Shermans engaged the now clearly visible 75-millimetre antitank gun and its covering two machine-gun positions. The lead tank under Corporal Ruff fired on the gun with a mixture of high-explosive and armour-piercing rounds, while also raking the German position with the co-axial machine gun. When one AP round punched a hole through the antitank gun's protective shield, return fire ceased and several Germans fled. The tankers took three prisoners, one of whom was mortally wounded. The body of another German lay next to the wrecked gun.

As it was now growing dark, the squadron commander considered any further advance too risky. At 1945 hours, he moved 'A' Squadron into a draw on the west slope of Monte Gallera. About six hundred yards southwest of the tankers' position was a platoon of the 46th British Infantry Division's 2nd Hampshire Regiment that had come up just before dusk. Soon the Germans discovered 'A' Squadron's position and started mortaring and shelling it. 'C' Squadron was meanwhile getting the same rough treatment back on the original hilltop objective. This contributed to an already confusing situation, as the Hampshires appeared to not have expected to find Canadians on the hill. When some of GGHG's assault troops started digging in on the forward slope, a Hampshire platoon cut off earlier from its company crept up on the digging soldiers and opened fire. A bullet struck Trooper Eaton in the head and killed him. The startled assault troop returned fire with Bren guns until Lieutenant Sockett recognized the typical silhouette of a Commonwealth soldier's helmet atop one of the "enemy" and brokered a ceasefire.[18]

Lieutenant Colonel Jordan and his tactical headquarters failed to catch up to his two squadrons, for the officer misread his map and strayed badly off course until finally becoming intermixed with the advancing companies of the 1st Canadian Light Anti-Aircraft Battalion. This unit was mopping up behind the Westminster and Strathcona

Regiments. The infantrymen were jumpy and at the slightest sound of shell or shot dived into the ditches alongside the road, a practice Jordan and his tankers found "a little disconcertingly earnest."[19]

For the "No-Name Battalion," the day had started terrifyingly when just twenty yards north of the Conca River the lead company confronted a Tiger tank, which "squealing and roaring, surged out of the stand of trees, its 88 belching fire.... The Tiger slewed left and clanked ponderously along the roadway, its 88 swung forty-five degrees and pumping armour-piercing and high-explosive shells as it moved. The vehicle commander was half out of the hatch, directing fire."[20]

Fortunately, several 8th Princess Louise New Brunswick Hussars' Shermans parked in covered positions nearby took on the Tiger. When two scored hits that bounced harmlessly off the tank's thick armour, the Tiger retaliated by blowing a wall out of the small farmhouse behind which one Sherman was hiding. The vaporized wall not only exposed the Canadian tank to the Tiger but also Sergeant Fred Cederberg and his carrier section who had been sheltering behind the building. "He gonna shoot at us?" one of the men squeaked.

"Would an elephant kill a fly when he's fighting lions?" another man replied.

The tank seemed more intent on fleeing, lumbering ponderously along the road towards a small bridge with shattered decking that couldn't possibly support its weight. Realizing this at the last moment, the tank halted and then started slowly backing up, "belching shells," as it went. "Gears clashed. The engine revved harder, a last shot was fired and the tank veered to its left and, sticking its lightly armoured rear high in the air, began snorting and chewing a path off the road down a dirt track that forded the creek.

"It was the moment the Sherman gunners had been waiting for. In rapid succession, three shells ripped into the Tiger. It coughed like a stricken rhino, and smoke and flame wreathed the turret, followed by a series of muffled explosions."[21] A couple of Canadian tanks approached the smoking wreck and two tankers dismounted to check it out. One of Cederberg's men asked if they saw any survivors and a tanker yelled back: "The Jerry tank commander. But I hope he dies. He cooked up one of our crews!" Looking back over the Conca, Cederberg saw that "the burning Sherman seemed to glow in the sunlight."[22]

The Tiger's appearance from a group of trees supposedly swept earlier by platoons of 1 CLAA's 'B' Company left everyone disconcerted. But units and individual vehicles were wandering lost all over the battlefront. So it was possible that the Tiger had blundered into the wood after 'B' Company had passed through. Still, the infantry warily watched their flanks and took cover at the slightest provocation.

Shortly before dusk, the leading company ran into a bypassed German position amid a cluster of farm buildings. The paratroopers poured out such heavy machine-gun and rifle fire that the company was unable to muster an attack. Seeing the difficulty the infantry faced, Lieutenant Hood, whose tank led the GGHG's headquarters section, offered to help. Hood hammered each house for an hour with high-explosive shells until the buildings were collapsed and burning. "The whole area was ringed with burning buildings and darkness had fallen" when the infantry declared the area secure at 2120 hours. Jordan had his HQ hunker down with the infantry for the night.[23]

[21]

A Sure-thing Gallop

On September 3, 1st Canadian Infantry Division's first priority was to push northward from the Conca River crossing it had won on the coastal highway. The Royal Canadian Regiment crossed the river at 0430 hours intent on simply brushing aside any opposition it might meet as it marched up the road to Rimini.[1] The infantry was followed by a composite 48th Royal Tank Regiment squadron consisting of three troops of Shermans and one of Churchills. Waiting to pass through whenever necessary were two companies of Hastings and Prince Edward Regiment infantrymen, supporting tanks, and two troops of tank destroyers. Brigadier D. Dawnay, the 21st Tank Brigade commander, remained in overall command of the attacking force. His orders were to "pursue the enemy, who were reported to be pulling back to Rimini, delaying only long enough to blow the bridges en route."[2]

Major Rick Forgrave's RCR 'C' Company advanced with Major Sandy Mitchell's 'B' Company right behind. Ranging well ahead of 'C' company was Lieutenant Jimmy Quayle's scout platoon. The rising sun dusted the beaches east of the road in a golden light.[3] As Quayle approached a built-up area of resorts south of Riccione, he "saw khaki figures in the road just ahead. They were strolling very casually and acted completely heedless of our presence. We halted and, when the lead rifle company came up, we pointed out the Germans.

To my amazement, our men went marching on up the road. They paid for this a few minutes later when there came a great spray from MG42S. Some of the men were hit and the rest belatedly took cover and began to return fire."[4] The scouts and 'C' Company were pinned down in front of the heavily defended German position. Men crawled to take cover behind buildings, rocks, low walls, and inside the bordering vineyards as a gunfight ensued.

Quayle's scouts crawled into a deep German-made recess cut into an embankment alongside the road, capable of simultaneously sheltering several vehicles from air attack. The scouts had already passed several such hides. Although well protected from the German machine-gun fire, whenever Quayle stuck his head out, "a great rip of machine gun fire . . . tore up the edges of our temporary home."[5]

As the entire regiment had been marching in column behind 'C' Company, Lieutenant Colonel Jim Ritchie managed to organize a hasty attack. But, worrying that the seaside resorts might house German pillboxes or tanks, he had Captain D.R. Martyn first deploy his antitank platoon's six-inch guns to cover the buildings. He then ordered Captain J. Birnie Smith to swing 'A' Company west of the road towards a point of high ground and roll up the Germans' right flank. Smith moved with No. 9 Platoon, commanded by Lieutenant H.L. Watson, and Lieutenant L.M. Miles's No. 7 Platoon out front and No. 8 Platoon, under Lieutenant P.B. Dickson, following.

Following a fold in the ground that was well concealed by the foliage of adjacent vineyards, 'A' Company attained the high ground undetected. As Miles's platoon closed on a large building, it was fired on by several German machine guns positioned inside. Watson's No. 9 Platoon moved to assist Miles, but the lieutenant and several of his men were wounded in the attempt. Wanting to prevent the Germans reinforcing the strongpoint, Miles led his platoon in an immediate direct assault. Although the Germans were quickly cleared out, a few of his men were killed or wounded in the short action.

Gathering the two platoons' wounded and a number of wounded prisoners inside the house, Miles assumed overall command and prepared to meet a counterattack. The fighting, the RCR war diarist noted afterward, "became extremely bitter as well as confused."[6] Two captured German stretcher-bearers, however, pitched in to help the Canadian stretcher-bearers tend the wounded. One of these Germans pleaded with Miles to let him fetch urgently needed medical supplies from his aid station. Miles finally relented, despite the probability the man was merely planning to escape. Surprisingly, however, the German returned, calling out to Miles from behind the cover of some nearby brush. Bemused, the lieutenant dashed to the position only to be confronted by a paratrooper armed with a Schmeisser. Helpless, Miles was hustled off as a prisoner.[7]

By the time Captain Smith reached the house with his No. 8 Platoon, the entire company had only fifty-four men capable of fighting. Ritchie ordered the survivors to "dig in and consolidate."[8] Captain George Hungerford's 'D' Company was sent with six Churchills in support to renew the advance by passing to the left of 'A' Company. Hungerford sent his platoons forward by bounds to a position six hundred yards beyond 'A' Company. During this advance, however, Lieutenant W. Powers suffered a severe wound and Lieutenant F.X. Boucher and Company Sergeant Major J.L. Goodridge were also wounded. Having lost most of its leadership and with four of the tanks also out of action, 'D' Company's attack stalled. Hungerford radioed Ritchie that further advance would render the company's position "untenable" and was told to "consolidate on the spot."[9] Only 'B' Company remained unengaged. It was 0900 hours and Rimini suddenly seemed far away.

Realizing the RCR was effectively blocked, Dawnay dispatched 'C' Squadron of the Royal Canadian Dragoons to follow a parallel secondary road left of the coastal highway in an attempt to outflank the German blocking force. The squadron's Staghounds and Dingoes initially enjoyed smooth running through a series of cuttings overlooked by small hills to the west. As the road curved back to intersect the highway a mile short of Riccione, however, the leading reconnaissance troop "ran into murderous machine-gun fire."[10]

It was an armoured car soldier's nightmare. Armoured cars, noted the regimental historian, "are bound to roads, and a resolute enemy who knows how to hold his fire can let them pass his position and then envelop a whole patrol. No skill can avoid this trap, for well-hidden positions two hundred yards to a flank are completely invisible. There is absolutely nothing to do but run down the roads and hope for the best."[11]

A Faustpatrone disabled the lead car commanded by Lieutenant Wilfred Percy Lawler and both he and the driver were killed attempting to bail out of the wrecked Dingo. Lieutenant Edward Samuel Stokes was meanwhile trying to reach the knocked-out vehicle, unaware that rescuing the two men was no longer possible, when a Spandau dug in beside the road tore into the passing Dingo. Stokes and his driver died instantly. The advance ceased as Captain P.J.H. LaVigne ordered 'C' Squadron to break off.[12]

IN A SMALL COTTAGE just north of the Conca, Brigadier Dawnay and 1st Canadian Infantry Brigade's Brigadier Alan Calder considered their options. At 1600 hours, they sent 'B' and 'D' companies of the Hastings and Prince Edward Regiment and their supporting tanks by a secondary track towards Santa Maria di Scacciano, which stood about two miles inland on a ridge spur extending eastward from Coriano Ridge. The infantry was to advance on foot while the tanks followed "as able."[13] As an after-action report recognized, it also failed to appreciate that the Hasty P's must move over ground that was "relatively flat, with numerous houses, and the enemy [holding] a commanding height... which afforded him good observation to all approaches."[14]

'D' Company led off at 1800 hours, supported by the tanks, and followed by 'B' Company. Only a half-mile out, a blown bridge blocked the tanks and their commander reported that "there was insufficient light for him to continue on in support of the infantry."[15] The Hasty P's went on alone and managed to reach the outskirts of the village unopposed, but were then forced to ground by fierce machine-gun fire emanating from positions inside the buildings.

Several Staghounds from the Royal Canadian Dragoons 'C' Squadron were still nearby and attempted to provide covering fire for the embattled infantry. No sooner had they rushed forward and opened up with their guns, however, than a Faustpatrone blasted the

Staghound commanded by Lieutenant Andrew J. Peterson. He was killed and one of his crewmen wounded. Captain LaVigne ordered the squadron to withdraw. Trundling back towards the coastal highway, the squadron passed in front of the sights of the 48th Royal Tank Regiment Churchills that had been stalled by the blown bridge. One tank fired an armour-piercing round into a Staghound's thin hull, mortally wounding two of its crew and injuring two others. RCD casualties in a day's action that the regimental war diarist termed "short, costly, and confused" totalled seven dead and three wounded.[16]

After dark, the Hasty P's slipped a reconnaissance patrol into Santa Maria that discovered three machine-gun positions "and observed considerable enemy movement in and about the village." Lieutenant Colonel Don Cameron accordingly ordered his men to "take up defensive positions overlooking the outskirts and consolidate."[17]

While the Hasty P's had fought their way towards Santa Maria, the Royal Canadian Regiment's 'B' Company had leapfrogged 'C' Company to carry out a frontal attack against the German blocking force. The hastily conceived plan ignored the fact that the blocking force showed no signs of weakening. Major Sandy Mitchell's 'B' Company had passed 'C' Company on the left at 1900 hours, with No. 11 Platoon moving down a narrow, dark track while No. 10 Platoon worked its way through a cluster of buildings west of the coastal highway. No. 12 Platoon and Mitchell's company HQ section followed a central axis directly between the two leading platoons. The men crept forward as quietly as possible, hoping to achieve surprise. As No. 10 Platoon approached a road crossing their line of advance, however, Private Millar triggered a mine that mangled his leg. The jig was up. German positions opened up with "a hail of machine-gun fire thickened up with rifle grenades, and [Faustpatrones]."[18] Scattering into cover, the platoon started shooting back.

To the left, No. 11 Platoon had followed a shallow ditch that led to two stout buildings, quickly transformed into a strongpoint. From there, they were able to support the rest of the company with sufficiently heavy covering fire that Mitchell had the chance to settle everyone into relatively secure positions. The company commander realized his company was virtually in the midst of the Germans' forward defences and destined to spend a night "trading bullets" with the paratroopers.[19]

The Hasty P's were likewise entangled in front of Santa Maria di Scacciano. Hoping to develop a better appreciation of the German strength, Cameron ordered Lieutenant Charlie Case's scout platoon to enter the village at 2200 hours. The scouts edged into the western outskirts, took a long, slow look, and returned to the Canadian perimeter at 0330 hours on September 4 without being detected. Case reported finding a covered approach by which the regiment might enter the village and that it seemed "only lightly held, probably by a screen of troops protecting a mortar and self-propelled gun located near the road junction."[20] Bolstered by this news, Cameron decided to attack at first light.

"OPPOSITION IS STIFFENING now and we wonder if the enemy is making a last stand before we reach the valley of the Po which now seems to be within our grasp," wrote 1st Canadian Infantry Division's war diarist at the close of September 3.[21] Major General Chris Vokes and I Canadian Corps's Lieutenant General Tommy Burns concurred that the Germans were merely conducting a delaying action to enable an orderly withdrawal into the fortified Rimini–San Fortunato line. Burns said he "didn't expect to have to mount a strong prepared attack until that position was reached."[22]

Staff officers at German Tenth Army, meanwhile, read events differently. "On 3 Sep[tember], when the enemy attacks were continued with increased severity," stated one after-action report, "the battle of Rimini reached its climax, and with it the critical stage for the defence." The divisions "which had up to now been fighting in the middle and left sector of [LXXVI] Panzer Corps were overstrained by the continuous service and the overwhelming superiority in matériel of the enemy, as well as greatly weakened by the heavy casualties suffered, especially by the infantry."[23] Only arrival of reinforcements in the form of regiments of the 98th Infantry Division and the 26th Panzer Division in British V Corps's sector had prevented disaster there. The commitment of the 29th Panzer Grenadier Division against 5th Canadian Armoured Division's flank near Misano was credited with preventing a collapse of the entire line in front of the Canadians."[24]

The close-run nature of this crisis and the confused and often contradictory news from the battlefront alarmed Commander-in-Chief Southwest Generalfeldmarschall Albert Kesselring. When General der Panzertruppen Traugott Herr raised the prospect of a full withdrawal to save his LXXVI Panzer Corps from destruction, Kesselring flew into an uncharacteristic rage and threatened to remove any corps or divisional commanders entertaining the idea of retreat.[25] Only after midnight was Tenth Army commander Generaloberst Heinrich von Vietinghoff able to calm Kesselring down and speak plainly to him about the high casualties Herr's corps had suffered. Herr's performance in the face of the determined and skillfully conducted Allied attacks, he said, had been exemplary. "Though not strong in numbers," von Vietinghoff said, "the Canadians are very good soldiers. I am told the 5th Canadian Armoured Division was excellent."[26] Somewhat mollified, Kesselring let Herr keep his job, but he urged von Vietinghoff to defend the Adriatic front vigorously, surrendering ground only when necessary. Kesselring knew that the long-range weather forecasts favoured the Germans, with the thunderstorm on the night of September 2–3 presaging rain.

Eighth Army's commanders, meanwhile, were giving little thought to the potential and possibly fatal delays a turn in the weather might deal their breakout to the Po. Eighth Army commander General Oliver Leese and V Corps's Lieutenant General Charles Keightley still expected the real breakout, believed imminent, would come not in front of the Canadians but on Keightley's right flank. The two officers had accordingly visited 1st British Armoured Division to emphasize this unit's key role in pursuing the German divisions. This, Leese warned, "might well be the last great battle of the Eighth Army." Keightley stressed that: "Speed was the factor on which success would depend and nothing must be allowed to stand in its way." As the generals departed in their staff car, Keightley called out to

Major General Richard Hull and Brigadier R.W. Goodbody that he would see them next "on the Po."[27] The two armoured division officers fully agreed. Goodbody thought the operation would be a "sure-thing gallop."[28]

That this great galloping charge was to be delivered by a division that had not seen battle since April 1943 and only then in Africa, where conditions differed greatly from Italy, failed to faze Leese and Keightley. The division's officers were largely untrained in the tactics evolved during more than a year of fighting in the close Italian country. Indeed, 1st Armoured Division had barely completed reorganizing to add more infantry clout at some loss to its armoured mobility, in order to conform to the new operational structure adopted by Eighth Army's armoured divisions. The armoured regiments were also still familiarizing themselves with the up-gunned 75-millimetre Shermans that had replaced their older tank models. And, having only assumed divisional command in mid-August, Hull hardly knew the officers serving under him.[29] He also barely considered the division combat-ready. He later said: "If a Staff College student had suggested that as a solution for reforming an armoured division, he'd have got nought out of ten."[30]

Even had the designated armoured division clearly been up to the task, the reported gap on V Corps's right flank adjacent to I Canadian Corps did not exist. Yet Major General J. Hawkesworth, commander of the 46th British Infantry Division fighting there, failed to admit this. Instead, he told Hull on September 3 that he would "hold the gate open for him."[31]

There was another problem neither Keightley nor Leese recognized. When Keightley inserted the 56th British Infantry Division into the front line to plug the gap developing between 4th Indian Division and the 46th Division, a misunderstanding had occurred between himself and Major General John Whitfield. The 56th Division commander believed he had been warned to keep out of the western hills on his left flank and bypass those dotting the relatively level plain on his right where his advance was being funnelled. He understood that the emphasis was speed and that these potential defensive strongpoints could be mopped up later. On September 3, Whitfield's division had accordingly bypassed to the east of a key position—Gemmano Ridge, which was a mile long and averaged a height of 1,500 feet.[32] On the ridge's eastern terminus stood the village of Gemmano protected by steep slopes, blanketed in thorny scrub that butted right into the village's thick twenty-foot-high wall. Gemmano was an ancient fortress, quickly transformed into a modern defensive bastion by the German 100th Mountain Regiment. Before Whitfield could recover from his error, the Germans concentrated three thousand men on the ridge, so that they dominated the upper reaches of the Conca Valley to the east and closed the very roads over which 1st Armoured Division was supposed to burst through Hawkesworth's imaginary gap.[33]

Whitfield failed to recognize the threat posed by Gemmano Ridge, for his eyes were fixed on reaching the Marano River and then pressing on from there. His operational order for September 3 stated his intention as being "to pursue the enemy to Bologna and destroy him." Whitfield was convinced that both V Corps and I Canadian Corps were engaged in a neck-and-neck race that he would win.[34]

FIRST LIGHT ON September 4 found RCR's 'B' Company "still trading bullets" with a bunch of determined paratroopers showing no signs of taking flight.[35] Out on the regiment's left flank, 'D' Company was similarly embattled. Despite its previous day's losses, Lieutenant Colonel Ritchie decided 'A' Company must break the stalemate by attacking the stronghold being used by the Germans pinning down 'D' Company. But it would be mid-morning before this attack was organized.

The Hasty P's, meanwhile, hoped to renew the division's advance sooner by infiltrating the scout platoon and 'B' Company into Santa Maria di Scacciano just before dawn. At 0430 hours, this small force crept into a clutch of small buildings on the village's south edge and hunkered down until dawn.

Ninety minutes later, company commander Captain Lazier judged it sufficiently light to begin the attack and ordered his men forward just as two Germans appeared on the road about one hundred yards ahead, ambling along and chatting back and forth unconcernedly. Someone shouted at the two men to surrender. The startled Germans dropped their weapons and dashed for cover, while the shout served to alert the paratroopers holding several nearby houses. Machine guns and rifles blazed out of windows and doorways and 'B' Company found itself ensnarled in a house-to-house melee. Although two houses were quickly captured, no further advance proved possible.[36]

When Lazier reported that he was stalemated, Lieutenant Colonel Don Cameron decided to move his tactical headquarters forward to enable him to make a personal assessment.[37] Cameron and the commander of a supporting squadron of 48th Royal Tank Regiment were soon lying in a position overlooking the village, but sniper fire aimed their way was so intense they could hardly take a look at things before being forced to duck for cover.[38] Realizing further frontal attacks were unlikely to succeed, Cameron ordered 'A' Company with a troop of tanks to move across country and seize a height of ground right of the village from which it could hit the defending Germans with flanking fire.

Captain Bill Graydon's 'A' Company marched forward at 0914 hours, but was stopped in its tracks about halfway to the objective by machine-gun fire from a heavily defended position in a nearby farmhouse. When several mortars started bracketing the company with rounds, Graydon rushed his men into the shelter of a farm building. Realizing the supporting tanks were unable to see the German position, Graydon ran over to where they were idling. Just as he grabbed the phone hooked to the back of the Churchill, which enabled infantry to communicate with the tankers inside, six machine gun slugs tore into his leg and knocked him flat. Unable to either stand to reach the phone or to yell loud enough to draw the attention of the tankers inside their armoured shell, Graydon could only painfully crawl back to the building housing his men and have 'A' Company try to neutralize the German strongpoint with small-arms fire.[39] Like the RCR on their right flank, the Hasty P's were now stalled.

Listening to the reports coming into his headquarters in Monte Albano, Brigadier Allan Calder knew the RCR and Hasty P's needed help. He also thought the attack currently planned by the RCR's 'A' Company must fail, so Calder cancelled it and froze the regiment in place.[40] Deciding it was time to commit his reserve regiment, he had summoned the 48th Highlanders of Canada's Lieutenant Colonel Don Mackenzie for an 0700 hours briefing.[41] The Highlanders had been waiting with 'B' Squadron, 48 RTR and three troops of M10 Tank Destroyers to dash through the gap the two leading regiments were to open all the way to the Marano River.[42] That plan, Calder said, was off and the reserve force must break through the enemy line left of the Hasty P's in a mid-afternoon attack.

At 1000 hours, Vokes, Brigadier Dawnay, and 1 CID's artillery brigadier, Bill Ziegler, bustled into Calder's headquarters. Vokes pronounced that the brigade was flagging and "stressed the importance of speed on our part," Calder later wrote.[43] Calder explained the difficulties presented by the terrain and reminded Vokes sharply that the German strength was "greatly in excess of that reported by intelligence, and on which [the] plan was based."[44]

Vokes acknowledged that Calder was right. He also knew the situation was only going to get worse, for his intelligence staff had just reported the 303rd Panzer Grenadier Regiment being rushed into the line facing the division to stiffen the defences. Further, because Coriano Ridge threatened 1 CID's left flank, Vokes believed the entire Canadian advance "may be stopped here for a few days."[45] Still, he urged Calder to pick up the pace. Vokes left Ziegler to help Calder organize supporting artillery for his forthcoming attack.[46]

Back at the rather sumptuous seaside villa headquarters at Cattolica in which Vokes had recently settled, the major general ordered 3rd Canadian Infantry Brigade commander Brigadier Paul Bernatchez, at 1400 hours, to move to a position overlooking the Conca River. He warned Bernatchez to be ready to take over the advance from 1 CIB on a moment's notice. When Bernatchez tried to reconnoitre the new battleground, he found the Conca River valley completely obscured by "the smoke ... of battle." Thinking an aerial view might reveal some sense of the terrain, Bernatchez and Captain D.F. Rankine arranged to go up in the corps's reconnaissance plane. The small plane was just starting its climb away from the runway, however, when it stalled and crashed. With his jaw fractured, Bernatchez was hospitalized.[47] Lieutenant Colonel Pat Bogert, former commander of the West Nova Scotia Regiment and currently Vokes's general staff officer, took over the brigade.

IN THE EARLY afternoon, Lieutenant Jimmy Quayle and his scouts joined the RCR's 'B' Company in the southern outskirts of Riccione and hotly engaged the German snipers there, killing ten in short order. As the sniper battle raged, Quayle realized false windows had been painted on some of the houses in an apparent attempt to lure the Canadians into betraying their positions by firing at these bogus openings, which would appear to provide a firing port for German snipers. On learning that 'B' Company's No. 11 Platoon was isolated far to the right in a couple of buildings opposite the road, three of Quayle's men dashed across the open ground between the company's main position and the platoon in an attempt to reinforce the vulnerable unit. Just as the scouts saw several men from the platoon trying to wave them off, a Spandau covering the open field opened fire. The lead soldier, Private D.E. Cake, fell to the first burst, and when privates R.R. Greenough and A.W. Burt tried to carry the wounded man to cover another burst cut them down.[48] Although volunteers from No. 11 Platoon eventually managed to drag Cake into their position, he died from his wounds.

With 'B' Company's situation increasingly perilous and its casualties mounting alarmingly, Ritchie ordered Major Sandy Mitchell to disengage, falling back on the regiment's tactical headquarters. The company would have to wait until nightfall, Mitchell reported, for No. 11 Platoon could not possibly escape its trap while it was light.[49] Ritchie concurred.

Ritchie knew he had no alternative but to pull 'B' Company out of the village, but having no intention of abandoning the overall attack, he ordered 'D' Company to seize the high ground it had failed to reach the previous day. 'A' Company, which had originally been tasked to carry out this assignment, was now obviously too shot up to succeed and so was assigned instead to covering 'D' Company's attack.

The slope up the hill lacked any cover, so Captain George Hungerford simply ordered his men to fix bayonets and then Company 'D' charged uphill with Lieutenant Danny Burns's No. 18

Platoon leading. A machine-gun round glanced off the lieutenant's helmet and knocked him down, but the dazed officer staggered to his feet and continued leading the charge. The platoon overran one machine-gun post and killed the paratroopers manning it, and was halfway to the objective before withering overlapping fire from several positions stalled their assault. Realizing the company was going to be chopped to pieces, Ritchie recalled Hungerford and his men back to the original start position. The lieutenant colonel decided there was nothing to do but tee up supporting artillery and try again in the morning.[50]

Left of the RCR, the Hastings and Prince Edward Regiment's 'B' Company and the scout platoon continued their lone fight on the edge of Santa Maria di Scacciano while waiting for nightfall and the opportunity to pull out. The slightest move attracted immediate swarms of sniper, machine-gun, mortar, and artillery fire that slowly decimated the ranks and an attempt by Major Alan Ross's 'D' Company to reinforce the embattled company was stopped cold well short of the village by well-entrenched and armed paratroopers. Lazier decided the situation was so desperate that the only hope for survival lay in mounting a probably suicidal spoiling attack in order to bring his platoons back together.

Precisely at noon, he led the survivors in a wild rush through heavy gunfire, with the two platoons linking up midway and then dashing on to seize a line of houses inside the village. A chaotic, confused melee ensued with Canadians and paratroopers fighting hand-to-hand and showering each other with grenades. Both platoon commanders died during the hour-long fight that ended with 'B' Company in possession of several buildings but so depleted that further advance was impossible. Both sides had taken a mauling and a truce was negotiated to enable evacuation of all the wounded. A German medic treated the most badly wounded Canadians, helping ensure they survived the trip back to the Hasty P's Regimental Aid Post.

Later, an officer advancing under the protection of a white flag called to the Canadians: "Surrender you English gentlemen—you are surrounded and will only die."

When sniper Private "Slim" Sanford barked back, "We *ain't* English. We *ain't* Gentlemen—and be Goddamned if we'll surrender," the fierce fight immediately resumed.[51] Lazier was counting on reinforcements, but Lieutenant Colonel Don Cameron had none to send. All the other companies were either committed or still reorganizing. Cameron ordered 'B' Company to abandon its hard-won gains and withdraw four hundred yards from the village, so he could soak the village and surrounding heights with artillery bombardments in preparation for a renewed dawn attack. Lazier led his men out of the village at nightfall. 'B' Company had suffered twenty-three casualties and lost four men missing. They brought twenty-five prisoners with them. Twenty-two men from the other companies had also been killed or wounded and another two were missing. Despite the heavy casualties, only six men had been killed.[52]

ON SEPTEMBER 4, the 48th Highlanders of Canada had been expected to rush through the gap opened by the other two regiments of 1 CIB with such verve and dash that the Canadians would, as set out in Calder's written order, be in "Rimini by noon!" This expectation was being turned to dust.[53] Instead, the Highlanders had marched towards battle on the left-hand side of the pinned-down Hasty P's and formed up behind Lieutenant Colonel Don Cameron's tactical headquarters, located inside a squat, stone hovel next to a crossroads overlooking Santa Maria di Scacciano.

From here, they watched the Hasty P's hard-fought battle develop through the early afternoon. There was a generally friendly rivalry between these two Ontario regiments, with the Highlanders calling the Hasty P's Plough Jockeys because most hailed from the farms and small towns of southern Ontario. The Hasty P's in response declared the Highlanders the Glamour Boys, largely young men from Toronto who were more at ease on sidewalks or in bars than fighting in the Italian hills and vineyards. This day, however, the Highlanders held their city tongues as a steady stream of wounded stumbled back to the nearby Regimental Aid Post.

At 1500 hours, Highlanders' commander Lieutenant Colonel Don Mackenzie called an O Group of 'C' and 'D' Companies in the dubious comfort and safety of Cameron's HQ. Arriving just as a stonk of German shells fell outside, 'D' Company's Captain L.G. Smith ducked frantically through the hut door for cover and saw Cameron grinning at him from across the room. "Shut the door, Smittie," the lieutenant colonel said, as if the thin, rough lumber might provide true protection from the shrapnel bouncing off the walls outside.[54]

A second salvo erupted outside, violently rattling the building and causing dust to pour from the walls and ceilings, just as the men inside heard the fall of footsteps approaching the closed door. Major Jim Counsell, who commanded the regiment's support company, whispered, "Ed Rawlings." As one, the men inside raced to the door only to find 'C' Company's commanding major lying in the dirt with blood pouring from a terrible wound. His runner, Private Willie Roberts, was dead. Although rushed to the Highlanders' RAP, Rawlings died a few minutes later. The major had joined the regiment in the fall of 1943 and was a veteran of its hardest fought battles.[55]

When Captain Pat Bates came up from the rear to assume command of 'C' Company, Mackenzie got down to business. The regiment's job was a tough one, he said, involving outflanking Santa Maria di Scacciano by advancing up a long sloping rise to a ridge. The intervening ground was thickly vegetated with vineyards, olive groves, and orchards; all cut by many narrow ditches and gullies. Dense hedges marked the boundaries of each farm from its neighbours. The entire line of advance was subject to enemy observation from both ridge and village. 'D' Company would lead, with 'B' Squadron of the 48th Royal Tank Regiment in support.

'D' Company jumped off at about 1630 hours, but was stopped cold by heavy machine-gun fire from a maze of positions one thousand yards short of the objective. Self-propelled guns firing from well-covered hides prevented the British tanks from clearing out the machine gunners. Captain Smith radioed Mackenzie, calling for a troop of M10 Tank Destroyers. Fifteen minutes after appearing on the scene, the M10s' heavy guns quelled the German SPGS.

At 1800 hours Mackenzie appeared at Smith's tactical headquarters and urged him to get moving, but the captain argued that the attack could not succeed without the cover of darkness.

Mackenzie relented but told Smith to make sure he got the job done. With the tanks withdrawing for the night, the infantry would attack alone. If the attack succeeded, the armour would return at first light.

'D' Company attacked on the heels of a short artillery concentration just before moonrise and by 0300 hours held a scatter of buildings on the ridge. 'C' Company, with the British tanks in tow, moved up behind Smith's position at dawn.[56] On the western flank, Coriano Ridge hulked darkly over the Highlanders and any further advance would face flanking fire from this daunting feature. Nobody thought anymore about being in Rimini by noon or, for that matter, anytime soon.

[22]

It Was Useless

SEPTEMBER 4 proved a day of blood-soaked frustration for 5th Canadian Armoured Division. Major General Bert Hoffmeister was determined to break through to the Marano River, but before the river stood Coriano Ridge and its namesake village. Coriano was a cluster of stone buildings grouped around a central square in which stood the inevitable steepled church. Leading the division's drive towards the village would be the 8th Princess Louise New Brunswick Hussars and the Westminster Regiment.

The tanks moved at 0600 hours with the reconnaissance troop and 'B' Squadron out front, followed by 'A' Squadron, then the regimental headquarters section, and finally 'C' Squadron. The Westminsters were right behind the tanks in their armoured cars and Bren carriers. Hoffmeister planned to strike the Germans with a blitzkrieg, whereby an entirely motorized force would punch through any roadblocks and bypass stubborn strongpoints, leaving them to be cleaned up by the 1st Canadian Light Anti-Aircraft Battalion following on foot.

But this was Italy rather than Poland or the open country of northern France, and although the upper valley of the headwaters of Besanigo River was unusually wide and open, it was also overlooked by Coriano Ridge from both ahead and the left flank. Still, things progressed well for the first thirty minutes. Captain Bob McLeod, who had taken over command of No. 1 Troop when Lieutenant Wally

Manley was wounded in the jaw, followed close behind the reconnaissance Honeys. The captain was just beginning to think it might be a drive in the country when an antitank gun opened up. McLeod frantically ducked his Sherman into a ditch, while ahead Corporal H.S. Fleming's tank exploded into flames. Trooper Duke Doucette was "blown to bits." Fleming was blinded, but managed to bail out. Another trooper named McCallum was wounded and tumbled from the tank with his clothes burning. Trooper Charlie Harvey, the tank's other survivor, managed to smother the fire and then guided Fleming and McCallum to the rear.[1]

About one hundred yards back of McLeod's position, 'B' Squadron's Major Howard Keirstead swung his tank down a slope with Sergeant Keith Fisher's tank right behind him in an attempt to evade the antitank guns that seemed to be firing from all around. The two Shermans sideswiped each other, bounced apart, and then careened down the slope. Several shells ricocheted off their sides as the two tanks skidded into the dry Besanigo streambed. Once in the stream, major and sergeant realized they had made a terrible mistake. Their tanks were sandwiched just ten feet apart, unable to turn sideways in the narrow streambed, and facing an insurmountably steep slope directly ahead. The slope behind was also far too steep to reverse up. They were stuck. Keirstead swivelled his turret to the left to cover that route of approach with his guns and Fisher did the same to cover the right approach.

The streambed and its banks were clogged with long grass, bamboo stands, and tangles of trees that offered perfect infantry cover. In fact, the streambed vegetation was so dense the tankers in one Sherman could barely see the other. No sooner had Keirstead and Fisher assessed the situation than several paratroopers crept up and fired on the tanks with Faustpatrones that failed to penetrate the armour. The Shermans ripped back with machine guns and several of the infantrymen fell dead.

Fisher's crew was pleading with the sergeant to let them abandon the tank before a Faustpatrone killed them all, but he replied they were safer in the tank than outside. It was only a matter of time before the regiment pushed the attack beyond the streambed and effected a rescue. Fisher still had radio contact with the squadron and was able to monitor the ebb and flow of the battle raging above the trapped tanks.

Although still mobile, the rest of the squadron was also in a bad way. Lieutenant McLeod and Sergeant Tom Robertson of No. 1 Troop were pinned well ahead and hoping to make a break for it back to the rest of the squadron. Heavy antitank fire from Coriano Ridge meanwhile was preventing the squadron from moving towards either pinned-down element. Knowing that before he could regroup the regiment 'B' Squadron had to be withdrawn, Lieutenant Colonel George Robinson ordered the recently promoted Major Lloyd Hill to bring up 'A' Squadron and extricate the embattled squadron.[2]

'A' Squadron clanked into the field of fire in which 'B' Squadron had been caught and within seconds Lieutenant J.H. Lackie's tank was knocked out.[3] Sergeant Billy Bell's Sherman crashed nose-first into a deep pit over which the Germans had placed a thin board covered with earth. It was the second tank Bell had lost in three days. He and his crew dodged from one ditch to another getting back to the assembly point where the regiment's second-in-command, Major G.R.H. Ross, gathered them in. The major knew the five tankers were exhausted from their latest mishap and three previous days spent with virtually no sleep. But there was a desperate shortage of crews and a perfectly operable Sherman back at rear echelon. You can have a rest, Ross told Bell, or you can take over that tank and go back into action. Bell looked at his men, who met each other's eyes in turn, and then everyone grinned and the five men went to collect the Sherman.[4]

RECOGNIZING THAT his tanks alone could never take Coriano Ridge, Robinson asked for the Westminsters' help at 1000 hours.[5] Lieutenant Colonel Gordon Corbould immediately sent Major Ian Douglas up to appraise the front. Thirty minutes later, he returned and suggested sending a single 'C' Company rifle platoon aboard three of the scout platoon's Bren carriers "hell bent for election" to seize a house in front of McLeod's No. 1 Troop, in order to take the pressure off the trapped tankers.[6] Then, when it got dark, the rest of 'C' Company could pass by and clear Coriano village. Lieutenant Tommy Forman's platoon boarded three carriers commanded by scout platoon Sergeant Ron Hurley.

The Bren carriers rolled at top speed past a German sign reading: "No vehicles of any type past this point" and headed along the narrow, flat top of a twelve-foot-high embankment belonging to an old railroad bed that was completely exposed to Coriano Ridge for its entire 1,200-yard length.[7] Fifty yards out, a German shell overturned the lead carrier. Everyone was thrown clear but suffered varying injuries. Private "Knobby" Clark's Lee Enfield had been fixed to a pintle-mount in front of his controls and when the carrier overturned the rifle's barrel was bent back like a cartoon image towards the stock. More shaken than injured, Clark stormed back to the start line with the ridiculous-looking rifle and shook it in Douglas's face. "What kind of asshole sent us to do this?" he screamed.[8] Clark was quickly evacuated. Hearing later of the man's behaviour, twenty-year-old Hurley thought it "pathetic" and typical of someone battle exhausted. Both the regiment's youngest sergeant and one of its youngest soldiers, Hurley believed war was about taking risks and never showing fear.[9]

He tried to maintain that resolve as his carrier took the lead. Perched on the seat beside him was the rifle platoon commander, Lieutenant Forman. All around the little vehicle exploding shells were tearing great chunks out of the embankment. Hurley's driver, Private Jim Goddard, swerved wildly from side to side to dodge smoking craters and present a difficult target. In the carrier's open cargo compartment, Forman's men clung grimly to any available handhold to keep from being thrown overboard. Suddenly Goddard made a skidding turn to avoid an exploding round and the carrier plunged off the embankment. It crashed with a great shriek of metal into the bottom of a ravine, landing upended. Hurley hit the surprisingly soft ground flat on his stomach and then the carrier's .50-calibre machine gun smashed down on the small of his back. The blow almost paralyzed him and blood poured out of a cut on his head. Sprawled all around the sergeant were men suffering broken shoulders, legs, or internal injuries. Amazingly, everyone was alive.

The few men who could walk helped the more badly injured to reach the shelter of a nearby stone hut, where an ancient Italian couple dressed in peasant black was huddled. Shortly after the least injured of the soldiers left for help, Hurley heard "all this singing and these Germans marched down the road, singing at the top of their lungs, as if on parade." Outside, a dog started barking. "Jesus Christ," Hurley hissed, "somebody shut him up or they'll come to check." A Native Canadian soldier ducked outside, located the animal behind the hut, cut its tether, and watched it run off. The Germans marched past without so much as a glance towards the hut.[10]

About an hour later, Hurley realized his paralysis was gone and that he could walk slowly, if painfully. Using a ditch for cover, Hurley and the Native soldier conducted a short reconnaissance and found near the hut a half-starved horse. The horse stood head down, with blood leaking from several shrapnel wounds to pool at its feet. Tears filling his eyes, the soldier told Hurley, "I'm going to shoot it."

"No, you're not," Hurley said. "It's tough, but there's nothing we can do."[11]

Soon after going back inside the hut, the soldier slipped out alone and Hurley knew he went to quietly put the horse out of its misery. He returned shortly with a German helmet under his arm brimming with fresh eggs. Following meekly behind was the helmet's owner, a blond, terrified German barely in his teens. "Christ, he's younger than we are," Hurley muttered. The Native soldier had found him hidden in a haystack.

The old woman's eyes lit up at the sight of the eggs and she was soon whipping up omelettes on the stove and pulling wine and bread from a locker for accompaniment. Taking a seat on a bench facing a rough wooden table, Hurley gestured for the German to join him. The woman shook her head and said, *"No Tedeschi,"* as the German started sitting down. Then more loudly: *"No Tedeschi. No Tedeschi."* Hurley pointed the muzzle of his Thompson at her and replied evenly, *"Si, Tedeschi. Si."* When the woman set an omelette before the German, she spit on it. Once the meal was finished, the Canadians could only await either the arrival of stretcher-bearers or Germans. With his limited ability to move and the severity of the injuries from which the others suffered, Hurley knew none of them could escape the ravine unaided. But they had their guns and ammunition and Hurley was determined that if the Germans found them there would be a fight before anyone surrendered. Late that night, a rescue party arrived and everyone was safely evacuated.[12]

Meanwhile, the remaining Westminsters had continued trying to reach Coriano, with 'C' Company managing to reach the banks of the Besanigo River on foot before being stopped by heavy German artillery and mortar fire. Thinking this a promising gain, Corbould sent 'A' and 'B' companies to broaden the foothold. 'B' Company started forming up behind the crest of a small hill and 'A' Company on a tree-sheltered road. Both companies were ready to move, the regimental war diarist wrote, when "shells came like all hell turned loose. For what seemed an eternity, Jerry pounded shell after shell upon the forming-up place. Casualties were light but nearly all fatal."[13]

Shoving off anyway at 1300 hours, the two companies came up alongside 'C' Company an hour later despite being relentlessly battered by artillery and mortar fire. But even with three companies in line, the advance could not be renewed in the face of the German opposition. At 1800 hours, elements of the Irish Regiment of Canada started filtering in to relieve the exhausted Westminsters, who were increasingly showing the effects of having been continuously on the move for nearly six days. In the early hours of September 5, they began withdrawing by platoon sections. As each group of men arrived in the rear area, they "just lay down and collectively went to sleep."[14]

While 5 CAD's main attack force had been trying to reach Coriano by crossing Besanigo River, the Governor General's Horse Guards 'A' Squadron had been trying to cover its left flank by staying up on the crest of the valley's southern ridge. The terrain was typically confused and No. 4 Troop, which was in the vanguard, strayed off course and headed almost due west rather than northeastward, with the result that the squadron's tanks were exposed on a downward slope to the German guns and observers on Coriano Ridge. Several 88-millimetres in front of Coriano village opened fire and pinned the squadron down. With one tank knocked out after another like ducks in a shooting gallery, 'A' Squadron was soon down to only three Shermans and those of its headquarters section. At 1130 hours, Lieutenant Colonel A.K. Jordan reported the dire situation to Major General Bert Hoffmeister and he ordered the squadron withdrawn.

That proved easier said than done. The slightest movement of one of 'A' Squadron's surviving tanks attracted immediate 88-millimetre fire and the squadron commander advised Jordan that the German gunners were so close they seemed to be firing over open sights. Finally, he asked for a fifteen-minute artillery concentration on the suspected antitank gun positions to cover the squadron's retreat. The artillery fire enabled the surviving tanks to regain the ridge crest and the entire regiment, which had been following the leading squadron, slinked back to its starting point at Monte Gallera. Jordan informed his weary officers that "the show was off" and he expected an order to stand down in the morning for a badly needed rest period.[15]

Hoffmeister's original plan had called for the Irish Regiment of Canada and the British Columbia Dragoons to pass through the Hussars and Westminsters once a crossing over the Marano River was won. The next phase of the attack would have carried the two relieving regiments through to San Fortunato Ridge. The initial advance, however, had ground to a halt just one thousand yards beyond the start line and so the Irish and BCDs were, noted the Dragoons' war diarist, left "in furious inaction all day."

All except for Major Dave Kinloch's 'B' Squadron that is, which became embroiled in a dogfight just before dark behind the main line of advance, while trying to support the 1st Canadian Light Anti-Aircraft Battalion's mopping-up operations.[16] When torrents of machine-gun and artillery fire struck the mopping-up force, the still shaky infantrymen hugged the ground and undertook only the most cautionary attempts to advance. 'B' Squadron at the time was being led forward by Lieutenant James P. Looney's troop. Spotting one of the main German positions dug in on the crest of a hill, Looney charged it with his three Shermans. No sooner had the tanks successfully overrun this position than German infantry counterattacked. Armed with his pistol and several grenades, Looney jumped out of his tank, killed two of the attackers and captured three others.

Looney's troop stood its ground, repelling repeated counterattacks until the infantry finally arrived an hour later. The lieutenant won a Military Cross.

A short distance away, Sergeant William Paul Fleck had engaged in a similar fray out front of the infantry. Around him several Shermans had been knocked out, mostly by Faustpatrones. It was so dark, Fleck could barely see the furtively dodging German soldiers operating between his location and that of the enemy positions on the crest of the hill. Knowing light was desperately needed, he set several nearby haystacks on fire with tracer rounds. Although he now had sufficient light to mount an attack, the sergeant realized that doing so with one tank unprotected by covering infantry would invite disaster. So Fleck decided to launch his own infantry-cum-tank operation by preceding the tank up the slope on foot accompanied by one crewman. Fleck raced up the hill alternately firing his submachine gun and chucking grenades at the German position. He single-handedly killed five Germans manning slit trenches blocking the approach to the hillcrest and once on the summit accepted the surrender of eight more dazed Germans. Moments later, the sergeant collapsed from loss of blood. He later confessed to being unaware that he had been wounded. Fleck survived to be awarded a Distinguished Conduct Medal.[17]

WELL BEYOND 5 CAD's official forward positions that evening, twenty tankers little expected to see the dawn. Major Howard Keirstead and Sergeant Keith Fisher's tanks remained trapped in the depths of Besanigo's streambed. Off to their right and eight hundred yards deeper in no man's land, Captain Bob McLeod and Sergeant Tom Robertson's Shermans huddled in a ditch by the side of a road still waiting vainly for the rest of the 8th New Brunswick Hussars to catch up.

Throughout the afternoon, McLeod and Keirstead had discussed plans by radio for withdrawing once night fell, although the major had no idea how he and Fisher would extract their tanks from the creek. Initially, things had been so quiet around McLeod's position that he had been able to conduct a reconnaissance on foot of the surrounding area and even took time out to harvest some grapes to take back to his crew. But in the afternoon the Germans discovered the presence of the two Shermans and subjected them to increasingly accurate artillery and mortar fire. Then a Faustpatrone round hissed overhead and a Spandau started raking the tanks. The tankers buttoned up the hatches for protection, with McLeod's crew resorting later in the afternoon to urinating into an empty 75-millimetre shell and then dumping the contents through the escape hatch in the hull's bottom. At 1730 hours, McLeod's anxiety increased as Keirstead abruptly ceased radio transmissions.

McLeod was loath to abandon the major's group. So at dusk, when Sergeant Robertson's tank left as planned, McLeod stayed, continuing to monitor the radio for a signal from Keirstead. With each passing minute, night drew closer and with it the inevitability of a close-up attack by German infantry, but McLeod still hesitated to leave.

Down in the creek, Sergeant Fisher had decided that the breakdown of Keirstead's radio precluded any chance of their being rescued and that prospects for surviving the night by staying inside their tanks were slim. When it was finally fully dark, he told his crew, they would evacuate the Sherman by the bottom escape hatch, crawl up a ditch that ran up the south slope to the ridgeline, then reach the road and make their way back to the rear. Wanting to abandon neither the major nor his own tank, Fisher stayed behind.

Meanwhile, McLeod had decided there was nothing he could do for Keirstead, so at 2020 hours he set his Sherman clanking slowly towards the rear. All around, haystacks were burning, but the light they cast was virtually smothered by thick smoke and dust boiling down from Coriano Ridge, which was being pounded by Allied artillery. McLeod sat in the open turret hatch with a Thompson and a handful of grenades at hand; ready to fight off any infantry that attacked the Sherman from the flanks or the rear. The roar of the tank's engines and grinding racket raised by its tracks was appallingly loud. He could imagine every German within miles being drawn in for the kill by the noise, but instead flushed only two of Fisher's crew who frantically waved the tank down. After mounting them on the back of the tank, McLeod pressed on and was soon relieved to reach the regiment's assembly point on Besanigo ridge.

McLeod, Sergeant Robertson, and Major Lloyd Hill gathered on the ridgeline and discussed ways of rescuing Keirstead and Fisher. The two tankers McLeod had brought in thought the two tanks had brewed up soon after they took flight, as there had been explosions behind them and some flames visible. Then the remaining two men from Fisher's tank had arrived safely and denied seeing the tanks destroyed. Finally, McLeod and Hill sought Lieutenant Colonel George Robinson's permission to take a foot patrol out to bring the missing tankers in. Admonishing the two officers that tankers were untrained in night-patrolling tactics and likely would get lost and end up getting some good men killed for nothing, Robinson refused. Instead, he reported the probable position of the two tanks to the Irish Regiment with a request that an infantry patrol be dispatched to the area. McLeod and Hill watched hopefully as the Irish patrol slipped slowly and stealthily into the valley.

Knowing nothing of the rescue effort, Keirstead and Fisher were both peering anxiously out of the turret hatches into the darkness when suddenly a Faustpatrone charge shrieked out of the night to explode in a fiery blast against the hull of Fisher's tank. Then another charge struck. Inside, Fisher stared fearfully at the hull, expecting at any moment that one of the rounds would slice through the armoured hull, but neither succeeded.

A third Faustpatrone charge, however, found a thinner chink in the steel sides of Keirstead's Sherman and was suddenly ricocheting about inside. "There was an explosion, a small one, the insane whirling of flying metal within that tight, compact world of a tank's interior, and then smoke and fire and the choked, tensed voice of the major telling them to bail out," the regimental historian wrote.[18]

They tumbled out into a nightmarish torrent of machine-gun and rifle fire. Driver Trooper E.R. Hilchey was shot dead while Trooper Charlie Stevens, the gunner, was paralyzed from the waist down. The impact of seven bullets tearing into Keirstead's left thigh and two into his left arm knocked the major to the ground. When assistant driver Lance Corporal John Wentworth tried shooting it out with the machine-gunner who had wounded Keirstead, a bullet hit him in the lower part of his left leg. As Wentworth rolled into the cover of one of the creek's banks, another bullet caught him above the right knee. Dazed and painstricken, the tanker screamed, "Shut that thing off!" Keirstead crawled painfully over to Wentworth and soon Sergeant C.M. Stevenson—the only unwounded crew member—wriggled in beside them. Stevenson tried to bandage the others' various bullet wounds.[19]

Unaware of the calamity that had befallen Keirstead and his crew, Fisher was still inside his tank and busy cursing himself for having not escaped with his men. A deadly lull outside was probably the prelude to a renewed attack and Fisher doubted the tank could withstand any more hits from Faustpatrones. He later wrote: "I decided to strike out myself. My chances, I figured, were not very good, so I tore off my stripes, hid my pay book in the tank, took off my boots and decided to go. By the time I got on the ground under the tank I could hear the Germans talking a yard or so away. They were right alongside the tank. All I could do was keep still. All I had with me was a .38 pistol and twenty-three rounds of ammunition. Somehow the Tommy gun barrel had been bent. It was useless."[20] Surprisingly, the Germans walked off without further inspecting the tank. Fisher lay still under the Sherman, fearing any move would betray his presence.

About seventy-five yards from the surviving tankers, the Irish patrol lay on the side of the hill peering down at the creek bed and hearing only the voices of what seemed to be a large party of Germans. Obviously outnumbered and sure that any Canadians down there must be either dead or prisoners, the patrol leader ordered his men to withdraw and the six unaccounted men from the two tanks were listed as missing in action.

Keirstead and his surviving three crewmen could hear Germans circling all around them, but surprisingly they failed to close back in on the two tanks. Talking in the softest of whispers, the four men tried to decide on a course of action. With Stevens and Wentworth virtually immobilized and the major little better off, Sergeant Stevenson was the only man fit enough to have a chance of reaching the Canadian lines. Keirstead agreed that the sergeant should make the attempt and passed him a white undershirt to use as a flag because nobody knew the password for the night. A few minutes after Stevenson crawled off, there was a long burst of machine-gun fire from the directon he had taken and then only silence.

Stevens and Wentworth were struggling not to moan from the terrible pain they suffered. Between whispering comforting words, Keirstead encouraged them with promises that the regiment would surely come to their rescue at dawn. The major steadfastly believed this was true. He had no idea that the offensive had collapsed and his shredded little party signified the deepest remaining penetration inside the German line.

Eventually the sun came up and Keirstead's gaze drifted to the turret of his tank and the sight of Stevenson's corpse dangling out of the top hatch. Instead of heading directly for the Canadian lines, as Keirstead had believed the sergeant had done, he apparently had tried to re-enter the Sherman either to get something or try the radio one last time. The Germans must have spotted him and that was the reason for the burst of fire he had heard.

Around Fisher's tank there was no movement or sign of life and Keirstead knew that at any moment the Germans, emboldened by the growing daylight, would soon start poking around the position. He decided there was nothing to do but try to reach the Allied lines by following the creekbed west towards where the British were on the Canadian flank and get help sent back to Stevens and Wentworth. There was no way in his condition that the major could crawl up the south bank to return to the Canadian lines. After lurching painfully along for several hundred yards, the shrill of an incoming mortar round caused him to flatten against the ground for cover. Shrapnel whirred through the air and one fragment struck his right shoulder, another his right leg, while a third gouged a furrow out of the side of his head. Keirstead's right arm was paralyzed. At first, carrying on seemed impossible, but somehow the major found the will to continue. He writhed onward like a snake, his useless arm dragging in the dust.

The creekbed stopped being a single channel, spreading out into a series of narrow ditches separated by narrow hummocks of ground and flood plains covered in long grass, brush, and thorny shrubs. Keirstead became completely disoriented in the resulting maze. He had lost his map when the mortar round struck. The hard thumping concussion of 25-pounder artillery fire echoed up and down the valley, but he was unable to use the sounds to fix a direction towards the Allied lines. Seeing a small farmhouse beside the creek, he dragged himself over to it. There was a bucket on a line next to a shallow well and he dumped it down and dragged it awkwardly up, then drank deeply. Inside the house a family of peasants huddled. Keirstead begged them to treat his wounds, but they just stared at him as if rendered dumb with fear. Then they made shooing gestures, obviously fearful of German retribution if he were discovered in their house.

On a little knoll not too far away there was another house, but it took several hours of agonized crawling for the major to reach it. He found it crowded with peasants, a gaggle of "gaunt, brown, ragged, chattering people."[21] They pressed a glass of grappa into his hand and then followed the fiery liquor with ladles of water dumped into his mouth. Amateurish and ill-equipped attempts were made to tend his wounds.

A grateful Keirstead was just beginning to relax when the hard sound of jackboots rang on stone outside and the front door was thrown open. Three Germans stomped in and looked down at him curiously. The major sighed, knowing he was captured. Then he realized they carried no guns, grenades, or any armaments. Quickly, efficiently, they stripped his tattered uniform off and cleansed his wounds with an alcohol mixture made by diluting wine with water. The three got the Italians cooking up a chicken broth while one took his temperature with a thermometer pulled from a pocket. Finally, they dug out all the bandages in their kits and fashioned others from sheets and bound his many wounds quite professionally. Keirstead realized by now that his German nurses were actually deserters wanting to surrender. The next morning, one of the Italians slipped off to the south and returned after dark with four Irish Regiment soldiers. They took the Germans prisoner and then had them carry the wounded major back to safety. After reporting what he knew of the fate of the rest of his troop, Keirstead was immediately sent to hospital. His war was over.[22]

About the time Keirstead was being treated by the Germans on the night of September 5, Lance Corporal Wentworth was drifting between bouts of delirium-ridden consciousness and troubled sleep punctuated by a recurring dream in which his Hussar comrades came to his rescue. Stevens was even worse off, spending his few moments of consciousness either screaming from pain or pitifully pleading that Wentworth brew a pot of tea. The lance corporal noted somewhat clinically that his leg wounds no longer bled and wondered if this was significant or not.

Venturing from under his tank at dawn, Fisher soon came upon the other two tankers. Wentworth was reading a pocket Bible and, seeing Fisher, started weeping softly. Stevens didn't recognize the sergeant and when Fisher examined the man's back he found four bullet wounds. One was next to the spine, which explained the lower paralysis. Bullets had broken both of Wentworth's legs. Retrieving a first-aid kit from his tank, Fisher treated the bullet holes with sulfa. He then stripped Stevens, treated his wounds, and managed to get his own coveralls on the man. A shot of morphine failed to lessen the soldier's pain.

There was no way Fisher could help these men to safety and he was unwilling to leave them, for they would surely die. Whenever he moved even a short distance away from the tanks, Fisher either spotted German positions or heard enemy soldiers talking. Why the Germans had yet to search the tanks puzzled him, but their lassitude was the only chance the surrounded tankers had. Fisher and Wentworth decided they would stay put and hope to be rescued. Even though it was clear that Stevens and Wentworth must surely die if their wounds went untreated for long, surrender was never considered. Neither Fisher nor Wentworth bothered consulting the delirious Stevens. Fisher's tank held a supply of bully beef, canned milk, jam, and some water, which they rationed. Stevens was unable to eat anything.

Fisher buried Hilchey in a shallow grave, but every time he tried retrieving Stevenson's body from where it dangled out of the turret the Germans immediately drove him off with machine-gun fire. This only left the sergeant more perplexed as to why the Germans, who obviously knew of their presence, were content to leave them alone.

Wentworth found he was unable to sort fantasy from reality, but he never lost hope of being rescued. Both he and Fisher had lost all sense of time and could no longer remember how many days had passed. They stopped trying to have conversations and spent most of their time just staring straight ahead into space.

On the fifth day of their ordeal when Allied planes droned overhead and bombed a nearby enemy position, one of the bombs exploded close by and knocked Fisher unconscious. Upon regaining consciousness, the sergeant found it hard to function and kept nodding off. He gave Wentworth the last of the morphine and then, caring little whether he lived or died, Fisher fell asleep.

Wentworth heard sounds of men approaching sometime that night. Then he heard an unmistakably Canadian voice say, "Christ, those are Shermans."

Wentworth croaked, "What outfit are you from?"

Soldiers skidded down the bank into the creekbed. A lieutenant bent over Wentworth and softly told him they were from the Perth Regiment and it was the night of September 9–10. Wentworth started weeping. Fisher, awakened by the noise, looked up dully to see a man standing over him with a rifle and didn't care whether the man was friend or foe. The tankers were quickly evacuated, but the rescue came too late for Stevens, who died soon after. After many months of hospitalization, Wentworth fully recovered. For deciding to stay initially with his tank and then with his wounded comrades, Sergeant Fisher was awarded the Military Medal.[23]

[23]

A Hard Row To Hoe

BECAUSE THE ALLIES had enjoyed overwhelming air superiority from the outset of the Italian campaign, German air squadrons seldom posed a threat. On the night of September 4–5, however, the Luftwaffe made a surprise attack that included remarkably accurate raids on the headquarters of both 1st Canadian Infantry Brigade and the Royal Canadian Regiment.

The raid against the RCR came right as its company officers and headquarters staff had gathered to await Lieutenant Colonel Jim Ritchie's return from brigade HQ with orders for renewed operations. A German fighter-bomber screamed down and scored a direct hit. "Glass and mortar flew everywhere but no one was hurt," Major Strome Galloway later wrote. As the plane circled back for a strafing run, the officers ran in an ever narrowing clump to the cellar door, with Galloway first to arrive. Halfway down the steps, he turned and shouted, "Don't panic, don't panic." The support company commander, Major Morgan John, wryly remarked that Galloway was the only one partially sheltered, "the others being held at the head of the stairs by [Galloway's] stopping halfway down and turning around to calm them down."[1]

Ritchie was caught in the same strafing run. He and his driver bailed out of their jeep and dived into a ditch moments before the vehicle was riddled by machine-gun slugs.[2] The lieutenant colonel calmly dusted his uniform off and walked on to headquarters, where by this time the panicked officers had recovered and were gathered around the map table for the briefing.

The attack inflicted no casualties. Elsewhere, however, the pilots of a German bomber spotted 'A' Company of the 48th Highlanders of Canada moving towards the front lines on a road bathed in moonlight and dropped a stick of bombs precisely on target. They then swept the road with machine guns before breaking off the attack. Although casualties were surprisingly light, when the smoke cleared and everyone emerged from the roadside ditches, Company Sergeant Major Gordon Keeler was found with legs so mangled that both had to be amputated. The company's morale was badly shaken as much from the loss of the veteran CSM as from the unfamiliar terror inherent to undergoing an aerial attack.[3] Nine men were killed and thirty-two wounded by Luftwaffe planes attacking 5th Canadian Armoured Division positions.[4]

Throughout I Canadian Corps, the air raids further rattled already exhausted front-line troops barely fit for continued combat. Yet 1st Canadian Infantry Division's Major General Chris Vokes still sought a breakthrough to the Marano River and ordered Brigadier Allan Calder to continue the advance. 1st Canadian Infantry Brigade would attack at dawn, while simultaneously the Royal Canadian Dragoons would use the coastal highway to drive through to Riccione.

The operational plan for 1 CIB remained little changed from the previous day, with the Hastings and Prince Edward Regiment again attacking Santa Maria di Scacciano and the tactically important ridgeline on its left. Simultaneously, 'D' Company would hit the village and 'A' Company the ridge. A heavy artillery program would immediately precede the attack. Moving in on the heels of the heavy shelling, the two companies reported with some surprise that they had easily taken both village and ridge. Several prisoners proved to be from the 162nd Turcoman Division rather than 1st Parachute Division, leading intelligence officers to speculate that the 162nd Division had been caught in the midst of a poorly executed relief of the paratroopers.[5]

On the Hasty P's right-hand flank, the RCR found the height of land previously held so doggedly by the paratroopers since September 3 manned only by a motley group of Turcoman troops. Even though still armed, eleven of these eastern European conscripts surrendered to Private J.W. Gardner without offering any resistance and then indicated to Gardner and Corporal R.W. Peters by sign language that they wished to keep their weapons. The two soldiers escorted the still-armed men back to the regiment's tactical headquarters where intelligence staff determined that the conscripts hoped to join the Canadians in fighting their former masters. They were gently coaxed into laying down their guns and then sent back to the prisoner cage.[6]

Racing up to the secured ridgeline, Ritchie and Galloway quickly examined the ground ahead and planned how to make a run for the Marano River. The only major obstacle was the Melo River, which flowed out of the hills and through the north end of Riccione. Immediately in front of the RCR position, the Melo became two parallel-running tributaries, both canalized, that merged at a coastal highway bridge crossing. On the north side of the bridge, the highway cut through the heart of San Lorenzo in Strada, but first it passed through a loose cluster of buildings clumped around a tall-spired church. Ritchie set this church as his next objective.

'B' Company led off under Major Sandy Mitchell, with Captain Rick Forgrave's 'C' Company tucked in close behind. Although Mitchell advanced cautiously, progress was good. By noon, the leading platoons were closing on the first tributary when some well-positioned heavy machine guns blocked the advance. It seemed 1st Parachute Division had reappeared.[7]

To 'B' Company's right, the Royal Canadian Dragoons also met scant resistance at first and slipped into Riccione at noon. The resort town had been a favourite Fascist haunt before the war, even boasting a villa owned by Benito Mussolini. The squadron's Dingoes and Staghounds slowly rumbled up streets littered with broken glass, fragments of furniture, torn clothing, empty wine bottles, shredded bedding, and the occasional civilian corpse. A few townspeople ducked furtively down alleys or into doorways as sporadic German mortar and artillery fire ripped up more cobblestones, stripped tiles off the roofs, and battered the sides of houses.

At the Melo River, the Dragoons found all the bridges blown and Germans dug in on the opposite bank. When a sergeant dismounted from his Staghound to check for a possible crossing, the Germans set the armoured car ablaze by firing a Faustpatrone across the canal. Two of the crewmen were wounded and the sergeant died trying to help his men escape the burning wreck. Unable to force a crossing, the RCD dismounted from its armoured cars and set up defensive positions inside a line of houses bordering the Melo for the length of its passage through Riccione.[8]

An odd war ensued, with each side stationed "in comfortable houses, served by bewildered but docile Italians. For a block or two on each side of the canal patrols slipped warily past street corners for fear of hostile MGS on fixed lines. Forward Observation Officers of various artillery units under command of I Canadian Corps lolled luxuriously on sofas in the upper storeys of the seaside hotels and called down fire on suspected buildings; while in the houses lining the canal snipers lay hopefully waiting for the day's 'kill.' Beyond maintaining strong street patrols to keep down looting, most of the RCD had a rest period, although sniping and mortaring caused occasional casualties."[9] With no idea how this standoff could be ended, the Dragoons seemed content to enjoy this unexpected respite from the dangers of an all-out offensive.

Things proved far more bloody when the RCR attacked the church south of San Lorenzo in Strada. Standing atop a bit of high ground, the church and its surrounding buildings had been transformed into a strong defensive position housing numerous machine guns. 'B' and 'C' companies hit the first resistance at 1935 hours and immediately started taking casualties. When 'B' Company got in among the buildings, its leading No. 10 Platoon came under intense fire from machine guns, rifle grenades, and Faustpatrones. "An additional hazard was that practically every building through which the platoon had to pass was either on fire or had been burned and consisted only of shells which were gradually demolished by enemy [Faustpatrones]," the regiment's war diarist wrote.[10] When the attack faltered, the two companies pulled back to regroup for an attempt to infiltrate the German positions under cover of darkness.

At 0045 hours on September 6, Lieutenant Dave Fisher went forward with two sections of No. 12 Platoon numbering less than twenty men, while the third section and the platoon headquarters section provided a covering base of fire. The tiny force sneaked through to the church undetected and slipped inside. Fisher hoped to establish a strong firebase here that the rest of the company could drive towards. No sooner had he swept out the few German defenders, however, than the paratroopers counterattacked in force. They fired Faustpatrones through the windows and blew doors open with explosives. Setting up an MG42 machine gun in a building facing the main doors, the paratroopers fired deadly streams of fire directly down the church's centre aisle. Rounds ricocheted wildly off the solidly constructed altar. Fisher was just considering aloud whether they should make a break for it when two paratroopers appeared at the top of the balcony stairs next to the altar.

Realizing they could bring the entire platoon under fire, Fisher rushed them. Halfway up the stairs; however, a Faustpatrone charge struck the wall next to the lieutenant and the blast killed him instantly. Corporal R. Duhaime took command and yelled to the rest of the men that they should make a break back to the company lines. Duhaime led the men towards a door through which a German suddenly appeared with a Faustpatrone shouldered in the ready firing position. When the corporal fired his Thompson at the man, the gun jammed. He then rushed the German, grabbed the Faustpatrone with his left hand, and wrenched it out of the paratrooper's grasp. Using his Thompson to bludgeon the man's head, Duhaime knocked the German unconscious. He then led the platoon back to the company's base in a narrow gully. Just twenty-five minutes had passed since Fisher first led his men towards the church. The platoon suffered just two casualties, with Fisher the only fatality.[11]

While the RCR were engaged at the church position, the 48th Highlanders of Canada and a supporting force of tanks had moved on the hamlet of Besanigo, standing on a ridge about a mile to the left. Meeting only scant resistance, the Highlanders closed on Besanigo by mid-morning and were surprised to find well-dug-in elements of 5th Canadian Armoured Division's Irish Regiment of Canada already strung out along the ridge.

Staying right of the Irish to avoid mingling divisional lines, Captain L.G. Smith's 'D' Company descended into the gully that formed the lower reaches of the Besanigo River prior to its juncture with the Melo River. Here the company smacked into a hard wall of German machine-gun positions and ground to a halt. Corporal Murray Percy Thomas was wounded in the abdomen and left shoulder. Although in great pain, Thomas charged across the thirty-five-yard open ground between himself and the Spandau gunner who had shot him. After killing the two-man crew with a long burst from his Thompson, the corporal collapsed. Surviving his wounds, Thomas won a Military Medal.[12]

The exploit failed to shatter the German defensive line, however, and 'D' Company was soon pinned down in the creek bed. Highlander commander Lieutenant Colonel Don Mackenzie was planning how to crack the German position when Lieutenant Colonel Bobby Clark of the Irish Regiment arrived and told him that he had just received a message from I Canadian Corps. The Highlanders, he said, having been ruled as being inside 5 CAD's designated territory, must pull back and then hook hard to the right to pass immediately south of the hamlet. From there, they were to execute a sharp left turn and cross the Melo River at a point that would place them back inside 1st Canadian Infantry Division's narrowing sector. This would leave 5 CAD free to swing around the choke point of Coriano Ridge.[13]

After extracting 'D' Company from the gully, the Highlanders carried out the realignment, managed to cross the Melo River, and even reached a point of high ground less than one thousand yards from the Marano River before nightfall and stiffening German resistance precluded further gains. Unknown to the Highlanders, they had achieved the deepest penetration into the German lines that would be won for another week. On every other front, Eighth Army was being blocked. And it was Coriano Ridge that presented the primary obstacle.

BY EARLY MORNING on September 6, it was apparent that the attempt to the west by 1st British Armoured Division to break through at Coriano Ridge had failed. But the situation reports by

Major General Richard Hull to his counterpart Major Bert Hoffmeister were "conflicting and confusing . . . and it was only possible to obtain from them the fact that the enemy was building up resources, particularly tanks, on the San Savino–Coriano ridge."[14]

In the midst of this uncertainty, Hoffmeister directed the Irish Regiment of Canada to "send patrols across River Marano and to try and build it up to company strength if possible."[15] Preparatory to this effort, Lieutenant Bobby Clark ordered the regiment advanced to a forward spur of Besanigo Ridge upon which stood the village of San Andrea. Upon arriving there, however, the Irish realized that Coriano, "a group of white houses, clustered about church spires atop its hill . . . prohibited any hope of crossing the Marano. For from that town," wrote the regiment's historian, "would come the artillery and perhaps the counterattack which would have spelled disaster to our venture."[16]

Clark established his headquarters in the whitewashed San Andrea church, intending to use its steeple as an observation point. No sooner had his staff set up tables, wired in the phones, and laid out the maps than the building started taking artillery and mortar fire accurately vectored in by German forward observation officers stationed on Coriano Ridge. Expecting the British to soon clear Coriano, Clark decided against repositioning the headquarters somewhere farther to the rear. Instead, he got busy sending patrols to test the resistance in front of the Marano River preparatory to pushing at least one company across that obstacle by day's end. A combination of fire from well-positioned German infantry in front of the river and a virtual rain of artillery and mortar fire, however, quickly drove these patrols back.[17]

At 1030 hours, Clark told Hoffmeister no further progress was possible so long as Coriano remained in German hands. Hoffmeister immediately arranged for the Desert Air Force to move its bomb demarcation line forward from the San Fortunato Ridge area to the north side of Marano River, so that targets there and on Coriano Ridge could be pounded from the air. But thickening cloud had settled over the entire area, which seriously hampered effective targeting and a planned attack by four hundred medium bombers was ultimately cancelled because the bombardiers could not see their targets.[18]

The Irish Regiment and the other two regiments of 11th Canadian Infantry Brigade positioned behind and on either flank endured a long, hard day of heavy shelling. Clark, who had earlier thought San Andrea was just a brief stop on the way to Rimini, issued orders in the afternoon for his staff to dig in as deeply as possible.

With the entire situation beginning to stagnate, I Canadian Corps commander Lieutenant General Tommy Burns arranged to meet Hull and Hoffmeister at 11 CIB's headquarters.[19] The three men agreed that until Coriano was taken, further advance by 5 CAD was impossible. Hull acknowledged that his division had the task of clearing the ridge, but was "being hampered by the high ground held by the enemy on his left and left rear."[20] Hoffmeister suggested that his division might clear Coriano by attacking from the east while Hull kept driving towards the village from the south. Although this plan looked feasible, the generals knew that Eighth Army commander General Oliver Leese must approve such a dramatic change in corps boundaries. Optimistic such approval would be granted, Hoffmeister started organizing the 12th Canadian Infantry Brigade to carry out such an attack against the ridge. At 1815 hours, Leese squelched the plan by instructing Burns that 12 CIB should "stand fast in its present positions."[21]

With each passing day of only painfully and slowly won gains, Leese had grown more hesitant and petulant. There would be no grand dash to the Po Valley. Indeed, his insistence on bringing Eighth Army over to the Adriatic for the decisive assault on the Gothic Line seemed increasingly ill thought. Even the weather was conspiring against him, for September 6 had been a day of cloud and intermittent showers that reduced the roads to mud-slick tracks. If the rain continued, the offensive could stall right where it was and the battle be lost.

To his wife, Leese complained: "This campaign is a hard row to hoe. It is the most difficult country in Europe, and yet we always get troops and equipment taken away from us for elsewhere. We have done all our fighting on a very narrow margin of relative strengths—I suppose it is all the more satisfactory to achieve." Things, Leese said, had "not been easy" with General Harold Alexander, Deputy Supreme

Commander, Mediterranean "since I decided not to go on slogging opposite Florence. I am sure I was right, and we've been partially vindicated since we've broken into the Plains, and I think there is disappointment. They don't realize what we are up against and that it takes time."[22]

But Eighth Army was not "into the Plains," and it would take a set-piece attack against Coriano Ridge to even renew its advance towards the Po. Leese met with Alexander, who, after studying the situation and considering the meteorological reports that called for short-term weather deterioration, agreed that a reorganization of several days was necessary.[23]

ORDERS MADE ON HIGH take time to filter down to the line units, however, and so the afternoon of September 6 saw two Canadian regiments still battering their way forward. At 0400 hours, Lieutenant Colonel Jim Ritchie mustered the seriously depleted companies of the Royal Canadian Regiment to try seizing the church fronting San Lorenzo in Strada. The job went to Captain J. Birnie Smith's 'A' Company, which, having lost 35 per cent of its strength, numbered only 75 men. The even more reduced 'C' and 'D' companies were to follow behind.

It was raining as the men moved out at 0600 hours. Smith was up front slogging through the gooey mud with his leading platoons when the same "murderous machine-gun fire" that had shredded 'B' Company's earlier attack ripped into his company. All down the company line, men fell dead or wounded. "In the face of this," wrote the RCR war diarist, "and showing contempt for danger Captain Smith kept going steadily forward, urging his men to within thirty-five yards of the enemy strongpoint determined to achieve his objective and carry out his commanding officer's intentions. By this time, the company was reduced to half its strength and was coming under withering fire from three sides. Rallying the remnants and personally hurling hand grenades at the enemy, Captain Smith kept leading his men forward.

"When last seen alive he was standing erect only a few yards from the final objective [of the church] throwing the grenades in the face of point-blank fire. Hit in the head by a German stick grenade he fell mortally wounded. So effective was the personal leadership and personal valour of this officer that his shattered company advanced steadily, inflicting many casualties, and he was instrumental in destroying many of the enemy by his own hand. The efforts of 'A' Company so employed the enemy that the remainder of the assaulting troops were saved from complete annihilation and were able to reorganize as fighting components."[24]

No amount of valour could save the attack, though, which crumbled. Thirty survivors of 'A' Company, however, were so far ahead they were unable to extricate themselves.[25] The highest surviving ranker among these was Sergeant C.R. Sweeney. Rushing and scattering a cluster of Germans, Sweeney threw a grenade after them but then, in his haste to catch the fleeing paratroopers, overran the explosive. The grenade exploded, killing him.[26] When night fell, eight of the isolated pocket succeeded in crawling back to the Canadian lines. The rest were believed taken prisoner. Only eighteen men from 'A' Company were present and accounted for when Company Sergeant Major I.A. MacDonald, now in command, formed them up that night.[27]

Left of the RCR, the 48th Highlanders of Canada had attacked the ridge overlooking Marano Ridge, where they had suffered heavy casualties the day before. 'A' and 'B' companies walked into a hail of fire at 1630 hours. The half-strength 'A' Company was too weak to make headway. 'B' Company did a little better, managing to close on the ridgeline before bogging down. Major D.B. Deeks radioed for 'C' Company to come up, but as its men rose to leave their slit trenches a heavy, unrelenting barrage of mortar fire poured down and they could only dive back into their holes for protection.

Lieutenant Colonel Don Mackenzie ordered Deeks to withdraw. Arrangements were made for the 3rd Canadian Infantry Brigade to relieve 1 CIB. In two days of fighting, the 48th Highlanders had lost four men killed and twenty-two wounded.[28] The RCR had been mangled, with two officers and twenty-six men dead, one officer and sixteen others missing, and five officers and ninety-one other ranks wounded.[29]

[24]

Five Minutes To Twelve

ON SEPTEMBER 7, Eighth Army commander General Oliver Leese relented. He summoned the Canadian corps commander Lieutenant General Tommy Burns, V Corps's Lieutenant General Charles Keightley, and Eighth Army Chief-of-Staff Major General George Walsh and informed them that the 4th British Infantry Division and 25th British Tank Brigade, less one regiment, were herewith under Burns's command. This was in addition to the 3rd Greek Mountain Brigade, which Burns had yet to utilize. The bulked-up Canadian corps was to cross the Marano and exploit onward to the Marecchia River and Rimini to realize Eighth Army's breakthrough to the Po Valley. With V Corps mired in a bloody fight to pry the Germans off Gemmano Ridge and out of the hilltop village of Croce, Leese knew he must switch the respective roles of his two corps or fail. So V Corps would now support a Canadian breakout directed up the Adriatic coastline. But before this could take place, Coriano Ridge must be cleared to secure the Canadian Corps's left flank.[1]

Leese developed a three-phase battle plan. In the first phase, V Corps's 46th Infantry Division, later supported by 4th Indian Division, would continue hammering away at Gemmano Ridge and Croce. Once these key objectives were won, 1st British Armoured Division and 5th Canadian Armoured Division would cooperatively clear Coriano Ridge. The 56th British Infantry Division would simultaneously pass through Croce to form alongside the British armoured division's left flank.

In phase two, 4th British Infantry Division would pass through 5 CAD to cross the Marano River with 1st British Armoured Division keeping pace to the left. On the right flank, 1 CID would march up the coastal highway.

During phase three, I Canadian Corps would seize San Fortunato Ridge and advance to the Marecchia River. Once a crossing was won, the army's reserve division, 2nd New Zealand Division, would drive into the heart of the Po Valley and liberate Bologna and Ferrara. If possible, 5 CAD would join the New Zealanders in this triumphal march.[2]

Leese told Burns to work up a plan using these resources and then meet with him again the following day, conceding that his plan would likely see 2nd New Zealand Division placed under Burns's command for the third phase. Burns "was impressed with the additional responsibility with which he proposed to entrust me, recalling that after the Liri Valley offensive one of the reasons for withdrawing the corps from the pursuit was his doubts as to our ability to handle divisions other than the Canadians. I felt that our success during the past twelve days had given him confidence in our competence. I was also glad that with the additional divisions it would be possible to withdraw the Canadian formations for rest and reorganization without halting the offensive."[3]

There would be no attack on Coriano Ridge until V Corps captured Gemmano Ridge. Repeated assaults had so far won only the barest of footholds on the ridge and inevitably each gain was met by fierce counterattacks that often succeeded in repelling the British units. Ground was taken, lost, retaken, and then lost again. Each passing day saw further deterioration in the weather as heavy rains transformed the hill country's formerly dusty ground into slimy mud and filled previously dry streambeds with thickly silted water.[4]

While this battle raged to the west, the regiments holding I Canadian Corps's front lines dug ever deeper shelters for protection from the incessant shelling. The Irish Regiment of Canada clung to Besanigo Ridge until being relieved by the West Nova Scotia Regiment on September 10. Lieutenant Colonel Bobby Clark was still headquartered in the shell-battered San Andrea church perched on its hilltop. The German gunners on Coriano Ridge enjoyed an excellent prospect over the Irish positions. In the four days that Clark and his headquarters were based in the little white church, the building took forty direct hits. Clark's intelligence officer, Major Gordon Wood, believed that perhaps "never before [had] a Tactical HQ remained so long in front of the remainder of the battalion."[5] The Irish paid the price in casualties. Wood later remembered "seeing the medical carriers dashing night and day, amid a thick hail of shells, picking up wounded men from the Church and from their trenches."[6]

When relieved, the Irish Regiment marched back to San Giovanni with the knowledge that they were to quickly reorganize, have only a brief rest, and then return to drive the Germans and their guns off Coriano Ridge. Even as his men trudged southward, Clark was at 11th Canadian Infantry Brigade headquarters with the brigade's other regimental commanders being briefed on the details of the forthcoming attack. The Irish, Perth Regiment, and Cape Breton Highlanders were to go forward on the night of September 12–13.

On September 10, Leese decided he could wait no longer for V Corps to clear Gemmano Ridge. The deteriorating weather served as a constant reminder that the autumn rains were drawing closer. As if only just noted, Leese declared that "the ground rose gradually inland from the sea, and thus there was always some higher feature on the left flank which interfered with the forward movement of the troops in the coastal sector. I decided," he later wrote, "to offset this advantage, which the enemy possessed by his occupation of the higher ground, by forcing him to dissipate his fire all along the front."[7] This decision made seizing Gemmano Ridge before attacking Coriano Ridge no longer imperative. It was enough for "V Corps ... to keep up the momentum necessary to maintain as many German divisions as possible throughout the battle on their front."[8]

Meanwhile, the Germans on Coriano Ridge were not restricting themselves to merely shelling and mortaring the Canadians placed so clearly on view below them. They took advantage of the lull to bolster their defensive positions. Numerous engineering battalions were withdrawn from sections of the Gothic Line to the west and, along with German and Italian construction battalions, put "under command of [LXXVI] Panzer Corps for the construction of positions in the rear adjoining the main battlefield and for keeping the supply lines open. Each day's delay in the enemy offensive represented a gain of several times that period for the defence. The hard-hit formations could rest and reorganize somewhat; fresh reserves flowed up, and the new positions became stronger."[9]

Burns figured as much. And he was going to deal with the strengthened positions in the time-tested Eighth Army manner by subjecting them to a terrific preponderance of artillery. Every gun in the corps was brought to bear and on September 8 the gunners opened up with concentrations on targets ranging from the Adriatic shore to the ridge. Some were pounded for hours, others only minutes. The intention was to confuse the Germans as to where the inevitable Eighth Army set-piece attack would occur.[10] In addition to the corps artillery, Burns had at his disposal four artillery field regiments of the 2nd New Zealand Division and an equal number of regiments from 4th British Infantry Division—all told, seven hundred guns.[11]

Once Leese declared his final intentions on September 10, Burns issued his corps plan to his divisional and brigade commanders. Ever one for details, the elaborate plan consisted of eight separate phases. Burns said that his "reasons for this detailed schedule were that our experience after the breakthrough of the Gothic Line showed that we should probably have to fight our way forward against continued and effective enemy opposition. Without careful coordination of the moves of the two divisions [4th British Infantry Division and 1st Canadian Infantry Division] and clear orders as to the objectives they would have to take, control of the operations and momentum could be lost."[12]

Burns was too cold a realist to think the plan would proceed as smoothly as developed on paper. He had carefully studied the maps of the terrain ahead and flown over them, making detailed notes regarding the high ground and key villages that likely served as enemy strongpoints. There was no shortage of possible positions and each must be taken in sequence or the kind of flanking fire that Coriano Ridge made possible would disrupt the advance's timing. That was why he insisted on such meticulous planning.

For one who always held his emotions and thoughts close to the chest, Burns made a surprise move by giving an off-the-record briefing to a clutch of newspaper correspondents. To do so, he acknowledged, was to stick his neck out. If the attack failed to go as planned—as likely to occur as not—he might be ridiculed and give Leese and Alexander precisely the ammunition they needed to fire him. Although developments had forced Leese to place British divisions under his control, the two men were never to be friends or even to trust each other. Perhaps due to this briefing of correspondents, Burns's operational instructions reverberated with the rhetoric favoured by Leese and his predecessor, Field Marshal Bernard Law Montgomery. Upon capturing Coriano, then forcing a crossing of the Marano River before Ospedaletto village, and then advancing north through San Martino, Burns wrote, the Canadians would "debouch into the Po Valley."[13]

When Major Strome Galloway, the ever skeptical Royal Canadian Regiment second-in-command, read this instruction, he said scornfully: "Debouch into the Po Valley. Crawl more likely."[14]

Over the course of September 11 and 12, Burns spent hours working through the divisional commanders' battle plans. He also confirmed details with Leese and Keightley in order to ensure everyone agreed on what was to happen the night of September 12–13. Burns was particularly pleased with Major General Bert Hoffmeister, whose plan was "simple and complete." Presenting his plan on September 11, Hoffmeister confided to Burns that he still wanted the majority of the next day to complete the details and asked for final approval to be withheld until then. Not wanting "another failure or partial success before Coriano," Burns agreed.[15]

Hoffmeister did not doubt that if he attacked with infantry during the night behind the weight of the promised artillery his division would gain a foothold on Coriano Ridge. The problem would come in the morning when the Canadians would face counterattacks supported by armour. To keep from being thrown off the ridge,

Hoffmeister must get tanks up on it in time to meet the counterattacks. But Besanigo River's deep bed, in which Major Howard Keirstead's tank had been trapped, stood in the way. The Germans had blown all crossings, so 5 CAD's engineers would have to build a fresh one. And there was no question that the crossing point the engineers had selected as feasible was also so noted by the Germans and would be registered by the German artillery and mortars on the ridge. Bridging Besanigo, Hoffmeister knew, would present the greatest challenge in the fight for the ridge.[16]

Otherwise his divisional plan was straightforward. As the British attacked the ridge's southern end from San Clemente, II CIB would cross the Besanigo, push westward up the narrow valley created by the stream, and then mount the slopes of Coriano Ridge. The Cape Breton Highlanders would go for the ridge's north end on the right, with the Perths five hundred yards to the left. Once both regiments were secure on the ridge, the Irish Regiment would pass through and mop up the village of Coriano. A squadron of 8th Princess Louise New Brunswick Hussars would support each regiment. Waiting in reserve would be the Westminster Regiment with a squadron of the Lord Strathcona's Horse. This regiment's other squadrons would be positioned in such a manner that they could serve as mobile, close-range artillery batteries capable of providing continuous fire.[17]

WHILE HOFFMEISTER was teeing up the forthcoming attack, his counterpart at 1st Canadian Infantry Division was able to pull his brigades out of the front line for a brief rest on the night of September 8–9, courtesy of the 3rd Greek Mountain Brigade. Although the relief itself proceeded smoothly despite the inevitable language difficulties, the Germans across the Melo River twigged to the fact that a changeover was being undertaken. Probing attacks ensued that resulted in the Greeks suffering an immediate battlefield blooding that left three men dead and sixteen wounded, followed the next night by two killed and ten wounded. Realizing that the Greeks, like the Poles, had no ready source of reinforcements and no significant reserves, Vokes had to cancel the Carleton and York Regiment's rest period on the night of September 9–10 to shorten the Greek line. At Hoffmeister's request, he also moved the West Nova Scotia Regiment into the line that night to free 11 CIB's Irish Regiment from front-line duties in order to allow it to regroup for the forthcoming operation against Coriano Ridge.[18]

These regiments aside, the rest of the division did the best they could to enjoy a brief hiatus from front-line duty. The RCR bivouacked around Gradara, and from the castle parapets Galloway enjoyed a view over "the most beautiful stretch of Adriatic coast" he had ever seen.[19] The regiments of 2nd Canadian Infantry Brigade were set up in Cattolica and despite the occasional German air raid experienced a grand time.

"Cattolica," wrote the Seaforth Highlanders of Canada war diarist, "was proving, perhaps, the best rest area the battalion had ever enjoyed." Lieutenant Colonel Syd Thomson's headquarters was in a seaside villa, 'B' Company was in a somewhat less grand, but pleasant building fifty yards to the north, while the other three companies had set up in the large naval barracks. Although the beach had been heavily mined, engineers had cleared paths through the German defensive barriers and lifted the mines in places so that the soldiers could swim and laze on the soft sand. "It was," the war diarist enthused, "an ideal place for swimming and this became our main pastime during the ensuing few days."[20]

"Adriatic is beautiful. Sand's lovely. Whole district evacuated by German orders. Every man gets his own villa to live in. Luxury for a day!" Seaforth Padre Roy Durnford recorded in his personal diary. "Yesterday killing and being killed, dodging from hole to hole, crawling in darkness and danger—today lolling on sands, swimming, lounging!!!"[21]

Among those in Cattolica who took advantage of the many abandoned buildings to establish unofficial billets was radio signaller Corporal Jack Haley. He and two others lived briefly in a seaside hotel. They found sheets in cupboards to put on mattresses that were in rooms looking out on the Adriatic. Days were spent swimming or sleeping, an activity always treasured by eternally tired front-line troops.[22] Wine was abundant, there were ample food stocks about with which to supplement the normal rations, and, as increasing numbers of civilians returned to reclaim their homes, a little money would get uniforms washed and mended.

Not all units were blessed with such luxurious quarters as the Seaforths, however. The Hastings and Prince Edward Regiment was assigned to several farms a couple of miles south of Cattolica, where Sergeant Basil Smith of the quartermaster's section, was billeted in "this damned shed... alive with fleas or chicken lice." His team spent as much time outside as possible. One day, he oversaw distribution of "an entire half bottle of beer per man." Smith ruefully noted later that "the officers had a big party tonight on the other half bottle and the rum which the men should have had. In my five years of soldiering this appears to be about the rawest deal yet, fortunately it isn't public knowledge."[23]

The men were allowed to visit Cattolica's beaches regularly. "It sure was nice," Smith wrote after one such visit. "The Adriatic was just the right temperature, the sand was hot, with a lovely fresh breeze blowing in from the sea. It is so peaceful and relaxing that this has really been a treat. A few destroyers blazing away at Rimini, from about ten miles out, some fighters on the roof and a bit of rusted wire along the beach, apart from that you'd never know there was a war on."[24]

But there was a war and it manifested itself almost nightly in the form of Luftwaffe raids on Cattolica. The September 9 raid was particularly fierce. Plaster from the ceilings in the Seaforths' headquarters villa showered down to cover everything, windows broke, and nearby houses were set alight by incendiary bombs. Durnford found the abrupt disruption of each peaceful day by the "hell of noise and shattering of the night" hard to take. He tried to buoy the men's spirits by holding nightly singsongs and quizzes with prizes awarded. Then he would spend the time before bed playing dominoes and drinking tea with his friend Lieutenant Wilf Gildersleeve, who was one of the signalling section officers and a man Durnford considered a true Christian.[25]

Captain Gerry Wheeler, a forward observation officer for the 2nd Field Regiment, Royal Canadian Artillery and who normally served with the Hasty P's, spent two evenings in Cattolica at the naval barracks.

Here, an officer's mess had been established. He was just settling down in the airy mess for lunch one day when someone noticed through the large plate-glass window facing the beach that an Italian civilian on the shore was pulling a wooden object out of the sand. Wheeler realized the man was gathering firewood, but this time he had grabbed hold of an elongated Italian box mine. An officer raced around the room shouting, "eight to five the guy's going to blow up," but nobody took up the bet. Another officer wearing the collar of a Roman Catholic padre was crossing himself and mouthing silent prayers. Then the mine exploded and the Italian vanished in a spray of red mist. The officer who had been trying to run a bet chastised the others for not joining in. Wheeler returned to his lunch with barely another thought about the man's death except to note in the recesses of his mind that the war was making them all terrifically "callous."[26]

Wheeler soon returned to his posting with the Hasty P's. The headquarters here was in a barn that had been subdivided, with one end holding a number of dead cattle and the other the headquarters. A door between was kept closed to somewhat stave off the rotting stench emanating from the carcasses. After the clean salt smells of Cattolica, Wheeler found the smell overwhelming, far stronger than seemed possible as long as the door was closed. Each passing day, the odour only worsened. Finally, as he sat down to eat some hardtack and bully beef with the other officers, Wheeler said, "It's like there's something dead right here. I can smell it."

Curious, one of the men started poking around in the corners. When he was just three feet from Wheeler, the man reached down and picked up an odd-looking object. "Here you are," he said, holding up a human arm.[27]

Any respite from the horrors of war was too good to last and so it came as no surprise to Padre Durnford when Seaforth Lieutenant Colonel Syd Thomson told him on September 12 that they would soon be back in the line and that "it might be fairly sticky." Durnford replied, "I just finished the letters to the bereaved from the last fighting."

"You will have a lot more soon," Thomson cautioned. Durnford noted the officer's "terrible grimness." The padre walked to the edge of the sea, where the early morning sun dappled the water and gently lit the sand. "The beach was all mine for ten minutes," he wrote. "It was the first chance I had of really getting wet feet. I suppose there are very few things on earth that set a man's thoughts along philosophical lines than when, sitting on a beach—away from sight and sound of human voice and presence, he watches and listens to the pounding of the eternal wave beats on the shore."[28]

Quartermaster Sergeant Basil Smith had seen artillery massing near the Hasty P's billet and noted that everyone knew there would soon come "a smashing blow on the high ground to the west of Rimini." Such an attack would add to the woes already being suffered by the Germans, he thought. In the most recent issue of the army newspaper, *Maple Leaf*, the American First Army was reported as five miles into the Rhineland, British troops were sending patrols over the Dutch border from a bridgehead behind the Albert Canal, and the Russians had broken into East Prussia. "Tomorrow is the day Kesselring gets his next jolt," Smith told his diary, "but whether we break out of here or not, it looks like it is about five minutes to twelve as far as Germany is concerned."[29]

IN PREPARATION FOR the artillery concentrations against Coriano Ridge, the Canadian gun regiments started stockpiling shells on September 9, with a buildup that day in the 17th Canadian Field Regiment's area to between 1,400 and 1,500 rounds per gun. On September 12, hours before the shelling was to commence, 6,000 more rounds were delivered to the regimental ammunition dump.[30]

The guns were concentrated at distances from the Canadian front lines that some gunners thought dangerously close. The 3rd Canadian Field Regiment occupied a position only about two miles south of Riccione, well within range of the German artillery and mortars positioned just to the north of the seaside town. Previously, it had been 5,000 yards from the assigned targets on Coriano Ridge, but this move had brought the regiment 1,500 yards closer. Burns wanted the guns so close to the front that it would be several days before the regiments had to shift their positions forward to keep up with the advance.

Because the corps's medium and heavy artillery was also positioned near the 3rd Field Regiment's guns, the Germans maintained constant shelling and mortaring on this wealth of targets throughout September 11. Anxious to get their own back with counter-battery fire, the regiment's gunners were dismayed to learn that they were limited to firing just fifty rounds per gun until the main fire plan started on the night of September 12–13.[31]

With the forward movement of the guns and the shifting of infantry and armoured divisions, there was little question that the Germans must know Coriano Ridge was due for an attack. The six regiments of the 26th Panzer Division and 29th Panzer Grenadier Division positioned there continued burrowing ever deeper into the ground, readying their defenses. The Panzer Grenadiers had three regiments strung along the ridge facing 11 CIB—the 67th Panzer Grenadiers, the 15th Panzer Grenadiers, and the newly arrived 71st Panzer Grenadiers.

On September 11, sixteen-year-old Oviglio Monti had also returned with his father and mother to Coriano. They had returned in the mistaken belief that the Eighth Army had already won the village and passed it by. Conditions in the railroad tunnels of the Republic of San Marino had deteriorated so badly due to overcrowding and food and water shortages that Monti's father, Paulo, had slipped down to Coriano a few days earlier and found the village seemingly empty. He found no traces of the Germans, who, unknown to him, were dug in to the front of Coriano. Then Monti had talked with several German soldiers who had passed through a section of the tunnels and were carrying a wounded man on a litter northward. One of the soldiers told him the battle in front of Rimini was lost and everyone was falling back.

So the Montis had decided to go home and walked across country down through the hills to their village. But they found Coriano shattered by the Eighth Army artillery and aerial bombardments that had started just two days earlier. Their home was destroyed and suddenly more shells started rocking the ruins of the village. Then dozens of Germans started dashing to and fro. It was as if they had just popped up out of the very earth. Paulo dragged his wife and sons into their home's basement and there they waited, too frightened to try returning to San Martino.[32]

The Montis were not the only ones moving towards danger that day. Westminster Regiment Sergeant Ron Hurley had undergone minor surgery for the back injury suffered when his Bren carrier rolled down the embankment at Misano on September 4. On September 10, he was considered sufficiently recovered to be kicked out of hospital. Issued with a nondescript British uniform that lacked both his regimental shoulder badges and sergeant's stripes, he was put on a train en route to a reinforcement depot. Hurley knew that the haphazard manner in which reinforcement depots operated meant there would be little likelihood that he would be reassigned to the Westminsters. Seated next to him was a guy the twenty-year-old Hurley thought looked like a "young kid." He was all kitted out in Seaforth Highlanders of Canada regalia replete with kilt and tam, as if headed for a parade. Except the Seaforths were in Cattolica and the young man was headed south. Hurley was popping codeine tablets to ease his back pains and growing more agitated with each southward mile. When he grumbled about wanting to return to his regiment, the Seaforth kid said he wanted the same thing. The train had just entered a valley and was starting to climb up a steep grade that was slowing it to a crawl. "You thinking what I'm thinking?" Hurley asked.

"Think we're thinking the same thing," the kid replied.

Just as the train edged over the crest, the two soldiers jumped down into a farm field. They rolled across the deep, soft dirt. Gaining his feet, Hurley watched the train chug off into the distance. He could see the Adriatic off across some hills and knew the coastal highway followed the sea, so the two men started walking that way across country. Soon they came to an empty farmhouse and found some wine in the cellar. They got a little drunk and then walked on to the highway.

Because their travel orders directed them to report to the replacement depot, Hurley knew they were technically deserters and had to be careful not to get picked up by the military police who would be patrolling the highway. He led the young Seaforth into a hide behind a sand dune and watched the passing traffic. Some hours later, Hurley saw what he wanted, a Royal Canadian Army Service Corps truck heading north. When he ran out on the road waving his arms, the driver stopped and hung his head out the side window. "Where you guys from? You been on leave?"

"Yeah, that's right," Hurley said with an incredulous laugh. The guy, he realized, had provided a perfect cover story. "On leave. Can you give us a lift?"

Jumping in the back, the two men were soon in the midst of I Canadian Corps. The driver dropped the Seaforth in Cattolica and then took Hurley to where the Westminsters were forming up for the attack on Coriano Ridge. When Hurley walked into headquarters, the sergeant major looked up and said, "Ron, Christ, where have you been?"

Hurley said he had been in hospital and had decided to return to the unit, but had done so without orders. "I need to tell the commander that I'm not a deserter and that I came back," he said.

The sergeant major grinned. "You find your pack, get yourself a tunic with some stripes on it, and get the hell back to your unit. We need you right now." Hurley did as ordered and the sergeant major put him officially back on the regimental strength roster.[33] A few hours after Hurley returned to his scout platoon, seven hundred guns opened up with one great thunderous roar at 2100 hours on September 12. The fight for Coriano Ridge was on.[34]

PART FIVE

THE RIDGES

[25]

This Is Our House

THE CORIANO RIDGE attack was timed so that two 1st British Armoured Division regiments struck the southern slopes at 2300 hours on September 12—two hours before 11th Canadian Infantry Brigade advanced into Besanigo Valley. By midnight, the 43rd Indian (Gurkha) Lorried Brigade had cleared the village of Passano while the 18th Lorried Infantry Brigade was entangled in a bitter house-to-house fight at San Savino.[1] An hour later, the Cape Breton Highlanders and Perth Regiment moved to battle. The Cape Bretoners were on the right flank headed towards the northern end of the ridge, with 'C' Company under Captain D.M. Chisholm to the right and Major Art Gale's 'D' Company left. Captain O.J. Price's 'A' Company followed Chisholm's men, while Major Tony MacLachlan's 'B' Company trailed 'D' company. The Highlanders formed up just behind the ridgeline crest overlooking Besanigo Valley. It was a warm night, the sky clear, the breeze gentle. The men watched the flash of explosions rocking Coriano Ridge.

It was a complex artillery program. A general soaking of the ridge and slope descending to Besanigo River preceded the infantry, which was to follow a timed creeping barrage that advanced through fifteen predesignated linear concentrations.[2] Each lift to the next concentration line was timed to match the infantry's estimated speed in covering the intervening ground. During the descent, the lift rate was one hundred yards every three minutes; across the valley floor, a hundred yards every five minutes; slowing to a hundred yards every six minutes for the long grind uphill to the summit.[3]

As the Highlanders entered the valley, the two leading companies crowded up so they were advancing almost in among the exploding shells. This tactic of "leaning into the barrage" offered the best protection from the inevitable counterbarrage the Germans would fire to disrupt the infantry attack.

Consequently, Company Sergeant Major Joe McIntyre, at the head of the leading platoon of 'C' Company, was not surprised when German shells and mortar bombs started exploding around him. A few men fell screaming, while others just crumpled soundlessly to the ground. Most kept going. Nobody stopped for the wounded; that job was for others. 'C' Company's task was to get up on the ridge whatever the cost.

As the Highlanders scrambled down the river's steep bank, 'D' Company plowed into a minefield that claimed more dead and wounded. The pace slowed, everyone gingerly placing one foot ahead of the other, while the barrage continued marching to the beat of the predetermined schedule. This left 'D' and the following 'B' Company nakedly exposed to German counterfire. 'B' Company's commander, Major MacLachlan, was killed. To avoid a deadly halt while a platoon commander was shifted to the company headquarters section, Company Sergeant Major Joe Oldford assumed command. His subsequent actions in this role won him a Distinguished Conduct Medal.[4]

It was 0130 hours when the Highlanders started sweating up the slope to the ridgeline, harassed every step of the way by German artillery. Then machine guns lashed at the leading platoons. Some men hit the dirt, but more pressed head-on into the storm of bullets. Everyone started bunching up and the four companies began getting mixed together. Platoon and company commanders were unable to use their radios to sort out the growing mess because the crazily cut-up terrain blocked signals. The officers could do nothing but keep climbing and hope that enough men followed to capture the ridge.

'A' Company's Company Sergeant Major Dave Bellefontaine realized there must be dazed and lost men scattered from halfway up

Coriano Ridge all the way back to the start line. He made five running trips under heavy fire to the start line, returning each time with a group of men gathered along the way. As he approached the forward lines on one return trip, Bellefontaine spotted the location of a machine gun holding up the advance. He rushed it, knocked the gun out, captured the crew, and then headed down the hill to collect more stragglers. Bellefontaine won a Military Medal.[5]

At 0230 hours, the Highlanders stalled well up the slope but short of the objective. Lieutenant Colonel Boyd Somerville sent a curt radio message to 11 CIB's Brigadier Ian Johnston. "We are held up, cannot put you in the picture." He then spent thirty minutes reorganizing the men under constant fire into some semblance of their proper companies before renewing the climb.[6]

Meanwhile, the Perth Regiment was closing on its objective about three hundred yards to the right of Coriano village and the small overlooking castle. There had been no minefield blocking their path and very little resistance offered by dug-in machine guns. The platoon of 'C' Company's Lieutenant H.C. Pattison had leaned into the barrage right to the summit and reported being on the objective at 0215. A few minutes later, 'A' Company's two leading platoons, under lieutenants T.S. Cooper and F. Culliton, arrived at their objectives just a few minutes later.[7]

At 0300 hours, a troop from 8th Princess Louise New Brunswick Hussars' 'C' Squadron clanked onto the forward slope of the ridge south of Besanigo Valley to support the attack by shelling Coriano village. Given their druthers, the tankers would have been set up in their firing position before nightfall, but the infantry officers had scuttled that notion for fear that the presence of the tanks would betray the attack's start line to the German artillery spotters. Realizing that finding the designated positions to ensure their 75-millimetre fire ranged accurately on the village would be impossible in the darkness unaided by lights, troop commander Lieutenant Ronald Lisson improvised an ingenious solution. While it was still light, he crawled down the slope and staked out each tank's position. Then, when he heard the tanks groping through the inky blackness towards him, Lisson lit cigarettes and placed one atop each stake. The tankers used the dull red glow of each cigarette to align their Shermans precisely where they were supposed to be, set their guns to the preset angle and range, and started shelling the village. Their four hundred rounds all landed among the badly battered buildings.[8]

The fire from the Shermans did little to aid the Highlanders in winning a foothold on the ridgeline, however. 'D' Company was completely stalled, so 'B' Company slipped to the right behind 'C' Company, which was closing on the objective. As 'B' Company undertook its hasty shift to the right, Lieutenant H.N. MacLeod assumed command of the company from CSM Oldford and then swung the men out in line to the left of 'C' Company. Ignoring the German machine-gun fire whipping around him, MacLeod doggedly led his men onto the ridge and both companies were digging in on the objective by 0400 hours.

'C' Company's CSM Joe McIntyre never made the ridge. He fell victim to the counter-artillery fire halfway up the slope when a chunk of shrapnel drove in under his helmet and deeply gouged his head. Dizzy and bleeding, McIntyre staggered for the shelter of a small house. As he entered the building, the CSM spotted and fired at a German soldier crouched in the shadows. The unharmed German ripped a board off a rear window, dived out, and ran into the night.

Sometime later, Captain Chisholm's batman, Private Fred Mallet, tracked the CSM down and was in the process of climbing into the house through a window when an artillery shell crashed through the roof and exploded in the room. The blast hurled Mallet seventy-five feet from the house and pierced his back with five pieces of shrapnel. Although both were evacuated as wounded, McIntyre and Mallet both returned to the regiment just ten days later.[9]

BACK AT BESANIGO RIVER, the 10th Field Squadron, Royal Canadian Engineers was trying to erect a crossing to enable the 8th Princess Louise New Brunswick Hussars to gain the ridge before daylight in order to repel the expected German counterattacks. It was a tough job made tougher by the incessant German shellfire and a grave man-power shortage. That morning, the men had been gathering around the cook's truck for breakfast when a shell struck and inflicted twenty-eight casualties, nine of which were fatal. Reinforcing the squadron with a platoon drawn from the 14th Field Company, RCE had still failed to bring it up to full strength.[10]

The major task the engineers had to accomplish was to scour diversions down the steep banks with Sherman tanks fitted with bulldozer blades. They started with three of these, but two quickly broke down. That left only the Sherman commanded by Lieutenant J.D. Graham to do the job under constant shelling. Despite the German attempts to stop the work, the sappers opened one crossing at 0544 hours.[11]

While the engineers laboured away, Major General Bert Hoffmeister was in his tactical headquarters, "biting my nails to my elbow. This was one of the most dramatic nights," he recalled later.[12] He started to relax when the engineers reported the crossing open. Hoffmeister figured this achievement clinched the fight for the Canadians. The rest, bloody as it might be, was just wrapping up the details.

The first tanks of 'A' Squadron ground across the creek at 0630 hours and clawed a path up the slope to the Perth Regiment. German artillery fire was incessant, but the Hussars knew their Shermans were virtually impervious to explosive or fragmentation rounds. The crewmates of Trooper Wallace Robert Bishop only slightly raised their eyebrows at the sight of him calmly reading a comic book as shrapnel clanged off the outside hull while his Sherman trundled along behind the Perths. Soon the infantry was locked in a stiff fight to clear a hospital turned into a German strongpoint. When a 75-millimetre antitank gun tried to disrupt the tank advance, it was quickly destroyed by return fire and seven Germans were taken prisoner.[13]

While the Hussars had been able to quickly reinforce the Perths, they had a harder time reinforcing the Cape Breton Highlanders. Only one Sherman bulldozer had been assigned to cut out the crossing that aligned with this regiment's line of advance and the machine soon broke down. 'B' Squadron was therefore stuck on the wrong side of the Besanigo. Knowing the need for tanks was urgent, Lieutenant

Colonel George Robinson ordered 'C' Squadron to use 'A' Squadron's crossing and then traverse the slope on an angle to reach the Highlanders. 'C' Squadron started crossing at 0730 hours.[14]

When he heard of the problem at the second crossing, Lieutenant Graham headed that way with his still operational Sherman bulldozer. The narrow valley was shrouded in dark shadows and the ground so rugged that he had to stand on the outside hull to guide the driver forward. It was one thousand yards from one crossing point to the other and Graham's machine was under artillery fire the whole way. Arriving safely, Graham had the crossing open by 0800 hours. 'B' Squadron began rolling towards the Highlanders and Graham won a Military Cross.[15]

The tanks arrived just as the Highlanders managed to secure their objective. Brigadier Johnston immediately ordered the Irish Regiment of Canada to pass through the Cape Bretoners and attack Coriano village with the tanks of Major Cliff McEwan's 'C' Squadron in support.[16] Captain Bill Mitchell's 'C' Company moved past the Highlanders into a stretch of open ground leading up to the village. The company was bracketed by withering shellfire and heavy casualties ensued. Still, the company managed to reach Coriano and started clearing houses one by one.[17]

Initially, the Irish found every house to be empty and Mitchell thought the 29th Panzer Grenadier Division had decided to bug out. With things progressing so well, two troops of 'C' Squadron pushed their tanks out past the infantry and down the eerily quiet streets alone. Sergeant D.I. Watkins was standing in the lead tank's turret when it rounded a corner and he spotted the long muzzle of a Mark V Panther's 75-millimetre sticking out of the cover of a building. The Panther opened fire and so did several infantrymen with Faustpatrones. Watkins screamed at his driver to reverse as explosive charges sizzled overhead. Then a sniper round killed the sergeant, and seconds later the Panther scored a direct hit. Trooper Emmett Hart was wounded, but the other three crewmen pulled him out as they evacuated the smouldering Sherman. Although a German machine gun bore down on the men, Trooper W.E. Fitzgerald managed to drag Hart into the safety of a house. There the crew hid until the Irish reached them.[18]

Their tank, however, blocked the entrance into the village's main plaza. So McEwan directed another tank to shove it out into the open. The tank rolled forward, only to be knocked out by a Faustpatrone. The surviving four tanks fell back on the infantry.

Coriano was rigged for defence. The panzer grenadiers had dug tunnels between houses and under the streets that allowed them to dodge unseen from one strongpoint to another. These tunnels also enabled the Germans to infiltrate back into buildings previously cleared by the Canadians. 'D' Company's Major Frank Southby fell to a sniper firing from a building that had been swept earlier. The major collapsed into a German slit trench and his company sergeant major was shot trying to reach him. The CSM sat on the edge of the slit trench, hands clutching his stomach wound.

Positioned behind the cover of a hedge, Lieutenant Lloyd Brown was unable to see the two wounded soldiers from his tank turret, but agreed to come to their aid when an Irish infantryman explained the situation. After bulling the Sherman through the hedge, Brown could see the wounded sergeant and realized the sniper was using him as bait to lure rescuers out into the open. The tank could reach the men easily enough, but anyone jumping down to lift the men into the tank would present easy targets. Suddenly, Brown remembered the Sherman's bottom escape hatch. He directed Sergeant Tug Wilson, who had brought his tank up alongside Brown, to cross over to the wounded men while Brown covered the move. Wilson manoeuvred his tank so it stood astride the slit trench. Trooper Roy Robertson then opened the hatch and dragged Southby inside.

Brown was frantically trying to signal the CSM with exaggerated gestures to lie down so Wilson's tank could repeat the rescue procedure. But the man appeared terrified of being crushed by the tracks. Finally he complied, was straddled and rescued by Robertson. Both men had been shot in the stomach and Major Southby's wound proved fatal, for he died several hours later in the Regimental Aid Post.[19]

Very quickly, the Canadians found they could permanently close one strongpoint after another by having the Shermans blow each building apart and then the infantry mop up any Germans found hiding in basements or underground embrasures. But the Panther in the square seemed indestructible. Major McEwan finally rounded up an Irish Regiment six-pound antitank gun team and had them push their gun by hand so its muzzle faced the wall of the building behind which the Panther crouched. The gun crew proceeded to knock the wall down on the tank, blocking its line of retreat with great piles of rubble. Unable to withdraw, the Panther crew lit a time-fused explosive charge inside the hull and bailed out. But the fuse fizzled out and the tank was captured intact.[20]

It took until midnight for the Irish and Hussars to wrest control of Coriano from the Panzer Grenadiers. Shortly thereafter, several Irish infantrymen brandishing flashlights entered the ruins of a small house on the edge of the village. Yanking open a door leading down to a cellar, they discovered Oviglio Monti, his brothers, and his mother and father crouched in blackness barely dispelled by the weak glow of a small, guttering candle. "What are you doing here?" one of the soldiers demanded. Monti's father, Paulo, looked up and said sadly, "This is our house." In the morning, the family stared at the smouldering wreckage of their home and village. Ever stoic and hard-working, Paulo told his sons they would rebuild.[21]

WHILE THE IRISH had been gaining control of Coriano, the Westminster Regiment and 'C' Squadron of the Lord Strathcona's Horse Regiment had passed the right flank of the Cape Breton Highlanders at 1315 hours. Their task was to clear the ridge's gradual downward slope to where the Fornaci River drained into the Melo River about two miles north of Coriano.[22]

The open fields here were overlooked from the west and north by hills and ridges being used by German artillery and mortar batteries or their spotters. To provide some cover for the Shermans and infantry, Hoffmeister directed the 17th Field Regiment to lay down a wall of smoke in front and to the west of the advancing force.[23]

'A' Company and 'C' Squadron were to lead, with the Westminsters' 'B' Company mopping up behind. The force began forming up adjacent to the Highlanders and immediately attracted a heavy artillery concentration. When the infantry started scattering for cover, their commander, Major Ernie Catherwood, bellowed at them to form up and move out. He figured they would be safer presenting moving targets than trying to hide in what meagre cover was available. No. 1 and No. 2 Platoon followed Catherwood forward, but the other platoon took a few minutes longer to reorganize. This left 'A' Company split into two distinct elements.[24]

The Strathcona's 'C' Squadron also split its strength, but deliberately so. Even though the 17th Field Regiment's 25-pounders were to drop nine hundred smoke rounds to screen the advance, 'C' Squadron's Major Jack Smith thought the smoke too far away to be completely effective. He therefore ordered No. 1 Troop to remain on the start line and fire smoke closer in. The other two troops then worked along opposite flanks of the ridge.[25]

Halfway to the objective, Catherwood realized that the lagging platoon was falling ever farther behind and told Company Sergeant Major Bill Smith to take Private B.L. Chase with him and chivvy them along. The two men were jogging back when they were ambushed by several panzer grenadiers in a house, who had allowed the leading elements to pass without betraying their presence and now thought to kill some easy game. Smith and Chase led the Germans in a desperately macabre game of ring-around-the-house as they scampered from one corner of the building to another, fired shots back at the Germans, then fled to the next corner with the panzer grenadiers in hot pursuit. For Chase, the game proved deadly. He was shot and killed, but Smith managed to break contact with the Germans when they appeared to run out of steam and gave up the pursuit.[26]

Just short of the objective and before Smith returned with the trailing platoon, Catherwood was wounded. He passed command to Lieutenant J.E. Oldfield. By 1500 hours, the two platoons and two troops of Strathconas' Shermans were on the objective. It was a hellish place next to a barely trickling stream. Strewn around were corpses of cows, horses, and many Germans. Shelling began almost immediately, and tankers and infantry both set to vigorously carving out deep slit trenches. Two hours later, the leading elements of the 4th British Infantry Division started passing on the left, a steady stream of Churchill tanks and marching Tommies. The British were all striking out for the Marano River and leaving II CIB and its supporting tank units to mop up the remaining German resistance on Coriano Ridge.[27]

By midmorning on September 14, the Irish finished clearing the last panzer grenadiers from Coriano and the nearby castle. With the village and surrounding terrain on the northern end of the ridge taken, II CIB blocked the retreat of German units to the south. When these elements attempted to slip first south and then west to link up with the main LXXVI Panzer Corps front line forming north of the Marano River, they ran into the advancing 1st British Armoured Division's brigades. The British snapped up 734 prisoners while the Canadians captured 202.[28] Once the mopping-up operation was complete, 5 CAD pulled back to San Giovanni for rest and reorganization.

Coriano Ridge had been a costly fight for the Canadians, with II CIB suffering 210 casualties. The Cape Breton Highlanders were hardest hit, losing 22 men killed and 63 wounded.

Throughout the two-day battle, the Germans had repeatedly tried to mass for counterattacks, only to have the forming-up units smashed into confusion by the Desert Air Force. Planes flying nine hundred sorties dropped more than five hundred tons of bombs. Seven hundred of these sorties were directed against targets on the ridge.[29]

Late on September 14, LXXVI Panzer Corps commander General der Panzertruppen Traugott Herr noted balefully that "two difficulties made themselves felt today. Firstly, the smokescreens which prevented aimed fire; secondly, the enemy's policy of destroying all daylight counterattacks from the air, so that reserves suffered great casualties. If the reserves are kept near the front they are decimated by the preparatory (artillery) fire; if held further back they are dispersed by attacks from the air."[30]

It was an anxious Commander-in-Chief Southwest Generalfeldmarschall Albert Kesselring who called Tenth Army's Generaloberst

Heinrich von Vietinghoff that evening. "I have just . . . heard the terrible news," Kesselring said. "Will you please inform me of the situation."

"The depth of the penetrations cannot be ascertained with accuracy yet. The front has been greatly weakened," von Veitinghoff reported.

"We must realize that tomorrow will be a day of great crisis," Kesselring mused.

"We are certain of this; all day we have been racking our brains about how to help, but we have nothing left."[31]

This was somewhat of an overstatement, for Kesselring was at the very moment rushing reinforcements to the Adriatic coast in the form of three divisions—356th Infantry Division, 20th Luftwaffe Field Division, and the elite 90th Panzer Grenadier Division. However, these divisions were still concentrating in the region and were badly delayed by the intense Allied bombing of rear areas. The railway running from Bologna to Rimini was so heavily bombed during daylight hours that the 356th Infantry Division gave up trying to move by train and marched towards the front. Kesselring therefore had no clear idea when these reinforcements would stiffen the front lines.[32]

[26]

A Carefully Coordinated Plan

ONE FINAL RIDGE blocked Eighth Army's entry into the Po Valley—San Fortunato. I Canadian Corps Lieutenant General Tommy Burns knew that, despite the fact that it stood only five hundred feet above sea level, the ridge would be a tough nut to crack.[1] Intelligence reported it "as honeycombed with dugouts and emplacements" augmented by several Panzerturms.[2] Then there was the intervening ground that 1st Canadian Infantry Division must first win to reach the ridge. On September 13, the division was still a mile south of the Marano River and two miles from the hilltop village of San Lorenzo in Corregiano. From San Lorenzo, it was another two miles to San Fortunato Ridge.[3] Burns knew he would have to wrest every foot of this ground, particularly the undoubtedly fortified village, from the Germans.

On the Canadian left flank, 4th British Infantry Division—still under Burns's command—was moving through 5th Canadian Armoured Division on Coriano Ridge and marching towards the Marano River at Ospedaletto. Directly under Major General Chris Vokes's command, the 3rd Greek Mountain Brigade was in the front line immediately west of Riccione. On September 13, the 22nd New Zealand (Motor) Battalion was added to support the Greeks. As had been the case throughout the Gothic Line Battle, 21st British Tank Brigade provided 1 CID's armoured support. The addition of these non-Canadian units allowed Burns to concentrate 1 CID's thinning ranks into a sharp arrowhead directed towards the ridge.

In the first phase of Vokes's operational plan, 3rd Canadian Infantry Brigade, supported by British tanks and elements of the 15th (Self-Propelled) Anti-Tank Battery, would cross the Marano River, capture San Lorenzo in Corregiano, and then win a bridgehead over the Ausa River in front of San Fortunato Ridge. At the same time, the Greeks would do their best to hold the Germans facing their front in place so 1st Canadian Infantry Brigade could hook across the Marano River and immediately to the left, to cut their line of retreat. The Royal Canadian Dragoons would clear Riccione and advance up the built-up coastline.

During phase two, 2nd Canadian Infantry Brigade would leap 1 CIB to capture first San Martino and then San Fortunato Ridge from the right flank while 3 CIB moved from the left against these same objectives. With the ridge secured, 2 CIB would establish bridgeheads over the Marecchia River and cut Highway 9, which ran northwest from Rimini to Cesena. The operation was to be completed by September 17, leaving time for Eighth Army's armoured divisions to rampage through the Po Valley before the fall rains began.[4] With Coriano Ridge secured by the night of September 13 and 4th British Infantry Division forming on 1 CID's left flank the following morning, Vokes's timing seemed not overly ambitious.[5]

THE FIRST STEP in carrying out the plan required the Greeks and 3 CIB's Carleton and York Regiment to clear out any Germans south of the Marano River before nightfall of September 13. Both forces attacked with gusto, but soon found their strength insufficient to hold ground won while also continuing to move towards the river. Behind the advancing forces, the Germans simply reinfiltrated their old fighting positions. Shortly after midnight, the Germans attempted to overrun the Carleton and York's forward companies with a force of self-propelled guns. Although these were driven off by a combination of artillery concentrations and individual attacks mounted by soldiers armed with PIAT guns, the regiment suffered sixty casualties, including five killed.[6] A frustrated Lieutenant Colonel Dick Danby could only report at 0145 hours on September 14 that the Carleton and York Regiment had cleared the way for the Royal 22e Regiment on the right, but that the West Nova Scotia Regiment should expect a rough fight to win a river crossing on the left.[7] Shortly after Danby filed this report, he was wounded while approaching 'B' Company's headquarters. Major Jack Ensor immediately took command of the regiment.[8]

Lieutenant Colonel Jean Allard thought Danby was dead wrong about the situation his Van Doos faced. When he and the Carleton and York commander took out a small reconnaissance party, Allard noted that the only suitable river crossing was 1,500 yards from the nearest of Danby's platoons. Even here, the riverbanks were "muddy, thick with reeds and difficult to reach." The bank on the opposite shore was steep and lined by tall, closely grouped poplars undergrown by dense thickets of brush and tall stands of bamboo—both ideal for concealing enemy gun positions.[9]

Van Doo patrols were soon stumbling on pockets of Germans dug in well south of the river. Then divisional intelligence gave Allard a map detailing "the new German layout north of the river, and it was hardly encouraging."[10] Allard considered delaying the attack to arrange artillery support. "If I were to launch this attack," he wrote later, "I could expect the worst. However, I had unbounded confidence in the quality of my officers and men and, in point of fact, no other choice; I therefore decided to go ahead."[11]

Major Tony Poulin's 'D' Company would lead the way to the river, with 'A' Company under Major Henri Tellier following. By dawn, the two companies were to have secured a bridgehead through which 'C' Company and 'A' Squadron of the 12th Royal Tank Regiment would pass to advance on the high ground east of San Lorenzo in Corregiano.[12]

Using the intelligence map, Allard had time before the attack to target forty-two likely machine-gun and mortar positions for possible counter-battery artillery fire. He told Poulin that, if his advance was contested at these points, he should radio in the coordinates and the artillery would immediately hit the Germans there. Skeptical that the silent night attack could succeed, Poulin took some heart in this news.

At 0345 hours on September 14, Poulin and his seventy-five men headed into the pitch-black night. The river lay two thousand yards away and the major hoped to reach it by following a narrow farm track. Reading his compass in the dark was impossible without the aid of a flashlight, but that would both destroy his night vision and betray the company's presence. He could only hope the track, which snaked through a series of ravines choked with thorns that snagged clothing and cut exposed flesh, went where the map said it did.

The company had just started out when someone tripped a flare that popped gently up into the night with a soft whistle and burst whitely overhead. Everyone froze, hoping to escape detection. It didn't help. The Germans had the coordinates of their flare traps marked on maps and responded immediately with fragmentation shells set for airbursts that exploded right above the French Canadians.[13]

"Shrapnel came down like razor blades," Poulin recalled later. Men ducked to escape the deadly rain, tore through thickets, and then found themselves lost and disoriented. Corporals tried frantically to keep the five or six men in their sections together, while lieutenants had three times that number to keep under control in the platoons, and Poulin "was just going crazy trying to maintain some order" in the company.[14]

He yelled into the radio, "Give me the artillery!" Allard apologized. The counter-battery program had been cancelled, with the guns shifted to other priority targets. "The Poor Blood Infantry alone as usual," Poulin muttered, but he also realized that "some sticky situation had likely come up elsewhere and the divisional commander had decided it was more important than my little sideshow. Accordingly, he had swung his artillery away from us. Should my advance and the subsequent attack be cancelled? As a lowly company commander of some seventy-five men at the time, I knew very little of what was going on within the companies of my own unit, let alone what was happening at brigade or divisional level." This, he knew, was the true "fog of war."[15] And all a company commander could do was carry on.

By the time 'D' Company escaped from the killing zone, Poulin and his officers had the men back under control. Two platoons were out front, followed immediately by Poulin's headquarters section and then the reserve platoon. They were almost at the river when a machine gun tore into the leading platoons, which immediately veered off the track to attack the position in a two-pronged assault. To Poulin, it seemed the men ahead of him just evaporated into the dense foliage. A firefight broke out somewhere in the brush, but he was unable to see muzzle flashes or use the echoing sounds of the gunfire to fix the location. Rather than blunder off into the brush with the rest of his men, Poulin trudged doggedly on down the track towards the river. It was about 0400 hours. In barely fifteen minutes, a company-scale attack had deteriorated into what Poulin considered the normal confusion of night combat.

It got worse. By the time Poulin reached the river, he had only his two-man headquarters section beside him. Then to his relief, the reserve platoon slipped out of the darkness. Fifteen minutes later, Major Tellier and his runner arrived. Tellier's company had been advancing by platoons in a long string down the track when the shellfire that had bracketed 'D' Company also set several haystacks on either side of his men on fire. Knowing the light from the fires would silhouette his men as they passed, Tellier swung right of the track to use the cover of the brush there to safely bypass the haystacks. This brought 'A' Company in range of a German machine-gun position, which allowed the first two platoons by and then ambushed the reserve No. 7 Platoon. Two section commanders and the platoon's sergeant had been killed, leaving only its commander and a wounded corporal in control of just ten men. The platoon went to ground and Tellier lost contact with them. He had no idea where they were and knew only that the ground through which his company was moving was lousy with Germans who were not supposed to be there.[16]

Tellier left Poulin to search for his lost men and returned a few minutes later with two platoons. But his reserve platoon and two of Poulin's platoons remained missing. Between them, 'D' and 'A' Company effectively mustered the strength of one company, less, of course, the normal deficiency that habitually sent companies into battle with seventy to eighty men.[17] Waiting for the missing men to show up was not an option, the two officers decided, as their position was being relentlessly mortared and sniped at from the opposite shore.

At 0610, the little force dashed through the virtually dry riverbed and pressed against the opposite bank directly below a stand of tall poplar trees just visible in the predawn light. They were two hundred yards from the initial objective of a road parallelling the river. Deciding to secure the road and hold it until the tanks and 'C' Company could come through, the two majors moved out, with Tellier's two platoons forward and Poulin's forming the reserve. While Tellier's left-hand platoon got through, a machine-gun position blocked the one to the right. When the platoon commander charged the gun with his leading section, they were all killed. Meanwhile, the left-hand platoon was caught on the road by two German tanks and, lacking PIATS, desperately tried to find cover from the machine-gun and high-explosive fire ripping through its ranks. Tellier ordered a retreat to the riverbed.[18]

Poulin was delighted to find his two lost platoons back at the riverbank. But Tellier had lost about forty men killed or wounded, so the Van Doos still had fewer than one hundred men across the Marano River at 0800 hours when hell suddenly broke loose overhead in the form of an 88-millimetre gun firing right down its barrel at them.[19] Each German shell exploded in a great flash of orange and red as it struck the poplar branches and trunks, spraying the men below with shards of wood and steel shrapnel. Eleven shells hammered into the trees directly over Poulin's head and as the hard concussion from each blast crushed down upon him, the major was each time rendered momentarily senseless. The thick stench of cordite was nauseating. Poulin and the others grimly hunkered in their holes, screaming into the radios for reinforcement.[20]

When help arrived, in the form of Tellier's reserve platoon and a troop from 12 RTR's 'A' Squadron, on the south bank at 0900 hours, no suitable crossing for the Shermans could be found. Engineers rushed a Sherman bulldozer to the site, however, and twenty-five minutes later three tanks moved across the river. One quickly suppressed the 88-millimetre gun by shelling its approximate location.

This enabled Tellier to evacuate his wounded to where jeeps waited across the river.[21]

Poulin, meanwhile, was able to establish radio contact with Allard via a static-garbled link and provide the lieutenant colonel with the gun's approximate coordinates. At 0948, following some hasty work by Allard, Canadian 25-pounders laid down a heavy concentration on the locations pinpointed by Poulin—mangling the gun.

A few minutes later, the rest of 'A' Squadron's operable Shermans arrived, boosting tank strength to seven and prompting the Germans to try smashing them with a concentration of shells from a devastatingly powerful 15.5-centimetre artillery piece. This fire was accompanied by the shrieking screams of incoming rounds fired by two Nebelwerfers. Casualties mounted. At 1010, Poulin's radio went off the air. Allard switched over to the tank squadron commander's net to regain contact to the bridgehead, and sent the scout platoon to bolster the infantry. Then Tellier, whose radio had been malfunctioning, suddenly came up on the air shouting that further advance was impossible and a Panther Mark V was bearing down on his position.[22]

The Van Doo commander restlessly paced his headquarters, trying to find a way to improve the perilous situation. There were, he thought, two options: "fall back and try again the next day or risk everything with a very slight chance of success." Allard fretted, trying to weigh the merit of each option, and hoped to hear soon that the West Nova Scotia Regiment had won a river crossing that would force the Germans to shift some of the pressure off his men. But the West Novas reported being badly bogged down well short of the river.[23]

Then Tellier's radio kicked back on momentarily at 1144, with the officer anxiously reporting 'A' Company "surrounded by the enemy" and requesting immediate reinforcement.[24] When Allard pressed the tank commander for details, he was told, "things are uncomfortable but can hold for awhile."[25] He decided that "the situation would be no better the next day, that I could not risk leaving 'A' and 'D' alone all night at the mercy of possible counterattacks, and that, after all, since the road was open, a breakthrough towards the northwest might still be possible. The best choice appeared to be an attack."[26]

Allard's two remaining rifle company commanders had been loitering impatiently outside his headquarters for instructions, so he called them in and ordered an attack at 1400 hours to the left of the current lodgement across the Marano River. Two tank troops and the regiment's Bren carrier platoon would be in support and artillery would provide covering fire in the form of a mixture of smoke and high-explosive shells.

Precisely on the hour, Captain Côme Simard led 'B' Company towards the river with Major Fernand Trudeau's 'C' Company behind. Simard's men advanced in an arrowhead formation, with Trudeau's company similarly spread out behind in order to protect the flanks and rear. The attack caught the Germans, who had shifted their strength to block 'A' and 'D' companies, off balance and the fresh Van Doo force punched out for a crossroads about a mile north of the river rather than trying to link up with the embattled two companies. Forced to pull men away from Poulin and Tellier, the Germans lost the initiative. Although antitank guns knocked out two of the tanks, the crossroads was taken at 1632 hours. Trudeau yelled into his radio that they could not "go further forward until someone else moves on to the ridge. Left flank is exposed."[27]

THAT SOMEONE should have been the West Nova Scotia Regiment, tasked with clearing San Lorenzo. Until this small gathering of stone buildings clustered around a stone church was secured, the Van Doos were stuck. But, as Lieutenant Colonel Danby had predicted, things had not gone well for the West Novas. At 0300 hours, 'A' and 'B' companies had headed for the riverbank and spent the first two hours making slow progress through confusing terrain. Well short of the river, the two companies had "encountered heavy resistance, which included small-arms fire, mortars, shelling, and [self-propelled] guns" at 0500 hours.[28] Positioned inside several wrecked houses, the SPGs were well protected from artillery fire.

Hoping to break the impasse, Lieutenant Colonel Ron Waterman pushed his other two rifle companies up and by daybreak—when 'C' Squadron of the 12th Royal Tank Regiment joined the fray—a tangled, confused firefight raged. From his tactical headquarters, Waterman could see dust and smoke rising from the battleground as both

Canadian and German artillery pounded the battlefield. Leaving his intelligence officer in charge of communications, Waterman walked out into the smoke, eventually made contact with his company commanders, and, by 0900 hours, had reorganized the attack. He then ordered his tactical headquarters section to meet him at a farmhouse in the middle of the battlefield and set up shop there.

The regimental commander's intervention had the desired effect and at 1000 hours, 'D' Company, under Captain W.H.P. David, entered into a house-to-house fight with bayonets, grenades, and machine guns for control of a small hamlet blocking the route of advance. Fifteen minutes later, it was in Canadian hands. But resistance remained fierce, to the point that when 3rd Canadian Infantry Brigade commander Brigadier Pat Bogert appeared at Waterman's farmhouse he was "greeted by a hail of enemy bullets and shells," as poignant explanation for the regiment's slow advance.[29]

Then suddenly the resistance eased and the forward pace accelerated. At 1300 hours, when Captain J.H. Jones's 'B' Company reached the river, the officer was stunned to see a bridge still spanning its banks. Lieutenant G.M. Hebb dashed out and tore the wires from demolition charges placed on the bridge before the Germans could react and set them off. Capturing a bridge intact was almost unheard of in Italy, but this day 'B' Company rushed over it by platoons and quickly dug in on the opposite bank.[30]

Ahead, the rising slope leading to San Lorenzo crossed recently harvested grain fields broken in small pockets by olive groves. The leaves of the trees had been stripped away by the force of shell blasts. Although the earlier fighting had cost 'C' Squadron many of its tanks, the British tankers did not hesitate to follow 'D' Company out into this barren ground for a blood-soaked climb towards the village. The infantry leaned into an ever increasing hail of small-arms fire and shrapnel thrown by exploding mortar rounds while antitank guns picked off the tanks.

When 'D' Company reached the village at 1500 hours, not a single tank remained and Captain David knew his company would be destroyed if it ventured on alone. He withdrew eight hundred yards to a fold and started digging in while Waterman requested another tank squadron to renew the attack.[31] Back at brigade headquarters, Bogert had no idea that Waterman had requested and subsequently believed he was going to receive more tank support, for no tanks were available.[32]

After a four-hour wait and no appearance by the phantom tanks, Waterman sent 'B' Company up on 'D' Company's left for a direct assault on San Lorenzo. Although the infantry got right up to the village, the attack stalled at 1940 hours. Waterman radioed Bogert with the puzzling report that his men were "rallying around" San Lorenzo.[33] Twenty minutes later, he informed Bogert that the entire regiment was retiring to concentrate near the river and that the village "was strongly held and that to capture it a carefully coordinated plan would be necessary."[34]

Just before midnight, Waterman advised an increasingly baffled Bogert that the attack could not possibly be renewed before 0500 hours on September 15. With Vokes urging him to get the advance moving, Bogert ordered Waterman to kick off the attack no later than 0200 hours. After a bit of dickering, this was finally pushed back to 0330 hours.[35] By the time this conversation concluded, the West Novas' support company had arrived among the infantry companies with trucks and half-tracks bearing the mortar and antitank platoons, ammunition, and, most welcome of all, the cookhouse. The cooks whipped up a hot meal.

"All ranks are now very tired," one West Nova after-action report recorded, "and, as a result of the fierce fighting, casualties were numerous and the fighting strength of the companies is dangerously low. However, we were told that as soon as the tanks arrive we will push on to our original objectives."[36]

HAVING WAITED in vain for the West Novas to eliminate the threat to his left flank, Allard arrayed the depleted Van Doos to hold the ground won. He brought Tellier's 'A' Company up from the river to provide security for his tactical headquarters, which he set up in a battered shack immediately behind 'B' and 'C' companies, and left 'D' Company holding the river crossing. Tellier sent a tank-hunting patrol out armed with PIATS to knock out some tanks lurking on the flanks, but it soon returned empty-handed. Everyone settled down in their slit trenches and broke out their hard rations. Allard planned to renew the attack at 0430 hours, with the next objective being Palazzo des Vergers, a massive seven-hundred-room palace with a high roofline that commanded the surrounding country.[37]

Both Allard and Royal Canadian Horse Artillery Forward Observation Officer Major George "Duff" Mitchell were too on edge to sleep, so they kept refining the regiment's dispositions to use the reduced ranks to maximum advantage. This led to Allard ordering Poulin to pull his company off the riverbank just before midnight and to bring it up to the tactical headquarters. Poulin was still being sniped and machine-gunned from his flanks and worried that his leaving would leave these German forces free to retake the river crossing. "If they don't have anyone to fight, they'll have to pull out," Allard argued.[38]

Although doubtful, Poulin did as ordered and was surprised when the Germans withdrew rather than seizing the crossing. Meanwhile, an equally worried Bogert sought and received permission from 1 CIB headquarters to draw a company from its nearby Hastings and Prince Edward Regiment supported by a squadron of the 48th Royal Tank Regiment to cover the crossing. Even though this improved the situation, Allard remained sleepless. So, too, did Bogert, who soon asked Allard if the Van Doos might assist the West Novas' morning attack on San Lorenzo. Allard replied that his position was "so precarious" he could not "take risks in that direction."[39] Looking up from where he had been restlessly trying to nap, Mitchell offered to direct artillery fire against the village. Except for that, Allard said, "the West Nova Scotias [will] have to take care of themselves."[40] When Bogert reminded Allard that he was to take the Palazzo and then the village of San Martino beyond, Allard declared he had insufficient strength for the latter phase because the supporting 'A' Squadron of the 12 RTR was too badly chewed up.[41] Bogert promised that he would be reinforced at dawn by a mixed force of Shermans and Churchills from the 48 RTR's 'A' Squadron.[42]

A coastal gun such as this one near Rimini was used by the Germans to fire on the Loyal Edmonton Regiment after it seized Monte Luro. Shortly before Rimini's capture by I Canadian Corps, the Germans abandoned the gun position and civilians used it as an air raid shelter. NAC PA-173428.

above · The many streams north of the Gothic Line had to be carefully forded by the Sherman tanks supporting the Canadians because of the risk of becoming mired in mud. NAC PA-204149.

top right · The relentless German artillery directed against the Canadians during the advance to the Po Valley made it wise to dig deep slit trenches. Note the grenade attached to the top of this soldier's pack and Thompson submachine gun beside it. NAC PA-185001.

right · A soldier inspects burnt rubber rollers on the tread of a Sherman. NAC PA-185002.

left · PIAT gun operator Private Stanley Rodgers of the 48th Highlanders of Canada takes a roadside break. NAC PA-189919.

above · A Canadian antitank gun crew with their six-pound gun set up in the middle of a village reduced to rubble during the battle. NAC PA-193850.

above · A heavily camouflaged Canadian tank crosses a Bailey bridge.
NAC PA-173514.

top right · The lead Sherman of a Canadian tank troop becomes heavily bogged down while trying to cross a narrow stream south of Rimini.
NAC PA-204159.

right · Brigadier D. Dawnay, 21st Tank Brigade commander, and Lieutenant General Tommy Burns (back to camera) hold a hasty roadside consultation during 1st Canadian Infantry Division's advance on the Metauro River. Note the goggles used as protection against the dust. NAC PA-205805.

above · The shelled-out ruin of San Lorenzo church, which the Royal Canadian Regiment fought to capture near Riccione on September 5, 1944. NAC PA-173438.

top right · German prisoners help carry Canadian wounded to a Regimental Aid Post. NAC PA-173520.

right · A file of Canadian infantry marches past the wreckage of German vehicles near Rimini. NAC PA-173437.

top left · The Arch of Augustus as it looked to Peter Stursberg when he visited Rimini shortly after its capture. NAC PA-193847.

left · A platoon of 48th Highlanders marches through the outskirts of Rimini. NAC PA-193845.

above · A Canadian patrol searches out a German machine-gun position in Rimini. NAC PA-136213.

above · A Greek patrol cautiously advances through the southern outskirts of the city. NAC PA-173430.

top right · The shell-battered ruin of Rimini's train station. NAC PA-173429.

right · A main street in Rimini near the central plaza, heavily damaged by Allied bombing and shelling. NAC PA-193846.

RIMINI

above · A group of civilians talks with Canadian and Greek troops in Rimini's central plaza. NAC PA-193852.

top right · The cleanup begins. Bulldozer clearing rubble a few days after Rimini's fall. NAC PA-142070.

right · As the Gothic Line Battle ended, Canadian infantry marched north from Rimini into the Po Valley with Ravenna and Bologna as their next objectives. NAC PA-173426.

RAVENNA · 52
R. A. C. I.

The fall rains quickly created a sea of mud that slowed the "debouch" into the Po Valley to a crawl. A Sherman tank wallows up a river embankment just north of Rimini. NAC PA-173521.

[27]

Little Reason for It

LIEUTENANT COLONEL Ron Waterman was also sleepless. At 0100 hours on September 15, the West Novas' three-inch mortars started chunking out rounds towards San Lorenzo from a pit dug in beside the farmhouse, ensuring his continued wakefulness. Waterman kept hoping for some tank support, but admitted at 0200 hours that this was unlikely. The unhappy lieutenant colonel told his officers at the subsequent O Group that "on instructions from higher authority . . . a further attack on the hill feature of San Lorenzo" would proceed.[1] 'B' and 'C' companies would lead, with 'A' and 'D' following.

Listlessly organized by the regimental commander, the attack fell apart within minutes of kicking off at 0230. Lines of advance became confused in the darkness and soon 'D' Company had ranged out ahead of the sluggishly advancing 'C' Company, so that this reserve company was formed up alongside 'B' Company when the leading elements reached the village at 0345 hours. Heavy fire from San Lorenzo stopped the leading platoons cold and Waterman ordered a withdrawal after forty-five minutes of fruitless attempts to push into the village. Among those wounded was 'D' Company's Captain W.H.P. David.[2]

Ordered to try again just after daylight, the West Novas were forming up for the attack when artillery supporting 4th British Infantry Division widely overshot their targets with a prolonged barrage that landed right on top of the hapless infantry. The men hugged the ground for thirty minutes before the barrage was finally lifted. By this time, an increasingly vexed Brigadier Dick Bogert had succeeded in rustling up 'B' Squadron, 48th Royal Tank Regiment and dispatched it to support a renewed attack.[3]

Meanwhile, the bridgehead won by the Royal 22e Regiment was in peril of being lost as the Van Doos only repelled a powerful German counterattack at 0730 hours by soaking the ground immediately to their front with artillery fire. Lieutenant Colonel Jean Allard advised Bogert that he had just two Shermans, two Churchills, and two M10 Tank Destroyers still operational.[4] The regiment had also lost sixty-eight wounded and ten dead since beginning the attack the previous day.[5] Help was desperately needed, he said. Bogert promised more tanks, but had no idea when these would actually arrive. He ordered Allard to sit tight until the West Novas cleared San Lorenzo, which would take the pressure off his flank.

The West Novas finally attacked at 0845 hours. But as 'C' and 'B' companies headed up the slope, two Tiger tanks roamed out in front of the village and started blasting away at the tanks and infantry with their powerful 88-millimetre guns. The tankers scuttled into hull-down positions and the infantry clawed out holes for shelter.[6]

'C' Company tried outflanking the tanks, but, in attempting to remain undetected, the platoons gravitated closely together and at 0930 hours attracted a cluster of mortar bombs. When every officer, including company commander Major C.W. Stohart, was wounded, the surviving men beat a disordered retreat. It took thirty minutes for the officers of Major R.G. Thexton's 'A' Company to reorganize 'C' Company and then lead their own company up alongside 'B' Company. As these two companies slowly climbed towards the village again, machine guns and self-propelled guns positioned on the lip of the ridge in front of San Lorenzo blocked their way. Meanwhile, 12th Royal Tank Regiment's Major J. Cornwell was trying to bring his 'B' Squadron up behind the infantry. But each attempt by the tankers was driven back by accurate fire from German SPGS. Finally, Cornwell requested deployment of the infantry regiment's six-inch anti-tank guns. Waterman immediately complied, but he also informed

Bogert that it would take several hours for the antitank guns supported by concentrations of artillery fire to break the German pocket of resistance sufficiently to enable the attack to continue.[7]

The situation soon worsened when a German 150-millimetre gun battery targetted Waterman's farmhouse headquarters. Many personnel were wounded or killed, the half-track containing the forward observation officer's two No. 22 radios was destroyed, and the No. 22 in Waterman's Bren carrier was also wrecked. That left the regiment with only a No. 18 set. Desperate to ensure its survival, the intelligence officer shouldered the unit and dashed through the smoke and flying shrapnel to the cover of a house standing outside the zone being shelled. Waterman formed up his surviving staff in this house at 1145 hours, but operations were seriously hampered by the fact that the one radio had to serve to communicate not only with the companies but also with brigade headquarters.[8]

From his position to the right of San Lorenzo, Allard watched the repeated failures to seize the village with a sense of dread. The Van Doo commander realized that there was little option but for his men to attack Palazzo des Vergers and the San Martino ridge spur with an exposed flank. Capturing these two objectives would cut the lines of reinforcement and resupply to the Germans, who were so doggedly holding San Lorenzo.

First, however, the Van Doos had to secure positions astride the road that could serve as start lines for such an attack. Although there was only a small number of German infantry defending this area, they were supported by a pack of tanks—mostly Tigers.[9] When 'A' Squadron, 12th Royal Tank Regiment engaged in a mismatched shootout with the German armour, all but three of the British tanks were knocked out. The infantry was also mauled, particularly Major Tellier's 'A' Company, which soon numbered only fifty-nine men after twenty-three of its ranks were wounded and five killed.

Having secured a tenuous hold on the road, Allard grimly ordered the attack to proceed at 1300 hours. He could see that the West Novas were still three hundred yards short of San Lorenzo, so there would be no help from that quarter. And repeated requests for more tanks only brought assurances from Bogert that both 'A' and 'B' squadrons of the 48th Royal Tank Regiment were en route. When the lieutenant colonel ventured out in a Honey tank to personally assess the condition of his three battered forward companies, he became even more discouraged. Still, he gathered the three company commanders together for a hasty O Group.[10]

As he started the briefing, the commander of 'A' Squadron, 48 RTR arrived in his tank. The officer climbed out of his turret hatch and was just starting to hop off the tank when an artillery shell tore his head off. When the dead man's subordinate, Major Robson, arrived, Allard returned to his briefing. Looking at his three company commanders, he saw the strain in their faces, the deep weariness. He knew they were "convinced that I had to be dissuaded from undertaking another attack on this next objective."[11]

Allard gave them no opportunity. "Today is September [15], the anniversary of the battle of Courcelette. Like our predecessors, and in memory of those among them who fell, we must make this one final effort." As expected, harking back to the honour that the French-Canadian regiment had won in the mud of the Somme in 1916 stifled any dissent. Allard explained that Captain Simard's 'B' Company, supported by one tank troop, would go straight for Palazzo des Vergers from the south while Major Fernand Trudeau's 'C' Company hooked around the right with the other tanks to take the objective from the rear. 'A' Company would be the reserve. The German positions would be heavily saturated by artillery directed on targets by Royal Canadian Horse Artillery FOO Major George Mitchell. Major Robson remarked that a delay to 1430 hours would be required to bring the tanks up.[12]

Mitchell radioed a series of initial targets to the artillery and provided coordinates for smoke concentrations. Then the two men climbed into the second storey of Allard's headquarters to study the line of attack through a window. Allard was pointing out several additional targets to Mitchell when a German shell exploded on the windowsill. Splinters hacked Mitchell's nose and cheek open and the concussion knocked both men flat. Allard helped the wounded artillery officer down the stairs and onto a stretcher. Although doped up on morphine, Mitchell tried to explain his fire plan to Allard. But his speech became increasingly slurred and after a few minutes of incoherent muttering, Mitchell passed out. Allard had the artillery radio moved up to the second storey and then scrunched up against a narrow window to direct the artillery himself as the Van Doos headed towards the Palazzo.[13]

The attack unfolded rapidly as the tankers, anxious to cross the open ground, dashed out ahead of the infantry. Despite coming under fire from two Tigers, the troop supporting Trudeau's rear-flanking move pressed on without pause. By 1515 hours, both attacking prongs were within two hundred yards of the objective and the infantry had managed to get alongside the tanks. Suddenly, antitank guns deployed in a triangular formation on the side of the hill below the Palazzo ripped into the tanks supporting Trudeau. Major Robson's tank took a direct hit that killed the officer.[14]

Allard watched three of Trudeau's men charge the gun positions. "The first fell almost at once; the second, carrying a Bren gun, had gone barely a hundred paces when he in turn was hit and dropped his weapon. The third quickly seized it and advanced towards the first casemate. I had just recognized him as Sergeant Yvon Piuze. In a few seconds, he wiped out the crew of the first casemate and moved on to the next, which he destroyed in less than five minutes.

"As he turned to come back to the third, he was hit by a burst of machine-gun fire and killed instantly. The firing had come from a fourth casemate, which had not been spotted. The destruction of the first two casemates had, however, opened the left flank. The company advanced and the other two casemates were raked by fire and destroyed."[15]

Allard recommended Piuze for a Victoria Cross, but the award was denied. The Van Doo commander believed this was because "the authorities failed to recognize the importance and valour of his action. Without his sacrifice, 'C' Company would probably not have achieved its objective . . . and the enemy would have had all night to reinforce its position and even to drive 'C' Company back down the hill."[16]

Piuze's gallantry enabled the Van Doos to win the Palazzo and the two attacking companies slugged uphill towards a cluster of buildings they thought represented San Martino while Major Henri Tellier's 'A' Company secured the Palazzo. By 1700 hours, the Van Doos reported San Martino secure.

Losing the Palazzo had unbalanced the Germans defending San Lorenzo and by the time the Van Doos secured San Martino, the West Novas' 'B' Company, under Captain J.C.H. Jones, fought its way into the village in the face of rapidly weakening resistance. 'A' Company quickly joined Jones's men and the village was secure at 1830. As the Germans dashed out of the village towards the rear, their artillery and mortars immediately brought it under fire. But the thick stone walls and many deep dugouts provided the West Novas with excellent shelter and most of the men immediately fell into a deep, exhausted sleep. They had been in almost constant combat for forty hours.[17]

Meanwhile, at last light the Van Doos held a jumbled landscape of small hills linked by numerous spiny ridges, over which a patchwork quilt of farmhouses, clustered buildings of large estates, and various small hamlets were scattered. All were surrounded by sprawling tangles of olive groves and vineyards. A road connecting San Martino to San Lorenzo in Corregiano cut across a saddle of ground between the two heights occupied by these villages. Every building, whether in a village or standing alone on the ridge, had been reduced to rubble.

On the ridge's reverse slope, the Germans had dug positions they could fall back to for protection from artillery concentrations. San Fortunato Ridge, upon which the Germans had positioned a strong contingent of artillery batteries, overlooked the entire height of land. As night set in, the whereabouts and strength of the paratroops remaining on the ridge in positions around the Van Doos remained undetermined. Throughout the night of September 15–16, German infantry and tanks were heard constantly roaming about in the darkness.

The Van Doos were beginning to appreciate that their hold on San Martino was at best tenuous and there was also some uncertainty regarding their precise whereabouts in this confused terrain. About a half-mile north of the Palazzo, a small cluster of ruined buildings surrounded the church of San Martino. It was this position that the Van Doos had won just before nightfall and reported as being San

Martino. A bit to the north stood another cluster of shattered buildings, which seemed of little strategic importance compared to the stoutly built church.[18]

ON THE NIGHT of September 14–15, the Germans had withdrawn from between the Melo and Marano rivers, allowing I Canadian Corps's right flank to form up that morning on the Marano's south bank. 1st Canadian Infantry Brigade was given the task of driving through to capture Rimini. While the 3rd Greek Mountain Brigade and the Royal Canadian Dragoons would advance up the coastline to support this attack, responsibility for capturing the city fell to the Royal Canadian Regiment and 48th Highlanders of Canada.[19]

The two regiments were to follow a line of advance bordered to the east by the Rimini airfield and to the west by the heights of San Martino until reaching the airfield's northwest corner. Here, the RCR would wheel right and cut sharply northeastward to pinch off German units engaging the Greeks while the 48th Highlanders pushed towards Rimini.[20] Lieutenant General Tommy Burns thought the Canadians were poised for a rapid breakout into the Po Valley. With the fall of San Lorenzo in Corregiano and San Martino, Burns expected the Germans to immediately withdraw behind the Ausa River to avoid having their flank turned. Believing Rimini all but taken, he turned that morning to discussing with 5th Canadian Armoured Division's Major General Bert Hoffmeister and 2nd New Zealand Division's Acting Major General C.E. Weir the forthcoming debouch beyond the Marecchia River.*[21]

Burns was premature. The Germans had neither intention nor need to surrender the ground south of the Ausa River because they still remained firmly ensconced among the ruins of San Martino. For the Van Doos were not where they thought they were. At 0315 hours on September 16, Lieutenant Colonel Bogert had advised Allard that

---

* Brigadier Weir had been temporarily promoted to divisional command after the New Zealand division's veteran commander, Lieutenant General Bernard Freyberg, was injured in a plane crash on September 3.

the 2nd Canadian Infantry Brigade's Seaforth Highlanders of Canada would relieve the Van Doos at 0700 hours.[22] The Van Doos were to pull back, reorganize, and then attack the final remaining feature between the Canadians and San Fortunato Ridge. This was a 150-foot-high, fingerlike, southward-trending spur crowned by farm buildings that was codenamed Whipcord.[23] Taking Whipcord was to be 3 CIB's last task. It would then move into divisional reserve while 2 CIB went on to capture San Fortunato Ridge.[24]

Allard initially intended to remain in place until the Seaforths arrived. But the 2 CIB regiment, having to march from a position well to the rear, was only passing Santa Maria di Scacciano three miles south of the Marano River by early morning.[25] By this time, Bogert was hectoring the Van Doo commander "to get my companies out of 2 CIB area and exploit with one company" towards Whipcord.[26] "With my completely exhausted regiment," Allard later wrote, "I could only think of ensuring the security of my men."[27] So the Van Doos marched off from the church while Allard sent several scouts to link up with the Seaforths and bring them up to the front line. All but one of these became lost, however. The Seaforths' 'D' Company linked up with the single remaining guide at 0915 hours. He led them to a large stone house with extremely thick walls positioned about one thousand yards south of the cluster of buildings the 'D' company commander believed his map indicated as San Martino.[28]

Meanwhile, 'B' Company passed by the great building containing 'D' Company and headed directly towards the cluster of buildings to the north, only to suddenly come under heavy fire from numerous positions to their front. The company commander radioed back to Lieutenant Colonel Syd Thomson that the village was in enemy hands and held in force. Heavy artillery and mortar fire also started zeroing in on all elements of the regiment with an uncanny accuracy made possible by spotters positioned on San Fortunato Ridge. In short order, the Seaforths suffered more than two dozen casualties from shellfire.[29]

Thomson set up his headquarters alongside 'D' Company in the Palazzo des Vergers. His radio signaller, Corporal Jack Haley, who was having trouble adjusting to being wrenched from a seaside villa in Cattolica and dropped back into combat, was unable to establish communications because the thick walls blocked transmissions.* So he strung a radio aerial through a window, trying to ignore the way Germans shells banging against the outside walls sent great shudders through the massive building. Once the aerial was in place, Haley decided the heavily constructed building was a pretty safe place to stay put in.

But Thomson had a habit of never wanting to stay where it was safe and the radio reports coming in were confused and spotty on details. The Seaforths seemed to be engaged in a fight for ground that was supposed to be secure and the lieutenant colonel was supposed to shortly send his men to attack San Fortunato Ridge. Thomson told Haley to grab his No. 18 set and the two men would take a jeep and see what was really going on.

Driving the jeep up a narrow track, Thomson parked behind an old powerhouse standing alone on a little pinnacle of rocky ground. Haley unloaded the radio and ran inside. Shells were exploding all around the building and bits and pieces of wall and ceiling kept collapsing. Shrapnel sizzled through the room. Haley thought they were in a "damned unsafe place."[30] Then the jeep was hit and blew up.

Thomson, who had until then been calmly studying the surrounding land, decided Haley was right. He told the signaller to whistle up tactical headquarters and request a tank to come fetch them. It soon clanked up next to the building. Thomson jumped aboard and pulled the radio into the turret with him. Haley started to follow, but the tank commander cheerily told him there was no more room inside. The increasingly terrified twenty-two-year-old radioman clung to the back of the tank, with dirt showering down upon him

---

* Haley, serving in the Royal Canadian Corps of Signals, had the distinction of serving in all three of 2 CIB's regiments in the role of the commander's signaller during pivotal battles. He served under PPCLI Lieutenant Colonel Cameron Ware at Villa Rogatti outside Ortona, Loyal Edmonton Lieutenant Colonel Rowan Coleman at the Hitler Line, and now with Thomson in his greatest test of arms. Haley, who was with the initial Canadian landing force in Sicily, ultimately marched through to war's end without ever being wounded.

from near misses that hurled great clots of earth into the air. As the tank rumbled through a farm, Haley saw a cow, one back leg shattered, struggling about on the remaining three. Finally, they reached the headquarters and Haley gratefully dragged his radio into the safety of its stout walls.[31]

It was noon and Thomson returned just in time to be advised by a liaison officer from 2 CIB headquarters that Brigadier Graeme Gibson wanted the Seaforths to attack San Fortunato at 1530 hours.[32] Grabbing Haley and his radio, Thomson had the liaison officer drive them back to brigade headquarters. He walked straight up to Gibson and told the brigadier an attack on San Fortunato was impossible until San Martino was secured. Gibson received this information dourly and then stared down at Thomson's feet, which were stuffed into running shoes rather than army-issue boots. "When the other ranks have to be wearing boots," Gibson sniffed, "you shouldn't be wearing running shoes." Thomson just ignored him.[33] He and Haley hitched a ride back to the Seaforths' headquarters, where the lieutenant colonel told his staff the San Fortunato attack was off until 0700 hours the next day.

Meanwhile, their task was to secure San Martino, but his company commanders reported all being pinned down and taking heavy casualties. Nobody was inside San Martino and the prospects of getting there looked poor. Thomson ordered everyone to fall back and then sent patrols out after dark to gather intelligence on the locations of the German positions. In the early morning hours of September 17, they confirmed that San Martino and its approaches were strongly held. When advised of this, Gibson agreed to postpone the San Fortunato attack until 0700 hours of September 18 to give Thomson a day to clear San Martino.[34]

AT 0300 HOURS on September 16, while the Seaforths and Van Doos were attempting to carry out the hand-off at San Martino, the 48th Highlanders set off from the north bank of the Marano River. They expected to pursue a demoralized enemy retreating to the fortified Rimini Line, which reportedly hinged on San Fortunato Ridge. So confident was 1st CIB's Brigadier Allan Calder that the operation would proceed smoothly that he had pulled all the regimental commanders out of the line to give their second-in-commands a chance at combat leadership. It came as a complete surprise therefore when 'B' Company crossed the start line on this cold, moonless morning and was instantly raked by three machine guns. This was Lieutenant Walter Moore's first action, and within seconds a bullet in the spine felled the young officer. More German machine guns opened up on the section of men he had been leading forward. There seemed to be enemy positions wherever they looked and German tanks were grinding about nearby. Moore was paralyzed and the section leader, Corporal Alex McCrae, feared that trying to move the officer without a stretcher might cause permanent injury. Forming a protective ring around their lieutenant, the section dug in.[35]

Seeing that his lead platoon was pinned down not just by infantry but by tanks, Captain Gordon Proctor requested that the antitank platoon's two six-inch guns cover a renewed attack. He told the Highlanders' second-in-command, Major Don Banton, that the company was also taking heavy casualties. Banton realized this was no exercise and that his command skills were about to be severely tested.

Fortunately, he had some good news for Proctor. Instead of antitank guns, the major promised tanks. Meanwhile, he sent 'D' Company, under Captain Lloyd Smith, to link up with Proctor and get ready to pass through once the rest of the regiment came up on line. 'B' Company would then slip into reserve and have the opportunity to retrieve and evacuate its wounded.

At 0405 hours, the Highlanders married up with tanks from 'B' Squadron, 48th Royal Tank Regiment and started moving out with three companies—'A,' 'C,' and 'D'—in line across with the tanks in similarly extended order behind.[36] Passing through 'B' Company, the strung-out force headed towards the obstructing machine-gun positions. It was growing light and San Martino overlooked the advancing troop to the northwest. From this height on their left flank, numerous machine guns, mortars, and Nebelwerfers opened up with a withering sheet of long-range fire to which seemingly countless snipers added their weight. 'A' and 'C' companies, with the tanks in tow, pushed on, leaving a trail of blood-soaked khaki figures lying dead or wounded in their wake. 'D' Company meanwhile met head-on the same machine guns that had forced 'B' Company to ground and Captain Smith quickly ordered his men to take cover alongside Proctor's troops. The right-hand flank of the attack was finished.

'A' Company's Captain George Fraser had marched from the tip of Sicily through Italy to reach this day. During that long journey he had never experienced such concentrated fire. Somehow the two companies on the left flank managed to get within three hundred yards of their initial objective, a dry streambed running west to east across their front roughly in line with the northwest corner of Rimini airfield. They were about a half-mile southeast of San Martino and the closer they came to the ridge the thicker the fire. Finally, it was too much. The two companies hit the dirt. Fraser established his company headquarters in a culvert and was joined there by Major Bill Joss, the squadron tank commander. When Joss directed a Churchill to blow down a house sheltering German positions, an 88-millimetre gun hidden inside returned fire and the tank was knocked out. Between paratroopers ambushing the tanks with Faustpatrones and the fire of the antitank guns, 'B' Squadron's tanks were almost all disabled by 1100 hours.

There was no going forward and no going back in broad daylight. Infantry and tankers hid as best they could and tried to endure. 'C' Company's Captain Pat Bates tried to tee up some artillery, but Banton confessed that none was available because all the artillery assigned to support the 1 CIB attack was committed to trying to help the Royal Canadian Regiment extract itself from similarly dire straits.

At 1300 hours, Lieutenant Colonel Don Mackenzie, having refused to stand by uselessly in the rear while his command died, burst into the regimental headquarters and took over from Banton. An hour later, Bates and Fraser reported that further advance was impossible. Bates said his position was becoming "untenable."[37]

'D' Company had meanwhile managed to reorganize and then bypass the enemy machine guns that had pinned it and 'B' Company down. When the company reached a position overlooking the dusty little streambed that was their objective, Lieutenant Murray Hoffman set up his platoon headquarters inside a stone building. Moments later, 88-millimetres firing from San Martino promptly blasted the little structure to pieces. Hoffman suffered a head injury from falling debris. Then Lieutenant D. Watson was shot in the hand by a sniper. Captain Smith told Mackenzie that the Germans had his company zeroed in.[38]

At 1600 hours, the few surviving 'B' Squadron tanks pulled back 150 yards to a position where they could get hull down from the German antitank guns.[39] Mackenzie ordered his three most forward rifle companies to fall back on this position as well. There was nothing to do but reorganize and try again next morning.

The Glamour Boys had been hard hit. Thirteen men were dead, another forty wounded. Four other men were missing and presumed captured. After midnight, Corporal McCrae organized a stretcher party and brought Lieutenant Moore in from where he had spent the day lying helplessly under the barrels of the still intact German machine guns.[40]

THE ROYAL CANADIAN REGIMENT had also passed the day creeping slowly into the face of determined resistance from 1st Parachute Division troops and the slashing fire from San Martino. As had been true for the Highlanders, the regiment's second-in-command, Major Strome Galloway, was initially in charge. But unlike the Highlanders, the RCR had trouble even reaching the initial start line.[41]

Captain J. Milton Gregg, a Permanent Force officer whose father, Milton Gregg, had won a Victoria Cross at Cambrai while serving as an RCR lieutenant on September 8, 1918, commanded 'A' Company. The entire route forward to the start line was bracketed by intermittent artillery and mortar fire that finally so grew in volume and duration that Gregg ordered his men into a weed-choked little irrigation ditch—fosso Rodello—and used it as a somewhat protected approach. With the dawn, the waist-deep ditch ceased to provide worthwhile cover and Gregg hurried his men into the cover of a culvert passing under a road crossing. His leading platoon, however, had already passed this point by and was unable to fall back, which Gregg thought probably for the best because his other men were crushed shoulder-to-shoulder in the cramped space. The officer had another worry. The Germans had planted demolition charges in the dirt above the culvert and the twenty-four-year-old officer feared an incoming shell might detonate these, which would undoubtedly either bury or kill them all. It was with some relief that Gregg received an order from Galloway to forget reaching the start line and fall back to a defensive position hidden from enemy view.[42]

Right of the regiment's line of advance was the wide-open three-hundred-acre expanse of Rimini airfield, which was bordered on all sides by a narrow line of mixed residential housing and pocket farms. The other three RCR companies followed a secondary road running from the Marano River to the airfield's northwest corner. Off to their right, the 3rd Greek Mountain Brigade was supposed to come straight up the airfield and its right boundary while the Royal Canadian Dragoons hugged the coastline on the Greeks' right flank.

It was 0630 hours when the leading RCR companies moved to the attack, with 'B' Company left and 'D' Company right. Within seconds, the two companies lost sight of each other in the thick vegetation and walked straight into the shredder of interlocked machine-gun positions and heavy shelling from the overlooking ridges to the west. Despite mounting casualties, Captain George Hungerford's 'D' Company pressed on relentlessly to the corner of the airfield before becoming pinned down. Major Sandy Mitchell's 'B' Company, however, was forced to ground right off the bat by the heavy fire coming from San Martino. Every attempt to continue was broken by a fusillade that left more men dead or wounded. Lieutenant Arnold Goode, a pre-war Permanent Force sergeant who had only rejoined the regiment four days previously, after spending the past five years of war as an instructor, was killed by a sniper bullet.[43]

At 1100 hours, Lieutenant Colonel Jim Ritchie arrived at the tactical headquarters Galloway had established in a stout building right behind the start line and resumed command. He teed up an attack that sent 'B' and 'D' companies towards a line of gullies cutting across the regiment's front, which the paratroopers were using like deep World War I trenches. Ritchie announced the attack would proceed without artillery support or tanks because whenever the supporting British tanks tried to join the infantry, a well-sited Panzerturm potshot them.

The tanks were reduced to sitting helplessly behind the tactical headquarters and offering indirect fire from their main guns.[44]

The two companies slogged off at 1430 hours and were immediately losing men at a steady rate. Just short of the first gully, a German shell exploded and Hungerford died. Captain Eric Hills took over.[45] Corporal N.J. McMahon's section came under fire from a house near the edge of the airfield. He led his men in a charge right into the teeth of the paratroopers' machine guns. Inside the house, a wild melee of hand-to-hand fighting ensued. Twelve paratroops were killed and two taken prisoner. McMahon personally accounted for five or six German fatalities, but there were only two soldiers in his section still on their feet at the end of the fight. The rest were dead or wounded.[46] He was awarded his third Distinguished Conduct Medal.[47]

On the left flank, 'B' Company was mangled. When Lieutenant Dave Little and his six-man platoon got too far forward, they were cut off and captured. Among 'B' Company's killed were Company Sergeant Major Anson Moore and Corporal E.G. Sullivan, both "July 10 men," as those who had landed on the beaches of Sicily were often called.[48]

Gregg's 'A' Company tried to back 'B' Company up, but his three platoon commanders were all slightly wounded in the effort. By late afternoon, the RCR had a tenuous hold on the northwest corner of the airport, but could go no farther. The Greeks were well back on their right and the Highlanders had withdrawn to a position several hundred yards behind the RCR, who were left forming the tip of a dull arrowhead.

Galloway confided to his diary at day's end that "George [Hungerford] and I joined The Regiment at Wolseley Barracks the same day, on March 9th, 1940. He joined us out here last March at Ortona, having been left in the U.K. as an instructor. Too many friends are going. There seems so little reason for it now."[49]

[28]

To the Last Man

COURTESY OF 'D' COMPANY, Royal 22e Regiment, September 16 did yield 1st Canadian Infantry Division mastery of one significant chunk of real estate—the fingerlike spur codenamed Whipcord, southwest of San Martino. Just after 1500 hours, Lieutenant Colonel Jean Allard had briefed Major Tony Poulin outside Allard's tactical headquarters. The lieutenant colonel pointed towards the mess of hills to their north and said, "You see that ridge there? That's your objective."

Squinting, Poulin peered along Allard's pointed arm. The incessant artillery fire had cloaked the countryside in a blue-grey smoke haze that cast everything in a watery, shimmering light. San Fortunato Ridge appeared as an inky black wall crowding the northwestern skyline. In front were a whole series of indistinguishable little hills. "I can't see it," the major confessed.[1]

"God, are you blind?" Allard demanded. Poulin glanced sharply at his lieutenant colonel. The outburst was unexpected. His commander's face was pale, drawn. Poulin thought: "He's exhausted, fed up to the teeth. Can't blame him. We all are. Too damned much."

Poulin replied carefully. "No, I'm not blind. Show me on the map." Allard rattled a map loose and stabbed a finger at the position. Poulin recognized the little knoll that stood fifty to seventy feet higher than the surrounding terrain from when the regiment had been on San Martino ridge. Except for four buildings and a couple of haystacks, Whipcord had been flat and clear as a billiard table.

"You've got to take it before nightfall," Allard cautioned. Poulin's watch showed he had just five hours.[2] Allard gave him "full freedom to plan his approach route, his supporting fire and the disposition of the tanks."[3]

With no time for reconnaissance, Poulin could only use the map to set out a plan. Using the promised assets lavishly, the major called for a heavy concentration fired by medium and field artillery to precede the attack and then concentrate on various, specifically assigned targets. Smoke shells would cover his flanks and the regiment's 4.2-inch and 3-inch mortars would provide covering fire. 'C' Squadron of the 48th Royal Tank Regiment would accompany the infantry. Once Whipcord was secure, the antitank platoon would rush the six-pounders up to bolster the night defence.[4]

Although rich in supporting arms, Poulin was poor in manpower. 'D' Company numbered only fifty-two men, twelve of whom were reinforcements the major had pieced off in fours to each of his three platoons. The company veterans—figuring the reinforcements inexperienced cannon fodder—hardly bothered learning their names.

Three minutes after the guns started firing at 1934 hours, Poulin waved his men forward with the tanks clanking along behind. He had two platoons out front, each numbering eighteen men, and the weaker third platoon behind. After firing a ten-minute general soaking program, the artillery would switch to hunting specifically designated targets. Despite the smoke screen dropped to conceal the company from the heights of San Martino, machine guns positioned there started slashing at his right flank. Hearing the snap of dozens of rounds passing overhead, Poulin urged the leading platoons to greater speed. But suddenly everyone up ahead stopped dead and dived to the ground. The two platoon commanders yelled at the men to get up, but nobody would budge.

A three-foot-high barbed-wire fence that looked as if it had been abandoned in mid-construction barred their path. "Mines," one man pleaded when Poulin ordered him up. Time was ticking by. The artillery would soon cease firing and, free to raise their heads, the Germans to their front would cut the company to pieces.

"Bunch of bastards," he yelled. "Don't you have any guts?"[5] Jumping the fence, Poulin stomped towards the objective with his small headquarters section scrambling along behind. Glancing over his shoulder, the major was relieved to see the two shamed platoons on their feet, coming on quickly to get ahead of their commander. One man was wounded when he tripped a mine that also injured two others. But these two men refused to go back. The rest of the company got through the field unmolested. They ran towards Whipcord "yelling like banshees and firing their weapons from the hip."[6]

Poulin and the Van Doos hit the summit at full tilt. There was fire coming from the buildings, so the men hugged the dirt and started shooting back. Seeing the tanks were still grinding a slow path up the hill, Poulin ran down towards them and waved his arm furtively to signal them forward. As the first Sherman passed him, its officer yelled, "Where am I going?"

"You're going right up there!" Poulin shouted back. "Shoot with all you can." The tank troop crested the hill and lit into the buildings. "Two of the houses were just coming to pieces," Poulin later recalled. "Dust and fire everywhere. The haystacks were burning."

Out of the corner of his eye, Poulin saw something move and shot it with his pistol. His runner snorted, "You just killed a fence post."[7] It was 1955 hours. Poulin told his men to start digging deep.[8] Whipcord was theirs, but now they had to hold it.

Thirty minutes later, the Germans started shelling the company's position with the same unerring accuracy hammering down on all of I CID's regiments close to the front lines because of the spotters on San Martino and San Fortunato. Even the Princess Patricia's Canadian Light Infantry, forming to the rear of the Seaforth Highlanders of Canada and the Van Doos, was in their line of sight. When Lieutenant Colonel David Rosser, only just recovered from a bout of malaria, had to be evacuated with a piece of shrapnel in his right calf, Major R.P. "Slug" Clark was promoted to acting lieutenant colonel and took over command.[9]

The PPCLI was to relieve Poulin's men on Whipcord, as part of

2nd Canadian Infantry Brigade's general takeover of the San Martino ridge from 3rd Canadian Infantry Brigade. 'C' Company's Captain L.G. Burton sent a twenty-one-man patrol up the slope at 2200 hours to contact Poulin. The small force quickly reported back that they had met "enemy in strength" two hundred yards short of Whipcord and were forced to return.[10] Burton realized Poulin's 'D' Company was surrounded.

There followed a night of confused, sharp small-scale firefights across the breadth of the Canadian front as Germans and Canadians probed each other's positions. A Seaforth Highlanders patrol commanded by Lieutenant Dave Fairweather was fifty yards from San Martino when heavy machine-gun and tank fire forced it to withdraw. Lieutenant Colonel Syd Thomson took this as a warning that the Germans were building up their strength there and decided to bounce them by having 'B' Company launch an immediate attack. At 0300 hours, Major "Ollie" Mace struck the village with his men while 'D' Company tried bypassing it on the left. In the pitch-black night, it was impossible for the two companies to coordinate operations. 'B' Company took a few buildings on the edge of the village only to be thrown out of them by a fierce counterattack, and 'D' Company was stopped cold by a wall of machine-gun fire. Both companies pulled back while Thomson reported to brigade that it was "evident that [San Martino] was the core of the enemy's positions south of Rimini, and that it would have to be secured by a heavier attack."[11]

AT 0400, the Germans hit Whipcord with a sharp probing counterattack quickly rebuffed by the well-positioned men of 'D' Company. But Poulin was relieved when the PPCLI's 'C' Company slipped through the Germans at his rear to form up alongside the Van Doos. This despite the fact that Captain Burton's company numbered just over forty men, which brought the infantry strength on Whipcord up to almost one hundred men. Poulin knew he needed every man possible, particularly as the tank troop—less one tank abandoned in the Van Doo position with mechanical problems—pulled out at dawn to resupply.[12]

The paratroopers returned in force with two tanks backing them up at 0920 hours, just as four tanks from the 145th Regiment, Royal

Armoured Corps were entering the PPCLI area.[13] When the tanks opened fire on the advancing Germans, the paratroopers sideslipped out of the tankers' line of sight and hit Poulin's position on an angle. Realizing he was about to be overrun, Poulin took a deadly gamble. Quickly positioning a platoon in positions on opposite flanks of the hill, he withdrew his remaining platoon and company headquarters two hundred yards to create a rectangular box on the summit itself. The Germans stormed into this seeming weak point "shouting and yelling. Pleased as punch that they were on the objective," the major recalled.[14] While the Germans had been entering the box, however, Poulin had radioed for every gun Allard could muster to fire right on top of Whipcord. Allard "asked no questions, and gave the order."[15]

An artillery forward observation officer with Allard brought the corps medium artillery to bear with devastating results. At the same time, two Van Doos climbed into the abandoned British tank and ambushed the Germans with its main gun. An observation plane was circling overhead minutes later and the artillery officer aboard corrected the fall of shot to keep the fire tightly concentrated on the now milling and cowering Germans. Finally at 1038 hours, Poulin told Allard to cease fire.[16] The only Germans left on Whipcord that he could see were dead.

Although the counterattack was smashed, there was nothing the Canadians on Whipcord could do to stave off the renewed shelling and mortaring. At 1400 hours, Poulin reported having only twenty-five men left and desperately wanting tanks and antitank guns.[17] Fifteen minutes later, the German shelling reached a fierce crescendo and Captain Burton was killed. Lieutenant H.E. Dalquist took over, was promptly wounded, and replaced by Lieutenant W.G. McNeil.[18] A flurry of movement three hundred yards northwest of his position warned Poulin another counterattack was forming. Allard said that a troop of three Sherman tanks was en route and for him to hold on.

At 1443 hours, Poulin radioed: "Two enemy tanks approaching. Send the tanks and antitank guns." Twenty-two minutes later, he told Allard: "Three tanks coming on us." Poulin provided coordinates for engaging the tanks with artillery. At 1513 hours, he reported, "Enemy tanks still coming towards us. Artillery is engaging them successfully." The shelling had the desired effect. The tanks stopped advancing and simply held in place. Poulin kept calling concentrations down on their armoured heads. The Panthers stalwartly endured the Canadian artillery and pounded the infantry with their 75-millimetre guns.[19]

From San Fortunato, a German self-propelled gun opened up on Whipcord with an 88-millimetre gun that proved dangerously accurate with each round. Poulin could see the gun on the ridge about eight hundred yards away. But every time he zeroed artillery on it, the SPG's commander seemed to divine what was about to happen and ducked the machine out of sight. Then it clanked back into view and started shooting the Van Doos until the next artillery concentration was teed up.

Noticing a flight of Kittyhawk fighter-bombers circling overhead in cab rank, Poulin asked for air support. To his surprise, Allard soon reported that it was on the way. Then a Kittyhawk streaked out of the dazzling blue sky and Poulin "saw this big silvery torpedo of a bomb detaching itself from the underside of the plane and thought it was coming for us, but it went over us very gracefully and hit the ridge. The men went crazy. They were yelling and jumping. We could see the pilot's face, he passed over so low." Two other planes swooped down for added strikes and then the three planes carried out several machine-gun strafing runs. "It was absolutely glorious," Poulin later remembered. Whether the SPG was destroyed, Poulin didn't know. But it never reappeared.[20] The stalemate with the tanks threatening his position, however, continued.

Worried that 'D' Company's dwindling ranks would be overrun during the night, Allard sent a platoon from 'C' Company up to Poulin at 2108 hours. It was all he could offer because the rest of the regiment had spent the day repelling repeated counterattacks aimed at turning Poulin's rear from the right and that of the Seaforths from the left. 'B' Company was particularly hard-pressed; a long day of shelling and sniping had left it badly reduced.

After telling Poulin that the 'C' Company platoon was en route to Whipcord, Allard ordered the major to "hold to the last man, last round."[21] Poulin acknowledged just as the Germans attacked in strength with three tanks. Having won the gamble once, Poulin could only try for another jackpot by ordering his men and the PPCLI remnants to slip back into the same box formation used earlier. The artillery opened up on call and again the German attack was thrown into disarray. Poulin's men stormed back onto Whipcord, driving the enemy out. Shortly thereafter, the 'C' Company platoon arrived to bulk up the badly thinned ranks.[22] Whipcord was still in Canadian hands as September 17 ended, but it had been a close call.

SAN MARTINO, however, still blocked the Canadian advance. In the early morning hours of September 17, 1st Canadian Infantry Brigade commander Brigadier Allan Calder had advised Major General Chris Vokes that "progress by RCR and 48th Highlanders could at best only be made at the expense of very heavy casualties as long as [San Martino] remained in enemy hands." Calder advocated a three-battalion-wide attack to overcome this position. His plan, which Vokes approved, was for his two regiments that were trying to push between the Rimini airfield and San Martino to renew their attack in conjunction with an all-out effort by the Seaforth Highlanders against San Martino itself. The Royal Canadian Regiment and 48th Highlanders of Canada advance would be preceded and supported by massive artillery concentrations that would include smoke to obstruct the German view from San Martino and San Fortunato. There would also be a twenty-five-minute barrage on San Martino immediately before the Seaforths attacked. The attack was scheduled for 1330 hours.[23]

Seaforth commander Lieutenant Colonel Syd Thomson called his company commanders together in the stronghold that 'D' Company had taken over from the Van Doos the previous day during the otherwise botched hand-off between the two regiments. His plan was for 'A' Company under Major Herbert Paterson and 'C' Company under Major Haworth Glendinning to carry out the attack.[24] They would have four troops of tanks—two each of Shermans and Churchills—from the 145th Royal Armoured Corps in support.[25] Paterson had not led a rifle company in some time and was largely unknown to the men in 'A' Company. Among these was Tennessee native Corporal

Charles Monroe Johnson, who had enlisted in the Canadian army in 1940 when it seemed the United States was going to steer clear of the war against fascism. Johnson understood that Paterson, "a tall, oldish man," was to lead this single attack and then be transferred back to England. To the American soldier, the major seemed very English in mannerisms and he crossed the start line with a walking stick in one hand, as if setting out on a stroll in the country.[26]

Johnson had no idea what they were supposed to do. The company commanders had not briefed the section leaders, and so no information had filtered down to the men. They just followed Paterson as he strolled towards San Martino, which was being battered by the last phase of the artillery program. Laid out in an arrowhead formation, 'A' Company moved through a vineyard and then started up a slope across open ground. At that point, the men started to run and the tanks ground along behind. They were about 150 yards from the edge of San Martino when Johnson noted that it was a clear, bright fall afternoon more suited for basking in sunlight than killing men. Just as this thought entered his mind, the dying began. A Faustpatrone round shrieked out of a slit trench dug in front of a building and Lieutenant G.F.F. Douse's tank went up in a ball of fire. None of the tankers got out. Having fired his charge, the German Faustpatrone man tried climbing through a hole in the wall of the house, but Lance Corporal Raymond C. Clarke threw a grenade on top of him first. An unseen German machine-gunner ripped a burst through Clarke, killing him. Then Private Walter Kadeniuk, who had won a Military Medal at the Hitler Line, was bowled over dead by a second burst. Johnson and the surviving members of his platoon hit the ground, desperately trying to locate the MG42 position.

Realizing he was completely out in the open, Johnson ran to the cover of a small olive tree only to discover that its trunk was barely four inches thick. The movement had attracted the machine-gunner's attention and slugs tore up the ground inches from his legs. Johnson scurried to a shallow shell hole "in which a six-year-old boy could not have hidden . . . and dug into the rock-like dirt with my hands until they began to bleed."[27] He kept waiting for orders from the company officers, instructions that would get the attack moving again. In frustration, he raised his rifle and snapped off some rounds at the buildings, but knew he was just wasting ammunition.

Johnson was unaware that Paterson was dead and Lieutenant Robert K. Swinton had assumed command of 'A' Company. But with four of the tanks that had been providing immediate support all knocked out, the others having stalled behind the infantry, and the Germans raking the company with intense machine-gun and mortar fire, going forward was impossible. Despite the intense opposition, one platoon from 'C' Company did work its way into San Martino. This was No. 15 Platoon, under command of Acting Sergeant Raymond E. Jenkins. The regiment's historian later wrote: "Doubling across the open field which the enemy had sited as a 'killing ground,' Jenkins and his men dashed into two houses barricaded and occupied by the enemy. He forced his way in, killing four of the enemy and taking the remainder prisoner. In the back garden were two slit trenches manned by the enemy. As the sergeant stepped out to deal with them he was shot through the neck and cheek. Bleeding and furious, Jenkins ran forward and killed those who were in the slit trenches."[28]

When Jenkins radioed Major Glendinning to report his men firm in the houses, the company commander ordered him to go back for medical treatment. Not wanting to further reduce his diminished platoon, Jenkins made his own way back without assistance.[29]

Back in 'D' Company's stone building, where his tactical headquarters was set up, Thomson was blessed with an opportunity that he expected was every battalion commander's dream. From his position, "the whole picture was laid out in front of me. There was a big slope in front of me and my companies were going up there and fighting the Germans. On my right, [Glendinning's] company was getting well ahead and was in fact going to outflank them, except he had lost all his tanks by that time."[30]

Thomson could see Germans fleeing from the buildings that Jenkins's platoon had managed to enter and believed if he could just get some tanks up there the battle would be turned. He got on the radio and asked Lieutenant Colonel E.V. Strickland, commander of 145 RAC, to release a squadron of tanks from where they were sheltered from the German antitank guns that had destroyed Douse's troop. "Oh, no, Syd," Strickland said, "you better have a talk to your brigade commander and do this through channels."[31]

The Seaforth commander explained the situation by radio to Brigadier Graeme Gibson at 2 CIB headquarters. "Don't get excited, Thomson," Gibson said. "If you want to discuss this, you come back and see me."

Thomson thought, "For Christ sake." He put the radio handset down without a reply. "Don't get excited," he muttered. "I've never got excited in my life."[32] But he knew an opportunity was lost. By the time he went back to brigade, received permission to deploy the tanks, made his way back to his tactical headquarters, issued the necessary orders, and actually got the tanks all the way up the hill to where they were needed, his two companies would most likely be destroyed. Thomson, who believed the heavy casualties 2 CIB had suffered at the Hitler Line had largely resulted from Gibson's refusal to listen to his regimental commanders' pleas that their right flank be covered during the attack, refused now to "sacrifice these troops for no gain." He ordered the remnants of 'A' and 'C' companies withdrawn.[33]

The platoons had to fall back over the same open ground they had gone up through, under heavy fire the entire way. There were many walking wounded who had to be helped out and most of the men requiring stretcher parties could only be left in sheltered hides for recovery after nightfall. Two sections of Jenkins's No. 15 Platoon never made it back and were presumed captured.[34] "Chased by bullets and shells," Corporal Johnson "ran to join the remnants of my company."[35] It was 1600 hours before the withdrawal was complete.

ON THE RIGHT FLANK of the Seaforths, the regiments of 1 CIB had fared no better. The 48th Highlanders had jumped off with Captain George Beal in command of 'A' Company on the left and 'C' Company under Captain Pat Bates on the right. 'C' Company was heading for a junction of narrow tracks that stood immediately below San Martino Ridge, while 'A' Company's objective was a ridge three hundred yards northeast of the road junction. The nine hundred yards of intervening ground both companies must traverse were flat, open, and sparsely vegetated. Despite the artillery concentrations, the two companies no sooner crossed the start line than they came under virtually continuous volleys of machine-gun fire from more positions than they could count. 'C' Company was immediately pinned down. Bates radioed back that the fire from San Martino that had murdered them the previous day was doing so again.

Sergeant Joe Gauthier, whose No. 13 Platoon was leading the company, stood up and led his men in a wild dash across the open ground to a covered position just three hundred yards from the objective. Bates meanwhile had been caught in the open by a burst of fire and was lying helplessly wounded. The rest of the company had failed to follow Gauthier's platoon and so it was now far out on its own in no man's land. Lieutenant Fred Williams took over the company and started working forward with the other two platoons, trying to reach Gauthier.

The sergeant decided that things were too much in the balance to wait for the rest of the company. He led his single platoon in another charge against the German positions dug in at the crossroads and was soon among them. Gauthier killed one of the paratroopers and possibly wounded or killed five more during the short firefight that followed as No. 13 Platoon cleared the positions. The sergeant was awarded the Military Medal.

Williams arrived with the other two platoons and radioed back to Lieutenant Colonel Don Mackenzie that 'C' Company was on the objective. But he also reported that there were Germans moving to his rear and that he was surrounded.

On the left, 'A' Company's Sergeant Stuart Montgomery managed to get the leading No. 8 Platoon to within thirty yards of the objective before raking machine-gun fire across the front of his leading sections drove everyone to ground. Paratroopers in slit trenches started popping up to throw grenades and fire Faustpatrones at Montgomery's men. The Highlanders replied with grenades of their own. Standing in the open, Montgomery chucked thirteen grenades into the German trenches as quickly as a corporal could hand them up to him. Then the platoon charged and overran the Germans who had survived the bloody exchange of explosives. The other platoons arrived moments later.

Although they had won their objective, Captain Beal realized that a farmhouse about fifty yards to their front dominated the position. He told Montgomery to take a section and secure it. The sergeant led another mad charge and captured the building after a sharp fight with some paratroopers. Looking back over the ground just covered, Montgomery saw that Private John Andrew was lying in the open after taking two bullets through his legs. He ran over, lifted the man in his arms, and carried him to the house. For all of his bravery, Montgomery was awarded the Military Medal.

As Montgomery brought Andrew inside, the Germans counter-attacked through the farm's courtyard. Sergeant Don Caswell, seeing that Montgomery's hold on the farmhouse was threatened, led a section over to reinforce him. Caswell burst into the courtyard, saw Germans occupying a stone stable, and charged it. One of the Germans spun and fired a Faustpatrone at close range that tore the sergeant apart.

When the paratroopers tried to rush the farmhouse from the stable, Montgomery's Bren gunner cut six of them down with a sustained burst. By now, the corpses of more than thirty Germans lay scattered across 'A' Company's objective and around the farmhouse.

Beal realized that without tank support 'A' Company could not hope to hold its ground much longer. Every tank that tried to reach them was knocked out one after the other by 88-millimetre guns firing from San Martino. There was no choice but to go back. But the ground over which they must withdraw was exposed to the German fire and the men's pace would be slowed by the need to carry out the wounded.

Company Sergeant Major Vic Jackson proposed a solution. He would stay behind with the two-inch mortar and all its rounds. As the others went out, he would lay down a screen of smoke bombs to cover them. There was no other viable option. Beal led the men out while the sergeant banged out a furious rate of fire with the tiny mortar. His fire drew the attention of machine guns on San Martino and then direct fire from an 88-millimetre on the ridge. He carried on firing smoke regardless until the last bomb was expended, then scooped up the mortar and made a run for it. The sergeant arrived back in the new company position unscathed and won a Military Medal for his valour.

Unfortunately, the new position was hardly safe. Minutes after the company formed there, it came under fire from behind. German paratroopers had infiltrated in between them and the original start line for the attack. Beal reported his predicament to Lieutenant Colonel Mackenzie, who said he was calling down an artillery smoke screen and that the moment it started 'A' Company should beat a retreat to the rest of the regiment. Mackenzie gave the same order to 'C' Company. When the smoke rounds started falling at 1520 hours, the two companies came back, fighting their way through several hastily thrown-up German blocking positions.

'C' Company's wounded commander, Captain Bates, was still out in the open. There was no way stretcher-bearers could reach him on foot and survive. Major Bill Joss, commander of the squadron of 48th Royal Tank Regiment that had been supporting the Highlanders, offered to send the lightly armoured scout car that the tankers used for an ambulance. One of 'C' Company's stretcher-bearers, Private James Gillard, volunteered to accompany the British scout car driver, who had also volunteered for the task. As the Red Cross–marked vehicle neared where Bates lay, some heavily armed paratroopers waved them down. The two men had no option but to stop. One of the Germans quickly searched the vehicle and men for weapons. Finding none, he signalled that they could continue on their errand of mercy. Bates was recovered and returned without interference from the Germans.

The butcher's bill for the Highlanders that day was less than that suffered on September 16. Surprisingly, only five men were dead, but twenty-seven were wounded. This brought the two-day tally to eighty-five casualties. And the regiment had gained no ground for the blood spilled.[36] Morale was at an all-time low. Everyone expected the next day would just bring a renewed attempt with the same futile tactics.

Nothing the Royal Canadian Regiment had tried yielded any significant gains either. Major Strome Galloway confided to his diary that it was "a day spent inching forward. It is very sticky going and our companies and the enemy are no more than 100 to 125 yards apart. The flat ground makes an 'up and at 'em assault' suicidal, so it is a firefight with small arms and artillery support. Neither will dislodge the enemy."[37]

Late in the afternoon, 'B' Company's Major Sandy Mitchell encountered scout platoon commander Lieutenant Jimmy Quayle outside the regimental tactical headquarters. "The bodies of three of your scouts are lying in a ditch beside us," he told Quayle. "They were hit by machine-gun fire earlier. The gun is still sweeping the area."[38] For a platoon that seldom numbered more than fifteen men, this was a terrible casualty toll.

Quayle went to the scene and a surviving scout told him what had happened. The first man had been crossing the road when an MG42 shot him. The second man in line ran to help his fallen mate and was killed trying to drag the injured soldier to safety. Then the third man had dropped all his webbing, ammunition, and weapons to show clearly that he was unarmed. With arms held away from his body, he had walked out on the road, expecting the German gunner to allow him to retrieve his fallen comrades. A burst of fire cut him down. After dark, Quayle led a party of scouts to reclaim their dead. As Quayle gently turned the body of the lead scout, he was startled by a soft voice. "I really messed up, Sir," the wounded man said. The scouts rushed him to the Regimental Aid Post but he soon died of his wounds.[39]

After two days of battle, the RCR had suffered seventy-four casualties. Brigadier Calder told Lieutenant Colonel Ritchie to prepare to launch an attack to capture Casa Rodella, a building standing alongside the little ditch of the same name that was situated on the extreme northwest corner of the Rimini airfield. The attack was to go in at 0230 hours. He restricted the Highlanders' operations for the night to patrolling and probing of the objectives that had failed to fall during the day.

LIEUTENANT COLONEL Syd Thomson was also receiving a new set of orders for yet another attack. Brigadier Graeme Gibson told him that the Seaforths should take San Martino by night assault. He made it clear that Thomson was failing to push the regiment as hard as the brigadier wanted. Neither officer was making any effort now to conceal his dislike for the other. Thomson thought Gibson—who would seldom come up to the sharp end—was once again refusing to accept that his regimental commanders were capable of appreciating a tactical situation and making sound recommendations that would not be apparent to regimental or divisional staff from their rearward positions. Because of this, there had been no tanks this afternoon and now just two companies of unsupported infantry would attack at night.[40]

Dissatisfaction with the performance of superiors and subordinates was not limited to Thomson and Gibson. All three of 1st Canadian Infantry Division's brigades were subject to escalating levels of friction between officers. Throughout the day, 48th Highlanders' Battle Adjutant Major Jim Counsell had endured constant calls from Brigadier Calder demanding to know if the attacking companies had secured their objectives. When Counsell passed these information demands down to the officers trying to get their companies forward in the face of mounting casualties, they would snap back: "Why don't the staffs of Brigade or Division, or both, get off their fat backsides and come up here and look at this country?" Thinking the same thing, Counsell offered no reply.[41]

September 17 ended with one regimental commander's replacement. Throughout the Gothic Line Battle, Lieutenant Colonel Ron Waterman's handling of the West Nova Scotia Regiment had ill pleased Brigadier Paul Bernatchez. After stepping in following Bernatchez's plane crash injury, Lieutenant Colonel Pat Bogert had been equally dismayed to see the West Novas he had once commanded repeatedly mauled while being ineffectually led. With every urging to move faster and more aggressively, Waterman seemed to become only more plodding, more cautious. Finally at 0920 hours on the 17th, Waterman had been called back to brigade headquarters. Then at 1100 hours, Major F.E. Hiltz, the West Novas' second-in-command took the regiment over.[42]

Waterman, by this time, was at divisional headquarters. Vokes had been concerned about him for some time, mainly because of his rumoured affair with an Italian contessa, possible heavy drinking, and his having taken to living in a caravan of the style used by divisional and corps commanders. When word of the problems with the regiment surfaced into open criticism from 3 CIB staff, including the brigadiers, Vokes had taken a closer look at the matter. He found that Waterman was running the regiment mostly from a headquarters two miles to the rear. Previously, Waterman had been noted for his courage, particularly at Ortona and the Hitler Line. In both cases, he had been right up on the front lines with his leading companies, roaming the battlefield in a jeep reinforced with a sandbag floor as protection against exploding mines. Vokes respected Waterman. But now he had the unpleasant duty of firing him.

For such a gruff, tough-acting commander, Vokes found the task surprisingly difficult. Without announcing his intention, he invited Waterman to join him for dinner. Before the meal, Vokes broke out a whiskey bottle. The two officers made a good dint in the liquor and then enjoyed a sumptuous roast goose. Finally, they adjourned from the dinner for a few more drinks in the comfort of Vokes's caravan. When both were comfortably settled with glass in hand, Vokes said: "Ronnie." The seriousness of his tone caused Waterman to sit a little straighter. "Ronnie," Vokes repeated, "I think you are getting tired."

Waterman shifted uneasily, but said nothing. "And so I think you should go, someone else assume the mantle of battalion commander. I hesitate saying this and doing this to you. You have been a first-class battalion commander. But now you seem to have gone to pieces." Vokes waited for Waterman's reaction.

The man sat taller yet. "Oh, that's all right, general," he said quietly. "That's fine. I started this war as a lance corporal in the Patricia's. As you know. I was commissioned. I've commanded a battalion in action. I've won the Distinguished Service Order. I'm quite happy to go."

Waterman left as soon as was politely possible. After he departed, Vokes reflected that the average time that most regimental commanders in the Eighth Army lasted was just three months. Waterman had served continuously since taking over the regiment in the midst of the Ortona battle on December 12, 1943. The pressure of the job had finally exhausted him and left him broken—"used up," in Vokes's words.

Returned to England, Waterman suffered the fate of many a replaced battalion commander. He got command of a training unit.[43]

Firing Waterman was not the only tough decision Vokes had to make on September 17. Earlier, I Canadian Corps commander Lieutenant General Tommy Burns had frankly asked him whether he "had doubts about the continued offensive power of his battalions."[44] If he did, Burns was willing to have the 2nd New Zealand Division—so strong in tank formations that it was really an armoured division without the official designation—pass through on September 18 and take over the corps's advance on the right flank of the 4th British Infantry Division. Vokes assured Burns "that his men were still able to carry out the tasks assigned to them."[45]

Accordingly, Burns issued instructions for a renewed effort. Regardless of the situation on San Martino, Burns expected 1 CID to attack San Fortunato Ridge early the next day with 4th British Infantry Division forming up alongside it to the left. On September 19, these two divisions must advance to a road that ran west out of Rimini and overlooked the Marecchia River. That night, they would both establish bridgeheads across the river and on the morning of September 20, the 2nd New Zealand Division and 5th Canadian Armoured Division would pass through and drive into the Po Valley.

Vokes laid out a new plan that night. On the right flank, 1 CIB, less the Hastings and Prince Edward Regiment, would continue pushing towards Rimini "to give the enemy the impression that the main attack" was coming in that brigade's sector. Both the RCR and 48th Highlanders were to advance beyond the airfield early on September 18. Meanwhile, the other two brigades would put in the true assault with 2 CIB on the right and 3 CIB the left. In 2 CIB's sector, the Loyal Edmonton Regiment would replace the Seaforths on the right and advance together with the PPCLI, which would be on the left. The Carleton and York Regiment was to initially lead the 3 CIB advance with both the West Novas and the Van Doos passing through at the Ausa River to make the actual assault on San Fortunato. Vokes told his brigadiers that before this attack went in the Seaforths "were to make an effort to clear San Martino, but if this were not successful, [the] Loyal Edmonton Regiment would have to fight for their start line." For San Martino was the line from which their attack towards the Ausa River must begin.[46]

[29]

Going To Bleed You

SHORTLY BEFORE MIDNIGHT on September 17, the Seaforth Highlanders of Canada's 'B' and 'D' companies, heavily equipped with PIATS with which to take on the tanks deployed in San Martino, attacked with neither artillery nor armoured support.[1] The moment the troops crossed the start line, all radio communication with them ceased. They simply disappeared into a landscape palely lit by the false moonlight created by a series of searchlights far off on the left flank. A new tactic, unleashed for the first time by Eighth Army, anti-aircraft searchlights positioned on nearby hills bathed the area of attack in a harsh white light to illuminate the ground and simultaneously blind the German defenders. Some of the beams were directed against hill features so they reflected back on the ground below, while others blazed directly onto the area designated for illumination.

The searchlights immediately hampered German movement. Within hours of their first use, the 29th Panzer Grenadier Division reported that having its front lit up by searchlights made "it most difficult to carry out moves."[2] Tenth Army's Generaloberst Heinrich von Vietinghoff told Commander-in-Chief Southwest Generalfeldmarschall Albert Kesselring: "Last night [the enemy] did the weirdest thing I ever saw. He lit up the battlefield with searchlights." Then he complained that there was no way to knock the lights out. "It's a great worry to the boys to be lighted up and blinded and not be able to do anything about it," von Vietinghoff concluded.

While the searchlights were intended to support 4th British Infantry Division's night attack, the intense light washed over into 1st Canadian Infantry Division's sector like light cast by a rising moon. But the intervening hills between the actual light positions and the advancing Seaforths cloaked the immediate ground around them in deep shadows.[3]

The Seaforths had hoped for surprise, but the paratroopers saw them coming up the slope and hit the leading platoons with long bursts of MG42 fire. Then, quickly withdrawing into deep bunkers dug under the buildings, they called artillery and mortar fire virtually on top of their own position. For four hours, the Seaforths unsuccessfully tried to get platoons around one flank or the other of San Martino, while the company commanders struggled to regain radio contact with headquarters in order to report and receive further instructions. Finally, at 0430 hours, contact was made and Lieutenant Colonel Syd Thomson told them to come home.

The two attacks by the Seaforths exacted a heavy toll. Almost one hundred men were killed or wounded in less than twenty-four hours. But still the Seaforths had to swallow the bitter pill of failure.[4] And the Loyal Edmontons would have to fight for their start line.

DOUBTING THAT THE Seaforths could possibly succeed, Loyal Edmonton Regiment commander Lieutenant Colonel Budge Bell-Irving had included a plan to take San Martino in his briefing of company commanders, delivered while the Seaforth attack was underway. Two companies, 'A' and 'C', would move in battle order towards the village. If the Seaforths held the village, they would simply relieve the other regiment. Alternatively, they would fight their way in and clear San Martino so the other two Edmonton companies could pass unhindered on the left flank and continue to the Ausa River.[5] As the O Group broke up, Bell-Irving walked over to 'C' Company commander Captain John Dougan. "This time I'm going to bleed you, Johnny," he declared in his typical breezy manner.[6]

The two companies learned the Seaforths had failed just as they crossed the start line at 0400 hours on September 18 with five tanks of 'C' Squadron, 145th Royal Armoured Corps in support. Dawn found the 140 infantrymen overlooking a small valley that lay between their position and San Martino. A typical Italian cemetery surrounded by a stone wall inset with family crypts crowded up against the long slope rising up to the village. Dougan looked over the ground with his binoculars as a stream of Seaforths staggered out of the valley to pass his position. Glancing over at them, Dougan decided they were all "shell-shocked."[7] One said the Germans had at least three self-propelled guns or tanks inside San Martino.

Dougan and Major David Blair decided that 'C' Company would attack on the left with two platoons forward and two tanks in support. Blair's 'A' Company would meanwhile be on the right, but without tanks because the officers wanted the remaining three to take up hull-down positions on the ridgeline and suppress the Germans in San Martino with main-gun fire. Dougan wished they had artillery or other fire support, but none had been offered.[8] The captain was uneasy. "To send two companies without a reconnaissance to take an objective that the Seaforths had not been able to take when they were on the ground, and knew the lay of it, seemed a bit impossible," he said later.[9]

Near the cemetery was a line of abandoned trenches that Dougan set as a rally point before his men started the long climb up to San Martino. At 0600 hours, the two companies and two tanks descended the slope. The morning was cloudy, with a cool breeze blowing off the Adriatic.

The Germans let them reach the slit trenches and "then opened up with a terrific fire. He had the gully absolutely covered—snipers, MGS, a tank on the right, one on the left. His 88's were firing at almost point-blank range. One section, which almost got into the village, was withered. The remainder of the forward platoons were pinned down."[10]

Dougan's two supporting tanks, commanded by an Anglo-Burmese lieutenant, rolled past the infantry on the left and started up the hill with guns blazing. Seconds later, both tanks were burning and the lieutenant was among the tankers killed.[11]

The German fire intensified, coming "down at a really tremendous rate. The gully was enfiladed from both sides. The defensive fire covered the area to within 150 yards of his positions on the crest."

Dougan called for smoke, "which came down eventually, but the enemy's fire was so intense that we could not advance. We stayed there from 0600 to 0930 hours, and all that time his fire never let up."[12] At 0900, Blair was killed. 'A' Company's second-in-command dashed over to where Dougan sheltered in one of the trenches. When he told the captain that 'A' Company was very hard hit, Dougan decided to use the covering smoke to pull back and reorganize.

One of Dougan's platoons, however, was well to the front of the rest of his company. By radio, Lieutenant Keith McGregor told the captain his men were safer remaining in a series of deep German dugouts they had found than trying to withdraw across such a long stretch of open ground. Dougan concurred. It rankled him badly enough to withdraw and to have to do so at great risk of more casualties made the matter all the worse. The captain, who had won a Military Cross in Sicily, had never before failed to capture an objective.

There was nothing dignified about the withdrawal. When the smoke arrived, everyone just ran towards the ridgeline from which they had advanced almost four hours earlier. Knowing that once men started running, their instinct would be to keep going as far as possible, Dougan sprinted to beat his men to the top. Winning the race, he spun around and started grabbing men, ordering them to assume a defensive position. Many of the soldiers coming in were bleeding from wounds, some were barely able to walk, and others were being dragged along or carried by their mates. Dougan realized then just what a mauling the two companies had suffered.[13] 'C' Company had fourteen casualties, but 'A' Company had forty-four either killed or wounded.[14] Including Major Blair, twenty-one men had died.[15]

As he finished steadying the men, Major Jim Stone strode up. The Edmontons' second-in-command lit into Dougan with "a real dressing-down for this disorganized withdrawal."

"I think that's unfair, Sir," Dougan responded stiffly. "I think we were very fortunate that the withdrawal was stopped here instead of a lot further back."

Stone relented slightly. "What happened to you?" he asked.

"Nothing," Dougan replied.

"Then why are you bleeding?"[16]

Dougan touched the side of his face and discovered it was covered in blood. A bullet or piece of shrapnel had gashed his forehead and blood was gushing from the wound. Stone ordered Dougan back to the Regimental Aid Post with the other wounded. "Goddamn it, no. I'm mad and I'm staying here," Dougan snapped.[17] Stone shrugged and called the medical officer up to dress Dougan's wound. Then Stone amalgamated the two companies into one and put Dougan in command of it, with orders to remain on the ridge while a new plan was developed.[18]

Bell-Irving and 2 CIB Brigadier Graeme Gibson decided that continued direct assaults on San Martino would only grind the Edmontons up like the Seaforths before them. Instead, they would try bypassing it on the left. While Dougan's combined company pressured San Martino from the front, 'B' and 'D' companies would swing to the village's left and follow either the Carleton and York Regiment or the Princess Patricia's Canadian Light Infantry. Both of these regiments had set off shortly after dawn with the intention of driving through to the Ausa River.

THE PPCLI HAD kicked off its attack at 0530 hours on September 18. 'B' Company under command of Major Colin McDougall and Major Pat Crofton's 'D' Company were to hook around the end of the narrow spur codenamed Whipcord and push northward. A railroad that bordered the Ausa River's south bank 1,500 yards away was the objective.[19]

On Whipcord itself, the PPCLI's 'C' Company and 'D' Company of the Royal 22e Regiment were surprised to find themselves alone. The Germans had withdrawn. At 0640 hours, Major Tony Poulin passed control of the knoll to the PPCLI's 'A' Company and marched the twenty-two men he had left back to the Van Doos' lines. From the base of the ridge, Poulin looked up at the "still smoking" summit that had cost so much blood to take and hold. "What the hell for?" he wondered.[20]

The strategic answer was: to enable the PPCLI to perform precisely the manoeuvre it was now making. Had the two companies been exposed to German fire from Whipcord, the attack would have crumbled as surely as had those struck in the flank from San Martino. As it was, the PPCLI reached the western corner of the narrow spur unmolested. The moment the two companies turned that corner and struck northward at 0700 hours, however, they came into view of the German guns on San Martino Ridge's reverse slope. Crofton thought it was as if "the Germans threw every shell they had left at us."[21] McDougall's company was out front, with 'D' Company following. Explosions sent men flying and hissing shrapnel cut down others.

The Shermans and Churchills of the 145th Royal Armoured Corps's 'B' Squadron mired in the thickly overgrown, rough terrain and fell far behind the infantry. McDougall and Crofton knew the best way to escape the shelling from San Martino was to get in among the Germans defending the Ausa River, so they urged their men to greater haste and let those who fell lie. At 0800 hours, the small force broke into a line of trees riddled with abandoned slit trenches and tumbled into them for cover. But the Germans had zeroed in the trenches and the shellfire directed their way only fell with more deadly accuracy.[22]

Seeing that the tanks were still coming on, the company commanders ordered the men to sit tight despite the shellfire so the armour could catch up. When Crofton returned from conferring with McDougall, he found the decision had resulted in several of his men being killed in the trenches and many others wounded.[23]

Any likelihood of the tanks reaching the infantry ended at 0920 hours when several well-concealed antitank guns ripped into them. The squadron commander's tank went up in flames and he was killed. With the tanks dying behind them and the two companies having lost about fifty per cent of their strength, Crofton and McDougall decided their only course was to run for the objective while they still had some men left. The soldiers dashed through a rain of artillery fire until reaching a brick building into which everyone piled for cover. A German tank could be heard grinding back and forth somewhere nearby. Crofton flopped down on a chair next to where McDougall was braced against the wall and the two officers started discussing how to reach the railroad with enough men still alive to take the objective.

There was a hellish crash overhead and a tank shell sliced through the roof and caromed into the wall right behind Crofton. Shrapnel flew around the room and a chunk of steel or masonry struck Crofton in the back of the head.[24] When he regained consciousness a few minutes later, Crofton had such a terrific headache and was so dizzy that McDougall told him to wait in the building for evacuation. There were so few men left in either company, McDougall said, that he could easily command them all.

At 1010 hours, McDougall led the sixty remaining combat effectives through to the railroad and a short distance past it to the cover of a ditch. From across the Ausa, Germans on the river's opposite shore opened up with antitank guns and machine guns. Several times over the next few hours, the Germans massed around the tiny force, but McDougall scattered them with artillery fire before a counterattack could be launched.

Meanwhile, a major effort to rescue the wounded strewn along the line of advance was underway. Under the watchful eyes and guns of the scout platoon, whose snipers were particularly vigilant, stretcher-bearers carried the wounded back to Whipcord. Here, they were loaded onto half-tracks and the regiment's ambulances for shuttling to a Regimental Aid Post set up in the Palazzo des Vergers. Crofton was among the evacuated, but his wound proved only minor and after being bandaged up he returned to duty.

At nightfall, the antitank and medium machine-gun platoons filtered through to shore up 'B' and 'D' companies. Several tanks arrived at 2230 hours. With the PPCLI on the Ausa River, the flank of San Martino was finally turned. Their casualties totalled seven dead and fifty-five wounded.[25]

THE PPCLI WERE NOT the only Canadians to reach the Ausa River that day. About 1,500 yards to the left, the Carleton and York Regiment's 'A' Company started digging in on the south bank at 0800 hours. In fact, 'A' and 'C' companies, which together had led the regiment's attack, moved so quickly at first that they overtook the supporting fire several times and were shelled by their own artillery or bombed by Kittyhawks. Fortunately, only a few casualties resulted.[26]

The artillery and aerial support provided for the Carleton and York attack was extensive—the result of their being on the boundary line between the operational areas of 1st Canadian Infantry Division and 4th British Infantry Division. The latter division was receiving massive support from Eighth Army's gunners and the Desert Air Force to enable it to push through the rugged, highly defensible terrain of the foothill country. Some of this fire was easily slopped over to support the Canadian regiment.

September 18 saw the culmination of a terrific gun battle between Eighth Army and the Germans defending the Rimini Line. The gun-for-gun ratio between the Germans and Allies here during the past five days had been virtually equal—an unusual situation because normally Tenth Army was greatly outgunned. But Kesselring had shifted every available artillery piece to the Adriatic, along with sufficient ammunition to keep them firing. The Germans routinely fired in excess of eleven thousand rounds each of these five days, a weight of fire just slightly lower than that of Eighth Army.

Tenth Army could not, however, match the Allies in air superiority or even challenge the Desert Air Force during the daytime. Allied flyers launched hundreds of strikes against San Fortunato Ridge and other parts of the German line. On September 18, the attacks on San Fortunato rose to a crescendo of 486 strikes by 24 light bombers, 228 medium bombers, and 234 fighter-bombers. Fighter-bombers alone dumped 128 tons of ordnance on the ridge. Tenth Army Chief of Staff Generalmajor Friedrich Wentzell reported that the massive Allied bombing of the ridge made it impossible for the German gunners to man their weapons. "And when the artillery is silenced fighting becomes a murderous mess," he complained.[27]

Despite the intensity of the fire that had backed up the two Carleton and York companies, they still found it impossible to cross the river because the Germans were holding in strength on the other side from fortified gun pits. With four of their six 12th Royal Tank Regiment tanks lost en route to mechanical breakdowns, one of the survivors was knocked out by an antitank gun just as it reached the riverbank. Crossing the river without help from an engineering unit was going to be impossible for any tanks because the wide streambed was cut down the centre by a steeply banked channel that formed a perfect tank obstacle.

Considering the Carleton and York Regiment safely on their objective, I Canadian Corps headquarters staff redirected the artillery and aerial cover back to 4th British Infantry Division. The German spotters on San Fortunato and San Martino crawled out of their holes, the gunners returned to their guns, and soon mortar and artillery fire began to rain down on the New Brunswick regiment. The resulting casualties were relatively light—six men killed and twenty wounded. At 1110 hours, the company commanders reported there were at least six tanks and many machine-gun positions ready to oppose any crossing. Major Jack Ensor estimated that the other riverbank "could not be cleared without 75 per cent casualties."[28]

But such a crossing was necessary, 3 CIB commander Lieutenant Colonel Pat Bogert told Ensor, in order to open the way for the assault on San Fortunato Ridge. Ensor replied that a daylight attack would "be suicidal alike for the infantry and for the sappers who would have to prepare the crossing."[29] Accepting Ensor's evaluation, Bogert ordered an attack just after nightfall and the construction of suitable tank crossings completed before dawn. Bogert promised heavy preparatory artillery fire to suppress the Germans holding the other riverbank.[30]

DESPITE THE CARLETON and York and PPCLI regiments reaching the Ausa on September 18, on the coastal plain between Rimini airfield and San Martino the 48th Highlanders of Canada and the Royal Canadian Regiment won only the slightest of advances. The Highlanders came face to face with a Panzerturm hidden in a farmhouse just three hundred yards from their front lines and no amount of artillery or mortar fire could silence the long-barrelled 75-millimetre Panther gun. The Highlanders hugged the ground out front of the gun and waited for nightfall.[31]

In the RCR sector, heavy casualties and the growing exhaustion of the men combined to hamper offensive operations. 'C' Company commander Major Rick Forgrave was so worn out, Lieutenant Colonel Jim Ritchie ordered him to take a forty-eight-hour rest. The officer walked back to regimental headquarters to spend the evening and get cleaned up before leaving for the rear the next morning.[32] Combining what was left of 'C' Company with his own 'A' Company, commander Captain J. Milton Gregg still had fewer men than would normally form a single company.

But Gregg detected a certain loosening ahead, and soon after a platoon under Lieutenant A.D. Egan captured a stone house the Germans had previously held with ferocious determination. Although the paratroopers counterattacked and wounded several of Egan's men, the platoon clung on until Gregg was able to reinforce them with the rest of his men.[33]

Meanwhile, Lieutenant Jimmy Quayle and his surviving scouts prowled the front, attempting to cause mayhem by sniping at the German positions. Quayle was creeping along the edge of Rimini airfield when a mortar bomb went off nearby. Metal fragments embedded his left leg and cut his forehead. "Apart from a slight limp, and some dramatic dried blood on my forehead," he later wrote, "I had no problems." Quayle refused evacuation not so much out of devotion to duty as out of fear of losing his special belongings, "particularly souvenirs like excellent German binoculars, a Luger pistol, a P-38 pistol and an Iron Cross. Theoretically your kit followed you back to hospital, but in practice it usually disappeared."[34]

As evening approached, RCR adjutant Captain Ted Shuter assumed temporary command of the regiment so that both the exhausted Ritchie and his second-in-command Major Strome Galloway could get some rest during what was anticipated to be an uneventful night. Radio traffic, which for many days and nights had been virtually constant and full of reports of desperate battle, suddenly hushed.[35] Wondering if the lack of activity might indicate that the paratroops were withdrawing, Shuter radioed Gregg at 2300 hours and asked that he send out a patrol. Gregg reported back at 0300 hours that the patrol had gone well forward without finding any enemy.[36]

Excited now, Shuter told Gregg to go as far forward with his entire company as possible before dawn. He then woke Ritchie and reported his actions. The lieutenant colonel grunted a couple of times by way of response and Shuter took this to mean his orders were endorsed.[37]

The RCR was not the only unit discovering that the paratroopers were falling back. At 0100 hours, a 48th Highlander patrol probed carefully up the slopes of San Martino expecting to trip an ambush. Instead, they got right through to the shattered ruins of the farm buildings there to be greeted only by a deadening silence. When Lieutenant Colonel Don Mackenzie learned that San Martino was empty, he immediately roused 'D' Company commander Lloyd Smith and told him to get his men up there. This time, the Germans would not be allowed to infiltrate back into the bastion without a fight. By dawn, Smith's men were dug in and San Martino was taken.[38]

The withdrawals by 1st Parachute Division were prompted by the advances I CID had gained on the left flank, particularly the Ausa River crossing made by the Carleton and York Regiment. At 2130 hours, 'D' and 'B' companies had moved down into the streambed just as the supporting artillery barrage lifted. They caught the Germans on the other side in the midst of a relief changeover and quickly scattered the disorganized opposition. By midnight, 'D' Company was dug in on the river's north bank and the engineers went to work with their bridging equipment.[39]

The necessary racket that No. 2 Platoon of 4th Field Company, Royal Canadian Engineers made with its mechanical equipment drew German artillery and mortar fire, but the work proceeded. Like the 10th Field Squadron a week earlier, 4th Field Company went into the bridging operation seriously depleted. This time, however, it had not been a German shell that had caught the engineers in the middle of forming up for breakfast. Rather, it was a bomb from a Kittyhawk that struck the church in which the sappers were preparing to take their morning meal. When the building collapsed, three men were killed and eight wounded.[40]

To build the river crossing, No. 2 Platoon had a D-4 bulldozer and a special bridging unit known as an Ark. This was a turretless Churchill with bridge decking built onto its body and long hinged steel ramps attached to either end. In this case, the incomplete Ark had only the rear ramp installed. As the sappers set to work, they were much assisted by the indirect illumination of searchlights once again lighting the night sky. They drove the Ark into the river channel and found its truncated span sufficient to bridge the river if the bulldozer cut the bank down on both sides to create adequate approaches. By 0320 hours, the engineers reported the crossing ready for traffic.[41]

BY DAWN OF SEPTEMBER 19, the Canadians were ready to finally mount a major attack against San Fortunato Ridge. Major General Chris Vokes ordered 2 CIB to assume a holding position while the West Nova Scotia Regiment expanded the Carleton and York Regiment's bridgehead and the Hastings and Prince Edward Regiment won another in front of the PPCLI. Once over the Ausa, both regiments were to push onto San Fortunato and clear that feature.[42] By day's end, Vokes wanted 1 CID firmly established on the heights of San Fortunato, ready to force a crossing of the Marecchia River and end this battle.

On the Canadian left, the 4th British Infantry Division had also crossed the Ausa and was consolidating its grip inside the major defensive fortifications of the Rimini Line at the extreme western end of San Fortunato Ridge. Farther inland, 1st British Armoured Division, 56th British Infantry Division, and 46th British Infantry Division were all either closing on or fighting through what constituted the final major German fortified line in Italy. The last section of the Gothic Line defence in depth was nearly broken. Once again, Eighth Army's commanders felt all it would take was one final hard shove to win entrance into the Po Valley.

That the entire army was worn out, both in physical and numerical strength, was not considered an impediment. Neither was the fact that the regiments given responsibility for carrying out the breakthrough had little idea of the state or strength of opposition they faced or the nature of the ground in which they must operate. Hastings and Prince Edward Lieutenant Colonel Don Cameron returned from the Orders Group at 3 CIB headquarters at 2045 hours on September 18 with orders that his men immediately march to battle. The start line was two miles away. While the soldiers gathered their battle packs, Cameron held a hasty forty-five-minute O Group with his company commanders. The entire attack plan was worked out purely by map consultation. There was no opportunity for on-the-ground reconnaissance.

Cameron had been warned he might have to fight for his start line on the Ausa's north bank, but that the main German defences were not expected to be met until he had crossed most of the 1,500 yards lying between the river and the base of San Fortunato Ridge. This was because the intervening ground was mostly grain fields that were completely commanded by the ridge. There were likely, however, to be some strong delaying forces dug in across the flat ground to ensure the defenders on the ridge had opportunity to brace to meet any attack.

Cameron decided to commit only two companies, 'A' and 'B', initially. His other two companies would remain at the start line and then leapfrog through the leading companies once they reached the base of the slope and set up a preliminary strongpoint there. Cameron thought it vital that his men be on the ridge "before light broke, as to be caught in the flat would prove extremely costly, therefore no 'mopping up' operations would be undertaken."[43] A squadron from the 48th Royal Tank Regiment would be in support. To help them cross the flats during the initial phase, 'A' and 'B' companies would follow a creeping barrage that lifted one hundred yards every six minutes.[44]

Throughout the briefing, Cameron kept his voice calm and moderated. He could have been discussing a simple militia training exercise back in Canada for all the anxiety his manner betrayed. When a newly assigned company commander, looking at the map and the open ground that must be covered, said, "Sir, we'll never make it," Cameron ignored him.[45] Orders finalized, the companies marched towards the Ausa River.

[30]

We'll All Be Heroes

THE HASTINGS and Prince Edward Regiment's 'A' and 'B' companies crossed the start line behind the creeping barrage on schedule at 0400 hours, September 19, after a night spent marching hard to get into position for the attack. Soon they were sweeping past empty trenches and unmanned machine guns. Not expecting a night attack, the 1st Parachute Division had pulled its men out of the valley and onto the ridge for a meal and some rest. Resistance was limited to a scattering of listening posts that the Hasty P's quickly pushed in. A few prisoners were disarmed and sent to the Canadian rear.

Hopes started running high that there would be no fight at all when the two forward companies reached the base of the ridge at 0530. Minutes earlier, Lieutenant Colonel Don Cameron had committed the two following companies into the plain to carry out their mission of passing through the leading companies and taking the ridge.[1] 'A' Squadron of the 48th Royal Tank Regiment, under command of Major J. Cromwell, bumped its Churchills across the Ark bridge in the Carleton and York Regiment's position and then started searching out in the plain for the infantry. The little valley was swathed in a thick cloud of smoke meant to screen the attack from German observation. While the smoke partially succeeded in this purpose, it also prevented the tankers from spotting the infantry companies that had spread out to avoid being detected by the enemy.[2]

The morning dawned brilliantly clear and the heat inside the tanks quickly became stifling. Despite the fine weather, the air pressure was lowering rapidly, which caused havoc with radio communication. The tankers' No. 18 sets stopped working, cutting them off from the Hasty P's. Every time either Cameron's tactical headquarters or the tank squadron commander tried calling the other on the No. 22 set, all they heard was a squall of static.[3]

Having realized they were under attack, the paratroopers were saturating the valley with artillery, mortar, and machine-gun fire. They also pushed men down the slope to meet the attack. The fire directed at 'B' Company's position on the left was so intense that 'C' Company was unable to pass through. Cameron ordered it to swing right and follow 'D' Company through 'A' Company's position.

The attack was staggering. Cameron worked frantically to maintain the momentum by bringing continuous artillery concentrations down on the ridge and cloaking the slope and valley in ever thickening layers of smoke. Finally, the tankers blundered upon the infantry and, with the artillery pounding the slope and ridge ahead, started climbing alongside 'D' Company.[4] Infantry and tanks clawed through shell-torn vineyards and orchards, while the British tankers anxiously remarked spotting several Tigers and self-propelled guns forming up on the very edge of the ridgeline to meet them.[5]

Moments later, one Churchill took a direct hit and started to burn. Then another died.[6] Others were falling by the wayside with thrown tracks or with tangles of the wire used to support grapevines jamming bogey wheels. 'D' Company reached a road running laterally across the slope and engaged a company-strength force of paratroopers dug in behind it. A short hand-to-hand fight was followed by a sudden German surrender. The Hasty P's had noticed on the way up the slope that whenever they closed with a pocket of resistance and a fight with bayonets, rifle butts, and fists seemed imminent that the paratroopers threw in the towel. This time, sixty prisoners were sent streaming down the hill. 'D' Company pressed on up the ever steepening slope, with the tanks now forced to use a single narrow track that switchbacked up the steep ridge face. Two hundred yards beyond the road, the infantry was finally halted by machine-gun fire. Left of

'D' Company, 'C' Company failed to get across the road before being forced to ground.[7]

The three remaining operable tanks pressed on alone until, at 1100 hours and just thirty yards from the ridgeline, a Faustpatrone knocked out the lead tank. Then the paratroopers swarmed the surviving Churchills. Tankers fought hand-to-hand to save their tanks and only narrowly managed to beat a hasty retreat to the comparative safety of a hull-down position behind a farmhouse near 'D' Company.[8] There was so little ammunition left for the main guns that the tankers reported they had to save these for their own defence.

Cameron, enjoying a momentary return of communications with the tankers, forwarded their ammunition needs to their brigade and asked for more tanks. Even with renewed munitions, two tanks were not going to be enough. He told his companies on the slope to dig in, but to be ready to advance again just before last light. The current 3rd Canadian Infantry Brigade plan was for the Hasty P's to push onto the ridge at dusk with the West Nova Scotia Regiment on the left flank. This, Cameron was assured, "would secure the whole feature and beyond on our front."[9]

Cameron was dubious because the West Novas were still in the valley, having barely left their start line. He figured the West Novas would still be trying to reach the base of the ridge when the Hasty P's had to try carrying the top. Back at brigade headquarters, a two-battalion attack might appear to be taking shape, but here at the front Cameron saw two regiments fighting individual battles.

There was another worry. On the maps, the regiment's final objective had appeared to be the ridgeline. But his two company commanders, who were on the slope just two hundred yards from the objective, reported that this position appeared to be a false summit completely dominated by the proper ridgeline. So even if his men got to the objective, Cameron doubted they would be able to hold it.[10]

They never had to try. Late in the afternoon, Cameron received word that "further tanks would not be forthcoming and that the [2nd Canadian Infantry Brigade] under heavy artillery support were going to infiltrate through to our right. This artillery plan, received on short notice, necessitated withdrawing from previous positions to clear the danger area."[11] When the shelling ended, the companies were to infiltrate back but not go any farther up the slope. The Hasty P's were to hold and let 2 CIB take over the advance.

In the valley, the West Novas had been pinned down three hundred yards north of their Ausa River start line. While the Hasty P's had attacked on schedule at 0400 hours, the West Novas had been an hour late.[12] This gave the Germans time to rush men from the ridge to their positions on the valley floor. As the two leading companies moved towards the river, they saw the enemy clambering into their forward gun positions. When the West Novas emerged from the Ausa channel, the Germans tore into them with close-range fire. No amount of smoke or artillery fire could suppress the enemy guns. Repeatedly, the infantry and tanks of 'C' Squadron, 48th Royal Tank Regiment tried and failed to push forward.

It soon became apparent "that the biggest thorn in the flesh of both infantry and tanks was a certain Tiger tank which moved about from fire position to fire position on the high ground above. One of its positions from which its spotted firing was practically unassailable was between two buildings protected in front by a brick wall, apparently some five or ten yards in front of the tank and below which the ground fell sharply. The only target which the Tiger presented was its gun barrel and the very top of the turret, which was just visible."[13]

By last light, the attack remained stalled and the regiment had suffered eighteen men killed and forty-five wounded.[14] The tanks, short of both ammunition and fuel, withdrew, leaving the West Novas to endure a night of intense shelling and mortaring in slit trenches zeroed in by the Germans.

AT 1600 HOURS, Vokes ordered 3rd Canadian Infantry Brigade to "exploit the success" of the Hasty P's by sending the Royal 22e Regiment to the left of the pinned- down West Nova Scotia Regiment to seize Villa Belvedere, a sprawling estate on the western flank of San Fortunato Ridge.[15] While the Van Doos distracted the Germans, 2 CIB's Loyal Edmonton Regiment would advance under cover of darkness onto the ridge between the West Novas and the Hasty P's. Rather than securing a strongpoint on the ridge itself, however, the

Eddies were to cross right over and split into two columns to capture the villages of San Lorenzo in Monte l'Abate and Le Grazie. Then they would advance across the flats beyond to win a bridgehead on the north bank of the Marecchia River. Once the Edmontons departed the ridge, the Seaforth Highlanders of Canada would follow through to the ridgeline and swing right to clear the Germans completely from the eastern flank.[16]

At no time did Vokes seriously turn his mind to developments on his right-hand flank and consider exploiting the glimmer of success realized there on September 19. His attention was entirely focused on bludgeoning a path over San Fortunato Ridge. Perhaps, however, this was due less to a failure to truly "exploit the success" won by one of his regiments than to the imposition of a political decision on his operations.

By dawn, the combined Royal Canadian Regiment company formed from the remnants of 'A' and 'C' companies was well north of the Rimini airfield. Captain J. Milton Gregg's men encountered only scattered opposition from forces obviously pulling back to Rimini or even the Marecchia River. From the city, the hard thumping sound of explosive demolitions indicated that the Germans were likely destroying anything deemed of tactical value preparatory to a withdrawal. Gregg's company was moving so fast he worried they might have moved north of the designated bomb line and be at risk of being strafed or bombed by the ever circling Desert Air Force planes. His radio had malfunctioned, so the captain was unable to contact headquarters to warn the planes off. When a couple of fighter-bombers roared low overhead to check the tiny force out, Gregg and his men dashed into a nearby house. Inside, they gathered up a stack of white bed sheets and threw these out on the road. Then the men hastily straightened and twisted sheets to etch out the letters CANADA. When the planes made a return pass, they waggled their wings and returned to their cab rank.[17]

Gregg's intrepid little band carried on and at 0610 hours were patrolling the outskirts of Rimini without finding any Germans. Realizing the city could fall with hardly a shot fired, Gregg sent a runner back to headquarters with the news while his men took up defensive positions in some houses.[18]

Back at RCR headquarters, adjutant Captain Ted Shuter, who had set the probe towards the city into action the previous night, was elated at the news. Orders were immediately issued for 'D' Company to move up on Gregg's left inside the city. 'B' Company's commander, Captain Len Courtin, was called back to headquarters to receive instructions to also move up to support the Rimini lodgement.[19]

It was 0730 hours and the officers at RCR headquarters were taking a few minutes to wash and shave while things were at a lull. Five officers and several other ranks were in the courtyard cleaning up. Shuter stood next to his friend, Captain Rick Forgrave, who was happily cleaning the muck of battle off his body and talking about his forthcoming forty-eight-hour rest period in Cattolica. Finished before Forgrave, Shuter playfully snapped a towel across the other officer's backside and then beat a hasty retreat into the headquarters to avoid Forgrave's legendary towel-snapping reflexive counterattack.[20] Suddenly a powerful explosion rocked the courtyard. A piece of shrapnel pierced Forgrave's skull. Lieutenant Jimmy Quayle had both legs and his right arm broken by the force of the blast, and shrapnel peppered his buttocks and thighs. Lieutenant Benny Potts took shrapnel in his chest and forehead. Courtin, who had just entered the courtyard en route to his briefing, had his face cut open in two places. Five other ranks suffered leg and back wounds. Everyone, except Courtin who was only slightly hurt, was quickly evacuated to the Regimental Aid Post.[21] A badly shaken Shuter realized that, had he not fled Forgrave's certain retaliation, he undoubtedly would have also been injured. Word came soon after that Forgrave's wounds had proved fatal.[22]

The cause of the explosion was never fully determined. While possibly the result of an incoming artillery or mortar round, the regiment's war diarist believed it was caused by someone accidentally triggering a loose grenade while moving it. The courtyard by this time was littered with packs and weapons belonging to evacuated wounded and a great deal of munitions was scattered about.[23]

While everyone was absorbing the shock of this tragedy, Shuter received a radio signal from brigade that rendered him speechless. He was to immediately direct Gregg's company to get out of Rimini and recall 'D' Company. Instead of stiffening the regiment's position in the city, the RCR was to withdraw from the coastal plain entirely to a holding position on San Martino. The 3rd Greek Mountain Brigade would occupy Rimini. Under no circumstances was any official record to mention RCR's foray into the city.*

Among the RCR, it was felt that an opportunity to achieve a decisive tactical gain was thrown away. The Greeks were neither in a position to quickly take over the RCR's line of advance nor inclined to vigorously engage the Germans. In the two weeks since coming into I Canadian Corps's front lines, the brigade had taken 314 casualties.[24] Like II Polish Corps, this brigade had no readily available source of reinforcements and such losses consequently reduced its combat effectiveness.

As Gregg's company tromped towards the northwest corner of Rimini airfield in order to swing left onto a road that would carry them to San Martino, it encountered a company of Greek soldiers huddled in the roadside ditch. Apparently startled by the appearance of about fifty men marching up the road straight at them from what was still reportedly German-controlled ground, the Greeks had taken cover. Gregg was unimpressed by the cautious pace of their advance.[25]

Had the RCR been allowed to mount an all-out attack on Rimini with support by the 48th Highlanders of Canada, the ancient Roman

---

* The decision that Rimini was to be "liberated" by the Greek brigade was made by Eighth Army and was intended to give this pro–Greek Monarchist unit a morale boost and also to generate support in Greece for the return of the monarchy after that nation's liberation from German occupation. Already, Greece was a focal point for conflict between a Soviet-backed Communist movement and the American-British backed monarchists. The RCR thus fell afoul of political manoeuvring. In fact, the length to which the military went to maintain the illusion that Canadian troops were never inside Rimini was extensive. All records were purged from official histories, except for the RCR's War Diary, which uses the codename 'Fulmar' for Rimini in its discussion of the orders given to Gregg's company and to 'D' Company prior to the order for those units to withdraw.

Ponte di Tiberio bridge spanning the Marecchia River could have been in 1st Canadian Infantry Brigade's hands by nightfall. Instead, the RCR marched eastward to occupy San Martino, while the Highlanders moved into the bridgehead over the Ausa that had been won on September 18 by the Princess Patricia's Canadian Light Infantry. Both were defensive moves intended to stabilize a front that was supposed to be ripped asunder that very night when 2 CIB and 3 CIB were to take San Fortunato Ridge.

AFTER IT MARCHED out of San Martino on the morning of September 18, Lieutenant Colonel Jean Allard had expected the Royal 22e Regiment to receive at least five days rest. The Van Doos were in rough shape, physically exhausted and badly depleted by casualties. What was needed was some time for officers and men to rest, eat decent meals, and clean themselves up. Instead, at 0530 hours on September 19, Allard received orders from 3 CIB headquarers to move up behind the attacking West Novas. Although asleep when this order arrived, Allard was still fully dressed. When his batman woke him and put the order in his hand, Allard immediately jumped into his jeep and drove back to brigade for an extensive briefing.

Lieutenant Colonel Pat Bogert, who had obviously delayed issuing Vokes's orders of almost twelve hours earlier in order to give the men a scant rest, was far from encouraging. The West Nova attack had faltered and the Hasty P's were in trouble. Then word came that the Van Doos were to carry out an assault. "That decision made me wonder," Allard later wrote. "We of the R22eR all believed that we had earned a good rest. We were now required to return to the front within six hours, in a sector where two battalions had just been broken. Disobeying orders was out of the question, but I quickly decided that, for my men, the time of the attack would be delayed as much as possible."[26]

Allard proceeded to the start line, where he found the situation of the brigade's other two regiments extremely confused. The West Novas seemed "in total disarray as a result of the complete failure of the attack it had attempted at dawn." The approaches across the valley that the Van Doos were to cross "were completely bare, more like a pool table than tactical terrain."[27] Allard asked for a delay, but

Vokes approved only a short one that would still necessitate a daylight advance. Allard pretended to accept this, but set about planning an attack at dusk.

'A' Squadron, 145th Royal Armoured Corps was assigned to support the Van Doos. Because he wanted a silent attack, Allard had no initial need for tanks. To ensure that a delay was necessary, Allard gave the 21st British Tank Brigade a false rendezvous point. At 1500 hours, he gathered his company officers together in a ditch one hundred yards behind the start line and briefed each man individually. 'A' and 'C' companies, under Major Henri Tellier and Major Fernand Trudeau respectively, would lead. Their target was a sumptuous estate on the western flank of San Fortunato Ridge, Villa Belvedere. Tellier's job was to secure a firm base on the road running in front of the villa, after which Trudeau would hook right around 'A' Company's position to seize the villa. 'B' Company would back 'A' Company up and Major Tony Poulin's 'D' Company provided the reserve.[28]

From the ditch, the company commanders enjoyed a good view of the ground to be crossed. The big villa was clearly visible on the skyline. "Do you see that house?" Tellier demanded of his platoon commanders. "That is our objective and this is the way we will go." He then traced out the route on the map while at the same time indicating physical points of reference on the ground itself.[29]

The planned artillery barrage started at 1550 hours, but Allard ordered no advance. Tellier and Trudeau had been told not to cross the start line until 1840 hours and just believed the artillery was softening the Germans up. Allard now reported to brigade that the tanks were late. When 'A' Squadron finally materialized at 1700 hours, Allard ordered the increasingly baffled tankers to conceal their Shermans and Churchills with camouflage nets in positions behind the cover of some buildings and await orders.[30]

Tellier thought the tanks could prove useful in the role of direct artillery, so he went over and asked the squadron commander to fire on the objective from the moment his company crossed the start line until he fired a Very light. At that time, the tankers should shift their fire well over the crest. To his men, Tellier said, concentrate on "speed, speed. Get through his [defensive fire]. Get close to him. Run until you are exhausted." Later he wrote: "The distance to be covered looked long and fearful." Villa Belvedere was just under a mile away, over half of this ground being up the ridge's steep slope.[31]

Just before 1830 hours, Allard reported that his attack had been unexpectedly delayed by the tardy arrival of the tanks and he would require the artillery concentrations repeated so that the attack could begin at 1840. As the shells resumed falling, the light of day was fast fading.[32]

Tellier's men sprinted across the start line. "Probably we did stop every three or four hundred yards to draw breath and cast an eye over our troops," he wrote, "but I remember only the running. The Germans spotted us as we started, but they could not be certain of our intentions, and we did make use of the dead ground, of which there was a fair amount beyond the flats as we began to climb. Whenever we passed a house, a couple of men were detached to chuck grenades into the window then to dash in one door, sweep the place with a Tommy gun if necessary and dash out another.... We went so fast that we kept ahead of the enemy [defensive fire], which chased us all the way up, but was always *behind* us. Only two men were wounded, and these were left behind, to be attended to later. I made no attempt at 'fire and movement' as such. Our fire was supplied by the tanks. All three platoons did the moving."[33]

As Tellier closed on the road, he could only see about twenty-five to thirty yards ahead. The men completed the last two-hundred-yard stretch "firing on the run and yelling like mad. It sounded as if a division were coming in."[34] Surprise was complete. Sentries had no time to sound the alarm before the Van Doos were in the defensive trenches rooting out dozing Germans or interrupting their meal. Eight men were captured in a trench, another sixteen in a small house. They were now past their original objective and closing on Villa Belvedere.

The right-hand platoon rushed the mansion and killed seven Germans manning a trench in front of it. "Then they put a bouquet of grenades into the house, at the same time yelling in Italian to anybody inside to come out and surrender. Apparently the inhabitants either understood Italian or the grenades, for out marched no fewer than forty-one armed enemy, including a captain."[35] Tellier set his tactical headquarters up in the villa and locked the Germans in the cellar.

Not all the Germans were so easily killed or captured. One of Tellier's privates, bayonet fixed on his rifle, rounded a tree and ran head on into a soldier coming out of a trench. Losing his rifle in the collision, the private kicked the German in the stomach. Unable to bring his Schmeisser to bear on the Van Doo, the German instead clubbed him on the head with the gun's butt. The force of the blow knocked the weapon from the German's hands, leaving both men with only their fists to fight with. As the two grappled, the private's section commander closed up with his Thompson machine gun, pressed the barrel against the side of the German's head, and blew it apart with a short burst.[36]

On Tellier's right, Trudeau's company had advanced by bounds from one preset objective to another. Each of these was a road junction, easily located in the gathering gloom. After passing the last preliminary objective, the right forward platoon went for a group of houses to the right of the already secured villa, while the left platoon filtered into some trees two hundred yards to the left of the mansion and mopped this area up.

Again the Germans had been surprised and the fighting was all at close quarters. More prisoners were taken at very little cost to the company.[37] By 2010 hours, Villa Belvedere was secure and 'B' Company was arriving on the objective. 'D' Company set out from the start line at 2340 hours with the regiment's antitank and medium-machine gun platoons in tow. This force arrived at 0210 hours on September 20.

For the past couple of hours, the two lead companies had been mopping up groups of Germans milling around in the woods, orchards, and vineyards. Because of the extent of the surprise achieved, the Germans had been unable to pull their support weapons out. They destroyed a Mark V Panther and an 88-millimetre gun in place.[38]

The Van Doos had achieved a stunning victory at very little cost. They also were the first Canadians to be firmly ensconced on San Fortunato Ridge. Most of the prisoners were identified as panzer grenadiers, with a few paratroopers mixed in. Allard warned the forward companies to expect a counterattack just before dawn or shortly thereafter.[39]

NOT ONLY THE Van Doos enjoyed success during the night of September 19–20. The Loyal Edmonton Regiment moved off from the edge of the Ausa River at 2100 hours, with the scout platoon leading 'D' Company onto the ridge. The company was to follow a path through the saddle that bisected the eastern and western high points of San Fortunato Ridge. The ridge itself contained about two thousand acres of vineyards, fields, and orchards crisscrossed by roads, many of them sunken. While the southern and western slopes to the summit were steep, to the north and east they fell away gently to the level plains beyond. Although only about 160 feet high, the last significant point of high ground on the north slope was topped by the hamlet of San Lorenzo in Monte l'Abate—the Edmontons' final objective. From the base of the south slope of San Fortunato Ridge to San Lorenzo was about 2,500 yards. The village itself was inconsequential, just a few little houses. But there was a large stone high-steepled church that dominated the northern slope of the ridge, which would serve as a defensible bastion and observation point.

'D' Company was to cover most of the intervening distance before stopping at a road junction, codenamed Bovey, and forming a firm base through which 'B' Company would pass and continue on to seize the hamlet, codenamed Moire. 'A' and 'C' companies would then come up and dig in on either flank of 'B' Company.[40]

Things started badly, as 'D' Company was shelled while forming up and had seven men wounded. Under command of Major F.H. McDougall, the company nonetheless got off on time. Travelling with it was a section of engineers whose services were soon required to clear strings of box mines that barred the company's path. By 2220 hours, these obstacles had been cleared and the company was moving again. The Germans seemed unaware of their presence. When 'D' Company came up on the ridge, it passed the scout platoon. Because the rifle companies would be moving over the horizon, it was expected that radio contact between the regimental headquarters and the company would be lost. The scouts were carrying a No. 18 set and were to set up a relay station on the ridgeline to maintain communications.[41]

Like many plans, this one failed immediately after 'D' Company passed the scouts and disappeared into the darkness. The scouts could raise neither the company nor headquarters on their radio. Lieutenant Colonel Budge Bell-Irving and his staff were left to fret and anxiously wait for any kind of news.

Meanwhile, 'D' Company moved carefully through the confusing terrain, trying to stay on course by use of compasses. Shortly after the company crossed the road running between San Fortunato and Villa Belvedere, its platoons became separated. The radios all failed and runners sent by each platoon to find the others ended up wandering lost. After finally linking up with each other, two platoons strayed into a German position. A sharp firefight left Lieutenant H.F. "Fritz" Hanson dead and Lieutenant J.S. Wood wounded. After breaking contact with the enemy, Lieutenant L.E. Taplin managed to get his radio working and relayed the news of the fight to Bell-Irving. He also said that Major McDougall was believed with the third platoon and "lost to them."[42]

Taplin was instructed to assume command of the two platoons, reorganize, and clear San Fortunato village instead of pressing on to the objective—it being thought that the company was now too weak to succeed in its original task. 'B' Company, by this time, had also passed over the ridgeline and vanished from the radio net. Its location was unknown.[43] At 0210 hours, however, radio contact was re-established and 'B' Company reported reaching Bovey and finding McDougall there with fifteen men.[44]

Heartened by this news, Bell-Irving reversed his earlier order to Taplin and urged him instead to press on to Bovey and reunite with 'D' Company. Captain John Dougan, whose 'C' Company had arrived on the ridgeline and engaged in a futile search for the scout platoon, was directed to jump through the two forward companies and secure San Lorenzo. 'B' Company and what was left of 'D' Company would dig in and establish a strongpoint on Bovey. 'A' Company, so badly beaten up during the previous failed San Martino operation that it fielded barely two platoons, remained at headquarters.[45]

Like the R22eR's Major Henri Tellier, Dougan believed speed would prove the key to success. This was no time for cautiously probing through the dark. If 'C' Company did that, the Germans would have time to throw an ad hoc defensive line between Bovey and San Lorenzo. With barely sixty men, Dougan knew he lacked the strength to fight through any determined defensive force.

Once again the searchlights were blazing to the west, this time reflected back to earth by bouncing the beam off a covering of cloud that had crept in early that evening. The resulting soft glow improved visibility enough for the men to move more quickly than would normally be possible.

No amount of artificial moonlight, however, could rationalize the reality of the ridge's terrain with what his map depicted. Finally, Dougan halted his men next to a little farmhouse and stepped inside to consult the map with a carefully hooded flashlight. The map and terrain remained at odds. There was supposed to be a road running to Bovey and from there to San Lorenzo. It was probably out there somewhere, but not near Dougan's position.

Blundering around in the dark with sixty men was asking for trouble, so, leaving the company at the house, he and his batman set off to reconnoitre the area. They soon stumbled upon a sunken road that the compass showed ran north to south. The two men walked carefully up it, listening for sounds. All Dougan heard was the soft muttering of voices coming from caves pocking the twenty-foot-high banks on either side of the track. Everyone in the caves seemed to be speaking Italian. Dougan thought they were civilians hiding in the scant shelter of holes dug to escape the heavy Allied bombardments. But he also knew that this kind of road was ideal for use by the Germans as a shelter or defensive position. The sound of gunfire up ahead told him that the other two companies were probably fighting to hold Bovey. He needed to get there quickly.

Time and again, Dougan had noted that the Germans were such creatures of doctrine they seldom could respond to any action that was unexpected or appeared illogical in terms of tactics. At Ortona, Dougan had led the first Edmonton platoon into the town's outskirts by charging up a ditch bordered on either side by open ground swept by machine guns. If the Germans had positioned a single machine gun at their end of the ditch, the platoon would have been slaughtered. But the paratroopers defending Ortona had never expected anyone to be crazy enough to use the ditch for an approach. Dougan had got into the town without losing a man and won the fight for control of the outskirts.

"Do the unexpected," he thought. "And do it quickly." Rushing back to the farmhouse, the captain told his men: "We're going to move very quietly. Don't speak. Don't shoot at anything and we may have a chance to get through. If we're successful, we'll all be heroes. If not, we'll all be dead."[46]

The company moved quickly up the sunken road without encountering any Germans, just a few Italians who poked heads warily out of their caves and then ducked back inside at the sight of the passing Canadians. 'C' Company emerged from the sunken road at an intersection with a road that led down to Bovey. As the infantry came astride the intersection, a Tiger tank clanked down the opposite slope and headed towards Bovey. Dougan's PIAT man tried to bring the weapon to bear, but the tank rolled out of range.

With the tank now between him and Bovey, and the road following a spine of ground that would leave his men silhouetted in the false moonlight, Dougan led his men down the west slope of the spine into a patch of bamboo that provided good cover. The company then circled northwest through the bamboo to come up on the road on the other side of Bovey. As they approached the road, Dougan signalled No. 13 Platoon off to the left and took the other two platoons to the right.

No sooner had the company split up than a column of men came marching up the road towards Bovey from San Lorenzo. Seeing coal-scuttle helmets, Dougan knew they were Germans. They were just forty yards away. The captain could see No. 13 Platoon getting into position beside the road to the front of the marching column and knew its commander would automatically form an anvil, while the men with him became the hammer in a classic ambush operation. No. 13 Platoon let the column almost into its midst before slamming the Germans in the front ranks with withering fire. At the same moment, Dougan brought his two platoons out of the road in a line and charged. Surprise was total. One German turned and started raising his gun towards Dougan, but the captain butt-stroked him to the ground. Most of the other Germans threw down their guns and surrendered. A few were killed, while a small number fled into the orchards on the other side of the road and disappeared into the night. Three officers were among the prisoners.[47]

'C' Company marched its prisoners up to Bovey, where at 0330 hours they found 'B' Company and the single platoon of 'D' Company. The other two platoons from 'D' Company had yet to arrive. As the company commanders started reorganizing and determining who would guard the prisoners, the Tiger tank Dougan had seen earlier rolled towards them. Some of the men brought up PIATS, but against the heavy armoured front the weapons would be useless. Sergeant H.O.W. Powell had what was needed. In his pack were several No. 75 Hawkins antitank grenades that he quickly armed and scattered across the road in a loose string. Intended to blow the tracks off tanks, the Hawkins grenades were fitted with a crush igniter fuse that set off an explosive charge when the tracks ground over the grenade.

The Tiger triggered one grenade and broke a track. Powell, now armed with a PIAT, circled behind the Tiger and fired a charge at its less heavily armoured rear. The round glanced off harmlessly. After reloading, Powell calmly advanced to within fifteen feet of the Tiger and punched a round through a weak chink in its armoured hide. Moments later, the crew bailed out and surrendered.[48]

Once the tank was dealt with, 'C' Company headed for San Lorenzo. A short distance from the objective, Dougan sent the lead platoon forward to probe the German strength. The platoon commander sent a runner back saying San Lorenzo was unoccupied. Dougan rushed the rest of the company in and established a strongpoint in the church and several of the houses. Because the Germans could come at him from any side, he faced men in every direction. It was 0430 hours and Dougan quickly realized he had secured the objective just in time, for coming up the road from the north was another German column obviously sent to occupy the village. Dougan strung his Bren gunners out to face them from covered positions. "Our Bren gunners had a grand time," he wrote later, "mowing them down right and left."[49]

Twenty minutes later, another counterattack struck from the west, with the Germans trying to infiltrate through the dense undergrowth on that flank. But Dougan had established radio contact with the Edmonton headquarters and was able to call artillery down. The shelling broke the counterattack before it began.

The sun was starting to rise and Dougan could see that the church was a shelled-out ruin. But he also saw that San Lorenzo was a "beautiful location" offering a 360-degree panoramic view over the German positions. To the north stretched the wide-open expanse of the Po Valley. In every other direction lay the German defensive positions on the northern slopes of San Fortunato Ridge. There were five Tiger tanks among the houses of Monticello, midway between the base of the ridge and the Marecchia River. Dougan hoped they remained unaware of his little band's presence. He had nothing with which to fight them.[50]

The Edmonton presence on San Fortunato Ridge was extremely precarious—less than two hundred riflemen concentrated in two isolated pockets more than two thousand yards inside German territory. Both Dougan and McDougall in their respective little outposts could hear tanks prowling around on their flanks, but were uncertain whether this meant the tankers knew their whereabouts. Their radio reports back to headquarters alarmed Major Jim Stone. If the tanks rustled up some infantry and seriously attacked Bovey and San Lorenzo, the positions would be overrun.

'C' Squadron, 145th Royal Armoured Corps was trying to move up the forward slope of the ridge to reach Bovey, but the tanks were having a tough time. Several had already thrown tracks on the steep grade and the rest were crawling painfully towards the ridgeline. They would be hours getting through, even if they were to escape being shot up by the Germans.

Never comfortable in the role of being regimental second-in-command—a duty that required long hours of administrative paperwork in the relative safety of headquarters—Stone decided he should directly help his rifle companies. He gathered the antitank platoon under Captain George Brown and had it hook one six-pounder up to a truck and another to a Bren carrier. With Stone in the lead vehicle, the small force headed up a narrow road leading to the ridgeline. It was another of the seemingly crazy gambles in which Stone and Dougan specialized. But Stone believed the odds tilted in his favour. The day before he had conducted a lone reconnaissance up onto the ridge and had discovered the same sunken road Dougan had used. His assessment had also been that the Germans had failed to tie the route into their defensive system. Instead, it was an open hole the bold might penetrate.[51]

This proved the case. At 0700 hours, Stone's antitank force pulled into Bovey without incident.[52] Their arrival, however, immediately drew the attention of a self-propelled gun lurking on the ridge above the Edmonton position. Its fire knocked out the two vehicles. Under the direction of Sergeant Bill Ross, the crews pushed the guns into safe positions from which they kept the SPG at bay and also engaged other German targets. The guns started shooting at German infantry and vehicle targets. Perhaps the most lucrative target was a battery of horse-drawn field guns, which the gunners prevented from escaping until they could be destroyed by fighter-bombers.[53] Ross's courageous efforts in moving the guns to safety earned him a Military Medal, while Stone took home a Distinguished Service Order, and Dougan added a bar to the Military Cross he had won in Sicily. Stone was pleased that his gamble had paid off, but he also knew the risk had been somewhat less than it might first seem. As his force had headed up the ridge, more Canadians had been moving up the slopes into the face of the German positions and forcefully brushing them aside. By mid-morning of September 20, control of San Fortunato Ridge had shifted decisively into Canadian hands.

[31]

The Gallant Attackers

AT 0220 HOURS on September 20, Lieutenant Colonel Syd Thomson was ordered to extend the Loyal Edmonton Regiment's foothold with a three-company assault in one hour's time against the eastern heights of San Fortunato Ridge. Thomson put the Seaforth Highlanders of Canada's 'D' Company out front, followed by 'B' Company, and then 'C' Company, with instructions to move up to the ridgeline immediately to the right of the Edmonton route and then hook around the rear of San Fortunato village. From here it would advance northeast to the village of Le Grazie, situated on the ridge's eastern edge.

Major Davey Fulton, the twenty-eight-year-old son of a British Columbia Member of Parliament and grandson of a former B.C. premier, commanded 'D' Company. His lead platoon was crossing the ridgeline when a German soldier popped up and fired a Faustpatrone. The exploding round caused eight casualties and smashed the platoon's single PIAT launcher.

When Fulton deployed his other platoons to the right to outflank the German position from which the Faustpatrone had erupted, they came under close-range machine-gun fire. Determined to prevent the attack bogging down, Fulton sent Sergeant Thomas Roberts to find a route around the German left flank. By 0430 hours, the sergeant guided the two leading companies in a sideslip move that turned the flank of the strong German position. Quickly reforming so that 'D'

Company was on the left and 'B' Company on the right, the Seaforths moved down the ridgeline in a two-company-wide assault that carried them through the few pockets of German resistance. By dawn, the Seaforths were firmly in control of Le Grazie.

When Fulton's company had been temporarily blocked on the ridgeline, Thomson had ordered 'C' Company to break away from the attack line, follow the highway parallelling the base of the ridge for about one thousand yards, and then swing up to seize a road junction west of Le Grazie. This objective was named Covignano. Having been badly mauled at San Martino, 'C' Company was hardly fit for combat. Just a few hours before Major Haworth Glendinning learned he was to go into an attack, the company commander had been trying to integrate twenty-four reinforcements into his depleted ranks. Two of these were platoon commanders—lieutenants S. Dickinson and J.H.F. Mara. Glendinning hastily arranged for the reinforcements to be armed, equipped, fed, and then shuffled into the platoons.

Lieutenant Mara, commanding No. 13 Platoon, led the advance along the road. After advancing just a short distance, the leading section came under mortar fire and Private J.H. Bohan was killed. Mara's men pressed on, fighting their way through a long string of houses bordering the road.[1] Then they started climbing up to the ridgeline, with Lance Corporal D.G. Skinner's section in the lead. When heavy machine-gun and rifle fire came from a house to the section's front, Skinner led his men into a draw and crept up on the building's blind side. The small force jumped the eight Germans inside and killed them with rifle fire and grenades. Skinner set his section inside the building, which provided a good position to cover 'C' Company's right flank during its uphill advance.[2]

Skinner's covering operation allowed Glendinning to attack Covignano crossroads. While the two inexperienced lieutenants spread their platoons in a line to keep the Germans occupied with gunfire, Glendinning took No. 14 Platoon and conducted a wide sweeping movement to get behind the enemy. Having set this platoon in the German rear, the major ran back to his other two platoons. Along the way he encountered a wounded Seaforth signaller, hefted the man over his shoulder, and carried him four hundred yards to safety.

By the time Glendinning reached the platoons, Skinner was desperately trying to stave off a fierce counterattack. If he lost the building, the right flank of the two platoons would be exposed to murderous fire. The little house was rocking from direct mortar hits and machine guns were ripping bursts through the windows and doors. One German crawled up close to the house and started blasting it with Faustpatrones. Skinner climbed out the back of the house, crawled around to where he could see the German, and killed him with a burst from his Thompson. Returning to the building, he continued to lead his men in fighting off one counterattack after another from 0830 to 1130 hours, maintaining the critical protection of Glendinning's flank until the Germans withdrew. For his action, Skinner was awarded the Distinguished Conduct Medal.

Glendinning meanwhile had set his anvil-and-hammer attack into motion, with the first two platoons serving as the hammer and No. 14 Platoon waiting in the German rear to be the anvil. The Germans were stunned by the ferocity of the Seaforth attack and forty surrendered almost the moment the two platoons charged. They pushed on, rooting Germans out of dugouts, until linking up with No. 14 Platoon. The final bag in this short operation was fifty-two German prisoners. They also captured a small hospital where a doctor and three orderlies were treating twenty-four wounded.

Opposition virtually collapsed and Glendinning's men pushed on to Covignano without further delay, scooping up another twenty prisoners en route. With the crossroads secure at 1130 hours, Glendinning sent a runner to bring Skinner's section in and soon the company was snug on its objective. In addition to the prisoners taken, Glendinning estimated they had killed another fifteen to twenty Germans. The company had suffered only one man killed and another wounded. It was a masterful operation and one that earned Glendinning a Distinguished Service Order.[3]

WHILE THE SEAFORTHS settled into a triangular-shaped defensive position that largely controlled the eastern flank of San Fortunato Ridge, the Royal 22e Regiment had fought to hold Villa Belvedere on the western flank. Using the cover of darkness, the Germans had established snipers in trees growing close to 'C' Company's position on the regiment's northwestern flank. The sniper fire directed at Major Fernand Trudeau's platoons was so heavy and accurate that any movement in 'C' Company's perimeter became almost impossible. Trudeau reported that his men were pinned down.[4]

The situation quickly became chaotic when the Germans struck the company with antitank and heavy machine-gun fire from positions to their front. Trudeau pulled back to reorganize, but was unable to withdraw one platoon of about fifteen men under Lieutenant P. Larochelle. This platoon holed up inside a little house next to a substantial mansion and was soon surrounded and in imminent danger of being overrun.

When Trudeau reported his situation to Lieutenant Colonel Jean Allard, the Van Doo commander immediately radioed 'D' Company's Major Tony Poulin and ordered a counterattack on the Germans threatening Larochelle's position. Poulin, who had only fifty men and was in a position well south of Trudeau's company, looked up the slope. He could hear Larochelle's men firing like mad to keep the Germans at bay and see the building they were in. A long swath of steeply rising open ground lay between. Trudeau's other platoons were down by Major Henri Tellier's 'A' Company on the left flank and a lot closer to the action. Poulin wondered why the hell Allard ordered him to counterattack, rather than Trudeau. It was Trudeau's platoon, after all, that had been abandoned and the 'C' Company commander at least had some idea of the ground. However, orders were orders.

Poulin had two choices. He could charge right up the hill to Larochelle's house or he could set off on a wide sweep to the left to strike the Germans in the rear. The first option was obviously suicidal, the second only somewhat less so. To balance the odds, Poulin hooked one of the six-pound antitank guns to a jeep. His company then began a long trek to the west that took them behind a line of trees and up a steep slope to the top of the ravine. His men had to push the jeep and gun up the last long, steep grade. Once they were astride the ridgeline, Poulin unhooked the gun and brought it to bear on the Germans surrounding Larochelle's house. So far he had escaped detection. It was a cool, cloudy day but every man was dripping sweat. The major told ten men to position themselves so they looked down the reverse slope of San Fortunato towards the Po Valley. "Keep your eyes open," he cautioned, "and shoot like hell if anything happens."[5] The gunners were told to open up in support the moment the Germans started opposing Poulin's attack.

From the ridgeline to where the German positions were formed around Larochelle's house, the ground was sparsely vegetated and flat. Poulin knew he could do nothing but dash across it and hope to close with the enemy before they saw the forty Van Doos coming. They went down the hill quietly, almost sprinting. By the time the Germans realized they were being attacked, 'D' Company was on top of them. The enemy fled into a house, but Poulin was ready for that. He had a man with a PIAT rip into it with an explosive charge that marked it for the antitank gun on the ridge. The gunners slammed the house with one round after another, "knocking it asunder." After a few minutes, the Germans still alive inside were signalling a desire to surrender. The PIAT man had meanwhile destroyed the enemy antitank gun, finishing the German resistance. Poulin hardly considered it a victory, however. He had gone into the attack with only three platoon and section leaders and the best of these had been killed by a machine-gun burst.[6]

The counterattack against the Van Doos was part of a desperate last-ditch German attempt to regain San Fortunato Ridge. But the situation was hopeless. From his position in San Lorenzo's church, Loyal Edmonton Regiment Captain John Dougan made it impossible for the Germans to reinforce the defenders on the ridge. Anytime he saw enemy forces gathering in the Po Valley, he directed artillery fire onto their heads.

On all sides of San Lorenzo, German troops and vehicles were trying to escape from the ridge. He counted twenty-four self-propelled guns or tanks rolling by at ranges varying from four hundred to a thousand yards, all in flight.[7] Then a sixty-strong party of German infantry emerged from an orchard and marched boldly down the slope with a white flag flying overhead. Still heavily armed, these Germans were retreating rather than surrendering. Dougan's men tore into the column with small-arms fire and inflicted heavy casualties.[8]

'C' Company's exposed position remained dangerous, however, for the British tanks had still not arrived and everyone was critically low on ammunition. Dougan feared that he might have to withdraw when an unusual source of help arrived in the form of two surrendering German soldiers, who told him that they had abandoned a Red Cross half-track in a gully below San Lorenzo. Thinking the half-track could be used to evacuate his wounded, Dougan had some men take the surrendered German driver and retrieve the vehicle. Inside the half-track they found a cache of about one thousand .303-calibre rounds that were useless to the Germans but exactly what the Canadians needed for their Lee Enfields and Bren guns. 'C' Company was back in business.[9] The half-track was used to shuttle the wounded, both Edmontons and German prisoners, from San Lorenzo and Bovey back to the Regimental Aid Post. Returning from the third trip to the RAP, a shell killed the German driver and knocked out the half-track.[10]

By noon, the German resistance on San Fortunato Ridge consisted of only scattered pockets of fanatics. The entire defensive line was collapsing as more Canadian regiments and British tank squadrons attacked the ridge. The badly shot-up West Nova Scotia Regiment had struck again at first light. This time, with the Van Doos having seized the ground to the left and the Seaforths clearing the right flank, the leading companies met only weak resistance and were able to quickly secure their objective—Palazzo Paradiso, another country estate like Villa Belvedere.[11] To the rear of the Seaforths, the Hastings and Prince Edward Regiment mopped up the Germans caught between the two companies.

Lieutenant General Tommy Burns, I Canadian Corps's commander, realized at noon that the battle for San Fortunato Ridge had been won by "the gallant attackers—every battalion of whom had suffered repulse and heavy casualties in the actions against San Martino and in the plain they now looked back upon."[12] It was time to exploit the success.

At 1330 hours, 2nd Canadian Infantry Brigade commander

Brigadier Graeme Gibson ordered the Princess Patricia's Canadian Light Infantry to advance with 'B' Squadron 48th Royal Tank Regiment in support to San Lorenzo. From there, they were to force a bridgehead over the Marecchia River.[13] When the combined infantry and tank force reached San Lorenzo at 1500 hours, Dougan warned its commanders about the five Tiger tanks still in Monticello. His attempts during the day to knock these out with artillery or air strikes had proved fruitless and they were so positioned as to be able to block any daylight attack across the open plain.

The British squadron commander deployed his Churchill troop behind the ridge with instructions to simultaneously roll into firing positions and attempt to hit the Tigers with armour-piercing shot. His Sherman troops were similarly positioned with instructions to fire high-explosive shells on the buildings that the Germans were using for protection. Each tank was to fire only one round at a time and then quickly pull back to cover before the Germans could retaliate. On the first attempt, one of the tanks scored a hit, but it was unclear if the Tiger was knocked out. The Churchills moved to new positions and popped up for another try. This time, one of the Tigers slammed an 88-millimetre shell into a Churchill. Although it failed to penetrate, the crew was stunned by the tremendous concussion. Although the British tankers kept this firefight going until nightfall, the Tigers never budged.[14]

If the PPCLI were to win a bridgehead over the river, it would have to do so under the cloak of darkness.

"SOMETHING UNPLEASANT has happened," Tenth Army's Generaloberst Heinrich von Vietinghoff told Commander-in-Chief Southwest Generalfeldmarschall Albert Kesselring at 1100 hours on September 20.[15] Less than two hours earlier, he had reported that the night's activities had resulted in no serious Canadian advances. Now he had to confess the loss of San Fortunato Ridge. The defending divisions were retreating in disarray and there had been heavy casualties.

Most of those losses were men taken prisoner, rather than killed. The Canadian prison cages were bursting. The Seaforths alone had taken 214 prisoners by 1400 hours.[16] The Van Doos also reported capturing more than 200 Germans and the Edmontons had another 300 in the cage at regimental headquarters. They reported having killed or wounded 150 Germans.[17] During mopping-up operations, the Hasty P's bagged 112 soldiers and killed about 40 more.[18]

LXXVI Panzer Corps commander General der Panzertruppen Traugott Herr wanted to pull his artillery north of the Marecchia, for some of his batteries were under direct machine-gun fire. Thinking Herr was once again succumbing to defeatism, Kesselring refused. He needed to consult first with his staff. Tenth Army Chief of Staff, Generalmajor Friedrich Wentzell, discussed the matter by phone with his counterpart at Kesselring's headquarters, Generalleutnant Army Group Chief of Staff Hans Röttiger. The situation on the Adriatic coast, he said, was "very strained." The 29th Panzer Grenadier Division had been practically wiped out on San Fortunato Ridge and the 162nd Turcoman division had disintegrated. Things were little better for the 1st Parachute Division or 26th Panzer Division. "I think it will be necessary to withdraw behind the river," he concluded.

"Yes, there is nothing else to do," Röttiger agreed. He asked Kesselring for permission to give the order. A moment later, the chief of staff said, "The Field Marshal agrees."

Although he knew the withdrawal necessary, Kesselring despaired of the consequences. "I have the terrible feeling that the thing is beginning to slide," he confided to his diary that evening.[19] There was no expectation that his torn-up divisions would be able to offer serious resistance from behind the Marecchia. The best he could hope for was to buy a little time. Time for the rains to come. Kesselring knew his best remaining defence was mud, mud to mire the inevitable Eighth Army armoured advance into the Po Valley. But the weather was unpromising. German meteorologists reported that the rains were two weeks late. And two weeks might be sufficient to allow the Allied tanks to drive the Germans back to Bologna or even farther.[20]

AT 0230 HOURS on September 21, a single infantry regiment moved cautiously out onto the marshy plain and headed towards the Marecchia. The PPCLI constituted not only the point of I Canadian Corps, but also the entire Eighth Army. They were pitifully few.

Lieutenant Syd Frost had rejoined the regiment on September 19 and been given command of a platoon in Captain Sam Potts's 'D' Company. Even after taking in some reinforcements, the company mustered only sixty men. Frost's No. 18 Platoon was twenty-one strong. The other companies and platoons were in similar straits.

Despite the collapse of the German forces on San Fortunato Ridge, the regiment's passage through to Bovey had not gone unchallenged. They were heavily shelled and mortared. By 1600 hours on September 20, Frost's platoon had lost two men. Of the remaining nineteen, two had slight wounds he worried would fester and another seemed to be suffering from malaria. None of the three would agree to be evacuated.

Frost had an additional worry. He had come to the regiment unarmed and had yet to find a gun. When he finally stumbled across a Thompson lying next to a dead PPCLI section leader, he was unable to get the bolt action to move. Figuring a gun that didn't work was better than nothing, Frost kept the weapon.[21]

The PPCLI had originally been ordered to occupy Monticello with two companies and establish a base of fire to support the bound to the river. With the village still presumably held by five Tiger tanks and undoubtedly some covering infantry, Lieutenant Colonel R.P. "Slug" Clark decided to bypass it. The leading companies would head instead for a little cluster of white buildings standing close to the river that was codenamed Pique. 'B' and 'D' companies were to secure this objective and then 'A' Company would pass through and effect the river crossing. It was a mile from Bovey to Pique, all crossing open ground.[22]

No. 18 Platoon led the way into the valley. As they moved out, it started to rain. Walking along, Frost tried distractedly to fix the Thompson. Finally, after an hour on the move, he threw the useless gun into a ditch. At that very moment, a guttural voice sounded ahead of him. Then a tank engine started, followed by another and yet another. The weaponless Frost jumped into the ditch, his men following suit while the tanks clanked off into the night towards the river.

'D' Company carried on, moving ever more cautiously as they drew closer to Pique. At 0445 hours, Frost's leading section commander materialized out of the soggy blackness and tapped him on the shoulder. He reported that they were almost on Pique. The man pointed out a white shape ahead that the lieutenant realized was indeed a building. Leaving one section behind with the two-inch mortar to cover their advance, Frost took the other two sections forward and found the buildings abandoned.

The two companies set up a defensive perimeter among the houses and Captain Potts tried to radio back that the leading companies were on the objective, but was jammed by static. Potts kept trying and finally reached Lieutenant Colonel Clark at 0545 hours.[23] 'A' Company set off immediately from Bovey towards Pique.

Major E.W. Cutbill and his company crossed the Marecchia at 0950 hours and took up a position astride Highway No. 9 running from Rimini inland to Cesena. The company came under sporadic shelling, but there was no response by either German infantry or armoured units. Clark ordered 'D' Company to move up to a position seven hundred yards west of 'A' Company.[24]

Frost was starting to feel the effects of lack of sleep when Potts told him the company was to cross the river. His men looked dead on their feet. Little wonder, they had been under almost constant shelling since September 16, whereas he had been in the front lines less than forty-eight hours. Still, the platoon gathered its gear and formed up without a word of complaint. "A great bunch of lads," he thought.[25]

Moments before the company set off, a Bren carrier came slipping and sliding up the muddy road from the direction of San Fortunato Ridge. The men inside had brought ammunition and, to Frost's delight, some extra weapons. Frost slammed a clip into a Thompson and headed towards the Marecchia.

The river was a wide, stony bed with only a little water running down a series of shallow channels separated by sand and gravel beds. But 'D' Company never had to get its feet wet, for the Germans had neglected to blow a wooden bridge spanning the channel. The soldiers ran across it and dug in frantically on the other side, expecting any moment to be shelled or counterattacked. Potts told them to get up and start moving again, this time to the highway. Frost's men were beginning to stagger with exhaustion.

By now, the Germans were throwing some artillery and Nebelwerfer fire their way, but it was still desultory. Finally, the roadway appeared ahead and Frost shouted at his section leaders to seize a white house and assume defensive positions around it. Firing from the hip, the platoon moved forward by sections with one covering the bound of the others. As the leading section stormed into the house, three Germans jumped out a back window waving a white flag and then clasped their hands behind their heads in surrender. Inside were two dead Germans and two others who were wounded. It was 1225 hours.

'D' Company's left flank was completely exposed to some other houses gathered alongside the road. German infantry in these buildings started harassing the company with small-arms fire. When Potts called an artillery concentration down on the buildings, the firing abruptly ceased. Frost set his headquarters up in the house he had stormed and positioned his sections to provide an all-round defence. Although he had two PIATS covering the road, Frost knew he would have little chance against an attack by Tigers. He also had too few men to send the German prisoners back under guard.

That problem resolved itself a few minutes later when the company started being shelled by 88-millimetre guns. Two of Frost's men were slightly wounded by shrapnel. He had them take the prisoners and go back for medical treatment. This left Frost with seventeen men. The whole company was barely fifty strong. Potts and Frost were the only officers left.[26] But 'D' and 'A' companies were across the Marecchia and, although they were unaware of it, by dusk another Canadian regiment was approaching their right flank.

THE 48TH HIGHLANDERS of Canada had received orders in the mid-morning to advance to the immediate west of Rimini, establish a bridgehead over the Marecchia, and capture Celle. This hamlet was situated at the junction of the coastal highway and Highway No. 9—an important objective for controlling the immediate northern approaches to Rimini. 'D' Company, under Captain Lloyd Smith, led off at 1000 hours with 'B' Company in trail. From their start point at the Ausa River to Celle was about two and a half miles. The regiment's diarist noted that "the weather was wet and the rain blowing in gusts, making the work all the more uncomfortable for the men."[27]

It was a rapid advance, slowed only by the presence of minefields and demolished crossings over the many little streams that were filling rapidly with runoff. At 1715 hours, Smith's company was on the banks of the Marecchia and Lieutenant Colonel Don Mackenzie ordered it across. Forty-five minutes later, Smith reported his company was over the river and had met no resistance. Mackenzie urged Smith on to Celle.

Dusk was falling as the company closed to within one hundred yards of the hamlet. German machine guns opened up from several of the buildings, forcing Smith's men to ground. Smith tried to work his platoons into Celle, but the enemy resistance was fierce. A protracted stalemate ensued that persisted into the early morning hours of September 22. At 0200 hours, Smith was personally so close to the German positions that he had to turn his radio set off for fear a signal from regimental headquarters would betray his location.

Finally, after three attacks on the hamlet, 'D' Company gained a foothold and started clearing houses. By 0530 hours, Smith radioed that Celle was secure. Mackenzie offered congratulations and then told the captain to hold firm until 2nd New Zealand Division passed through later that day. After this happy event occurred, the regiment was to pull back from the Marecchia to a rest position south of Rimini.

WHILE THE HIGHLANDERS experienced a quiet day in Celle until being relieved by the New Zealanders at 1700 hours, the PPCLI companies on their left endured heavy shelling. Lieutenant Syd Frost wondered if any of them would survive. One shell after another struck the house in which his platoon headquarters and one section sheltered in a large downstairs room. The second storey was being torn apart and plaster, bricks, and chunks of supporting timbers were falling from the ceiling. Outside, stonks from Nebelwerfers were blasting the yard so thickly that Frost could see none of the men from his other two sections. He hoped they were all deep inside their slit trenches.

Suddenly, one of the men outside burst in with a shattered arm pumping blood. He said the bombardment was the worst he had ever seen and that Frost should pull the men into the farmhouse or they would all be killed. Thinking the house a poor refuge at best, but better than the yard, Frost agreed and signalled the section commanders outside to bring their men inside.

By now, the entire two rooms of the upstairs had been blown clean away and the three downstairs rooms were receiving the full attention of several 88-millimetre guns. But the stout stone walls held. Then a mortar round pierced the ceiling and ripped one room, fortunately unoccupied, to pieces. Frost gathered everyone together in the big room, which he thought was better protected than the other smaller remaining room. The little room soon disintegrated when a large shell broke through the ceiling and exploded.

Frost bent down to speak to one of his wounded men just as an armour-piercing round ripped through the wall where his head had been moments before and exited out the rear wall in a flash of sparks. Everyone flattened on the floor as another AP round flashed through the room. A Nebelwerfer stonk fell on the house and chunks of the ceiling collapsed, with only some strong beams overhead providing any protection. Smoke and dust filled the room. One man started sobbing hysterically. More holes were punched into the walls by AP rounds. It seemed impossible that the shattered structure could stand any more damage.

Frost heard the hard grinding noise of approaching tank tracks—coming from the left flank where the Germans held the buildings. He figured they were going to be overrun. Warily, Frost raised his head and peeked out a window. The tanks were Churchills. Frost staggered outside, waving and shouting greetings to the New Zealanders.[28] It was 1100 hours, September 22. For the Canadians, the Gothic Line Battle was over.

[32]

Well Done, Canada

THE CANADIANS WALKED out of the smoking wasteland of San Fortunato Ridge or back from the still contested north bank of the Marecchia River by companies or regiments. It all depended on how the final hours of battle found them deployed. To a man, they were nearly dead with exhaustion. Uniforms were ragged and torn, caked with filth and dried blood. Many sported grimy bandages that covered various cuts, burns, holes opened in flesh by bullets or shrapnel—wounds insufficiently serious to warrant evacuation. Others had graver injuries, but had refused evacuation so as not to leave their buddies short a man who might make all the difference. There were those who carried deeper injuries of the mind that might never heal, the product of all they had seen and done during twenty-six days in hell. They were unshaven, hair stiff with dirt, fingernails broken and bloody from working weapons. Hunger gnawed at their guts. But they still lived and, for the moment, that was all that mattered.

Italy's fickle fall weather had brought rain that left their uniforms sodden, their bodies chilled. As the men trudged to the rear, quartermasters and other headquarters staff worked frantically to secure billets where the men might lie down with at least a roof over their heads to keep them dry. It was a difficult task in a land devastated by more than a month of shelling and bombing. Everywhere they looked, buildings sat with roofs blown in by direct hits, or with no roof and walls shattered and jagged as broken teeth.

The Seaforths marched from San Fortunato to Palazzo des Vergers on the San Martino Ridge. Here, its rear echelon headquarters had been established late on September 19, joined the next day by Brigadier Graeme Gibson's 2nd Canadian Infantry Brigade headquarters.[1] At the time, the building had seemed no more than some luxurious mansion badly shot up by artillery, but afforded with a good view of the Ausa River valley and the southern slopes of San Fortunato Ridge. There had been shell holes in the walls and the roof and the great expanses of gardens had been reduced to a mess of craters. Padre Roy Durnford initially thought it was "a marvelous place. I do not sleep in the dungeons or wine cellars below but sleep on ground floor surrounded with oil paintings of fabulous worth."[2]

But the rifle companies on September 19 had enjoyed no pleasant sleep. Earlier they had prepared for battle and then marched into the gathering darkness towards the Ausa River. Durnford had watched their departure anxiously, worried by the high number of fresh reinforcements who all seemed "inadequately armed and fed . . . and some few, wholly inexperienced. I go to sleep thinking of dead faces I had seen and oil paintings and magnificent furniture and ornaments."[3]

It was sometime later on September 20 that the destruction began. Durnford watched in horror as exhausted soldiers yanked aged oil paintings from the walls and threw them out flat on the floor to serve as beds. Some of the canvases were strong and supple enough to bear the weight of men who "lay on old masterpieces boots and all."[4] Others, as Major Jim Stone of the Loyal Edmonton Regiment witnessed later that day, "smashed into a thousand pieces."[5]

Durnford collected many of the paintings, thinking that he must either rescue them or they would surely be destroyed. "Many works of art have gone through sheer Philistinism," he noted. "If I had taken them at the start that would not have happened." Durnford gave some paintings that he "recovered" to other chaplains in the Canadian regiments. Meanwhile, some Seaforth and 2 CIB staff officers cut paintings from frames, put them in rolls, and arranged their shipment to Canada. Among them was a young lieutenant, Norman DePoe, who had only joined the Seaforths on August 21, 1944.[6]

Between attempts to rescue artwork from the destruction or looting by the respective Seaforth and 2 CIB headquarters staffs, Durnford attended to the grim business of burying the many dead Seaforths. On September 20, twenty men killed by shellfire were interred in the palace grounds. "It was too horrible to describe," he wrote. "I feel sick in body and heart. Go to bed . . . out of temper and weary of it all."[7]

The looting of the palace, which was owned by the House of Ripoli, continued in fits and spurts until the Seaforths and 2 CIB headquarters left for Cattolica on the morning of September 23. The two headquarters staffs wound "up a successful op[eration with] an impromptu party . . . in the officers mess which was located in the main ballroom of the Palace," noted the 2 CIB war diarist. "The palace had proved an admirable brigade headquarters and in spite of the great damage done to the building there were still sufficient rooms to house all of brigade headquarters and [the rear echelon] of the Seaforths of Canada."[8] Come the morning, however, most officers and men were glad to see the back of the place. The Seaforths' war diarist described it as a "battle-scarred, devastated backwash . . . which . . . was only mitigated by the knowledge that a move to a rest area was imminent."[9]

Soon after the regiment and brigade headquarters left for Cattolica, reports circulated about the extent of the looting and, given the property owners' noble connections, an investigation was undertaken. The investigation focused on the Seaforths, with no note made of the presence of brigade headquarters staff. It was not a vigorous investigation and nothing came of it. Stone, who became aware of the investigation, was unsurprised that no action was taken against any soldiers looting from a family "of dubious political leanings." He figured the family had probably been fascists, a point that would explain why the Germans had left the contents intact. Certainly the Germans had usually stripped other Italian mansions clean of anything valuable, the booty added to their government's massive holdings or to the personal collections of individual Nazi leaders.[10]

THERE WAS NO SHORTAGE of devastation elsewhere in the region, which may have made pursuing one rumoured looting incident not worth undertaking. Having endured ninety-two bombing raids—more than any other Italian city—Rimini was a ruin. A further 1.47 million rounds of artillery shells had been fired on it. This represented 14,000 tons of explosives. Ninety per cent of Rimini was either destroyed or heavily damaged.[11] Seaforth Highlanders of Canada commander Lieutenant Colonel Syd Thomson briefly considered bivouacking his regiment there, but after a brief visit pronounced it in too "ruinous state."[12]

Canadian Broadcasting Corporation's radio correspondent Peter Stursberg reported that he found the city's central plaza, named after Julius Caesar, "utterly desolate" and told listeners at home his impression perhaps arose "due to the dull, menacing sky and the gallows out there in the middle of the empty square."[13] The gallows had been used by fascists and Germans to hang suspected partisans.

"We drove," he added, "to Rimini across the airfield over which the Canadians and Greeks had fought so hard, over a flat straight road littered with boughs and branches. The heavy clouds made the flat fields dank and dark and foreboding and the shattered buildings of Rimini seemed in keeping with them. The town has ... suffered heavily from shellfire and bombing and the Germans, before they left, blew up many buildings as roadblocks. Yet the Arch of Augustus is untouched and the statue of Julius Caesar and the Renaissance clock tower in the main square are miraculously undamaged for all the buildings around are in ruins."

Stursberg got out of his jeep and climbed "over piles of rubble and debris to reach the centre of town here. Near the Arch of Augustus, I found a Canadian mortar platoon, its mortars all set up for action. Private Charles Little of Toronto said to me, 'Boy, this place is a junk heap.'"[14]

That junk heap was home to fifty thousand people before war visited it with such tragic consequence. Twenty-one-year-old newspaper journalist, Amedeo Montemaggi, soon returned to his beloved Rimini from hiding in the country and was appalled. Except for a couple of small rooms at its front, a bomb had destroyed his family home. The neighbouring houses had all been levelled. He managed to prop up a badly sagging corner of the remaining structure with a log and scrounged enough usable roof tiles from those blown into the streets and yards to adequately repair the roof over the remaining rooms to keep out the winter rains. One room served as a rough kitchen area, the other a bedroom. Like most of Rimini's surviving population, Montemaggi turned his thoughts to rebuilding.

The English-speaking Montemaggi found temporary work as an interpreter for the string of Allied units that subsequently used Rimini as a temporary base.[15] In a land where food and shelter remained scarce, he was not alone in seeking work with the Allies, who were blessed with plenty of the former and able to offer the latter if needed.

Sixteen-year-old Oviglio Monti also worked as an interpreter for the Allies and found the duty far preferable to his enforced time serving the Germans. Shortly after the fighting rolled past Coriano, Monti had walked to Riccione. He secured work initially in the officer's mess of a British unit, but found the tea they insisted he both constantly serve and drink a foul concoction. He learned there were Canadians nearby, who might need a hand. Knowing Canadians were supposed to be like Americans, Monti figured they must drink coffee, something he yearned for. He was fortunate; the Royal Canadian Regiment took him in. Although he spent time in the kitchen, Monti's chief duty was as a guide and interpreter.

This did not mean going out with Canadians and showing them the sights around Rimini. It meant ensuring none of the men ran afoul of the many fascists living in Riccione. Monti, knowing a soldier who stayed too late in a bar or restaurant owned by a fascist or took his pleasure in the boudoir of a woman similarly persuaded might not live to see the dawn, took his job seriously. He scouted the various places that were opening and determined which were safe and which not. Then he shepherded the soldiers to and from their billets with a watchful eye. At one point, some officers arranged with a group of locals to hold a dance. The locals promised many willing young women would attend. Instantly suspicious, Monti soon learned that the locals involved were fascists. He reported this to the provosts and the dance was quickly scuttled. With each passing week and war's fortune tilting more decisively against the possibility of some fascist miracle recovery, Monti was bemused to see Riccione's fascists reshape themselves into communists, democrats, or monarchists.[16]

AFTER EVERY MAJOR battle, there followed a period of evaluation. Everyone agreed that I Canadian Corps had performed brilliantly and come very close to winning the decisive breakout. Had 1st British Armoured Division or even the 4th British Infantry Division been under the corps from the outset, Burns might have had the strength to break through without the long delay suffered while Coriano Ridge was cleared so slowly and at such cost in blood. Eighth Army commander General Oliver Leese—who had finally given Burns the added formations when it was too late—demonstrated his usual penchant for widely distributing effusive praise. During the battle's last stages and immediately thereafter, messages burned across the radio wires to the many headquarters of I Canadian Corps. Each message referred to one or two specific moments where a particular formation had performed masterfully. All ended with personal thanks, best wishes, and a "Well done, Canada" salutation.

Major General Chris Vokes wrote of 1st Canadian Infantry Division that, "throughout the whole operation the division fought gallantly and well. The spirit of cooperation and teamwork between all supporting arms, services and infantry was of a high order. Although we suffered local reverses at times, they were few in number. We gained our objectives one by one, throughout five complete phases and over a period of twenty-six days, and in so doing we advanced a total of thirty-two miles."[17]

Brigadier D. Dawnay of the 21st British Tank Brigade, whose regiments had fought with 1 CID throughout, offered similar praise. He described the advance from the Metauro River to the Marecchia as "most successful" and one "during which the infantry have fought with great skill and dash. The battle for the San Martino and San Fortunato features was an epic struggle." He ended by saying that his brigade was "proud to have fought with such a splendid division."[18]

The British tankers had paid their price in blood during the battle, reporting 306 casualties. Of these, 9 officers and 53 other ranks died.[19]

Tanker casualties were usually far lower than those suffered by infantry. Certainly this proved true at the Gothic Line. From August 25 to September 22, 1 CID had 2,424 Canadian casualties. Of these, 30 officers and 412 other ranks were killed, 97 officers and 1,691 other ranks wounded, with 5 officers and 189 other ranks reported missing. The 3rd Canadian Infantry Brigade was hardest hit, reporting 781 casualties as compared to 692 in 2nd Canadian Infantry Brigade and 689 in 1st Canadian Infantry Brigade. The division's other units, including the artillery regiments, had 262 men killed, wounded, or missing at the close of September 22. For 5th Canadian Armoured Division, the battle had been a little shorter—from August 25 to the final clearing of Coriano Ridge on September 19—and it lost 28 officers and 293 other ranks killed, 70 officers and 961 other ranks wounded, one officer and 15 other ranks missing.[20]

In all, Canadian casualties from August 25 to September 22 totalled 4,511—the highest casualty rate experienced by Canadians during any battle in Italy.[21] Throughout the entire corps during the same period, another 1,005 men were evacuated because of illness. Many of these were soldiers who succumbed to exhaustion, either straight physical fatigue or battle fatigue.[22]

Eighth Army as a whole had been through the grinder. Including the Canadians, it had 14,000 men killed, wounded, or missing after the twenty-six-day battle. More than two hundred tanks were destroyed. But as General Harold Alexander, Deputy Supreme Commander, Mediterranean, ruefully noted: "Tanks were easily replaceable, but the men were not."[23] The British infantry divisions were so badly mauled that every regiment could field only three companies instead of the normal four. Several brigades were completely disbanded, their complement used to reinforce others.[24]

The Germans also suffered heavily. Up to September 15, LXXVI Panzer Corps, which had faced the Eighth Army on the Adriatic coast, reported 14,604 casualties. No records after that period to the end of the battle survived, but Lieutenant General Tommy Burns had ample justification in believing that the Germans "must have lost many more before withdrawing across the Marecchia."[25] The Canadians alone had taken 2,500 prisoners over the twenty-six days.

While the loss of men was great, even greater perhaps was the loss of experience. At the end of the day, the commanders of almost every Canadian regiment noted that the veteran ranks had been decimated. The West Nova Scotia Regiment had suffered the highest casualties of all—75 dead and 255 wounded, half its strength, with a disproportionately high number of these being soldiers who had landed in Sicily. The West Novas would march towards the next battle without their hard-earned combat experience and skill. They would also march under the command of a new officer, Lieutenant Colonel A.L. Saunders.[26]

Not all losses to the regiments resulted from shot or shell. The West Novas' Lieutenant Colonel Ron Waterman was not the only commander sacked in the battle's aftermath. The intense feud between Seaforth Highlanders of Canada Lieutenant Colonel Syd Thomson and 2 CIB Brigadier Graeme Gibson proved too much. As Thomson later put it: "We fired each other."[27]

Burns called Thomson into his headquarters shortly after the battle. "I gather you and Gibson aren't getting along too well," he said. Thomson agreed that was the case. "Gibson is a Permanent Force soldier and this is his life," Burns said. That meant Gibson could not be fired for failure of command. "So I'm going to send you both home."[28]

In Thomson's case, this meant a transfer to Britain and relatively speedy appointment to command of the Black Watch (Royal Highland Regiment of Canada). Lieutenant Colonel Budge Bell-Irving, a Seaforth Highlander before being posted to command of the Loyal Edmonton Regiment, returned to command his original regiment. This paved the way for Major Jim Stone's promotion to lieutenant colonel and ascendancy to command of the Eddies. Gibson's replacement would not come until October 6 and he would ostensibly be evacuated on medical grounds.[29] Lieutenant Colonel Pat Bogert, who had commanded 3 CIB skillfully after stepping in for the injured Paul Bernatchez, assumed the helm as 2 CIB's brigadier.

By the time the final shakeout of command changes was concluded within the ranks of I CID, Eighth Army was itself in the throes of adjusting to a new commander. Chief of the Imperial General Staff, Field Marshal Sir Alan Brooke had never believed General Oliver Leese up to the task. The decision to shift the focus of the offensive against the Gothic Line from the central Apennines to the Adriatic remained controversial and lack of decisive success little enhanced Brooke's estimation of the general. Brooke considered Leese "a serious disappointment." He gave Brooke the "impression of stickiness and lack of thrust."[30] When Brooke won Prime Minister Winston Churchill's ear, Leese's replacement was agreed.

Firing an army commander could, however, adversely affect the morale of both a nation and those serving in its ranks. So Leese moved to another job, ostensibly a promotion. An able administrator, if in the informal manner of English Old Boys, Leese was appointed Commander in Chief, Allied Land Force Southeast Asia under Supreme Allied Commander, Southeast Asia, Lord Louis Mountbatten. Thus, Leese was gently removed from direct hands-on command of combat troops. He received the news on September 28 from General Sir Harold Alexander, Deputy Supreme Commander, Mediterranean during a walk on the beach south of Rimini.

"I am to be an Army Group Commander," he wrote after, "in the final fight against the Japanese.... It's a wonderful command in war time, and I pray for the strength and wisdom and guidance to carry it through." Alexander, he added, "was so nice about it, and said I was the only person."[31]

Lieutenant General Tommy Burns had fewer friends, uncompromising foes in his two divisional commanders, and could claim no membership in the Canadian Army's Old Boys' network. Hence, his fate proved grimmer than Leese's. Despite the accolades Leese and Alexander grudgingly offered for his handling of the Gothic Line breakthrough and Alexander's recommending him for a DSO, Burns never won the latter's confidence. The new Eighth Army commander, General Richard McCreery, thought Burns cautious and methodical when dash and verve were necessary to debouch across the Po Valley.

Burns could no longer count on support from the Canadian government. Following Defence Minister James Layton Ralston's late September inspection of Canada's forces in Italy, he left convinced that Burns had to be replaced.

McCreery dropped the axe in person on October 24. He informed Burns "that he was not satisfied with me as corps commander, and had recommended that I be replaced."[32] While Burns had survived the loss of command following a similar recommendation in the wake of the Liri Valley Battle, this time his fate was sealed. On November 2, Burns went on leave to Rome. While there, he was summoned to England by Canadian 1st Army commander, General Harry Crerar, and posted as senior Canadian officer at the Twenty-first Army Group Headquarters. Lieutenant General Charles Foulkes replaced him as I Canadian Corps commander.

The 5th Canadian Armoured Division was spared significant leadership bloodletting. Major General Bert Hoffmeister had been generally pleased with the performance of his brigade and regimental commanders. He was also too busy to think of replacing men. For as the Gothic Line Battle ended, there was no rest for his division. The long-anticipated debouch into the Po began immediately, with 5 CAD crossing the Marecchia and driving into the valley to the west of 2nd New Zealand Division. Debouch turned into mud-soaked slog as the rains at last fell in torrents and the Germans erected one defensive line after another behind every ditch and river. The tank country of the Po Valley proved as illusory as the belief that a quick and decisive victory was at hand in Western Europe and the end of the war possible before year's end. Soon 1 CID was back in the line alongside its armoured division colleagues, and week after week of fighting awaited the entire Canadian Corps as Eighth Army crept slowly northward.

More Canadians must die in Italy, with the only certainty that there would be another river and, behind it, more Germans surely waiting. Fall would give way to another bitter mud-drenched winter that would culminate in the last major Canadian battle in Italy. From December 2, 1944 to January 5, 1945, I Canadian Corps would be entangled in a battle on the outskirts of Ravenna as it attempted to advance from the Montone River to the Senio River. The butcher's bill for winning a patch of ground barely ten miles by fifteen miles would ultimately tally 2,581 killed or wounded—the fourth bloodiest Canadian battle of the campaign. And the advance would continue to grind on for another two months before the Canadians were withdrawn from the Italian front for transfer to new battles in Holland and Germany itself. Far too few of the young men who, on July 10, 1943, had landed on the beaches of Sicily to begin the long journey through Italy would escape unscathed to see the final victory on May 7, 1945. As for Bologna—the tactical target towards which the Allies in Italy had undertaken the great offensive against the Gothic Line—it did not fall until April 21, less than three weeks before the war's end.

[EPILOGUE]

The Gothic Line in Memory

IT'S A WARM FALL DAY and I look out across the 1,940 white marble headstones of Commonwealth troops buried at Coriano Ridge War Cemetery. A breeze is rising and the leaves are shaking out of the trees in a gentle red, orange, yellow rain onto the graves of soldiers who have lain here under Italian soil for more than fifty-five years. Most were half that number of years in age before they fell during the Gothic Line Battle.

As has proved the case at every Commonwealth cemetery visited over the last few years, Coriano is well tended. Pretty arrangements of flowers grow around and between the headstones. The sweeps of grass running between the orderly rows of graves and down the entrance concourse are freshly mowed to meticulous perfection.

The tilling of the flowerbeds at times creates small hillocks around the gravestones, which obscure the lowest line of the inscriptions carved in the marble. For no particular reason, as I pass between the rows of headstones of Canadian dead that are concentrated on the cemetery's southern flank, I scrape back the earth at the base of Captain George Richard Corkett's grave. Later, I learn that the twenty-eight-year-old Corkett had the misfortune to rejoin the Princess Patricia's Canadian Light Infantry on September 22, 1944, the very last day of the Gothic Line Battle. An exploding German shell killed him. The inscription reads: "Beloved husband of Aileen. Father of Georgina Anne, born in England 1944." And so I learn that Corkett had taken a bride in England and fathered a child in the same year he perished. Was he able to hold her in his arms after her birth? Or was he already bound for Italy? Or had he already perished on the banks of the Marecchia River?

Here, walking from headstone to headstone and reading the names of the dead, their ages, their hometowns, the regiments in which they served, and the epitaphs that family have had etched in the marble, it is impossible to remain unmoved by the sacrifice these Canadians made. It is particularly poignant to see the headstones of men with whose death I am familiar. There is Major Herbert William Paterson, the Seaforth Highlander officer that Corporal Charles Monroe Johnson thought an elderly English gentleman and who led his company towards San Martino on September 18 with a walking stick in his hand. Paterson was only forty-one and hailed from Kelowna, B.C.

There is also Captain Jack Birnie Smith, who died at San Lorenzo in Strada's church. He was thirty on September 6, 1944. Nearby is the grave of another Royal Canadian Regiment soldier who died that day—Private Lyall F. Douglas, aged twenty-two. The epitaph on his headstone reads: "To those at home in Winnipeg, he is just away until the daybreak."

I have come to Coriano this day with Oviglio Monti, whose home in Coriano was just a short distance south of this cemetery. He insists on being called Monti, rather than Oviglio or, heavens forbid, Signor Monti. I soon learn that even his children refer to him by his last name. Because it was Canadian troops who liberated Coriano and also gave Monti a job after, Monti has great affection for us. He has penned a short article, reprinted at one time in the *Canadian Legion*, on "Why I Am a Lucky Man." His luck was in surviving the battle that rolled over Coriano and then having the opportunity to build a life after. Monti still is grateful for his liberation from the fascists and the German Nazis.

He has a good life, too. The skills he learned working with the Royal Canadian Regiment sparked an interest in providing service to people, which resulted in his becoming a hotelier. Today, he owns two seaside hotels—one in Rimini, the other in Riccione. There is also a guesthouse in the country near Coriano.

Monti has often had Canadian dignitaries stay at his hotel and has acted as host and interpreter for them. On several occasions, his hotel has been the base for the Canadian Staff College tours of the Gothic Line held every couple of years. For the Canadian military, the Gothic Line Battle has become a textbook case for the study of battlefield tactics and strategy. Usually, a few veterans have accompanied the tours as resource personnel.

John Dougan and Henri Tellier have served in this role. Dougan was called on so often he eventually bowed out, having, he said, "gone back to the cemeteries of dead friends too many times." In addition to Canadian veterans, staff college tour planners have drawn upon the expertise that German veterans bring to understanding the battle. One of the most regular former German officers so involved is Oberst Gerhard Muhm. A company commander in the 29th Panzer Grenadier Division during the battle, Muhm fought immediately opposite Tellier at Villa Belvedere and was caught in the artillery concentrations that Dougan called down on the Germans pulling off the ridge on September 20. Tellier and Muhm became friends, while Dougan's relationship with his ex-enemy proved more guarded. There is respect, but there is also the barrier of dead Canadian friends who died in a war that was, in the final analysis, Germany's making.

Today, the Italians in the Rimini area have largely forgotten the war. Most were not even born when this land felt the blast of explosions and witnessed the struggle of thousands of soldiers for its mastery. Tourists are today's invaders. They come by the tens of thousands to the longest-stretching beach resort in Europe, where they sit in beach chairs lined up in regimented rows ten to twenty deep in front of their hotels and bronze themselves under an Adriatic sun. Germans mostly, and this invasion is generally welcomed.

There are still Italians who remember the battle, of course. One has even made it his lifetime calling. Amedeo Montemaggi, the once young journalist, is undoubtedly the world's leading expert on the Gothic Line and author of several books in Italian on the subject.

When I meet him, he is working to a publisher's deadline and has the inevitable glazed look in his eye caused by too little sleep, too many pages yet to write, and too many questions that remain unresolved. He still takes time out to provide his analyses of the Canadian role in the great battle for the last German defensive line. Hoffmeister, he believes, demonstrated "a touch of genius" in seeing that he could bounce the Gothic Line. But there was a following inability of I Canadian Corps—due to its weakness—to exploit the breaches won through each defensive line quickly enough. So the breakout from the Rimini Line came too late to give Eighth Army the decisive victory required.

Montemaggi's summary seems accurate. It is doubtful, of course, that a breakout into the Po Valley two or three weeks earlier would have resulted in the great armoured blitzkrieg that the Allies sought. Travelling from Bologna to Ravenna and from there down the coastline to Rimini is a sobering experience. The canals, rivers, and ditches that must be crossed unfurl in an endless parade. Many are substantial enough to present major barriers to the attackers and provide fine antitank ditches from behind which a defender could offer stiff resistance. This proved the case for Eighth Army when it did move out into the plain, and it was not just the mud that slowed the advance to a crawl. The Germans fought with their normal defensive skill from behind these rivers and canals. In doing so, they frustrated Allied intentions in Italy. Ultimately, the goal of the campaign became more to keep German divisions pinned down there and grind them up—an operation in attrition—rather than seeking any major offensive breakout. Campaigns of attrition are costly for both sides. Certainly this was the case with the Italian campaign. It is estimated that the Allies suffered 320,955 casualties while inflicting 658,339 on the Germans prior to the surrender of all German forces in Italy on May 2, 1945.[1]

By the time of the surrender, I Canadian Corps was gone from Italy. It had left at the end of March 1945 for northwestern Europe. In all, 92,757 Canadians saw service in Italy and more than a quarter became casualties. The total numbers of casualties has been set at

26,254. Of these, 5,399 were killed. About sixty per cent of the casualties occurred in five major operations, of which the Gothic Line Battle exacted the highest price.[2]

It's sunset when I visit Montecchio War Cemetery, the southernmost of the Commonwealth cemeteries where Gothic Line dead are buried. With 582 graves, it is comparatively small by the standards that guide the burying of war dead. Among the Canadian graves is an uninterrupted row of a dozen men from the West Nova Scotia Regiment. They all died in the minefield on August 31, during that regiment's failed attack on the Gothic Line proper.

There is also the grave of a twenty-one-year-old Irish Regiment of Canada private, William Winslow. His wife, Patricia, had recently visited the cemetery. She noted in the register, "You are always in my heart." As I walk from the cemetery, I carry with me the hope that Private Winslow and all the others who lie in graves scattered across Italy and Sicily shall always have a place deep in the heart of a nation's memory.

APPENDIX A: EIGHTH ARMY ORDER OF BATTLE AT THE GOTHIC LINE

V BRITISH CORPS (Lieutenant General C. Keightley)
1st British Armoured Division
4th British Infantry Division
4th Indian Infantry Division
46th British Infantry Division
56th British Armoured Brigade
25th British Tank Brigade

I CANADIAN CORPS (Lieutenant General E.L.M. Burns)
5th Canadian Armoured Division
1st Canadian Infantry Division
21st British Tank Brigade

II POLISH CORPS (Lieutenant General W. Anders)
3rd Carpathian Infantry Division
5th Kresowa Infantry Division
2nd Polish Armoured Brigade
Army Group Polish Artillery

2nd New Zealand Armoured Division

3rd Greek Mountain Brigade

APPENDIX B:
CANADIANS AT THE GOTHIC LINE
(NOT ALL UNITS LISTED)

I CANADIAN CORPS

7th Anti-tank Regiment

No. 1 Army Group, Royal Canadian Artillery:

1st Survey Regiment

11th Army Field Regiment

1st Medium Regiment

2nd Medium Regiment

5th Medium Regiment

1ST CANADIAN INFANTRY DIVISION

1st Canadian Armoured Car Regiment (Royal Canadian Dragoons)

The Royal Canadian Artillery:

1st Field Regiment (Royal Canadian Horse Artillery)

2nd Field Regiment

3rd Field Regiment

1st Anti-tank Regiment

2nd Light Anti-Aircraft Regiment

Corps of Royal Canadian Engineers:

1st Field Company

3rd Field Company

4th Field Company

2nd Field Park Company

Brigade Support Group:

The Saskatoon Light Infantry

1st Canadian Infantry Brigade:

The Royal Canadian Regiment (permanent force)

The Hastings and Prince Edward Regiment
48th Highlanders of Canada Regiment
2nd Canadian Infantry Brigade:
Princess Patricia's Canadian Light Infantry Regiment (permanent force)
Seaforth Highlanders of Canada Regiment
Loyal Edmonton Regiment
3rd Canadian Infantry Brigade:
Royal 22e Regiment (permanent force)
Carleton and York Regiment
West Nova Scotia Regiment

5TH CANADIAN ARMOURED DIVISION
Reconnaissance Troops:
3rd Canadian Armoured Reconnaissance Regiment (Governor General's Horse Guards)
Brigade Support Group:
Princess Louise Fusiliers
The Royal Canadian Artillery:
17th Field Regiment
8th Field Regiment (Self-Propelled)
4th Anti-tank Regiment
5th Light Anti-tank Regiment
5th Canadian Armoured Brigade:
2nd Canadian Armoured Regiment (Lord Strathcona's Horse) (permanent force)
5th Canadian Armoured Regiment (8th Princess Louise New Brunswick Hussars)
9th Canadian Armoured Regiment (British Columbia Dragoons)
11th Canadian Infantry Brigade:
Perth Regiment
Cape Breton Highlanders
Irish Regiment of Canada
12th Canadian Infantry Brigade:
Westminster (Motorized) Regiment
Princess Louise Dragoon Guards

1st Light Anti-Aircraft Regiment (The Lanark and Renfrew Scottish Regiment)

Corps of Royal Canadian Engineers:

1st Field Squadron

4th Field Park Squadron

10th Field Squadron

APPENDIX C:
CANADIAN INFANTRY BATTALION
(TYPICAL ORGANIZATION)

HQ COMPANY:
No. 1 Signals Platoon
No. 2 Administrative Platoon

SUPPORT COMPANY:
No. 3 Mortar Platoon (3-inch)
No. 4 Bren Carrier Platoon
No. 5 Assault Pioneer Platoon
No. 6 Antitank Platoon (6-pounder)

A COMPANY:
No. 7 Platoon
No. 8 Platoon
No. 9 Platoon

B COMPANY:
No. 10 Platoon
No. 11 Platoon
No. 12 Platoon

C COMPANY:
No. 13 Platoon
No. 14 Platoon
No. 15 Platoon

D COMPANY:
No. 16 Platoon
No. 17 Platoon
No. 18 Platoon

APPENDIX D: CANADIAN MILITARY ORDER OF RANK (LOWEST TO HIGHEST)

Private (Pte.)
Gunner (artillery equivalent of private)
Trooper (armoured equivalent of private)
Lance Corporal (L/Cpl.)
Corporal (Cpl.)
Lance Sergeant (L/Sgt.)
Sergeant (Sgt.)
Company Sergeant Major (CSM)
Regimental Sergeant Major (RSM)
Lieutenant (Lt. or Lieut.)
Captain (Capt.)
Major (Maj.)
Lieutenant Colonel (Lt. Col.)
Colonel (Col.)
Brigadier (Brig.)
Major General (Maj. Gen.)
Lieutenant General (Lt. Gen.)
General (Gen.)

APPENDIX E: GERMAN MILITARY ORDER OF RANK (LOWEST TO HIGHEST)

Because the German Army and the Luftwaffe ground forces had a ranking system where rank also usually indicated the specific type of unit in which one served, only basic ranks are given here. The translations are roughly based on the Canadian ranking system, although there is no Canadian equivalent for many German ranks.

Schütze Private, infantry
Grenadier Private, infantry
Kanonier Gunner
Panzerschütze Tank crew member
Pionier Sapper
Funker Signaller
Gefreiter Lance Corporal
Obergefreiter Corporal
Unteroffizier Lance Sergeant
Unterfeldwebel Sergeant
Feldwebel Company Sergeant Major
Oberfeldwebel Battalion Sergeant Major
Leutnant Second Lieutenant
Oberleutnant Lieutenant
Hauptmann Captain
Major Major
Oberstleutnant Lieutenant Colonel
Oberst Colonel
Generalleutnant Lieutenant General
Generalmajor Major General
General der Artillerie General of Artillery

General der Infanterie General of Infantry
General der Kavallerie General of Cavalry
General der Pioniere General of Engineers
General der Panzertruppen General of Armoured Troops
Generaloberst Colonel General
Generalfeldmarschall General Field Marshal
Oberbefehshaber Süd Commander-in-Chief South

APPENDIX F: THE DECORATIONS

Many military decorations were won by soldiers in the Gothic Line Battle. The decoration system that Canada used in World War II, like most other aspects of its military organization and tradition, derived from Britain. A class-based system, most military decorations can be awarded either to officers or to "other ranks," but not both. The exception is the highest award, the Victoria Cross, which can be won by a soldier of any rank.

The decorations and qualifying ranks are:

VICTORIA CROSS (VC): Awarded for gallantry in the presence of the enemy. Instituted in 1856. Open to all ranks. The only award that can be granted for action in which the recipient was killed, other than Mentioned in Despatches—a less formal honour whereby an act of bravery was given specific credit in a formal report.

DISTINGUISHED SERVICE ORDER (DSO): Officers of all ranks, but more commonly awarded to officers with ranks of major or higher.

MILITARY CROSS (MC): Officers with a rank below major and, rarely, warrant officers.

DISTINGUISHED CONDUCT MEDAL: Warrant officers and all lower ranks.

MILITARY MEDAL: Warrant officers and all lower ranks.

GLOSSARY OF COMMON CANADIAN MILITARY TERMS AND WEAPONRY

ANTITANK GUNS: Canadian forces used two antitank guns. The six-pounder was the main antitank gun attached directly to infantry battalions. Each battalion had its own antitank platoon. This gun had a range of one thousand yards and fired a six-pound shell. Also available were the seventeen-pounder antitank guns of the antitank regiments. This was basically an up-gunned version of the six-pounder, with greater range and greater hitting power because of the seventeen-pound shell.

BATTALION: *See* Regiment

BREN CARRIER: Also known as the universal carrier. A lightly armoured tracked vehicle capable of carrying four to six soldiers and their weapons. Provided no overhead protection, but was walled on all sides by armour. Top speed of thirty-five miles an hour. This was the Commonwealth forces battlefield workhorse. Its open design enabled it to be used for carrying just about any kind of military gear used by infantry. Some were converted into weapons carriers and played a combat role by being fitted with Vickers .303 medium machine guns, Bren light machine guns, or two-inch mortars, or were used as the towing vehicle for six-pounder antitank guns.

BREN GUN: Standard light machine gun of Commonwealth forces. Fired .303 rifle ammunition held in thirty-round magazines. An excellent, although slow-firing weapon, it had a range of about five hundred yards and weighed twenty-two pounds.

BROWNING 9-MILLIMETRE AUTOMATIC: The standard pistol used by Canadian forces. Officers in the line rifle companies generally kept their pistols hidden or even threw them away to avoid being easily identified as officers by German snipers.

CBH: Cape Breton Highlanders.

CIB: Canadian Infantry Brigade.

CO: Any commanding officer, regardless of unit size.

COY: Company.

EDDIES: Loyal Edmonton Regiment.

FAUSTPATRONE: A hand-held, disposable German antitank rocket launcher that proved quite effective against Western Allied armour. The first model Faustpatrone 1 (Fist-Cartridge) fired a 5.5-pound projectile capable of penetrating armour 140 millimetres thick at a range of less than thirty yards.

Soon Faustpatrone 2 appeared on the battlefield. This was heavier both in terms of physical weight and its punch against armour. The 6.39-pound charge fired by the new weapon could slice through armour 200 millimetres thick. The biggest flaw in both weapons was their effective range of only about one hundred feet, which brought the soldier employing it perilously close to the target and any infantry that might be screening it. However, the Faustpatrone was simpler to use, lighter, and more powerful than the PIAT or the American bazooka, both of which were more cumbersome, nondisposable weapons. The Faustpatrone was soon nicknamed Panzerfaust (Tank Fist) by the soldiers using them and later, even more powerful models were officially designated as such.

FORMING-UP POINT (FUP): A geographical point where a unit of any size gathers in preparation for an attack or other form of movement.

FORWARD AID POST (FAP): Most advanced aid post to which casualties could be withdrawn for treatment.

FORWARD OBSERVATION OFFICER (FOO): Artillery batteries had two officers, usually captains. During a battle, one officer remained with the guns to oversee their operation. The other, the FOO, accompanied the infantry regiment that was being supported. He usually was part of a three-man team that included the FOO, a radio signaller, and a Bren carrier driver. The FOO was in charge of calling for artillery support and directing the fire towards enemy targets that were threatening or holding up the infantry.

GGHG: Governor General's Horse Guards.

GLAMOUR BOYS: Nickname for 48th Highlanders of Canada.

GUNNER: The artillery regiment equivalent to a private.

HASTY P'S: Hastings and Prince Edward Regiment.

HE: High explosive.

HMG: Heavy machine gun.

HQ: Any form of headquarters.

JERRY: Common term for Germans. Also spelled Gerry. Canadians seldom if ever used the harsher term Kraut, which was favoured by American soldiers. *Tedeschi*, the Italian word for German, was also popular. As an alternative to Jerry, Canadians occasionally used Hun or Boche.

LEE ENFIELD RIFLE, NO. 4, MARK I: Standard rifle of Commonwealth forces. The Mark I was made in Canada for Canadian personnel. It fired .303 ammunition contained in five-round clips. Effective range was nine hundred yards, but most accurate when fired at ranges under six hundred yards. A highly reliable, rugged weapon, and capable of being mounted with an eight-inch spike bayonet.

LMG: Light machine gun.

LOYAL EDDIES: Loyal Edmonton Regiment.

MG: Machine gun.

MO: Medical Officer.

MORTARS: The Canadians had three weights of mortars: two-inch, three-inch, and 4.2-inch. The latter was a heavy mortar and operated by the Saskatoon Light Infantry in support of the infantry regiments. The three-inch was operated by a mortar platoon attached to each battalion, while two-inch mortars were carried directly into battle by a section attached to each company. A mortar lobs a bomb on what is usually a high trajectory towards a target. The bombs can be high-explosive, shrapnel, or phosphorous (smoke). Range and firepower varied according to the size of the gun. The bigger the mortar, the greater its range and firepower. The three-inch could engage targets as close as 125 yards and as far away as 2,800 yards. Its bomb weighed ten pounds. The 4.2-inch fired bombs of twenty pounds and had a much greater range. The small two-inch put out only a 2.5-pound bomb, but was extremely useful for laying smoke screens.

NBH: 8th Princess Louise New Brunswick Hussars.

NCO: Non-Commissioned Officer. All warrant officers, sergeants, and corporals are considered non-commissioned officers. NCOS provide the leadership backbone of infantry platoons and armoured troops.

NEBELWERFER: A launcher system that fired either fifteen-centimetre or twenty-one-centimetre rockets in a rapid, ten-second sequence. The most common launch carriage used in Italy resembled a two-wheeled artillery gun carriage, but was mounted with six tubes rather than a single gun. A Nebelwerfer crew could routinely load and fire a volley every ninety seconds, but to avoid injury from the significant exhaust backblast had to take shelter in a trench at least fifteen feet from the weapon before firing. Maximum Nebelwerfer range varied according to launcher size. The fifteen-centimetre Nebelwerfer 41 had a maximum range of 6,900 metres, while the twenty-one-centimetre Nebelwerfer 42 could reach out 7,850 metres. Known as "Moaning Minnies" because of the loud howling noise the rockets emanated during flight, Nebelwerfers were quite inaccurate. But when a stonk landed near or on target, casualties were almost inevitable because of the concentration of explosive and large chunks of shrapnel created when the rocket casing shattered.

OPS ORDERS: Operational orders.

ORDERS GROUP (O GROUP): A session at which the orders setting out the tactics to be used in a forthcoming action are given to participating commanders. Most actions entail multiple O Groups starting at the highest level and descending downward. A brigade planning an attack, for example, will have its first O Group called by the brigadier. He and brigade HQ staff will brief regimental commanders and the commanders of included supporting arms (artillery, heavy mortars, etc.). Regimental commanders then brief the company commanders, who in turn brief platoon commanders, who pass the information down to individual sections. What will start as a broad-stroke tactical plan at the brigade level will, by the time it hits platoon and section stages, become a set of intensely specific tasks that must be accomplished for the overall attack to succeed. A process of filtering out nonessential detail occurs all down the line until the section leader will have little idea of the purpose of the tasks his section must achieve.

PIAT: Projector Infantry Antitank. The hand-held antitank weapon of Commonwealth forces, weighing thirty-two pounds and firing a 2.5-pound hollow-charge explosive bomb. Difficult to load, prone to mechanical failure, and complicated to operate, the PIAT was an unpopular weapon. Effective against German tanks only if fired against the thinner side and rear armour plate, or against the tracks.

PIONEERS: Engineering personnel who were members of an infantry battalion's pioneer company. Pioneers had a higher level of expertise with regard to handling explosive, laying charges, carrying out demolitions, and defusing enemy mines and booby traps than the average soldier.

PLOUGH JOCKEYS: Nickname for Hastings and Prince Edward Regiment.

PPCLI: Princess Patricia's Canadian Light Infantry.

RAP: Regimental Aid Post. This first aid post was usually located near the forward regimental HQ.

RCA: Royal Canadian Artillery

RCE: Royal Canadian Engineers.

RCEME: Royal Canadian Electrical and Mechanical Engineers.

RCHA: Royal Canadian Horse Artillery (1st Field Regiment).

RCR: Royal Canadian Regiment.

RECCE: Abbreviation of reconnaissance. Recce units are reconnaissance units, such as the Royal Canadian Dragoons or Governor General's Horse Guards.

REGIMENTS: As a Commonwealth force, the Canadian Army follows the British organizational model, of which the regimental formation is heart and soul. The armouries of each regiment are based in a distinct region and generally its members are locally recruited, ensuring an immediate bond. This bond is further enhanced by immersing recruits into an organization possessed of a distinguished history, unique traditions and symbols, and a familial culture in which loyalty to the regiment and one's regimental comrades is expected.

In World War II, mobilized regiments provided the manpower from their ranks to form individual battalions of the divisional brigades. These brigades were also generally organized on broad geographical lines. The 2nd Canadian Infantry Brigade, for instance, was manned by regiments that hailed from British Columbia and Alberta. Technically, the regiment serves as the home of its personnel and a working contingent remains behind at its Canadian station (usually an armoury) to continue the intake of new recruits and otherwise maintain normal regimental routine while most of its strength is deployed overseas and serving as a battalion. The terminology can become complicated, however, since the Royal Canadian Regiment, for example, continues to use the designation of regiment when overseas rather than calling itself a battalion in its records. For this reason, the term regiment and battalion have been used synonymously throughout.

SAPPER: Explosive and engineering personnel in the Royal Canadian Engineers, equivalent to private in the infantry.

SHERMAN TANK: The standard tank used by Canadian forces was the Sherman M-4A2, usually called the M-4. It weighed just under thirty-five tons. The Sherman had a five-man crew, consisting of commander, gunner, loader, driver, and assistant driver. Its main armament was a 75-millimetre gun. Fixed into the front of the tank was also a .30-calibre machine gun and a .50-calibre machine gun could quickly be mounted on top of the turret for use as an anti-aircraft weapon. The Sherman had a top speed of about twenty-nine miles per hour and a maximum range without refuelling of 150 miles. Although the Sherman would undergo only slight modifications over the course of the war, it was generally considered inferior to most German tanks in terms of both firepower and armour. It also had a higher profile, which made it harder to get into a hull-down (protected) stance than German tanks.

SLI: Saskatoon Light Infantry Regiment. The more official, but less commonly used, abbreviation was Sask LI.

SPG: Self-Propelled Gun. A standard artillery piece mounted on a tracked body. Lacking a turret, it could only fire directly at targets by wheeling the entire vehicle to face it. They also had no overhead cover to protect the crew and so were more vulnerable than tanks. The Allies generally used SPGS as mobile artillery that operated close to, but behind, the front lines. In many cases, the tank-deficient Germans attempted to deploy SPGS in a tank role, but their open-top design and inability to turn quickly to face a new threat left them highly vulnerable to both tank and infantry attack.

START POINT (SP): Also called the Start Line (SL) or Jumping-off Point, the spot where a unit of any size forms up immediately before going into an attack.

TANK DESTROYER (MIO): By sacrificing some of the armour protection provided by the standard Sherman M4, the western Allies were able to field heavier guns that were mobile and could be used in an antitank role. The standard model used by Canadian forces in Italy fitted an American three-inch high-velocity gun in an open-top revolving turret onto the chassis of a Sherman M4.

THOMPSON SUBMACHINE GUN: Fondly referred to as the Tommy Gun by those who carried it, the Thompson was a .45-calibre submachine gun. The favoured submachine gun of Canadian forces and the only American weapon they respected, the Thompson could fit either a box or drum-shaped magazine. The use of .45-calibre ammunition gave the gun tremendous stopping power.

TROOPER: The armoured corps equivalent to a private. Trooper harks back to the armour's cavalry heritage.

TWENTY-FIVE POUNDER: The workhorse artillery gun of Commonwealth forces. Incredibly durable and reliable, the 25-pounder was manned by a crew of six. It was generally used as a howitzer—firing high-explosive shells at a high angle—but could also fire armour-piercing shot at flat trajectories. Effective range of 12,500 yards. Weighed four tons.

TYPE 36 GRENADE: Standard grenade of Commonwealth forces. Its metal case was ribbed, leading to its being called the "pineapple." Each of the eighty ribs broke into a separate shrapnel piece upon exploding. This type of grenade was usually thrown overhand in a lobbing manner.

VAN DOOS: Semi-official nickname for Royal 22e Regiment. Derived from *vingt-deux*.

VICKERS .303 MACHINE GUN, MARK I: Remarkably, the medium machine gun that the Canadians used throughout World War II was essentially the same gun Canadian forces had used in World War I. With a simple gas-assisted recoil system, the gun was water-cooled and fired belts of .303 ammunition. Its accurate range was 1,100 yards, but it could fling bursts much farther. At full automatic, the Vickers put out bursts of ten to twenty rounds. Rate of fire varied from 60 rounds a minute to 250 rounds, depending on whether the gunner was using slow or rapid fire. The Vickers weighed in at forty pounds. It had amazing endurance, seldom failing to operate in even the most adverse conditions.

Although an adequate weapon, the Vickers was outclassed in performance by its German counterpart. The MG42 was rated the best gun of its type in the world for years after the war. Introduced in 1942, it had an impressive firing rate of 1,200 rounds a minute. The MG42 had another advantage over the Vickers. It was actually a light machine gun, weighing only 25.35 pounds. When fired using a bipod, the gun had a light-machine gun range of about 600 yards. On a tripod, the range more than doubled and the weapon proved effective as an anti-aircraft gun.

WEST NOVAS: West Nova Scotia Regiment.

NOTES

1: SOJOURN IN FLORENCE

1 Strome Galloway, interview by author, 6 May 2000, Ottawa.
2 G.W.L. Nicholson, *The Canadians in Italy: 1943–1945*, vol. 2 (Ottawa: Queen's Printer, 1956), 484.
3 Ibid.
4 Galloway interview.
5 Reginald Roy, *The Seaforth Highlanders of Canada, 1919–1965* (Vancouver: Evergreen Press, 1969), 323.
6 Farley Mowat, *The Regiment*. 2nd ed. (Toronto: McClelland & Stewart, 1973), 198.
7 James Riley Stone, interview by William S. Thackray, 13 and 20 May; 3, 10, and 17 June 1980, University of Victoria, Special Collections.
8 G.R. Stevens, *A City Goes to War* (Brampton, ON: Charters, 1964), 303.
9 Stone interview.
10 Strome Galloway, *A Regiment at War: The Story of the Royal Canadian Regiment, 1939–1945* (Royal Canadian Regiment, 1979), 150–51.
11 Strome Galloway, *Bravely Into Battle: The Autobiography of a Canadian Soldier in World War Two* (Toronto: Stoddart, 1988), 205.
12 Ibid.
13 Galloway, *A Regiment at War*, 151.
14 J.T.B. Quayle, *In Action: A Personal Account of the Italian and Netherlands Campaigns of WW II* (Abbotsford, BC: Blue Stone, 1997), 192–93.
15 Howard Mitchell, *My War: With the Saskatoon Light Infantry (M.G.) 1939–1945* (n.p., n.d.), 100.
16 Quayle, 189–91.
17 Galloway, *A Regiment at War*, 151.
18 Roy, 324.
19 Quayle, 193.
20 Bill Worton, interview by author, 4 Oct. 2000, Vancouver.

2: A VERY HAPPY FAMILY

1 E.L.M. Burns, *General Mud: Memoirs of Two World Wars* (Toronto: Clarke, Irwin, 1970), 162–63.
2 J.L. Granatstein, *The Generals: The Canadian Army's Senior Commanders in the Second World War* (Toronto: Stoddart, 1993), 134.
3 Ibid., 135–36.

4 Burns, 163.
5 Ibid.
6 Crerar Papers, vol. 7, file 958C.0009 (E157), "Notes by Lt-Gen K. Stuart Regarding His Trip to Italy," 21 July 1944, MG30, National Archives of Canada, 1–4.
7 Vokes Papers, Royal Military College of Canada Massey Library, n.p.
8 Ibid.
9 Crerar Papers, "Notes by Lt-Gen K. Stuart," 4.
10 Ibid.
11 Ibid., 4–5.
12 Ibid., 5–6.
13 Crerar Papers, vol. 7, file 958C.0009 (E157), "Oliver Leese Letter to Ken Stuart," 14 July 1944, MG30, National Archives of Canada, 1–2.
14 Granatstein, 138–39.
15 Ibid., 140.
16 E.L.M. Burns, "Canadian Operations in the Mediterranean Area, May–June 1944: Extracts from Memoranda (Series 23)," Department of National Defence, 14.
17 G.W.L. Nicholson, *The Canadians in Italy: 1943–1945*, vol. 2 (Ottawa: Queen's Printer, 1956), 479.
18 Ibid.
19 Ibid., 480.
20 Ibid., 465.
21 Ibid., 480–81.
22 E.L.M. Burns, *Manpower in the Canadian Army, 1939–1945* (Toronto: Clarke, Irwin, 1956), 175–76.
23 Vokes Papers, n.p.
24 Nicholson, 480.
25 H.M. Jackson, *The Princess Louise Dragoon Guards: A History* (Ottawa: The Regiment, 1952), 196–97.
26 Daniel Dancocks, *The D-Day Dodgers: The Canadians in Italy, 1943–1945* (Toronto: McClelland & Stewart, 1991), 292.
27 Jackson, 197.
28 Dancocks, 293.
29 Gordon McGregor, interview by author, 3 Jan. 2001, Victoria, BC.
30 Vokes, n.p.
31 Bert Hoffmeister, interview by Greenhous and McAndrew transcript, Directorate of History, Department of National Defence, n.d., 90.
32 Brig. D.C. Spry, "Letter regarding 1 LAA Regt RCA, July 20 44," 264C12.049 (D1), National Archives of Canada.
33 Fred Cederberg, *The Long Road Home: The Autobiography of a Canadian Soldier in Italy in World War II* (Toronto: Stoddart, 1985), 138.

34 Ibid., 141.
35 Ibid., 143.
36 Ibid., 143–44.
37 Ibid., 144.
38 Ibid., 144–47.
39 Col. C.P. Stacey, "Report No. 187 Historical Section Canadian Military Headquarters: Operations of 1 CDN Corps, 4 Jun 44 to 24 Sep 44—The Breaking of the Gothic Line and the Capture of Rimini," Department of National Defence, n.d., 5.
40 Ibid., 6.
41 Nicholson, 484.
42 Vokes Papers, n.p.

3: INEVITABLE WRANGLES

1 Field Marshal Harold Alexander, "The Allied Armies in Italy," National Archives of Canada, n.d., 3–4.
2 G.W.L. Nicholson, *The Canadians in Italy: 1943–1945*, vol. 2 (Ottawa: Queen's Printer, 1956), 463.
3 Trumbull Higgins, *Soft Underbelly: The Anglo-American Controversy over the Italian Campaign, 1939–1945* (New York: Macmillan, 1968), 184–85.
4 Douglas Orgill, *The Gothic Line: The Italian Campaign, Autumn 1944* (New York: W.W. Norton, 1967), 20.
5 Higgins, 183.
6 Ralph Bennett, *Ultra and Mediterranean Strategy: 1944–1945* (London: Hamish Hamilton, 1989), 292.
7 Higgins, 172.
8 Bennett, 289.
9 Ibid., 290.
10 Higgins, 174.
11 Ibid., 175.
12 Ibid., 177.
13 Ibid., 179.
14 Orgill, 22.
15 Alexander, 4–5.
16 Rowland Ryder, *Oliver Leese* (London: Hamish Hamilton, 1987), 183.
17 Dominick Graham and Shelford Bidwell, *Tug of War: The Battle for Italy, 1943–1945* (New York: St. Martin's Press, 1986), 348.
18 Col. C.P. Stacey, "Report No. 187 Historical Section Canadian Military Headquarters: Operations of 1 CDN Corps, 4 Jun 44 to 24 Sep 44—The Breaking of the Gothic Line and the Capture of Rimini," Department of National Defence, n.d., 7.
19 Ibid.

20 Orgill, 31.
21 Alexander, 7.
22 Eric Morris, *Circles of Hell: The War in Italy, 1943–1945* (New York: Crown Publishers, 1993), 341–42.
23 Ryder, 184.
24 Graham and Bidwell, 348.
25 Alexander, 8–10.

4: WITH THE GREATEST ENERGY

1 G.W.L. Nicholson, *The Canadians in Italy: 1943–1945*, vol. 2 (Ottawa: Queen's Printer, 1956), 488.
2 Ibid., 470.
3 Ibid., 188.
4 Douglas Orgill, *The Gothic Line: The Italian Campaign, Autumn 1944* (New York: W.W. Norton, 1967), 12.
5 Ibid., 12–13.
6 Nicholson, 460.
7 Orgill, 24.
8 Nicholson, 461.
9 Ibid., 460.
10 Orgill, 24.
11 Ibid., 459.
12 Carl Bayerlein, "Retreat through Central Italy, 1944," account in possession of author, translated from German (Alex MacQuarrie, trans.), n.d., 1–2.
13 Ibid., 2.
14 Ibid., 2.
15 Ibid., 3.
16 Orgill, 26.
17 Ibid.
18 Albert Kesselring, *The Memoirs of Field Marshal Kesselring* (Lynton Hudson, trans.), (London: William Kimber, 1953), 207.
19 Ibid.
20 Nicholson, 460.
21 Field Marshal Harold Alexander, "The Allied Armies in Italy," National Archives of Canada, n.d., 1–3.
22 Ibid.
23 Nicholson, 266.
24 Ralph Bennett, *Ultra and Mediterranean Strategy: 1944–1945* (London: Hamish Hamilton, 1989), 288.
25 Nicholson, 494–95.
26 Bayerlein, 8.

27 Ibid., 9.
28 Ibid., 9–10.
29 Nicholson, 497.

5: UNDER THE BOOT HEEL

1 Richard Lamb, *War In Italy, 1943–1945: A Brutal Story* (London: John Murray, 1993), 206–7.
2 Ibid., 207.
3 Albert Kesselring, *The Memoirs of Field Marshal Kesselring,* (Lynton Hudson, trans.), (London: William Kimber, 1953), 227–28.
4 Oviglio Monti, interview by author, 22 Oct. 2000, Rimini, Italy.
5 Amedeo Montemaggi, interview by author, 23 Oct. 2000, Rimini, Italy and correspondence 25 May 2001.
6 Lamb, 316.
7 Ibid.
8 Ibid., 316–17.
9 Len Deighton, *Blitzkrieg: From the Rise of Hitler to the Fall of Dunkirk* (London: Jonathon Cape, 1979), 175.
10 Monti interview.
11 Ibid.

6: A TREMENDOUS NUT TO CRACK

1 William McAndrew, "Canadian Land Forces Staff Course: Operation Olive Battlefield Study, Eighth Army at the Gothic Line," (Kingston, ON: Department of National Defence, 1984), 6.
2 Col. C.P. Stacey, "Report No. 187 Historical Section Canadian Military Headquarters: Operations of 1 CDN Corps, 4 Jun 44 to 24 Sep 44—The Breaking of the Gothic Line and the Capture of Rimini," Department of National Defence, n.d., 9.
3 McAndrew, 7.
4 Ibid.
5 Ibid., 8–9.
6 Ibid., 9.
7 E.L.M. Burns, *General Mud: Memoirs of Two World Wars* (Toronto: Clarke, Irwin, 1970), 177.
8 William McAndrew, "Eighth Army at the Gothic Line: Commanders and Plans," *RUSI*, March 1986, 54–57.
9 Ibid., 178.
10 Stacey, 9–10.
11 G.W.L. Nicholson, *The Canadians in Italy: 1943–1945,* vol. 2 (Ottawa: Queen's Printer, 1956), 492.
12 Stacey, 10.

13 Bert Hoffmeister, interview by Greenhous and McAndrew transcript, Directorate of History, Department of National Defence, n.d., 93.
14 John Ellis, *Brute Force: Allied Strategy and Tactics in the Second World War* (London: Andre Deutsch, 1990), 336.
15 Stacey, 10–11.
16 Ibid., 11.
17 "History: Royal Canadian Engineers First Canadian Infantry Division, 1 August 1944–1 October 1944," National Archives of Canada, 3.
18 Ibid.
19 Stacey, 11.
20 "History: Royal Canadian Engineers First Canadian Infantry Division, 1 August 1944–1 October 1944," 4.
21 A.J. Kerry and W.A. McDill, *History of the Corps of Royal Canadian Engineers,* vol. 2 (Ottawa: The Military Engineers Assoc. of Canada, 1966), 225.
22 3rd Canadian Field Regiment, Royal Canadian Artillery War Diary, Aug. 1944, National Archives of Canada, n.p.
23 Stacey, 11–12.
24 Thomas A. Loten, correspondence with author, April 24, 2001.
25 British Columbia Dragoons War Diary, Aug. 1944, National Archives of Canada, 6.
26 Headquarters 5th Canadian Armoured Brigade War Diary, Aug. 1944, National Archives of Canada, 6.
27 4th Canadian Princess Louise Dragoons Guards War Diary, Aug. 1944, National Archives of Canada, 4.
28 Nicholson, 498.
29 3rd Canadian Field Regiment, Royal Canadian Artillery War Diary, Aug. 1944, n.p.
30 Governor General's Horse Guards War Diary, Aug. 1944, National Archives of Canada, 3.
31 Strome Galloway, *Bravely Into Battle: The Autobiography of a Canadian Soldier in World War Two* (Toronto: Stoddart, 1988), 206.
32 Royal Canadian Regiment War Diary, Aug. 1944, National Archives of Canada, n.p.
33 Nicholson, 498.
34 Stacey, 12.

7: WE BEGIN THE LAST LAP

1 W.G.F. Jackson, *The Mediterranean and Middle East,* vol. 6, part 2 (London: Her Majesty's Stationery Office, 1987), 122.
2 E.L.M. Burns, *General Mud: Memoirs of Two World Wars* (Toronto: Clarke, Irwin, 1970), 177.

3 Ibid., 178.
4 Ibid.
5 Ibid., 180.
6 Ibid.
7 Field Marshal Harold Alexander, "The Allied Armies in Italy," National Archives of Canada, n.d., 13.
8 Strome Galloway, *Bravely Into Battle: The Autobiography of a Canadian Soldier in World War Two* (Toronto: Stoddart, 1988), 207.
9 Ibid.
10 Royal Canadian Regiment War Diary, Aug. 1944, National Archives of Canada, n.p.
11 Ibid.
12 1st Canadian Infantry Division (GS Branch) War Diary, Aug. 1944, National Archives of Canada, 19.
13 Ibid.
14 3rd Field Regiment, Royal Canadian Artillery War Diary, Aug. 1944, National Archives of Canada, n.p.
15 17th Field Regiment, Royal Canadian Artillery War Diary, Aug. 1944, National Archives of Canada, 5.
16 Ibid.
17 Ibid., 6.
18 Alexander Ross, *Slow March to a Regiment* (St. Catharines, ON: Vanwell Publishing, 1993), 148.
19 Ibid.
20 Ibid., 149.
21 17th Field Regiment, Royal Canadian Artillery War Diary, Aug. 1944, 6.
22 Ibid., 7.
23 Col. C.P. Stacey, "Report No. 187 Historical Section Canadian Military Headquarters: Operations of 1 CDN Corps, 4 Jun 44 to 24 Sep 44—The Breaking of the Gothic Line and the Capture of Rimini," Department of National Defence, n.d., 23.
24 T.G. Gibson, "Account by Brig. T.G. Gibson, Commander 2 Canadian Infantry Brigade on the Action of 2 Canadian Infantry Brigade from 23 Aug to 22 Sep 44," Ottawa: Directorate of History, Department of National Defence, n.d., 1.
25 2nd Canadian Infantry Brigade Headquarters War Diary, Aug. 1944, National Archives of Canada, n.p.
26 Douglas Orgill, *The Gothic Line: The Italian Campaign, Autumn 1944* (New York: W.W. Norton, 1.967), 40–41.
27 Stacey, 20.
28 Ibid.
29 G.W.L. Nicholson, *The Canadians in Italy: 1943–1945*, vol. 2 (Ottawa:

Queen's Printer, 1956), 500.
30 Stacey, 26.
31 Ibid.
32 "Battle History 1 Canadian Infantry Brigade 25 Aug to 19 Oct 44," National Archives of Canada, 10.
33 Ibid., 4.
34 Ibid.
35 Stacey, 27.
36 Ibid.
37 Ibid., 28–29.
38 Nicholson, 503.
39 Ibid., 504.
40 C. Sydney Frost, *Once a Patricia* (St. Catharines, ON: Vanwell Publishing, 1988), 276.

8: AH, CANNON!

1 Kim Beattie, *Dileas: History of the 48th Highlanders of Canada, 1929–1956* (Toronto: 48th Highlanders of Canada, 1957), 604.
2 G.R. Stevens, *The Royal Canadian Regiment, vol. 2, 1933–1966* (London, ON: London Printing, 1967), 150.
3 G.R. Stevens, *The Princess Patricia's Canadian Light Infantry, 1919–1957* vol. 3 (Griesbach, AB, Historical Committee of the Regiment, n.d.), 180–81.
4 Beattie, 604–605.
5 J.T.B. Quayle, *In Action: A Personal Account of the Italian and Netherlands Campaigns of WW II* (Abbotsford, BC: Blue Stone, 1997), 194.
6 Major G.D. Mitchell, *RCHA–Right of the Line: An Anecdotal History of the Royal Canadian Horse Artillery from 1871* (Ottawa: RCHA History Committee, 1986), 136.
7 Ibid.
8 Ibid.
9 Rowland Ryder, *Oliver Leese* (London: Hamish Hamilton, 1987), 187–88.
10 3rd Canadian Field Regiment, Royal Canadian Artillery War Diary, Aug. 1944, National Archives of Canada, n.p.
11 17th Canadian Field Regiment, RCA War Diary, Aug. 1944, National Archives of Canada, 7.
12 Princess Patricia's Canadian Light Infantry War Diary, Aug. 1944, National Archives of Canada, 21–22.
13 Beattie, 606.
14 Col. C.P. Stacey, "Report No. 187 Historical Section Canadian Military Headquarters: Operations of 1 CDN Corps, 4 Jun 44 to 24 Sep 44—The Breaking of the Gothic Line and the Capture of Rimini," Department of National Defence, n.d., 32.

15 Beattie, 606.
16 G.W.L. Nicholson, *The Canadians in Italy: 1943–1945*, vol. 2 (Ottawa: Queen's Printer, 1956), 504.
17 Ibid., 503.
18 Ibid.
19 Douglas Orgill, *The Gothic Line: The Italian Campaign, Autumn 1944* (New York: W.W. Norton, 1967), 47.
20 Stacey, 31.
21 Orgill, 47.
22 Stacey, 33.
23 Nicholson, 505.
24 "Battle History 1 Canadian Infantry Brigade 25 Aug to 19 Oct 44," National Archives of Canada, 5.
25 Nicholson, 505.
26 Beattie, 607.
27 Ibid., 608.
28 Quayle, 188–89.
29 Ibid., 194.
30 Gordon Potts, "Battle Narrative, 25 Aug–29 Aug 44: The Royal Canadian Regiment," Directorate of History, Department of National Defence, n.p.
31 Royal Canadian Regiment War Diary, Aug. 1944, National Archives of Canada, n.p.
32 Ted Shuter, correspondence with author, 27 Mar. 2001.
33 Strome Galloway, *Bravely Into Battle: The Autobiography of a Canadian Soldier in World War Two* (Toronto: Stoddart, 1988), 207.
34 Shuter correspondence.
35 Stevens, *Royal Canadian Regiment*, 151.
36 Ryder, 188.

9: QUITE AN AFFAIR

1 "Account of the action of the Seaforth of Canada from River Metauro to River Marecchia–25 Aug to 21 Sep 44," Directorate of History, Department of National Defence, n.p.
2 Seaforth Highlanders of Canada War Diary, Aug. 1944, National Archives of Canada, n.p.
3 Major H.L. Glendinning, "Report on the action by 'C' Coy from 26 August to 2 September," Appendix to Seaforth Highlanders of Canada War Diary, Aug. 1944, National Archives of Canada, n.p.
4 Ibid.
5 "Battle History 1 Canadian Infantry Brigade 25 Aug to 19 Oct 44," National Archives of Canada, 6.

6 Hastings and Prince Edward War Diary, Aug. 1944, National Archives of Canada, n.p.
7 Farley Mowat, *The Regiment,* 2nd ed. (Toronto: McClelland & Stewart, 1973), 203.
8 Hastings and Prince Edward War Diary, n.p.
9 "Report on the action by 'B' Coy from 26 Aug to 31 Aug," Appendix to Seaforth Highlanders of Canada War Diary, Aug. 1944, National Archives of Canada, n.p.
10 "Account of the action of the Seaforth of Canada from River Metauro to River Marecchia–25 Aug to 21 Sep 44," n.p.
11 "Report on the action by 'B' Coy from 26 Aug to 31 Aug," n.p.
12 Reginald Roy, *The Seaforth Highlanders of Canada, 1919–1965* (Vancouver: Evergreen Press, 1969), 328.
13 James Riley Stone, interview by William S. Thackray. 13, 20 May and 3, 10, 17 June 1980, University of Victoria Special Collections.
14 Ibid.
15 Loyal Edmonton Regiment War Diary, Aug. 1944, National Archives of Canada, n.p.
16 Lt. Col. D.C. Cameron, "The Pursuit to the Gothic Line—22 Aug to 29 Aug," The Hastings and Prince Edward Regiment, Canadian Army Overseas, Directorate of History, Department of National Defence, 2.
17 Ibid.
18 Royal Canadian Regiment War Diary, Aug. 1944, National Archives of Canada, n.p.
19 Strome Galloway, *A Regiment at War: The Story of the Royal Canadian Regiment, 1939–1945* (Royal Canadian Regiment, 1979), 154.
20 RCR War Diary, n.p.
21 Loyal Edmonton Regiment War Diary, n.p.
22 Gibson, T.G., "Account by Brig. T.G. Gibson, Comd 2 CDN INF BDE, on the Action from 23 Aug to 22 Sep 44," n.d., National Archives of Canada, 2.
23 Loyal Edmonton Regiment War Diary, n.p.
24 G.W.L. Nicholson, *The Canadians in Italy: 1943–1945*, vol. 2 (Ottawa: Queen's Printer, 1956), 507.
25 Col. C.P. Stacey, "Report No. 187 Historical Section Canadian Military Headquarters: Operations of 1 CDN Corps, 4 Jun 44 to 24 Sep 44—The Breaking of the Gothic Line and the Capture of Rimini," Department of National Defence, n.d., 36.
26 Nicholson, 507.
27 Ibid., 508.
28 Ibid., 505.
29 Ibid., 511.

10: A GALLANT DO

1 "Battle History 1 Canadian Infantry Brigade 25 Aug to 19 Oct 44," National Archives of Canada, 10.
2 Ibid.
3 2nd Canadian Infantry Brigade War Diary, Aug. 1944, National Archives of Canada, n.p.
4 Ibid.
5 Princess Patricia's Canadian Light Infantry War Diary, Aug. 1944, National Archives of Canada, 23.
6 Alon Johnson, interview by author, 6 Oct. 2000, Victoria, BC.
7 Alon Johnson, interview by Ken McLeod, n.d., Victoria, BC.
8 Loyal Edmonton Regiment War Diary, Aug. 1944, National Archives of Canada, n.p.
9 Alon Johnson, interview by author, 9 Jan. 2002, Victoria, BC.
10 "Battle History 1 Canadian Infantry Brigade 25 Aug to 19 Oct 44," 6.
11 Hastings and Prince Edward Regiment War Diary, Aug. 1944, National Archives of Canada, n.p.
12 Col. C.P. Stacey, "Report No. 187 Historical Section Canadian Military Headquarters: Operations of 1 CDN Corps, 4 Jun 44 to 24 Sep 44—The Breaking of the Gothic Line and the Capture of Rimini," Department of National Defence, n.d., 36.
13 Farley Mowat, *The Regiment*. 2nd ed. (Toronto: McClelland & Stewart, 1973), 206.
14 Stacey, 36.
15 Hastings and Prince Edward Regiment War Diary, n.p.
16 Ibid.
17 1st Canadian Infantry Brigade War Diary, Aug. 1944, National Archives of Canada, 14.
18 Gordon Potts, "Battle Narrative, 25 Aug–29 Aug 44: The Royal Canadian Regiment," Directorate of History, Department of National Defence, n.p.
19 1st Canadian Infantry Brigade War Diary, 14.
20 2nd Canadian Infantry Brigade War Diary, Aug. 1944, National Archives of Canada, n.p.
21 1st Canadian Infantry Division (GS Branch) War Diary, Aug. 1944, National Archives of Canada, n.p.
22 2nd Canadian Infantry Brigade War Diary, n.p.
23 E.L.M. Burns, *General Mud: Memoirs of Two World Wars* (Toronto: Clarke, Irwin, 1970), 183.
24 "Olive: The Battle for the Gothic Line and the Advance into the Po Valley: 1 CDN Corps Narrative of Events," National Archives of Canada, 1.
25 Ibid.
26 Burns, 183.

27 Princess Patricia's Canadian Light Infantry War Diary, 23.
28 "21st Tank Brigade (British) report on 1 CID support at Gothic Line," National Archives of Canada, 2.
29 Princess Patricia's Canadian Light Infantry War Diary, 23.
30 Ibid., 24.
31 "21st Tank Brigade (British) report on 1 CID support at Gothic Line," 2.
32 Loyal Edmonton Regiment War Diary, n.p.
33 J.T.B. Quayle, *In Action: A Personal Account of the Italian and Netherlands Campaigns of WW II* (Abbotsford, BC: Blue Stone, 1997), 194–95.
34 Royal Canadian Regiment War Diary, Aug. 1944, National Archives of Canada, n.p.
35 Stacey, 38.
36 "21st Tank Brigade (British) report on 1 CID support at Gothic Line," 2.
37 Mowat, 206.
38 Hastings and Prince Edward Regiment War Diary, n.p.
39 Kim Beattie, *Dileas: History of the 48th Highlanders of Canada, 1929–1956* (Toronto: 48th Highlanders of Canada, 1957), 615.
40 48th Highlanders of Canada Regiment War Diary, Aug. 1944, National Archives of Canada, n.p.
41 Mowat, 208.
42 Ibid., 208–9.
43 G.W.L. Nicholson, *The Canadians in Italy: 1943–1945*, vol. 2 (Ottawa: Queen's Printer, 1956), 509.
44 Ibid., 510.

II: MOST DIFFICULT AND UNPLEASANT

1 Loyal Edmonton Regiment War Diary, Aug. 1944, National Archives of Canada, n.p.
2 Alon Johnson, interview by author, 9 Jan. 2002, Victoria, BC.
3 Loyal Edmonton Regiment War Diary, n.p.
4 Col. C.P. Stacey, "Report No. 187 Historical Section Canadian Military Headquarters: Operations of 1 CDN Corps, 4 Jun 44 to 24 Sep 44—The Breaking of the Gothic Line and the Capture of Rimini," Department of National Defence, n.d., 40.
5 Kim Beattie, *Dileas: History of the 48th Highlanders of Canada, 1929–1956* (Toronto: 48th Highlanders of Canada, 1957), 617–19.
6 48th Highlanders of Canada Regiment War Diary, Aug. 1944, National Archives of Canada, n.p.
7 Stacey, 39.
8 Princess Patricia's Canadian Light Infantry War Diary, Aug. 1944, National Archives of Canada, 25.
9 48th Highlanders of Canada Regiment War Diary, n.p.

10 Beattie, 621.
11 "21st Tank Brigade (British) report on 1 CID support at Gothic Line," National Archives of Canada, 2.
12 Hastings and Prince Edward Regiment War Diary, Aug. 1944, National Archives of Canada, n.p.
13 "Battle History 1 Canadian Infantry Brigade 25 Aug to 19 Oct 44," National Archives of Canada, 8.
14 48th Highlanders of Canada Regiment War Diary, n.p.
15 Stacey, 41.
16 "21st Tank Brigade (British) report on 1 CID support at Gothic Line," 3.
17 48th Highlanders of Canada Regiment War Diary, n.p.
18 Loyal Edmonton Regiment War Diary, n.p.
18 "21st Tank Brigade (British) report on 1 CID support at Gothic Line," 3.
20 Loyal Edmonton Regiment War Diary, n.p.
21 Johnson interview, 9 Jan. 2002.
22 G.R. Stevens, *A City Goes to War* (Brampton, ON: Charters, 1964), 308.
23 Loyal Edmonton Regiment War Diary, n.p.
24 Alon Johnson, interview by Ken McLeod, n.d., Victoria, BC.
25 "21st Tank Brigade (British) report on 1 CID support at Gothic Line," 3.
26 Johnson interview, 9 Jan. 2002.
27 Loyal Edmonton Regiment War Diary, n.p.
28 Seaforth Highlanders of Canada War Diary, Aug. 1944, National Archives of Canada, n.p.
29 Stacey, 41.
30 Ibid., 42.
31 "Battle History 1 Canadian Infantry Brigade 25 Aug to 19 Oct 44," 9.
32 "3rd Canadian Infantry Brigade Account of The Operations in Italy, 29 Aug – 21 Sep 44," National Archives of Canada, 2.
33 Lt. Col. D.C. Cameron, "The Pursuit to the Gothic Line – 22 Aug to 29 Aug," The Hastings and Prince Edward Regiment, Canadian Army Overseas, Directorate of History, Department of National Defence, 3.

12: SOMETHING RADICALLY WRONG

1 Stan Scislowski, *Not All of Us Were Brave* (Toronto: Dundurn, 1997), 236.
2 Perth Regiment of Canada War Diary, Aug. 1944, National Archives of Canada, n.p.
3 Scislowski, 237.
4 Perth Regiment War Diary, n.p.
5 Scislowski, 237–38.
6 Ibid., 238.
7 Ibid., 239.
8 Ibid., 241.

9 Ibid., 242.
10 Ibid.
11 Col. C.P. Stacey, "Report No. 187 Historical Section Canadian Military Headquarters: Operations of 1 CDN Corps, 4 Jun 44 to 24 Sep 44—The Breaking of the Gothic Line and the Capture of Rimini," Department of National Defence, n.d., 57–58.
12 Ibid., 51.
13 Ibid., 49.
14 Howard Mitchell, *My War: With the Saskatoon Light Infantry (M.G.), 1939–1945* (n.p., n.d.), 101.
15 Stacey, 49.
16 Ibid., 54–55.
17 Bert Hoffmeister, interview by B. Greenhous and W. McAndrew transcript, Directorate of History, Department of National Defence, n.d., 93–94.
18 Alex Morrison and Ted Slaney, *The Breed of Manly Men: The History of the Cape Breton Highlanders* (Toronto: The Canadian Institute of Strategic Studies, 1994), 221–22.
19 Perth Regiment War Diary, n.p.
20 Lt. W.F. Dean, "Report on Recce Patrol to Montecchio," Ops-11 Canadian Infantry Brigade, National Archives of Canada, 1–2.
21 Ibid., 52–53.
22 Hoffmeister interview, 95.
23 Stacey, 54.
24 11th Canadian Infantry Brigade War Diary, Aug. 1944, National Archives of Canada, n.p.
25 Chris Vokes, Operations 1st Canadian Division, "The Gothic Line—Phase Three: The Break-through the Gothic Line and the Pursuit to the Conca," National Archives of Canada, 9.
26 Ibid.
27 Ibid., 10.
28 "3rd Canadian Infantry Brigade Account of the Operations in Italy, 29 Aug – 21 Sep 44, Part Two: Attack on the Gothic Line," National Archives of Canada, 1.

13: GO DOWN, BOYS

1 "The West Nova Scotia Regiment, Part I: Gothic Line," National Archives of Canada, 2.
2 "3rd Canadian Infantry Brigade Account of the Operations in Italy, 29 Aug – 21 Sep 44, Part Two: Attack on the Gothic Line," National Archives of Canada, 2.
3 Chris Vokes, *My Story* (Ottawa: Gallery Books, 1985), 170.

4 "The West Nova Scotia Regiment, Part I: Gothic Line," 2.
5 West Nova Scotia Regiment War Diary, Aug. 1944, National Archives of Canada, n.p.
6 "The West Nova Scotia Regiment, Part I: Gothic Line," 3.
7 "3rd Canadian Infantry Brigade Account of the Operations in Italy, 29 Aug – 21 Sep 44, Part Two: Attack on the Gothic Line," National Archives of Canada, 3.
8 Ibid.
9 West Nova Scotia Regiment War Diary, n.p.
10 "3rd Canadian Infantry Brigade Account of the Operations in Italy, 29 Aug – 21 Sep 44, Part Two: Attack on the Gothic Line," 3–4.
11 Ibid., 4.
12 Ibid.
13 Ibid.
14 Ibid., 5.
15 Arthur Bishop, *Courage on the Battlefield: Canada's Military Heritage, vol. 2* (Toronto: McGraw Hill-Ryerson, 1993), 260–61.
16 "HQ 11th Canadian Infantry Brigade: The Attack on the Gothic Line and the Capture of Coriano, 20 Aug–14 Sep 44," National Archives of Canada, 2.
17 Cape Breton Highlanders of Canada War Diary, Aug. 1944, National Archives of Canada, n.p.
18 Alex Morrison and Ted Slaney, *The Breed of Manly Men: The History of the Cape Breton Highlanders* (Toronto: The Canadian Institute of Strategic Studies, 1994), 226–28.
19 Ibid., 229.
20 Ibid.
21 Cape Breton Highlanders of Canada War Diary, n.p.
22 Douglas How, *The 8th Hussars: A History of the Regiment* (Sussex, NB: Maritime Publishing, 1964), 230.
23 Ibid., 230–31.
24 Cape Breton Highlanders of Canada War Diary, n.p.
25 The Perth Regiment of Canada War Diary, Aug. 1944, National Archives of Canada, n.p.
26 Stan Scislowski, *Not All of Us Were Brave* (Toronto: Dundurn, 1997), 249.
27 Ibid., 250.
28 Col. C.P. Stacey, "Report No. 187 Historical Section Canadian Military Headquarters: Operations of 1 CDN Corps, 4 Jun 44 to 24 Sep 44—The Breaking of the Gothic Line and the Capture of Rimini," Department of National Defence, n.d., 58–59.
29 Scislowski, 250.
30 Ibid., 251–52.
31 Ibid., 255–56.

32 Stacey, 59.
33 Perth Regiment of Canada War Diary, n.p.
34 G.W.L. Nicholson, *The Canadians in Italy: 1943–1945*, vol. 2 (Ottawa: Queen's Printer, 1956), 515.
35 How, 233.
36 Morrison and Slaney, 227–28.
37 1st Canadian Infantry Division (GS Branch) War Diary, Aug. 1944, National Archives of Canada, n.p.
38 Stacey, 62–63.
39 Princess Patricia's Canadian Light Infantry War Diary, Aug. 1944, National Archives of Canada, 27.
40 G.R. Stevens, *Princess Patricia's Canadian Light Infantry, 1919–1957*, vol. 3 (Griesbach, AB: Historical Committee of the Regiment, n.d.), 185.

14: A DEFINITE BREACH

1 "The West Nova Scotia Regiment, Part I: Gothic Line," National Archives of Canada, 3.
2 Ibid.
3 "3rd Canadian Infantry Brigade Account of the Operations in Italy, 29 Aug – 21 Sep 44, Part Two: Attack on the Gothic Line," 5.
4 "The West Nova Scotia Regiment, Part I: Gothic Line," 4.
5 Jean V. Allard, *The Memoirs of General Jean V. Allard* (Vancouver: University of British Columbia, 1988), 84.
6 "The West Nova Scotia Regiment, Part I: Gothic Line," 4.
7 Ibid.
8 "5th Canadian Armoured Brigade: I–Account of Ops from 30 Aug to 14 Sep 44," Reginald Roy Collection, Special Collections, University of Victoria, 1.
9 Reginald Roy, *Sinews of Steel: The History of the British Columbia Dragoons* (Kelowna, BC: Charters, 1965), 287.
10 Eric Waldron, correspondence with Reginald Roy, 21 Sept. 1962, Reginald Roy Collection, Special Collections, University of Victoria, 1.
11 Chris Vokes, *My Story* (Ottawa: Gallery Books, 1985), 165.
12 David Kinloch, correspondence with author, 23 Nov. 2000.
13 David Kinloch, interview by author, 3 April 2000, Vernon, BC.
14 Stan Scislowski, *Not All of Us Were Brave* (Toronto: Dundurn, 1997), 259.
15 Ibid., 260–61.
16 Ibid., 261.
17 Ibid., 262.
18 Gordon Wood, *The Story of the Irish Regiment of Canada, 1939–1945* (Heerenveen, Holland: Hepkema, 1945), 42.
19 8th Princess Louise New Brunswick Hussars War Diary, Aug. 1944, National Archives of Canada, n.p.

20 Ibid.
21 Douglas How, *The 8th Hussars: A History of the Regiment* (Sussex, NB: Maritime Publishing, 1964), 235–39.
22 "Report on Operations, 5th Canadian Armoured Regiment (8NBH): Gothic Line to Fiumicino Rubicone, 24 Aug 44 to 13 Oct 44," Reginald Roy Collection, Special Collections, University of Victoria, 1.
23 How, 233–34.
24 Ibid., 239.
25 Wood, 42–43.
26 Irish Regiment of Canada War Diary, Aug. 1944, National Archives of Canada, n.p.
27 Ibid.
28 Princess Patricia's Canadian Light Infantry War Diary, Aug. 1944, National Archives of Canada, 29.
29 "21st Tank Brigade (British) report on 1 CID support at Gothic Line," National Archives of Canada, 4.
30 Jack Letcher written account, 1962, Reginald Roy Collection, Special Collections, University of Victoria.
31 Gerry Eastman, correspondence with Reginald Roy, 14 Nov. 1962, Reginald Roy Collection, Special Collections, University of Victoria, 3.
32 Roy, 292.
33 Letcher written account.
34 Tom Blake, interview by Ken McLeod, n.d., Vancouver.
35 Eastman correspondence.
36 "Report by Major Colin McDougall, OC B Coy, PPCLI," Directorate of History, Department of National Defence, n.p.
37 Col. C.P. Stacey, "Report No. 187 Historical Section Canadian Military Headquarters: Operations of 1 CDN Corps, 4 Jun 44 to 24 Sep 44—The Breaking of the Gothic Line and the Capture of Rimini," Department of National Defence, n.d., 62.
38 Princess Patricia's Canadian Light Infantry War Diary, 29.
39 Ibid.
40 G.R. Stevens, *Princess Patricia's Canadian Light Infantry, 1919–1957*, vol. 3 (Griesbach, AB: Historical Committee of the Regiment, n.d.), 185.

15: A BITTER DAY

1 Eric Waldron, correspondence with Reginald Roy, 21 Sept. 1962, Reginald Roy Collection, Special Collections, University of Victoria, 3–4.
2 Reginald Roy, *Sinews of Steel: The History of the British Columbia Dragoons* (Kelowna, BC: Charters, 1965), 293.
3 Perth Regiment of Canada War Diary, Aug. 1944, National Archives of Canada, n.p.

4 David Kinloch, correspondence with author, 23 Nov. 2000.
5 Gerry Eastman, correspondence with Reginald Roy, 14 Nov. 1962, Reginald Roy Collection, Special Collections, University of Victoria, 6.
6 Zeke Ferley, correspondence with Reginald Roy, 12 Nov. 1963, Reginald Roy Collection, Special Collections, 12.
7 Roy, 293.
8 Ferley correspondence, 13.
9 Ibid.
10 Roy, 295.
11 Ferley correspondence, 14.
12 Ibid., 15–17.
13 Eastman correspondence, 14 Nov. 1962, 4.
14 Ferley correspondence, 17.
15 Ibid., 18–19.
16 Ibid., 19.
17 Ibid., 20–21.
18 David Kinloch, interview with author, 3 April 2001, Vernon, BC.
19 Kinloch correspondence.
20 R.W. Green correspondence, 11 Sept. 1962, Reginald Roy Collection, Special Collections, University of Victoria, 2.
21 Raymond E. Stubbs correspondence, 7 Aug. 1963, Reginald Roy Collection, Special Collections, University of Victoria, 1.
22 Ibid.
23 Waldron correspondence, 7–8.
24 Ferley correspondence, 22.
25 Ibid., 23.
26 Ibid., 24.
27 Ibid., 26–31.
28 Gerry Eastman, correspondence with Reginald Roy, 8 March 1962, Reginald Roy Collection, Special Collections, University of Victoria, 6.
29 Green correspondence, 3.
30 Eastman correspondence, 8 March 1962, 3.
31 Stubbs correspondence, 2.
32 Eastman correspondence, 8 March 1962, 4.
33 Stubbs correspondence, 2.
34 Eastman correspondence, 8 March 1962, 4.
35 Roy, 303.
36 Ibid., 302.
37 Stubbs correspondence.
38 Chris Vokes, *My Story* (Ottawa: Gallery Books, 1985), 169.
39 Ibid.
40 Waldron correspondence, 12.

41 Kinloch correspondence.
42 Kinloch interview.

16: PURE BLOODY MURDER

1 J. M. McAvity, *Lord Strathcona's Horse (Royal Canadians): A Record of Achievement* (Toronto: Brigdens Limited, 1947), 120–21.
2 Gerry Eastman, correspondence with Reginald Roy, 14 Nov. 1962, Reginald Roy Collection, Special Collections, University of Victoria, 6.
3 McAvity, 120–21.
4 John Marteinson and Michael R. McNorgan, *The Royal Canadian Armoured Corps: An Illustrated History* (Toronto: Robin Brass Studio Inc., 2000), 210.
5 Zeke Ferley, correspondence with Reginald Roy, 12 Nov. 1963, Reginald Roy Collection, Special Collections, 12.
6 Reginald Roy, *Sinews of Steel: The History of the British Columbia Dragoons* (Kelowna, BC: Charters, 1965), 305.
7 Ibid., 306.
8 Arthur Bishop, *Courage on the Battlefield: Canada's Military Heritage, vol. 2* (Toronto: McGraw Hill-Ryerson, 1993), 262.
9 Stan Scislowski, *Not All of Us Were Brave* (Toronto: Dundurn, 1997), 266.
10 Perth Regiment of Canada War Diary, Aug. 1944, National Archives of Canada, n.p.
11 Scislowski, 266–67.
12 G.W.L. Nicholson, *The Canadians in Italy: 1943–1945*, vol. 2 (Ottawa: Queen's Printer, 1956), 519–20.
13 Col. C.P. Stacey, "Report No. 187 Historical Section Canadian Military Headquarters: Operations of 1 CDN Corps, 4 Jun 44 to 24 Sep 44—The Breaking of the Gothic Line and the Capture of Rimini," Department of National Defence, n.d., 67.
14 Douglas Orgill, *The Gothic Line: The Italian Campaign, Autumn 1944* (New York: W.W. Norton, 1967), 64–65.
15 Reginald Roy, *The Seaforth Highlanders of Canada, 1919–1965* (Vancouver: Evergreen Press, 1965), 330–31.
16 Seaforth Highlanders of Canada War Diary, Aug. 1944, National Archives of Canada, n.p.
17 Roy, *The Seaforth Highlanders of Canada*, 331.
18 Jean V. Allard, *The Memoirs of General Jean V. Allard* (Vancouver: University of British Columbia, 1988), 84.
19 "History—Royal Canadian Engineers, First Canadian Infantry Division: 1 August 1944–1 October 1944," National Archives of Canada, 9.
20 Royal 22e Regiment War Diary, Aug. 1944, National Archives of Canada, n.p.

21 "3rd Canadian Infantry Brigade: Account of the Operations in Italy, 29 Aug – 21 Sep 44," National Archives of Canada, 6.
22 Ibid.
23 Allard, 85–86.
24 Scislowski, 267.
25 Ibid., 268.
26 Ibid.
27 Ibid., 269.
28 Ibid.
29 McAvity, 122–24.
30 [Stafford Johnston] *The Fighting Perths: The Story of the First Century in the Life of a Canadian County Regiment* (Stratford, ON: Perth Regiment Veteran's Assoc., 1964), 92.
31 Scislowski, 271.
32 Ibid., 271–72.
33 Ibid., 272.
34 [Johnston,] 92.
35 Ibid.
36 Ibid.
37 Gerry Eastman, correspondence with Reginald Roy, 13 June 1963, Reginald Roy Collection, Special Collections, University of Victoria, 4.

17: A GREATER SORROW

1 Tony Poulin, *696 Heures d'enfer avec le Royal 22e Régiment,* trans. Tony Poulin (Quebec City: Éditions A-B, n.d.), n.p.
2 Tony Poulin, correspondence with author, 28 Sept. 2000, 1.
3 Tony Poulin, interview by author, 10 May 2000, Ottawa.
4 Ibid.
5 Ibid.
6 Ibid.
7 Royal 22e Regiment War Diary, Sept. 1944, National Archives of Canada, n.p.
8 Tony Poulin, *696 Heures d'enfer avec le Royal 22e Régiment,* n.p.
9 Tony Poulin, interview.
10 Royal 22e Regiment War Diary, n.p.
11 Tony Poulin, *696 Heures d'enfer avec le Royal 22e Régiment,* n.p.
12 Royal 22e Regiment War Diary, n.p.
13 Tony Poulin, *696 Heures d'enfer avec le Royal 22e Régiment,* n.p.
14 Ibid.
15 Ibid.
16 Ibid.
17 Tony Poulin interview.

18 Jean V. Allard, *The Memoirs of General Jean V. Allard* (Vancouver: University of British Columbia, 1988), 86–87.
19 Tony Poulin, *696 Heures d'enfer avec le Royal 22e Régiment,* n.p.
20 Ibid.
21 Royal 22e Regiment War Diary, n.p.
22 Tony Poulin, *696 Heures d'enfer avec le Royal 22e Régiment,* n.p.
23 Ibid.
24 Royal 22e Regiment War Diary, n.p.
25 Ibid.
26 Tony Poulin, *696 Heures d'enfer avec le Royal 22e Régiment,* n.p.
27 Royal 22e Regiment War Diary, n.p.
28 2nd Canadian Infantry Brigade War Diary, Sept. 1944, National Archives of Canada, n.p.
29 Martha Gellhorn, *The Face of War* (London: Granta Publications, 1998), 143.
30 Ibid.
31 Seaforth Highlanders of Canada War Diary, Sept. 1944, National Archives of Canada, n.p.
32 Alex Morrison and Ted Slaney, *The Breed of Manly Men: The History of the Cape Breton Highlanders* (Toronto: The Canadian Institute of Strategic Studies, 1994), 235.
33 Douglas How, *The 8th Hussars: A History of the Regiment* (Sussex, NB: Maritime Publishing, 1964), 242.
34 "Report on Operations: 5th Canadian Armoured Regiment (8NBH), Gothic Line to Fiumicino Rubicone–24 Aug 44 to 13 Oct 44," Reginald Roy Collection, Special Collections, University of Victoria, 2.
35 8th Princess Louise New Brunswick Hussars War Diary, Sept. 1944, National Archives of Canada, n.p.
36 How, 242–43.

18: ABSOLUTE BEDLAM

1 "HQ 11th Canadian Infantry Brigade: The Attack on the Gothic Line and the Capture of Coriano, 30 Aug – 14 Sep 44," Directorate of History, Department of National Defence, 4.
2 Princess Louise Dragoon Guards War Diary, Sept. 1944, National Archives of Canada, 1–2.
3 Col. C.P. Stacey, "Report No. 187 Historical Section Canadian Military Headquarters: Operations of 1 CDN Corps, 4 Jun 44 to 24 Sep 44—The Breaking of the Gothic Line and the Capture of Rimini," Department of National Defence, n.d., 69.
4 Princess Louise Dragoon Guards War Diary, 1.
5 J.M. McAvity, *Lord Strathcona's Horse (Royal Canadians): A Record of Achievement* (Toronto: Brigdens, 1947), 125.

6 Princess Louise Dragoons Guards War Diary, 2.
7 Arthur Bishop, *Courage on the Battlefield: Canada's Military Heritage, vol. 2* (Toronto: McGraw Hill-Ryerson, 1993), 262–63.
8 Gordon McGregor, interview by author, 3 Jan. 2001, Victoria, BC.
9 G.W.L. Nicholson, *The Canadians in Italy: 1943–1945*, vol. 2 (Ottawa: Queen's Printer, 1956), 521.
10 McAvity, 125.
11 Princess Louise Dragoon Guards War Diary, 2.
12 McAvity, 125.
13 Jackson, H.M. *The Princess Louise Dragoon Guards: A History* (Ottawa: The Regiment, 1952), 206.
14 Irish Regiment of Canada War Diary, Sept. 1944, National Archives of Canada, 1.
15 Douglas How, *The 8th Hussars: A History of the Regiment* (Sussex, NB: Maritime Publishing, 1964), 243.
16 Ibid.
17 Ibid., 244.
18 Gordon Wood, *The Story of the Irish Regiment of Canada, 1939–1945* (Heerenveen, Holland: Hepkema, 1945), 44.
19 How, 244.
20 Wood, 44.
21 The Irish Regiment of Canada War Diary, 1.
22 Loyal Edmonton Regiment War Diary, Sept. 1944, National Archives of Canada, n.p.
23 John Dougan, interview by author, 9 Oct. 2000, Victoria, BC.
24 Loyal Edmonton Regiment War Diary, n.p.
25 Nicholson, 522.
26 Dominick Graham and Shelford Bidwell, *Tug of War: The Battle for Italy, 1943–1945* (New York: St. Martin's Press, 1986), 356–57.
27 Stacey, 71.
28 Ibid., 70.
29 I Canadian Corps (GS Branch) War Diary, Sept. 1944, National Archives of Canada, 1.
30 Stacey, 71–72.
31 Ibid., 72.
32 E.L.M. Burns, *General Mud: Memoirs of Two World Wars* (Toronto: Clarke, Irwin, 1970), 188.
33 Ibid., 188–89.
34 I Canadian Corps (GS Branch) War Diary, 1.
35 Dr. William McAndrew, "Eighth Army at the Gothic Line: The Dog-Fight," *RUSI*, June 1986, 58.
36 Ibid., 60.
37 Graham and Bidwell, 360.

19: A LONG CHANCE

1 W.R. Freasby (ed.), *Official History of the Canadian Medical Services, 1939–1945, vol. 1: Organization and Campaigns* (Ottawa: Queen's Printer, 1956), 194.
2 Waldo E.L. Smith, *What Time the Tempest: An Army Chaplain's Story* (Toronto: The Ryerson Press, 1953), 267.
3 Ibid., 268.
4 Ibid., 269.
5 Ibid.
6 1st Canadian Infantry Division (GS Branch) War Diary, Sept. 1944, National Archives of Canada, 1.
7 Royal Canadian Dragoons War Diary, Sept. 1944, National Archives of Canada, 1.
8 Col. C.P. Stacey, "Report No. 187 Historical Section Canadian Military Headquarters: Operations of 1 CDN Corps, 4 Jun 44 to 24 Sep 44—The Breaking of the Gothic Line and the Capture of Rimini," Department of National Defence, n.d., 75.
9 G.R. Stevens, *Princess Patricia's Canadian Light Infantry, 1919–1957*, vol. 3 (Griesbach, AB: Historical Committee of the Regiment, n.d.), 188.
10 "21st Tank Brigade (British) report on 1 CID support at Gothic Line," National Archives of Canada, 5.
11 Loyal Edmonton Regiment War Diary, Sept. 1944, National Archives of Canada, n.p.
12 "21st Tank Brigade report," 5.
13 John Dougan, "Account Given to Historical Officer on 11 Oct 44," Directorate of History, Department of National Defence, 1.
14 Loyal Edmonton Regiment War Diary, n.p.
15 G.R. Stevens, *A City Goes to War* (Brampton, ON: Charters, 1964), 311.
16 Seaforth Highlanders of Canada War Diary, Sept. 1944, National Archives of Canada, n.p.
17 "21st Tank Brigade report," 5.
18 G.W.L. Nicholson, *The Canadians in Italy: 1943–1945*, vol. 2 (Ottawa: Queen's Printer, 1956), 522.
19 John Marteinson and Michael R. McNorgan, *The Royal Canadian Armoured Corps: An Illustrated History* (Toronto: Robin Brass Studio Inc., 2000), 201.
20 Ibid., 197.
21 Royal Canadian Dragoons War Diary, 2.
22 Ibid.
23 Ibid.
24 Stacey, 76.
25 *Royal Canadian Dragoons: 1939–1945* (Montreal: The Regiment, 1946), 105.
26 Royal Canadian Dragoons War Diary, 2.

27 *Royal Canadian Dragoons*, 106.
28 Ibid.
29 Royal Canadian Dragoons War Diary, 3.
30 *Royal Canadian Dragoons*, 108.
31 Ibid.
32 Ibid., 108–109.
33 Brereton Greenhous, *Dragoon: The Centennial History of the Royal Canadian Dragoons, 1883–1983* (Ottawa: Guild of the Royal Canadian Dragoons, 1983), 354.
34 Ibid.
35 Fred Cederberg, *The Long Road Home: The Autobiography of a Canadian Soldier in Italy in World War II* (Toronto: Stoddart Publishing, 1985), 151.
36 Ibid., 152.
37 Lanark & Renfrew Scottish Regiment War Diary, Sept. 1944, National Archives of Canada, n.p.
38 Stacey, 72.
39 Westminster (Motorized) Regiment War Diary, Sept. 1944, National Archives of Canada, n.p.
40 J.E. Oldfield, *The Westminsters' War Diary: An Unofficial History of the Westminster Regiment (Motor) in World War II* (New Westminster, BC: n.p., 1964), 118.
41 Stacey, 72.
42 Ibid., 77.
43 Nicholson, 523.
44 Stacey, 77.
45 Carl Bayerlein, "Retreat through Central Italy, 1944," account in possession of author, translated from German (Alex MacQuarrie, trans.), n.d., 10.
46 Ibid., 11.
47 Ibid.
48 von Austerman, *Eben Emael–Edewichter Damm* (Alex McQuarrie, trans. from passage provided by Carl Bayerlein), (n.p., n.d.), n.p.
49 Leutnant Hobeck, "Letter to Mr. Bayerlein," Dec. 12, 1944 (Alex McQuarrie, trans.), letter provided by Carl Bayerlein.
50 Nicholson, 523.
51 Douglas Orgill, *The Gothic Line: The Italian Campaign, Autumn 1944* (New York: W.W. Norton, 1967), 94.
52 Stacey, 88.

20: ALL THIS UNPLEASANTNESS

1 G.W.L. Nicholson, *The Canadians in Italy: 1943–1945*, vol. 2 (Ottawa: Queen's Printer, 1956), 526.
2 Col. C.P. Stacey, "Report No. 187 Historical Section Canadian Military

Headquarters: Operations of 1 CDN Corps, 4 Jun 44 to 24 Sep 44—The Breaking of the Gothic Line and the Capture of Rimini," Department of National Defence, n.d., 78–79.

3 "5 Canadian Armoured Brigade: I–Account of Ops from 30 Aug to 14 Sep 44," Reginald Roy Collection, Special Collections, University of Victoria, 3.

4 J.M. McAvity, *Lord Strathcona's Horse (Royal Canadians): A Record of Achievement* (Toronto: Brigdens, 1947), 130.

5 Lord Strathcona's Horse War Diary, Sept. 1944, National Archives of Canada, 3.

6 McAvity, 131.

7 Lord Strathcona's Horse War Diary, 3.

8 McAvity, 133.

9 Ibid., 131–33.

10 Ibid., 133–35.

11 Ibid., 135.

12 J.E. Oldfield, *The Westminsters' War Diary: An Unofficial History of the Westminster Regiment (Motor) in World War II* (New Westminster, BC: n.p., 1964), 118–19.

13 Ibid.

14 Westminster (Motorized) Regiment War Diary, Sept. 1944, National Archives of Canada, n.p.

15 Oldfield, 119.

16 Westminster Regiment War Diary, n.p.

17 McAvity, 135.

18 Governor General's Horse Guards War Diary, Sept. 1944, National Archives of Canada, 7–11.

19 Ibid.

20 Fred Cederberg, *The Long Road Home: The Autobiography of a Canadian Soldier in Italy in World War II* (Toronto: Stoddart Publishing, 1985), 154.

21 Ibid., 155.

22 Ibid.

23 Governor General's Horse Guards War Diary, 11.

21: A SURE-THING GALLOP

1 Gordon Potts, "Battle Narrative, 3 Sep–6 Sep 44: The Royal Canadian Regiment," Directorate of History, Department of National Defence, 1.

2 "21st Tank Brigade (British) report on 1 CID support at Gothic Line," National Archives of Canada, 6.

3 Royal Canadian Regiment War Diary, Sept. 1944, National Archives of Canada, 2.

4 J.T.B. Quayle, *In Action: A Personal Account of the Italian and Netherlands Campaigns of WW II* (Abbotsford, BC: Blue Stone, 1997), 196–97.

5 Ibid., 197.
6 Royal Canadian Regiment War Diary, 3.
7 Ibid.
8 Ibid., 3–4.
9 Ibid.
10 Royal Canadian Dragoons War Diary, Sept. 1944, National Archives of Canada, 3.
11 *Royal Canadian Dragoons: 1939–1945* (Montreal: The Regiment, 1946), 112.
12 Royal Canadian Dragoons War Diary, 3.
13 1st Canadian Infantry Brigade War Diary, Sept. 1944, National Archives of Canada, n.p.
14 Hastings and Prince Edward Regiment War Diary, Sept. 1944, National Archives of Canada, n.p.
15 Ibid.
16 Royal Canadian Dragoons War Diary, 3–4.
17 Hastings and Prince Edward Regiment War Diary, n.p.
18 "B 55, B Coy: Log Book–2 Sept 44 – 6 Sept 44, Appendix to Royal Canadian Regiment War Diary, Sept. 1944, National Archives of Canada, 2.
19 Ibid.
20 Hastings and Prince Edward Regiment War Diary, n.p.
21 1st Canadian Infantry Division (GS Branch) War Diary, Sept. 1944, National Archives of Canada, 3.
22 E.L.M. Burns, *General Mud: Memoirs of Two World Wars* (Toronto: Clarke, Irwin, 1970), 190.
23 Col. C.P. Stacey, "Report No. 187 Historical Section Canadian Military Headquarters: Operations of 1 CDN Corps, 4 Jun 44 to 24 Sep 44—The Breaking of the Gothic Line and the Capture of Rimini," Department of National Defence, n.d., 88.
24 Ibid.
25 G.W.L. Nicholson, *The Canadians in Italy: 1943–1945*, vol. 2 (Ottawa: Queen's Printer, 1956), 528.
26 Daniel Dancocks, *The D-Day Dodgers: The Canadians in Italy, 1943–1945* (Toronto: McClelland & Stewart, 1991), 326.
27 Dr. William McAndrew, "Eighth Army at the Gothic Line: The Dog-Fight," *RUSI*, June 1986, 60.
28 Dominick Graham and Shelford Bidwell, *Tug of War: The Battle for Italy, 1943–1945* (New York: St. Martin's Press, 1986), 360.
29 Ibid., 351.
30 McAndrew, 59.
31 Ibid., 58.
32 Ibid., 58.

33 Douglas Orgill, *The Gothic Line: The Italian Campaign, Autumn 1944* (New York: W.W. Norton, 1967), 106–7.
34 Ibid., 70.
35 "B 55, B Coy: Log Book–2 Sept 44–6 Sept 44," 2.
36 Farley Mowat, *The Regiment*, 2nd ed. (Toronto: McClelland & Stewart, 1973), 215–16.
37 Hastings and Prince Edward Regiment War Diary, n.p.
38 "21st Tank Brigade (British) report on 1 CID support at Gothic Line," 6.
39 Mowat, 216.
40 Royal Canadian Regiment War Diary, n.p.
41 1st Canadian Infantry Brigade War Diary, n.p.
42 "21st Tank Brigade (British) report on 1 CID support at Gothic Line," 7.
43 1st Canadian Infantry Brigade War Diary, n.p.
44 Ibid.
45 1st Canadian Infantry Division (GS Branch) War Diary, 4.
46 1st Canadian Infantry Brigade War Diary, n.p.
47 3rd Canadian Infantry Brigade War Diary, Sept. 1944, National Archives of Canada, n.p.
48 Royal Canadian Regiment War Diary, n.p.
49 "B 55, B Coy: Log Book–2 Sept 44 – 6 Sept 44," 3.
50 Royal Canadian Regiment War Diary, n.p.
51 Mowat, 217.
52 Hastings and Prince Edward Regiment War Diary, n.p.
53 Kim Beattie, *Dileas: History of the 48th Highlanders of Canada, 1929–1956* (Toronto: 48th Highlanders of Canada, 1957), 630.
54 Ibid., 631.
55 Ibid., 632.
56 48th Highlanders of Canada War Diary, Sept. 1944, National Archives of Canada, 3.

22: IT WAS USELESS

1 Douglas How, *The 8th Hussars: A History of the Regiment* (Sussex, NB: Maritime Publishing, 1964), 249–50.
2 Ibid., 250–51.
3 8th Princess Louise New Brunswick Hussars War Diary, Sept. 1944, National Archives of Canada, 3.
4 How, 252.
5 8th Princess Louise New Brunswick Hussars War Diary, 3.
6 Westminster (Motorized) Regiment War Diary, Sept. 1944, National Archives of Canada, n.p.
7 J.E. Oldfield, *The Westminsters' War Diary: An Unofficial History of the Westminster Regiment (Motor) in World War II* (New Westminster, BC: n.p., 1964), 120.

8 Ron Hurley, interview by author, 4 Oct. 2000, Vancouver.
9 Ibid.
10 Ibid.
11 Ibid.
12 Ibid.
13 Westminster Regiment War Diary, n.p.
14 Oldfield, 121–22.
15 Governor General's Horse Guards War Diary, Sept. 1944, National Archives of Canada, 13–16.
16 British Columbia Dragoons War Diary, Sept. 1944, National Archives of Canada, n.p.
17 Reginald Roy, *Sinews of Steel: The History of the British Columbia Dragoons* (Kelowna, BC: Charters, 1965), 313–14.
18 How, 253–55.
19 Ibid., 255.
20 Ibid., 256.
21 Ibid., 256–59.
22 Ibid., 259–60.
23 Ibid., 260–62.

23: A HARD ROW TO HOE

1 Strome Galloway, *Sicily to the Siegfried Line: Being Some Random Memories and a Diary of 1944–1945* (Kitchener, ON: Arnold Press, n.d.), 18.
2 Royal Canadian Regiment War Diary, Sept. 1944, National Archives of Canada, n.p.
3 48th Highlanders of Canada Regiment War Diary, Sept. 1944, National Archives of Canada, 3.
4 "Operations, 5th Canadian Armoured Division: 'The Gothic Line,'" Directorate of History, Department of National Defence, 7.
5 Hastings and Prince Edward Regiment War Diary, Sept. 1944, National Archives of Canada, n.p.
6 Strome Galloway, *A Regiment at War: The Story of the Royal Canadian Regiment, 1939–1945* (Royal Canadian Regiment, 1979), 158.
7 Royal Canadian Regiment War Diary, n.p.
8 *Royal Canadian Dragoons: 1939–1945* (Montreal: The Regiment, 1946), 11.
9 Col. C.P. Stacey, "Report No. 187 Historical Section Canadian Military Headquarters: Operations of 1 CDN Corps, 4 Jun 44 to 24 Sep 44—The Breaking of the Gothic Line and the Capture of Rimini," Department of National Defence, n.d., 82–83.
10 Ibid., 83.
11 "B 55, B Coy: Log Book–2 Sept 44 – 6 Sept 44, Appendix to Royal Canadian Regiment War Diary, Sept. 1944, National Archives of Canada, 6–7.

12 Kim Beattie, *Dileas: History of the 48th Highlanders of Canada, 1929–1956* (Toronto: 48th Highlanders of Canada, 1957), 637.
13 Stacey, 85.
14 "Operations, 5th Canadian Armoured Division: 'The Gothic Line,'" 7.
15 Ibid.
16 Gordon Wood, *The Story of the Irish Regiment of Canada, 1939–1945* (Heerenveen, Holland: Hepkema, 1945), 46.
17 Ibid.
18 "Operations, 5th Canadian Armoured Division: 'The Gothic Line,'" 7.
18 Ibid.
20 I Canadian Corps War Diary, Sept. 1944, National Archives of Canada, 2–3.
21 5th Canadian Armoured Division War Diary, Sept. 1944, National Archives of Canada, n.p.
22 Rowland Ryder, *Oliver Leese* (London: Hamish Hamilton, 1987), 189.
23 Ibid.
24 Royal Canadian Regiment War Diary, n.p.
25 Ibid.
26 Strome Galloway, *Sicily to the Siegfried Line,* 19.
27 Strome Galloway, *A Regiment at War,* 160.
28 48th Highlanders of Canada Regiment War Diary, n.p.
29 Gordon Potts, "Battle Narrative: 3 Sep – 6 Sep 44, The Royal Canadian Regiment," Directorate of History, Department of National Defence, 2.

24: FIVE MINUTES TO TWELVE

1 Douglas Orgill, *The Gothic Line: The Italian Campaign, Autumn 1944* (New York: W.W. Norton, 1967), 112.
2 Ibid., 118.
3 E.L.M. Burns, *General Mud: Memoirs of Two World Wars* (Toronto: Clarke, Irwin, 1970), 192.
4 Orgill, 119.
5 Gordon Wood, *The Story of the Irish Regiment of Canada, 1939–1945* (Heerenveen, Holland: Hepkema, 1945), 47.
6 Ibid.
7 Col. C.P. Stacey, "Report No. 187 Historical Section Canadian Military Headquarters: Operations of I CDN Corps, 4 Jun 44 to 24 Sep 44—The Breaking of the Gothic Line and the Capture of Rimini," Department of National Defence, n.d., 94.
8 Ibid.
9 Ibid.
10 "Olive: The Battle for the Gothic Line and the Advance into the Po Valley: I Canadian Corps Narrative of Events," National Archives of Canada, 10.

11 G.W.L. Nicholson, *The Canadians in Italy: 1943–1945*, vol. 2 (Ottawa: Queen's Printer, 1956), 532.
12 Burns, 193–94.
13 Stacey, 94.
14 Strome Galloway, interview by author, 6 May 2000, Ottawa.
15 Burns, 194.
16 Bert Hoffmeister, interview by Greenhous and McAndrew transcript, Directorate of History, Department of National Defence, n.d., 100.
17 Nicholson, 533–34.
18 Stacey, 99.
19 Strome Galloway, *Sicily to the Siegfried Line: Being Some Random Memories and a Diary of 1944–1945* (Kitchener, ON: Arnold Press, n.d.), 20.
20 Seaforth Highlanders of Canada War Diary, Sept. 1944, National Archives of Canada, n.p.
21 Major Roy C.H. Durnford, diary, National Archives of Canada, 82.
22 Jack Haley, interview by author, 24 Aug. 2000, Victoria, BC.
23 Basil Smith, "Memoirs of a Quarterbloke," unpublished manuscript, Directorate of History, Department of National Defence, n.d., 104.
24 Ibid., 105.
25 Durnford, 83.
26 Gerry Wheeler recollections, audiotape provided by family, 2002.
27 Ibid.
28 Durnford, 84.
29 Smith, 105.
30 17th Canadian Field Regment, RCA War Diary, Sept. 1944, National Archives of Canada, 4.
31 3rd Canadian Field Regiment, RCA War Diary, Sept. 1944, National Archives of Canada, n.p.
32 Oviglio Monti, interview by author, 22 Oct. 2000, Rimini, Italy.
33 Ron Hurley, interview by author, 4 Oct. 2000, Vancouver.
34 Nicholson, 534.

25: THIS IS OUR HOUSE

1 Col. C.P. Stacey, "Report No. 187 Historical Section Canadian Military Headquarters: Operations of I CDN Corps, 4 Jun 44 to 24 Sep 44—The Breaking of the Gothic Line and the Capture of Rimini," Department of National Defence, n.d., 95.
2 Alex Morrison and Ted Slaney, *The Breed of Manly Men: The History of the Cape Breton Highlanders* (Toronto: The Canadian Institute of Strategic Studies, 1994), 249.
3 HQ II Canadian Infantry Brigade, "The Attack on the Gothic Line and the Capture of Coriano: 30 Aug–13 Sep 44," National Archives of Canada, 8.

4 Morrison and Slaney, 250.
5 Ibid., 252.
6 Ibid.
7 [Stafford Johnston] *The Fighting Perths: The Story of the First Century in the Life of a Canadian County Regiment* (Stratford, ON: Perth Regiment Veteran's Assoc., 1964), 96–97.
8 Douglas How, *The 8th Hussars: A History of the Regiment* (Sussex, NB: Maritime Publishing, 1964), 265.
9 Morrison and Slaney, 252–53.
10 A.J. Kerry and W.A. McDill, *History of the Corps of Royal Canadian Engineers*, vol. 2 (Ottawa: The Military Engineers Assoc. of Canada, 1966), 231.
11 Ibid.
12 Bert Hoffmeister, interview by Greenhous and McAndrew transcript, Directorate of History, Department of National Defence, n.d., 100.
13 How, 265.
14 8th Princess Louise New Brunswick Hussars War Diary, Sept. 1944, National Archives of Canada, 6.
15 Kerry and McDill, 232.
16 Irish Regiment of Canada War Diary, Sept. 1944, National Archives of Canada, n.p.
17 Gordon Wood, *The Story of the Irish Regiment of Canada, 1939–1945* (Heerenveen, Holland: Hepkema, 1945), 48.
18 How, 268–69.
19 Ibid., 266–67.
20 Ibid., 269–70.
21 Oviglio Monti, interview by author, 22 Oct. 2000, Rimini, Italy.
22 J.M. McAvity, *Lord Strathcona's Horse (Royal Canadians): A Record of Achievement* (Toronto: Brigdens, 1947), 139–40.
23 Westminster (Motorized) Regiment War Diary, Sept. 1944, National Archives of Canada, n.p.
24 J.E. Oldfield, *The Westminsters' War Diary: An Unofficial History of the Westminster Regiment (Motor) in World War II* (New Westminster, BC: n.p., 1964), 123.
25 McAvity, 140.
26 Oldfield, 124.
27 McAvity, 140–41.
28 Stacey, 96–97.
29 G.W.L. Nicholson, *The Canadians in Italy: 1943–1945*, vol. 2 (Ottawa: Queen's Printer, 1956), 535.
30 "The Battle of Rimini from German telephone logs and War Diaries," Directorate of History, Department of National Defence, 52.

31 Nicholson, 536.
32 Ibid., 536–37.

26: A CAREFULLY COORDINATED PLAN

1 Col. C.P. Stacey, "Report No. 187 Historical Section Canadian Military Headquarters: Operations of I CDN Corps, 4 Jun 44 to 24 Sep 44—The Breaking of the Gothic Line and the Capture of Rimini," Department of National Defence, n.d., 100.
2 "Olive: The Battle for the Gothic Line and the Advance into the Po Valley: I Canadian Corps Narrative of Events," National Archives of Canada, 10.
3 G.W.L. Nicholson, *The Canadians in Italy: 1943–1945*, vol. 2 (Ottawa: Queen's Printer, 1956), 537.
4 Chris Vokes, Operations 1st Canadian Infantry Division, "The Gothic Line—Phase Five: The Crossing of the T Marano–The Battle for S. Lorenzo and S. Fortunato Features–The Capture of Rimini," National Archives of Canada, 16–17.
5 Ibid., 16–18.
6 Robert Tooley, *Invicta: The Carleton and York Regiment in the Second World War* (Fredericton, NB: New Ireland Press, 1989), 273.
7 3rd Canadian Infantry Brigade War Diary, Sept. 1944, National Archives of Canada, 16.
8 Tooley, 274.
9 Jean V. Allard, *The Memoirs of General Jean V. Allard* (Vancouver: University of British Columbia, 1988), 88–89.
10 Ibid., 89.
11 Ibid.
12 "Royal 22e Regiment account: Part Two–Crossing of the Marano," National Archives of Canada, 2.
13 Tony Poulin, correspondence with author, 23 Feb. 2001, n.p.
14 Tony Poulin, interview by author, 10 May 2000, Ottawa.
15 Poulin correspondence, 23 Feb. 2001.
16 Henri Tellier, "Account by Major H. Tellier, OC 'A' Company R22e Regiment," Directorate of History, Department of National Defence, 1.
17 Poulin correspondence, 23 Feb. 2001.
18 Tellier, "Account by Major H. Tellier, OC 'A' Company R22e Regiment," 1.
19 Ibid.
20 Poulin interview, 10 May 2000.
21 Royal 22e Regiment War Diary, Sept. 1944, National Archives of Canada, n.p.
22 Ibid.
23 Allard, 89.
24 Royal 22e Regiment War Diary, n.p.

25 Ibid.
26 Allard, 89.
27 Royal 22e Regiment War Diary, n.p.
28 West Nova Scotia Regiment War Diary, Sept. 1944, National Archives of Canada, n.p.
29 Ibid.
30 Ibid.
31 Ibid.
32 "3 Canadian Infantry Brigade, Account of Operations in Italy: 29 Aug–21 Sep 44," National Archives of Canada, 10.
33 3rd Canadian Infantry Brigade War Diary, Sept. 1944, National Archives of Canada, 16.
34 "3 Canadian Infantry Brigade, Account of Operations in Italy: 29 Aug–21 Sep 44," 10.
35 Ibid.
36 "The West Nova Scotia Regiment, Part Two: Battle for Rimini," National Archives of Canada, 13.
37 Allard, 90.
38 Ibid.
39 Ibid.
40 Ibid.
41 Stacey, 105.
42 "21st Tank Brigade (British) report on 1 CID support at Gothic Line," National Archives of Canada, 9.

27: LITTLE REASON FOR IT

1 West Nova Scotia Regiment War Diary, Sept. 1944, National Archives of Canada, n.p.
2 "The West Nova Scotia Regiment, Part Two: Battle for Rimini," National Archives of Canada, 13.
3 3rd Canadian Infantry Brigade War Diary, Sept. 1944, National Archives of Canada, 17.
4 Ibid.
5 Royal 22e Regiment War Diary, Sept. 1944, National Archives of Canada, n.p.
6 3rd Canadian Infantry Brigade War Diary, 17.
7 West Nova Scotia Regiment War Diary, n.p.
8 "The West Nova Scotia Regiment, Part Two: Battle for Rimini," 14.
9 Royal 22e Regiment War Diary, n.p.
10 Jean V. Allard, *The Memoirs of General Jean V. Allard* (Vancouver: University of British Columbia, 1988), 91.

11 Ibid.
12 Ibid.
13 Ibid., 91–92.
14 Royal 22e Regiment War Diary, n.p.
15 Allard, 92.
16 Ibid.
17 Thomas H. Raddall, *West Novas: A History of the West Nova Scotia Regiment* (n.p., 1947), 228.
18 Col. C.P. Stacey, "Report No. 187 Historical Section Canadian Military Headquarters: Operations of 1 CDN Corps, 4 Jun 44 to 24 Sep 44—The Breaking of the Gothic Line and the Capture of Rimini," Department of National Defence, n.d., 109–110.
19 "Battle History 1 Canadian Infantry Brigade 25 Aug to 19 Oct 44," National Archives of Canada, 20.
20 Ibid.
21 I Canadian Corps (GS Branch) War Diary, Sept. 1944, National Archives of Canada, 7.
22 Ibid., 111.
23 Allard, 93.
24 Stacey, 112.
25 Reginald Roy, *The Seaforth Highlanders of Canada, 1919–1965* (Vancouver: Evergreen Press, 1969), 334.
26 "Royal 22e Regiment account: Part Three–Battle of the San Martino Ridge," National Archives of Canada, 2.
27 Allard, 94.
28 Seaforth Highlanders of Canada War Diary, Sept. 1944, National Archives of Canada, n.p.
29 Roy, 335.
30 Jack Haley, interview by author, 24 Aug. 2000, Victoria, BC.
31 Ibid.
32 Seaforth Highlanders of Canada War Diary, n.p.
33 Haley interview.
34 Seaforth Highlanders of Canada War Diary, n.p.
35 Kim Beattie, *Dileas: History of the 48th Highlanders of Canada, 1929–1956* (Toronto: 48th Highlanders of Canada, 1957), 650.
36 48th Highlanders of Canada War Diary, Sept. 1944, National Archives of Canada, 11.
37 Ibid.
38 Beattie, 652–53.
39 "21st Tank Brigade (British) report on 1 CID support at Gothic Line," National Archives of Canada, 10.

40 Beattie, 653.
41 Royal Canadian Regiment War Diary, Sept. 1944, National Archives of Canada, n.p.
42 J. Milton Gregg, correspondence with author, Oct. 2001.
43 Royal Canadian Regiment War Diary, n.p.
44 Gordon Potts, "Battle Narrative: 14 Sep–22 Sep 44, The Royal Canadian Regiment," Directorate of History, Department of National Defence, 1.
45 Royal Canadian Regiment War Diary, n.p.
46 G.R. Stevens, *The Royal Canadian Regiment, vol. 2, 1933–1966* (London, ON: London Printing, 1967), 157.
47 Strome Galloway, *A Regiment at War: The Story of the Royal Canadian Regiment, 1939–1945* (Royal Canadian Regiment, 1979), 163.
48 Strome Galloway, *Sicily to the Siegfried Line: Being Some Random Memories and a Diary of 1944–1945* (Kitchener, ON: Arnold Press, n.d.), 22.
49 Strome Galloway, *Sicily to the Siegfried Line*, 22.

28: TO THE LAST MAN

1 Tony Poulin, interview by author, 10 May 2000, Ottawa.
2 Ibid.
3 Jean V. Allard, *The Memoirs of General Jean V. Allard* (Vancouver: University of British Columbia, 1988), 93.
4 Royal 22e Regiment War Diary, Sept. 1944, National Archives of Canada, n.p.
5 Poulin interview.
6 Ibid.
7 Ibid.
8 Royal 22e Regiment War Diary, n.p.
9 Princess Patricia's Canadian Light Infantry War Diary, Sept. 1944, National Archives of Canada, 15.
10 Ibid., 16.
11 Seaforth Highlanders of Canada War Diary, Sept. 1944, National Archives of Canada, n.p.
12 Royal 22e Regiment War Diary, n.p.
13 Princess Patricia's Canadian Light Infantry War Diary, 17.
14 Poulin interview.
15 Allard, 93.
16 Royal 22e Regiment War Diary, n.p.
17 Ibid.
18 G.R. Stevens, *Princess Patricia's Canadian Light Infantry: 1919–1957*, vol. 3 (Griesbach, AB: Historical Committee of the Regiment, n.d.), 192.
19 Royal 22e Regiment War Diary, n.p.
20 Poulin interview.
21 Royal 22e Regiment War Diary, n.p.

22 Ibid.
23 Col. C.P. Stacey, "Report No. 187 Historical Section Canadian Military Headquarters: Operations of 1 CDN Corps, 4 Jun 44 to 24 Sep 44—The Breaking of the Gothic Line and the Capture of Rimini," Department of National Defence, n.d., 112.
24 Seaforth Highlanders of Canada War Diary, n.p.
25 "21st Tank Brigade (British) report on 1 CID support at Gothic Line," National Archives of Canada, 10.
26 Charles Monroe Johnson, *Action with the Seaforths* (New York: Vantage Press, 1954), 319.
27 Ibid., 320–21.
28 Reginald Roy, *The Seaforth Highlanders of Canada, 1919–1965* (Vancouver: Evergreen Press, 1969), 338.
29 Ibid., 338–39.
30 Syd Thomson, interview by author, 27 May 2000, Salmon Arm, BC.
31 Ibid.
32 Ibid.
33 Thomson interview.
34 Roy, 339.
35 Johnson, 321.
36 Kim Beattie, *Dileas: History of the 48th Highlanders of Canada, 1929–1956* (Toronto: 48th Highlanders of Canada, 1957), 654–58.
37 Strome Galloway, *Sicily to the Siegfried Line: Being Some Random Memories and a Diary of 1944–1945* (Kitchener, ON: Arnold Press, n.d.), 22.
38 J.T.B. Quayle, *In Action: A Personal Account of the Italian and Netherlands Campaigns of WW II* (Abbotsford, BC: Blue Stone, 1997), 199.
39 Ibid.
40 Thomson interview.
41 Beattie, 656–57.
42 West Nova Scotia Regiment War Diary, Sept. 1944, National Archives of Canada, n.p.
43 Chris Vokes, *My Story* (Ottawa: Gallery Books, 1985), 170–71.
44 E.L.M. Burns, *General Mud: Memoirs of Two World Wars* (Toronto: Clarke, Irwin, 1970), 202.
45 Ibid., 202.
46 Stacey, 117–18.

29: GOING TO BLEED YOU

1 Reginald Roy, *The Seaforth Highlanders of Canada, 1919–1965* (Vancouver: Evergreen Press, 1969), 340.
2 Douglas Orgill, *The Gothic Line: The Italian Campaign, Autumn 1944*, (New York: W.W. Norton, Inc, 1967), 137.
3 Col. C.P. Stacey, "Report No. 187 Historical Section Canadian Military

Headquarters: Operations of 1 CDN Corps, 4 Jun 44 to 24 Sep 44—The Breaking of the Gothic Line and the Capture of Rimini," Department of National Defence, n.d., 114–15.

4 Roy, 340–41.
5 John Dougan, "Account Given to Historical Officer on 11 Oct 44," Directorate of History, Department of National Defence, 1.
6 John Dougan, interview by author, 9 Oct. 2000, Victoria, BC.
7 Ibid.
8 Dougan, "Account Given to Historical Officer on 11 Oct 44," 2.
9 Dougan, interview by author.
10 Dougan, "Account Given to Historical Officer on 11 Oct 44," 2.
11 Dougan, interview by author.
12 Dougan, "Account Given to Historical Officer on 11 Oct 44," 2.
13 Dougan, interview by author.
14 Dougan, "Account Given to Historical Officer on 11 Oct 44," 2.
15 G.R. Stevens, *A City Goes to War* (Brampton, ON: Charters, 1964), 314.
16 John Alpine Dougan, interview by Tom Torrie, 27 July 1989, University of Victoria Special Collections.
17 Ibid.
18 Dougan, interview by author.
19 Princess Patricia's Canadian Light Infantry War Diary, Sept. 1944, National Archives of Canada, 19.
20 Tony Poulin, interview by author, 10 May 2000, Ottawa.
21 Pat Crofton, interview by Ken McLeod, n.d., Vancouver.
22 Princess Patricia's Canadian Light Infantry War Diary, 19.
23 Crofton interview.
24 Ibid.
25 Princess Patricia's Canadian Light Infantry War Diary, 20.
26 Carleton and York Regiment War Diary, Sept. 1944, National Archives of Canada, 11.
27 G.W.L. Nicholson, *The Canadians in Italy: 1943–1945*, vol. 2 (Ottawa: Queen's Printer, 1956), 548.
28 Carleton and York Regiment War Diary, 12.
29 Nicholson, 551.
30 Ibid.
31 48th Highlanders of Canada War Diary, Sept. 1944, National Archives of Canada, 13.
32 Royal Canadian Regiment War Diary, Sept. 1944, National Archives of Canada, n.p.
33 J. Milton Gregg, correspondence with author, Oct. 2001.
34 J.T.B. Quayle, *In Action: A Personal Account of the Italian and Netherlands Campaigns of WW II* (Abbotsford, BC: Blue Stone, 1997), 200.

35 Ted Shuter, correspondence with author, 27 Mar. 2001.
36 Royal Canadian Regiment War Diary, n.p.
37 Ted Shuter, correspondence with author.
38 48th Highlanders of Canada War Diary, 13.
39 Carleton and York Regiment War Diary, 12.
40 A.J. Kerry and W.A. McDill, *History of the Corps of Royal Canadian Engineers*, vol. 2 (Ottawa: The Military Engineers Assoc. of Canada, 1966), 235.
41 Ibid., 236.
42 Stacey, 120.
43 Lt. Col. D.C. Cameron, "The Battle for San Fortunato Ridge," The Hastings and Prince Edward Regiment, Canadian Army Overseas, Directorate of History, Department of National Defence, 2.
44 Hastings and Prince Edward Regiment War Diary, Sept. 1944, National Archives of Canada, n.p.
45 Farley Mowat, *The Regiment*, 2nd ed. (Toronto: McClelland & Stewart, 1973), 226.

30: WE'LL ALL BE HEROES

1 Lt. Col. D.C. Cameron, "The Battle for San Fortunato Ridge," The Hastings and Prince Edward Regiment, Canadian Army Overseas, Directorate of History, Department of National Defence, 2–3.
2 "21st Tank Brigade (British) report on 1 CID support at Gothic Line," National Archives of Canada, 11.
3 Cameron, "The Battle for San Fortunato Ridge," 3.
4 Ibid.
5 "21st Tank Brigade (British) report on 1 CID support at Gothic Line," 11.
6 Farley Mowat, *The Regiment*, 2nd ed. (Toronto: McClelland & Stewart, 1973), 227.
7 Cameron, "The Battle for San Fortunato Ridge," 3.
8 "21st Tank Brigade (British) report on 1 CID support at Gothic Line," 11.
9 Cameron, "The Battle for San Fortunato Ridge," 3.
10 Ibid., 2.
11 Ibid., 3.
12 3rd Canadian Infantry Brigade War Diary, Sept. 1944, National Archives of Canada, 20.
13 "21st Tank Brigade (British) report on 1 CID support at Gothic Line," 11.
14 G.W.L. Nicholson, *The Canadians in Italy: 1943–1945*, vol. 2 (Ottawa: Queen's Printer, 1956), 553.
15 "Phase Five: The Crossing of the T Marano–The Battle for S. Lorenzo and S. Fortunato Features–The Capture of Rimini," National Archives of Canada, 19.

16 Ibid., 554.
17 J. Milton Gregg, correspondence with author, Oct. 2001.
18 Ibid.
19 Royal Canadian Regiment War Diary, Sept. 1944, National Archives of Canada, n.p.
20 Ted Shuter, correspondence with author, 27 Mar. 2001.
21 Royal Canadian Regiment War Diary, n.p.
22 Shuter correspondence.
23 Royal Canadian Regiment War Diary, n.p.
24 Nicholson, 559.
25 Gregg correspondence.
26 Jean V. Allard, *The Memoirs of General Jean V. Allard* (Vancouver: University of British Columbia, 1988), 95.
27 Ibid.
28 Ibid., 96.
29 Henri Tellier, "Account by Major H. Tellier, OC 'A' Company R22e Regiment," Directorate of History, Department of National Defence, 2.
30 Allard, 96.
31 Tellier, "Account by Major H. Tellier," 2.
32 Allard, 96–97.
33 Tellier, "Account by Major H. Tellier," 2–3.
34 Ibid., 3.
35 Ibid.
36 Ibid.
37 L.F. Trudeau, "Account by Major L.F. Trudeau, OC 'C' Company R22e Regiment," Directorate of History, Department of National Defence, 1.
38 Col. C.P. Stacey, "Report No. 187 Historical Section Canadian Military Headquarters: Operations of 1 CDN Corps, 4 Jun 44 to 24 Sep 44—The Breaking of the Gothic Line and the Capture of Rimini," Department of National Defence, n.d., 124.
39 Allard, 97.
40 G.R. Stevens, *A City Goes to War* (Brampton, ON: Charters, 1964), 316.
41 Loyal Edmonton Regiment War Diary, Sept. 1944, National Archives of Canada, n.p.
42 Ibid.
43 Ibid.
44 Nicholson, 556.
45 Loyal Edmonton Regiment War Diary, n.p.
46 John Dougan, interview by author, 9 Oct. 2000, Victoria, BC.
47 Ibid.
48 Stevens, 317.
49 John Dougan, "Account Given to Historical Officer," Directorate of History, Department of National Defence, 3.

50 Dougan, interview by author.
51 James Riley Stone, interview by William Thackray, 13, 20 May and 3, 10, 17 June 1980, University of Victoria Special Collections.
52 Loyal Edmonton Regiment War Diary, n.p.
53 Stevens, 318.

31: THE GALLANT ATTACKERS

1 Reginald Roy, *The Seaforth Highlanders of Canada, 1919–1965* (Vancouver: Evergreen Press, 1969), 344–45.
2 G.W.L. Nicholson, *The Canadians in Italy: 1943–1945*, vol. 2 (Ottawa: Queen's Printer, 1956), 557.
3 Roy, 346–47.
4 L.F. Trudeau, "Account by Major L.F. Trudeau, OC 'C' Company R22e Regiment," Directorate of History, Department of National Defence, 1.
5 Tony Poulin, interview by author, 10 May 2000, Ottawa.
6 Ibid.
7 John Dougan, "Account Given to Historical Officer," Directorate of History, Department of National Defence, 3.
8 Loyal Edmonton Regiment War Diary, Sept. 1944, National Archives of Canada, n.p.
9 Dougan, "Account Given to Historical Officer," 3.
10 Loyal Edmonton Regiment War Diary, n.p.
11 West Nova Scotia Regiment War Diary, Sept. 1944, National Archives of Canada, 22.
12 E.L.M. Burns, *General Mud: Memoirs of Two World Wars* (Toronto: Clarke, Irwin, 1970), 206.
13 G.W.L. Nicholson, *The Canadians in Italy: 1943–1945*, vol. 2 (Ottawa: Queen's Printer, 1956), 557.
14 "21st Tank Brigade (British) report on 1 CID support at Gothic Line," National Archives of Canada, 12.
15 Nicholson, 557.
16 Seaforth Highlanders of Canada War Diary, Sept. 1944, National Archives, n.p.
17 Loyal Edmonton Regiment War Diary, n.p.
18 Hastings and Prince Edward Regiment War Diary, Sept. 1944, National Archives of Canada, n.p.
19 Nicholson, 558.
20 Ibid., 565.
21 C. Sydney Frost, *Once a Patricia* (St. Catharines, ON: Vanwell, 1988), 282–84.
22 Princess Patricia's Canadian Light Infantry War Diary, Sept. 1944, National Archives of Canada, 24.
23 Frost, 285–87.

24 Princess Patricia's Canadian Light Infantry War Diary, 24.
25 Frost, 287.
26 Ibid., 288.
27 48th Highlanders of Canada War Diary, Sept. 1944, National Archives of Canada, 15.
28 Frost, 288–90.

32: WELL DONE, CANADA

1 2nd Canadian Infantry Brigade War Diary, Sept. 1944, National Archives of Canada, n.p.
2 Major Roy C.H. Durnford, diary, National Archives of Canada, 87.
3 Ibid.
4 Ibid.
5 James Riley Stone, interview by William Thackray, 13, 20 May and 3, 10, 17 June 1980, University of Victoria Special Collections.
6 Ian MacLeod, "Did Canadians Steal the Treasures?" *National Post* 17 March 2001, A16.
7 Durnford, 87.
8 2nd Canadian Infantry Brigade War Diary, n.p.
9 Seaforth Highlanders of Canada War Diary, Sept. 1944, National Archives of Canada, n.p.
10 Stone interview.
11 Amadeo Montemaggi, correspondence with author, 25 May 2001.
12 Seaforth Highlanders of Canada War Diary, n.p.
13 Peter Stursberg, CBC Radio broadcast, 22 Sept. 1944, CBC Radio Archives.
14 Ibid.
15 Amadeo Montemaggi, interview by author, 23 Oct. 2000, Rimini, Italy.
16 Oviglio Monte, interview by author, 21 Oct. 2000, Rimini, Italy.
17 "Phase Five: The Crossing of the T Marano–The Battle for S. Lorenzo and S. Fortunato Features–The Capture of Rimini," National Archives of Canada, 22.
18 "21st Tank Brigade (British) report on I CID support at Gothic Line," National Archives of Canada, 13.
19 Ibid., 17–18.
20 Col. C.P. Stacey, "Report No. 187 Historical Section Canadian Military Headquarters: Operations of I CDN Corps, 4 Jun 44 to 24 Sep 44—The Breaking of the Gothic Line and the Capture of Rimini," Department of National Defence, n.d., 135–36.
21 G.W.L. Nicholson, *The Canadians in Italy: 1943–1945*, vol. 2 (Ottawa: Queen's Printer, 1956), 681.
22 Stacey, 136.

23 Douglas Orgill, *The Gothic Line: The Italian Campaign, Autumn 1944* (New York: W.W. Norton, 1967), 159.
24 E.L.M. Burns, *General Mud: Memoirs of Two World Wars* (Toronto: Clarke, Irwin, 1970), 208.
25 Ibid.
26 Thomas H. Raddall, *West Novas: A History of the West Nova Scotia Regiment* (n.p., 1947), 232.
27 Syd Thomson, interview by author, 27 May 2000, Salmon Arm, BC.
28 Ibid.
29 Nicholson, 579.
30 W.G.F. Jackson, *The Mediterranean and Middle East,* vol. 6–Part 2 (London: Her Majesty's Stationery Office, 1987), 361–63.
31 Rowland Ryder, *Oliver Leese* (London: Hamish Hamilton, 1987), 191.
32 Burns, 218.

EPILOGUE

1 G.W.L. Nicholson, *The Canadians in Italy: 1943–1945,* vol. 2 (Ottawa: Queen's Printer, 1956), 679.
2 Ibid., 681.

BIBLIOGRAPHY

BOOKS

Allard, Jean V. *The Memoirs of General Jean V. Allard*. Vancouver: University of British Columbia Press, 1988.

Beattie, Kim. *Dileas: History of the 48th Highlanders of Canada, 1929–1956*. Toronto: 48th Highlanders of Canada, 1957.

Bennett, Ralph. *Ultra and Mediterranean Strategy: 1944–1945*. London: Hamish Hamilton, 1989.

Bishop, Arthur. *Courage on the Battlefield: Canada's Military Heritage. Vol. 2*. Toronto: McGraw Hill-Ryerson, 1993.

Boissonault, Charles-Marie. *Histoire du Royal 22e Régiment*. Québec: Éditions du Pélican, 1964.

Burns, E.L.M. *General Mud: Memoirs of Two World Wars*. Toronto: Clarke, Irwin, 1970.

———. *Manpower in the Canadian Army, 1939–1945*. Toronto: Clarke, Irwin, 1956.

Cederberg, Fred. *The Long Road Home: The Autobiography of a Canadian Soldier in Italy in World War II*. Toronto: Stoddart, 1985.

Copp, Terry and William McAndrew. *Battle Exhaustion*. Montreal: McGill-Queen's University Press, 1990.

Dancocks, Daniel G. *The D-Day Dodgers: The Canadians in Italy, 1943–1945*. Toronto: McClelland & Stewart, 1991.

Deighton, Len. *Blitzkrieg: From the Rise of Hitler to the Fall of Dunkirk*. London: Jonathon Cape, 1979.

Duquemin, Colin K. *Stick to the Guns: A Short History of the 10th Field Battery, Royal Regiment of Canadian Artillery, St. Catherines, Ontario*. St. Catherines, ON: Norman Enterprises, 1996.

Ellis, John. *Brute Force: Allied Strategy and Tactics in the Second World War*. London: Andre Deutsch, 1990.

———. *The Sharp End of War: The Fighting Man in World War II*. London: David & Charles, 1980.

Fraser, W.B. *Always a Strathcona*. Calgary: Comprint Publishing Company, 1976.

Freasby, W.R., ed. *Official History of the Canadian Medical Services, 1939–1945. Vol. 1: Organization and Campaigns*. Ottawa: Queen's Printer, 1956.

———. *Official History of the Canadian Medical Services, 1939–1945. Vol. 2: Clinical Subjects.* Ottawa: Queen's Printer, 1953.

Frost, C. Sydney. *Once a Patricia.* St. Catherines, ON: Vanwell, 1988.

Galloway, Strome. *Bravely into Battle: The Autobiography of a Canadian Soldier in World War 2.* Toronto: Stoddart, 1988.

———. *A Regiment at War: The Story of the Royal Canadian Regiment, 1939–1945.* Royal Canadian Regiment, 1979.

———. *Sicily to the Siegfried Line: Being Some Random Memories and a Diary of 1944–1945.* Kitchener, ON: Arnold Press, n.d.

Gellhorn, Martha. *The Face of War.* London: Granta Publications, 1998.

The Governor General's Horse Guards, 1939–1945. Toronto: Canadian Military Journal, 1954.

Graham, Dominick and Shelford Bidwell. *Tug of War: The Battle for Italy, 1943–1945.* New York: St. Martin's Press, 1986.

Granatstein, J.L. *The Generals: The Canadian Army's Senior Commanders in the Second World War.* Toronto: Stoddart, 1993.

Greenhous, Brereton. *Dragoon: The Centennial History of the Royal Canadian Dragoons, 1883–1983.* Ottawa: Guild of the Royal Canadian Dragoons, 1983.

Higgins, Trumbull. *Soft Underbelly: The Anglo-American Controversy over the Italian Campaign, 1939–1945.* New York: Macmillan, 1968.

History of 17th Field Regiment, Royal Canadian Artillery: 5th Canadian Armoured Division. Groningen, Holland: J. Niemeijer's Co., 1946.

How, Douglas. *The 8th Hussars: A History of the Regiment.* Sussex, NB: Maritime Publishing, 1964.

Hurley, Ron. *Ritorno in Italia: Thirty Years After.* New Westminster, BC: n.p., 1976.

Jackson, H.M. *The Princess Louise Dragoon Guards: A History.* Ottawa: The Regiment, 1952.

———. *The Royal Regiment of Artillery, Ottawa, 1855–1952.* n.p., 1952.

Jackson, W.G.F. *Alexander of Tunis: As Military Commander.* London: B.T. Batsford, 1971.

———. *The Mediterranean and Middle East. Vol. 6, Part 2.* London: Her Majesty's Stationery Office, 1987.

Johnson, Charles Monroe. *Action with the Seaforths.* New York: Vantage Press, 1954.

[Johnston, Stafford.] *The Fighting Perths: The Story of the First Century in the Life of a Canadian County Regiment.* Stratford, ON: Perth Regiment Veterans' Assoc., 1964.

Kerry, A.J. & W.A. McDill. *History of the Corps of Royal Canadian Engineers. Vol. 2.* Ottawa: The Military Engineers Assoc. of Canada, 1966.

Kesselring, Albert. Lynton Hudson, trans. *The Memoirs of Field Marshal Kesselring.* London: William Kimber, 1953.

Kitching, George. *Mud and Green Fields: The Memoirs of Major General George Kitching*. Langley, BC: Battleline Books, 1985.

Lamb, Richard. *War in Italy, 1943–1945: A Brutal Story*. London: John Murray, 1993.

Landall, K.D. *Royal Canadian Dragoons*. Montreal: The Regiment, 1946.

McAndrew, Bill. *Canadians and the Italian Campaign, 1943–1945*. Montreal: Éditions Art Global, 1996.

McAvity, J.M. *Lord Strathcona's Horse (Royal Canadians): A Record of Achievement*. Toronto: Bridgens, 1947.

Marteinson, John and Michael R. McNorgan, *The Royal Canadian Armoured Corps: An Illustrated History*. Toronto: Robin Brass Studio, 2000.

Mitchell, G.D. RCHA*—Right of the Line: An Anecdotal History of the Royal Canadian Horse Artillery from 1871*. Ottawa: RCHA History Committee, 1986.

Mitchell, Howard. *My War: With the Saskatoon Light Infantry (M.G.), 1939–1945*. N.p., n.d.

Montemaggi, Amedeo and Bill McAndrew. *The Gothic Line: Linea Gotica*. Tavullia, Italy: Comune di Tavullia, 1997.

Morris, Eric. *Circles of Hell: The War In Italy, 1943–1945*. New York: Crown Publishers, 1993.

Morrison, Alex and Ted Slaney. *The Breed of Manly Men: The History of the Cape Breton Highlanders*. Toronto: The Canadian Institute of Strategic Studies, 1994.

Mowat, Farley. *The Regiment*. 2nd ed. Toronto: McClelland & Stewart, 1973.

Nicholson, G.W.L. *The Canadians in Italy: 1939–1945. Vol. 2*. Ottawa: Queen's Printer, 1956.

——. *The Gunners of Canada. Vol. 2*. Toronto: McClelland & Stewart, 1972.

The North Irish Horse, Battle Report: North Africa and Italy. Belfast: W. & G. Baird, 1946.

Oldfield, J.E. *The Westminsters' War Diary: An Unofficial History of the Westminster Regiment (Motor) in World War II*. New Westminster, BC: n.p., 1964.

Orgill, Douglas. *The Gothic Line: The Italian Campaign, Autumn 1944* New York: W.W. Norton, 1967.

Perrett, Bryan. *Tank Warfare*. London: Arms & Armour Press, 1990.

———. *Through Mud and Blood: Infantry/Tank Operations in World War II*. London: Robert Hale & Co., 1975.

Poulin, Tony. *696 Heures d'enfer avec le Royal 22e Régiment*. Trans. Tony Poulin. Quebec City: Éditions A–B, n.d.

Quayle, J.T.B. *In Action: A Personal Account of the Italian and Netherlands Campaigns of WW II*. Abbotsford, BC: Blue Stone, 1997.

Raddall, Thomas H. *West Novas: A History of the West Nova Scotia Regiment*. N.p., 1947.

Ross, Alexander. *Slow March to a Regiment*. St. Catherines, ON: Vanwell, 1993.
Rowland, David Parsons. *The Padre*. Scarborough, ON: Consolidated Amethyst Communications, 1982.
Roy, Reginald H. *The Seaforth Highlanders of Canada, 1919–1965*. Vancouver: Evergreen Press, 1969.
———. *Sinews of Steel: The History of the British Columbia Dragoons*. Toronto: Charters, 1965.
Royal Canadian Dragoons: 1939–1945. Montreal: The Regiment, 1946.
Ryder, Rowland. *Oliver Leese*. London: Hamish Hamilton, 1987.
Scislowski, Stan. *Not All of Us Were Brave*. Toronto: Dundurn Press, 1997.
Smith, Waldo E.L. *What Time the Tempest: An Army Chaplain's Story*. Toronto: Ryerson Press, 1953.
Stevens, G.R. *A City Goes to War*. Brampton, ON: Charters, 1964.
———. *Princess Patricia's Canadian Light Infantry: 1919–1957. Vol. 3*. Griesbach, AB: Historical Committee of the Regiment, n.d.
———. *The Royal Canadian Regiment. Vol. 2, 1933–1966*. London, ON: London Printing, 1967.
Tooley, Robert. *Invicta: The Carleton and York Regiment in the Second World War*. Fredericton, NB: New Ireland Press, 1989.
Vokes, Chris. *Vokes: My Story*. Ottawa: Gallery Books, 1985.
von Austerman. *Eben Emael–Edewichter Damm*. Trans. Alex McQuarrie. n.p., n.d.
Wallace, John F. *Dragons of Steel: Canadian Armour in Two World Wars*. Burstown, ON: General Store Publishing, 1995.
Westphal, Siegfried. *The German Army in the West*. London: Cassell & Co., 1951.
Wood, Gordon. *The Story of the Irish Regiment of Canada, 1939–1945*. Heerenveen, Holland: Hepkema, 1945.

MAGAZINES AND NEWSPAPERS

McAndrew, William. "Eighth Army at the Gothic Line: Commanders and Plans." *RUSI*. March 1986: 50–57.
———. "Eighth Army at the Gothic Line: The Dog-Fight." *RUSI*. June 1986: 55–62.
MacLeod, Ian. "Did Canadians Steal the Treasures?" *National Post*. 17 March 2001: A16.

UNPUBLISHED MATERIALS

"Account of the action of the Seaforth of Canada from River Metauro to River Marecchia–25 Aug to 21 Sep 44." 145.255.011. Directorate of History, Department of National Defence.
Alexander, Harold Rupert Leofric George (Field Marshal). "The Allied Armies in Italy." Vol. 3. MG27 III A1, vol. 6. National Archives of Canada.

"Battle History 1 Canadian Infantry Brigade 25 Aug to 19 Oct 44." RG24, vol. 10883. National Archives of Canada.
"The Battle of Rimini from German Telephone Logs and War Diaries." Directorate of History, Department of National Defence.
Bayerlein, Carl. "Retreat through Central Italy." Trans. Alex McQuarrie. In possession of the author.
British Columbia Dragoons (9th Canadian Armoured Regiment) War Diary, Aug.–Sept. 1944. RG24, vol. 14229. National Archives of Canada.
Burns, E.L.M. (Lt. Gen.). "Canadian Operations in the Mediterranean Area, May–June 1944: Extracts from Memoranda" (Series 23). Directorate of History, Department of National Defence.
———. "Olive Planning Notes No. 1," RG24, vol. 10779. National Archives of Canada.
Cameron, Don (Lt. Col). "The Pursuit to the Gothic Line–22 Aug to 29 Aug" and "Leading up to the Battle for S. Fortunato Ridge." The Hastings and Prince Edward Regiment, Canadian Army Overseas. 145.2H1013 (D2), Directorate of History, Department of National Defence.
Canadian Land Forces Command and Staff College: Kingston. "Operation Olive: Battlefield Study," Department of National Defence.
Canadian Operations in the Mediterranean Area, May–Sept. 1944: Extracts from War Diaries and Memoranda (Series 27). Directorate of History, Department of National Defence.
Canadian Operations in the Mediterranean Area, May–Sept. 1944: Extracts from War Diaries and Memoranda (Series 28). Directorate of History, Department of National Defence.
Cape Breton Highlanders War Diary, Aug.–Sept. 1944. RG24, vol. 15048. National Archives of Canada.
Carleton and York Regiment War Diary, Aug. 1944. RG24, vol. 15050. Sept. 1944. RG24, vol. 15051. National Archives of Canada.
Crerar Papers. Vol. 7, file 958C.0009 (E157). National Archives of Canada.
Dean, W.F. (Lt.). "Report on Recce Patrol to Montecchio," Ops—11 Canadian Infantry Brigade, RG24, vol. 10982. National Archives of Canada.
Dougan, John. "Account Given to Historical Officer on 11 Oct 44." 145.2E2 (D1), Directorate of History, Department of National Defence.
Durnford, Roy C.H. Diary of Maj. Roy Durnford, Chaplain (Padre), the Seaforth Highlanders of Canada, June 1943–June 1945. National Archives of Canada.
8th Canadian Field Regiment (Self-Propelled), Royal Canadian Artillery War Diary, Aug.–Sept. 1944. RG24, vol. 14451. National Archives of Canada.
8th Princess Louise's New Brunswick Hussars. "Report on Operations, 5th Canadian Armoured Regiment (8NBH): Gothic Line to Fiumicino Rubicone, 24 Aug 44 to 13 Oct 44." University of Victoria, Special Collections, Reginald Roy Collection.

8th Princess Louise's New Brunswick Hussars War Diary, Aug.–Sept. 1944. RG24, vol. 14209. National Archives of Canada.
11th Canadian Infantry Brigade. "The Smashing of the Gothic Line." University of Victoria, Special Collections, Reginald Roy Collection.
11th Canadian Infantry Brigade Headquarters. "The Attack on the Gothic Line and the Capture of Coriano, 30 Aug–14 Sep 44." RG24, vol. 10982. National Archives of Canada.
11th Canadian Infantry Brigade (Headquarters) War Diary, Aug.–Sept. 1944. RG24, vol. 14159. National Archives of Canada.
5th Canadian Armoured Brigade. "I—Account of Ops from 30 Aug to 14 Sep 44." University of Victoria, Special Collections, Reginald Roy Collection.
5th Canadian Armoured Brigade (Headquarters) War Diary, Aug.–Sept. 1944. RG24, vol. 14056. National Archives of Canada.
5th Canadian Armoured Division (GS Headquarters) War Diary, Aug.–Sept. 1944. RG24, vol. 13796. National Archives of Canada.
5th Canadian Armoured Division. "Operations: The Gothic Line." Directorate of History, Department of National Defence.
1st Canadian Infantry Brigade (Headquarters) War Diary, Aug.–Sept. 1944. RG24, vol. 14077. National Archives of Canada.
1st Canadian Infantry Division War Diary (GS Branch), Aug. 1944. RG24, vol. 13728 and Sept. 1944. RG24, vol. 13729. National Archives of Canada.
48th Highlanders of Canada Regiment War Diary, Aug.–Sept. 1944. RG24, vol. 15297. National Archives of Canada.
Gibson, T.G. (Brig.), "Account by Brig T.G. Gibson, Comd 2 CDN INF BDE, on the Action from 23 Aug to Sep 44." RG24, vol. 10883. National Archives of Canada.
Governor General's Horse Guards (3rd Canadian Armoured Reconnaissance Regiment) War Diary, Aug.–Sept. 1944. RG24, vol. 14200. National Archives of Canada.
Hastings and Prince Edward Regiment War Diary, Aug.–Sept. 1944. RG24, vol. 15073. National Archives of Canada.
"History: Royal Canadian Engineers First Canadian Infantry Division, 1 Aug. 1944–1 Oct. 1944." RG24, vol. 10883. National Archives of Canada.
Hobeck, Leutnant. "Letter to Mr. Bayerlein." 12 Dec. 1944. Trans. Alex McQuarrie. In possession of the author.
Horsey, R.M. (Maj.). "Account by Maj. Horsey, OC 'D' Company Carleton & York Regt of action in area of R Marano 7–14 Sep 44 and action at R Ausa, 18–19 Sep 44." 145.2C6.011 (D1), Directorate of History, Department of National Defence.
Irish Regiment of Canada War Diary, Aug.–Sept. 1944. RG24, vol. 15086. National Archives of Canada.
Italian Campaign–Sicily and Southern Italy, July 1943–April 1945. Condensed from an Official Historical Sketch prepared by the Canadian Army

Historical Section. N.d., n.p. Directorate of History, Department of National Defence.

Johnston, I.S. (Brig.). "Appreciation on a possible attack by 11 Cdn Inf Bde Gp on Montecchio posns on the Gothic Line." RG24, vol. 10983. National Archives of Canada.

Lanark and Renfrew Scottish Regiment (1st Light Anti-Aircraft Regiment) War Diary, Aug.–Sept. 1944. RG24, vol. 14587. National Archives of Canada.

Landell, K.D. (Lt. Col.). "Report on Ops 1 CACR 28 Aug–20 Oct 44." 141.4A1011 (D1). Directorate of History, Department of National Defence.

Lord Strathcona's Horse Regiment (2nd Canadian Armoured Regiment) War Diary, Aug. 1944. RG24, vol. 14192 and Sept. 1944. RG24, vol. 14193. National Archives of Canada.

Loyal Edmonton Regiment War Diary, Aug.–Sept. 1944. RG24, vol. 15115. National Archives of Canada.

McAndrew, William. "Canadian Land Forces Staff Course: Operation Olive Battlefield Study, Eighth Army at the Gothic Line." Kingston: Department of National Defence, 1984.

McDougall, Colin (Maj.). "The Crossing of the Foglio and the Minefield–31 Aug 44 and Crossing the River Marrecchia–20/21 Sep & 21 Sep 44." 145.2P7011(D3). Directorate of History, Department of National Defence.

McDougall, Colin. (Maj.). "Report by Major Colin McDougall, OC B Coy, PPCLI." Directorate of History, Department of National Defence.

Mackenzie, Don (Lt. Col.). "Report on Ops of 48 Highlanders from 25 Aug 44 to 8 Sep 44." 145.2H3013 (D1). Directorate of History, Department of National Defence.

"Olive: The Battle for the Gothic Line and the Advance into the Po Valley—1 CDN Corps Narrative of Events." RG24, vol. 10779. National Archives of Canada.

I Canadian Corps War Diary (Gen. E.L.M. Burns), Sept. 1944. RG24, vol. 17507. National Archives of Canada.

I Canadian Corps War Diary (GS Branch Headquarters), Sept. 1944. RG24, vol. 13687. National Archives of Canada.

Perth Regiment of Canada War Diary, Aug.–Sept. 1944. RG24, vol. 15136. National Archives of Canada.

Potts, Gordon. "Battle Narrative: 25 Aug–29 Aug 44, Royal Canadian Regiment" and "Battle Narrative: 14 Sep–22 Sep 44, Royal Canadian Regiment." 145.2R13.011 (D3). Directorate of History, Department of National Defence.

Princess Louise Dragoon Guards (4th Canadian Regiment) War Diary, Aug.–Sept. 1944. RG24, vol. 14205. National Archives of Canada.

Princess Louise Fusiliers War Diary, Aug.–Sept. 1944. RG24, vol. 15154. National Archives of Canada.

Princess Patricia's Canadian Light Infantry War Diary, Aug.–Sept. 1944. RG24, vol. 15157. National Archives of Canada.

Robinson (Maj.). "Report of Conversation which Historical Officer had with Maj. Robinson BM 3 Cdn Inf Bde, on the subject of S Martino–S Lorenzo Fighting 16 to 18 Sep 44 on 8 Oct 44." 145.2R19011 (D1). Directorate of History, Department of National Defence.

Royal Canadian Artillery, I Canadian Corps. "Report on Operations During Period 25 Aug–28 Oct 44." 142.2013 (D1). Directorate of History, Department of National Defence.

Royal Canadian Dragoons (1st Canadian Armoured Regiment) War Diary, Aug.–Sept. 1944. RG24, vol. 14188. National Archives of Canada.

Royal Canadian Horse Artillery (1st Canadian Field Regiment) War Diary, May 1944. RG24, vol. 14409. National Archives of Canada.

Royal Canadian Horse Artillery (1st Canadian Field Regiment) War Diary, Aug.–Sept. 1944. RG24, vol. 14410. National Archives of Canada.

Royal Canadian Regiment War Diary, Aug.–Sept. 1944. RG24, vol. 15210. National Archives of Canada.

Royal 22e Regiment. "Account." RG24, vol. 10883. National Archives of Canada.

Royal 22e Regiment War Diary, Aug.–Sept. 1944, RG24, vol. 15329. National Archives of Canada.

Seaforth Highlanders of Canada War Diary, Aug.–Sept. 1944, RG24, vol. 15257. National Archives of Canada.

2nd Canadian Infantry Brigade (Headquarters) War Diary, Aug.–Sept. 1944. RG24, vol. 14079. National Archives of Canada.

2nd Field Regiment, Royal Canadian Artillery War Diary, Aug.–Sept. 1944. RG24, vol. 14419. National Archives of Canada.

17th Field Regiment, Royal Canadian Artillery War Diary, Aug.–Sept. 1944. RG24, vol. 14528. National Archives of Canada.

Smith, Basil. "Memoirs of a Quarterbloke." Hastings and Prince Edward Regiment, Canadian Army Overseas. Directorate of History, Department of National Defence.

Spry, D.C. (Brig.). "Letter regarding 1 LAA Regt RCA, 20 July 44." RG24, vol. 10983. National Archives of Canada.

Stacey, C.P. (Col.). "Report No. 141 Historical Section Canadian Military Headquarters: Situation of the Canadian Military Forces Overseas, Progress in Equipment (Jan.–Dec. 1944)." 18 July 1945. Directorate of History, Department of National Defence.

———. "Report No. 143 Historical Section Canadian Military Headquarters: Canadian Operations in Italy, 4 Jun 44–23 Feb 45." Directorate of History, Department of National Defence.

———. "Report No. 187 Historical Section Canadian Military Headquarters:

Operations of I CDN Corps, 4 Jun 44 to 24 Sep 44—The Breaking of the Gothic Line and the Capture of Rimini." Department of National Defence. University of Victoria, Special Collections, Reginald Roy Collection.

Steiger, A.G. (Capt.). "Headquarters Corps Witthoeft (Venetian Coast Command)." SGRII 207 (Steiger). Directorate of History, Department of National Defence.

____. "The Fight for the Apennine Position and the Improvement of the Western Alps Position." SGRII 255 (Steiger). Directorate of History, Department of National Defence.

Stursberg, Peter. Broadcasts from 14 Sept. 1944 to 4 Oct. 1944. CBC Radio Archives, Toronto.

Tellier, Henri (Maj.). "Account by Maj. H. Tellier, OC 'A' Company R22e Regt." 145.2R19011 (D3). Directorate of History, Department of National Defence.

3rd Canadian Infantry Brigade. "Account of the Operations in Italy, 29 Aug–21 Sep 44." RG24, vol. 10883. National Archives of Canada.

3rd Canadian Infantry Brigade (Headquarters) War Diary, Aug.–Sept. 1944. RG24, vol. 14085. National Archives of Canada.

3rd Field Regiment, Royal Canadian Artillery War Diary, Aug.–Sept. 1944. RG24, vol. 14435. National Archives of Canada.

Trudeau, L.F. (Maj.). "Account by Maj. L.F. Trudeau, OC 'C' Coy R22 Regt." 145.2R19011 (D3). Directorate of History, Department of National Defence.

12th Canadian Infantry Brigade (Headquarters) War Diary, Aug.–Sept. 1944. RG24, vol. 14162. National Archives of Canada.

21st Tank Brigade (British). "Report on I CID Support at Gothic Line." RG24, vol. 10990. National Archives of Canada.

Vokes, Chris (Maj. Gen.). "The Adriatic Front–Winter 1944." Vokes Papers, Royal Military College of Canada Massey Library.

———. Canadian Operations in the Mediterranean Area, July–Sept. 1944: Extracts from War Diaries and Memoranda (Series 27). 20 July 1944. Directorate of History, Department of National Defence.

———. Operations 1st Canadian Infantry Division. "The Gothic Line—Phase Three: The Break-through the Gothic Line and the Pursuit to the Conca." RG24, vol. 10883, National Archives of Canada.

Westminster Regiment (Motorized) War Diary, Aug.–Sept. 1944. RG24, vol. 15283. National Archives of Canada.

"The West Nova Scotia Regiment," RG24, vol. 10883. National Archives of Canada.

West Nova Scotia Regiment War Diary, Aug.–Sept. 1944. RG24, vol. 15289. National Archives of Canada.

INTERVIEWS AND CORRESPONDENCE

Blake, Tom. Interview by Ken McLeod. Vancouver. N.d.

Brown, Ted. Correspondence with author. 30 July 2000.

Bulger, Victor. Correspondence with author. 13 April 2001.
Creighton, Donald. Interview by author. Richmond, BC. 4 Oct. 2000.
Crofton, Pat. Interview by Ken McLeod. N.d.
Dodd, G.T. Memo to Dr. Reginald Roy. University of Victoria, Special Collections, Reginald Roy Papers. 15 Sept. 1962.
Dougan, John Alpine. Interview by author. Victoria, BC. 9 Oct. 2000.
———. Interview by Ken MacLeod. Victoria, BC. N.d.
———. Interview by Tom Torrie. University of Victoria, Special Collections, Reginald Roy Papers. Victoria, BC. 27 July 1987.
Eastman, Gerald. Correspondence with Dr. Reginald Roy. University of Victoria, Special Collections, Reginald Roy Papers. 8 March and 14 Nov. 1962, 13 June and 15 Aug. 1963.
Ferley, Zeke. Correspondence with Dr. Reginald Roy. University of Victoria, Special Collections, Reginald Roy Papers. 12 Nov. 1963.
Galloway, Strome. Correspondence with author. 8 June 2001.
———. Interview by author. Ottawa. 6 May 2000.
Gildersleeve, Wilf. Interview by author. West Vancouver, BC. 5 Oct. 2000.
Gower, Don. Correspondence with author. 25 June 2000.
Green, R.W. Correspondence with Dr. Reginald Roy. University of Victoria, Special Collections, Reginald Roy Papers. 11 Sept. 1962.
Gregg, J. Milton. Correspondence with author. Oct. 2001.
Haley, Jack. Interview by author. Victoria, BC. 24 Aug. 2000.
Hammerstrom, Percy. Correspondence with Dr. Reginald Roy. University of Victoria, Special Collections, Reginald Roy Papers. 12 Sept. 1964.
Hoffmeister, Bert M. Interview by B. Greenhous and W. McAndrew. Directorate of History, Department of National Defence. N.d.
Hurley, Ron. Interview by author. Vancouver. 4 Oct. 2000.
Johnson, Alon. Interview by author. Victoria, BC. 6 Oct. 2000, 9 Jan. 2002.
———. Interview by Ken McLeod. Victoria, BC. N.d.
Kinloch, David. Memo to Dr. Reginald Roy. University of Victoria, Special Collections, Reginald Roy Papers. 1962.
———. Correspondence with author. 23, 30 Nov. 2000.
———. Interview by author. Vernon, BC. 3 April 2001.
Letcher, Jack. Transcript of taped recording. University of Victoria, Special Collections, Reginald Roy Papers. 1962.
Logan, Rodman. Correspondence with author. 28 June 2000.
Loten, Thomas A. Correspondence with author. 24 April 2001.
McGregor, Gordon. Interview by author. Victoria, BC. 3 Jan. 2001.
Milroy, W.A. Correspondence with author. 5 Sept. 2000.
Montemaggi, Amedeo. Correspondence with author. 19 Nov. 2000, 25 May 2001.
———. Interview by author. Rimini, Italy. 23 Oct. 2000.
Monti, Oviglio. Interview by author. Rimini, Italy. 21, 22 Oct. 2000.

Mortensen, Gordon. Correspondence with author. 8 May 2001.
Nikiforuk, Dan. Interview by author. Sidney, BC. 27 Dec. 2000.
Poulin, Tony. Correspondence with author. 23 Feb., 28 Sept. 2001.
Poulin, Tony. Interview by author. Ottawa. 10 May 2000.
Rankin, Harry. Interview by author. Vancouver. 15 Oct. 2000.
Reid, Donald. Correspondence with author. Oct., 6 Dec. 2000.
Reynolds, Garnet. Correspondence with author. Oct. 2000.
Sawdon, Robert. Correspondence with author. 2 Nov. 2001.
Shuter, Ted. Correspondence with author. 27 March 2001.
Smith, Don. Correspondence with author. 15 Aug. 2000.
Stone, James Riley. Interview by William S. Thackray. Victoria, BC. University of Victoria, Special Collections. 13, 20 May, 3, 10, 17 June 1980.
Stubbs, Raymond E. Correspondence with Dr. Reginald Roy. University of Victoria, Special Collections, Reginald Roy Papers. 7 Aug. 1963.
Tellier, Henri. Correspondence with author. 18 July, 22 Aug., 23 Sept. 2000.
Thomson, Sydney. Interview with author. Salmon Arm, BC. 27 May 2000.
Trépanier, Fernand. Correspondence with author. Oct. 2001.
Waldron, Eric. Correspondence with Dr. Reginald Roy. University of Victoria, Special Collections, Reginald Roy Papers. 21 Sept. 1962.
Warton, Bill. Interview by author. Vancouver. 4 Oct. 2000.
Wheeler, Gerry. Taped recollections provided to author by family. 2000.

INDEX

INDEX OF FORMATIONS, UNITS, AND CORPS

ABOUT THE AUTHOR

THE GOTHIC LINE is the final volume of Mark Zuehlke's trilogy on Canada's involvement in the World War II Italian Campaign. The first two volumes, *Ortona: Canada's Epic World War II Battle* and *The Liri Valley: Canada's World War II Breakthrough to Rome,* were published to wide critical acclaim both within military circles and without. With mapmaker C. Stuart Daniel, he co-authored *The Canadian Military Atlas: The Nation's Battlefields from the French and Indian Wars to Kosovo*. His other books include *The Gallant Cause: Canadians in the Spanish Civil War, 1936–1939* and *Scoundrels, Dreamers, and Second Sons: British Remittance Men in the Canadian West.*

Also a novelist, Zuehlke is the author of a popular mystery series based on the adventures of a coroner in the Pacific Coast town of Tofino. *Hands Like Clouds* and *Carry Tiger to Mountain* are the first two titles, with a third, *Sweep Lotus,* soon to be published. *Hands Like Clouds* won the 2000 Arthur Ellis Award for Best First Novel.

Zuehlke lives in Victoria, British Columbia, where, when not writing, he enjoys backpacking, cycling, kayaking, cooking Italian food, and gardening.